C0-ALR-928

MAC OS 8.5

Black Book

Mark R. Bell
Debrah D. Suggs

Publisher
Keith Weiskamp

Acquisitions Editor
Stephanie Wall

Marketing Specialist
Gary Hull

Project Editor
Don Eamon

Technical Reviewer
Paul Cory

Production Coordinator
Wendy Littley

Layout Design
April Nielsen

Cover Design
Anthony Stock

CD-ROM Developer
Robert Clarfield

Mac OS 8.5 Black Book

Copyright © The Coriolis Group, 1999

All rights reserved. This book may not be duplicated in any way without the express written consent of the publisher, except in the form of brief excerpts or quotations for the purposes of review. The information contained herein is for the personal use of the reader and may not be incorporated in any commercial programs, other books, databases, or any kind of software without written consent of the publisher. Making copies of this book or any portion for any purpose other than your own is a violation of United States copyright laws.

Limits Of Liability And Disclaimer Of Warranty

The author and publisher of this book have used their best efforts in preparing the book and the programs contained in it. These efforts include the development, research, and testing of the theories and programs to determine their effectiveness. The author and publisher make no warranty of any kind, expressed or implied, with regard to these programs or the documentation contained in this book.

The author and publisher shall not be liable in the event of incidental or consequential damages in connection with, or arising out of, the furnishing, performance, or use of the programs, associated instructions, and/or claims of productivity gains.

Trademarks

Trademarked names appear throughout this book. Rather than list the names and entities that own the trademarks or insert a trademark symbol with each mention of the trademarked name, the publisher states that it is using the names for editorial purposes only and to the benefit of the trademark owner, with no intention of infringing upon that trademark.

The Coriolis Group, Inc.
An International Thomson Publishing Company
14455 N. Hayden Road, Suite 220
Scottsdale, Arizona 85260

602/483-0192
FAX 602/483-0193
http://www.coriolis.com

Library of Congress Cataloging-in-Publication Data
Bell, Mark R.
   Mac OS 8.5 black book/by Mark R. Bell and Debrah D. Suggs.
      p. cm.
   Includes index.
   ISBN 1-57610-304-8
   1. Mac OS. 2. Operating systems (Computers) 3. Macintosh
(Computer)--Programming I. Suggs, Debrah D. II. Title.
QA76.76.063B448   1999
005.4'469--dc21

                 98-33996
                 CIP

Printed in the United States of America
10 9 8 7 6 5 4 3 2 1

an International Thomson Publishing company

Albany, NY • Belmont, CA • Bonn • Boston • Cincinnati • Detroit • Johannesburg • London • Madrid
Melbourne • Mexico City • New York • Paris • Singapore • Tokyo • Toronto • Washington

14455 North Hayden, Suite 220 • Scottsdale, Arizona 85260

Dear Reader:

Coriolis Technology Press was founded to create a very elite group of books: the ones you keep closest to your machine. Sure, everyone would like to have the Library of Congress at arm's reach, but in the real world, you have to choose the books you rely on every day *very* carefully.

To win a place for our books on that coveted shelf beside your PC, we guarantee several important qualities in every book we publish. These qualities are:

- *Technical accuracy:* It's no good if it doesn't work. Every Coriolis Technology Press book is reviewed by technical experts in the topic field and sent through several editing and proofreading passes in order to create the piece of work you now hold in your hands.

- *Innovative editorial design:* We've put years of research and refinement into the ways we present information in our books. Our books' editorial approach is uniquely designed to reflect the way people learn new technologies and search for solutions to technology problems.

- *Practical focus:* We put only pertinent information into our books and avoid any fluff. Every fact included between these two covers must serve the mission of the book as a whole.

- *Accessibility:* The information in a book is worthless unless you can find it quickly when you need it. We put a lot of effort into our indexes, and we heavily cross-reference our chapters, to make it easy for you to move right to the information you need.

Here at The Coriolis Group we have been publishing and packaging books, technical journals, and training materials since 1989. We're programmers and authors ourselves, and we take an ongoing active role in defining what we publish and how we publish it. We have put a lot of thought into our books; please write to us at **ctp@coriolis.com** and let us know what you think. We hope that you're happy with the book in your hands, and that in the future, when you reach for software development and networking information, you'll turn to one of our books first.

Keith Weiskamp
President and Publisher

Jeff Duntemann
VP and Editorial Director

Mark dedicates this book to Virginia, and absolutely no one else.

Debrah dedicates this book to her husband Mark and their son Anthony.
Without a single complaint, they let Mommy peck at the computer all summer.

❧

About The Authors

Mark R. Bell (Chapel Hill, NC) is a best-selling author of over a dozen computer books and software manuals, including The *Mac OS 8 Book* and *The Mac Web Server Book*. He is also a technical editor and contributing author for such publishers as Netscape Press, Ventana Press, AP Professional, Maxum Development Corporation, and Bare Bones Software. Mark also speaks at conventions and workshops, including Mactivity/Web and, most recently, Macworld Expo.

Debrah D. Suggs (Durham, NC) is a software trainer, system administrator, and technical editor. She has contributed to several books in the past, and currently serves as the Macintosh Specialist for the Office of Information Technology at Duke University.

Acknowledgments

Computer books are the products of teams, not just authors, and good teams make all the difference between just another product and a truly useful tool. In particular, we extend our thanks to our project editor Don Eamon, Ellen Strader (copy editor), Bob LaRoche (proof reader), Paul Cory (technical reviewer), Robert Clarfield (CD-ROM specialist), Wendy Littley (production coordinator), Tony Stock (cover design), April Nielsen (layout design), Stephanie Wall (acquisitions editor), Tristan Reid (who wrote Chapter 15), Caerwyn Pearce (who contributed the error codes information), Jeremy Hall (for the HTML Resource Guide), and Apple Computer (for permission to reprint the Apple Spec Chart).

We also would like to thank the many friends and developers in the Mac community who gladly give their advice, software, and precious time to help us make this a much better book than it would have been otherwise: Rob Terrell (always), Bailey Smith, Gregg Johnson and Mary Catherine Bunn, Keith Hatounian and Staci Sheppard (Apple Computer), E. Kenji Takeuchi, Alex Trottier, Bob Fronabarger, John O'Fallon, Thorsten Lemke, Cal Simone, Sandra Schneible, Humayun and Mihail Lari, Mathew Caughron, Snorri Gudmundsson, Luke van der Westhuyzen, Greg Landweber, and many others who are too numerous to mention.

Finally, we would like to acknowledge the vision and hard work of Steve Wozniak and Steve Jobs, without whom 26 million people wouldn't be as productive as they could be. Thinking different has its merits.

Contents At A Glance

Table Of Contents

Chapter 3
The User Environment 55

In Depth

Immediate Solutions

Chapter 4
Installation And Basic Configuration 103

In Depth

Immediate Solutions

Chapter 5
Disk And File Systems..**131**

Introduction

This book is intended for experienced users of Mac OS 8, or those of you who have significant experience with an earlier version of System 7 and who are considering upgrading to OS 8.5. For the most part, this book covers all the main features of Mac OS 8, including 8.1, as well as relevant portions of System 7. If you're new to 8.5, however, this book is a goldmine of information. This book guides you through all the features of Mac OS 8.5. It shows you how to perform all the tasks necessary for the care and feeding of a single user, as well as groups of users connected over a Local Area Network or the Internet.

How To Use This Book

In this book, each chapter is divided into two sections:

- A technical section, "In Depth," which covers the main topics found in each chapter and is designed to lay the groundwork for the other two sections or serve as a stand-alone section that can be reviewed at any time.

- A practical section, which consists of "Immediate Solutions," which cover the steps necessary to administer the Mac OS. Immediate Solutions is usually the largest section and may be used as a refresher course to test your skills for a particular topic.

The Tools You Need

What do you need to use this book most efficiently? First, this book assumes that you have significant experience with the Macintosh family of computers, the Internet, and some level of interest in cross-platform connectivity and interoperability. This last point may not seem too relevant, but we suggest that all Mac users need to realize that the Mac OS probably never will reach the usage level that the Microsoft Windows enjoys. Also, the successful OS is often the one that gets along best with all the others. To this end, we assume that you share this view on the state of things, that you want to use the Mac OS to communicate and share data with other operating systems, and that you have some experience with these operating systems.

Next, we assume that you have a PowerPC-based Mac or a Mac clone. Previous versions of Mac OS 8 could run on a Motorola 68040-based computer, but Mac OS 8.5 requires a PowerPC. However, it doesn't matter if it is an older PPC 601, or the latest G3 processor. Any PowerPC will do just fine.

Finally, this book assumes that you have experience with—and connectivity to—the Internet. You may have a permanent Internet connection through your computer at work, or you may be one of the lucky few with access through cable modem, DSL, ISDN, or frame relay. Nevertheless, even us poor souls with a modem and a PPP connection still qualify.

How This Book Is Structured

Each chapter in the *Mac OS 8.5 Black Book* is self-contained, but the first paragraph or so will make it clear if you need to read a previous chapter before you proceed with the present chapter. The following overview of the book's chapters will help you to see that we've organized the material so that you will feel free to jump right into the middle of the fray, if this is what you think is needed:

- **Chapter 1** introduces the latest version of Mac OS 8 and all its recent additions. The Immediate Solutions shows how to use its most significant features.

- **Chapter 2** covers everything you need to know to successfully launch and quit the Mac OS. The Immediate Solutions provides detailed examples of how perform these tasks and how to correct the most common problems associated with starting and stopping the OS, such as Extension conflicts.

- **Chapter 3** introduces the main elements of the Mac OS's many user environment options. The Immediate Solutions explains how to make changes to the user environment, including the new Appearance Manager and Application Switcher.

- **Chapter 4** covers how to install, add, and remove portions of the Mac OS, as well as the default configuration settings. The Immediate Solutions takes you through the exact steps required to add, modify, or delete the Mac OS.

- **Chapter 5** provides details on the disk and file systems used by the Mac OS. The Immediate Solutions covers everything you need to know to administer both fixed and removable media and how to use the HFS and HFS+ formats of the Mac OS.

- **Chapter 6** explores the memory management capabilities of the Mac OS. The Immediate Solutions provides examples on how to configure and maximize the efficiency of your computer's physical and virtual memory.

- **Chapter 7** covers all the issues of mobile computing for PowerBook and Duo users. The Immediate Solutions shows users how to take advantage of the Mac OS built-in security features and the improved Location Manager.

- **Chapter 8** details the printing capabilities of the Mac OS. The Immediate Solutions shows you how to select, configure, and print to a variety of local and networked printers.

- **Chapter 9** introduces the Mac OS's built-in multimedia capabilities. The Immediate Solutions shows users how to best use the audio and video features on the Mac OS, paying close attention to the latest release of QuickTime and its many components.

- **Chapter 10** explores the many ways in which the Mac OS is compatible with the various version of Microsoft Windows. The Immediate Solutions shows users how to exchange data with users of Windows 3.1, 95, 98, and NT, as well as how to run these versions of Windows on their own Macs.

- **Chapter 11** covers the many networking capabilities of the Mac OS. The Immediate Solutions shows users how to connect to Local Area Networks and the Internet by using AppleTalk and TCP/IP by using the Mac OS and several other popular applications.

- **Chapter 12** explores how to connect the Mac OS to the Internet using TCP/IP. The Immediate Solutions explains how install the most popular network adapters and modems, as well as configure TCP/IP communication software.

- **Chapter 13** covers the many types of Internet and intranet services that can be provided by using the Mac OS. The Immediate Solutions covers how to install and configure software to serve Web, FTP, email and other services.

- **Chapter 14** covers the built-in scripting capabilities of the Mac OS, as well as those added to Mac OS 8.5. The Immediate Solutions shows users how to use AppleScript to perform routine tasks, as well as what other alternative script editors are available to Mac OS users.

- **Chapter 15** explores the Java capabilities on the Mac OS. The Immediate Solutions demonstrates several Java applets and how they work.

- **Chapter 16** covers all the aspects of system security that are important for single users, network users, and Internet access. The Immediate Solutions explains how to make your Mac as safe as possible.

- **Chapter 17** covers the tools you'll need to monitor your Mac's internal events and system integrity. The Immediate Solutions shows users how to use the tools necessary to patrol the state of the OS, its RAM, and network usage.

- **Chapter 18** covers how to troubleshoot the Mac OS. The Immediate Solutions explains how to resolve Extension conflicts, overcome boot problems, fix disk errors, and more.

- **Appendix A** lists most popular shortcuts for the Mac OS.

- **Appendix B** lists the best tools to help administer the Mac OS.

- **Appendix C** covers the changes and enhancements to the Mac OS.

- **Appendix D** provides explanations for the most common Mac OS error codes.
- **Appendix E** provides an overview of all the makes and models of Apple Macintosh and Macintosh clone computers.
- **Appendix F** covers the terminology and elements of HTML.
- **Appendix G** provides several additional resources for getting help.

Chapter 1

Using Mac OS 8.5

In Depth

This chapter introduces the key components of version 8.5 of the Mac OS. A number of differences exist between 8.5 and previous versions of Mac OS 8; if you use System 7, you will simply be amazed at the speed, stability, and features of the latest version of the Mac OS. If you are familiar with previous versions of the Mac OS, you will be able to use 8.5 with very little difficulty, because all the main concepts remain intact. This chapter will help explain how to utilize the enhancements introduced in the latest version of the Mac OS.

What's New In Mac OS 8.5?

Mac OS 8.5 builds on previous versions of the Mac OS, as well as incorporates new features that are welcomed enhancements to what has long been known as one of the easiest operating systems to use in the world. What's new in Mac OS 8.5 can be summarized into the following categories:

- Improved Mac OS features

- New Mac OS features

- New applications

There are too many tweaks and new features to mention, but the following list captures the significant changes to Mac OS 8.5:

- More PPC-native code.

- Virtual memory improvements.

- Feature-rich content.

- User-interface themes and sounds.

- Font smoothing (anti-aliasing).

- Window title bars now have icons (icon proxies).

- Multiple scroll bar options (double scroll and proportional thumbs).

- New Sherlock find command powered by V-Twin engine allows you to find-by-content, search the Internet, index a local drive, and using AppleScript.

- Revised Applications Menu supports tear-off menus, and is both sizable and scriptable.

- PPC-Native AppleScript 1.3 has more scriptable applications.
- Open Transport 2.0 supports SNMP and better DHCP.
- Control Strip 2.0.
- New navigational services (Open/Save dialogs).
- QuickDraw rewrite.
- AppleGuide Help in HTML and new Help Menu items.
- Unicode and European character support by LaserWriter 8.
- Desktop printer browser.
- Network Browser for file server and TCP/IP services.
- Personal Web Server update.
- Application Switcher (Alt+Tab).
- List View enhancements.
- Monitors and Sounds rewrite.
- Monitor Calibration rewrite.
- New icons for files and folders.
- JPEG files that are dropped onto the System Folder are redirected to the Desktop Pictures folder.
- New Get Info window.
- Disk cache improvements.
- Pervasive zoom recticles.
- Date & Time control panel rewrite adds synchronizing and time server capabilities.
- File Exchange control panel replaces Mac OS Easy Open and PC Exchange.
- File Sharing.
- General Controls.
- Internet control panel integrates Internet Config 2.0 capabilities.
- Keyboard.
- Launcher.
- Revised Location Manager control panel.
- Revised Memory control panel.
- Modem.
- Revised Monitors & Sound control panel.

- Mouse.

- Numbers.

- PowerBook/Energy saver replaces several PB control panels.

- QuickTime Settings.

- Remote Access Control Panel/Apple Remote Access 3.1 replaces OT/PPP and ARA 2.1.

Mac OS Components

The components of the Mac OS (not including the third-party applications that come bundled with the OS, such as Microsoft Internet Explorer) perform the tasks necessary to allow you to display, input, and store data. These components are typically stored in the System Folder, although some of their associated parts may be located in other folders on your computer's hard drive.

TIP: *Never attempt to store essential OS components on removable media such as floppy disks or Zip cartridges, as well as on network volumes or fileservers.*

The System Folder, shown in Figure 1.1, contains many folders (and a few files) that must be properly named; it also contains the programs necessary for the operation of the OS.

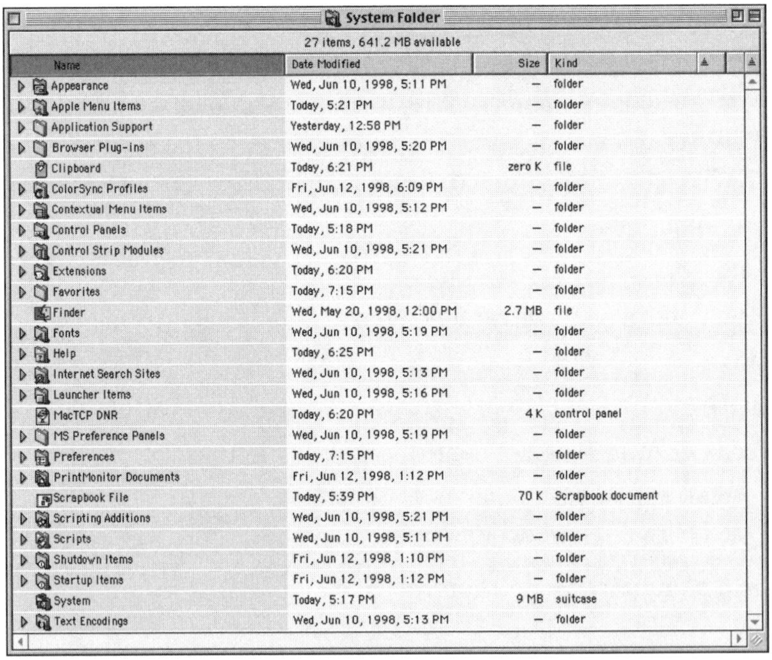

Figure 1.1   The typical System Folder for Mac OS 8.5.

The System Folder on your computer may look a bit different, depending on which OS components you installed. (Your folder also may have files and folders added by other software you have installed.)

The components that are most critical to the booting of the OS are the Finder and the System suitcase. They constitute the kernel of the OS and work in conjunction with control panels, Extensions, and System Extensions to provide access to the computer, network services, and disk and files, as well as to printing and other kinds of input and output.

TIP: *For a detailed description of all the components of the System Folder, please see Chapter 2.*

In addition to the OS itself and its associated files and folders, a default installation of Mac OS 8.5 includes many additional applications, utilities, and documentation. It includes over 2,000 files that fall into several broad categories:

• Help files, documentation, and Assistants

• Multimedia applications, such as QuickTime

• Internet applications, such as Netscape Navigator and Microsoft Internet Explorer

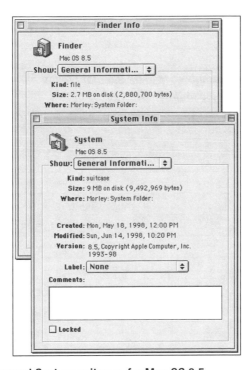

Figure 1.2   The Finder and System suitcase, for Mac OS 8.5.

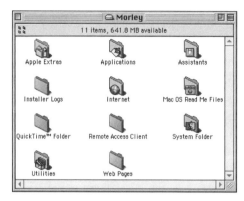

Figure 1.3   A typical installation of Mac OS 8.5 looks much like this, but your installation depends on your computer and the options you installed.

• Utilities for printing and disk drive repair

A typical installation is shown in Figure 1.3.

The components of the Mac OS that are not directly responsible for the low-level operation of your computer (the Finder and System suitcase) are usually modular and upgraded by Apple once the initial release of the OS has reached consumers. These components add valuable functionality in areas such as networking and multimedia support; in Mac OS 8.5, they include the components listed in Table 1.1.

Table 1.1   The modular components of Mac OS 8.5 that are not part of the low-level OS and which may be updated in the future.

Component	Version	Purpose
Open Transport	2.0	Networking and SNMP capabilities
QuickTime	3.0	Multimedia support
AppleScript	1.3	Scriptability of applications
AppleShare	3.8	File sharing services over AppleTalk and TCP/IP
Mac OS Runtime for Java	2.0	Java applications to run on a Mac
QuickDraw 3D and VR	1.5.4	Variety of screen drawing routines
Apple Remote Access	3.1	Remote access
Personal Web Sharing	1.5	HTTP serving capability
Appearance Manager	1.1	Display of different user interface themes
Speech Manager	1.5.2	Speech recognition and playback

User Interface Objectives

The objectives of the user interface under Mac OS 8.5 remain much the same as with Mac OS 8.0 and 8.1, but with improvements that bring the interface itself and access to information on the Internet closer to the user. The Mac OS has always been extremely easy to use, with icons and a mouse instead of a command line interface, and now Internet access via the Mac OS is equally important. Mac OS 8 introduced the Internet Setup Assistant (see Figure 1.4), but now you have closer ties to the Internet via several user interface options.

The following elements of the Mac OS user interface show just how easy it can be to access the Internet from the Mac OS.

Internet Access Tools

Mac OS 8.5 comes with many tools to assist in connecting to the Internet. For example, Figure 1.5 shows several tools to assist in the creation or modification of an Internet Service Provider account, including shortcuts to the Internet Setup Assistant and a utility to convert account information from the Apple Internet Connection Kit (AICK).

In Figure 1.5, notice the folder titled Internet—actually a subfolder within the Apple Menu—and the shortcuts it provides to Web and email services.

Sherlock (Search Internet)

The old Find application has undergone a serious upgrade and now allows you to find information by name, by content on an indexed hard drive, or on the Internet, using the new Sherlock application. These new capabilities, shown in Figure 1.6,

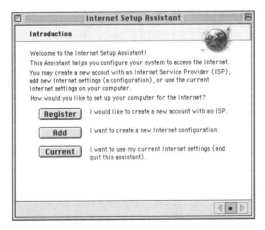

Figure 1.4   The Internet Setup Assistant helps you connect to the Internet without third-party connection software.

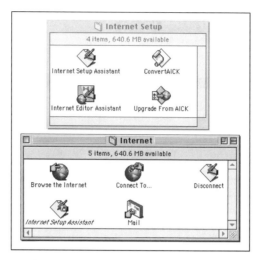

Figure 1.5   Mac OS 8.5 provides several options to access the Internet.

show exactly how Apple has extended the reach of the Mac OS to incorporate its trademark ease of use to control information beyond the local file system.

Internet-Style Help

Apple has appropriated HTML technology to its new Help Center to allow you to seek help using a Web browser-like interface in place of the AppleGuide of yore. The searchable Help Viewer, shown in Figure 1.7, uses frames to display help topics on the left and detailed information on the right, using clickable hyperlinks that direct you to additional information on a topic.

Icons And Metaphors

Mac OS 8.5 uses new icons and listing metaphors for volumes, files, folders, applications, and aliases, making it easier to navigate and display the contents of your hard drive. Many of the icons have been updated to make them more appealing and easier to view. For example, Figure 1.8 shows the System Folder with its new icons viewed as small buttons and as large icons.

Two new additions to the Mac OS icon family include translucent file names and the addition of an arrow to the alias icon, both of which are shown on Figure 1.9. Translucent file names are much easier to read when viewed against a colored background (they are invisible against a white background), and the new alias icon helps distinguish it as an alias when viewed in conjunction with almost any font. Aliases still used italicized text for the file name, but this was not as clear as it could have been because some listview fonts made it difficult to distinguish between regular and italicized text.

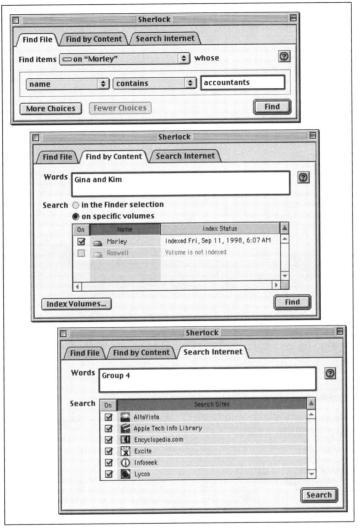

Figure 1.6   You can now search the Internet right from the Mac OS itself.

Pointing, Clicking, Dragging, And Dropping

Mac OS 8.5 supports all the traditional elements of manipulating text and objects—such as files and folders—that have been present in the Mac OS for many years, including:

- Pointing with the mouse
- Clicking and Shift+clicking
- Shift+dragging
- Dragging selections
- Dropping selections

Figure 1.7 The Mac OS now uses the new Help Viewer and HTML technology in place of the AppleGuide.

Mac OS 8 introduced two enhancements that continue in OS 8.5 that help clarify the copying of a selected object or the creation of an alias of the object. Figure 1.10 shows the Utilities folder being copied (left) and aliased (right).

Summarizing Text

Mac OS 8.5 adds two new features that use the OS's capability to simmarize text. First, text clippings are now automatically named using the first 18 characters of text plus the word "clipping," as in Figure 1.11. Not all applicaitons support this capability, however. Those that don't will create text clipping named "SimpleText clipping", or no clipping at all.

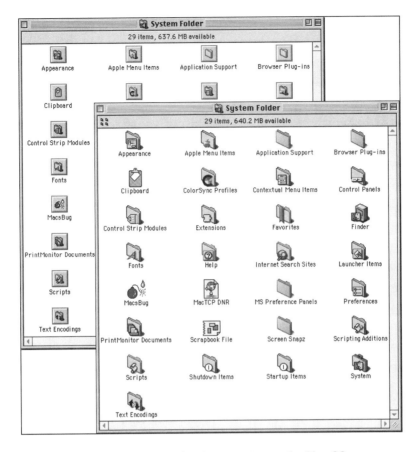

Figure 1.8   New folder icons make it easier than ever to use the Mac OS.

Figure 1.9   An example of translucent file names and the new alias icon.

Figure 1.10   Visual clues help you manage file copying and alias creation.

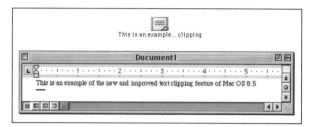

Figure 1.11   A text clipping summary.

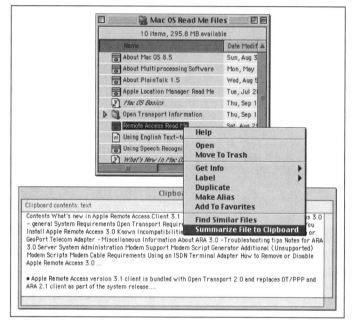

Figure 1.12   The new Summarize File to Clipboard command.

Also, a summary of a file may be created and sent to the clipboard by using the contextual menu. For example, Figure 1.12 shows a ReadMe document that has been sumamrized.

Windows And Menus

The most dramatic change in Mac OS 8.5, of course, is the addition of the new Appearance Manager and its capability to display sets of themes (appearance, font, Desktop picture, and pattern preferences). The new Appearance Manager also has the capability to display Kaleidoscope-like appearances, but Mac OS 8.5 only installs the Apple Platinum appearance. System 6 and 7 users were stuck

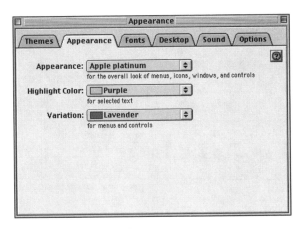

Figure 1.13   The Appearance control panel

with the old "System 7" appearance, Mac OS 8 introduced the new "Platinum" appearance, but OS 8.5 creates a framework for third-party software developers to create entirely new appearances. Figure 1.13 shows the Appearance tab of the new Appearance control panel and the Apple Platinum options.

Windows, menus, and all mouse actions work the same, no matter which theme you are using, so apart from the visual aspect of the new user experience, nothing has really changed. For more information on the Appearance Manager and themes, see Chapter 3.

The Finder And Desktop

The Finder and Desktop views have undergone significant changes since OS 8.1. These provide a much better user experience than in previous versions of the OS and include the following changes:

- New menu items
- More PowerPC-native code for faster performance and stability
- Additional scriptability

You can find new menu items in the File menu (Add To Favorites), the View menu (Reset Column Positions and Standard Views), the Help menu (Help Center and Mac OS Help), and the Application menu (this has short or long names and you can "tear it off" and place it on the Desktop). Figure 1.14 shows how the new menus appear in Mac OS 8.5.

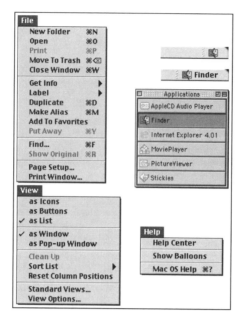

Figure 1.14   The Finder gets a few menu tweaks in Mac OS 8.5.

The Preferences and View Options menus have also been modified to consolidate several preferences configuration options into a single location. This also allows you to create a "Standard Views" option for each disk drive or folder that you then use to control the view preferences for all enclosed folders. (This was possible in System 7, but not in Mac OS 8.0 or 8.1.) See Figure 1.15.

This much-needed enhancement not only allows you to control the view options of a series of enclosed folders, but also to easily change the options for one or more of the enclosed folders on a folder-by-folder basis while retaining the default view for the others. For additional information on how to customize your Desktop, file, and folder views, turn to Chapter 3.

Managing Menus

Some people prefer to use the Mac OS's menus with a mouse for making menu selections, but some of us prefer to use any and all keyboard shortcuts whenever they are available. The menu changes do not affect keyboard equivalents, and Mac OS 8.5 uses faster routines to draw hierarchical menus on screen, which makes navigating the Apple Menu seem faster than ever before. Figure 1.16 shows one of our personal favorite keyboard equivalents, throwing a selected item in the Trash by pressing Command+Delete.

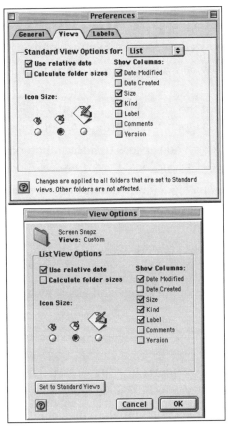

Figure 1.15   New Finder view options allow you to have more control over how you view
the contents of your computer.

Figure 1.16   Keyboard shortcuts like this one can be great time-savers (to some of us,
anyway).

Quick Reference Specifications

The following list shows the essential facts about using Mac OS 8.5:

- Mac OS 8.5 runs only on PowerPC processors, including Apple Macintosh and Macintosh clones.

- The core elements of the Mac OS are not updated as frequently as its modular components, such as Open Transport and QuickTime.

- Mac OS 8.5 seeks to provide access to information on the Internet as seamlessly as it does to your local hard drive.

- New icons help you navigate more quickly and accomplish tasks.

- New themes and appearances allow you to customize your environments to suit your own tastes.

- You can arrange files and folders, with visual clues provided by the OS to make navigating your hard drive easier.

- You can run numerous applications and easily switch among them in a variety of ways.

Utilities To Use

The utilities or elements of the Mac OS discussed in this chapter are listed here as a memory aid for the busy user or system administrator:

- *Finder*—Arrange, store, and manipulate files and folders.
- *Finder Preferences*—Control general preferences, list views, and labels.
- *Internet Setup Assistant*—Access an Internet Service Provider account.
- *Sherlock*—Search local drives or the Internet for information.
- *Help Viewer*—Search for assistance on the Mac OS or application.
- *Appearance Control Panel*—Change appearance and theme views, fonts, Desktop pattern and picture, as well as scroll bar options.
- *View Options*—Change folder views for icons, buttons, and lists.
- *Duplicate*—Copy files and folders on local file system or server volume.
- *Hierarchical Menus*—Navigate collections of subfolders with a single mouse click.
- *Application Menu*—Switch among applications, as well as move them to and from the background.

Immediate Solutions

The following sections describe how to implement the latest, or most popular, features of Mac OS 8.5.

Changing Theme Views

You can change the theme view on your computer in at least two different ways: Select Appearance from the control panels or click on the Desktop while holding down the Control key to open the Finder's contextual menu and then select Change Desktop Background. The latter option also opens the Appearance Control Panel.

Some confusion may exist between the following terms, but to you as an end user, they essentially control the same thing—how your computer displays windows, menus, and backgrounds:

- *Themes*—A collection of user-defined preferences for your computer's appearance, font, desktop pattern, soundtrack, and scroll bar options. You can mix, match, and save elements of each for quick activation as a set.

- *Appearance*—A set of window and menu definitions created by a software programmer for use by the Mac OS, such as the Apple Platinum theme.

Using The Appearance Control Panel

To change to another theme view using the Appearance control panel:

1. Go to the Apple Menu, navigate down to Control Panels, and select Appearance.

2. Select a theme from the Themes panel or an appearance from the Appearance panel, as in Figure 1.17.

Using The Contextual Menu

To change to another theme view using the contextual menu:

1. Click anywhere on the Desktop while holding down the Control key.

2. Choose Change Desktop Background, as shown in Figure 1.18.

3. Select a theme from the Appearance panel, such as Roswell, shown in Figure 1.19. The selected theme takes effect immediately without your having to quit the Appearance control panel or restart the computer.

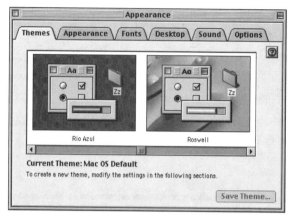

Figure 1.17   Selecting a theme, which is a collection of appearance preferences saved as a set, such as Rio Azul or our personal favorite, Roswell.

Figure 1.18   Using a contextual menu to change a theme view.

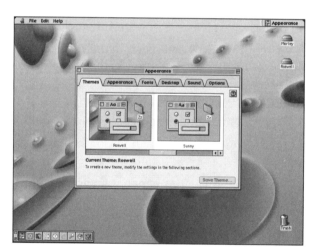

Figure 1.19   Selecting an appearance causes the change to go into effect immediately.

Changing Desktop Views

In addition to themes and appearances, you can still change several elements of the Desktop experience independently of the other Appearance settings. Mac OS 8.5 supports patterns and pictures as in the past, as well as the viewing of icons on the Desktop in several ways.

To change the Desktop pattern or to place a picture on the Desktop:

1. Select the Appearance control panel from the Apple Menu or via a contextual menu as described previously.

2. Select the Desktop tab, as shown in Figure 1.20.

3. Select a Pattern from the scrolling list on the right to preview how it will look on the Desktop.

4. To activate the pattern, double-click on the preview window or select the Set Desktop button.

5. To select a picture instead of a pattern, click on the Place Picture button and select a picture from the scrolling list on the left, as in Figure 1.21.

6. Select the Choose button to return to the Desktop tab, then select the Set Desktop button. Figure 1.22 shows how this example looks when set as a Desktop picture.

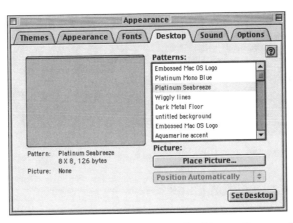

Figure 1.20   Selecting the Desktop tab to change the Desktop pattern or picture.

Figure 1.21   Selecting a picture for use on the Desktop.

Figure 1.22   A picture used as a Desktop picture.

Changing Your Desktop Icons

Finally, you can view your Desktop icons as icons (large or small) or as buttons (large or small), but not as a list. Buttons require only a single click to open, whereas icons require a double click.

To change your Desktop view to icons or buttons:

1. Activate the Desktop in the finder by clicking anywhere on the Desktop.

2. Select View as Icons or View as Buttons from the View menu.

3. Select Options from the View menu to select a size (small or large) for the icons or buttons.

Figure 1.23 shows the Desktop viewed as small buttons (left) and large icons (right).

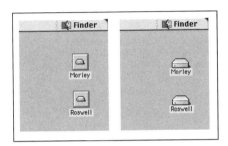

Figure 1.23   Two views of a portion of the same Desktop.

Arranging Files And Folders

Mac OS 8.5 allows you to customize how files and folders are viewed through the Finder, the portion of the OS that provides access to the contents of all storage devices. We've already seen how you can change the Desktop views using icons and buttons, but you can't view the contents of the Desktop as a list. This capability is reserved for folders that reside on your hard or floppy drives, fileserver volumes, and other storage devices.

List View

To change a folder to a list view:

1. Select a folder by clicking anywhere in the folder.

2. Select View as List from the View menu.

3. Select View Options from the View Menu, as in Figure 1.24.

4. Select any of the View Options you want to activate, such as Use Relative Dates and which columns to show.

5. Click on OK to make the changes, or select Set to Standard Views to revert this—and all enclosed folders—to the default settings.

Standard View

To set the standard view options for lists (as well as icon and button views):

1. Select Preferences from the Edit menu, as in Figure 1.25.

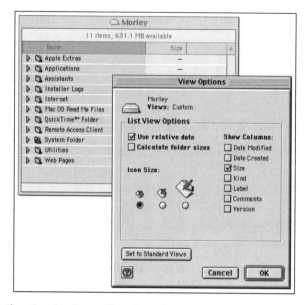

Figure 1.24   Selecting the viewing options for a folder.

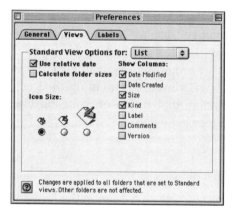

Figure 1.25   Setting the standard view options for list views.

2. Make sure the Views tab is selected, as well as the List option in the pop-up menu within the Views tab.

3. Select the desired configuration options and close the Preferences window.

The next time you view a list window's View Options and select Set to Standard Views, these options will be activated for any given list window.

Copying Files And Folders

You can copy files and folders in Mac OS 8.5 in at least three ways: by issuing the Duplicate command (Command+D), by dragging items from one volume to another, and by Option+dragging items from one folder to another on the same or another volume.

To copy a file or folder using the Duplicate command:

1. Select one or more files and/or folders in the Finder.

2. Choose File|Duplicate (or Command+D).

The items will be duplicated with their original file names followed by the word "copy" at the end.

Copying To Another Volume

To copy items from one volume to another:

1. Select one or more files and/or folders in the Finder.

2. Drag them to another volume.

The items will be copied with no change in file name.

Using The Option+Drag Method

To copy items using the Option+drag method:

1. Select one or more files and/or folders in the Finder.

2. Drag them to the same or another volume while holding the Option key.

The addition of the small plus sign on the file icon is a visual clue that a Copy command has been issued.

Manipulating Windows

The Mac OS has two main types of windows: normal and pop-up windows. We're all familiar with normal windows and pop-up windows have been around since Mac OS 8.0 (or earlier, with a little help from certain third-party utilities). Pop-up windows are very cool and easy to use.

To create a pop-up window, take these steps:

1. Select any folder or volume in the Finder.

Figure 1.26   Creating a pop-up window.

2. Drag it to the bottom of the screen until it turns into a pop-up window, as in Figure 1.26.

3. Alternatively, you may select a window and choose View|As Pop-up Window.

To access the contents of a pop-up window, just click on the window's tab.

You can resize windows in the usual way, but pop-up windows can be resized by dragging the top-left or -right corners. You can also still roll up non-pop-up windows using the Windowshade button (see Figure 1.27).

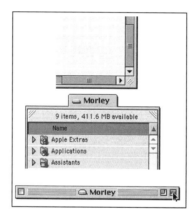

Figure 1.27   All your favorite window-manipulation tools are present in Mac OS 8.5, including new scroll bar options.

Launching Applications

Mac OS 8.5 allows you to launch applications in a variety of ways, enabling you to customize the user interface experience to best suit your needs. You can launch applications by performing any one of the following options:

• Double-clicking on an application's icon

• Double-clicking in a document belonging to an application

• Double-clicking on an alias to an application or document

• Selecting an application, alias, or document from the Apple Menu, Recent Applications, or Recent Documents menu

- Selecting an application, alias, or document from the Launcher
- Selecting an application, alias, or document in the Finder and choosing File|Open (or Command+O)

Switching Among Applications

The Mac OS has long been a multitasking operating system; starting with Mac OS 8, it has been multithreaded as well. These two features enable multiple applications to run at the same time while returning mouse and keyboard control to the user. Now, you can switch among open applications by the following four methods:

- Select an application through the Application menu (see Figure 1.28)
- Select an application through the tear-off Application menu (see Figure 1.28)
- Press Command+Tab to cycle through the applications alphabetically
- Click on an application's window

Figure 1.28   Two of the three ways you can switch among running applications.

Running Foreground And Background Processes

Most applications can run in the foreground or background under the Mac OS. However, to provide user input, an application almost always needs to be in the foreground. Some applications are actually designed to run specifically in the background and are referred to as "faceless" applications, such as the HotSync application for use with the PalmPilot.

To switch an application between the foreground and background, take these steps:

1. Select an application like Internet Explorer from the Application menu, as shown in Figure 1.29.

2. Select Hide (application name).

3. Select Hide Others to move all but the current application into the background.

4. Select Show All to display all the applications that are currently running, leaving the selected application in the foreground.

Only one application at a time can be in the foreground; all others are considered to be in the background, whether or not they are hidden.

Figure 1.29   Selecting an application to move to the background.

Chapter 2

System Startup And Shutdown

In Depth

Startup Options

You have several choices available when starting a Macintosh. The options you use depend on the task or tasks you are attempting to do (or undo). In some cases, you will be improving system performance; in others, you will be dealing with a machine incapable of running in its current condition, and that requires intervention on your part—ranging from a simplistic to an heroic effort.

Your first option is to boot normally and allow the computer to load all system components. For most users, this procedure is standard. During startup, you should see a small computer icon—named the happy Mac—in the center of the gray screen. As the first system diagnostic, this icon indicates that the computer hardware is in working order and that an operating system has been found. Any other icon indicates problems with the computer. The most common error icon is the floppy disk with a blinking question mark, which indicates that no working operating system has been found. Any other icon indicates possible serious problems, which probably are hardware-related. Older Macintosh computers will also make an *arpeggio* sound that is very distinctive. It has been said, the prettier the startup sound, the sicker the Mac. Although not totally true, any change in the starting sound a Macintosh makes does indicate computer hardware problems. Figure 2.1 shows some of these startup icons.

You are not limited to launching the system installed on the hard drive. By inserting a floppy disk with a smaller system loaded, you can run diagnostics on the internal hard drive and make repairs. You can also launch the operating system

Figure 2.1   Samples of some startup icons.

from a CD-ROM. External hard drives, DVD disks, floppy disks, and CD-ROMs can all boot a Macintosh computer.

After the happy Mac icon appears, proceed to the "Loading The OS" section in this chapter for the rest of the booting process. However, if you know that problems exist with the system, you can opt to change some of the startup options; the most basic of these options is to load with Extensions off. To do so, hold down the Shift key during startup. The startup screen will display the message "Welcome to Macintosh. Extensions off". At this point, you can release the Shift key. This option allows only the most basic system components to load. In many cases, a system that hangs during startup is indicative of a system component conflict. You can also activate the Extensions Manager control panel during startup by holding down the spacebar. This action allows you to choose which Extensions and control panels you want to load.

Several key combinations are available that modify the way the OS loads. Table 2.1 lists the most common combinations.

Loading The OS

After an operating system has been located, a startup screen appears. Unless you or another user have changed this screen to reflect personal tastes, you should

Table 2.1   Startup key combinations.

Key Combination	Usage	Function
Shift	Hold until startup screen appears	Disables all Extensions
Spacebar	Hold before Extensions begin loading	Launches the Extensions Manager
Option+Command	Hold until dialog box (Figure 2.2) appears	Rebuilds the Desktop file
Command+Shift+P+R	Press and hold down before startup	Zaps the PRAM
C	Hold if bootable CD-ROM is in the drive until happy Mac appears	Commands the computer to boot from the CD-ROM
Shift+Option+ Command+Delete	Press before startup	Boots from an alternate SCSI device

Figure 2.2   The dialog box for rebuilding the Desktop file.

Figure 2.3   The Mac OS startup screen.

see the logo for the Mac OS (Figure 2.3) with a progression bar, indicating how much of the system components has loaded. Icons for several of these components appear at the bottom of the screen and, depending on the amount of software installed, may wrap upward several lines. Near the end of the booting process, the various portions of the Desktop appear, including the hard drive, trashcan, and all additional drives or files stored on the Desktop.

Finally, File Sharing, if you have enabled it, will begin loading. Depending on the size of the hard drive and how many partitions exist on the system, File Sharing may take some time to finish launching. However, the system should be useable while File Sharing is loading.

Elements Of The System Folder

The System Folder contains many of the components that load by default as well as the brains of the operating system. These components include system Extensions, Extensions, control panels, Preferences, Startup and Shutdown folder contents, and Apple Menu items. The following sections cover these components.

System Extensions

While there are not many system Extensions, they are among the first to load during the booting process. One of the most useful is MacsBug. In the past, when a system crashed or froze, the only user alternative was to immediately reboot. The user was given no chance to reboot gracefully, or—even more important—to know exactly what caused the crash. Today, you routinely run multiple applications at the same time, especially Internet-based ones that can cause a system crash while running in the background. MacsBug is a valuable tool that can tell you what process caused the system malfunction. You can even quit the offending program from the MacsBug command line. For more in-depth information on MacsBug, refer to the Troubleshooting information in Chapter 18.

Extensions

Rather than write a new operating system every time a software program is released or a system component is tweaked, developers create extensions that plug into the system to increase functionality or improve performance. You will find that the Extensions folder, more than any other folder, has a tendency to get out of control, containing unknown files with cryptic names that eat away at precious system and memory resources.

The files stored in the Extensions folder load after system Extensions. Most Extension icons have the distinct puzzle-like appearance similar to those shown in Figure 2.4 (even the folder sports a puzzle-piece graphic). The most well known Extensions are printer, peripheral, CD-ROM, video, and network drivers, but there are facetious ones as well, including singing trashcans.

Occasionally, Extensions or control panels fail to load properly and cause the system to hang. This condition is termed an *extension conflict*, although the problem may be isolated to a control panel. Previously, we discussed options for booting the system and one of these options is to boot with Extensions off. For clarification, this actually entails disabling both Extensions and control panels.

Weed out those useless Extensions. If for no other reason than to tighten your system performance, it's one of the best things that you, as a user or administrator, can do. Several Web sites define what these Extensions do and whether you can live without them. The Extensions Manager also can provide some information about these files, such as the creator and version number.

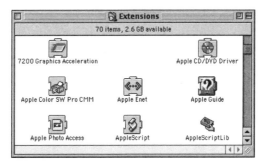

Figure 2.4   Some sample Extension icons.

Control Panels

One of the biggest differences between control panels and Extensions is that control panels have windows or dialog boxes that allow you to change control panel settings. Control panels are the last system components to load. They often deal with the way that the system looks and behaves and include some screen savers, appearance managers, network configuration applications, and monitor settings. Control panels, like Extensions, also have a distinctive appearance, as shown in Figure 2.5.

If a programmer wants you to have some control over how an application runs within the system, he will write the code as a control panel. Otherwise, the code is written as an Extension.

Preferences

Every application that launches on a Macintosh creates a preference. Even if you used the application only once, decided that it didn't meet your requirements, and dragged it straight to the trashcan, there is still a file in the Preference folder that indicates how the program should be run in the future.

Information stored in a preference file can include options input by the user, such as preferred email address, custom toolbars, default views, and so on, as well as window positioning of a particular document. Applications that keep a list of recently used documents store this information in the preference file.

Most users do not need to interact with the Preference folder unless something has stopped working within a particular application. Programs that hang when launching (and those that are not functioning normally) may have a corrupt preference file. In most cases, removing the preference and allowing the program to create a new one will fix the problem. You do need to input some user preferences again. Make sure that important information—such as the IP number assigned to the machine, serial numbers for software, and configuration options—are available or documented, should you have to delete important preferences.

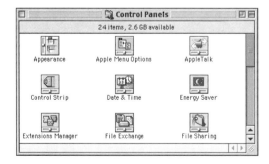

Figure 2.5   Some sample control panel icons.

Startup Folder

If you have applications that you use every time you launch the machine (such as Web server software, email applications, or client programs), you may want to take advantage of the Startup folder. As the operating system nears the end of the booting process, it looks to this folder to see if any applications need to be launched. You can place the actual application in the folder, but for better system security, you will find that an alias functions just as well (see Chapter 5 for more information on creating and using aliases).

You can place multiple items in the Startup folder. These items are launched alphabetically and by manipulating the first character, you can control the launch order (a space will launch before the letters of the alphabet and a bullet character will launch after).

Shutdown Folder

Just as the Startup folder runs the programs within it during the boot process, the Shutdown folder runs applications during shutdown. Common applications that run at this time are disk utilities, optimization programs, and virus protection—although any application within the folder will run.

Apple Menu Items

The System folder also includes the Apple Menu Items folder. This folder contains the applications or aliases that appear under the Apple menu located in the top-left corner of the screen. This menu is special because you can launch applications from it simply by selecting them. Figure 2.6 shows the Apple menu under Mac OS 8.5.

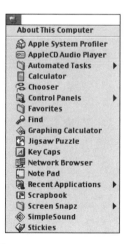

Figure 2.6   The contents of the Apple menu.

Shutting Down

As with any graphical interface, you must exercise care in properly shutting down the operating system. In fact, you can shut down a Macintosh in several acceptable ways.

The most common method is to go to the Special menu as shown in Figure 2.7. The system will begin closing open programs. If any applications have open documents that have been changed, the system will display a dialog box that gives you an opportunity to save changes to the file. When all applications are closed, the system will shut down and turn off the power for most Macintosh computers. Older models with a power button will display a window, indicating that you can now turn off the computer.

A second method of shutting down the computer is to press the power key on the keyboard (this method is often discovered by accident). The dialog box shown in Figure 2.8 will appear, asking if you are sure that you want to shut down the computer. You also have the option to restart, sleep, or cancel the command. Notice that the default shuts down the system. If you should press the Return or Enter keys at this point, the system will begin the shutdown process.

Finally, some Macintosh systems have an option under the Apple menu named Shut Down. This option will also effectively bring down the operating system gracefully. This option is not included by default in Mac OS 8.5, but it is often found on systems as legacy software.

Should you turn your computer off every time it is not in use? It depends on your situation. For most work situations, it's perfectly fine to leave a system running. In many environments backup systems work during the night and cannot back up

Figure 2.7   The Special menu with Shut Down selected.

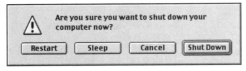

Figure 2.8   The Reboot Options dialog box.

a computer that is not running. For the home computer, it would be better to turn off the system. Most home computers have long periods of inactivity during which running them wastes energy.

Quick Reference Specifications

The following list shows the essential facts about System Startup and Shutdown:

- Macintosh computers are turned on by pressing the power button located on the keyboard.

- A happy Mac icon indicates the system is ready to load. Anything else indicates problems with the computer or system.

- Any change in the startup sound indicates problems with the computer that are probably hardware related.

- System Extensions such as MacsBug are loaded first during startup.

- The difference between control panels and Extensions is that control panels have dialog boxes and windows, allowing you to configure the program, while Extensions usually lack windows and dialog boxes.

- Control panels load after Extensions.

- When a system hangs or fails to finish launching during the startup sequence, we refer to this problem as an extension conflict.

- To restart the computer without Extensions, hold down the Shift key until the system indicates Extensions are disabled.

- Applications that you wish to launch automatically during startup should have an alias in the Startup folder.

- Applications that you want to launch during shutdown should have an alias in the Shutdown folder.

- Preferences are kept for every program ever launched on the computer unless you manually remove the file within the Preferences folder.

- You can launch an operating system from multiple media, including floppy disks, CD-ROMs, DVDs, and other hard drives.

- If your system freezes or crashes, you can perform a warm reboot by pressing the Control+Command+Power keys on the keyboard.

- You can use the Force Quit key sequence to shut down applications that are no longer responding by typing Option+Command+Escape.

Utilities To Use

The utilities or elements of the Mac OS discussed in this chapter are listed here as a memory aid for the busy user or system administrator:

- *Extensions*—Adds functionality to the core system without releasing a system update.

- *Control panels*—Extensions that can be configured.

- *Extensions Manager*—The built-in utility that allows you to turn Extensions on or off and create or delete custom extension sets.

- *Conflict Catcher*—A commercial package that allows you to manage troublesome or large extension sets.

- *About This Computer*—The built-in system function that informs you how memory is being allocated, as well as what system is installed on the computer.

- *MATM*—A shareware utility that clarifies information found in the "About This Computer" window.

- *System Profiler*—The utility included with Mac OS 8.5 that gives extensive information about the software and hardware in your computer.

- *Chooser*—The application located in the Apple menu that allows you to access other servers on your network and attach to them automatically.

- *Network Browser*—A new utility included in Mac OS 8.5 that allows you to browse the network in the same way that you view your hard drive and maintain a list of favorite servers.

Immediate Solutions

Starting The Computer

So, you have the packing material removed from the computer. You've got the monitor, keyboard, mouse, and whatever else will fit plugged into the back of the CPU. If you normally use a PC, at this point you may be looking for the power button. However, a Mac is different (of course). To start the computer, take the following steps:

1. Make sure the computer has a power cord plugged into the CPU.

2. Locate the power button on the keyboard. The power button has an arrowhead pointing to the left (refer to Figure 2.9 for a picture).

3. Press the power button.

4. You should hear some kind of musical sound, indicating that the computer has started.

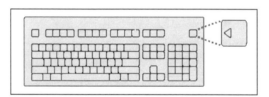

Figure 2.9   The power button on the keyboard.

TIP: *A few Macintosh models actually do have a power button that you must push to turn on the computer. Some of these models are the Centris 610 and Power Macintosh 6100/66 (we refer to these models as the "pizza box" design). If you press the power button on the keyboard and the computer fails to start, you may want to locate the power button on the CPU.*

Monitoring Startup Progress

You've started the computer. Do you have time for a coffee break while the system launches? You can tell by the progress bar. This bar acts as a thermometer that lets you know how much of the system has launched. This is the first time you will see this progress bar, although you will see it often during regular functions within the Finder (for example, copying files from one folder or drive to another). As Extensions and control panels load, the progress bar will begin to fill. When the bar is full, the window will disappear and begin loading the Desktop. Figure 2.10 shows a typical progress bar in action.

Figure 2.10   The progress bar.

Disabling Extensions

If you have a Mac that can't seem to finish the boot process, then you probably have an extension conflict. Symptoms include freezing immediately on startup, hanging while the Extension and control panel icons are flashing across the bottom of the screen, and just plain hanging.

Before you can fix this problem, you have to determine if the computer will boot at all. You need to start with Extensions off. You won't be able to do much productive work on a Mac in this condition, but at least you can determine your next step in the troubleshooting process by taking these steps:

1. Start or restart the Macintosh.

2. Hold down the Shift key.

3. Continue holding down the Shift key until you see the Mac OS startup screen. It should say "Welcome to Mac OS. Extensions Off". Figure 2.11 shows this screen.

If the computer boots successfully, you have a conflict with your INIT programs. If it does not boot, you may have fundamental problems with your installed system. Refer to Troubleshooting in Chapter 18 for additional steps you can take to resolve this problem.

Figure 2.11   The Extensions Off startup screen.

Using The Extension Manager To Load Only System Extensions

In the stone ages of conflict diagnosis, you had to create an Extensions backup folder, move all your Extensions into that folder, and then begin a painful process of loading a few Extensions at a time. After multiple (and we mean multiple) restarts, you may or may not have discovered the offending application.

Now, thankfully, we have the Extensions Manager. If you have determined that you do indeed have an Extensions conflict, the Extensions Manager is the first place you should go to begin resolving this problem. Your first step is to load only the extensions necessary for the system to run. The following instructions are written with the assumption that you have had to restart your computer with Extensions off:

1. Go to the Apple menu and select Control Panels.
2. Double-click on the Extensions Manager control panel.
3. Click on the tab at the top of the columns to view a drop-down menu. See Figure 2.12 for assistance.
4. Select Mac OS 8.5 base.
5. Restart the computer.

The computer will now be booting with a basic extension set. If you still have trouble booting, then you may have a fundamental problem with your system.

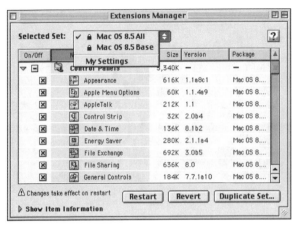

Figure 2.12   The drop-down menu in Extensions Manager.

Saving Custom Extension Sets Using The Extensions Manager

In the previous section, we covered loading only necessary extensions. However, one of the more powerful uses of the Extensions Manager is the capability, based on the situation, to load certain extensions. This is accomplished by creating extension sets. For example, you may have a PowerBook computer that you use at work and at home. You could have two extension sets—one for work, where you can directly access the Internet, and one for home, where you use a dial-up software program.

Follow these steps for saving a custom extension set:

1. Go to the Apple Menu|Control Panels and select Extensions Manager.

2. Turn on or off the desired control panels and extensions.

3. Go to the File menu and select New Set.

4. Give this set a name (Figure 2.13 shows an extension set named Home Extensions) and click on Okay.

Manipulating Load Order

You have determined that there is an extension conflict on your system. You have reinstalled the software and still the programs are fighting like two sumo wrestlers, yet you have to have both applications running.

2: System Startup And Shutdown

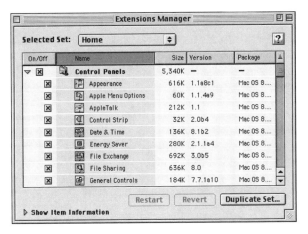

Figure 2.13   A custom extension set named Home Extensions.

Extensions load alphabetically. You can take advantage of this by naming your Extensions so that they load first or last. Sometimes, you can fix an extension conflict by changing the order that the programs load. To make an Extension load first, take these steps:

1. Locate the file.

2. Click once on the name of the file to put the name in an edit mode.

3. Click at the beginning of the file name and insert one of the characters that will make the file load first (some examples are the space or the numerical characters).

To make an Extension load last, repeat the preceding steps, but insert a tilde (~) or a bullet (•) or any other character that will force the file to load last.

Disabling Extensions At Startup

Just think of this little gem as a solution to the "uh oh" situation. "Uh oh" situations include the moment you slam the car door as you realize that the keys are in the ignition. For Mac users, the "uh oh" situation happens when you know you have an Extensions conflict and restart the computer, but forget to hold down the Shift key. In case you've forgotten, this key combination disables Extensions.

Not all is lost. If you have not begun loading Extensions, simply hold down the spacebar until the Extensions Manager control panel launches, as shown in Figure 2.14. However, if you wait until the icons begin appearing at the bottom of the screen, it is too late.

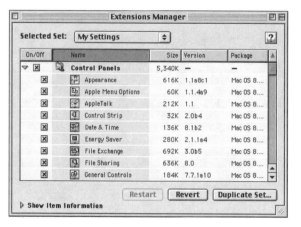

Figure 2.14   The Extensions Manager when called during startup.

Conflict Catcher

If you have continual extension conflicts, you may want to invest in software named Conflict Catcher by Casady & Greene, Inc. Conflict Catcher goes beyond Extensions Manager in that it can scan files and locate damaged resources, lock sets so they cannot be modified, and show the program file names during startup. You can also stop or pause the system during startup, as well as restart or shut down while Extensions are being loaded.

You can find more information at **www.casadyg.com/products/conflict-catcher/ default.html**, including system requirements and latest version information.

Checking For Available Resources By Using About This Computer

You may occasionally sit down to a computer and be unsure of some important information, such as how much memory is installed, how it is allocated, what system is running, and so on.

An excellent tool for accessing this information quickly is named About This Computer. It is very easy to access—just take these steps:

1. Make sure that you are within the Finder (if not, go to the Application menu and select Finder).

2. Go to the Apple menu and select About This Computer.

Figure 2.15   The About This Computer window.

Figure 2.15 shows a sample window that contains several applications that are running and shows how memory is allocated to each.

Using MATM

MATM (pronounced "madam") is an acronym for "More About This Macintosh." This shareware utility builds and expands on the information shown in the section "About This Computer." Figure 2.16 gives an excellent overview of this utility.

In MATM, not only can you see what applications are running, you can also see exactly how the memory is being allocated. For example, in About This Computer, you may only see that the largest unused block of memory is 15MB. In

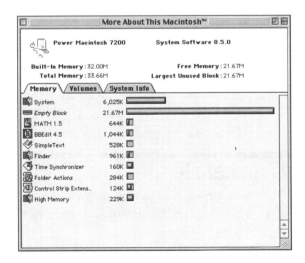

Figure 2.16   The MATM window.

MATM, you also see if this memory is fragmented and even what application is causing the break. How many times have you been told by the system that there is not enough memory to launch a particular application and that you must close open programs? MATM can tell you exactly what application to close, and in the case of applications that cause memory leaks, MATM can provide a valuable warning to restart the computer to fix the fragmented memory. Finally, MATM also includes volume and system information.

For more information on MATM, visit its Web site at **pobox.com/~albtrssp** or email it at **albatross@kagi.com**.

Checking For Available Resources By Using The System Profiler

One of the best tools in the release of Mac OS 8.5 is the revamped System Profiler. It certainly gives some commercial programs a run for their money. The System Profiler will be covered in depth in other chapters in this book, including Chapters 5 and 18.

Figure 2.17 shows an overview of the System Profiler. The System overview includes information about the system and the Finder and installed and virtual memory. Device and Volume information includes installed devices and their numbers on the SCSI chain. This is very useful when adding external SCSI devices such as scanners and external drives. You can also see what Control Panels and Extensions are installed, as well as the applications on the hard drive.

To launch the System Profiler, do the following:

1. Go to the Apple Menu.
2. Select Apple System Profiler.
3. Click on the appropriate tab to retrieve the desired information.

Shutting Down Gracefully

There is a right way and a wrong way to shut down a Macintosh. This is because of the tight integration between the hardware and the system software.

Figure 2.17   The Apple System Profiler window.

To properly shut down a Macintosh, choose either of the following options:

• Go to the Special menu and choose Shut Down, as shown in Figure 2.18.

• Press the power button on the keyboard to bring up the Shut Down options menu (see Figure 2.19).

Figure 2.18   The Special menu with Shut Down selected.

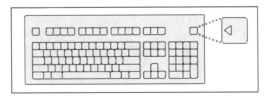

Figure 2.19   The power button on the keyboard.

Managing Abnormal Endings (Crashes And Freezes)

Although some users believe that Macintosh computers are perfect machines incapable of any wrongdoing, those of us in the real world know that it isn't always possible to shut down or restart the machine gracefully. In this section, you will learn what to do when your Macintosh crashes or freezes.

First, let's define our terms. When we say *crash*, we refer to an occasion when the system will no longer function, but tells you this in the form of a "bomb" dialog box (see Figure 2.20). In some cases, you will retain mouse control, be granted mercy, and be allowed to restart the Mac—or you may not be so lucky.

A *freeze* is also a system failure, but unlike the crash, a freeze occurs with-out warning or dialog box. A freeze is also different from a *hang* in that no mouse control remains, and thus, you have no recourse but to force a computer restart.

If you are faced with an unresponsive or frozen screen, you will probably have to force a restart. The following steps explain how:

1. Determine whether you must force a restart. If you still have mouse control, go to the next section entitled "Managing Abnormal Endings (Hanging Applications)."

2. Hold down the Control key.

3. While holding the Control key, press the Command key.

4. While holding the Control and Command keys, press the power key on the keyboard.

5. You should hear the computer restart.

This keystroke combination feels much like the PC three-fingered salute (Control+Alt+Delete). If you support PCs as well, you will feel right at home using this keyboard shortcut.

Some Macintosh models also have a restart button on the front of the computer. This small button should have a small left-pointing triangle that looks the same as the power key on the keyboard. This button will also restart the computer.

Figure 2.20   A system bomb window.

Managing Abnormal Endings (Hanging Applications)

In the preceding section, we talked about system crashes or freezes. However, occasionally an application will cause the system to stop reacting to mouse clicking and dragging. You can still move the mouse around the screen but cannot seem to do much else. Your first impulse may be to do the Macintosh version of the three-fingered salute. However, when an application is hung, you still have an opportunity to gracefully restart your computer.

What you need to do is force the application that is running to quit. However, because you don't have mouse control, you need to do this via a keystroke combination, as follows:

1. Hold down the Option key.

2. Press the Command key.

3. Unless you are double-jointed, reach with your other hand and press the Escape key. (This is one of the few times that you use the Escape key.)

4. The dialog box shown in Figure 2.21 will appear. Choose Force Quit.

WARNING!   The dialog box in Figure 2.21 also indicates which application has developed problems, including Finder. If an application is causing the problem, you have a much better chance of closing down the offending program and gracefully restarting your system. However, don't panic if Finder happens to have difficulties. Sometimes, a process within the Finder is not responding (such as a print command). You can still force the process to quit and properly restart the computer. However, we have seen a force quit dialog box lead to a freeze or crash, so this solution can cause problems.

Finally, after forcing an application to quit, your computer may seem to function just fine. However, the warning in the dialog box for a forced quit does remind you that you should restart your computer. Don't ignore it; restart your computer to reduce chances of a system freeze or crash.

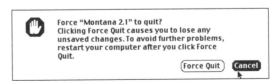

Figure 2.21   The dialog box that you use to force an application to quit.

Connecting To A File Server At Startup By Using The Chooser

Remember when a 250MB hard drive seemed ridiculously large? That was in the old days when Microsoft Word in its entirety was roughly 5MB. Today, the Microsoft Web site says to allow 56MB for the easy installation of MS Word. More and more system administrators are deciding to run huge office applications from a central server, in spite of the fact that computers have larger hard drives. If you find that you need to connect to the same server every time you start your computer, you may want to connect to the server automatically by taking these steps:

1. Go to the Apple menu and select the Chooser.

2. Click on AppleShare and locate the server you wish to access automatically. Click on Okay (refer to Figure 2.22).

3. Enter your username and password or select the guest button if that is an option. Click on Okay.

4. In the third dialog box, if there are multiple volumes available on the server, choose the one you need.

5. While still in this dialog box, click in the small box beside the volume you choose to access this server each time your computer is restarted. You can also decide to save your name or save your name and password. Most system administrators prefer that you not opt for the latter.

6. Click on Okay and close the Chooser.

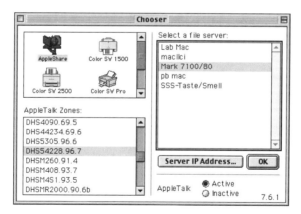

Figure 2.22   The Chooser.

You will now automatically attach to this server each time you start your computer. If you want to learn more about how to work with non-AppleShare networks, see Chapter 10.

Connecting To A File Server By Using The Network Browser

One of the most striking updates to Mac OS 8.5 is the inclusion of the Network Browser. It breaks the limitations of the Chooser and allows you to browse your network in the same way that you browse your computer. Figure 2.23 shows a sample view of the network. The Network Browser will be covered in depth in Chapter 11.

One of the most promising aspects of the Network Browser is the capability to keep a list of commonly accessed servers. This is called your Favorites list. If you've used Microsoft's Internet Explorer, you are familiar with this term and with Web sites. To add a server to your favorites list:

1. Open the Network Browser.

2. Locate the server you want to add to the favorites list.

3. Click on the button with the Book icon (refer to Figure 2.23), and choose Add To Favorites.

You can now access this server quickly, as well as any other server on this list.

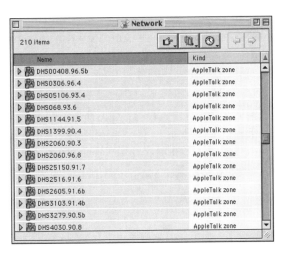

Figure 2.23   The Network Browser.

Choosing A Reboot Option

If you push the power key on the keyboard while the system is active, you bring up the special Reboot Options dialog box, shown in Figure 2.24. You have the following four options:

- Choose Restart to close open applications and perform a warm reboot on the system.

- Choose Sleep to put the system in a low energy mode. Push the spacebar to wake the system.

- Choose Cancel to close the dialog box without making any changes to the system status.

- Choose Shut Down to close all open applications and shut down the system.

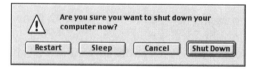

Figure 2.24   The Reboot Options dialog box.

Choosing A Startup Disk

In this age of large hard drives, we find that power users often divide a large drive into multiple partitions either by choice or by necessity (older versions of the Mac OS had a size limit for drive partitions). Users can also easily add additional internal or external storage devices such as hard drives, which also mount separately on the Desktop. Mac OS 8.5 also changes the appearance of hard drive icons to indicate that a system is installed. Darker gray icons have a system installed; lighter ones do not.

You can install an operating system on any partition. This is an excellent solution if you are testing alpha or beta software applications and are concerned about the integrity of your system. To do so, take these steps:

1. Go to the Apple Menu|Control Panels and choose Startup Disk.

2. Select the volume you wish to use for starting the computer and close the window.

3. Restart the computer to use the chosen drive or partition.

Figure 2.25 shows the Startup Disk control panel.

Figure 2.25   The Startup Disk control panel.

You can also choose an alternate SCSI drive as the startup disk by pressing Shift+Option+Command+Delete while starting the computer.

Booting From A CD-ROM

The latest Macintosh computer, the iMac, doesn't contain a floppy drive. Although this may seem frightening to the average user, most of us rarely use a floppy disk unless we are practicing "sneaker" networking. For newer Macs, it's more efficient to boot from a CD-ROM. These discs have a larger system because of the greater disk size. It may even be worthwhile to create a custom CD boot disc if you have access to a CD burner.

Follow these steps to boot from a CD-ROM:

1. Insert the CD-ROM in the drive.

2. Start or restart the computer.

3. Hold down the C key.

4. You should hear the CD-ROM drive grinding as the system launches from the CD-ROM.

5. If you have successfully booted from the disk, you should see the CD-ROM icon in the top-right corner of the screen as shown in Figure 2.26.

You can also use the Startup Disk control panel to choose the CD drive as the starting volume (refer to the section "Choosing A Startup Disk," covered previously in this chapter, for instructions).

Figure 2.26   The CD-ROM as the primary boot volume.

Booting From A Floppy Disk

Booting from a floppy disk is one of the ancient methods of getting a computer to a useable state. For some, the old ways are still the best ways. This especially applies to old Macs. Reasons for booting from a disk would include situations where hard drive repair could not occur while the disk was active. You may also want to use a disk for starting a computer that had lost its ability to boot.

To boot from a floppy disk, take these steps:

1. Locate or create a disk with a system installed.

2. Insert the system disk while the computer is not up (either while it is off or in the dark screen phase during a warm reboot).

3. Start the computer.

4. You should hear the floppy drive grinding, and if you are using a disk with System 8 or later, you should see the "Welcome to Mac OS" screen.

5. If the floppy disk icon is in the top-right corner as shown in Figure 2.27, you have successfully booted from disk.

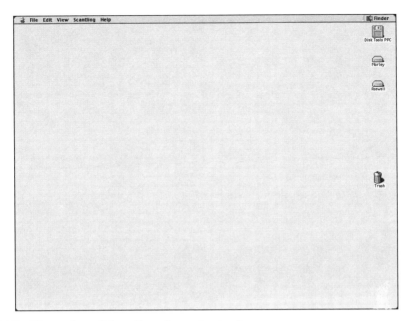

Figure 2.27   The system disk as the primary boot volume.

Booting From Other Removable Media

You can boot from other media, including popular storage devices currently in use such as the Iomega Zip and Jaz drives and Syquest removable hard drives. There are also peripherals and drives that are poised to be just as common, including the Imation Superdrive with its USB interface and the DVD disks, that can hold much more data than CD-ROMs. No matter the media, if an operating system is installed on the device, you can boot from it. Simply select it in the Startup Disk control panel.

WARNING!   Do not attempt to remove a cartridge, Zip disk, or other removable media that serves as the startup disk while your system is running.

Chapter 3
The User Environment

In Depth

The most compelling aspect of the Mac OS is the user environment: Mac OS 8.5 adds many new features for users to explore. This section highlights the essential aspects if the user environment, discusses its many configuration options, explains where to find software and resources for enhancing the user environment, and provides tips to help you organize the contents of your computer.

Essential Configuration Options

You need to configure or check several elements of the user environment for accuracy immediately after installing Mac OS 8.5. The sky won't fall if these matters are not attended to promptly, but you may experience some degree of frustration if they are not. We consider the following items to be essential configuration options:

- *Hardware-related options*—Energy saving settings, auto wake up and shutdown, monitor resolution, sound-in and sound-out, removable drive settings (such as Zip, Jaz, or SyQuest), virtual memory, local and networked printers, and mouse tracking and clicking speed.

- *Software-related options*—Languages, color control, text and numbers, Internet preferences, and speakable alerts.

These configuration options allow the computer to accurately store data on your hard drive (using the proper date, time, time zone, and Daylight Savings Time options, for example), as well as wake up or shut down on schedule (using Energy Saver or Auto Power On/Off, for example).

Optional Configuration Options

What sets the optional configuration options apart from the essential options is that once configured, the essential options are rarely modified. You can frequently change the following configuration options however, to suit your (or your users') individual needs or whims:

- Appearance (themes, fonts, scroll bars, collapsible windows, Desktop pictures and patterns), sounds, and Desktop views

- Shortcuts (Apple menu, Application menu, Control Strip, Launcher, and Favorites)

- Speech recognition
- File and Web sharing
- Finder elements (Spring-loaded folders, View, Labels, and other preferences)

These options are most of what we consider alternative configuration options that are part of the Mac OS, but you may have other ideas as to what is essential and what is optional.

Enhancing The User Environment

The Mac OS has never had a shortage of utilities and applications to enhance its usability, and many of these enhancements will run under Mac OS 8.5. Those that won't run either have been incorporated into the OS and may no longer be needed, or are being upgraded to add new features. Over the years, Apple has incorporated many of these utilities and features because it was easy to do, as with Kaleidoscope themes, hierarchical menus, and pop-up windows. Simultaneously, Apple has helped developers create even more enhancements by providing Application Programming Interface (API) specifications. By using these specifications, developers can write applications to take advantage of OS features, such as the new Sherlock search engine and the navigational services (Open and Save dialog windows).

We discuss a few of the more popular user-environment utilities in the "Immediate Solutions" section later in this chapter. Visit the Web sites of your favorite software developers for more information on the status of Mac OS 8.5 compatibility for their applications and utilities. For general information about enhancing the user environment, see these URLs:

- **www.kaleidoscope.net**
- **www.iconfactory.com**
- **www.clixsounds.com**
- **macworld.zdnet.com**
- **www.macweek.com**
- **www.zdnet.com/mac/download.html**
- **hyperarchive.lcs.mit.edu/HyperArchive/HyperArchive.html**

Organizing Content

Aside from the user interface itself, one of the chief ways you can organize and customize the user environment is by organizing your files into folders using a plan that is logical to you. Our Macs consistently hold between 10,000 and 40,000 files apiece, and Mac OS 8.5 installs some 2,000 files. So, it just makes good sense to organize the contents of storage devices in some way.

The Mac OS creates several folders at the root level of the startup disk (see Figure 3.1) that serve as a good starting point, including the following:

- *Apple Extras*—Additional applications, utilities, and OS components
- *Applications*—QuickTime, SimpleText, and other applications
- *Assistants*—Internet Setup and Mac OS Setup assistants
- *Installer Logs*—An optional folder that contains logs files created by the Mac OS installer and others
- *Internet*—Internet applications and utilities
- *Mac OS Read Me Files*—Documents containing important information about the Mac OS and any optionally installed software, such as Speech Recognition
- *System Folder*—The Mac OS and other system resources
- *Utilities*—Hard disk utilities, including Drive Setup and Disk First Aid
- *Web Pages*—HTML documents for use with the Web Sharing personal Web server

These folders are a good start, but you'll want to add folders and subfolders as necessary, for example, for your documents, images, projects, downloads, and games. When you open a folder, the Mac OS has to read information from the Desktop database pertaining to that folder, including file names, sizes, modification dates, and the like. The more items that are in a folder, the longer it takes the folder to open. Therefore, we recommend that if you have more than several dozen items in a folder, you consider creating subfolders. For example, we have about 150 different utilities stored in the Utilities folder, so we create subfolders that allow us to divide the utilities evenly among them, as shown in Figure 3.2.

Of course, no "correct" way exists to organize the contents of your hard drives. Do what you feel is best for you and what makes it easiest to find your files.

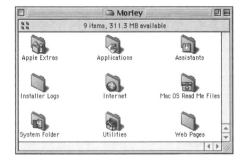

Figure 3.1   Folders created by the Mac OS.

Figure 3.2   A customized approach to organizing over 150 utilities.

Immediate Solutions

This section describes the elements of Mac OS 8.5 that you can configure to affect the user environment, as well as a few utilities and applications to make the user interface more fun and useful.

Using The Setup Assistant

The Mac OS 8.5 installer places an alias to the Mac OS Setup Assistant in the Startup Items folder, so that when the computer reboots after installation, the Mac OS Setup Assistant is automatically launched. A clean installation of Mac OS 8.5 will cause several of the default environments to lose their configuration; the Mac OS Setup Assistant will help users enter these configuration options, including:

- Keyboard layout
- Username and organization
- Date, time, and time zone
- Standard or Simple Finder
- File sharing username, password, and sharing folder
- Printer configuration

The Mac OS Setup Assistant alias will be automatically deleted from the Startup Items folder after the first time it is run, but you can always run it again from the Assistants folder if necessary. Figure 3.3 shows how the user interface appears in the Mac OS Setup Assistant.

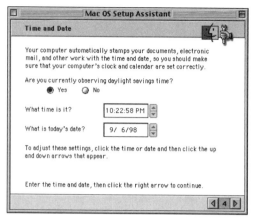

Figure 3.3   The Mac OS Setup Assistant.

Configuring Energy Saver

The Energy Saver control panel is installed only on PowerMacs that are Energy Star-compliant, including all PCI-bus Macs and PowerBooks. First-generation PowerMacs that are not Energy Star-compliant can use the Auto On/Off control panel instead. Both control panels allow you to configure the Mac OS to automatically start up and shut down the computer on selected days of the week and at certain times. You can also configure computers that are Energy Star-compliant to go into power-saving mode by:

- Putting the entire computer to sleep (CPU, hard drive, and monitor)
- Putting the monitor to sleep
- Putting the hard drive to sleep

For all these features to work, of course, each component must have power-saving features as well, in addition to the CPU itself.

Power Down Configuration

To configure the Energy Saver to power down:

1. Open the Energy Saver control panel.

2. Select the Sleep Setup button, as well as the Show Details button (see Figure 3.4).

3. Configure the options you want.

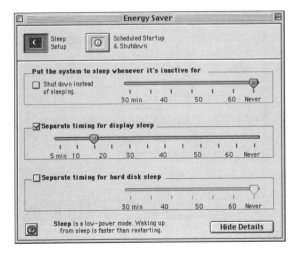

Figure 3.4   Configuring the Energy Saver control panel.

4. Review the Notification and Server Settings, which are located in the Preferences menu. If your computer is acting as a file sharing or Internet server, be sure to check both the settings shown in Figure 3.5.

5. Close (or quit) the control panel.

Startup And Shutdown Configuration

To configure any PowerMac to automatically start up or shut down:

1. For Energy Star-compliant computers, open the Energy Saver control panel.

2. Select the Scheduled Startup & Shutdown button (see Figure 3.6).

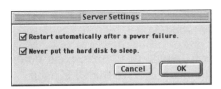

Figure 3.5   The Server Settings preferences are for computers that act as servers on a network.

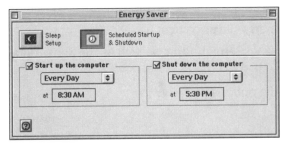

Figure 3.6   Configuring the Energy Saver control panel.

3. Configure the options you want, then close (or quit) the control panel.

4. For non-Energy Star-compliant computers, open the Auto Power On/Off control panel.

5. Configure the desired options, then close the control panel (see Figure 3.7).

Note that the Auto Power On/Off control panel isn't an application and has all its configurable options in the same window, unlike the Energy Saver, which has menu options.

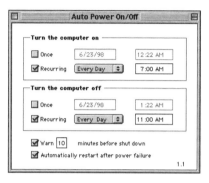

Figure 3.7   Configuring the Auto Power On/Off control panel.

Configuring Date & Time

Configuring the computer's date, time, and time zone settings is important because you can track documents according to the date and time they were created or last modified. Therefore, a file with an incorrect date and time stamp may very well elude you in a search for a file created on an incorrect date. Also, some applications, such as databases, may not function properly if some of their files are incorrectly time-stamped.

To configure the Date & Time control panel:

1. Open the Date & Time control panel (see Figure 3.8).

2. Enter the current date and time.

3. Make the appropriate Daylight Saving Time option and select a time zone.

4. To use a network time server to automatically set the time on your computer, select the checkbox and click on the Server Options button (see Figure 3.9).

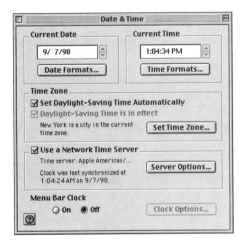

Figure 3.8   The new Date & Time control panel in Mac OS 8.5.

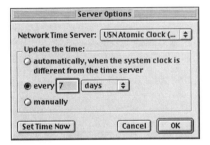

Figure 3.9   The time server option allows the computer's time to be set automatically by any time server on the Internet, including various atomic clocks.

5. Select a time server from the list, such as Apple's time server (**time.apple.com**), or choose edit List from the menu and enter another selection, as in Figure 3.10. For example, the U.S. Naval Observatory maintains two atomic clocks (**tick.usno.navy.mil** or **tock.usno.navy.mil**) that are used to set the time for U.S. military operations worldwide and many astronomical observatories. Setting the time using a time server is very quick and only takes a few seconds. It connects to a time server only when Internet connectivity is available.

6. Finally, you may choose to display the time and date in the menu bar, as well as select several clock display options by selecting the Clock Options button and making any appropriate configuration options.

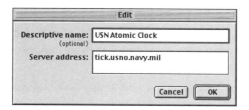

Figure 3.10   For the most accurate time possible, select a time server powered by an atomic clock, such as those of the U.S. Naval Observatory.

Configuring Monitors & Sound

As we describe later in the chapter about multimedia, Mac OS 8.5's Monitors & Sound control panel is where you configure several features that have a big impact on how you interact with the OS. Most monitors built in the past two to three years are capable of displaying at multiple resolutions and more users than ever are equipping their computers with external speakers (and subwoofers). Use Monitors & Sound control panel to configure the basics of what you see and hear from the Mac OS.

To configure the Monitors & Sound control panel:

1. Open the Monitors & Sound control panel. Depending on what model of CPU and monitor you have, different options display. AV-equipped computers generally have more options to allow for the configuration of the speakers and the positioning of the picture, as shown in Figure 3.11.

2. Use the Monitor button to select the bit-depth (colors) and resolution options you want.

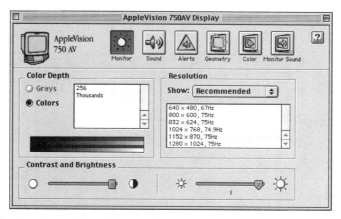

Figure 3.11   The Monitor portion of the Monitors & Sound control panel for a G3/266 CPU with an AppleVision 750AV monitor.

3. Use the Sound button to choose an appropriate volume level as well as to select sources for sound input and output (see Figure 3.12). Again, different computers display different options depending on the monitor and any additional installed AV hardware.

4. Use the Alerts button to select or record your own system alert sound (see Figure 3.13). Sounds are stored in the System suitcase in the native sound format for the Mac OS.

5. Make any additional selections that may be appropriate for your situation, then close the control panel.

The most important step in this whole process is selecting a proper resolution, refresh rate, and bit-depth for your level of comfort. If the refresh rate is too low, causing the screen to flicker, the human eye can detect this. We suggest a resolution that supports a refresh rate of at least 75Hz, but a higher rate is always better and never worse. If possible, select as many colors as possible, and purchase additional VRAM if possible (it is very inexpensive at this time, costing only a few dollars per megabyte).

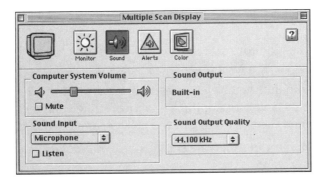

Figure 3.12   The Sound configuration options for a 7100/80 CPU with an Apple Multiple Scan 15 Display.

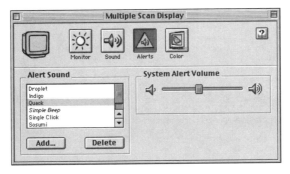

Figure 3.13   The Alerts section of the Multiple Scan Display.

Configuring The Mouse And The Keyboard

After you have configured your monitor, you'll want to check your mouse and keyboard mapping options. Most users will have the standard Apple mouse and keyboard, but if you have purchased a third-party keyboard or mouse, such as a Kensington mouse, you need to refer to any additional software that may have been installed by that item.

Mouse Configuration

Figure 3.14, for example, shows the application that comes with the popular four-button Kensington mouse.

To configure a standard Apple mouse, take these steps:

1. Open the Mouse control panel (see Figure 3.15).
2. Select a speed for mouse tracking and double-clicking.
3. Close the Mouse control panel.

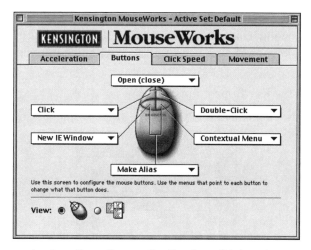

Figure 3.14   An example of configuration application for a third-party mouse from Kensington.

Figure 3.15   The Mouse control panel.

Changes made to the Mouse control panel go into effect immediately, but remember to never unplug an ADB device such as a mouse or keyboard while the computer is powered on. iMacs use the new Universal Serial Bus (USB) instead of ADB and are free to plug and unplug devices without shutting down the computer.

Keyboard Configuration

Many American users will be unfamiliar with the keyboard layout options that are part of the Mac OS. A keyboard layout assigns what we consider special characters, such as the German umlaut (¨) or an accented character (ò), to keys on the keyboard. The Mac OS supports multiple languages through WorldScript and keyboard layouts; you can adjust these on the fly.

To configure the Keyboard control panel:

1. Open the Keyboard control panel (see Figure 3.16).

2. Select a script family (Roman is the default).

3. Select a keyboard layout. Selecting multiple options causes a new option to appear in the menu bar that allows you to select a keyboard layout from a pull-down menu. Click on the Options button at the bottom of the window to select a keyboard menu shortcut for switching between keyboard layouts.

4. Configure the Key Repeat options.

5. Close the Keyboard control panel.

Figure 3.16   The Keyboard control panel.

Configuring Numbers And Text

Like previous versions of the Mac OS, Mac OS 8.5 lets you configure preferences for the display of numbers, currency, and text. For example, some people prefer to have a comma separate the hundreds from the thousands when viewing rows of numbers (e.g., 1000 versus 1,000).

Number Configuration

To configure the Numbers control panel, take the following steps:

1. Open the Numbers control panel (see Figure 3.17).
2. Choose a predefined format from the Number Format menu, such as U.S.
3. Optionally, you can edit the Separator or Currency fields and use your customized preferences in place of the predefined formats.
4. Close the control panel and the changes will go into effect immediately.

To see how your choices will appear on screen, look at the Sample field after making your selections, but before closing the control panel.

Text Configuration

Similarly, you can configure the Mac OS so that text items behave according to the rules of a particular language, which affect things such as case conversions and sort order.

To configure the Text control panel, take these steps:

1. Open the Text control panel (see Figure 3.18).
2. Choose a language from the Script menu.
3. Choose a language from the Behavior menu (each script system might support multiple languages).
4. Close the control panel and the changes will go into effect immediately.

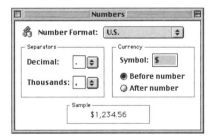

Figure 3.17   The Numbers control panel.

Figure 3.18   The Text control panel.

Configuring General Controls

The General Controls control panel, shown in Figure 3.19, allows you to config-ure several aspects of the user environment, including ones that are discussed in other chapters. To make any of the following changes, open the General Controls control panel, make your selections, then close the control panel:

- *Show Desktop When In Background*—When unchecked, the Desktop and its contents are hidden from view, leaving only the windows of unhidden appli-cations (see Figure 3.20).

- *Show Launcher At System Startup*—Opens the Launcher (described later in this chapter) when the computer is started up without placing an alias to the Launcher in the Startup Items folder.

- *Warn Me If Computer Was Shut Down Improperly*—When checked, the OS warns you with a dialog window and verifies the integrity of the startup disk when the computer is restarted following a crash or abnormal ending (*abend*). The warning dialog self-dismisses after a few moments, unlike in previous versions of the OS when it would stay on screen until dismissed by the user.

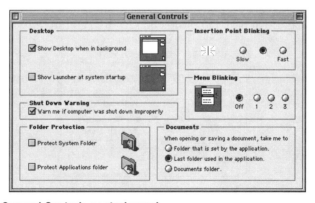

Figure 3.19   The General Controls control panel.

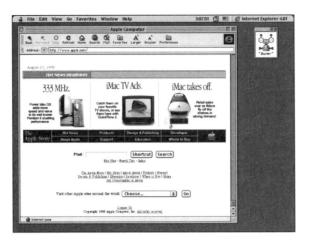

Figure 3.20   Hiding the Desktop when in the background can help clear up a messy environment.

- *Protect System Folder*—When checked, the OS locks down critical areas of the System Folder to prevent unwanted items from being installed into the folder and to prevent critical items from being deleted. This option is only available when File Sharing is turned off.

- *Protect Applications Folder*—Similar to the Protect System Folder option, but for the Applications folder instead.

- *Insertion Point Blinking*—Chooses the blink rate of the insertion point (where you may enter text in a window or document) as slow, medium, or fast.

- *Menu Blinking*—Controls whether or not an item in the Apple menu blinks when selected, and if so, how many times it should blink before opening the selected item. This is a cosmetic feature. Turn it off to enable the fastest response time when selecting an item in the Apple menu.

- *When Opening Or Saving A Document, Take Me To*—Selects the location where the OS will open automatically. If you select Documents folder, a folder will be created at the root level of the startup disk called *Documents if it does not already exist.*

Configuring The Apple Menu

The Apple menu is probably the most recognized avenue for shortcuts and easy access to the contents of your hard drive. In some earlier versions of the OS, the

Apple menu was not hierarchical and therefore displayed only the contents of the Apple Menu Items folder, located in the System Folder, but not subfolders. Fabien Octave wrote a great shareware utility named BeHierarchic (**www.artecnet.com/ BeHierarchic/BeHierarchic.html**) in the early 1990s that provided hierarchical capabilities to the Apple menu, the most basic features of which were included in the Apple menu itself several years ago. Figure 3.21 shows the Apple menu and the Apple Menu Items folder, which holds the contents of the Apple menu.

The Apple menu in Mac OS 8.5 remains the same from previous versions of Mac OS 8. To configure the Apple menu:

1. Open the Apple Menu Options control panel (see Figure 3.22).

2. Turn the Submenus option on or off.

3. Turn the Remember Recently Used Items option on or off and select how many items are to be remembered for each (0 through 99).

4. Close the Apple Menu Options control panel.

Of course, you can add items you want to the Apple menu by moving the original or an alias to the Apple Menu Items folder. Be aware, however, that the OS must cache information about each item or the contents of each folder; therefore, large numbers of items can slow the responsiveness of the Apple menu. Figure 3.23 shows a side-by-side comparison of the Apple menu and the Apple Menu Items folder, including subfolders.

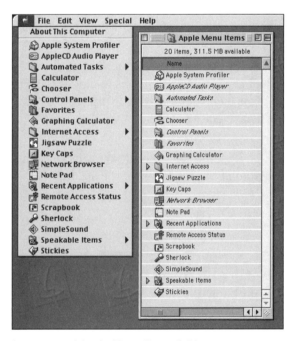

Figure 3.21   The Apple menu and Apple Menu Items folder.

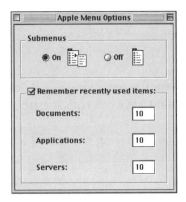

Figure 3.22   The Apple Menu Options control panel.

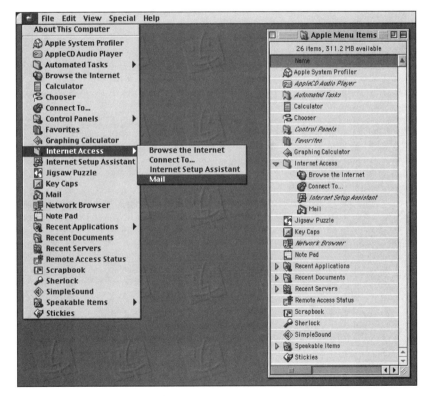

Figure 3.23   A subfolder of the Apple menu.

Using GoMac

GoMac from Proteron, LLC is a great shareware compliment (or replacement) to the Apple menu. It provides all the functionality of the Apple menu; additionally, it adds several features found in other popular operating systems, including a list of active applications. It also has numerous shortcuts to frequently used configuration options and utilities, such as the Sherlock search engine. Figure 3.24 shows several of GoMac's features, including its hierarchical menus, active applications, minimized applications, clock, and calendar (when clicked).

GoMac consists of a control panel and a folder named Start Menu Items (located in the System Folder) that contains the files, folders, and documents that are accessible through the Start menu. Any items placed in this folder appear in the uppermost portion of the Start menu in alphabetical order, with files at the top and folders at the bottom.

To configure GoMac, take these steps:

1. Open the GoMac control panel from the Start menu by choosing Start|Settings|Program Bar (see Figure 3.25).

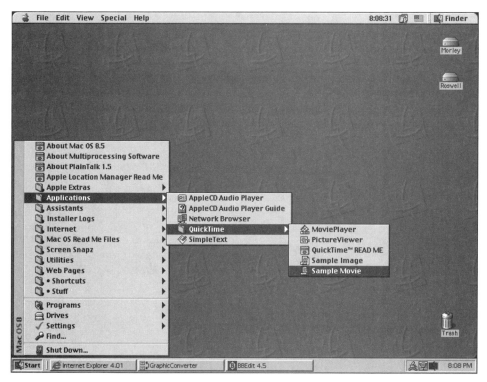

Figure 3.24   GoMac is a great alternative to many of the features of the Apple menu.

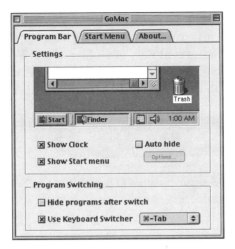

Figure 3.25   The Program Bar configuration tab of the GoMac control panel.

2. Make the configuration options you want in the Program Bar section, such as to show the clock and start menu, as well as to automatically hide the program bar until activated by the mouse.

3. Click on the Start Menu tab, shown in Figure 3.26, and make any configuration options, such as adding a Drives menu to the Start menu and selecting an alternative find utility in place of Sherlock.

4. Close the GoMac control panel and the changes will take place immediately.

GoMac comes with very good documentation and has too many features to cover here. The GoMac installer is located on this book's companion CD-ROM. You can

Figure 3.26   The Start Menu configuration tab of the GoMac control panel.

also download it from the Proteron Web site at **www.proteron.com** along with LiteSwitch, an alternative to Mac OS 8.5's keyboard Application Switcher, which is also on the CD-ROM and is part of GoMac itself. Figure 3.27 shows the program-switching feature of GoMac and LiteSwitch, which uses the key combination of Command+Tab to toggle between applications (which is customizable).

Figure 3.27   The program-switching feature of GoMac and LiteSwitch.

Configuring The Appearance

The new appearance features of Mac OS 8.5 are bound to get the most attention from users because they provide many of the features currently available from the wildly popular Kaleidoscope program (**www.kaleidoscope.net**). Although Kaleidoscope wasn't compatible with Mac OS 8.5 at the time this book went to press, it is reported to be in beta testing and available about the time Mac OS 8.5 ships.

The new Appearance Manager consolidates several features in earlier versions of the Mac OS that affect the user environment, such as the Desktop Pictures and Appearance control panels, into the new Appearance control panel, shown in Figure 3.28.

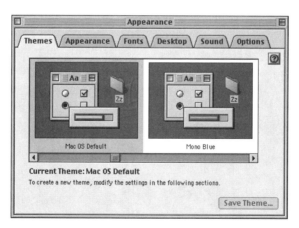

Figure 3.28   The new Appearance control panel consolidates most of the features that affect the look and feel of the Mac OS.

To change the appearance of windows, the Desktop, fonts, and sounds, open the Appearance control panel and select from among these options:

- *Themes*—A collection or set of appearance, font, Desktop pattern or picture, and sound options that can be saved and reloaded. To select a theme, scroll through the list of available themes and click on the theme you want to activate. Figure 3.29 shows the default collection of themes installed by Mac OS 8.5.

  To save your own theme, choose from the available appearances, fonts, Desktop patterns and pictures, and sounds, then return to the Themes tab, choose the Save Theme button, and assign it a name.

- *Appearance*—Choose an appearance that comes with the Mac OS, which forms the basis upon which a theme is created. Currently, only the Apple Platinum appearance is available, but more will become available shortly (see Figure 3.30).

- *Fonts*—Choose fonts (large and small) for system menus and for viewing window lists and underneath icons. Also, Mac OS 8.5 introduces a font-smoothing option that allows fonts over 12 pt. to be anti-aliased for a smooth appearance on the screen (see Figure 3.31).

- *Desktop*—Choose a Desktop pattern or picture to replace the Mac OS Default pattern that displays automatically after installation. To create your own

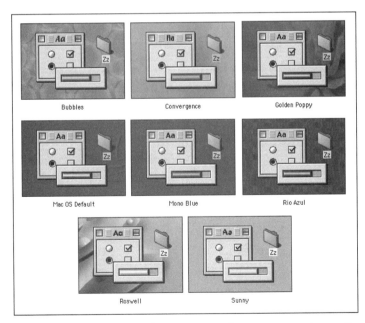

Figure 3.29 Choose from one of these themes, or create your own and save them for quick activation using the Appearance control panel.

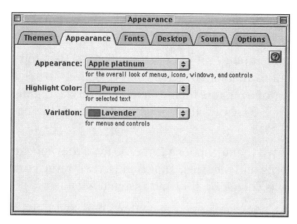

Figure 3.30   Choose an Appearance as the basis of a theme.

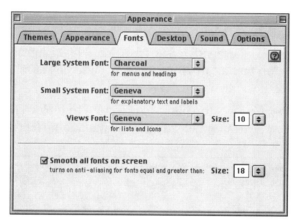

Figure 3.31   The Fonts configuration tab of the Appearance control panel.

pattern, drag a picture to the Desktop preview area shown in Figure 3.32, then choose Edit|Pattern Name to edit the pattern name. To place a picture on the Desktop, repeat this step, or select the Place Picture button and locate a picture, such as those in the Desktop Pictures folder in the Appearance folder in the System Folder. Also, you may drag and drop pictures in several file formats—such as PICT, GIF, and TIFF—onto the System Folder and they will be automatically directed into the Desktop Pictures folder.

To place a different picture on the Desktop every time your Mac is restarted, drag and drop a folder of images in the JPEG format onto the Desktop preview area.

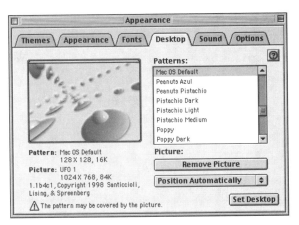

Figure 3.32   The Desktop configuration tab of the Appearance control panel.

- *Sound*—Choose a *sound track*, a collection of optional sound effects that play in conjunction with changes to user environment, including the following:
  - Opening and selecting menu items
  - Dragging and resizing windows
  - Clicking buttons, checkboxes, or scrollbars
  - Finder actions such as clicking, dragging, and dropping

Mac OS 8.5 includes a sound track for the Apple Platinum appearance, as shown in Figure 3.33.

- *Options*—Miscellaneous options that control scrolling and collapsible windows (also called the WindowShade feature), shown in Figure 3.34.

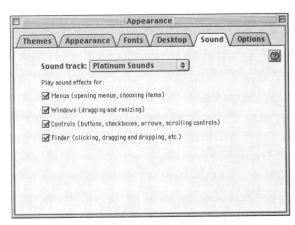

Figure 3.33   The Sound configuration tab of the Appearance control panel.

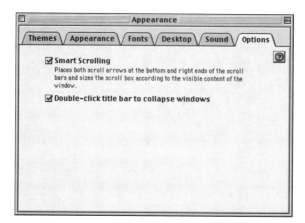

Figure 3.34   The Options configuration tab of the Appearance control panel.

The Smart Scrolling feature has been around for some time, thanks to several third-party utilities, but this marks the first time it has been a part of the Mac OS. This feature places vertical and horizontal scroll arrows in both the bottom and right corners of a window; it also uses *proportional thumbs* to indicate how much of a window's vertical and horizontal areas are visible. These features make navigating windows considerably easier. For example, Figure 3.35 shows two views of the same window with Smart Scrolling off (top) and Smart Scrolling on (bottom). A large proportional thumb indicates that more of a window's contents is visible than not.

The scroll bars are scriptable, and it is possible to add double scroll arrows at both ends of each scroll bar, not just in the lower and right corners, as does the following AppleScript by Mitch Crane:

```
tell application "Appearance"
    set scroll bar arrow style to «constant ****dubl»
    quit
end tell
```

For more AppleScript solutions for the scroll bars and other Appearance features, see Bill Reising's Web site at **www-scf.usc.edu/~reising/**.

Figure 3.35 The Smart Scrolling option provides more scrolling options and visual clues as to the size of a window.

Using The Control Strip

The Control Strip was originally designed to provide PowerBook users with quick access to several of the more frequently used user environment configuration options, such as changing the sound volume or selecting a printer. The Control Strip became so popular that it was included as part of the Mac OS standard installation. Mac OS 8.5 introduces version 2.0 of the Control Strip; you configure it through the Control Strip control panel, shown in Figure 3.36.

Configuring The Control Strip

To configure the Control Strip, take the following steps:

1. Open the Control Strip control panel and select how you want to show, hide, or activate the Control Strip.

2. Select a font for viewing the contents of the Control Strip, then close the control panel.

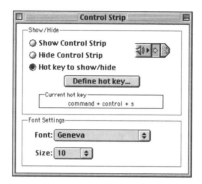

Figure 3.36   The Control Strip control panel.

Many applications and utilities install a Control Strip module to allow you to interact with that application via the Control Strip. To do so, such applications and utilities must install the module in the Control Strip Modules folder located in the System Folder. To disable a particular module, remove it from this folder and restart the computer.

Working With The Control Strip

To use the Control Strip, take these steps:

1. Activate the Control Strip and move it to a desired location on your screen by Option+dragging the Control Strip tab (the end of the strip closest to the center of your screen).

2. Resize the Control Strip horizontally by dragging the tab to show as much or as little as you need.

3. Hide all but the tab by clicking on the square box closest to the screen border.

4. Access a Control Strip module by clicking on any of the items in the Control Strip, as shown in Figure 3.37, which displays a monitor's bit-depth options.

Figure 3.37   The BitDepth Control Strip module.

Configuring The Launcher

The Launcher has also been around for some time, but it has not changed under Mac OS 8.5. It provides quick access to files, folders, and drives in a user-configurable palette. To activate the Launcher, double-click on the Launcher control panel or choose "Show Launcher at system startup" in the General Controls control panel and it will appear as a Finder-like window, as in Figure 3.38.

To configure the contents of the Launcher:

1. Open the Launcher Items folder in the System Folder.

2. Add as many items as you like.

3. To create subcategories in the Launcher, create folders with a bullet (Option+8) as the first character and place them in the Launcher Items folder.

Any items in the root level of the Launcher Items folder (but not in a subfolder) will be accessible in the Applications section of the Launcher. Folders not preceded by a bullet will simply open on the Desktop when clicked in the Launcher. For example, Figure 3.39 shows the Launcher with two items at the root level (Script Editor and SimpleText) and three new subfolders (Apps, Docs, and Utilities).

Figure 3.38 The Launcher and its default contents.

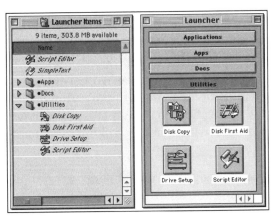

Figure 3.39 A customized Launcher with items at the root level and several customized subcategories.

Using The Simple Finder

The Simple Finder is a feature that removes Finder menu items that aren't used as frequently by some users. This is an ideal user-environment feature for schools and computer clusters where people with low skill levels have inquiring minds and want to explore all of the Mac OS menus and features. Figure 3.40 shows the File menu before (left) and after (right) the Simple Finder option has been activated.

To activate the Simple Finder, follow these steps:

1. Activate the Finder and select Edit|Preferences.
2. Select the General preferences tab and select the Simple Finder option.
3. Close the Preferences window.

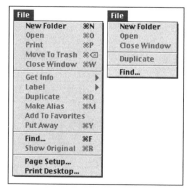

Figure 3.40   The Simple Finder deactivates several menu options in the Finder, which is useful for young or inexperienced users.

Configuring The Applications Switcher

The Application Switcher has been enhanced in several ways in Mac OS 8.5, as we've already seen in "Switching Among Applications" in Chapter 1. You can select, hide, and show applications in the Application Switcher, as well as "tear off" the menu and place it elsewhere on the Desktop as a floating window, as shown in Figure 3.41.

However, you may also change the configuration of the Application Switcher once it has been torn off, as well as use AppleScript to change its appearance even more. Some of the actions to change the Application Switcher include the following (after tearing off the menu):

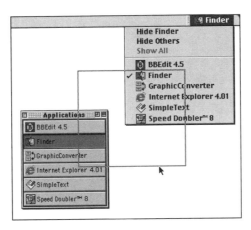

Figure 3.41   Tearing off the Application Switcher.

- *View by small icon and name*—(Default).
- *View by small icon*—Click on the Zoombox.
- *View by large icon and name*—Option+click on the Zoombox.
- *View by large icon*—Click on the Zoombox, then Option+click the Zoombox.
- *View horizontally by small icon and name*—Shift+Option+click on the Zoombox.
- *View horizontally by small icon*—Shift+Option+click on the Zoombox, then click on the Zoombox.
- *View horizontally by large icon and name*—Shift+Option+click on the Zoombox, then Option+click the Zoombox.
- *View horizontally by large icon*—Shift+Option+click on the Zoombox, click on the Zoombox, then Option+click on the Zoombox.

This may be a bit confusing, but remember that you can view the Application Switcher by name and icon, large or small, and vertically or horizontally. You can also hold down the Option key and resize the width (but not height) of the applications menu. Figure 3.42 shows all the viewing options previously listed.

You can also use AppleScript to hide the title bar, display items in the order they were launched (rather than alphabetically), as well as position the Application menu in a specific location on the screen, such as the lower left. You can also Command+drag the Application Switcher anywhere on the screen.

To test these options, open the Help Viewer and search for the term "Application Switcher." Scroll to the bottom and select the options entitled "Open the Application Switcher in a horizontal row in the lower-left corner of the screen and make

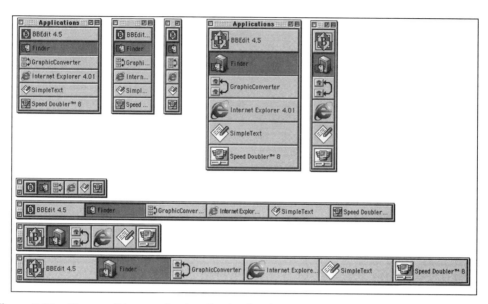

Figure 3.42   The possible ways to view the Application Switcher without using an AppleScript.

the window always remain on screen" and "Open the Application Switcher in icon view in the lower-right corner and list programs in the order in which they were opened". Figure 3.43 shows how these two options appear when clicked from within the Help Viewer. For more information on scripting the Application Switcher, follow the links provided.

The AppleScripts that control these actions are located on your hard drive as compiled scripts. To find them, search for the term "AppSwitcher" and open them using the Script Editor. See the AppleScript chapter for more details on using the Script Editor.

To use the Application Switcher:

1. Click on any of the buttons that appear in the Application Switcher to switch to that application.

2. Option+click on any of the buttons that appear in the Application Switcher to switch to that application and hide all the others. Option+selecting an

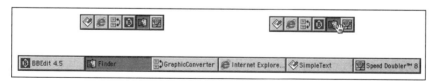

Figure 3.43   You can use AppleScript demos in the Help viewer to further enhance the
Application Switcher.

item from the normal Application menu also automatically hides all other applications as well.

3. Click on the close box to hide the Application Switcher from view.

Finally, if you want to try an application to perform most of these tasks, try Mitch Crane's Switcher PowerUp at **www.mindspring.com/~sublink/swpu.html**.

Configuring Speech Recognition

The Speech Manager is installed as part of Mac OS 8.5, which allows the computer to speak alerts in one of several voices. Speech recognition, which isn't installed by default, has the capability to recognize human speech and execute commands in response. You can install it from the Mac OS 8.5 CD-ROM at any time by using the Add/Remove feature (choose English Speech recognition), and you can temporarily disable it by using the Extension Manager control panel.

Setting Up Speech Recognition

Speakable alerts requires the basic speech software to be installed (Speech Manager extension and the Speech control panel). Speech recognition requires the full speech package to be installed (the Speakable Items folder, Speech Manager extension, and Speech control panel), as well as a PlainTalk microphone. To configure speech recognition once it has been installed:

1. Open the Speech control panel, shown in Figure 3.44.

2. Select a voice for the computer from the Voice section, clicking on the speaker icon to hear a sample of the chosen voice.

3. Configure a hotkey combination to enable/disable speech recognition on a temporary basis in the Listening section, as well as to give the computer a name. You may require the computer to listen for a command when the hotkeys are pressed and only after you first speak the computer's name.

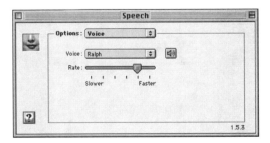

Figure 3.44   The Speech control panel.

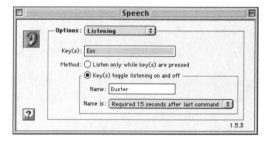

Figure 3.45   Speech recognition options for how the computer should listen for commands.

Please note that some names, especially monosyllabic names like Ralph, are difficult for the Mac OS to recognize, so it will prompt you to assign the computer a different name (see Figure 3.45).

4. In the Feedback section of the control panel, select a character (or persona) to go along with the voice you have already selected; also, select what the computer should do to let you know that the command you have issued was understood and will be executed. Figure 3.46 shows the Feedback section of the Speech control panel.

5. Finally, configure the Speakable Items section (see Figure 3.47) to allow you to issue commands located in the Speakable Items folder (see Figure 3.48), which is installed in the System Folder. Close the control panel when you are finished.

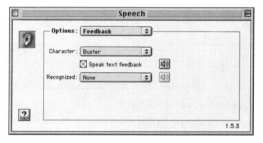

Figure 3.46   The Feedback section of the Speech control panel.

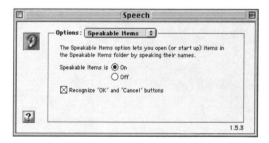

Figure 3.47   The Speakable Items section provides access to the Speakable Items folder.

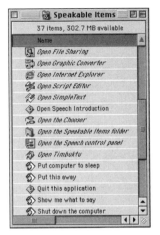

Figure 3.48   The Speakable Items folder contains commands that the Speech Manager
can execute.

Using Voice Commands

To issue a voice command, follow these steps:

1. Place the microphone above the speech character window, shown in Figure 3.49.

2. Speak clearly and in a normal tone and ask the computer "What time is it?"

3. Sound waves will appear beside the character's ears to indicate the microphone is working, and if the command is understood, it will be displayed in the window and then executed, as shown in Figure 3.50 on page 90.

To add an item to the list of executable commands, place an alias to the command in the Speakable Items folder and rename it "Open <application, document, or folder>." To have the command executed by saying *"Open* <application, document, or folder>". Or, to create an easy command, open the Script Editor and type *say "Howdy, partner!"* and save it as an application named "Hello". When you say "Hello" to the computer, it will respond with "Howdy partner!"

Figure 3.49   The speech character window displays your computer's persona and gives visual
clues to its ability to listen for and execute voice commands.

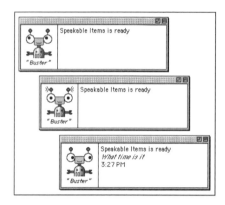

Figure 3.50   A command is successfully understood and executed.

Changing Finder Window Views

You can view Finder windows for folders and disks in the Mac OS as regular or pop-up windows; you can view the contents of each window as icons, as a hierarchical list, or as buttons, depending on the options selected for that window in the View menu.

To change the viewing options for a window, take these steps:

1. Open a folder or disk in the Finder.

2. Activate the View menu, shown in Figure 3.51, and select one of the following:

   • As Icons

   • As Buttons

   • As A List

3. Next, select one of the following options:

   • As A Window

   • As A Pop-Up Window

You can optionally drag any window to the bottom of the screen that is free of other pop-up window tabs and it will automatically turn into a pop-up window.

3: The User Environment

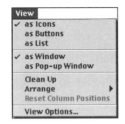

Figure 3.51   Selecting a window view.

Setting Finder Window Preferences And Views

One of two new Mac OS 8.5 features relating to viewing Finder windows is the capability of setting viewing preferences for icon, button, and list views of Finder windows. In pre-Mac OS 8 versions of the OS, it was possible to set a global view for windows, but this ability was lacking in 8.0 and 8.1.

Configuring Finder Window Preferences

Now, you can set global preferences, such as setting all button views to use large buttons, as well as allow any particular window to override such a preference and use small buttons instead. To set Finder window view preferences, follow these steps:

1. In the Finder, choose Edit|Preferences.

2. Select the Views tab, shown in Figure 3.52.

3. Make any desired view preferences, then close the Preferences window.

Figure 3.52   Setting default view preferences for windows viewed as a list.

Overriding Window View Preferences

To override the preferences for a window view, follow these steps:

1. Select a window in the Finder.

2. Select View|Arrange and choose to arrange (with icons) or sort (with lists) the contents of the folder accordingly, as shown in Figure 3.53.

3. Next, select View|View Options, as shown in Figure 3.54, and fine-tune your icon, button, or list window.

Reverting To The Default Window View Preferences

To revert to the viewing preferences for a specific type of window (icon, button, or list), take the following steps:

1. Select a window.

2. Choose View|View Options.

3. Select the Set to Standard Views button (which will be inactive if the current window is already viewed using the preferences defined in the Views tab of the Edit|Preferences menu).

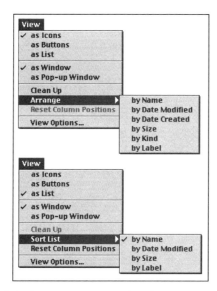

Figure 3.53   Arranging and sorting the contents of a window.

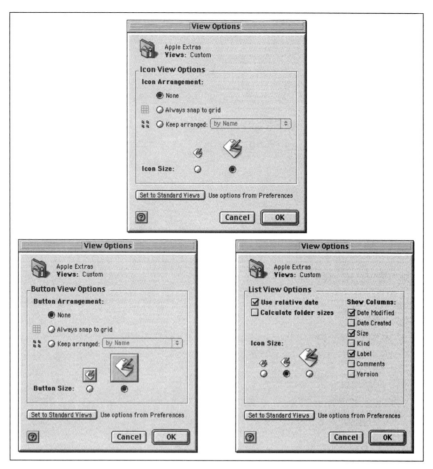

Figure 3.54   The options for viewing icon, button, and list windows.

Rearranging And Resizing Window Columns

A second—and very cool—feature that is new to Mac OS 8.5 is the capability to resize and reorder columns of list view windows, not just sort them by clicking on the column heading (Name, Date Modified, Size, and so on). Third-party utilities such as CoolViews from Quadratic Software (**www.quadratic.com**) have offered these features before; now, you can drag and drop columns to reorder them, as well as click and drag column margins to resize their widths.

Reordering Columns

To reorder columns in a list window, take the following steps:

1. Open a folder or disk window and view it as a list.

2. Drag a column heading such as the Date Modified or Kind and drop it onto any other heading except the Name heading, which will always appear first (on the left) in a list window.

For example, Figure 3.55 shows the Kind heading before, during, and after it has been reordered to appear second in the list instead of fourth.

You may also resize the width of a column, and like with rearranging their order, the changes you make to the columns' widths will remain until you select the Set to Standard Views button.

Resizing Column Width

To resize the width of a column:

1. Open a folder or disk window and view it as a list.

2. Drag the right margin indicator in a column heading to the desired width, then release it.

For example, Figure 3.56 shows a before (top) and after (bottom) view of a window whose columns have been resized. Note the changes in the date formats from long, where room is available for it to be viewed and abbreviated to short, where not enough room is available.

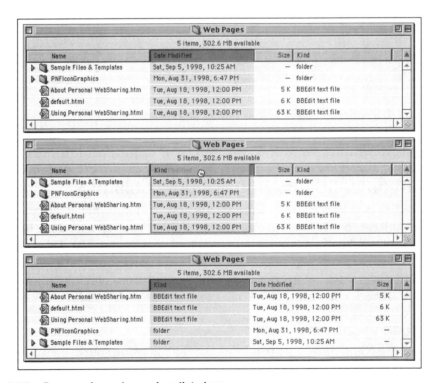

Figure 3.55   Rearranging columns in a list view.

3: The User Environment

Figure 3.56   Resizing columns.

Using Window Shortcuts

We've already seen how to view folder windows under Mac OS 8.5 in Chapter 1, but here are a few shortcuts and new features that make the user environment even more useful in Mac OS 8.5.

Collapsing Windows

You can collapse one or all open windows (the old WindowShade feature) to save room on your Desktop for viewing other elements, such as the Desktop itself, or simply to unclutter your screen. This feature works with all Finder windows, as well as with most application windows.

To collapse a window, follow these steps:

1. Select a window.
2. Double-click on the title bar (if enabled in the Options tab of the Appearance control panel).
3. Optionally, single-click on the collapse box (see Figure 3.57).

Figure 3.57   Collapsing a single window.

3: The User Environment

To collapse multiple windows, take the following steps:

1. Select any open window.

2. Option+double-click on the title bar (if enabled in the Options tab of the Appearance control panel).

    Alternatively, Option+click on the collapse box.

To undo this action, just repeat it.

Navigating Backwards Within A Folder

Another shortcut that has been available for some time but isn't well known to many users is the capability to navigate backwards through a folder hierarchy. To do so, hold down the Command key on the title bar, as shown in Figure 3.58.

To navigate backwards from within a folder, take these steps:

1. Command+click on the window title until a pop-up menu appears.

2. Select a folder, then release the mouse button.

3. Choose Option+Command+click to navigate and close the current folder when the mouse is released.

Manipulating The Icon Proxy

Another new shortcut is the capability to move, copy, or alias a folder (by dragging, Command+dragging, or Option+Command+dragging the icon proxy—the small icon in the title bar) to another location, as in Figure 3.59.

To use an icon proxy, do the following:

1. Open a window.

2. Click and hold the mouse on the icon proxy.

3. While holding down the mouse, you can do one of the following:

    • Drag the icon proxy elsewhere to move the folder.

    • Drag the icon proxy to another volume to copy it to that volume.

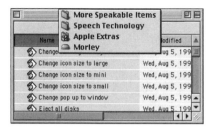

Figure 3.58   Command+click the window title to reveal the folder's path and to navigate backwards through it.

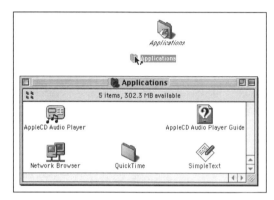

Figure 3.59   Using an icon proxy to create an alias of a folder on the Desktop.

- Option+drag the icon proxy to copy the folder onto the same volume as the original.
- Option+Command+drag the icon proxy to make an alias of the folder.

Using The Command Key To Scroll

Mac OS 8.5 also introduces a new way to scroll through windows without using the scroll bar, an example of which can be seen in the hand-style cursor in place of the traditional pointer in Figure 3.60. This can be useful if you have a multi-button mouse. You can assign a secondary mouse button to emulate the Command key, which allows you to more easily target the entire window region for scrolling rather than the narrow scroll regions at the left and bottom of each window.

To scroll by using the Command key, take these steps:

1. Open any window to an icon, button, or list view.

2. Command+drag any portion of the active window region (but not the title, scroll, or header areas).

3. Drag along the vertical or horizontal axes, and the window will scroll as if you were moving the window itself instead of its contents. The scroll bars will move in the reverse direction, which is a little confusing at first.

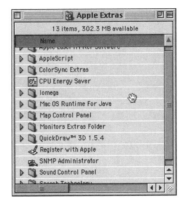

Figure 3.60   Command+dragging a list view allows you to scroll.

Additional Sorting Options

Finally, you can also reverse the order in which a list is viewed by clicking on the small triangle (the *Sort button*) in the upper-right side of the window as shown in Figure 3.61.

When selecting the Sort button:

- Lists viewed by Name will be alphabetized in reverse.

- Lists viewed by Date Modified will be sorted in reverse chronological order (newest to oldest).

- Lists viewed by Date Created will be sorted in reverse chronological order (newest to oldest).

- Lists viewed by Size will be sorted smallest to largest, with folders listed first.

- Lists viewed by Kind will be alphabetized in reverse by kind (utility, document, application).

- Lists viewed by Comments will be alphabetized in reverse according to the first character in the Comment field in the Get Info dialog window.

- Lists viewed by Version will be in reverse numerical order (3.3, 2.2, and 1.1).

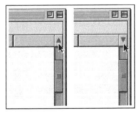

Figure 3.61   Reverse the sort order of any list by clicking on the Sort button.

Using Navigational Services

Mac OS 8.5 uses a new dialog window for opening and saving files that is a tremendous improvement over previous versions of the Mac OS. However, only those applications and utilities that have been specifically programmed to take advantage of these features will be able to display the new dialog windows. For example, Figure 3.62 shows the new navigational services in the Appearance control panel (top) and the standard Open dialog window of SimpleText (bottom).

The advantages to the open and save dialog windows provided by the new navigational services are as follows:

- The entire dialog window is resizable, vertically and horizontally.

- The dialog box is no longer modal, which allows you to move to another application or view the Desktop while the Open or Save dialog window is still active.

- A more window-like interface displays your current location and the path to the folder, such as Option+clicking on a window's title bar.

- List items are sortable by name and date modified and are hierarchically expandable.

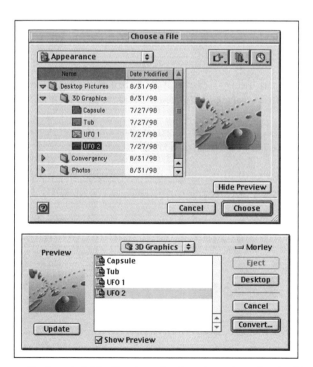

Figure 3.62   The new (top) and old (bottom) navigational services for the Mac OS.

- You can easily jump to the Desktop, mounted volumes, AppleTalk and AppleShare IP server and volumes by using the Shortcuts button.

- You can easily access your Favorites folder by using the Favorites button.

- You can quickly locate recently used files and documents by using the Recent button.

- You can easily access the Help viewer.

Using Default Folder And ACTION Files

Two great Mac OS supplements to the open and save dialog windows are Default Folder from St. Clair Software (**www.stclairsoft.com**) and ACTION Files! from Power On Software (**www.poweronsoftware.com**). Each provides some rather unique features to enhance the user environment, including all the features of the new navigational services, and many more.

Default Folder has a small control panel that adds three buttons to every open and save dialog window to allow highly configurable shortcuts to sets of your favorite folders. Webmasters and HTML developers will especially appreciate the ability to create multiple sets of favorite folders for different projects, for example. Figure 3.63 shows how the Default Folder shortcut buttons appear when using SimpleText to open a file.

The three buttons added by Default Folder are shown at the center of Figure 3.64, with their respective menus, to better illustrate some of its features.

Default Folder is highly configurable, of course, and may look different depending on the features that are enabled or disabled.

ACTION Files also provides many more features than does Mac OS 8.5's new navigational services, but the user interface alone is worth trying it out. Shown in

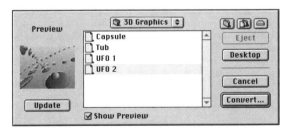

Figure 3.63   Access Default Folder's shortcuts and menu items, using the three small buttons added to every open and save dialog window and dialog box.

3: The User Environment

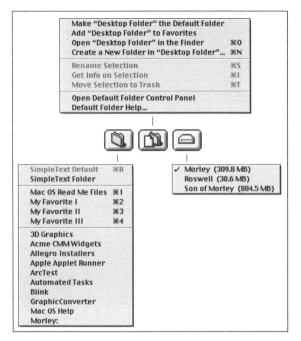

Figure 3.64   Default Folder's three menus.

Figure 3.65, ACTION Files uses a whole new way of displaying dialog windows by adding a much more Finder-like list view to represent the contents of a folder. It even comes with a Find utility that allows you to search for a file even while the open or save dialog window itself is open.

Both Default Folder and ACTION Files have far too many features to mention here. They are, however, on this book's CD-ROM, and we urge you to try them out, along with GoMac, to sample ways in which you can further enhance the Mac OS user environment.

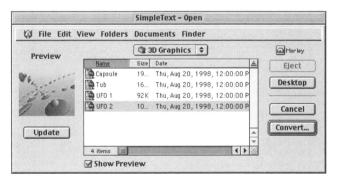

Figure 3.65   ACTION Files greatly enhances all Open and Save dialog boxes.

Chapter 4

Installation And Basic Configuration

In Depth

Operating systems have gotten larger and more complicated. Components must be in the proper place within the structure of the operating system. If they aren't, the system or programs installed on the computer may not run properly. The days are gone when you could drag a couple of folders onto your hard drive and upgrade the operating system. You now launch an Installer that is scripted to place the parts of the system in the proper places and install the operating system appropriate for your computer. Of course, some users still try to cheat and copy a System Folder to the hard drive, only to see a range of problems from constant system errors to a computer that will not boot.

In spite of the complexity of the system, Apple has made it very easy to install Mac OS 8.5. Although the installer has automated the process, you still need to do some things to prepare for the upgrade and make certain decisions during the installation process.

Before You Install

It's tempting to snap that Mac OS 8.5 CD-ROM in the drive and launch the installer, but you need to take steps to prepare your computer. Most Mac OS installations do run quite smoothly in spite of the lack of preparation by the user, but in some cases you can experience serious problems or conflicts. You can reduce the odds of serious problems with the new installation by getting your computer in the best possible shape.

Repair Your Disk

Make sure that your hard drive is as free as possible of system problems. If you have been experiencing problems with your system, run Disk First Aid or some kind of disk repair and recovery utility and repair these problems. Disk First Aid can repair many problems, but some are beyond this program's abilities and you may need to use a commercial utility such as Norton Utilities or TechTool Pro. Disk errors can carry over to the new system and continue to cause problems.

Even if your system has been operating well, you should run a disk repair utility to check system integrity. Your hard drive may contain lots of little errors that haven't been severe enough for you to notice.

Clean Your System Folder

Go through the System Folder and remove files that you no longer need. Check the folders containing disabled extensions or control panels first. These files are not in use, possibly because you disabled the file, or more importantly, because the program disabled itself (which means the program can't run at all). Remove these files if you no longer need them, and contact the software company for an upgrade.

Check the Preferences folder as well. Remember that almost any program that you run on your computer generates a preference, even if you immediately delete the application. The items in this folder can be extensive, especially if you have used the computer for a while or have lots of little programs and utilities running. Your best approach with the Preferences folder is to remove preferences for programs that you know you have removed. If you don't recognize the file name, don't remove the preference. You may be tempted to just drag the entire contents of the Preferences folder to the trash, but avoid this unless your system is hopelessly corrupted. Many applications require that you enter a serial or registration number before the program will run. This information is often stored in the program's preference file. If you don't have this number handy, you may not be able to run your application again.

Be cautious when you check the Extensions and control panels folders. Don't delete a file unless you know what it does. Some of the file names can be rather cryptic, especially extensions. If you have a program that you want to delete, try running the installer for the program again. Many of these installers allow you to remove the application as well as install it. This option is usually located within the custom options for the program installer. You may also want to use a utility that can intelligently search the hard drive for all the files that accompany an application. Yank from Maui Software can remove an application and the files associated with it to the trash. It can also find outdated or orphaned preferences and move them to the trash.

Check Your Hardware

Take the time now to check out your hardware and make sure that you can meet the system requirements for Mac OS 8.5. Some changes from Mac OS 8 have occurred. One of the biggest changes with Mac OS 8.5 is that the computer itself must be a Power Macintosh. The 68K architecture is no longer supported. Apple also indicates that the computer must have been manufactured as a Power Macintosh computer. Mac OS 8.5 is not supported for 68K systems upgraded to a Power Macintosh. You may also want to watch out for problems if you have installed an accelerator card in an older Power Mac such as the 6100, 7100, 8100, or 9150. The main installer may not run. If so, Apple recommends that you run the installer for each part of the system individually. These installers are available in the Software Installers folder. If you have a Performa model in the 5200, 5300, 6200, or 6300 series, you need to run a program called 5xxx/6xxx Tester that is included with Mac OS 8.5. This test determines if your computer needs a hardware repair. You don't need to run this test on the Performa 5260, 6320, or 6360 models.

Check your available disk space. The Mac OS 8.5 installation requires approximately 180MB of disk space (even more if you install additional software utilities). The amount of disk space you have free determines the kind of Mac OS installation you perform. Also, make sure that you have adequate memory installed on your computer. Most Macintosh computers sold today include at least 32MB of memory. If you have less, you can purchase additional memory at very competitive prices. In all fairness, you can install Mac OS 8.5 on systems with less than 32MB of memory, but you need to run Virtual Memory to make up the memory difference. Be prepared for a system-wide performance hit if you run Mac OS 8.5 under these conditions.

Back Up Your Hard Drive

In most cases, upgrades are relatively painless and simple. But you should prepare for problems by at least backing up your System Folder. You may not know which third-party software will conflict with the new system. By backing up the System Folder, you can restore the computer to its original state if you find that you must run the conflicting software. You can also plan to perform a Clean Installation of Mac OS 8.5. If you encounter problems after the upgrade, you can easily remove the new system and return to the older operating system. Clean Installation instructions are included in the section "Performing A Clean Installation."

Review Your Documentation

If documentation accompanies the installation software, make sure that you read and review it. It may contain important information that was not included in the printed manual (usually due to publishing time constraints). These documents may indicate possible conflicts between Mac OS 8.5 and other kinds of applications.

Installation Media

Usually, you will install Mac OS 8.5 from a CD-ROM. This medium is excellent for installing the operating system because the CD-ROM includes its own System Folder, which allows you to boot from the CD-ROM drive. You can also run the installation from other removable media such as Zip, Jaz, or Syquest cartridges.

4: Installation And Basic Configuration

Be aware that the Mac OS install program accesses individual installers for each component of the system. If you use a Zip cartridge, you need to bypass the main installer program and run individual installers.

You can also install Mac OS 8.5 from a network server. The software may be stored on the server itself, or the Mac OS 8.5 installation CD-ROM may be accessible from the network. In either case, running the Mac OS 8.5 installation from a network server behaves almost the same as installing it from the local CD drive.

Mac OS 8.5 is a major system release. However, Apple will release a slight update to the Mac OS within the next six months. When this update is ready, you will be able to download it from the Apple software archive. The update includes an Installer similar to the one used with a major system release. This update usually fixes program bugs and provides system enhancements; you may not see major system changes with an update. However, the Mac OS will be undergoing major revisions over the next year and updates may include major system changes as the Mac OS moves toward release 10 (Mac OS X).

Booting For OS Installations

If possible, boot from a media or partition other than the disk of the system you want to upgrade. You have the best chance of overwriting all the components successfully. You can boot from another hard drive partition if it has a system or a floppy, CD-ROM, or other removable media, as long as a system is on the media. If you must boot from the system you intend to upgrade, make sure that the following factors are in place:

- Boot with all non-Apple extensions off. This reduces the risk that a third-party program will interfere or conflict with the installation process.

- Disable all security software such as At Ease or FolderBolt Pro. They interfere with the installation of the new software.

- Disable all virus protection software. If you are paranoid, run a virus check on the media that contains the Mac OS installation software as well as on your own system, then reboot with the virus protection disabled.

- If you are upgrading the system on a PowerBook, make sure that you have the power adapter plugged into the computer. The installation process can be rather long and you don't want the battery to die in the middle of your system upgrade.

- Don't attempt to install Mac OS 8.5 on a PowerBook operating in SCSI mode. The installer retrieves information about the computer and tailors the operating system to the type of computer during the installation. The Installer treats the PowerBook the same way as the computer to which the PowerBook is attached.

One other step in the installation process that you should watch is the task of updating the hard-disk driver. In the past, most hard drives were formatted at the factory by Apple. Today, many users purchase larger hard drives without upgrading the system and probably use a non-Apple hard disk driver. During the installation, the installer will attempt to upgrade the hard disk driver. If the Installer cannot upgrade the driver, contact the company that manufactured your hard drive for a driver update.

Installation Options

Now that you are ready to upgrade the system, you want to take steps to ensure that the upgrade is accomplished as simply and as quickly as possible. Two kinds of installation methods are possible—reinstallation and clean installation—and each method has merits.

Reinstallation

The most popular and easiest upgrade method is to install the upgrade on top of your existing system, allowing it to overwrite and update files. This is the simplest and fastest of the upgrade methods. When you restart your computer, your operating system will be upgraded and still have the additional software that you installed.

By default, the installer reinstalls the software. All old versions of existing programs are overwritten by newer versions. When you launch the Mac OS Install program, you are greeted with a Welcome window that generally explains the steps you follow to upgrade your software. Figure 4.1 shows the install Welcome window.

Figure 4.1   The Welcome window for installing Mac OS 8.5.

The Select Destination window shows a destination disk. You can indicate another partition or medium. You can even install a minimum system on a Zip disk. The Mac OS install software displays information about the destination disk, such as the current operating system version and how much disk space is free, as shown in Figure 4.2. You can see if you have enough disk space available to perform a basic installation. Don't despair if this screen indicates that you don't have enough disk space. You can still perform a minimum system installation. Instructions are included later in this section.

If you are reinstalling Mac OS 8.5 on top of an existing Mac OS 8.5 system, you will see the dialog box shown in Figure 4.3. You can choose to cancel the installation, reinstall Mac OS 8.5, or add or remove components of Mac OS 8.5.

After you have selected an installation disk, the Mac OS Install program gives you an opportunity to read some information about installing Mac OS 8.5. This document is very important because it contains late-breaking information about changes in the operating system or possible conflicts with older software. You should read this document carefully to confirm that you can install Mac OS 8.5. If you don't like to read long documents on a monitor, print the document.

Figure 4.2   Selecting a destination disk.

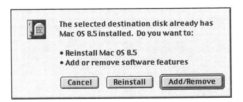

Figure 4.3   The dialog box for overwriting the same operating system.

As you continue through the installation, you will be presented with the license for using this software. You must agree to this license to install Mac OS 8.5. Although much of the license is filled with legal terms and written in "legalese," you should review it. For example, if you purchased Mac OS 8.5, the license says you can install the program on only one computer. Don't be annoyed with this screen; when you install Windows 98 you must enter a 16-digit product code before you can use the operating system. Apple is being extremely nice; for the sake of all Mac OS users, you should abide by this license.

After you accept the terms of the license, you can begin installing the software. However, you can set some additional parameters. When you perform the installation of a new operating system over an existing one, you may not know what files have been changed or upgraded. You can track this in the following two ways:

- Before you run the installation, change the labels on your system files, especially extensions and control panels, to something other than *none*. After the installation, files that were changed will no longer have the label you designated.

- Set the option in the Mac OS install program to create an Installation Report. This report lists all changes to files on your computer during the installation. This option is enabled by default. To confirm it, simply click on the Options button on the Install Software window (see Figure 4.4). You should see a check in the Create Installation Report box.

The other parameter within this window is the option to update the hard disk driver. If your hard drive was formatted with a non-Apple utility, you should disable this option. If you leave it enabled, you will receive an error message that the hard disk driver could not be updated (you can still continue with the installation). If you know the formatting utility used on your hard drive, you should contact the company that developed the utility for information on updated hard-disk drivers. You can then update your disk driver manually. However, if you

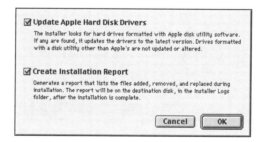

Figure 4.4   The option is enabled to create an installation report.

formatted your hard disk with an Apple utility, you should leave this option enabled. Updating the driver improves the interaction between the hard disk and the operating system, and in some cases, if you don't update the hard disk driver, you could experience serious problems with the new operating system.

By default, the following system components are installed with a basic Mac OS 8.5 installation:

- *Mac OS 8.5*—Includes the basic operating system.

- *Internet Access*—Installs software used for accessing the Internet, such as Web browsers and email software.

- *Apple Remote Access*—Installs software used for establishing PPP connections using a modem.

- *Personal Web Sharing*—Installs software that allows you to easily enable Web services on your Mac.

- *QuickDraw 3D*—Installs software that allows you to manipulate and view 3D images.

- *Text-to-Speech*—Installs software that allows your computer to read alert messages and other documents to you.

- *Mac OS Runtime for Java*—Installs software that allows your Mac to run Java applications.

- *ColorSync*—Installs software that allows you to produce accurate color images both on screen and in print.

At this point, you can begin the Mac OS 8.5 installation. You can also customize the installation and add or remove components. Instructions for customizing the installation are included in "Customizing The Installation" later in this chapter. As the installation begins, the Installer program gathers information about your system and installs the appropriate operating system for it. When this installation is finished, the operating system will be upgraded.

You must restart the computer to begin using it. Upon restart, the Desktop File may be automatically rebuilt and the Mac OS Setup assistant may run. You can use this program to configure your Mac with your network parameters or exit the program and perform the tasks manually. After the Mac OS Setup assistant has finished running, you can begin using Mac OS 8.5. Your previous extensions and control panels should be enabled. If not, you can use the Extensions Manager control panel to enable them and restart the computer. If these system files are compatible with Mac OS 8.5, you should see little or no difference in their function.

However, reinstallation can produce unexpected results. Control panels and extensions may not run under the new system. Ram Doubler and Speed Doubler (from Connectix) usually require an upgrade to the software to run successfully under a major upgrade. Screen savers such as After Dark from Berkeley Systems also may have problems. If you encounter conflicts with your software, contact the manufacturer for upgrade information.

Clean Installation

If you are concerned about possible conflicts with existing software on your computer and Mac OS 8.5 or if you want to start off the era of Mac OS 8.5 on your computer with a clean slate, you should consider performing a *clean installation*. A clean installation differs from a reinstallation in that your old system software components are not overwritten or carried over to the new Mac OS. The Mac OS Install program disables your current System Folder and renames System Folder to Previous System Folder. All of your software will be located in this folder and will be inactive.

Differing schools of thought exist on whether you should perform a clean installation or not. Some feel it is only necessary if you performed a reinstallation but encountered problems with the new system. Others feel you should do it with every major upgrade. The reason for this disagreement is that performing a clean installation is very easy. Reconfiguring your System Folder afterwards is not. It is quite labor-intensive and is definitely not something that new users should attempt without clear instructions. We recommend that you consider a clean installation if you are performing a major upgrade (for example: from System 7.X to Mac OS 8.X) or if you have not thoroughly cleaned out your system in the last 18 months. Of course, you would also want to consider it as a troubleshooting method for an unsuccessful installation of Mac OS 8.5 on a previous operating system.

The option to perform a clean installation is encountered early in the installation process, but may not be very obvious. You will find it within the Options button on the Disk Selection window. Figure 4.5 shows the option that allows you to perform a clean installation. By default, it is not enabled. You must manually choose this option to create a completely new System Folder.

After you enable this option, the rest of the installation process is the same as a reinstallation. However, after you restart your computer, begin placing the items from within the Previous System Folder into the new System Folder. Before you begin moving items, label all the files in your clean System Folder. This differentiates them visually from the files you will be adding. As we said, this process takes time and if you are not careful, you may forget to move an item from one folder to the other. Compare each System Folder, and move files that are found in

4: Installation And Basic Configuration

Figure 4.5   The option to perform a clean installation.

the Previous System Folder—but not in the new System Folder—to the newer folder. Do not overwrite files in the new System Folder. The exception to this suggestion is preferences files. For example, you can replace the new TCP/IP preference with the TCP/IP preference file from your Previous System Folder. This eliminates having to reconfigure TCP/IP. When you have placed the items in the new System Folder, restart the computer and see if you encounter problems. For example, you may need to reenter the serial number for some of your applications (some developers attempt to prevent software piracy by disabling the capability to move a preference to another System Folder). You should also try reinstalling the software program that is causing your problems. Some software applications will not function if they are moved from one System Folder to another. If you encounter severe system extension conflicts, contact the manufacturer of the software for an upgrade.

Minimum Installation

You may have removed every piece of extraneous fluff from your hard drive, yet not have enough disk space available to do a basic Mac OS 8.5 installation. Or, perhaps you want to create a bootable Zip disk. Zip disks have only 100MB of total space and could not contain a basic Mac OS 8.5 installation. You can instead perform a minimum installation. You won't have many of the fancy bells and whistles of Mac OS 8.5, but you can at least boot a computer with the disk.

Although the Mac OS install program will tell you if you do not have enough space for a basic installation, it will allow you to proceed with the installation. You will eventually reach the Install Software window. Normally, you would click on the Start button, but to perform a minimum installation, you click on the Customize button. A window lists all components of Mac OS 8.5 that are being installed. Beside each component is a pop-up menu, which allows three options: Recommended Installation, Customized Installation, and Customized Removal. To perform a minimum installation of Mac OS 8.5, click on the pop-up menu beside Mac OS 8.5 and choose Customized Installation. The window shown in Figure 4.6 appears. Select Core System Software, which uses a little more than 13MB of disk space. If you are installing Mac OS 8.3 on a removable disk such as a Syquest, Imation, or Zip disk, you have a lot more space and can probably do a Universal

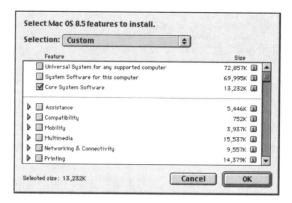

Figure 4.6   The Customized Installation options for Mac OS 8.5 system software.

system installation. You can then boot almost any computer supported by Mac OS 8.5.

Customizing The Installation

Previously in this chapter, we showed you the list of components that the Mac OS Install program includes by default. You may not need some of the listed components. Perhaps you are satisfied with your email and browser programs and would prefer to disable that option. You must also manually enable other components that are not enabled by default. Each of these software components has its own Installer and installation options. You can configure each component with the settings you desire. Simply push the Customize button on the Install Software window. You will see the listing shown in Figure 4.7.

You can find out general information about each component by clicking on the small "*i*" button. In a small window, an explanation appears of what is being

Figure 4.7   The Customize window.

installed and how much space the installation will take. To enable or disable a component, simply add or remove the checkmark beside it. You can further customize all these options. An installation mode pop-up menu lies beside each option. Click on the menu and select Customized Installation to see exactly what will be included with or can be added to the individual component installation. For example, the default Web browser installed with Mac OS 8.5 is Microsoft Internet Explorer. However, by customizing the Internet Access installer options, you can select Netscape Navigator instead, as shown in Figure 4.8.

You can also use the Mac OS Install program to remove software. Rather than choosing Customized Installation, choose Customized Removal from the pop-up menu beside the software component. Suppose that you use your home computer and don't need Personal Web Sharing. Go to the Customized Removal options and select each portion you want removed, as shown in Figure 4.9. To remove the entire software component, select All from the pop-up menu at the top of the Customized Removal window.

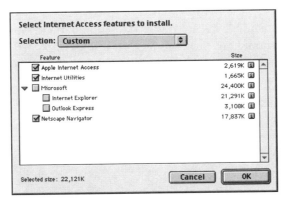

Figure 4.8   The custom installation options for Internet access.

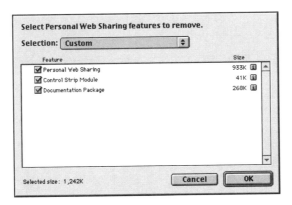

Figure 4.9   Removing Personal Web Sharing system components.

Basic Configuration Issues

After you have installed Mac OS 8.5, you may need to do some basic system configuration. This is the case if you did a clean installation. You also may have just purchased a Macintosh computer that did not have Mac OS 8.5 installed and you have performed the upgrade before using the computer.

When the installation is completed, your hard drive window may look something like the one shown in Figure 4.10. You will also have icons on the Desktop, including icons for browsing the Internet and checking your email, as well as Assistants for configuring your computer and Internet settings. If you support other Mac users, you may recommend to them that they configure the system by running these Assistants. (The questions asked are easier to understand and less confusing than those found in the TCP/IP control panel.)

Quick Reference Specifications

The following are the essential facts about Event And System Monitoring Tools:

- Most Mac OS installations are tailored to a machine logic board and processor type. You should not drag the System Folder of a particular type of Macintosh computer onto the hard drive of a different Macintosh computer unless it is a Universal System Folder.

- Prepare your disk for a system upgrade by running Disk First Aid and backing up your System Folder.

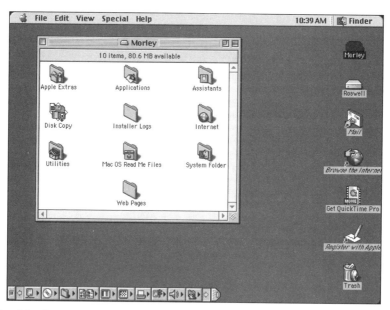

Figure 4.10   A basic Mac OS 8.5 hard drive installation.

- Remove unused software from your System Folder before an upgrade.

- Mac OS 8.5 will run only on a Power Macintosh computer.

- Accelerator cards that change 68K machines to Power Macintosh aren't supported.

- Run the testing utility included with the Mac OS 8.5 installation software for Performas in the 5200, 5300, 6200, and 6300 series. You may have a hardware problem that must be fixed before installation can take place.

- You will achieve the best results if you boot from a system other than the one you intend to upgrade (boot from CD or floppy).

- If you must boot from the system you intend to upgrade, boot with non-Apple extensions off, security and virus protection software disabled, and the power adapter plugged in on PowerBook computers.

- Reinstalling Mac OS 8.5 on top of an existing system is the easiest upgrade method.

- You can determine what changes were made within your System Folder by labeling all System Folder components before the upgrade or by configuring the installer to create a log report.

- A clean installation renames the System Folder to Previous System Folder and creates an entirely new System Folder. You must manually move the items in the older System Folder to the newer one.

- You can perform a minimum installation by customizing your Mac OS 8.5 installation options and selecting Core System Software.

- Each component of the Mac OS has its own installer and you can customize each installation.

Utilities To Use

The utilities or elements of the Mac OS discussed in this chapter are listed here as a memory aid for the busy user or system administrator:

- *Disk First Aid*—A disk repair utility included with Mac OS 8.5

- *Norton Utilities*—A commercial disk repair and system management software suite from Symantec

- *TechTool*—A free diagnostic utility from MicroMat

- *TechTool Pro*—A commercial diagnostic utility from MicroMat

- *Yank*—A shareware utility that can search a hard drive and remove all components associated with a particular application

- *5xxx/6xxx Tester*—A utility included with Mac OS 8.5 that checks the Performa 5200, 5300, 6200, and 6300 for hardware problems
- *RAM Doubler and Speed Doubler*—System improvement programs from Connectix that may need upgrading to work with Mac OS 8.5
- *Apple System Profiler*—An accessory that you will find under the Apple menu provides important information about the computer's hardware and software

Immediate Solutions

How To Determine Your Hardware Configuration

You have that Mac OS 8.5 CD-ROM in your hot little hands, but before you run the installation program you need to check out your hardware. Do you have enough disk space? Is your computer supported for Mac OS 8.5? How much memory do you have? Follow these steps to find out your hardware configuration:

1. Go to the Apple menu and launch Apple System Profiler. The window in Figure 4.11 will appear.

2. Confirm that the computer is a Power Macintosh. This information is located in the first field. Non-Power Macintosh machines aren't supported for Mac OS 8.5.

3. Verify that you have enough memory installed to run Mac OS 8.5. Most new Macintosh computers come with at least 32MB of memory. You can run Mac OS 8.5 on systems with less than 32MB of memory, but you may need to run virtual memory to make up the difference.

4. Go to Select|Volume Information and choose the drive you want to use for your Mac OS 8.5 installation. If you plan to do a basic installation, verify that you have approximately 160MB of free disk space.

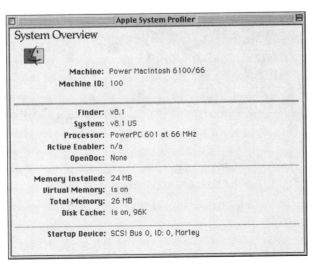

Figure 4.11   The Apple System Profiler.

5. If you do not have the Apple System Profiler, you can download TechTool from **www.micromat.com** and retrieve the hardware and processor information. Download the program, then launch TechTool. Click on the Hardware button. The window shown in Figure 4.12 will appear.

6. Confirm that your CPU type is Power PC chip (PPC), then exit TechTool.

7. From within Finder, go to the Apple menu and select About This Computer or About This Macintosh to determine the amount of memory you have (see Figure 4.13).

8. Check free disk space by clicking on the drive icon and selecting File|Get Info.

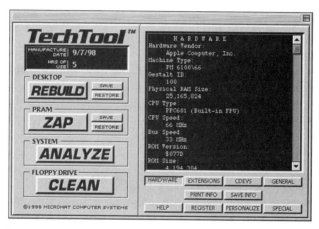

Figure 4.12   The TechTool hardware information window.

Figure 4.13   About This Computer memory information.

How To Pick The Best OS Version

Now that you have analyzed your hardware, you'll determine what operating system would be best for your computer or the computer you are supporting. Not all Macintosh computers can run Mac OS 8.5. That doesn't mean that you cannot upgrade the system at all. Many computers are running older operating systems when they could be enjoying the benefits of an upgrade. Table 4.1 indicates the operating system best suited for these different Macintosh models.

If you are not sure which system should run on your computer, search Apple's Technical Information Library at **til.info.apple.com**. You can determine the latest system for your computer.

Be aware that the computer must have been manufactured as a Power Macintosh computer in order to run Mac OS 8.5. Support is not available for 68K machines that were upgraded to Power Macintosh.

Table 4.1   The best operating system for older Macintosh computers.

Processor	Example Models	Operating System
68000	Mac Plus, Classic, PowerBook 100	System 7.5.5
68020	Mac II, LC II	System 7.6.1
68030	Mac SE/30, IIx, IIcx, IIci, PowerBook Duo 210	Mac OS 7.6.1
68040	Quadra 610 and Centris 650	Mac OS 8.1
PPC	All Power Macintosh models	Mac OS 8.5

Preparing For Installation

Now that you have verified that Mac OS 8.5 can run on your system, take the following steps to prepare for the installation. While it is not necessary to perform these tasks, you will increase your chances of a successful installation if you do. Some of these tasks should be done on a routine basis anyway:

1. Run Disk First Aid on the disk on which you intend to install Mac OS 8.5. Disk First Aid should report any errors and whether it can fix them. If you encounter errors that cannot be repaired, run Disk First Aid repeatedly to see if the utility is fixing the problem bit by bit.

2. If you cannot repair the drive with Disk First Aid, run a commercial utility such as Norton Utilities Disk Doctor or TechTool Pro. If possible, fix the disk before you upgrade, or you may continue to have problems with it. You may also want to defragment the hard drive.

3. Read the documentation that accompanies Mac OS 8.5, especially the files included with the Installer. They contain important compatibility issues and installation guidelines. Doing so helps reduce compatibility issues.

4. If possible, back up the contents of your hard drive. If this is not possible, at least back up your System Folder in the event that the Mac OS 8.5 installation fails and you need to restore the original configuration.

5. If you are going to install Mac OS 8.5 over your current system, it's a smart idea to label all the files within the System Folder (for example, assign the color red to all files within the folders). After the installation, you can quickly see what was replaced because those items will not be labeled. This process also helps when you need to troubleshoot an extension conflict if you are having difficulties booting with Mac OS 8.5.

Booting Correctly For The System Upgrade

You could probably boot your computer normally, run the Mac OS Install program, and install Mac OS 8.5. But in doing so, you could run into problems with compatibility issues, Energy Saver problems, and system protection software. Any of these can severely interfere with your upgrade process. Follow these steps to boot your computer for a Mac OS upgrade:

1. Boot from the Mac OS 8.5 installation CD-ROM. You should be able to do this by holding down the C key during startup. If this doesn't work, choose the CD-ROM as the primary disk from the Startup Disk control panel.

2. If you must boot from the system that you intend to upgrade, boot with non-Apple extensions off. Do so by going to Control Panels|Extensions Manager and choosing the Mac OS Base set as shown in Figure 4.14.

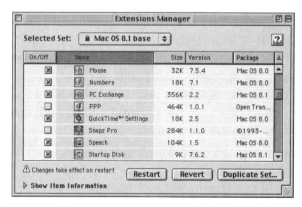

Figure 4.14   The Extensions Manager control panel with Mac OS 8.1 base extensions enabled.

3. Disable all virus protection and security software; these programs interfere with the installation.

4. Make sure that screen saver and the Energy Saver control panels are disabled. The installation process can be quite lengthy; if you have configured these options to activate after short periods of inactivity, you may increase your installation time.

5. On PowerBooks, make sure that the power adapter is plugged in. This eliminates the risk of the battery dying during installation.

Remember that you will achieve the best results if the system you want to upgrade is not active. If possible, boot from a disk other than the one you need to upgrade.

Performing A Basic Installation

It's time to install Mac OS 8.5. You will probably be running the Mac OS Install program from the CD-ROM. However, some businesses or institutions may have the software available on a server. For either method, the process is the same. Follow these steps to install Mac OS 8.5:

1. Launch the Mac OS Install program. This is a "master" installer that interacts with all the individual installers for each of the system components. You can customize all of these installations from within the Mac OS Install application.

2. The first screen that requires your input is the Welcome window, as shown in Figure 4.15. This window provides a brief overview of what you will be doing during installation. Click on the Continue button to proceed.

Figure 4.15   The Welcome window and installation overview.

3. The Select Destination window shown in Figure 4.16 allows you to choose the destination disk for your new software. It indicates what system software, if any, is currently installed and advises you if you have enough space to perform a basic installation. Choose the disk and click on Continue (if you choose a disk that already has Mac OS 8.5 installed, you will be given the option to reinstall Mac OS 8.5 or add or remove system components). Note that you can continue with the installation even if you are warned that you do not have enough disk space. You may need to see the section "Performing A Custom Installation" to install Mac OS 8.5.

4. The Important Information window displays. This is a text file containing important information about installing Mac OS 8.5; it indicates any compatibility issues. Review this file and click on Continue.

5. The Software License Agreement is listed next. If you need to read this in a language other than English, select that language from the pop-up menu in the top right of the window. After you click on Continue you are asked if you agree to accept the terms of the license. You must click on Agree to proceed.

6. The Install Software appears. By default, the program will attempt to update your hard disk driver and create a report of changes to your system folder. These settings are accessed by clicking on the Options button. Figure 4.17 shows these options enabled. You may want to disable the setting to update your driver if you know that a non-Apple utility was used to format it. Contact the manufacturer of the formatting utility to update your hard disk driver.

7. Click on the Start button to begin installing your software. A progress bar indicates how much time remains before the process finishes. When the installation is finished, restart your computer to use the new operating system.

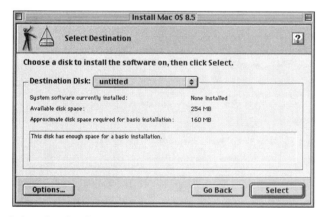

Figure 4.16   The Select Destination window.

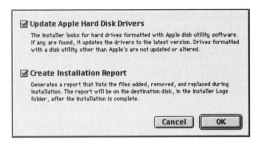

Figure 4.17   The options for the Install Software window.

Performing A Clean Installation

Perhaps you are nervous about the integrity of your System Folder, or maybe you installed Mac OS 8.5 and ran into problems when restarting the computer. In these and other situations, you may want to perform a clean installation of Mac OS 8.5. This process is almost identical to the instructions for a basic installation:

1. Launch the Mac OS Install program.

2. You will be greeted with a Welcome window listing the steps you will be taking to install Mac OS 8.5. Click on the Continue button.

3. The Select Destination window indicates what disk is selected, the current operating system on the selected disk, and if enough space exists to perform a basic installation. Click on the Options button.

4. A dialog box will appear similar to the one shown in Figure 4.18. Place a check in the box beside the Perform Clean Installation option.

5. Finish the installation by following the instructions starting at Step 3 in the "Performing A Basic Installation" section.

6. After you have completed the installation of the Mac OS 8.5 software and restarted the computer, you will notice that your customized settings are

Figure 4.18   The option to perform a clean installation.

gone. All system preferences are set to their defaults, and your third-party software is inactive. Label the files in your new System Folder to differentiate them from the files that you will be adding, then locate and open the Previous System Folder.

7. Compare each folder within each System Folder and move items from the old to the new System Folder (for example, compare the Apple Menu Items folders, then the control panels, and so on). Do not overwrite any files in the new System Folder if you are prompted.

8. After you move the items from the old to the new System Folder, restart the computer. If you experience any conflicts, see the "What To Do If Something Goes Wrong" section later in this chapter.

TIP: As the Mac OS is upgraded, some control panels and extensions are removed and their functionality combined with other control panels or extensions. For example, the PC Exchange control panel has been removed and its functionality included with the File Exchange control panel. For this reason, you probably shouldn't move control panels or extensions that were installed with the previous Mac OS version.

Performing A Custom Installation

Perhaps you only want to upgrade the system, you don't want all the other components that are installed along with Mac OS 8.5, or you would like the English Speech software installed so that you can control your computer by voice. Whatever the situation, you can customize all parts of the Mac OS 8.5 installation. When you launch the main installation program, what you may not know is that this program interacts with lots of other smaller installer programs for each system component. In previous methods of installing the Mac OS, you were sometimes interrupted by these individual installers, asking for you to interact with them to continue the installation. The Mac OS 8.5 main installer program bypasses all this. You can set your options for each of these individual installers from the main installation program. Follow these steps to customize the Mac OS 8.5 installation:

1. Launch the Mac OS Install program.

2. Choose a destination disk, and if you want, click on Options to perform a clean installation; otherwise, click on Continue.

3. Read the installation documentation window and click on Continue.

4. Click on Continue on the License Agreement window and when prompted agree to the terms of the license.

5. You should now be at the Software Install window. Normally you would click on the Start button and begin the installation, but you can control what is and isn't installed by clicking on the Customize button. The window shown in Figure 4.19 will appear.

6. You can disable entire system component installations by removing the checkmark beside the system component. To add system components to the installation, add a checkmark to the option.

7. You can customize each system component. Beside each component is a pop-up menu that allows you to choose Recommended Installation, Customized Installation, or Customized Removal. Choose Customized Installation beside the system component you want to customize.

8. Decide what parts of a system component to add. Options with a triangle beside them can be expanded to include additional choices. Select the options you wish to install and click on Okay.

9. You can now click on Start to begin your software installation. The new operating system will now be active until you restart your computer.

Figure 4.19   The Customize window, which lists all the individual installer programs.

Performing A Universal Or Minimum System Installation

If you provide support for several Macintosh computers, you may support more than one type of computer. Each type of Macintosh requires a unique operating system geared to the hardware specifications of that computer. This means you should not drag a System folder from one type of Macintosh computer to another. However, you can create a boot disk that should start almost any type of Power Macintosh computer. This is called *creating a Universal System Folder.*

Perhaps you do not have enough disk space free to install the entire Mac OS 8.5 installation. You can perform a Minimum System installation. Both of these options involve the same steps:

1. Launch the Mac OS Install program.

2. Choose the destination disk and if you want, click on Options to perform a clean installation; otherwise, click on Continue.

3. Read the installation documentation window and click on Continue.

4. Click on Continue on the License Agreement window and when prompted agree to the terms of the license.

5. You should now be at the Software Install window. Click on the Customize button.

6. Disable all the other software component installations so that only Mac OS 8.5 is selected.

7. Click on the pop-up menu beside Mac OS 8.5 and choose Customized Installation. The window shown in Figure 4.20 will appear.

8. Determine what type of system you need installed. If you want a minimum system installation, select Core System Software. If you want to create a disk that can boot almost any computer (in this case, a removable media such as a Zip disk or Syquest cartridge), choose Universal System installation and click on Okay.

9. Click on the Start button to begin the software installation. When the installation has finished you should have upgraded your system or created a Universal System Folder.

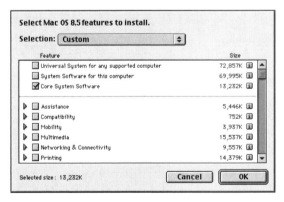

Figure 4.20   The customized installation options for the Mac OS 8.5 installer.

What To Do If Something Goes Wrong

If everything goes right with your installation, you will reboot your computer and be able to use Mac OS 8.5 and your existing applications. Sometimes, however, you may encounter problems. Table 4.2 provides some suggestions for handling problems with your new software installation.

Table 4.2   Troubleshooting the Mac OS installation.

Problem	Resolution
Computer hanging upon restart	If your computer hangs after restarting, reboot with extensions off (hold down the Shift key). If the computer still will not boot, try booting from another system disk. If it can boot, run Disk First Aid and see if the hard drive has problems. If you cannot boot with another system disk, you may have hardware problems. Try zapping the PRAM (boot and hold down Option+Cmd+P+R until the computer restarts). If you still cannot boot, you may need to have an authorized repair shop look at your computer.
Extension conflict	If the computer can boot with extensions off, launch the Extensions Manager control panel and select the Mac OS 8.5 Base set from the pop-up menu at the top of the window. Restart your computer. If you can boot successfully, you have an extension conflict. Return to the Extensions Manager and enable a few extensions or control panels and restart the computer. If you diagnose the conflicting software, contact the manufacturer for an updated version of the software that is compatible with Mac OS 8.5.
Cannot boot with extensions enabled	If you cannot isolate an extension conflict but are still having problems with your system, try performing a Clean Installation (refer to the "Clean Installation" section in this chapter). See if you can successfully boot with this new System Folder. If you can, gradually add items from the Previous System Folder to the new System Folder and restart the computer until either you isolate the problem or can successfully boot with the third-party programs enabled.
System will not load	If you cannot boot after a Clean Installation, try performing a minimum installation. Customize your installation options and install only Mac OS 8.5. Restart and see if you can boot. If you can, go back and run the installers for each system component you wish to add noting if any cause conflicts upon restart. If they do, customize your installation again, choosing Customized Removal, then remove the component.

(continued)

Table 4.2   Troubleshooting the Mac OS installation (continued).

Problem	Resolution
Upgrade needs to be removed	If you still cannot boot your computer with only Mac OS 8.5 installed, you may not be able to run Mac OS 8.5 on your hard drive in its current condition. You may need to restore the System Folder from the backup you performed before upgrading. If you did not do this, run the Mac OS Install program and customize your installation. On each component that was installed, select Customized Removal and remove the component. Then, reinstall your previous operating system version (for example, reinstall Mac OS 8.1). If you performed a clean installation of Mac OS 8.5, you can boot from another medium and delete the current System Folder, then open and close the Previous System Folder. Reboot to see if the old Mac OS will load. If not, reinstall the previous Mac OS that ran successfully on your computer.

4: Installation And Basic Configuration

Chapter 5

Disk And File Systems

In Depth

Creativity and productivity occur within the memory or RAM portion of the computing environment, but when it's time to preserve your efforts, you will probably access a permanent storage device. Moreover, if you want to locate that file you just saved, you will probably be using some method of file organization. In this chapter, we discuss different kinds of storage media and file formats, file organization methods, and remote storage options.

Hard And Floppy Disk Options

The floppy disk has gone through many transformations. It used to be the size of an LP album. One of the most interesting and unintentionally funny scenes in the motion picture *War Games* involves the main character inserting an 8" floppy disk into the drive. As technology improved, the disks were able to hold more data in smaller sizes. The last of the truly "floppy" disks was the 5.25" size. Protective envelopes kept the Mylar disk from being damaged, yet data was still in a fragile state because the disk media was exposed. The next step in the floppy disk revolution was the format that we see today: the 3.5" disk. Not only can this disk hold more data, it also has a hard, protective, plastic shell with a metal shield to protect the actual disk until you insert it into the drive. This particular size has endured. The most popular ones were, of course, the PC formats. The double-density disks hold 640KB of data, and the high-density disks hold 1.4MB. However, double-density disks in a Macintosh format can hold 800KB of data.

The floppy disk has been one of the most reliable media when used to boot a computer unable to boot by the hard drive. However, this disk has begun the road to obsolescence. Application programs are routinely larger than the storage capacity of one disk. (Imagine installing the standard Mac OS 8.5 system from floppy disk. By the time you have finished, you would have a repetitive-motion injury to report.) Documents created by these larger programs have also increased in size so that even a high-density disk is inadequate for file storage. Moreover, floppy disks are fragile when used for long-term storage—many of us have experienced the frustration that arises from discovering that a disk has become corrupted and that no backup storage exists.

Today, the floppy disk has two major uses:

5: Disk And File Systems

- It boots up computers that are either unable to boot from the existing system or are suffering from hard drive problems. In the latter case, the disk can verify and repair hard disk problems.

- It is the primary component of the "sneaker" network. Data is stored on the disk and exchanged with coworkers; this often occurs when users do not know all their storage options. This chapter should help reduce the necessity of the sneaker network in favor of more reliable data storage media.

The more reliable alternative to the floppy disk is the hard drive. Considering the 1.4MB storage limit of one floppy disk, a hard drive with 40MB of storage was huge. Inevitably, however, hard drives became larger. Today, many computers contain an internal hard drive with a minimum size of two gig-abytes. Power users—especially graphic designers—insist on even greater storage capacity.

One of the most interesting issues with large capacity hard drives has been the inability of operating systems to handle the larger partitions. On older Macintosh systems, this problem resulted in inaccurate statements of how much hard drive space was free. To resolve this issue, users would break or partition the hard drive into smaller chunks that the operating system could handle. Today, the Mac OS can handle drive partitions of two terabytes, a vast improvement for users with large hard drives.

External hard drives are also common, especially for novice Macintosh users who dread the thought of opening the computer case. External hard drives are more expensive than internal drives and can cause problems for older Macs; they may spin faster than the internal ones, causing system stalls. Also, by purchasing an external drive, users may find themselves exploring the wonderful world of SCSI devices.

SCSI Issues

Most external devices are attached to the computer via the SCSI port. SCSI, or Small Computer System Interface, is a processor-independent standard for communication between the computer and SCSI devices such as printers, scanners, hard drives, and CD-ROM drives. A SCSI chain can contain up to seven devices and each device is assigned a number in the chain. The number 7 is reserved for the Macintosh, and the number 0 is reserved for the internal hard drive. All other devices use the remaining numbers. Some Macintosh computers have more than one SCSI bus and can contain even more devices (up to 14). If you have added a device to the SCSI chain and are experiencing difficulties accessing the device or if your system fails to boot, then you may have a SCSI conflict. That is why the Apple System Profiler is so invaluable for diagnosing these conflicts. Figure 5.1 shows the Apple System Profiler, reporting the devices on a SCSI chain. It searches the bus and tells you what devices are found for each associated number. In many cases, just changing the number of the device may resolve the conflict.

Removable Media

We've discussed the floppy disk, which is one of the first methods of removable media. However, you can use a wide variety of other media to keep your data accessible and secure.

Zip Disks

Other removable storage devices were around before the Zip drive from Iomega. However, Iomega made this device accessible to all users. Before the Zip disk, removable media was big, clunky, ugly, expensive, and occasionally unreliable. The Zip disk was small, flat, economically priced, and stable. It is only slightly larger and heavier than a 3.5" disk. It holds 100MB of data and you can format it for the Macintosh or the PC. You can install it internally or externally. (In fact, the external drive is very popular for its portability.) The Zip drive is so popular that the Mac OS has included the driver since release 7.6.1. If you are looking for a new computer, the inclusion of an internal Zip drive is very desirable.

SuperDisks

The SuperDisk drive from Imation is an emerging device that goes a step beyond the Zip drive. Its greatest feature is its backward compatibility. While this drive's

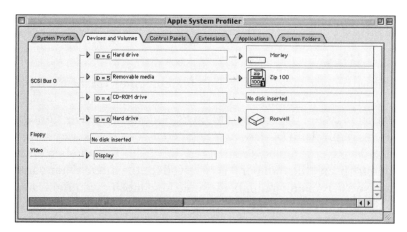

Figure 5.1   Apple System Profiler, showing the SCSI configuration.

main feature is the SuperDisk that can hold 120MB of data, it also can read and write to conventional 3.5" disks. The SuperDisk media looks and feels much like a conventional floppy disk. Several major computer manufacturers have begun including the SuperDisk as a built-in device; most computer retail stores also carry it.

The greatest potential benefit of the SuperDisk is that Imation will be releasing it with a USB, or Universal Serial Bus interface. This interface, the main feature of the new iMac computer, gives iMac users access to their old floppy disks as well as to the large capacity SuperDisks. (Its release also solved the mystery of releasing a computer without a floppy drive.)

Jaz Drives

The Jaz drive from Iomega can hold even more data than the Zip and SuperDisk media disks. Jaz drives initially held one gigabyte of data, but recently their capacity has been upgraded to two gigabytes. However, unlike the previous media we discussed, Jaz disks are somewhat large and clunky in comparison. Nevertheless, if you are faced with shrinking hard drive space and are debating whether to purchase another hard drive or go with a removable media device, the Jaz drive is very attractive in price and storage capacity.

Syquest

An established name in the business of removable media is Syqest. Its drives come in a variety of sizes that range from 135MB in storage to 1.5 gigabyte cartridges. The one drawback of using a Syquest drive is its lack of popularity compared to the Iomega Zip and Jaz drives. If you don't anticipate sharing data with others, then Syquest is certainly a reliable name in the removable hard drive business.

Magneto-Optical Disks

When the first magneto-optical systems were released, some in the industry thought it would be the technology to replace floppy disks. Magneto-optical disks are a cross between a floppy disk and a fixed hard drive. They can hold large amounts of data and can write information to the disk many times. One tremendous advantage they have over other storage media is their stability around magnetic fields. Magneto-optical disks also have an extended storage life of 10 to 20 years.

The drawback of the magneto-optical disk over a fixed hard drive is the relatively slow data access rate of the magneto-optical drive. For this reason, you may want to consider this system if you have large data files or information that you may not need to access on a regular basis.

Tape Backup Drives

If you are the manager of a network of Mac users or if you just want to protect your existing data, then you may want to consider the purchase of a tape backup system. Tape cartridges can hold huge amounts of data and with the right software can perform data protection and recovery functions without interfering with your daily routine. While tape backup systems are more expensive than other media that we have discussed, they are indispensable when you are faced with a corrupted database or a sobbing user who just overwrote an important file.

CD-ROM Disks

By far, the most popular form of removable media is the CD-ROM disk. It has become the standard format for software purchasing. One CD-ROM disk can hold both PC and Macintosh data. One of the problems with the myth that no software is out there for the Mac is the fact that many titles do contain both system formats, but are grouped with other PC titles.

TIP: When buying software, don't limit yourself to the Macintosh software section in your local Computers-R-Us retail store. Look at all the software. Many titles contain both Mac and PC formats but are grouped in the PC section to save space. More software is available for the Mac than most people realize.

One of the drawbacks of the CD-ROM drive is that in most computers the device is read-only. However, CD-writing devices (also known as "toasters") have become economically priced. In our environment, we often use toasters to write an image of a hard drive to a CD-ROM so we can configure multiple workstations at once. If you need to make copies of software to additional CDs, keep a central resource of departmental fonts or move installation programs from floppies to CD-ROMs; then, you may want to consider purchasing a CD read-write drive.

DVD Disks

Today's computer games and software have pushed the CD-ROM disk to its limit. DVD-ROM is the next generation of the digital storage format. DVD or *digital versatile disks* look exactly like CD-ROM, but because the player angles the laser a little differently, a second layer of data on the disk can be read. DVD disks can be double-sided, enabling them to hold much more data than CD-ROMs. However, this new industry has taken a while to agree upon a data format. The first DVD drives are just now emerging, and the capability to write to DVD disks may still happen in the future. Finally, while the software companies and advertising agencies are looking happily at the DVD format, the entertainment industry has been the real force behind this new standard. Thousands of motion pictures are

5: Disk And File Systems

available in DVD format. You can play these movies on a computer that has the proper equipment (a DVD drive and a specialized video card) installed.

Understanding File Formats

The Macintosh file structure is unique from other systems. Each file in the operating system consists of two parts. The *data fork* contains what a user would normally see in a file. The *resource fork* contains information about the file such as its creator, icon bitmap, and program segments. Information about the files on the Macintosh is stored in a hidden file named the *Desktop Database*. This database is a "roadmap" of the storage system, whether it is the hard drive, CD-ROM, or floppy disk. This lets you double-click on a file and have the appropriate software launch that reads the document. Occasionally, this database becomes confused. Symptoms of this problem include scrambled icons, poor performance, an inability to connect to the network (if all cabling and network parameters have been correctly set), and an obvious failure of association (for example, you double-click on a plain text document and receive an error that the software creator for the document cannot be found). To rebuild this database file and fix some of these problems, refer to "Troubleshooting" in Chapter 18 in the section entitled "Rebuilding The Desktop File."

The resource fork includes information about the file creator. A broad category of creators exists; a good example is the **ttxt** category, which includes all plain-text documents. However, even more specific creator information is available. Every Macintosh software program uses a unique four-character annotation to assign to any document it creates. For example, Microsoft Word uses the creator identification of MSWD. You can find out this information by using specialized utilities such as ResEdit, File Buddy, or Cool Views. You can also search for documents by creator with the File Find or Sherlock utility; this is very useful if you have trouble remembering information about a file, such as its name or where you saved it.

Standard Vs. Extended Formats

The Macintosh standard format was revolutionary when it was first released in 1986. Until that point, the Macintosh file system could not even support the use of folders. By using allocation bits on a volume, the Macintosh standard format could support partitions up to two gigabits in size (remember, at this time, large hard drives were 20MB). However, a standard number of allocation bits per volume was assigned. For example, for smaller volumes such as 256MB, the allocation bit for a file could be 4KB. However, for a two-gigabyte volume, this allocation is 64KB. Therefore, the same file on both volumes would take up vastly different

5: Disk And File Systems

amounts of space, in spite of the fact that the files are identical. This was trouble-some for very small files, especially text-only documents.

With the release of Mac OS 8.1, a new file storage format was made available to Macintosh users. The Macintosh extended format increases the number of al-location bits from 65,536 to over four billion, thus enabling disks to accurately represent and store files by their true size. Figure 5.2 shows a file listing on a standard format volume and Figure 5.3 shows the same files on the extended format volume.

However, the Macintosh extended format has some problems. Companies have been slow to supply disk-management programs for it, and this new format causes disk fragmentation at a much greater rate. Although tools are gradually being released that can defragment a hard drive, the most popular tool, Norton Utili-ties, has been slow to meet this demand. The question also arises as to whether you need to move to the Macintosh extended format at all. If the volume in ques-tion stores primarily large documents such as graphics files, then the extended format will not make much of a difference. However, if you maintain a file system that has many small or plain-text files such as a Web server, then you may want to consider the Macintosh extended format. You can recover several megabytes of additional storage by using the newer format. You should also know that comput-ers must be running Mac OS 8.1 or greater to see extended format disks on the local system. However, extended format volumes accessed over a network can be mounted on pre-Mac OS 8.1 systems.

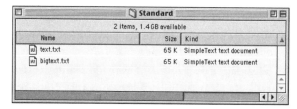

Figure 5.2   Files in the standard format volume.

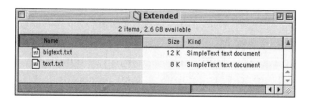

Figure 5.3   The same files in the extended format volume.

Finally, if you support several computers that a user could modify, you need to know how you can determine if a disk is formatted which the Mac OS standard or extended format. Instructions are available later in this chapter, in the section "Determining Mac OS Standard Or Extended Format."

Maintaining Large File Systems

We discussed disk fragmentation briefly in the previous section. Disk fragmentation occurs when gaps occur in the hard drive between stored files as well as when files are broken up and stored over multiple areas of the disk. When a hard drive has barely been used, each new file is stored one after the other in neat alignment. However, as you make changes to files, delete them, save them under new names, and append data to them, data storage becomes messy. As you delete files, new files—rarely the same size as the old—are saved in their places and spread out over the disk. Eventually, you end up with gaps throughout your hard drive, with each gap too small for new data storage and, therefore, wasted. Worse, the tables that track the location of the parts of a file may become corrupt, rendering the files tracked effectively lost. Defragmentation utilities manually rewrite the data back to the volume and in the process remove these gaps, therefore restoring disk space for data storage. Performing this function also improves hard drive performance.

Several software makers provide disk defragmentation utilities. The most popular is Norton Utilities Speed Disk. Not only can it defragment the hard drive, it can also organize files by type so that documents are immediately recognizable. Speed Disk is part of the Norton Utilities package, which also includes Disk Doctor; this fixes volumes that need repair. Disk Doctor can repair volumes that Apple's Disk First Aid cannot fix. Norton Utilities also has a program to recover deleted files, as well as crash-protection software. If you are a system administrator, you should have some kind of disk or volume utility software. These programs can at least warn you that a drive is about to fail. At some point, every data storage volume needs maintenance. It is not a matter of *if*, but *when*.

Server Storage

Several years ago, most computing environments featured a series of networked computers, sharing data with a central file server. Today, the server environment is still very strong; many benefits result from storing data remotely. Most servers feature some kind of backup process that protects data. As a system administrator, you know that it is more economical to purchase five copies of a software program and meter them, rather than buying and installing one hundred copies of the program on each hard drive.

Problems develop, depending upon the type of server and the server software. Of course, if the server is an AppleShare device, then access is easy. The server should be accessible from the Chooser or Network Browser. However, reality tells us that most servers will be running either Novell NetWare or Windows NT. Both of these platforms allow Macintosh access by running certain processes on the server. Figure 5.4 shows files stored on a remote Novell server.

However, you may be working in an environment that is not friendly to the Mac. Don't despair; programs are available that allow you to access the servers without running special processes on the server itself. For Windows NT servers, you can use a software utility from Thursby software called DAVE. This program not only allows you to access NT servers, but also other Windows systems, including Windows 95. Another benefit is the ability to access other Macintosh servers using TCP/IP rather than AppleTalk. We will be discussing utilities such as DAVE in more detail in Chapter 10, which covers Microsoft Windows compatibility issues.

Using The Multithreaded Finder

The Finder was improved in Mac OS 8 to include multithreading capabilities. This is most dramatic when you are doing file manipulation. For example, you can copy files from one volume to another and while this copy is in progress, continue performing functions in the Finder, including copying additional files to other folders or volumes. Figure 5.5 shows multiple copies in progress. Mac OS 8.5 has been improved to also include multiple searching sessions by using the Find or Sherlock utility.

Quick Reference Specifications

The following are the essential facts about Disk And File Systems:

- Floppy disks are used most frequently to boot computers and manually exchange files with colleagues.

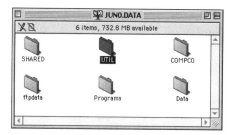

Figure 5.4   Files stored on a remote server volume.

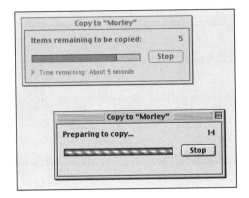

Figure 5.5   Multiple copies in progress.

- You can format hard drives into multiple partitions.
- SCSI chains, both internal and external, are limited to seven devices on each chain.
- SCSI devices must have unique numbers between one and six.
- Removable media provide greater storage capacity than floppy disks and may need special drivers installed to be recognized by the system.
- The Zip Drive driver extension is included in Mac OS 8.5.
- Macintosh files consist of two parts: the data fork and the resource fork. Only the data fork is readable on a PC.
- The resource fork of a file contains icon information as well as creator information, both general and specific.
- The greatest benefit of the Macintosh Extended format is the increased amount of hard disk space available due to smaller allocation blocks.
- Drives with mostly large image files or with partitions smaller than one gigabyte may not benefit from the Extended format for disks.
- You must perform routine maintenance and hard drive defragmentation to protect and improve disk performance.
- Macintosh computers can access remote servers either via AppleTalk or through special utilities, such as DAVE or the Macintosh Novell client.
- You can perform multiple functions within the Finder at the same time, including copying and moving files.

Utilities To Use

The utilities or elements of the Mac OS discussed in this chapter are listed here as a memory aid for the busy user or system administrator:

5: Disk And File Systems

- *Removable Media*—Expands disk space without installing additional hard drives.

- *Remote Servers*—Provides remote storage and access to shared software applications.

- *Get Info*—Provides information about files and folders.

- *Sherlock*—Search utility that locates files by several criteria, including name, kind, size, and creation/modification date (also known as Find).

- *Find By Content*—Additional search function in the Sherlock utility that allows the searching of file contents.

- *Labels*—Expands file organization by providing a file label structure that can be customized.

- *Aliases*—Small files that act in the place of, and point to the original file, application, folder, or volume.

- *Disk Defragmentation*—A commercial utility that removes gaps in the data storage structure on a volume.

- *Disk Cache*—A portion of memory reserved for frequently performed instructions.

- *Disk Copy*—A free utility from Apple that allows you to create disks from images and create disk images for distribution.

- *Disk First Aid*—A free utility from Apple that diagnoses and repairs damaged disks.

- *Norton Utilities and TechTool Pro*—Commercial packages that include several programs that go beyond Apple's Disk First Aid to repair damaged volumes.

Immediate Solutions

Mounting And Dismounting Floppy Disks

Floppy disks are still commonly used in the workplace. An administrator of multiple platforms who may be new to the Mac may not be aware of the method of ejecting disks (the eject command for removable disks can cause many problems in public clusters. Here are some simple guidelines for working with this media:

1. Insert the disk in the drive.
2. The Mac OS will mount the disk on the Desktop.
3. Use the disk for storing files or run programs from it.
4. When you are finished, dismount or eject the disk by any of these methods:
   - Drag the disk's icon to the trashcan.
   - Click once on the disk's icon, go to the File menu, and select Put Away, as shown in Figure 5.6.
   - Click once on the disk's icon, go to the Special menu, and select Eject Disk, as shown in Figure 5.7.

Figure 5.6   Using the Put Away command.

Figure 5.7   Using the Eject Disk command.

5: Disk And File Systems

An Eject Disk Caveat

Although this book covers the Mac OS 8.5 system, you should know that the Eject Disk command worked differently in systems previous to release 8. Eject Disk dismounted a disk while it was in use. The "ghost" image of the disk was still present on the Desktop even while the disk was outside the disk drive. You would most commonly use the Eject Disk command when a disk booted the computer. This allowed you to insert other disks while the system on the disk was still present in RAM. You could run other applications stored on the second disk by inserting the appropriate disk as the system asked for it (although this process took a long time and a lot of disk swapping to complete).

However, many users did not know that Eject Disk performed this special function; they would select this command when they were finished with the disk. When the time came to shut down the computer, they would be frustrated by a series of requests for the disk. Because of the confusion over the Eject Disk command, the function was changed to behave the same as the Put Away command.

Using Removable Media

As a Macintosh user, you have access to many different removable media, including Zip and Jaz disks and removable hard drives. But installing, mounting, accessing, and dismounting any one of these media is very much the same:

1. Turn off the computer and devices.
2. Attach the device (you'll probably use the SCSI port).
3. Turn on the computer.
4. Insert the device's software disk and install the driver for the device.
5. Restart the computer and insert the disk or cartridge in the drive.
6. The icon of the media should appear on the Desktop; you can use it to store documents or run applications (see Figure 5.8 for an example of a mounted Zip disk).
7. Drag the icon of the media to the trash or use File|Put Away to dismount the media.

TIP: *The Mac OS 8.5 system includes the Iomega Zip disk driver. You can attach the device, insert the disk, and start the computer. The Zip disk should be mounted on the Desktop automatically.*

Figure 5.8   A Zip disk mounted on the Desktop.

Accessing Remote Servers And Volumes

You've had to use some cost-cutting measures and now have software stored on a local server rather than on each hard drive. You can use the Network Browser to access a remote server:

1. Go to the Apple menu.

2. Select the Network Browser utility (use this once, and you'll never use the Chooser for accessing servers again).

3. If applicable, locate and double-click on the zone where your server resides (see Figure 5.9).

4. To open your server, double-click on its icon within the browser (you'll probably be prompted for a password, as shown in Figure 5.10).

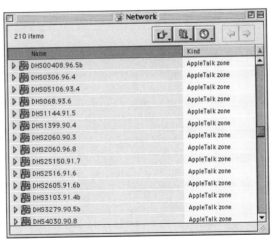

Figure 5.9   The Network Browser window listing zones.

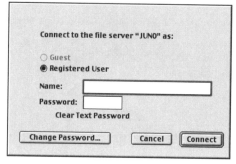

Figure 5.10   A password prompt.

Getting Information About Files And Folders

You need to retrieve information about a particular file such as its status, path, creation and modification date, and version of the application. Much of this information is available in the Get Info window. Follow these directions to retrieve this information:

1. Click once on the file or folder to select it.

2. Go to the File menu and select Get Info|General Information.

Figure 5.11 shows a standard Get Info window.

TIP: *You can also access this information by pressing the Command key as you click the object. This action brings up a contextual menu with the Get Info option.*

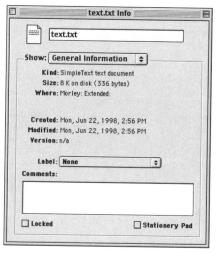

Figure 5.11   The Get Info window.

5: Disk And File Systems

Making A File Read-Only

You have a particular file that you want to protect from changes. At a rudimentary level you can lock the file so that it is read-only. Be aware that this protects the document from changes within an application and does not allow the user to save a file of the same name to the locked file location. However, by following these steps in reverse you can easily disable the locked setting:

1. Click once on the document you wish to make read-only.

2. Go to the File menu and select Get Info|General Information.

3. Locate the small box in the bottom left of the Get Info window beside the word "Locked".

4. Click in the small box, placing an X within it. The file is now read-only (see Figure 5.12).

TIP: *While the file is locked, it keeps this setting, even if you drag the file to the Trashcan. If you attempt to empty the trash that contains this locked file, the dialog box in Figure 5.13 appears. You can easily bypass this warning and delete the file by holding down the Option key and selecting Empty Trash.*

You can also save a file as stationary. Rather than read-only, the file will open in an untitled window but will still contain the information you added. This option is great for creating templates.

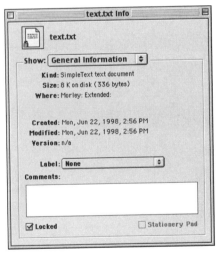

Figure 5.12   The Get Info window with the locked file setting.

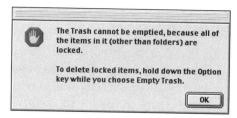

Figure 5.13   The warning for a locked file in the trash.

Determining Mac OS Standard Or Extended Format

You are unsure as to whether a particular volume has been formatted with the Mac OS Standard or Extended System. Follow these steps to determine the format of the volume:

1. Click once on the icon of the volume in question.
2. Go to the File Menu and select Get Info.
3. Look in the section entitled "format".

The term *Mac OS Standard* refers to the typical Macintosh file storage format as shown Figure 5.14. The term *Mac OS Extended* refers to the new file allocation format as shown in Figure 5.15.

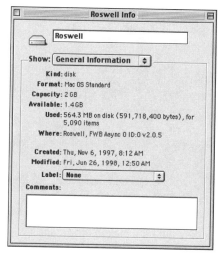

Figure 5.14   A standard format volume.

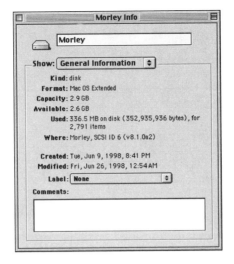

Figure 5.15   An extended format volume.

Finding Files And Folders

In spite of your extraordinary organizational skills, you will often need to locate a particular file or document. Perhaps you need to locate a file on a remote server. Your best friend is the Sherlock or Find utility. Remember that this utility was previously called Find (for clarity, we refer to the utility by both names). For example, in the Apple menu, you would select Sherlock, and in the File menu, you would choose Find). Sherlock is an improved version of the Find utility, and it is included in Mac OS 8.5.

1. Select either File|Find or Apple|Sherlock.

2. Determine all the volumes that you want searched (see Figure 5.16).

3. Set your search options. You can search by name, size, kind, label, date created, date modified, version, comments, lock attribute, folder attribute, file type, and creator.

Figure 5.16   Searching volumes selection menu.

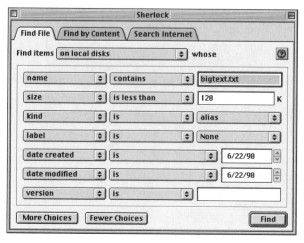

Figure 5.17   A wide variety of search options in the Sherlock utility.

4. If necessary, click on More Choices to limit your search results, especially if you are searching a large file system or are searching by a common name. Figure 5.17 shows an extensive search window.

5. Click on Find.

6. The results are shown. Click on a file in the upper window and the path displays in the lower window (see Figure 5.18).

You can perform many of the functions in the Items Found window that you do in Finder. You can launch applications, drag files to the trash, and perform the menu option Get Info.

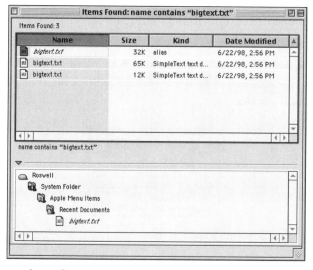

Figure 5.18   The search results.

Indexing Content

Indexing content is the first and biggest step in the process to search volumes by file content. In fact, you cannot access the full power of this search style until you have created an index of the volume. You can also program your Mac to do this indexing routinely by taking these steps:

1. Select either Apple|Sherlock or File|Find.

2. Click on the Find By Content window tab to view a window similar to Figure 5.19.

3. Click on the Index Volumes button (if you have not done this before, you will see a warning that no volumes are indexed).

4. Select the volume you want indexed and click on the Create Index button (see Figure 5.20).

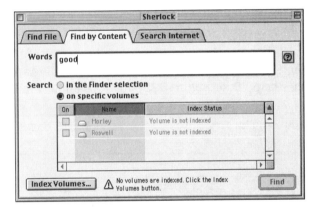

Figure 5.19   The Find By Content window.

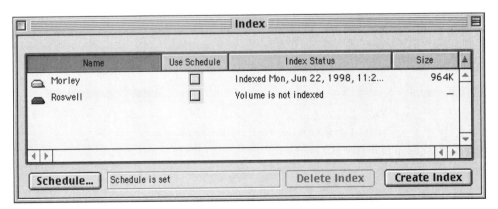

Figure 5.20   Creating an index.

A progress bar indicates how much of the volume has been indexed. If you can read quickly, you will see file names appear under the progress bar. After this has finished, you can find files by their content, not just by their names.

Finding Files By Content

No longer do you need to buy software for searching the content of files the way you can with the Unix **grep** command. Finally, the Mac OS contains the ability to search the contents of the file, not just the name of it.

1. Launch the Sherlock or Find utility from the Apple or File menu.

2. Click on the Find By Content window tab.

3. Enter the text you want to locate.

4. Determine if you want the search limited to the Finder selection or by specific volumes. If you search by volume, choose the name or names as shown in Figure 5.21.

5. Click on Find. A window indicating your search results appears with the best matches listed first. Figure 5.22 shows a sample window.

TIP: *You can search via Finder selection if you have manually selected the files in Finder before conducting the search.*

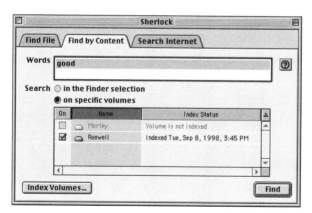

Figure 5.21   Setting the Find parameters.

5: Disk And File Systems

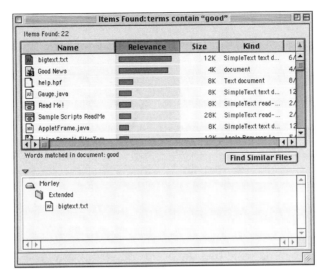

Figure 5.22   The search results.

Scheduling Content Indexing

Unless you fancy creating an index every time you wish to conduct a file content search, you may want to schedule this indexing on a regular basis. You can take the following steps to schedule indexing during the evening hours, so that you can work undisturbed:

1. Launch the Find or Sherlock utility.
2. Select the tab labeled Find By Content.
3. Click on the Index Volumes button.
4. Place a check in the box under the column Use Schedule.
5. Click on the Schedule button, as shown in Figure 5.23.

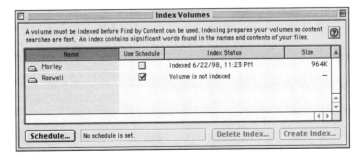

Figure 5.23   Choosing a volume to index routinely.

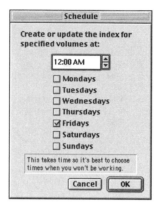

Figure 5.24   Setting the schedule.

6. Set the time of day and the day of the week you want the automatic index-ing to occur (see Figure 5.24) and choose Okay.

7. Close all windows for the settings to take effect.

Automatic volume indexing will now occur. If you watch this process, you will see the same progress bar that displays when you manually create an index. This feature will vastly improve your accuracy in searching by content.

Searching The Internet

The revamped Sherlock utility also includes an interface to search all the popular search engines on the Web. To do so, take these steps:

1. Launch the Find or Sherlock utility located under the Apple or File menu.

2. Click the Search Internet tab to see the window, as shown in Figure 5.25.

3. Enter the information you seek.

4. Choose the search engines you want to use.

5. Click on Search.

5: Disk And File Systems

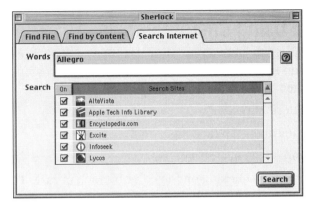

Figure 5.25   Searching the Internet within the Sherlock utility.

Labeling Files And Folders

You can organize your files by type or by labels. You can use these labels for searching via the Sherlock utility, and you can group files in the list view by label.

1. Select the item or items you want to label.

2. Choose File|Label.

3. Choose the most appropriate phrase or color.

4. The item now has a special property for organizational structure. Figure 5.26 shows a group of files organized by label.

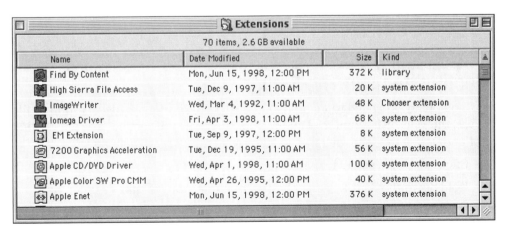

Figure 5.26   Files with labels.

Creating And Using Custom Labels

Okay, so now you can label icons. Your next question is, "How can I change the phrases to mean something?" After all, wouldn't it better if the label Project 2 could be changed to ACME or something more intuitive?

1. Select Edit|Preferences.

2. Click on the Labels tab (see Figure 5.27).

3. Edit the phrases as necessary.

4. Edit the colors by clicking on the color by each phrase. This brings up the standard color selection window. Choose the color you want.

5. Save changes by closing the window.

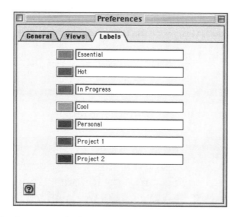

Figure 5.27 The Label Preference window.

Selecting Items In The Finder

Occasionally you need to manipulate, label, copy, or open a file or group of files (yes, the Mac OS is wonderful in that you can open multiple files and applications at once). Use the following methods for selecting files in the Finder:

- Click once on a single icon to select it.

- Hold down the Shift key and click on multiple icons within a Finder view such as a window or the Desktop.

- Click and drag the mouse just outside a group of files to form a lasso and catch them (the icons darken as you select them).

- Combine the Shift and drag to select noncontiguous groups of icons.

Creating Comments

You can enter additional text in the resource fork of a file by adding custom comments. Some examples of useful comments might be the reason the document was created or relevant Web sites; you can also create other comments by taking these steps:

1. Select a file.

2. Choose File|Get Info.

3. In the Comments text box, enter whatever text you deem relevant to the file (see Figure 5.28).

4. Close the window.

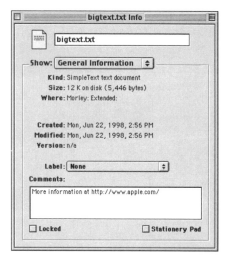

Figure 5.28   Adding comments to a file.

Creating And Using Aliases

Aliases are already heavily used in the operating system. If you see files with italicized text, you are looking at an alias of an original file or folder. The Apple menu often employs aliases. In fact, when you select the Control Panels option, you are actually selecting an alias that points to the original located in the System Folder. Aliases are very easy to create:

1. Select the file that needs an alias.

2. Choose File|Make Alias.

3. Move the newly created file to the location where you need access to the original file.

You can also press the Command key as you click on the object to bring up the contextual menu with an option to make an alias.

Figure 5.29 shows the difference between an alias and the original file.

TIP: Make an alias in one swift motion by clicking the item, pressing the Command+Option keys, and dragging the file to the folder where the alias will reside. The file will not be moved; instead, an alias will be placed in the selected folder.

Broken Aliases

One of the problems with aliases has been that you could put the alias almost anywhere you chose, but if you moved the original, the alias no longer functioned. Mac OS 8.5 now includes a feature that fixes broken aliases.

Figure 5.29   An original (top) and an alias (bottom).

Cataloging Removable Media

One of the handy tools included with a Zip drive is a function named FindIt. With this utility, you can create your own "library" catalog of what information is stored on each Zip disk. When you access this utility and search for a particular file, FindIt tells you which Zip disk to insert so you can access the data.

Almost all of the removable media devices include this type of utility. It certainly is better than inserting each disk and conducting a search from within Finder.

Increasing Disk Performance

A volume without routine maintenance performed on it is an accident waiting to happen. You can take several steps not only to prevent accidents, but also to improve disk performance:

- Defragment your hard drive. Several commercial products do an excellent job, including Norton Utilities and Disk Express Pro.

- Run Disk First Aid at the first sign of trouble. Disk First Aid can now repair active volumes.

- Use a commercial utility to repair damaged volumes. Norton Utilities has an excellent program named Disk Doctor that can repair volumes beyond the capabilities of Disk First Aid. However, if you have disks that are formatted with the Macintosh extended format, make sure that your version of Norton can repair them. Other utilities, such as TechTool Pro, can repair extended format volumes.

- Use some sort of virus protection. Symantec, McAfee, and Dr. Solomon all carry excellent virus protection packages.

Configuring Disk Cache

You can improve system performance by setting your disk cache to a suitable level. The cache contains a history of commonly used commands. The smaller this file is, the more often the application must consult the hard drive for instructions on how to perform a function. A larger cache stores more of these common instructions. To set your cache, take the following steps:

1. Go to the Apple menu and choose Control Panels|Memory.

2. Locate the cache section at the top of the window (see Figure 5.30).

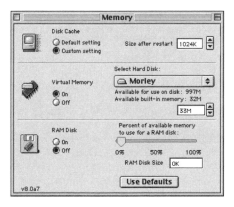

Figure 5.30   Setting the disk cache.

3. Set the cache using this formula: Multiply 32 kilobytes by the amount of RAM installed (for example, someone with 16MB of memory would set the cache to 512K).

4. Close the Memory control panel.

Accessing Damaged Disks

If you are experiencing strange system errors or your machine seems to be crashing frequently, you may have a damaged disk. Another obvious symptom is that your computer doesn't seem to recognize the drive and wants to initialize it. You can utilize Disk First Aid as a first attempt at fixing the program. To do so, take the following steps:

1. Launch Disk First Aid (see Figure 5.31).

2. Select the volume that may be damaged (if you are using a floppy disk, insert it now).

3. Choose Repair to attempt to repair the volume (Verify will only tell you what is wrong).

4. When the process is finished, you will receive a report in the Disk First Aid window.

If Disk First Aid does not work, you may need to invest in a commercial disk-utility package, such as Norton Utilities.

Figure 5.31   Disk First Aid.

5: Disk And File Systems

Creating A Disk Tools Disk

Although the floppy drive is almost an antique, it has tremendous troubleshooting value when your computer cannot boot and when you cannot seem to locate the system CD-ROM. Creating a disk-tools disk is easy because Apple always includes a disk image with each system release. Before you can create a disk tools disk, you need two things: the latest disk tool image and the program Disk Copy. Both of these items are available on the Apple Web site at **www.apple.com**. To create the disk, take the following steps:

1. Launch Disk Copy.

2. Choose Utilities|Make A Floppy.

3. Locate the disk image that you downloaded from Apple (you can also find disk tool disk images on your system CD-ROM).

4. After the image has loaded into Disk Copy, you will be prompted to insert a floppy disk. Be aware that all the data on the floppy disk will be erased.

5. Disk Copy will copy the disk image onto the floppy disk (Figure 5.32 shows the process in action).

When this process is finished, you will now have a disk suitable for booting your computer.

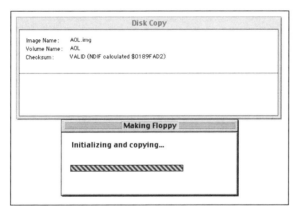

Figure 5.32   Disk copy in action.

Creating Disk Images

In the past, disk images were used to copy installation programs onto floppy disks. Today, disk images are used to simplify distribution of installer programs. You can create your own disk images using the Disk Copy utility available from Apple:

1. Launch Disk Copy.

2. Go to the Image menu and select Create Image From Folder or Create Image From Disk.

3. Locate the folder or disk and click on the Select button.

4. A Save dialog box displays. Choose a name for the image, and set the appropriate options such as image status (read-only) and image location.

5. Click on Okay. The program will create and mount the image. See Figure 5.33 for the results.

This format is an appropriate method for distributing files.

TIP: *Do you want to increase game performance? Create a disk image of a game CD-ROM, and mount the image rather than the CD. The game will play more smoothly and the movies and multimedia will load faster because a hard drive is much faster than a CD.*

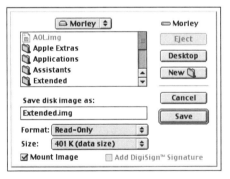

Figure 5.33   Creating a disk image.

Chapter 6

Memory Management

In Depth

This chapter explains the ways in which the Mac OS uses Random Access Memory for the OS itself and for applications that run on top of the Mac OS; it also discusses Read-Only Memory and Video Random Access Memory. Memory management is very different among operating systems, but the model used by the Mac OS has been consistent over the years, and users of Mac OS 8.5 shouldn't see any major changes. You will notice, however, that memory usage is faster, especially in the case of virtual memory; it's also more stable than ever before.

How The Mac OS Uses Memory

The Mac OS uses one contiguous Random Access Memory (RAM) pool for both system resources and applications. (Windows 95, 98, and NT use a similar approach to memory allocation, but earlier versions of Windows and MS-DOS use a very different method that caused many headaches for system administrators). When the Mac OS boots, it loads most system resources into two areas in the memory pool: the System Heap and the High Memory area. The System Heap, the first section of the memory pool, contains everything that is located in the System suitcase, such as fonts, sounds, and keyboard mappings, as well as icons and Desktop database resources. The last section of the memory pool is occupied by the contents of the High Memory area, including disk cache data and other system resources. The area between the System Heap and the High Memory is available for use by applications, desk accessories, control panels, and extensions.

The About This Computer feature offers basic information on how your computer has allocated memory, as shown in Figure 6.1, but the level of information here only scratches the surface.

TIP: *For an overview of the most popular applications and RAM-related utilities, see the "Immediate Solutions" section that follows in this chapter.*

Understanding how the Mac OS uses memory can help you run more concurrent applications, avoid problems with memory fragmentation, recover unused and fragmented memory, as well as handle errors and crashes that occur as a result of memory-related issues.

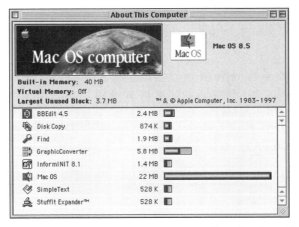

Figure 6.1   You can obtain basic information on memory allocation from the About This Computer command.

Physical Memory

RAM chips comes in various sizes and speeds, and memory intended for one type of computer cannot necessarily be used in another computer. Macintosh computers enjoy a higher level of hardware interoperability than most other computers, and RAM chips can usually be interchanged among families of computers, such as the first-generation PowerMacs (6100, 7100, 8100), second-generation PowerMacs with a PCI bus (7200, 8500, and 9500), and also the new G3 line.

Today, Macs use several types of RAM chips, including the following:

• 30- and 72-pin SIMMs (Single Inline-Memory Modules)

• 168-pin DIMMs (Dual Inline-Memory Modules)

• 168-pin EDO (Extended Data Out) DIMMs

• 168-pin SDRAM (Synchronous Dynamic Random Access Memory)

PowerBooks use similar types of RAM chips, but come in fewer configurations because most PowerBooks have very limited expansion slots (usually just a single slot).

Moreover, different RAM chips are capable of transmitting data through the chip at different speeds, usually measured in nanoseconds, although some manufacturers and retailers list speed in megahertz:

• SIMMs: 80-120ns

• DIMMs: 60-70ns

• SDRAM: 10ns

6: Memory Management

RAM speed is important because it is easy to mix chips with different speeds. This can generally slow the computer or cause it to be unable to recognize one or more of the chips.

Desktop Macs have either one or two banks of RAM expansion slots. When two banks are present, memory is best installed in like pairs to take advantage of memory interleaving. Interleaved memory isn't required, but even Apple recommends that memory be interleaved when possible because a significant performance boost (some say up to 7 percent) can occur.

TIP: *See the Apple spec chart in Appendix E for information about how much memory ships with which Macintosh, the maximum amount of RAM it will accommodate, and how many expansion slots are available. Also, when you order memory, it's important that your vendor understand Mac memory and whether matched-pairs are required. If they are not sure, at least verify that you can return or exchange the memory if it isn't acceptable for your computer.*

You use memory not only to store applications while they are in use, but also to assist the processor by serving as a temporary storage area for processing instructions. All PowerPC processors include an on-chip memory chip known as a *cache*, and most computers utilize additional cache chips on the processor daughter card or the motherboard, including the following:

- Level 2 (L2) cache
- Level 3 (L3) cache
- Backside cache
- Inline cache
- Look-aside cache

A typical on-chip cache is very small, usually 16- or 32K, and very, very fast when compared to the type of memory used for application data and the operating system. L2 and L3 cache chips are also faster, and they range in size from 256K to 1MB. Backside, inline, and look-aside cache are sometimes referred to as types of L2 cache, but they are really more like an L1.5 cache because they sit on or very near the processor card (or near the processor on the motherboard), but before the L2 cache. The G3 and upcoming G4 processors use these types of cache and are so fast, they make any other L2 or L3 cache superfluous. Cache chips can significantly increase the overall speed of just about any computer; check the Apple Spec Chart later in Appendix E of this book to see if your model ships with a cache and if you can increase its size to further increase the performance of your computer.

Physical Vs. Virtual Memory

Long before the first Mac came on the scene, mainframe, mini, and Unix computers were using hard drive space to mimic RAM to provide a very cheap substitute for it. Virtual memory—often abbreviated as VM—is a well-known concept to Mac users, even in the face of cheaper-than-ever RAM prices. It takes inactive RAM, writes it to the hard drive in a protected and hidden file, and then exchanges it back into active memory in place of inactive data. The Mac OS has long had the capability to use virtual memory and it has gotten more efficient over the years. Many third-party developers have created alternatives to Apple's virtual memory routines, including Ram Doubler from Connectix and RAM Charger from the Jump Development Group. Figure 6.2 shows the Memory Control Panel, where you can configure Apple's built-in virtual memory capabilities.

Debates persist on whether or not to use virtual memory. It is our opinion that if you need or want to use it, then do so. The two most important reasons for using virtual memory are as follows:

• You can launch more applications.

• Applications launch faster and require less memory to load.

The downside to using virtual memory includes the following:

• The effect VM has on the speed of the Mac OS

• System instability (some say it has increased, others say it has decreased)

Every user's situation is different, of course, and at times, virtual memory is more useful than at others. Some applications such as Adobe Photoshop have a built-in

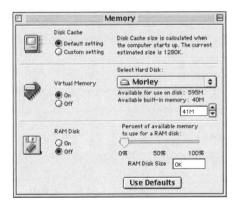

Figure 6.2   You can configure virtual memory through the newly revised Memory Control Panel.

virtual memory routine that enables very large files to be opened and temp files written to disk rather than being held in memory. So, even if you're not specifically using virtual memory, some of your applications may use it anyway.

TIP: *Virtual memory relies on writing data to, and reading from, your hard disk. A fast hard drive (7200 RPM or faster) and a SCSI accelerator will help speed things up when virtual memory is in use.*

Two of the most popular virtual memory utilities, Ram Doubler and RAM Charger, are discussed in the "Immediate Solutions" section later in this chapter.

Other Types Of Memory

In addition to RAM, the Mac OS uses at least four other types of memory:

- Read-Only Memory (ROM)
- Parameter RAM (PRAM)
- Video RAM (VRAM)
- Synchronous Graphic RAM (SGRAM).

All Macintosh computers rely on what is referred to as an *Apple ROM*, a chip that is several megabytes in size and contains essential data for the operation of the Mac OS. As a read-only chip, Apple ROM cannot be altered and doesn't lose its contents when the power is shut off. Apple ROMs are hardware-specific; each model of computer uses a ROM designed for use with that particular model. If the ROM is removed from the motherboard, the computer will not boot.

Parameter RAM is a very small chip, about 8K in size, that stores information about several of your computer's settings, including the time and date, as well as the startup disk. These settings are preserved by the computer's internal battery when it is off or when the computer is lacking a power source such as a battery (for PowerBooks) or an external power source. The information stored in PRAM is needed by the computer when it is powered on; it is not deleted when the computer is turned off, as long as the battery is charged (referred to as *nonvolatile memory*).

VRAM and SGRAM are two type of RAM that enable your computer's monitor to display at a higher bit depth (more colors) and faster refresh rate, which is easier on the eyes and reduces stress. Most new G3 PowerMacs come with 2MB of VRAM and can accommodate up to 6MB, but third-party graphics cards often come with 8MB or more, enabling monitors to display at higher resolutions and more colors. See your computer's "Technical Information" pamphlet for a

6: Memory Management

breakdown of how much VRAM or SGRAM is required to display various resolutions and colors.

Determining Memory Requirements

While it is possible to run Mac OS 8.5 with as little as 8MB or 16MB or RAM, it certainly isn't recommended. A good rule of thumb is to have at least 32MB of physical RAM for any PowerMac. (RAM is so cheap these days that you're really doing yourself or your users a disservice by having anything less.)

How much RAM do you really need? It boils down to your answers to the following questions:

- How many applications do you need to run at one time?
- How much RAM does each application require?
- How will you configure your Memory Control Panel to use virtual memory and the disk cache?

Unlike other operating systems, the Mac OS allows you to allocate a predetermined amount of RAM for exclusive use by a particular application. To determine how much RAM you need, add up the minimal amount of RAM that is required for each application that must be run simultaneously, then add about 16MB for the Mac OS. You can determine how much RAM each application needs by selecting it in the Finder and choosing Get Info from the File menu, as in Figure 6.3.

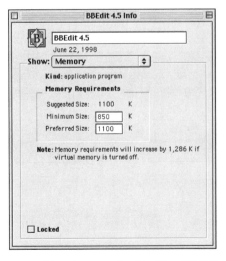

Figure 6.3   The Get Info command has been revised in Mac OS 8.5, but it still allows you to set memory requirements for applications.

To get the best possible estimate of an application's RAM requirements, turn off virtual memory, launch your applications, and see how much memory they actually use versus how much they have been allocated. Remember that PowerPC-native applications take into account the presence of virtual memory when recommending memory requirements.

Typical Memory Issues

You need to be aware of a small handful of memory-related issues as you explore Mac OS 8.5. Some of these issues are manageable to some extent, some are mere limitations of the Mac OS itself, and some are the fault of computer programmers who create the applications we love so dearly (grin).

Not Enough Memory

The most common error message you are likely to encounter is the "not enough memory errors." Two of these kinds of errors are shown in Figure 6.4.

The solution for this type of error is simple: Quit one or more applications to free up memory for another application (we'll cover this in detail in the "Immediate Solutions" section).

Memory Fragmentation

Many Mac users are unaware of the memory fragmentation issue. Memory can be fragmented similar to the fragmentation of files on a hard disk, resulting in the inability of programs to launch or function properly once they are loaded into memory. Fragmented memory takes up memory that would otherwise be available for other programs. Because all programs need to be loaded into a contiguous memory space, the Mac OS will report less memory available for applications than would be available if fragmentation were not present. Figure 6.5 shows five

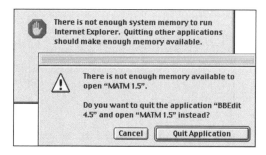

Figure 6.4   A good sign that your computer needs more RAM.

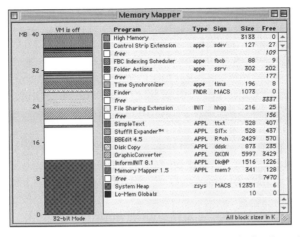

Memory Mapper				
Program	**Type**	**Sign**	**Size**	**Free**
High Memory			3133	0
Control Strip Extension	appe	sdev	127	27
free				*109*
FBC Indexing Scheduler	appe	fbcb	88	9
Folder Actions	appe	ssrv	302	202
free				*177*
Time Synchronizer	appe	tims	196	8
Finder	FNDR	MACS	1073	0
free				*3337*
File Sharing Extension	INIT	hhgg	216	25
free				*156*
SimpleText	APPL	ttxt	528	407
Stuffit Expander™	APPL	SITx	528	437
BBEdit 4.5	APPL	R*ch	2429	570
Disk Copy	APPL	ddsk	873	235
GraphicConverter	APPL	GKON	5997	3429
InformINIT 8.1	APPL	Dk@P	1516	1226
Memory Mapper 1.5	APPL	mem?	341	128
free				*7470*
System Heap	zsys	MACS	12351	6
Lo-Mem Globals			10	0

MB 40 — VM is off — 32 — 24 — 16 — 8 — 0 — 32-bit Mode — All block sizes in K

Figure 6.5   Fragmented memory can prevent applications from being launched.

fragments of free memory in an application called MemMapper. Two of the fragments are large enough to prevent many applications from being launched.

Identifying memory fragmentation is one thing, but how do you prevent it? Future versions of the Mac OS will probably eliminate most of these types of problems, but for now here are a few tricks to keep in mind:

• Don't quit applications unless necessary.

• Load applications first that are less likely to be quit before the next restart of your computer.

• Quit applications in reverse order in which they were launched.

• Install Apple's MacsBug to identify problematic applications.

• Manipulate the load order of applications in the Startup Items folder to load applications last that may crash or need to be restarted, such as Web browsers.

• Use as little virtual memory as possible or none at all.

Memory-Related Errors

You may have encountered several other memory-related errors while using the Mac OS, some of which you may not have known were actually memory errors. These errors usually result in an application crash and the display of a Mac OS error code such as "The application SuperApp has unexpectedly quit because of a Type 25 error," or a similar message. Memory errors occur when an application tries to read to, or write from, an invalid address space. Some applications are programmed to be more tolerant of such errors, but others can not only crash the current application, but the entire Mac OS as well.

Another "popular" error involves the need for System Heap to creep upwards in the memory pool. When an application occupies the space immediately above the System Heap, it cannot grow any larger and the Mac OS returns a "not enough memory" error. However, you sometimes will still get the error even after you have quit all the running applications. Why? If the address space directly above the System Heap is fragmented, it cannot grow and the error will persist until you reboot the system. Similarly, if an application attempts to write to an address space that is occupied by the Mac OS, it probably will crash the entire computer. However, if the address space is occupied by another application, it might crash only one or both applications, and not the entire computer.

TIP: *Quitting applications in reverse order from which they were launched can help prevent memory fragmentation.*

Finally, the System Heap itself can become fragmented, the consequence of which is that the Memory Manager can no longer do its job and the Mac OS will crash. This type of error is usually the result of flawed programming, and the only solution is to try a utility that purges it of unused blocks. This frees up more memory for use by the System Heap.

Quick Reference Specifications

The following list describes the essential facts about how Mac OS 8.5 uses memory:

- Macintosh computers use several different types of memory, including Random Access Memory (RAM), Read Only Memory (ROM), Parameter RAM (PRAM), Video RAM (VRAM), and Synchronous Graphic RAM (SGRAM).

- RAM comes in various sizes, speeds, and configurations; some of these are interchangeable with other computers.

- The Mac OS can employ virtual memory in place of physical memory, but it is much slower than RAM.

- Several conditions can lead to memory-related errors in Mac OS 8.5, including memory fragmentation and undeleted memory in and around the System Heap.

Utilities To Use

The utilities or elements listed here either are part of the Mac OS, are included on the book's accompanying CD-ROM, or are easily located on the Web:

- *Memory Control Panel*—Change how memory is handled on your Mac (allocate memory for use as a disk cache, enable and adjust virtual mem-ory by using any physically attached hard drive, and create and adjust a single RAM disk).

- *About This Computer*—View basic information about how allocated memory is used by active applications and the Mac OS.

- *More About This Macintosh*—View detailed information about how allocated memory is used by active applications and the Mac OS, as well as mounted volumes and basic hardware information. A Pro version is also available.

- *MemMapper*—View very detailed information about how allocated memory is used by active applications and the Mac OS.

  Get detailed information about running applications, as well as quit selected applications.

  View how data is paged to disk when using virtual memory.

- *Cache Saver*—Save the contents of your disk cache in case of system crashes.

- *Ram Doubler*—Create and adjust virtual memory that is more efficient than the Mac OS's virtual memory.

  View detailed information on memory allocation for running applications and the Mac OS.

- *AppDisk*, *ramBunctious*, *RamDisk+*—Create custom RAM disks.

- *Get Info*—View an application's suggested memory requirement, as well as adjust its minimum and preferred allocation.

  View how much more or less memory will be required or saved if virtual memory is enabled or disabled, respectively.

- *RAM Charger*—Optimize and highly customize memory usage and allocation for applications.

- *Mac OS Purge*—Purge the System Heap of stale data to decrease the number of blocks occupied.

- *RAM Handler*—View memory usage.

  Purge and compress memory used by applications and Mac OS.

6: Memory Management

Immediate Solutions

Viewing Memory Allocation

It's a hard fact of life that few of us actually have enough RAM in our computers, which leaves us wondering how the memory we do have is being used, and also if it is being used efficiently. Knowing how memory is allocated is the first step toward optimizing your system for peak performance.

About This Computer

Mac OS 8.5 offers limited information on how your system's memory is currently allocated. The About This Computer command (see Figure 6.6) gives a broad overview of allocated memory, but that's about it. This command used to be known as About This Macintosh in earlier versions of the Mac OS.

To issue the About This Computer command, follow the same steps you used in the past:

1. Select the Finder from the application menu.

2. Choose About This Computer from the Apple Menu.

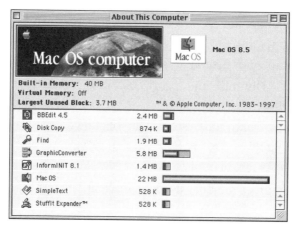

Figure 6.6   The About This Computer command offers only an overview of your system's memory allocation.

Information about your system's memory will appear in the upper half of the window, and running applications will be listed (in alphabetical order) in the lower half of the window, as well as memory usage of the Mac OS itself.

TIP: *The amount of memory used by the Mac OS, as reported by About This Computer, is equal to the memory occupied by the Finder, System Heap, High Memory area, and miscellaneous memory partitions used by the Mac OS.*

The upper half of the window displays the following information about your computer's memory usage:

- *Built-in Memory*—The amount of physical RAM installed on your logic board.

- *Virtual Memory*—The amount of memory emulated by using disk space.

- *Largest Unused Block*—The largest contiguous allocation of RAM (physical or virtual) available for use by an application.

Looking at the lower half of the window, the actual amount of memory used by the Mac OS and applications will vary, depending on whether you are using virtual memory and if you've reconfigured the amount of memory each application is allowed to use. For example, Figure 6.7 shows the same set of applications as in the previous figure, but with virtual memory turned on (and set to its default settings).

Several utilities and applications provide much more information about how your computer is using memory.

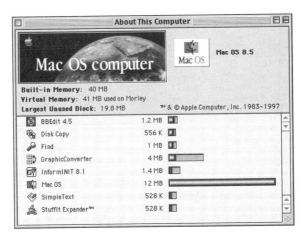

Figure 6.7   The About This Computer command with virtual memory turned on.

More About This Macintosh

Kevin Tieskoetter's application, More About This Macintosh (MATM), provides exactly what it says, more information about your computer (remember, the command used to be called About This Macintosh). You can download the latest version from Kevin's Web site at **pobox.com/~albtrssp** (the standard version is bundled with RAM Charger, which we'll discuss in just a few minutes, and a demo of MATM Pro is included as well).

MATM provides a more detailed level of information about your computer's memory allocation, including free blocks of RAM. Visit Kevin's home page to obtain the latest version of MATM, then install it. To use it, just double-click on the MATM application icon, and a window like the one shown in Figure 6.8 will appear.

MATM's interface describes four main features about your computer, information about the operating system, memory usage, disk usage, and general information about your computer's hardware. The upper portion of the window shows similar information found in About This Computer, as does the Memory tab, at first glance.

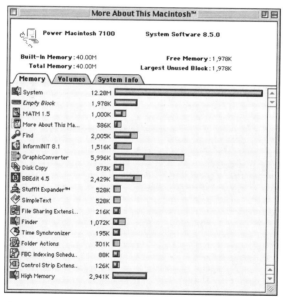

Figure 6.8   Kevin Tieskoetter's More About This Macintosh application provides more details on your computer's allocation of available memory.

As you can see in Figure 6.8, however, MATM shows much more about how your computer is using memory:

- Memory used by applications
- Memory used by major extensions, such as File Sharing
- Free blocks of memory
- Percentage of memory used by each entry

Double-clicking on an application's entry while holding down the Option key will cause that application to quit and automatically update the MATM Memory tab to show newly freed blocks of RAM. For example, quitting all the applications shown in the previous example is shown in Figure 6.9 as discongruent "Empty Blocks."

Finally, the demo of the Pro version of MATM that ships with RAM Charger uses a different interface than does the standard version of MATM, but it allows you to customize the information about your memory. For example, you can reorder the list of items that have memory allocated to them in several ways. Figure 6.10 shows the same information as in the previous examples, but here it is ordered so that the items requiring the most RAM are listed first.

MemMapper

Another solution for exploring how your system is using memory is MemMapper, by R. Fronabarger. This is a freeware utility that shows more information than

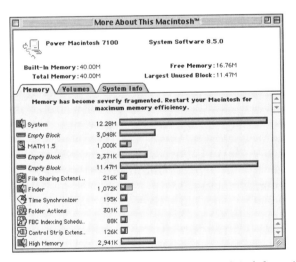

Figure 6.9   You can quit applications from within MATM to update information about empty blocks of memory.

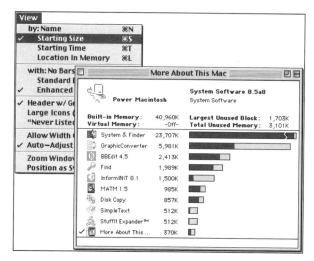

Figure 6.10   The Pro version of MATM that comes bundled with RAM Charger offers different views and is customizable.

About This Computer shows; it draws a map of your computer's memory, which is a real bonus in understanding how the Mac OS allocates memory.

For example, Figure 6.11 shows the same applications running as in the previous examples as viewed through MemMapper. It does a great job showing how portions of the Mac OS are loaded into the High Memory area at the top of the map and the System Heap at the bottom. It is especially useful for detecting fragmented free memory blocks, four of which are shown in this example.

Double-clicking on an entry reveals detailed information about a process, as in Figure 6.12, including the type of process and how much CPU time lapsed since it was launched. Also, like with MATM, you can exit an application from within MemMapper by choosing File plus Send Quit Event.

Another very useful feature of MemMapper becomes visible when virtual memory is enabled, either through Apple's built-in virtual memory scheme or by using an application like Ram Doubler, shown in Figure 6.13. MemMapper displays memory blocks that have been paged out to disk using a black vertical line on the right side of the memory map.

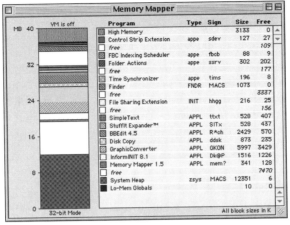

Figure 6.11   MemMapper lists applications and processes, as well as maps them out for an easy-to-read diagram of allocated memory.

Figure 6.12   MemMapper provides detailed information about each process.

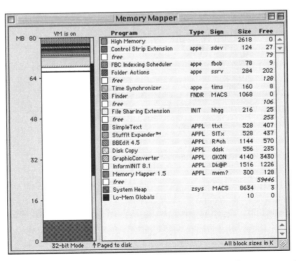

Figure 6.13   MemMapper also tracks memory blocks that have been paged to disk through virtual memory.

6: Memory Management

Allocating Disk Cache

Mac OS 8.5 allows you to set aside a portion of your RAM as a hard disk cache, which speeds up many applications that need to access your hard drive for information on a frequent basis. Some programs are not disk intensive, but a large disk cache can really boost those applications that are. Keep in mind, however, that any memory you set aside for use by the disk cache will be unavailable for use by the operating system or by applications. The Memory Control Panel in Mac OS 8.5 provides two choices for allocating disk cache.

Default Disk Cache Settings

The Default setting for the disk cache takes the guesswork out of allocating memory for the disk cache. Debates still rage over how much RAM is enough, but the engineers at Apple have consistently suggested using about 32K of RAM for every megabyte of physical RAM installed on your computer. Therefore, for a computer with 32MB of RAM, a default disk cache setting would be 1024K, or 1/32 of your installed physical RAM.

To allow the Mac OS to make this calculation for you, choose the Default setting in the Memory Control Panel, as shown in Figure 6.14.

Customizing Disk Cache Settings

At times, of course, you need to customize the disk cache settings to gain a performance advantage. This advantage can be either to increase the cache to speed things up or to decrease the size of the cache to optimize other aspects of your computer.

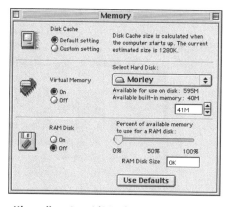

Figure 6.14   The Default setting allocates 1/32 of your physical RAM for use as a disk cache.

To customize your disk cache, follow these steps:

1. Open the Memory Control Panel.

2. Select the Custom Settings button.

3. Select Custom again when the warning dialog appears, reminding you that changing the settings may cause poor system performance.

4. Increase or decrease the size of the cache using the Up or Down buttons shown in Figure 6.15.

5. Restart the computer to force the changes to take effect.

One drawback to having a large disk cache is that if your computer crashes while in a word-processing document, for example, the changes to your document may not get written to disk fast enough. Consequently, you may lose some of your work. To help in these situations, St. Clair Software makes a fine utility, CacheSaver, that allows you to flush the cache to disk—at predetermined intervals or manually—when the computer has been idle for an extended period (see Figure 6.16 for an example).

You can download the latest version of CacheSaver from the St. Clair Software home page at **www.stclairsw.com/**.

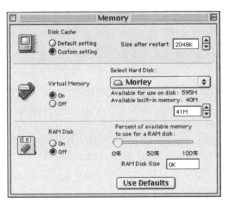

Figure 6.15   Customize your disk cache settings as needed, or allow the Mac OS to calculate the standard setting size for you automatically.

Allocating Virtual Memory

Mac OS 8.5 improves the speed and stability of virtual memory, but until the Mac OS is revised to allow for protected memory space, virtual memory will not ever

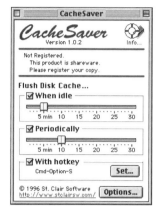

Figure 6.16   CacheSaver writes the contents of your disk cache to disk to prevent data loss in case of a system failure.

6: Memory Management

be as efficient as it could be. Many experienced Mac users shy away from using virtual memory if at all possible because it slows some aspects of the Mac OS and introduces issues of system stability. The majority of us, however, use virtual memory because we have limited amounts of physical RAM and we run so many applications. Luckily for us, several virtual memory solutions are available for use with Mac OS 8.5.

The following two main reasons exist for using virtual memory:

• Virtual memory enables more applications to run on a computer at the same time.

• Virtual memory takes advantage of file mapping with PowerPC-native applications and allows them to be launched using significantly less RAM.

System degradation that results from using virtual memory varies widely, depending on your computer's speed, hard drive speed and throughput, system bus speed, and SCSI or IDE adapter.

Mac OS Virtual Memory

The virtual memory options have changed very little under Mac OS 8.5. You can still select to turn virtual memory on or off, select a hard disk to use, and the amount of disk space to use for virtual memory. The Memory Control Panel shown in Figure 6.17 is configured to use 1MB of virtual memory on the drive named Morley, providing 41MB of total system memory and consuming 41MB of disk space.

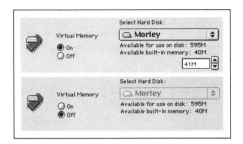

Figure 6.17   Customizing the Mac OS's built-in virtual memory options.

How much virtual memory you need is a matter of personal choice and depends on how much memory you need, how much speed you're willing to sacrifice by using virtual memory, and how much disk space you have available for use with virtual memory. Keep in mind that any performance decrease could be offset by the lower memory requirements of most applications when virtual memory is active and file mapping is therefore enabled.

Ram Doubler

Ram Doubler, from the Connectix Corporation, is a great improvement over Apple's virtual memory capabilities in Mac OS 8.5 for several reasons. First, it is reported to be faster and more stable than Apple's virtual memory. Also, Ram Doubler allows you to use virtual memory only for file mapping, which is what allows applications to be opened using less allocated memory than if virtual memory were turned off. Ram Doubler has few configuration options; Figure 6.18 shows its interface.

With Ram Doubler, you can perform the following tasks:

• Enable file mapping only, which saves the time of having to page data to and from disk.

• Double or triple your computer's RAM using virtual memory, or adjust the amount of virtual memory in increments of 20MB (typically).

• Default to doubling the amount of RAM by selecting the Use Default button.

Remember, the more disk space you use as virtual memory, the more time your system will spend paging data to and from disk. Use the setting that best meets your needs.

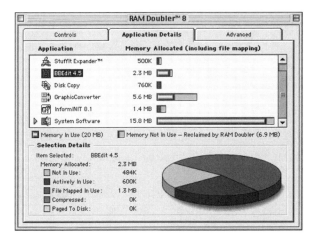

Figure 6.18   Ram Doubler is an appealing alternative to Apple's virtual memory routine in
Mac OS 8.5.

Another nice feature of Ram Doubler is the way it displays information about
how your memory has been allocated to a running application and to the operating system. For example, Figure 6.19 shows some of the same applications as in
previous examples, as seen through the Ram Doubler Control Panel configuration window.

Unlike MATM, you can only view the memory allocation for each item; you cannot send a Quit Apple Event to quit an application and unload it from memory.
However, it's nice to see exactly how much RAM is in use by the various elements
of your operating system. For the latest information about Ram Doubler, see the
Connectix Web site at **www.connectix.com**.

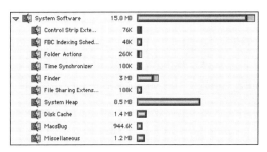

Figure 6.19   Ram Doubler provides detailed information on your operating system and
application's memory usage.

Allocating Memory For RAM Disks

RAM disks are really the opposite of virtual memory because they use physical RAM to emulate a hard disk. RAM disks are typically used to store files and folders that are frequently accessed, such as databases or Web server documents, because the speed at which a RAM disk can be accessed is several times higher than with a disk drive mechanism. RAM disks are used much less frequently than virtual memory, but several solutions are available for those who need RAM disks. Mac OS 8.5 has a built-in capability to allocate a portion of your computer's RAM to serve as a RAM disk, but you have other options as well.

RAM Disk

The RAM disk portion of the Memory Control Panel, shown in Figure 6.20, allows you to allocate a portion of your system's RAM for use as a RAM disk. As with virtual memory, any RAM used for a RAM disk is unavailable for use by the operating system and applications.

To create a RAM disk, take these steps:

1. Open the Memory Control Panel.

2. Turn the RAM disk on and select a size for the disk.

3. Restart the computer.

RAM disks work just like other disks on the Mac OS. You can share them, you can save files and folders on them, and (when you restart the computer) the contents of the RAM disk are saved and will reappear for continued use. However, remember that when the RAM disk is being shared, you cannot change the settings in the Memory Control Panel, and the memory used to create the RAM disk will be unavailable for use by other applications. Figure 6.21 shows a 5MB RAM disk with a few items that will be restored after the computer is rebooted.

Other RAM Disks

Here are a few other RAM disks that might be of use to you. Each has its own strengths and all are excellent alternatives to the RAM disk features of the Mac OS. Figure 6.22 shows some of the options available with these RAM disk alternatives.

Figure 6.20   Open the Memory Control Panel to create and adjust RAM disk settings.

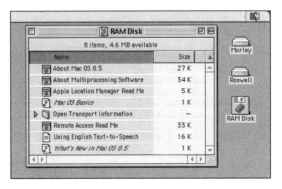

Figure 6.21   RAM disks function like any other disk, but much faster.

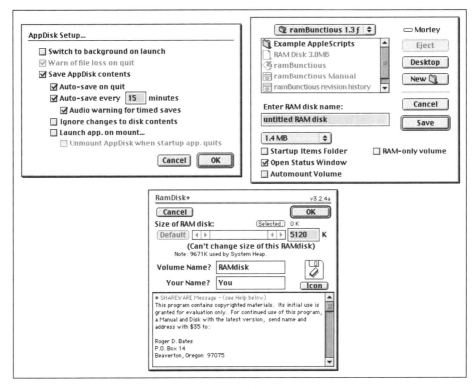

Figure 6.22   A few alternatives to the Mac OS's RAM disk.

6: Memory Management

- *AppDisk*—An easy-to-use RAM disk by Mark Adams that automatically saves the contents of the disk at predefined intervals and allows you to mount and unmount multiple RAM disks without restarting. You can find this at **members.aol.com/mavsftwre**.

- *ramBunctious*—An AppleScriptable RAM disk by Elden Wood and Bob Clark that is more feature-rich than most other RAM disk utilities, and even supports write-through to disk just in case the computer crashes. You can find this at **www.kagi.com/rambunctious**.

- *RamDisk+*—A system INIT from Roger D. Bates that supports booting from the RAM disk and can automatically copy files and folders from a hard disk onto the RAM disk on startup. You can find this at **www. teleport.com/ ~rbates**.

Allocating Application Memory

The Mac OS is rather unique among mainstream operating systems because you can decide how much memory an application may use. You are no doubt accustomed to this concept from previous versions of the Mac OS, and little has changed under Mac OS 8.5 except the revised Get Info command, shown in Figure 6.23.

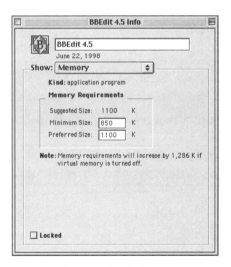

Figure 6.23 The memory section of the new Get Info command.

The Memory portion of the Get Info command is only an active option for applications (foreground and background), and isn't available for documents and folders. The Memory Requirements section provides the following information and allocation options:

- *Suggested Size*—The amount of memory the author of the program suggests should be allocated for normal use.

- *Minimal Size*—The smallest allocation that is advisable to sustain functionality.

- *Preferred Size*—The amount of memory you want to allocate to an application, if available for use.

The Note section advises users how much RAM will be saved or lost if virtual memory is turned on or off, respectively. Applications that are not PowerPC-native or FAT binary (for both PowerPC and 68K computers) will not have a Note section.

A good rule of thumb is to only increase the Preferred Size setting if you get an error message that indicates the application is running low on memory, or if you get persistent system-level errors such as Type 1 or 10 errors. Try doubling the amount of suggested memory, and then scale back if necessary. Also, keep in mind that some applications do not return portions of allocated memory back to the Finder after they have been quit. This is a leading cause of Memory fragmentation and will persist until the computer is restarted.

To increase the amount of memory allocated to an application, take these steps:

1. Quit the application.

2. Select the application and choose File|Get Info (or Command+I).

3. Increase the Preferred Size to a figure higher than the Suggested Size.

4. Close the Info window and relaunch the application.

TIP: *Applications are able to report errors, including memory-related errors. The programmer also has enabled them to report errors, so persistent crashing of an application may or may not be the result of a lack of memory allocation.*

Reducing Memory Requirements

You can reduce the memory requirements of applications in Mac OS 8.5 in several ways. The first way is to manually reduce the amount of RAM in the Get Info command. Alternatively, you can get shareware and commercial applications that do the job automatically.

Get Info

Computers with low physical memory can take advantage of the Memory Requirements section of the Get Info command to reduce the amount of memory allocated to an application. However, this may cause problems, and you should reduce memory requirements only if necessary.

To reduce the memory requirements for an application:

1. Quit the application.
2. Select the application and choose File|Get Info (or Command+I).
3. Change the Preferred Size to a figure higher than the Minimum Size but smaller than the Suggested Size.
4. Close the Info window and relaunch the application.

You can change the Minimum Size to an amount smaller than the default, but a warning dialog will inform you that this could cause the application to crash. Do this only if absolutely necessary.

RAM Charger

RAM Charger, a commercial application from the Jump Development Group, is a comprehensive solution for reducing and optimizing memory requirements for applications on the Mac OS. Do not confuse this application with virtual memory applications such as Ram Doubler, however, because it is an optimization tool rather than a virtual memory tool. You can use RAM Charger in conjunction with Ram Doubler, the Mac OS's virtual memory scheme, or with no virtual memory at all. To get the latest version of RAM Charger, including a fully functional demo version, visit the Jump development Web site at **www.jumpdev.com**.

RAM Charger evaluates an application's memory requirements and intercepts certain Apple Events between the application and the Mac OS to dynamically allocate additional memory when necessary that prevents the application from running out of memory. Moreover, it adds many configuration options to the get Info command and allows you to preconfigure your applications for optimal memory usage.

6: Memory Management

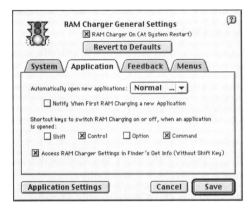

Figure 6.24   You can open the General Settings Control Panel for RAM Charger from the Control Panels menu or from the newly installed RAM Charger menu next to the Application menu.

RAM Charger has too many features to go into much detail here, but the following example of how to "charge" an application will illustrate how it might help you with your needs:

1. Install the latest version of RAM Charger, reboot, and open the RAM Charger General Settings Control Panel, as in Figure 6.24.

2. Make sure that the Access RAM Charger Settings in Finder's Get Info is selected, then select Get Info for an application such as BBEdit and note the new RAM Charger Memory Requirements section. Figure 6.25 shows before and after versions of this section.

3. Click on the More button to access the RAM Charger Application Settings menu, shown in Figure 6.26, to configure the application for use with RAM Charger.

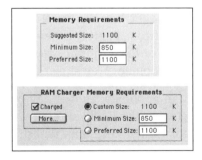

Figure 6.25   RAM Charger replaces the Memory Requirements section of the Get Info command with several new options.

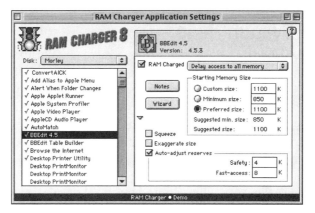

Figure 6.26   You can configure applications to work with RAM Charger one at a time, or select RAM Charger Application Settings from the RAM Charger drop-down menu and configure them *en masse*.

4. Confirm the current settings, or select the Wizard button and follow the instructions to have RAM Charger evaluate your usage of the application against its actual memory usage. This is a very good option and the folks at Jump Development have already evaluated many applications and noted their peculiar memory requirements when necessary.

RAM Charger does an excellent job evaluating memory allocation usage and re-quirements for most applications; you may have to try a thing or three to optimize RAM Charger to work with your applications. For example, Figure 6.27 shows the result of our use of the RAM Charger Wizard with BBEdit.

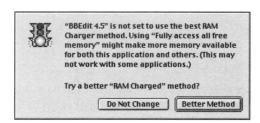

Figure 6.27   The RAM Charger Wizard evaluated how BBEdit is used and recommended a different approach for allocating memory.

Purging The System Heap

We mentioned earlier that the System Heap grows and shrinks dynamically, and that it sometimes runs into trouble when an application residing in the lower region of the memory pool blocks its upward growth. One way to temporarily fix this problem is to run Kenji Takeuchi's freeware application Mac OS Purge before launching—and after quitting—applications that rely upon system extensions. It deletes or purges stale data from memory and allows more room for the Mac OS.

To run Mac OS Purge, take these steps:

1. Copy Mac OS Purge anywhere onto your hard drive (we suggest the Apple Menu).

2. Launch Mac OS Purge.

3. Mac OS Purge will run, quit, and then display the About This Computer window.

You will see a decrease in the amount of memory used by the Mac OS that is proportional to the amount of stale data that was purged. For example, Figure 6.28 shows an excerpt from MemMapper after Mac OS Purge has been run (it offers detailed information on the System Heap). Notice that the System Heap now has twice as much free memory.

See the Info-Mac HyperArchive at **hyperarchive.lcs.mit.edu/HyperArchive/ HyperArchive.html** for updates to this and many other programs.

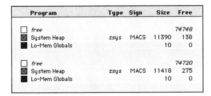

Figure 6.28   Mac OS Purge rids the System Heap of unused data, which can lead to "out of memory" error messages from the Finder when the System Heap cannot expand upward into the memory pool.

Purging Unused Memory

Mac OS 8.5 doesn't allow users to purge unused memory from the System Heap, let alone applications. Another great utility that allows you not only to view memory use but purge unused memory as well is RAM Handler, by Mike Throckmorton. RAM Handler is similar to MemMapper in that it displays detailed memory allocation information; it is similar to Mac OS Purge because it allows you to purge unused memory. However, it also allows you to purge unused application memory. RAM Handler is copyrighted by the Ziff-Davis Publishing Company, and you can download it from **www.macdownload.com**.

To use RAM Handler:

1. Copy RAM Handler anywhere onto your hard drive (we suggest the Startup Items folder).

2. Launch RAM Handler.

3. RAM Handler will run, opening a floating palette like the ones shown in Figure 6.29.

Configure RAM Handler by choosing the items you want displayed from the Options menu. You can configure two views, a Maximized Window view and a Minimized Window view (see Figure 6.30).

In this example, RAM Handler is configured to display:

• The name of the application or process (left)

• The amount of memory in use (middle)

• The amount of free memory (right)

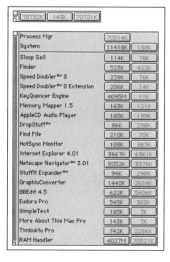

Figure 6.29 RAM Handler's floating palette gives you quick access to memory allocation information in two different views, a Minimized Window view and a Maximized Window view.

6: Memory Management

Figure 6.30   Configure RAM Handler's floating palette to display as much information as you need.

TIP: *The Process Manager lists only the amount of RAM that is free for use by other applications.*

To purge and compact memory usage, just click on any of the buttons that list an application or a process.

Chapter 7

Mobile Computing

In Depth

It seems that the quest for almost any electronic device is to make it smaller without relinquishing any power. Notebook computers and devices are no exception. The first computers filled entire rooms. Gradually the tubes gave way to circuits, which gave way to chips and microchips. One of the reasons Apple elected to move away from the 68K architecture was that the Reduced Instruction Set Computer (RISC) chip manufactured by Motorola was smaller and cooler, yet faster. Meanwhile, the X86 architecture or Complex Instruction Set Computer (CISC) chip was growing larger and running hotter. Intel, the dominant manufacturer of the X86 chips, occasionally aired commercials with the brightly colored technicians, also known as "bunnies." In one such commercial, the Intel Pentium chip was thrust toward the viewer, and it is the size of a chalkboard eraser. Imagine fitting that into a notebook computer.

Portable Vs. Desktop Computing

One of the driving forces of portable computing is mobility. This may involve traveling great distances or taking a device to work and home. Whatever the reason, busy people increasingly find themselves out from behind a desk and hating to leave the computer behind. Fortunately the PowerBook provides excellent portability options. A quick comparison shows that these PowerBooks are almost as good as desktop systems.

Expansion

In the expansion arena, desktop systems definitely have an advantage. Size allows the desktop systems to easily improve storage, memory, and performance. PowerBooks also have the ability for expansion but in different ways. PowerBooks increase capabilities by using expansion bays that can hold different devices. The latest G3 models allow you to use two devices at once by removing the battery, but you have to plug the computer to a power source, so that may not suit your needs. PowerBooks do have the PCMCIA card option for expansion. Additional storage and RAM as well as Ethernet and modems are available. See the section on "Cards" for additional information on these devices.

7: Mobile Computing

Fragility

When Compaq first developed portable computers, it would demonstrate the quality of the device by dropping it, then picking it up and turning it on—something no manufacturer of portable or desktop computers would even dream of doing today. Portable computers are especially vulnerable to damage. Desktop systems are just as fragile, but except for the rare earthquake or other disaster, they are not often in motion.

Portability

If portability is a deciding factor in your computer purchase, you should buy a PowerBook. Thanks to the PowerPC processor chip, PowerBooks can run at speeds comparable to Macintosh desktop machines. So, if you find yourself on the go, and you need a computer that can go with you, a PowerBook would definitely fit your needs.

PowerBook Limitations

A PowerBook can do just about anything a desktop computer can do, but PowerBook users must recognize certain limitations.

A PowerBook is truly portable when it's using the battery. Batteries have come a long way from the first PowerBooks, running from two and up to three and one-half hours (even longer, if you practice some of the energy saving techniques covered in this chapter). Many of the hardware components have been manufactured to use as little power as possible. Still, on a long airplane flight, invariably the battery begins to fade. The PowerBook G3 Series computers now allow you to plug two batteries into the expansion bays—a helpful feature, but that limits your options with other devices. If you plan on watching a DVD movie by using the DVD-ROM expansion device, don't expect the battery to last as long as the movie.

Two G3 PowerBooks

It may seem confusing, but two PowerBook models have the G3 chip. The PowerBook G3 computer is an older model. Apple recently announced the PowerBook G3 *Series* computer, which contains the G3 chip, but has been redesigned. The difference is visible on the case. The PowerBook G3 computers have the familiar color Apple logo on the cover, while the PowerBook G3 Series computers have a sleek design with a large white Apple logo on the cover. Apple is moving away from the color Apple and moving toward a solid Apple logo. The new iMac computer also follows this convention.

7: Mobile Computing

Energy Saving

Much research has been done to find the correct deadly chemical combination that will provide the longest battery life, and many advances have been made. In some cases, you can enjoy up to seven hours of computer usage without recharging the battery (this is accomplished using batteries in both expansion bays of the PowerBook G3 Series computer). You can take certain steps to increase battery life. The computer also takes some steps on its own to preserve power.

Screen Dimming

By default, the computer dims the screen after a certain period of inactivity. The screen appears to darken slightly, although icons and the Desktop still display. Screen dimming is an important feature because the display itself uses a significant percentage of battery power: Black-and-white or grayscale display uses roughly twenty percent; the color display uses a whopping fifty percent.

Previous versions of the Mac OS used a control panel called PowerBook Settings to configure many of the energy saving features. In Mac OS 8.5, these options are found within the Energy Saver control panel. Figure 7.1 shows the Energy Saver control panel in its default view.

You can configure screen dimming to occur at different time intervals or have the screen never dim. By default, the time has been set to one minute of inactivity during battery usage and five minutes while using the power adapter. You can also change these to have separate settings for battery versus power adapter usage.

You can also save battery power by manually dimming the screen by adjusting the brightness and contrast of the display. If you do this to save energy, a better choice is to put the system to sleep instead.

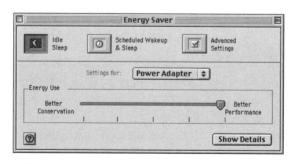

Figure 7.1   The Energy Saver control panel default view.

Hard Disk

The hard drive spins in order to access data stored on it. This spinning and data access use an estimated fifteen percent of the battery power. Much of the work you do on the computer is held in memory until you need to store the data in a more permanent location (like the hard drive), especially if you are working in a word-processing package. All this hard drive activity may not be necessary. You can cause the hard drive to "spin down" (which means that it stops spinning). The Energy Saver control panel can do this automatically. Figure 7.2 shows the settings for hard disk spindown.

You can use any of the following methods to conserve hard drive usage:

- Reduce I/O usage by using memory-resident applications.
- Turn off Virtual Memory. It is enabled by default to improve memory performance. If you are really in need of extended battery life, turn it off.
- Use the Energy Saver control panel. It contains a setting that causes the hard drive to spin down after a period of inactivity.
- Use the Control Strip button for instantly stopping the hard drive.
- Press the key sequence: Command+Shift+Control+0 to stop the hard drive from spinning.
- Create a RAM disk (see the instructions later in this chapter in "Creating A RAM Disk").

How often should you spin down the hard drive? Consider that the energy expended to bring the hard drive back up to speed equals the energy expended by

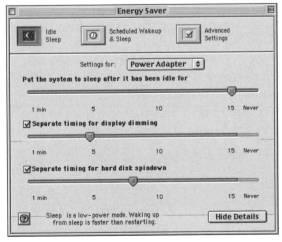

Figure 7.2   The Settings for hard drive spindown.

thirty seconds to one minute of routine spinning. If you have loaded a long Web page that will take several minutes to read, energy saving might be an option. Otherwise, you may want to let the computer do this feature automatically via the Energy Saver settings.

Sleep

Computer *sleep* is a state where very little energy is used. The sleep option was first developed for notebook computers such as the PowerBook as a way of conserving battery power, but owners of desktop systems also found that it was desirable, and so it was included in the Mac OS. However, systems that are in a sleep state have some differences. Desktop systems do conserve energy, but the hard drive continues to spin. PowerBooks shut down everything, but keep the contents of memory protected.

When a PowerBook is sleeping, the screen darkens completely and the hard drive ceases to spin. The computer looks as though it has been turned off, with the exception of a blinking light at the top of the monitor. However, pushing any key—with the exception of the Caps Lock and trackpad button—brings the system back to full power.

You can use any of the following methods to put the PowerBook to sleep:

- Use the Energy Saver control panel. You can configure sleep to occur after a period of inactivity.
- Select the Energy Saver Control Strip button to sleep immediately.
- Go to the Special menu and select Sleep as shown in Figure 7.3.
- Use the key sequence Command+Shift+0.

Your computer will also go to sleep when the battery power is at such a low level that the system can no longer function. You will receive a series of warnings that instruct you to plug in the adapter immediately and charge the batteries. If you ignore these warnings or cannot begin charging immediately, the system will eventually go into a sleep state and will not "awaken" until adequate power has been provided. If you have information stored within RAM and the computer has reached this level of power deprivation, be aware that the contents of RAM may only be

Figure 7.3   The Sleep option in the Special menu.

held for a limited time. Check the user's manual that came with your PowerBook for more information.

RAM Disk

You can designate part of your hard drive to function as additional memory; this function is called *virtual memory*. You can also allocate a section of memory to function as a high-speed storage disk called a *RAM disk*. The RAM disk was designed for PowerBooks as a method of extending battery life by reducing reading and writing to the hard drive during a computing session. You can also create a RAM disk on desktop systems. The one drawback of a RAM disk is that the contents are lost when the computer is shut down. However, you can configure the system to save the contents of a RAM disk to the hard drive upon system shutdown. Figure 7.4 shows the RAM disk options in the Memory control panel.

Network Access

In the business environment, PowerBooks need to be able to access a network. To this end, the latest PowerBook G3 Series computers come with built-in Ethernet. You can also have an internal modem. However, even the earliest PowerBooks had methods of accessing the network, and these devices still work today.

A SCSI solution is available for network access. The early PowerBooks used this method, and you can still purchase this option today. SCSI Ethernet options are discussed in the following section.

Companies such as Farallon manufacture PCMCIA cards that provide Ethernet access to the PowerBook. These solutions are more portable than the SCSI network device and a wide variety of cards are available for Ethernet access.

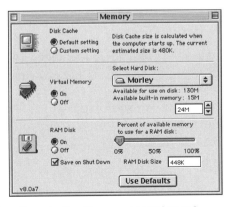

Figure 7.4 The RAM Disk options in the Memory control panel.

Finally, newer PowerBooks have an infrared port. Data can be exchanged between two computers in this fashion (if the second computer also has an infrared port).

When you have enabled network access, your computer functions the same way a desktop system does. You can use the Chooser or the Network Browser to access network services and enjoy rapid file transfer between computers.

SCSI Ethernet

The SCSI Ethernet device plugs into the SCSI port in the back of the computer and uses this alternate method to access the network. Asante manufactures this solution. If you have an older PowerBook, this in an excellent device for getting the computer on the network. The device is larger than PCMCIA cards, but products are available that use the computer's power supply and thus allow you some mobility. Other devices have their own power supply but still provide network access.

Cards

A technology that has greatly improved expansion capabilities of PowerBooks is *PCMCIA cards*. PowerBooks with this capability have two PCMCIA ports, usually located on the left side of the computer. PCMCIA cards, also known as *PC cards*, are the size of credit cards—except for a greater thickness—and come in three types:

- Type I cards are 3.3 millimeters thick and can be placed in either the top or bottom slot.

- Type II cards are 5 millimeters thick and can be placed in either the top or bottom slot.

- Type III cards are 10.5 millimeters thick and can be placed only in the bottom slot (because of size limitations).

PC cards perform a variety of functions, including Ethernet, modem, Ethernet and modem, and additional disk storage. And because they are so small, you can carry several of these cards. Their small size, however, can also be a drawback. The connection cables for the cards are especially fragile and should be handled with care. If you should damage the connection, you may have to purchase a replacement from the manufacturer.

Infrared

Today's network environment is full of cabling and connections. Each device is hardwired into the chain, limited like animals on a leash. Infrared promises to

7: Mobile Computing

change that. We use infrared technology in everyday life. Millions use a device that sends signals to a receiver each time they watch television and ambitious plans are in the works for wireless networks. PowerBooks have included infrared ports for several years and have expanded this capability to the iMac. You can exchange data between devices that contain these wireless connectivity ports.

The Apple IR File Exchange application allows you to exchange information between Macintosh devices with infrared ports. Apple even has a network protocol called IRTalk that facilitates this communication. The devices need to be no more than three feet from each other with their IR windows facing. Infrared communication can be enabled within the AppleTalk control panel by selecting the Apple IR Talk protocol.

Modem

The majority of us do not enjoy fast Ethernet in our homes, at least not yet. Future Internet access technologies include ADSL, ISDN, and cable modems; each of these technologies makes great promises for speedy Internet access. Until that time, most of us use modems to access the Internet.

Modems use analog telephone lines to transmit digital information. In the beginning, modem connections were slow and were primarily used to access text-based systems such as bulletin boards and terminal servers. As modem speeds increased, it became feasible to use network protocols that could function within a modem connection. Point-to-Point Protocol (PPP) and Serial Line Interface Protocol (SLIP) connections allowed users to function remotely in almost the same way as they could when directly connected to an Ethernet network. Even as some of the advanced technologies become more common, PowerBook users will probably still rely on modems when traveling, so we will discuss modem options.

In the previous section, "Cards," we talked about PC cards. One of the most popular PC card purchases is the PC card modem. These are excellent solutions for PowerBooks that have PC card ports. Installation is as simple as installing some software drivers and inserting the card in a free PCMCIA slot. Older PowerBooks have both internal and external modem options. In fact, external modems should work with all PowerBooks. Be aware that the more recent models use a printer and modem combination port, which means that printing becomes a more creative option while you are trying to surf the Web. If you must use an external modem in this port, you may have to print offline.

Automatically Remounting Servers

As you are working on your PowerBook and accessing servers and file systems right and left, you find that server volumes are mounted on your Desktop. Now, suppose that you go and take a coffee break. When you return to work, your PowerBook has gone to sleep. Those remote volumes are unmounted, leaving you with the prospect of locating and logging in to each one of them again.

As a solution to this problem, PowerBooks had a special control panel called *AutoRemounter*. Desktop systems, which could also go to sleep, did not need this feature because servers were not dismounted. You could set options for automatically remounting servers upon system wakeup. If you are familiar with the AutoRemounter, you will find that its options have been combined with the Energy Saver control panel. In the Advanced Options section you can enable automatic remounting of servers and determine whether the password will be saved or not. If you are in an open or unsecure environment, you should not enable saved passwords for security reasons. Figure 7.5 shows the automatic remounting options in the Energy Saver control panel.

Processor Cycling

Another routine PowerBook system activity that eats up your battery power is processor activity. Not all applications need full processor power; for example, a graphic-rendering program such as Adobe PhotoShop uses more of the processor than a word processor such as Microsoft Word. By default, an option is set in the Energy Saver control panel to enable processor cycling. This happens when little keyboard, mouse, or trackpad activity has occurred. The processor slows

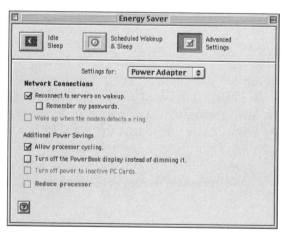

Figure 7.5   Automatic remounting options.

down to an absolute crawl, but immediately returns to normal speed when system activity resumes. In many cases, a user is unaware that the processor has cycled. And unlike the spindown of the hard drive, the processor returns to normal much faster.

Because this process happens quickly and is normal, Apple suggests that you leave it enabled. You can also manually reduce the processor speed from the Energy Saver control panel in the Advanced Settings panel. See the example in Figure 7.6 for the processor cycling features.

If you feel that you need the processor running constantly at top speed, you can disable processor cycling by removing the check next to the Allow Processor Cycling option.

File Synchronization

One of the biggest problems with mobility is that files located on more than one computer end up with different versions; thus, they are "out of synch." You begin working on a file on your desktop computer and transfer it to the PowerBook for additional changes, only to end up manually synchronizing the files on the different systems. You can ease this process by utilizing the File Synchronization control panel; it has an extensive menu system and several options and configurations. You can synchronize files on different systems, as well as documents on the same system that are located in different folders.

You can choose among several options for synchronizing files. Links can be one-way with a master copy determining how the other file is updated. Links can also

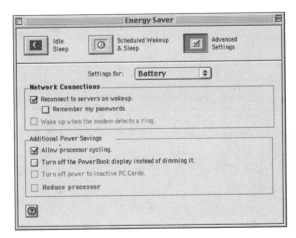

Figure 7.6   Processor cycling in the Energy Saver control panel.

Table 7.1   File Synchronization Table

File On Left	File On Right	Synchronization Results
Changed	Unchanged	The file on the right is updated.
Unchanged	Changed	For a left-to-right arrow, the right file is updated. For a right-to-left and two-way arrow, the left file is updated.
Unchanged	Deleted	For a left-to-left arrow, the right file is updated. For a right-to-left and two-way update, you are asked if you want to delete the left file.
Deleted	Unchanged	For a left-to-right and two-way arrow, you are asked if you want to delete the right file. For a right-to-left arrow, the left file is updated.

be two-way, enabling both copies to remain identical. Table 7.1 shows what happens in the synchronization process between files. This process depends upon the direction of the arrow between the files or folders.

Figure 7.7 shows the File Synchronization control panel. File Synchronization occurs whenever you open the control panel; you can also synchronize manually. When you select files for updating, the documents must have the same name. However, folders can have different names. You can add files to the right or left by either dragging the files to the window or by manually selecting the file. You can also see the path of the folders by clicking on the arrow by the volume name.

The File Synchronization control panel has a Preferences window that allows you to configure the application. You can decide when and if error messages should

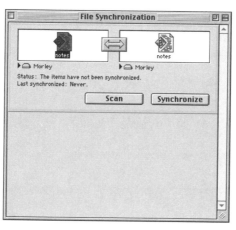

Figure 7.7   The File Synchronization control panel.

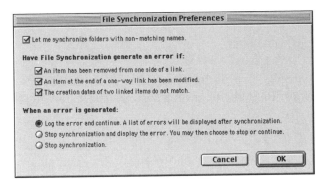

Figure 7.8   The File Synchronization Preferences window.

be generated, as well as how the synchronization process should function when errors are encountered. You can see more of the File Synchronization preferences in Figure 7.8.

If you use more than one computer, one of which is a PowerBook, and you want to keep information accurate, then you should familiarize yourself with the File Synchronization functions. Life isn't always this easy.

Control Strip

We've discussed a few options that were originally developed for the PowerBook that, because of their popularity, were added to the standard Mac OS installation for all systems. Sleep and Control Strip are two of these options. The Control Strip is a strip of icons containing shortcuts to standard system functions. So, rather than having to go to the Monitors control panel to switch your system colors from color to grayscale, you could now click on a Control Strip button and choose the new color palette. The shortcuts enabled you to conserve battery power. Of course, users with desktop systems began scheming to get their hands on this great utility and soon it became a part of the Mac OS operating system.

Figure 7.9 shows a sample Control Strip for PowerBooks, using Mac OS 8.5. Your configuration may differ, depending on the following factors:

- A clean installation versus an upgrade.

- Your PowerBook model.

- Additional programs you may have installed (some of them add buttons to the Control Strip).

7: Mobile Computing

Figure 7.9   A sample Control Strip.

Each Control Strip button performs a particular task that can also be executed from another location in the operating system. The following list defines the buttons shown in Figure 7.9:

- *AppleTalk Switch*—Turn AppleTalk on and off.

- *Battery Monitor*—This section shows the battery charge level (you may also see a button indicating current battery activity; this displays only if you are using a battery for your power source).

- *CDStrip*—Control your audio CD play program and eject CD-ROMs.

- *Energy Settings*—Choose your system performance levels and put your system to sleep.

- *File Sharing Strip*—Turn File Sharing on and off and see who is connected to your computer.

- *HD Spin Down*—Spin down the hard disk.

- *Location Manager Controls*—Switch to a different location document.

- *Monitor BitDepth*—Choose the color depth of the system.

- *Monitor Resolution*—Choose the screen resolution (this setting is limited on PowerBooks due to the display technology).

- *Printer Selector*—Change printers.

- *Remote Access Control Strip*—Open a remote access connection.

- *Sound Volume*—Set the system volume.

- *Web Sharing CS*—Enable or disable Web sharing.

Don't worry if the strip crosses the whole screen. Arrows are at either end so that you can access buttons that are no longer visible. If you do not like the location of the Control Strip you can move it: Hold down the Option key and move the mouse to the strip until the cursor changes to a hand. Then, drag the strip to the preferred location. You can also customize Control Strips. Many software applications add icons to the Control Strip and Web sites provide a host of buttons that you can add.

Location Manager

Before the Location Manager, PowerBook users had to manually switch settings between environments. For example, at work you have an Ethernet connection and use certain extensions and protocols to support it. But while traveling or at

7: Mobile Computing

home, you utilize a modem for Internet access. You may also turn off File Sharing while traveling to conserve system memory. Remembering all these configurations can be frustrating. The Location Manager allows you to tell the system which way you want to perform tasks. Figure 7.10 shows the Location Manager.

You can have multiple configurations; each configuration can be organized by whatever method you need, for example, configurations for network protocols or for particular applications. Setting a location document can take some time, but once each setting is completed, you can change locations easily from the Control Strip button or the control panel.

Additional Devices

Newer PowerBook devices such as the 1400, the 3400, the PowerBook G3, and PowerBook G3 Series have expansion bays that can take multiple devices. Two devices are included with the initial purchase: the floppy disk drive and the CD-ROM drive. Only the PowerBook G3 Series allows you to use both devices at once, although you must give up battery power.

The devices that go in the expansion bays are hot-swappable; you can switch the devices while the computer is up and running (older PowerBooks are sleep-swappable in that the computer must be in sleep mode to switch the devices). You can purchase additional devices, as well: Zip drives are available; Apple has also released a DVD-ROM drive capable of playing DVD movies with the appropriate translator card. And those creative folks at Apple have developed a wonderful control interface that includes standard playback buttons and parental control options. When Steve Jobs, Interim CEO of Apple, announced the new device, he joked that it would be the coolest way to watch an in-flight movie.

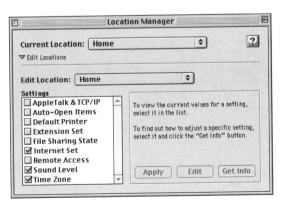

Figure 7.10   The Location Manager.

More devices are being manufactured every day. Between the expansion bays, the PC card ports, and the built-in serial and SCSI ports, your PowerBook has access to as many devices as you can afford.

Video Displays

Multimedia and animated slide presentations are some of the more common uses for a PowerBook computer. No longer are you limited to an overhead projector and transparencies. Your creative side can be unleashed in colorful presentations that can include special effects, as well as sound and movies, to drive home your point. Many PowerBooks have an external video port; if your computer lacks one, you can purchase an expansion card to give you this capability. With video out, you can project the PowerBook display to another video device such as a projection device or another monitor (in some cases special cables may be needed to connect the PowerBook to the other video device).

When you connect another monitor to the PowerBook, you have one and possibly two display options (check your manual to confirm what options you have). You can use *video mirroring*, allowing you to see the same image on both displays. This is useful if you are using a projection device to display a presentation. You don't have to perform interesting acrobatic moves to see the screen image and still talk to the audience. What you see on your display will be the same as what is projected on the screen. You can use the PowerBook Display control panel shown in Figure 7.11 to enable video mirroring. You may also have an *extended Desktop*, allowing you to continue your Desktop to the next monitor, giving you twice as much screen area.

Security Issues

As we have mentioned, portability is one of the strengths of the PowerBook. It is also one of its greatest weaknesses. Portable computers are more expensive compared to comparable desktop systems and are very attractive to thieves. PowerBooks are small enough to conceal and one left unattended could very likely be stolen. You may feel you need to handcuff your PowerBook to your body

Figure 7.11   The PowerBook Display control panel.

like some secret agent, but by using common sense as well as available tools, you can protect your investment.

Password

One of the hallmarks of computing is the password. Passwords secure a wide variety of systems, including network access, email accounts, and ATM machines. Apple also includes password protection for your PowerBook. You activate the password feature by accessing the Password Security control panel as shown in Figure 7.12. After a password has been activated on the computer, it will no longer boot without the appropriate password. In fact, the computer's hard drive is no longer functional without it. In older PowerBooks, you had to reformat the hard drive to bypass this security, but newer PowerBooks go a step further: The drive cannot be reformatted without this password, because the password is assigned at the disk's driver level.

This is an excellent feature unless you happen to forget your password. If this happens and you absolutely cannot remember it, you have to go to an Apple Certified repair technician who has been entrusted with a password that will boot the computer and bypass the security.

TIP: *Regarding passwords, make sure that you keep the rules of good passwords in mind:*

- *Do no use any word in the dictionary.*
- *Do not use telephone numbers, license plates, or other phrases that can be easily seen and guessed.*
- *Do not use names.*
- *If the system is case-sensitive, make some of the letters uppercase for extra security.*
- *Mix numbers and letters, as well as other non-alphabetical characters.*
- *The more secure the system must be, the longer the password needs to be.*

So, not only does the password security system protect your data, it also protects your hard drive. You can also use third party products such as CryptDisk or MacLocksmith to provide file encryption.

Figure 7.12   The Password Security control panel.

Security Packages

When you are not mobile, you can lock your PowerBook down by using security cables. A security slot is located in the back of the PowerBook; you can attach cables and lock the PowerBook to a fixed object. Depending upon your environment, you can even include the PowerBook in an alarm system. By utilizing both password and cabling options, you can protect your system against both data and physical theft.

Airport Issues

Walk through any airport during a weekday and you will see literally thousands of business travelers carrying some sort of portable computer. Some users misunderstand airport security systems and the impact they could have on portable devices. Apple has stated that it is safe to allow PowerBooks to pass through a properly tuned X-ray machine. However, some conveyor belts utilize magnetic components. For this reason, you should place your PowerBook close to the entrance or "tunnel" of the device and remove it immediately when it passes through the other end. PowerBooks are not damaged by metal detectors, but if these devices make you nervous, you can have the airport security personnel inspect your PowerBook by hand. Be aware that some airports personally inspect portable computers and request that you turn the computer on. Make sure that you have a fully charged battery ready to power the computer. You may even want to leave the computer in sleep mode rather than shut it down. For some reason, the time-space continuum disrupts while you're waiting for the darn laptop to turn on, and you may find yourself having visions of your computer being torn apart by airport security in search of smuggled items or worse.

Many airlines do not allow portable computers to run while the airplane is taking off or landing, because airlines suspect that these devices may interfere with certain airplane instruments, especially guidance systems. Although this has not been conclusively proven, you should respect this request and not run your computer during flight until the captain gives permission to do so.

Quick Reference Specifications

The following are the essential facts about Mobile Computing:

- PowerBooks can run faster than Pentium notebooks because of their smaller size and lower heat factors of the RISC chip.

- The average PowerBook battery runs two to three and one-half hours.

- The PowerBook G3 is a different computer from the PowerBook G3 Series computer.

- Screen dimming and a lower monitor bit depth extend battery life.

- You can set the energy saver options so that the hard drive will cease spinning after a set period of inactivity (this extends battery life).

- You can configure PowerBooks to go into a low-energy mode called *sleep* after a set period of inactivity.

- A blinking light at the top of the monitor indicates that the computer is in sleep mode.

- A RAM disk uses a portion of the installed memory to act as a temporary storage drive, enabling you to save documents without accessing the hard drive until the end of the computing session.

- PowerBooks can use several Ethernet options, including an expansion card, built-in Ethernet, SCSI device, or PC card.

- PowerBooks can exchange files with other computers that have infrared ports.

- PowerBooks dismount remote volumes when they go into a sleep mode unless the option to reconnect upon wakeup is selected in the Energy Saver control panel.

- Processor cycling occurs when a set period of computer inactivity causes the processor to go to an extremely slow speed. Computer activity will cause the processor to immediately return to normal.

- File synchronization allows files on different systems to remain identical.

- PowerBooks can have multiple configurations within the Location Manager.

- Expansion bays can be switched, but must not contain any media (it will be difficult to dismount the volume and remove the media from the expansion device).

- PowerBooks can project images on external video devices if the appropriate video port is installed.

- When password protection is enabled, the system will not boot and the hard drive cannot be formatted without it.

- PowerBooks will not be damaged by airport security measures provided you take a few precautions.

Utilities To Use

The utilities or elements of the Mac OS discussed in this chapter are listed here as a memory aid for the busy user or system administrator:

- *Energy Saver*—The control panel that sets screen dimming, hard drive spindown, and system sleep options.

7: Mobile Computing

- *RAM Disk*—A portion of memory allocated for file storage.

- *SCSI Ethernet*—An alternative Ethernet that exchanges data packets and translates them via the SCSI port.

- *PCMCIA Cards*—Also known as PC cards, these are portable hardware devices that become computer components such as a modem or network card when installed.

- *IR Talk*—The network protocol for infrared data exchange.

- *File Synchronization*—The control panel that keeps files on different systems or folders updated and identical.

- *Control Strip*—The customizable grouping of icons stored on a strip that provides shortcuts to system functions.

- *Location Manager*—The control panel that sets and enables different computer configurations.

- *PowerBook Display*—The control panel that enables video mirroring.

- *Password Security*—The control panel that enables system security.

- *PowerBook SCSI Disk Mode*—The control panel that sets a PowerBook's SCSI number when the PowerBook is used as a device on a SCSI chain.

- *RAM Disk*—A setting in the Memory control panel that enables a RAM disk that stores files during a computing session.

Immediate Solutions

Increasing Battery Performance (Simple Details)

Consult your user documentation to see how long your estimated battery life is. Then, try some of the following methods to make it last a little longer, especially when you are in situations where you cannot recharge the battery.

Setting energy conservation takes place within the Energy Saver control panel. You can also configure power adapter settings with this control panel. To do so, take these steps:

1. Go to the Apple Menu|Control Panels and select Energy Saver or click the Energy Saver button on the control strip and select Open Energy Saver control panel.

2. If it is not selected, click on the Idle Sleep button.

3. In the Settings for: pop-up menu, select Battery.

4. To allow the system to determine the appropriate battery conservation methods, slide the tab to Better Conservation (choose Better Performance if battery usage doesn't matter). Figure 7.13 shows the Energy Saver control panel with these simple settings.

TIP: *You can use your PowerBook without running batteries. However, when you are transporting batteries, make sure that you use the cover to cover the metal contacts. Do not touch the metal contacts. This will preserve and prolong the life of the battery.*

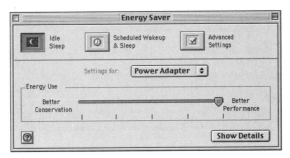

Figure 7.13   The Energy Saver control panel, hiding details.

Increasing Battery Performance (Customization)

You can be a weenie and let the system decide when the system sleeps, dims, and spins down, or you can take charge of your PowerBook and show it who's boss. In the previous section, we showed you how to access and set the Energy Saver control panel. However, you can control each function that saves battery power by going a little deeper:

1. Go to the Apple Menu|Control Panels and select Energy Saver.

2. If it is not selected, click on the Idle Sleep button.

3. In the Settings for: pop-up menu, choose Battery.

4. Click on the Show Details button. You will see the control panel shown in Figure 7.14.

5. On the Sleep Time slide bar, slide the tab to a preferred sleep time (one minute minimum). This will take effect when the system is idle for the time you chose.

6. If you prefer a different screen dimming time, click on the checkbox and slide the tab. Notice that the maximum time allowed is the setting you chose for the sleep time.

7. If you prefer a different hard disk spindown time, click the checkbox and slide the tab. Notice that the maximum time allowed is the setting you chose for the sleep time.

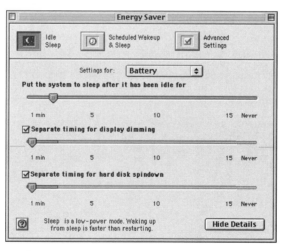

Figure 7.14   The Energy Saver control panel showing details.

You can follow these same steps for the Power Adapter settings which are accessed via the Settings for: pop-up menu. You will notice that the settings for the Power Adapter are somewhat longer (see Figure 7.15) because energy saving is not as critical.

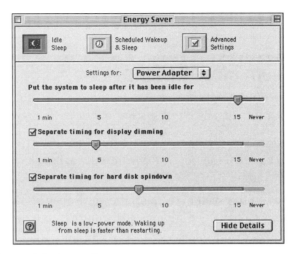

Figure 7.15   The Power Adapter settings.

Using CD-ROMs

For most PowerBook models, you must choose whether to run the CD-ROM or the floppy drive. Only the PowerBook G3 Series allows you to use both devices at once and even then you must give up battery power. See the tip after the instructions to determine which computer you have.

CD-ROMs are inserted and mounted on a PowerBook the same way they are mounted on a desktop. However, if the CD-ROM does not mount and you do not hear the drive spinning, you may have improperly inserted the CD-ROM drive into the expansion bay. To correct this, take these steps:

1. If necessary, put the system to sleep (newer PowerBook models may not need this step: check your computer manual).

2. Use a straightened paper clip to eject the CD-ROM manually (carefully insert a straightened paper clip into the small hole located at the front of the drive and push gently until the CD-ROM bay glides out).

3. Remove the entire CD-ROM drive and insert it into the expansion bay again (push carefully but firmly).

4. Wake up the system and attempt to mount the CD-ROM disk again.

7: Mobile Computing

TIP: *Remember that a difference exists between the PowerBook G3 and the PowerBook G3 Series. The latter is a newer and completely redesigned system all the way down to the exterior case. To determine which system you have, look at the outside of the display case. The PowerBook G3 has the familiar multi-colored logo while the PowerBook G3 Series computer has a white Apple logo.*

Ejecting Problem Floppy Disks

Mounting and ejecting floppies in a PowerBook is very similar to the way you mount and eject them on a desktop system.

If the disk icon does not appear and you do not hear the drive spinning, you may have improperly inserted the floppy drive into the expansion bay. To correct this, take the following steps:

1. If necessary, put the system to sleep (newer PowerBook models may not need this step: Check your computer manual).

2. Use a straightened paper clip to eject the floppy manually (carefully insert a straightened paper clip into the small hole located at the front of the drive and push gently until the disk comes out)

3. Remove the entire floppy drive and insert it into the expansion bay again (push carefully but firmly).

4. Wake up the system and attempt to mount the disk again.

Apple recommends that you push firmly on the floppy drive to insert it in the expansion bay. Remember the "firmly" part. For some reason, the floppy drive is more difficult to insert than other expansion devices (this is perhaps due to the location of the contact pins). You should hear a reassuring "click" when the drive is properly seated.

Swapping Removable Devices

You have been busily playing *Myst* when a colleague gives you a file on a disk that you are expected to open immediately. Follow these steps to do this quickly and properly:

1. Eject any media in the expansion bay drive.

2. If necessary, put the system to sleep (this step may not be required for later PowerBooks: check your PowerBook manual).

3. Remove the existing expansion bay device.

7: Mobile Computing

4. Insert the new expansion bay device. Ensure that you use a gentle but firm touch. The device should click into position.

5. Wake the system up.

You can now use other media.

TIP: *You can use the DVD-ROM expansion device to play DVD movies, but you must also insert a PC card that acts as a translator to view the movies.*

Configuring Energy Saver Scheduled Options

You can configure the PowerBook to start up and shut down on a regular schedule. This feature can eliminate accidentally leaving the system up all night. Business travelers may find this function especially useful.

1. Go to the Apple Menu|Control Panels and select Energy Saver.

2. Click on the Wakeup & Sleep button.

3. Place a check in the box beside Wake Up The Computer.

4. Choose the daily schedule (for example, you could choose to make the system wake up on Monday mornings and sleep on Friday afternoons).

5. Set the hour and minute you prefer for system wakeup.

6. Place a check in the box beside Put The Computer To Sleep.

7. Choose the daily schedule and set the hour and minute you prefer for putting the system to sleep.

8. Close the control panel to save changes.

The PowerBook will now sleep and wake up at the times and days you selected. Figure 7.16 shows a sample configuration.

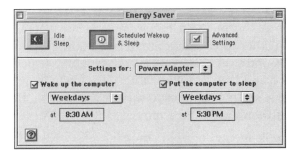

Figure 7.16   The sleep and wakeup schedule.

Controlling Processor Cycling

We don't always run at top speed from one task to another, so why should we expect this from a computer? You may be reading a Web page and need less horsepower. You can configure the system to slow down the processor when it has been idle for a certain length of time:

1. Go to the Apple Menu|Control Panels and select Energy Saver.

2. Click on the Advanced Settings button.

3. Locate the section for Additional Power Savings.

4. Put a check in the box Allow Processor Cycling (see Figure 7.17).

You can also manually reduce processor functions, but it is best to let the system determine this energy saving option.

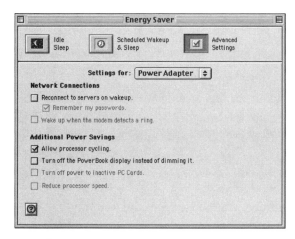

Figure 7.17   Processor cycling.

Automatically Remounting Shared Disks

Suppose you are talking on the telephone and decide it is time for a nap. You tell the party on the other line, "I'm going to sleep now." Normally the other party would tell you "Good-bye" and hang up. You wouldn't expect him or her to stay on the other line and listen to you snore. PowerBooks behave the same way. When they go to sleep, connections to servers are broken. However, you can tell the PowerBook to automatically reconnect to these servers upon system wakeup:

1. Go to the Apple Menu|Control Panels and select Energy Saver.

2. Click on the Advanced Settings button.

3. Locate the Network Connections section.

4. Place a check in the box beside Reconnect Servers On Wakeup.

5. If you work in a very secure environment or security is not a concern, place a check in the box Remember My Passwords. If you do not do this, you will be prompted to enter your password for each shared disk you are mounting.

6. Your system should now automatically remount these volumes. Figure 7.18 shows this process enabled.

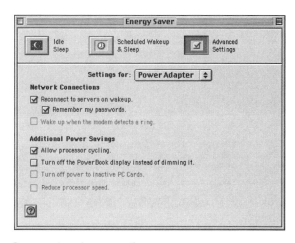

Figure 7.18   Energy Saver network connections.

PowerBook SCSI Disk Mode

You can use your PowerBook as an external hard drive to another computer. You can then install, copy, and move software rapidly. Be aware that if you don't use the proper equipment you will not be able to treat the PowerBook as another device on the SCSI chain:

1. Purchase an Apple HDI-30 SCSI Disk Adapter cable. This is not a standard SCSI cable; it is designed specifically for this function. Additionally, third-party cables that can switch between SCSI disk mode and a standard SCSI adapter cable.

2. If you have enabled password security on your PowerBook, disable it. You cannot mount a hard drive that has password protection.

3. Go to the Apple Menu|Control Panels and select PowerBook SCSI Disk Mode (see Figure 7.19).

7: Mobile Computing

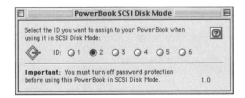

Figure 7.19   The control panel for SCSI Disk Mode.

4. By default, the ID is "2". If you know that a device on the desktop system will conflict with this number, select another number, then close the control panel.

TIP: *Remember that a SCSI chain can only have six additional devices and each device on the chain must have a unique ID. If two devices have the same number, many strange problems can occur.*

5. Shut down the PowerBook.

6. Attach the HDI-30 SCSI Disk Adapter cable to the PowerBook and a SCSI system cable from the adapter to the other computer, then connect these two cables.

7. Turn the PowerBook on. You should see the icon in Figure 7.20 on your PowerBook display (the number may be different if you chose a different SCSI ID number).

If your PowerBook begins booting normally or generates an error while booting, shut off the PowerBook, remove it from the SCSI chain, and repeat Steps 5 through 7. Make sure that you have the correct cables. You should also verify that password protection has been turned off. This action isn't necessary for all PowerBooks, but may be required on your particular model.

TIP: *Make sure that you plug in the power adapter when you are using the PowerBook in SCSI mode. This mode is more intensive on the batteries. Also, you will not get a warning when battery power is almost gone; instead, the computer will simply shut down.*

Figure 7.20   The SCSI Mode icon on the PowerBook display.

Creating A RAM Disk

If you are really serious about conserving battery power and you have memory to spare, then create a RAM disk. It behaves like a hard disk. You can save files to it, reducing the spinning of the hard drive and ultimately saving some battery juice. Just make sure that you save any documents stored in the RAM disk to a permanent storage location or you may experience data loss. To create a RAM disk, take this step:

1. Go to the Apple Menu|Control Panels and select Memory.

2. Locate the RAM disk section at the bottom of the window.

3. Click on the On radio button.

4. Use the slide bar to indicate what percentage of RAM you want allocated to the RAM disk. Notice that the minimum RAM disk size shown is 448K and as you move the slide tab this figure increases. Figure 7.21 shows the Memory control panel with the RAM disk enabled.

5. The Save On Shut Down option is checked by default. If you disable this, you will have to manually move the contents of the RAM disk to a permanent storage device. If you shut down the computer with files stored in the RAM disk, you will see the error message shown in Figure 7.22.

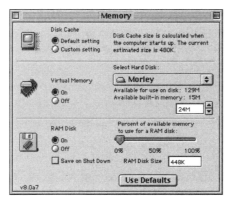

Figure 7.21   The Memory control panel with RAM Disk enabled.

Figure 7.22   The warning for files in the RAM disk.

7: Mobile Computing

6. Close the Memory control panel and restart the computer.

7. You should see a RAM disk icon on the Desktop as shown in Figure 7.23. You can now use this disk to save documents within computing sessions.

For additional information on RAM disks, refer to Chapter 6.

Figure 7.23   A RAM Disk icon.

Removing A RAM Disk

A RAM disk is wonderful for helping to extend battery life, but you may find that you need to remove it. This may especially be true if you need every scrap of memory you have. Also, some systems will behave better if the RAM disk is removed.

To remove a RAM disk:

1. Go to the Apple Menu|Control Panels and select Memory.

2. Locate the RAM Disk section.

3. Click on the Off radio button. The RAM disk should disappear immediately. In fact, if you really didn't intend to click on the On button, you will find that you'll have to restart your computer to enable the RAM disk again.

TIP: *If you go into the Memory control panel, and the On and Off buttons are grayed out, you will notice a message indicating that the RAM disk has files in it and cannot be modified (see Figure 7.24). (This includes files that have been placed in the trash.) You must remove these files from the RAM disk and empty the trash before you can remove the RAM disk.*

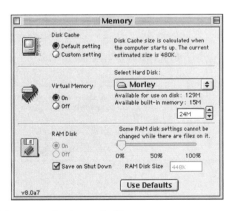

Figure 7.24   The RAM disk cannot be turned off.

Enabling Password Protection

One of the simplest things you can do to protect your PowerBook against intruder access is to require that users enter a password. This password works at the driver level and cannot be bypassed, even by formatting the hard drive; you cannot do so without entering the password. To set up a password:

1. Go to the Apple Menu|Control Panels and select Password Security.

2. If you have not set up password protection, click on the Setup button to view the dialog box shown in Figure 7.25.

3. Follow the on-screen directions by entering a password in the first field, then retyping the password in the second field.

4. For extra convenience, Mac OS 8.5 provides a space to enter a hint that will help you remember your password (optional).

5. If you want password prompting both at system startup and upon wakeup, place a check in the Also Ask When Waking From Sleep box.

6. Click on the Okay button to continue setting up your security, or click on the Cancel button to stop the process.

7. At the Mail window, click on the On radio button to enable password protection (see Figure 7.26).

If you want to delete password settings, go into the Setup section of the Password Security control panel and click on Reset.

Figure 7.25   Setting up password security.

Figure 7.26   Password security enabled.

Configuring The Control Strip

The Control Strip is a handy group of icons placed on a long tab that enables you to perform system functions with the push of a button. You can rearrange the order of the Control Strip icons, as well as add and remove them. The Control Strip behaves like an Apple Guide window: It remains in the front (it cannot be placed in the background).

To access Control Strip settings, follow these steps:

1. Go to the Apple Menu|Control Panels and select Control Strip.

2. You have three options:

   • You can show the Control Strip.

   • You can hide the Control Strip.

   • You can use a hotkey to toggle between show and hide within the Finder.

3. Select your preferred option and if necessary define a hotkey combination for the show/hide function.

4. Select the font for the Control Strip menu options. Figure 7.27 shows the Control Strip control panel window.

Figure 7.27   The Control Strip control panel.

Customizing The Control Strip

Did you know that you can add many more icons to the Control Strip? In fact, many applications add a button to the Control Strip during installation. You can also remove buttons that you don't use. And if you don't like the location of the Strip, you can move it or compress it easily.

To rearrange the order of the icons on the Control Strip:

1. Hold down the Option key.

2. Move the mouse over the icon you wish to move. It will assume the shape of a hand.

3. Click and drag the icon to the preferred location (the hand will appear to grab the icon).

4. Release the icon. You have now customized the strip.

To add new icons or remove existing ones:

1. Open the hard drive and the System folder.

2. Locate and open the Control Strip Modules Folder.

3. Drag the icon out of the folder to the trash or drag new modules into the folder.

4. Changes will take effect only after you restart the computer.

TIP: *You can use a new method for customizing the Control Strip. Option+click+drag the button off the control strip to a new location and it disappears from the strip immediately. Use the same key combination to add buttons. This method has the benefit of immediately reflecting the Control Strip changes. The traditional method forces you to restart to see the changes.*

To move the Control Strip within Finder:

1. Hold down the Option key.

2. Move the mouse over the tab at the end of the strip. The cursor will assume the shape of a hand.

3. Drag the strip to its preferred location. You can even move it to the right side of the screen.

TIP: *Occasionally, when you switch screen resolutions (especially lower to higher resolution), the Control Strip will end up stationed where the bottom of the screen used to be. Just use the previous instructions to relocate the strip.*

7: Mobile Computing

Configuring The Trackpad

The Trackpad control panel now allows you to tap the trackpad for mouse control. (Previously, you had to drag with the pad and click with the trackpad button.) Now, you can tap the trackpad to initiate a click, relieving the stress on your thumb joint.

To configure the trackpad:

1. Go to the Apple Menu|Control Panels and select Trackpad. See Figure 7.28.

2. Set the tracking speed in the first section. Use slower trackpad speeds for drawing applications and faster speeds to effectively use the track-pad space. For example, in some conditions you run out of trackpad before you reach your destination. Faster tracking helps reduce this predicament.

3. Set the double-click speed. This determines the time lapse between clicks. If you are new to a mouse or trackpad device, you may want to increase this gap until you get used to the art of double-clicking.

3. Determine the trackpad uses. You can use the trackpad for clicking (tap the pad), dragging, and drag lock. If you choose nothing else, use the trackpad for clicking. Your thumb will appreciate it.

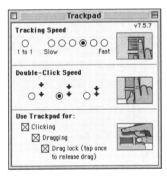

Figure 7.28   The Trackpad control panel.

Configuring The Location Manager

It's a fact of life for PowerBook users. You bought it to take it to multiple locations—even if this means only between work and home, a lot of hard work is involved in switching between network and remote access. In Mac OS 8.5, you can use the Location Manager to expedite this process by using different extension sets for different locations or applications:

1. Go to the Apple Menu|Control Panels and select Location Manager or click the Location Manager button on the Control Strip and select Open Location Manager. If this is the first time the Location Manager is being launched, you will see Figure 7.29. Open the window to its full view by clicking on the triangle by Edit Locations.

2. Go to the File menu and select New Location.

3. Give a name to your new location and click on Save. For our example, we'll use *Home*.

4. In the pop-up menu by Edit Location, select a location. See Figure 7.30 for an example.

5. Set your options such as Sound Level, Default Printer, and Extension Set. As you set the values for each option, the right side of the dialog box will display each setting.

Configuration Sets

Setting up the locations involves more work than what appears in this window. For example, in the AppleTalk and TCP/IP option, you need to go into each of these control panels and create configuration sets with names other than *default*. To use the Extension Sets option, you must have gone previously into the Extension Manager and saved sets with names other than *My Settings*. Several of these options listed in the Location Manager require configuration beforehand, but the Mac OS will tell you what you need to do to use each option. Simply select the option and click on the Get Info button.

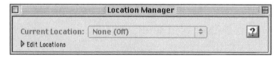

Figure 7.29 The Location Manager unconfigured.

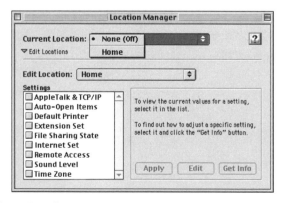

Figure 7.30 Selecting a location.

6. When you have set the options for the location, go to the File menu and choose Save Location (if you forget this step, you'll be prompted to save when you close this control panel).

7. To make a location active, select it from the pop-up menu beside Current Location (a restart may be necessary if you've specified custom extension sets).

Using PCMCIA Ethernet Cards

The latest PowerBooks from Apple come with a built-in Ethernet port. However, many PowerBook users do not have this luxury and must use one of the other methods for network access, including the installation of a network expansion card, an external SCSI Ethernet device, or a PCMCIA (PC) card. Of the three options, the PC card is the most economical and expandable. To set up a PC card:

1. Purchase an Ethernet PC card (make sure that Macintosh drivers are available).

2. Install the drivers for the card and restart the computer.

3. Insert the PC card into a PCMCIA slot and attach the Ethernet cable (some cards use a small cable with the 10Base-T jack on the end; others include the Ethernet cable that attaches directly to the PC card). The icon of the PC card appears on the Desktop (see Figure 7.31).

4. Go to Control Panels|AppleTalk and choose Alternate Ethernet as your network option (if AppleTalk is disabled, you will be asked to enable it).

5. Close the AppleTalk control panel and save changes. You should now be able to access your network.

If you fail to access the network, try disabling AppleTalk, then re-enabling it.

Figure 7.31   The Ethernet PC Card icon on the Desktop.

Using PCMCIA Modem Cards

Not every computer owner has access to a fast network; most of them must rely on modem connections to access the Internet. Internal modems can be installed, but lack easy expandability. External modems lack portability. PC card modems are an excellent and economical alternative. To install and set up a PCMCIA modem card:

1. Install the PC card modem software (most important, make sure that you install any modem scripts).

2. Restart the computer.

3. Insert the PC card modem into a PCMCIA slot. An icon of the PC card should appear on the Desktop.

4. Go to the Apple Menu|Control Panels and select the Modem control panel.

5. In the Connect via: section choose Upper or Lower PC Card slot as shown in Figure 7.32.

6. Choose the correct modem script for your PC card.

7. Close the control panel and save the settings.

You can continue setting the remote access options as detailed in Chapter 11.

TIP: *You can eject PC cards while the system is active by dragging them to the trash. The card will automatically pop out. If the computer is off, push the small button beside the PCMCIA slot to eject the card. However, if the system is in sleep mode you must wake it to eject the card: pushing the button on the card slot will not work.*

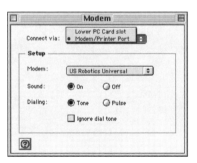

Figure 7.32   Choosing a modem port.

7: Mobile Computing

Chapter 8

Printing

In Depth

Printing Technologies

Everyone who has worked in computing technology has heard the term "paperless" work environment. It seems to be the Utopian state of computing. Printers would become obsolete and we would instead read and manage everything using an electronic display *à la* Captain Kirk. You may even have wished that this dream was reality when a frantic administrative assistant called because a report due in five minutes would not print. The painful fact is that the paperless work flow has generated a greater need to print.

Many users take printing for granted and may use the same printer for several years. They may even purchase an entirely new computer system, but keep an old printer. At the other end of the spectrum, graphic designers use expensive, specialized printers for high-quality output. Amazingly, much of the technology across the spectrum has remained consistent. In this chapter, we hope to provide information about printers, printing technology, and drivers, to achieve the best printing results. We will also cover font technology, for both printing and text types are intertwined. Once a method was developed to print text clearly, font usage exploded.

PostScript

Before PostScript, printers used a simple method of output. A series of tiny blocks would compose or build a "bitmap" of images or text. Fonts of this type are often called *fixed size*. The results of this method were images and text with jagged edges. The technology of the time seemed to concentrate on making these blocks as small as possible, thus making the jagged edges minimal. Moreover, the printing device most commonly used was a dot-matrix printer. Apple's version of this printer was called the ImageWriter. Since these printers used small dots generated by a print head to reproduce the data from the computer, the output was less than desirable for business. Many times, the information on the screen differed from the output because of the inability to reproduce the displayed image on the printer. Then came the laser printer; these devices used toner and heat rollers instead of print heads and ribbons to print. A font revolution was soon in the making.

8: Printing

Before PostScript, fonts were installed with a range of standard sizes. A set might include 9-, 10-, 11-, 14-, 18-, and 24-point sizes. In the earlier versions of the Macintosh operating system, these fixed-sized fonts were often represented by city names (Chicago, Geneva, and New York). If you wanted to use a size other than those previously listed, the output was not as attractive, especially the larger point sizes. The computer attempted to redraw the font, but instead, it produced hugely jagged text. When printed on a laser printer, the results were still unsatisfactory.

Then, Adobe developed an entirely new method of printing. Rather than using a series of squares, it developed a language for printing by creating a smooth outline of the curves and lines of the font or image based on mathematical equations. This language not only improved the quality of text, but also allowed graphic images to print with smooth, continuous lines and shading. This language took advantage of the printer's ability to smoothly spread the toner over the page rather than generate output by a series of ribbon punches. Output was even better if you used PostScript fonts (fonts that were written for the printer so that it handled the output faster, better, and more easily). It makes sense if you think about it. Using bitmap technology to print to a laser printer would be like trying to dry your hair in a clothes dryer: You may get the job done, but the results won't be pretty.

However, PostScript had problems within the operating system, which became a big mess of font files. Read the "Fonts" section later in this chapter to learn more. Later, we will also discuss printing to a file; this feature utilizes PostScript technology.

TrueType

Competition is good because the consumer benefits from choices. In fact, TrueType technology arose from a need for competition. When laser printers with PostScript technology were first released, they were a great success. The business community could print in-house, thanks to the tremendous improvement in quality. Adobe knew this and charged a hefty licensing fee to include PostScript technology in the printers. Laser printers were already expensive, and Apple began to explore developing its own font technology. This would allow it to save money and fix the problems inherent with PostScript fonts.

Now, you know how TrueType came to be. This printing language produced text output as good as PostScript and it was free. It used a similar method of outlining the font with curves and lines instead of bitmaps to eliminate the jagged edges. TrueType was also embraced by Microsoft (who says two companies can't get along). Unlike PostScript fonts, TrueType housed all of the font information in a single suitcase file (both the display and the printing information).

However, TrueType didn't cause the death of PostScript. First, many users had invested money in PostScript fonts and were not inclined to spend additional money on TrueType. Second, Adobe became very generous in light of the competition and gave the PostScript technology away for almost nothing. Third, the two technologies actually coexisted quite nicely. Both, however, are very different in one important aspect: TrueType is font-based while PostScript is graphics-based. You still need PostScript for printing clipart and images.

QuickDraw GX

We are mentioning QuickDraw GX briefly because you may see vestiges of it through system upgrades on Macs. QuickDraw GX is no longer included with Mac OS 8, but as a printing technology, it had great potential. However, during the period when Apple developed a hybrid of Mac OS and Rhapsody (now known as Mac OS X Server), QuickDraw GX became a casualty to standardization.

QuickDraw GX used such components as desktop printer icons, simplified page-setup windows, printer sharing, and portable digital documents or PDDs (one of its best features). Specialized drivers and extensions provided much of this functionality. Other aspects were built-in to QuickDraw GX itself.

QuickDraw GX Features

Before QuickDraw GX, you had to change printers by using the Chooser. This method was rather annoying if you frequently used more than one printer. QuickDraw GX used the Chooser to install printer icons on the desktop; you switched printers via the Finder. When you selected a printer icon, a new menu would appear called *Printing*; you could set the default printer from this menu. This functionality is still included in Mac OS 8.5.

One feature provided by specialized extensions is *portable digital documents* (PDD). This extension provided the capability to print a PDD document by dragging its icon over the printer icon. Regardless of the fonts used in the document or the application that created it, you could print the document.

As for PDD technology, you can have the same functionality by using the *portable document format* (PDF) from Adobe. The catch, of course, is that you must purchase Adobe Acrobat to create these files. However, you will find that this file format preserves your fonts, images, and formatting so that the printed output will be what you intended.

As we discuss aspects of printing, you'll see that much of the functionality of QuickDraw GX has been included with Mac OS 8.5.

8: Printing

Printer Drivers

When personal computing was still new, PC printing was often a nightmare. You usually had to have a printer driver installed with each application. No centralized place existed to which all applications could send their data. Thank goodness for the Macintosh. Each application went its merry way and created documents; when it came time to print, the application simply sent the data to a driver within the system. The driver spooled the information and sent it to the printer, downloading fonts if the printer did not have them installed, and storing large files in parts until the printer was ready to handle the next piece.

Today, many types of printers are available. You'll still find legacy dot-matrix printers around, but the more prominent types are laser and ink-cartridge printers. Consumers purchase the ink-cartridge printers because of cost. Ink-cartridge printers can produce excellent printed output and many have color capability. Supplies for ink cartridge printers are reasonable and the more expensive ink cartridge printers are competitive to laser printer quality.

The business world is the domain of the laser printer. Although it is possible to share ink cartridge printers, the laser printer has been developed for the networked environment. Many laser printers include PostScript technology, which results in excellent print quality. Color laser printers are also available and produce excellent printouts. However, laser printers are not cheap, although they are much lower in price today than when they were first introduced. Toner cartridges also contribute to the ongoing costs of owning a laser printer.

One of the best things Apple does for its customers is to provide printer drivers that will run almost any Mac-compatible printer. In fact, the driver for the ImageWriter (an Apple-manufactured dot-matrix printer) is still included with Mac OS 8.5, despite the fact that this printer is no longer in production.

Ink Technology Drivers

Many different manufacturers make ink-technology printers. For many years, Apple manufactured the StyleWriter and Color StyleWriter printer family. Ranging from black and white to color, the StyleWriter was aimed toward the consumer. Apple no longer manufactures the StyleWriter printers, but many are still in use. Canon also has the Bubble Jet family of printers (this printer used the same form factor as the StyleWriters). Hewlett Packard also manufactures a line of Macintosh-compatible printers called the DeskWriter. Epson also develops Macintosh-compatible printers and drivers.

The ink technology printer drivers included with Mac OS 8.5 are Color SW 1500, Color SW 2500, Color SW Pro, and StyleWriter 1200 (see Figure 8.1). These

8: Printing

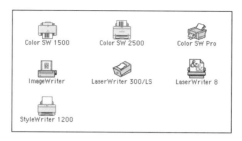

Figure 8.1   The printer drivers included with Mac OS 8.5.

drivers can communicate with most StyleWriter printers. You also have the option of using the driver that shipped with your computer. If the driver that shipped with your printer is also available in Mac OS 8.5, check the version numbers of the drivers and use the one with the latest driver. This enables you to take advantage of new printing options for your printer and reduces the risk of system errors when printing.

Unlike laser printer drivers, ink cartridge printers do require a specific driver that may not be included with Mac OS 8.5. If you do not see a compatible driver, install the one that came with the printer (printer drivers are placed in the Extensions folder) or download the latest driver from the manufacturer's Web site.

You should also check your printer's technical specifications to see if the printer has PostScript technology installed. If it does, you can use the PostScript drivers included with Mac OS 8.5 to achieve higher print quality. Be aware, however, that some programs using PostScript objects may not translate to the printer well. If you should encounter this problem, a software program called StyleScript is available from InfoWave that serves as a PostScript interpreter for ink-technology printers that don't have PostScript hardware interpreters.

Laser Printer Drivers

All the manufacturers previously listed manufacture laser printers. In fact, Apple now makes only laser printers. Laser printers provide speed, versatility, and durability to users. Most are manufactured with the intent of sharing them in a work environment, although personal laser printers are also a desirable item. Personal laser writers are usually slower and may not have PostScript technology installed (check your printer manual). Industrial laser printers frequently have several levels of PostScript installed (the count is currently at level 3).

Mac OS 8.5 includes drivers for many other printers, but usually two drivers are included for laser printers—a driver for the non-PostScript personal laser printer and a driver for the laser printers with PostScript capability. In most cases, you will use the latter driver (if you are in doubt, check your printer manual to verify if PostScript is a feature).

The driver included with Mac OS 8.5 that is used with PostScript printers is LaserWriter 8 (you can also use the Adobe PostScript driver). Although it is named for the brand of laser printers manufactured by Apple, the LaserWriter 8 driver can communicate with most PostScript printers. If AppleTalk protocol is enabled or if the printer can be reached via TCP/IP, then you should be able to print to it. However, to take full advantage of each printer's capabilities, you must have a PPD or a PostScript printer description file, which allows you to use special features of the printers, such as bypass trays or custom paper sizes. PPD files usually come bundled with the driver installation software; they are located within the Extensions folder in the Printer Descriptions folder. Figure 8.2 shows some of the PPD files in this folder.

The latest LaserWriter 8 driver is version 8.6. Use the latest printer driver if possible. However, if you develop system problems you should keep the older driver handy so that you can restore it. The latest LaserWriter 8 drivers are available at **www.apple.com**. If you have a non-Apple printer, you may also want to retrieve the latest driver from the manufacturer's Web address. Printer companies are usually very good at distributing drivers for their printers.

Non-Macintosh Printers

If you have a PC-compatible printer, especially one that is non-PostScript printer, you should know that software packages are available that will enable you to use the printer. One of the more well-known of these packages is PowerPrint, a hardware and software solution. The package ships with an adapter cable and software that contains hundreds of printer drivers.

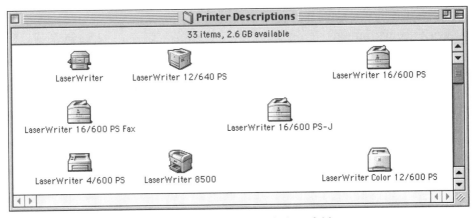

Figure 8.2   Printer description files in the Printer Descriptions folder.

Connecting To Printers

Now that you have the appropriate driver, you can set up Mac OS 8.5 to print to the appropriate printer. Several files are involved in printing beside the driver and printer. Desktop PrintSpooler, Desktop Print Monitor, and Print Monitor work together to manage the printing process. These files are located in the Extensions folder.

Chooser

Chooser has been a part of the printing process for years. This utility lists not only the drivers, but also AppleTalk zones and the printers within them (if the computer is connected to an AppleTalk or Ethernet network). Initially, the process is simple: Select the icon of the printer driver you will be using, the AppleTalk zone (if necessary), and the name of the printer or its port (printer or modem).

For non-PostScript printers such as the ImageWriter or StyleWriter, you select a port (printer or modem). If you are not on a network, you also need to disable AppleTalk within the Chooser. Figure 8.3 shows the Chooser with AppleTalk disabled. In most cases, you plug the printer into the printer port, but if you must run AppleTalk, you can use the modem or Ethernet port to reduce conflicts (especially if the modem port is unused). Just make sure to choose the modem port within Chooser.

You don't choose a port for PostScript printers. Instead, the printer appears by name when you select the LaserWriter 8 icon. In some cases, especially if you are not on a network, it is the only name to appear. However, if you are part of a local area network, you may see many printers listed in many zones. Figure 8.4 shows an extensive listing of PostScript printers available in a particular networked environment.

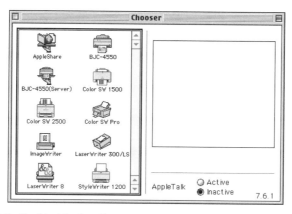

Figure 8.3   AppleTalk disabled in the Chooser.

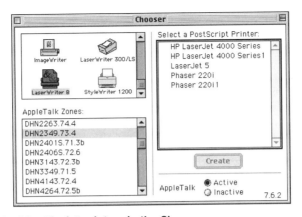

Figure 8.4   Networked PostScript printers in the Chooser.

When you select a printer, regardless of whether it's PostScript or not, you next have the option of setting up the printer. Simply click on the Create button to initiate a connection to the printer. You can then choose from a variety of options, such as updating the printer information and customizing options.

Desktop Printing

In the previous section, we discussed selecting printers via the Chooser. But that's only half of the story. Before Desktop Printing, every time you wanted to change printers you had to go to the Chooser. Frequently, you would change printers, then forget to switch back to the preferred printer. Soon, you would be reporting lost printing jobs, when in reality you were not checking the Printer dialog box to see which printer was selected. Desktop printing makes all this much easier. You still need to use the Chooser to access a printer the first time. When you select a new printer, however, an icon for the printer is created on the Desktop, as shown in Figure 8.5.

As each printer is chosen, an icon is created on the Desktop. The default printer has a heavy black border. When a printer icon is selected, a new menu appears within the Finder called Printing (see Figure 8.6). This menu replaces much of the function of the old Print Monitor. (Print Monitor was an application that launched when you sent something to print—you could also launch it manually. Print Monitor appeared in the Application menu and allowed you to perform such tasks as deleting print jobs or halting the print queue. All these tasks and more can be accessed from the Printing menu.)

Figure 8.5   A printer icon on the Desktop.

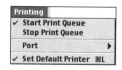

Figure 8.6   The Printing menu.

When documents are sent to print, the application prepares the document and sends it to the Print Spooler, which then prepares the document for the printer. When the Desktop Print Spooler is active, you will see a graphic of a document appear over the printer icon. Double-clicking on the icon reveals the Print Queue window. This window provides information, such as how much of the document has been processed and where it is located in the queue. You can rearrange and delete print jobs within this window. Figure 8.7 shows an active Print Queue window.

Note: You can drag a document over a particular desktop printer icon. The Mac OS will launch the application that created the document, bring up the print dialog box, and close the application when printing is finished.

You may find yourself using a locally attached laser printer that is plugged in to the printer port. If you are a home user, this is usually not a problem because AppleTalk is not normally needed in a non-networked environment. But if you must keep AppleTalk active, yet still use the printer port for the printer, you may need a copy of LaserWriter Bridge available at **www.apple.com**. This control panel enables you to use the printer and AppleTalk at the same time. A side benefit is that the printer can be seen and shared by multiple users with this software.

Note: If you are not using a particular printer any longer, you can drag its icon to the trash. However, you must have at least one Desktop printer icon. If you attempt to drag the default printer to the trash, the icon will be re-created.

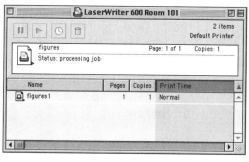

Figure 8.7   The Print Queue.

Fonts

Fonts and printing seem to go hand-in-hand. Fonts are used to communicate information in an attractive, legible, and eye-catching manner. Thousands of fonts are available, and fonts are used both by the System as well as for printing (the default system font in Mac OS 8.5 is Charcoal). Several types of fixed-size fonts also exist.

Fixed-Size

The earliest computing fonts were *fixed-size* or *bitmap* fonts. Don't confuse fixed-size with mono-spaced. *Monospaced* fonts are those that allocate the same amount of space to every character (Courier, the "typewriter" font is a good example). Fixed-size fonts are those that have a picture of every character in the font set. Each character is created by a series of blocks (kind of like the electronic highway communication signs). If you look closely at your monitor you can see that the pixels help build the letters. These fonts are installed in size sets; if you use one of these sets for your font size, your printout and on-screen display looked reasonably well, because the blocks have been arranged for the best effect. Fixed-size fonts were easily printed on dot-matrix printers, because the printer head also used dots that corresponded with the squares. However, on laser printers, you ended up with a jagged effect on the text.

Quality significantly diminishes when you choose a size that does not have a font set. The computer and printer must guess at the arrangement of the squares to create the character. When laser printers were developed, a new language managed to radically improve font printing. However, fixed-size fonts are still used today (in many cases, in conjunction with PostScript fonts).

PostScript

As we discussed earlier, PostScript used a different method for creating text and images. Consequently, print quality was radically improved. By outlining the font and filling in the white area, the text looks smooth and professional. PostScript also improved graphic printing. PostScript fonts were written so that the printer could understand and correctly produce the desired text, and PostScript fonts looked good at any size or resolution.

Literally thousands of PostScript fonts are available. In fact, that is part of the problem. PostScript display fonts must have a file for each formatting style. It's common to see separate files for bold, italics, and bold italics. In addition to the display fonts, you also must have a printer font corresponding to the display fonts. The display fonts are stored in the Fonts folder, but printer fonts are often scattered through the System Folder.

TrueType

Instead of using a fixed-size font, TrueType uses a variable-size font technology. TrueType was developed by Apple to reduce costs on LaserWriters. It also produces excellent output on many printers, including non-PostScript ones. TrueType's font files are one of the biggest improvements over PostScript. TrueType stores all of the font information in a suitcase file within the System Folder. You don't need additional files for special formatting or a printer font. Everything is stored in one place. TrueType also has wide acceptance with the printing community and thousands of fonts are available for purchase or download from any of the software archives, including the Info-Mac archive at **www.pht.com/info-mac**.

Quick Reference Specifications

The following are the essential facts about Printing:

- Fixed-size or bitmap fonts use squares (or pixels) to compose each character and are created in sets.

- PostScript uses lines and curves to create the outline of a character, producing smoother text and graphics. PostScript must be installed on a printer to be used.

- TrueType is a variable-size font system that can be used on most printers.

- In order to access a printer, the appropriate driver must be installed.

- Not all laser printers have PostScript installed.

- Most inkjet printers do not have PostScript installed.

- If possible, use the latest version of a printer driver.

- Chooser is used to initially set up a printer connection.

- Desktop Printing creates icons of printers on the Desktop from which printing options can be set.

- In Desktop Printing, the default printer has a heavy black border around the icon.

- Desktop printer icons can be placed in the trash; however, you must have at least one printer on the Desktop once you have enabled Desktop Printing.

Utilities To Use

The utilities or elements of the Mac OS discussed in this chapter are listed here as a memory aid for the busy user or system administrator:

- *PostScript*—A font and imaging technology developed by Adobe that produces smooth text and graphics and is installed on the better printers.

- *TrueType*—A font technology developed by Apple in competition to PostScript.

- *QuickDraw GX*—The printing technology developed by Apple that is no longer included with Mac OS 8.5 but may be found on upgraded systems (especially GX printer drivers).

- *LaserWriter 8*—The printer driver used to print to PostScript printers.

- *PPD*—PostScript Printer Description files are stored in the Extensions folder and contain information about each printer's capabilities.

- *PowerPrint*—A commercial utility that Macintosh computers use to print to non-Macintosh or incompatible printers.

- *Chooser*—The application included with Mac OS 8.5 for connecting to printers and servers.

- *Print Monitor*—The software application that is launched when documents are sent to print that contains information about the printer queue.

- *LaserWriter Bridge*—A Control Panel that allows AppleTalk to be active with a locally attached printer by using the printer port.

- *Apple Printer Utility*—An application that communicates directly with the printer and allows the user to make changes to the printer's configuration.

8: Printing

Immediate Solutions

Configuring Local Printers

A *local printer* is a printer that is physically attached to your machine. Consult your manual for instructions on how to attach the printer. Be aware that some printers do not include the printer cable; you must purchase one separately. To configure your printer, take these steps:

1. While all devices are turned off, connect the printer to the computer. If you will not need AppleTalk, use the printer port. However, if you need AppleTalk, try using the modem or Ethernet port instead.

2. Turn on the computer and printer.

3. Install the software that came with the printer, unless it's a PostScript printer or the driver for the printer is included with Mac OS 8.5. (You can still install the software; just be watchful for warnings that indicate your drivers are older than existing drivers.)

4. If you had to install new drivers, restart the computer. Otherwise, go to the Apple Menu|Chooser menu option.

5. Select your printer icon.

6. Select the port (the same physical port that you chose in Step 1). Figure 8.8 shows the printer and port selected.

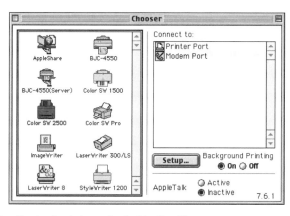

Figure 8.8   A locally attached printer selected in the Chooser.

7. Click on the Create button to set printer options and create a Desktop printer icon.

8. Close Chooser.

Configuring Networked Printers

Two kinds of networked printers are in use: those that have a built-in Ethernet port and those that are locally attached to a computer but visible over the network (some of these printers can be converted to Ethernet with an adapter). The printers with built-in Ethernet ports have special software utilities that allow you to set options such as an IP address and printer name. You also use printer utility software for locally attached laser printers if you need to change printer options such as the printer name or disabling of the banner page. Some older or personal laser printers may need LaserWriter Bridge, a control panel that allows the printer to be visible on a network. LaserWriter Bridge is available from **www.apple.com**. You may also need LocalTalk cables if your printer does not have an Ethernet port.

1. Launch the printer utility (in this example we will use the Apple Printer Utility).

2. Locate the zone where the printer resides (optional).

3. Select the printer you need to configure (the Apple Printer Utility has a series of dialog boxes indicating that the computer is communicating with the printer).

4. Set the printer options such as the printer name or IP number. Figure 8.9 shows the Apple Printer Utility accessing a LaserWriter 16/600 and the options available.

Note: *By default, when a printer is turned on or restarted and ready to print, a banner page appears. The most useful information on this page is the page count. If you maintain many printers, you can use this information to see how many printed pages you are getting from each toner cartridge. It can also warn you if the printer has lost its name or IP number. However, many users disable the banner page option as a method of saving paper. Either option is fine. Many printers allow you to print this page "on the fly" so you may want to selectively enable it.*

8: Printing

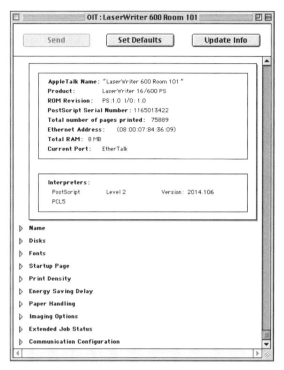

Figure 8.9   The Apple Printer utility.

Selecting A Network Printer

Selecting a network printer is much easier than configuring one. And you can set up several printers at once while you are still in the Chooser. To select a network printer:

1. Go to the Apple Menu and open Chooser.

2. Select the LaserWriter 8 driver.

3. Select the AppleTalk zone that houses the printer (optional).

4. Select the printer by name from the list that appears.

5. If this is the first time you have accessed this printer, click on the Create button that displays (see Figure 8.10).

6. You will see a series of dialog boxes as the computer communicates with the printer. You can also select the PPD file by clicking on the Select PPD button.

7. When the printer and computer have finishing communicating, you will be returned to the Chooser. An icon will now appear by the printer within the

8: Printing

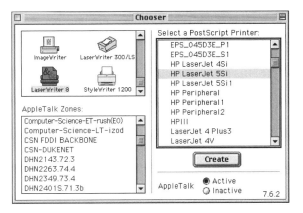

Figure 8.10   Choosing a new network printer within the Chooser.

Chooser and on the Desktop. You can continue setting up printers; close the Chooser when you are finished.

Changing Page Attributes

Most documents are printed in portrait orientation. Occasionally, landscape is required (for example, printing PowerPoint transparencies). Paper orientation is specific to the application; the setting will remain as you chose it until you select a new orientation. You may also need to indicate a different paper size or scale. To change the orientation:

1. Go to File|Page Setup.

2. By default, the Page Attributes window should appear, as shown in Figure 8.11.

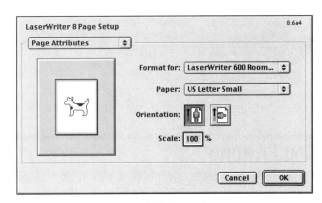

Figure 8.11   The Page Attributes window within Page Setup.

3. Select your orientation, printer format (this lists all your desktop printers), or scale.

4. Click on Okay to close the window.

Remember that these settings will remain this way until you go back into Page Setup and change them.

Setting PostScript Options

If you are printing to a PostScript printer you can set specialized options such as inverting the image. These options are expanded, depending upon the driver you are using. Note also that although some of these options can greatly increase printing time, they will produce better quality documents.

1. Go to File|Page Setup.

2. Locate the Page Attributes button. Select PostScript Options (see Figure 8.12).

3. Select or deselect the options you prefer. When you are finished, click on Okay to initiate the options. For an explanation of the PostScript options, refer to Table 8.1.

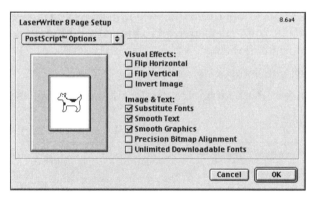

Figure 8.12   PostScript Options within Page Setup.

Using Desktop Printing

The nice thing about Desktop Printing is that much of it is done automatically. When you choose a printer within the Chooser, a printer icon is placed on the

Table 8.1   *PostScript options.*

Option	Purpose
Flip Horizontal	This option produces a mirror image of the original document.
Flip Vertical	This option produces an upside-down mirror image of the original document.
Invert Image	White areas are printed black and black areas are left white.
Substitute Fonts	Replaces certain fonts by better printing fonts (for example: Monaco will be replaced by Courier). However, this can produce disappointing results in that the text output may result in repagination of the document or overlapping text).
Smooth Text	PostScript will smooth fixed-size or bitmap fonts.
Smooth Graphics	PostScript will smooth graphic images.
Precision Bitmap Alignment	PostScript will reduce the image size to prevent image distortion.
Unlimited Downloadable Fonts	PostScript will download all the fonts needed for the document. This option will increase print time.

desktop. The default printer is denoted by a bold border. Figure 8.13 shows the default printer beside an additional printer.

When you send a document to print, the icon changes to reflect that it is spooling the document to the printer (see Figure 8.14).

If you want to see the progress of your document, double-click on the printer icon to launch the window for the Desktop Print Monitor; this window lists all documents in the queue. You can rearrange your jobs, cancel jobs, or halt the print queue. Figure 8.15 shows the Desktop Print Monitor.

You can also print by dragging a document over any printer icon. The Mac OS will launch the application for that document, open the print command window, and quit the application after the document is printed.

Figure 8.13   Desktop printer icons.

Figure 8.14   A Desktop printer icon in action.

8: Printing

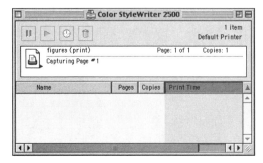

Figure 8.15   The Desktop Print Monitor.

Setting The Default Printer

You use the printer icons when you set the default printer, but the action brings up the Printing menu. This menu only appears when a printer icon is selected. Several options are available under the print menu, but if you have more than one printer chosen, the most common action will be setting a new default printer. To set the default printer:

1. Click on the icon of the printer that you want to be your default printer (if it doesn't exist, go to Chooser and select the printer).

2. The Printing menu displays. Select the option Set Default Printer.

3. A heavy black border should appear around the icon you chose.

You can also perform this task by pressing the Control key as you click on the printer icon. A contextual menu appears with an option to Set Default Printer. Figure 8.16 shows the contextual menu for Desktop Printing.

Figure 8.16   The Desktop Printing contextual menu.

Foreground Vs. Background Printing

When you send something to print, you will be using either foreground or background printing. By default, background printing is enabled. It allows you to continue working in an application while the document is sent to the printer. You will notice that the application may bog down as the two programs (the application and the print queue) use system resources to accomplish their tasks. The size and type of document being printed will also affect system performance.

Foreground printing is faster than background printing. Foreground printing means that you allow the print driver to take over the computer while the document is printed. When the information has been sent to the printer and the queue is empty, you will be allowed to continue working in an application. Most users prefer background printing. Background printing is slower, but it allows them to continue using the application. If the speed of printing does become a factor, you can easily disable background printing. To do so, take these steps:

1. Go to Apple|Chooser.

2. Select the printer driver and port or printer name.

3. Locate the Background section and click on the Off radio button. Figure 8.17 shows the Chooser window with Background printing disabled.

Be aware that background printing may not be an option for some printers. If that is the case, you will not see the background settings in Chooser.

Note: *If you do not have Desktop Printing installed or enabled, then background printing is handled by the Print Monitor application. When you send information to print, the Print Monitor is automatically launched. You can see what print jobs are in the queue, and you can remove print jobs from the queue.*

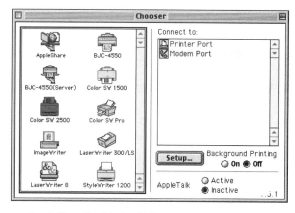

Figure 8.17   Background printing disabled within the Chooser.

Halting The Print Queue

Occasionally, you may need to disable printing from a particular computer. When you halt the print queue, print requests will stay resident on your computer until you are ready to begin printing again. You may also want to be aware that some users halt the print queue accidentally and may call you when nothing they send to the printer will print. This may be one of the first places you check.

Halting The Queue With Desktop Printing

To halt the Print Queue in Desktop Printing, follow these steps:

1. Click once on the printer icon.
2. Go to Printing|Stop Print Queue.
3. To resume printing, select Start Print Queue.

You can also stop printing by holding the Control key and clicking on the printer icon. A contextual menu will appear with Stop Queue as a menu option. To start printing again, select Start Queue.

Halting The Queue With Print Monitor

To halt the Print Queue in Print Monitor, take the following steps:

1. Launch the Print Monitor application.
2. Go to File|Stop Printing.
3. To resume printing, select File|Resume Printing.

Printing To A File

When you are using a PostScript printer and the proper LaserWriter driver, you can print documents to a file rather than print them immediately on paper. Why would you do this? You could save the files in a format that can be printed on another printer. Therefore, you could print a document to file and exchange it with a colleague who also has a PostScript printer. The output would be almost the same, depending on the options you chose. Printing to a file is also the first step in creating an Acrobat file. You can also create one-page PostScript files that can be placed in another document (such as Quark XPress or PageMaker).

To print to a file, take these steps:

1. Select File|Print.

2. Locate the unmarked pop-up menu under the General button. Select Save as File.

3. Select the Format pop-up menu and choose your option. Table 8.2 defines each option.

4. Determine your PostScript level. Level 1 will communicate with the most printers, but Levels 2 and 3 will provide better quality and handling.

5. Determine the Data Format. ASCII will print on most printers, but binary will provide greater speed on a compatible printer.

6. Determine the Font Inclusion option. None uses the least disk space, but may print incorrectly. The All option imbeds every font used in the document, thus creating a larger file. The All But Standard 13 option indicates that fonts, other than the 13 installed on all PostScript printers, will be included, and the All But Fonts In PPD File option includes fonts not listed in the printer description file.

7. In the top right of the window, change the Destination option to File. The Print button will change to a Save button (see Figure 8.18).

Table 8.2   Format options for printing to a file.

Option	Results
PostScript Job	Creates a normal PostScript file for later printing.
EPS Mac Standard Preview	Creates a black-and-white bitmapped preview image of the graphic.
EPS Mac Enhanced Preview	Creates a color PICT preview image of the graphic.
EPS No Preview	Creates the graphic with no preview image.
Acrobat PDF	Creates PDF files, working with Adobe Acrobat. (Adobe Acrobat Distiller must be installed).

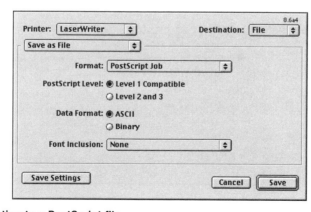

Figure 8.18   Printing to a PostScript file.

8. Click on the Save button. The Save dialog box will appear. Provide a name and location for the file and click on the Save button.

The computer will behave as if it is spooling a document, but instead of sending the output to a printer, a file will be created at the location you specified.

Sharing A Printer

Ethernet- or LocalTalk-enabled printers are not the only printers that can be shared over a network. You can also share StyleWriters. Software is installed on the system that allows for print sharing. One drawback is that the computer that is attached to the printer becomes a print server. Any jobs sent to print on this printer will slow the host computer, especially if fonts are used that are missing from the host computer. This option is practical if you have a dedicated computer used as the printer server (no one is using the computer as a personal workstation), or if you are setting up a home network and want to share the printer. Check your printer manual to see if printer sharing is an option.

To share a printer, take these steps:

1. Go to Apple|Chooser.

2. Select the printer you want to share.

3. Click on the Setup button.

4. The window in Figure 8.19 will appear. Select the option to Share This Printer.

5. Set a distinctive name for the printer (this name will be visible over the network). Optionally, you can designate a password that must be entered before anyone can print to the printer.

6. If desirable, select Keep Log of Printer Usage. Click on Okay.

Figure 8.19   Sharing a printer.

The printer is now visible over the network. Other users can access it by selecting the printer driver within Chooser. Not only will the printer and modem ports appear, but also any printers using that driver that are being shared over the network.

Getting Configuration Information

One of the printing improvements in Mac OS 8.5 is the ability to get printer information without obtaining special printer utility software. You can't make changes to the printer, but you can find out valuable information such as the IP number, memory installed, PPD file in use, printer type, and printer name.

To retrieve status and configuration information:

1. Go to the File|Get Info menu option. In the menu that branches to the right, select Status & Configuration.

2. The system will attempt to communicate with the printer to display the status in the upper window.

3. The lower window will contain printer information. Click on the Update button to retrieve configuration information from the printer. Figure 8.20 shows Status and Configuration information.

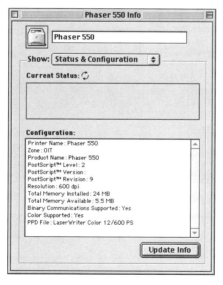

Figure 8.20   The status and configuration of a laser printer.

Getting Font Information

Most users don't know much about fonts and printers. They believe fonts are files installed within their system. Fonts, however, are also part of a printer's "operating system." In fact, you can purchase and install additional fonts to printers.

When a font is installed on a printer, the printer can recognize and more quickly print the document containing the font. However, when fonts are missing from the printer, they must be downloaded, which increases printing time and the risk of poor output. Mac OS 8.5 now includes an updated printer driver that allows you to see what fonts are installed on a PostScript printer. To determine the fonts installed on a Postscript printer:

1. Go to File|Get Info. In the menu that appears to the right, select Fonts.

2. The computer will communicate with the printer and produce a list of installed fonts. Figure 8.21 shows the fonts installed on a LaserWriter 16/600.

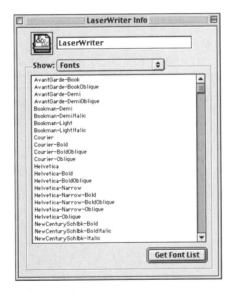

Figure 8.21   The font information window.

Chapter 9

Multimedia

In Depth

Some of you Macintosh old-timers may remember a saying that goes like this: "Macintosh *is* multimedia." This chapter covers everything in Mac OS 8.5 that makes this statement as true today as it was in 1984, including details on the latest versions of QuickTime, the Internet standard for multimedia, and ColorSync (Apple's color management architecture for the Mac OS).

Defining Multimedia

We define *multimedia* as the convergence of text, images, audio, and video in a single broadcast medium, in this case a computer. Not too long ago, we thought about multimedia only in terms of CD-ROM games, but now, more people associate multimedia with the Internet and the Web than with anything else. This re-thinking is good because the Mac OS is supremely adapted for viewing multimedia over the Internet, thanks to QuickTime, a standard part of the Mac OS.

QuickTime is a series of extensions and a control panel that enable you to view all the most popular multimedia file formats, including QuickTime, QuickTime VR, AVI, and MPEG. With the professional version of QuickTime, you can access additional file formats and even edit QuickTime movies. Numerous applications from third-party companies allow you to create complex movies and save them in QuickTime format for viewing over the Web or on CD-ROM. For the latest information about QuickTime, see the official Web site at **www.apple.com/ quicktime**.

Audio And Video Capabilities

All Power Macintosh computers have the ability to play basic audio and video, and some come with additional hardware components that provide more robust multimedia capabilities. The G3 series of computers has various optional *personality* cards that add serious audio and video (AV) capabilities, including:

- 16-bit sound
- 128-bit graphic acceleration
- 2D and 3D acceleration
- 8MB of EDO VRAM

- Microphone connector
- Speaker connector
- Telephony port
- NTSC, PAL, S-video, and composite support
- Dual-monitor support with 1,600 by 1,200 resolution at 85Hz

Of course, you can always purchase alternative AV hardware from any number of companies to provide these—and additional—capabilities. The basic AV capabilities of all PowerMac computers are sufficient for viewing most of the Web's content, with the exception of a good set of speakers (for those of us without an AV-capable monitor, which lacks speakers).

TIP: *Mac OS 8.5 takes the speed of your Internet connection into account when downloading and viewing QuickTime files, retrieving an optimized version of a file when available.*

Most Macs also allow you to record sounds from either a microphone or a CD player. Older Macs such as the Plus, II series, and Classic, don't include a sound-in port, but these models aren't capable of running Mac OS 8.5. Those that do, however, accept a monophonic microphone such as the Apple Microphone and the PlainTalk microphone. Some models have a microphone built into the computer or monitor, but these, too, are not capable of recording in stereo, for which you'll need to purchase third-party hardware and software.

QuickTime Vs. QuickTime Pro

QuickTime is the heart of Mac OS 8.5's ability to play multimedia, and like most everything else these days, it comes in two versions, QuickTime and QuickTime Pro. QuickTime is free and comes with Mac OS 8.5; QuickTime Pro, on the other hand, will cost you about $30 and enable you to perform significantly more tasks. Our discussion here pertains to QuickTime Pro.

Note: *QuickTime Pro doesn't require additional installation; a decryption key unlocks features installed as part of the standard version of QuickTime.*

We think the Pro version is worth the money: Besides, it stops that pesky advertisement that pops up—reminding you to purchase the Pro version—every time you launch MoviePlayer. Seriously, though, it does provide some cool features, including:

- Create and edit QuickTime movies
- Play and export more than 30 types of multimedia file formats

9: Multimedia

- Use the QuickTime Plug-in to view almost all the multimedia types on the Web
- Create slide shows

The standard version is fine if you only view movies over the Web, but the Pro version opens several new doors to the world of multimedia.

QuickTime Essentials

QuickTime has several components that provide just about all the multimedia capabilities you'll ever need, including the ability to open files to do the following:

- Play movies
- Navigate QuickTime VR panoramas
- View pictures
- Play audio
- Explore 3D worlds using QuickDraw 3D

QuickTime's general preferences are configured through a control panel, as well as a Web browser plug-in. These options enable you to use the applications in the following sections to view multimedia content on your Mac.

Note: *QuickTime performance speed will no doubt increase several times over when the next generation of PowerPC processor debuts next year. The G4 processor will include a new 128-bit data path, add new AltiVec instructions, and be able to create multiple virtual FPUs to handle 2D and 3D imaging.*

MoviePlayer

The venerable MoviePlayer application has been revised to support not just the playing of movies, but the customized presentation and export of movies as well. When playing a movie, as in Figure 9.1, it looks much the same as in previous versions.

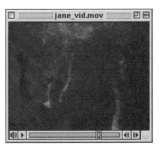

Figure 9.1   The MoviePlayer application, part of QuickTime 3.0.

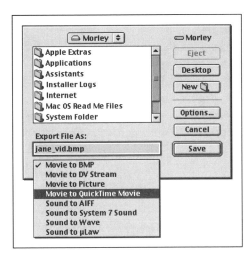

Figure 9.2   The Export options enabled as part of QuickTime Pro.

The Pro version allows you to selectively play the audio or video track of a movie, for example, as well as export it as a Digital Video (DV) stream, among other formats (see Figure 9.2).

PictureViewer

QuickTime 3 also introduced the PictureViewer application, which used the QuickTime component of Mac OS 8.5 to view, manipulate, and convert images into several popular file formats, including BMP (for Microsoft Windows) and Photoshop. It is a no-frills application, but an essential one for anyone who uses the Web and downloads images. Figure 9.3 shows a sample JPEG image as viewed through the PictureViewer application.

Figure 9.3   The PictureViewer application is a handy utility and a good alternative to the popular (and no longer supported) JPEGView.

9: Multimedia

QuickTime Plug-In

The QuickTime Plug-in, also a standard part of Mac OS 8.5, enables some of the features found in the MoviePlayer application for use in a Web browser, including Microsoft Internet Explorer and Netscape Navigator. The plug-in has its own set of controls that are configured independently of the control panel. Each browser may need a bit of assistance to work properly with the plug-in. Figure 9.4 shows some of the new options associated with the QuickTime Plug-in.

QuickTime VR

A new twist to QuickTime 3 is the incorporation of the QuickTime VR (QTVR) player into the MoviePlayer and QuickTime Plug-in, which enables you to view QuickTime and QTVR movies and panoramas using the same application and plug-in. For example, Figure 9.5 shows a sample QTVR file viewed in a Web browser (left) and the same file downloaded to hard disk and viewed in MoviePlayer.

QuickDraw 3D

Not as many people are as familiar with QuickDraw 3D as QuickTime. This situation will probably change in the near future, because the QuickDraw 3D metafile format (3DMF) has been chosen as the basis for the next generation of Virtual Reality Modeling Language (VRML). QuickDraw 3D, now a part of QuickTime, is a cross-platform application programming interface (API) that allows Mac, Windows, and Unix users to view one version of a document on any of these platforms without modification. QuickDraw 3D images can be exported to the QuickTime movie format or viewed using SimpleText, like the examples shown in Figure 9.6.

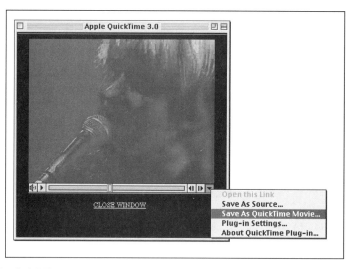

Figure 9.4   The QuickTime Web browser plug-in, as viewed through Internet Explorer.

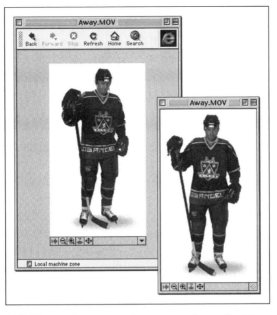

Figure 9.5   QuickTime VR files no longer require a separate application.

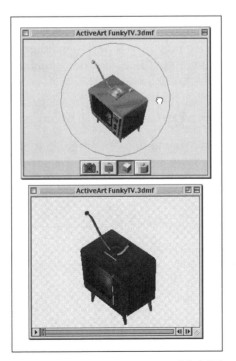

Figure 9.6   QuickDraw 3D's 3DMF file format is now part of QuickTime, as well as the basis for VRML 2.0 and Live3D.

9: Multimedia

QuickTime Streaming

An earlier version of QuickTime introduced the capability to stream movies over the Internet and to allow recipients to start viewing the files before they completely downloaded (sometimes referred to as a "quickstart" feature). Streaming multimedia files over the Internet is becoming increasingly important, because companies have found ways to market products and services by using this type of technology. QuickTime has positioned itself very well as a standard file format to suit this purpose. Currently, QuickTime movies may only be streamed using the Hypertext Transfer Protocol (HTTP), but Apple has already given a public demonstration, showing how QuickTime can be streamed live. Moreover, rumors abound that QuickTime will be interoperable with Real Network's RealPlayer and RealSystem G2 later this year, allowing MoviePlayer and the QuickTime Plug-in to play Real streams, and perhaps vice versa. QuickTime Pro enables you to save multiple versions of a document for streaming over the Web at different connection speeds.

QuickTime For Java

Apple announced in March 1998 that it was developing a version of QuickTime for Java, a programming language that allows applications to run on a wide variety of computing platforms, by porting QuickTime functions into Java class libraries. This could be a tremendous boost to the Java programming language, as well as to Apple, because they both stand to gain increased interoperability. At this time, however, QuickTime for Java is not in public beta and, therefore, not available for further consideration in this book.

Other File Formats

QuickTime is the Swiss Army knife of multimedia tools because it can open just about anything. Some of the more than 35 popular multimedia file formats that QuickTime can open and view include:

- MIDI
- AVI
- MPEG
- WAV
- BMP
- DV Stream
- Cinepak
- DV NTSC
- DV PAL
- mLaw
- AIFF

9: Multimedia

- JPEG/JFIF
- Photoshop
- PNG
- Targa
- TIFF

Moreover, the QuickTime file format has been chosen as the basis for the MPEG-4 format by the International Standard Organization (ISO), as well as being the new format of choice by Silicon Graphics (maker of the multimedia powerhouse SGI workstations). It's a safe bet that if QuickTime doesn't support a certain file type now, either it will in the future or that specific file format isn't long for this world.

Color-Matching Issues

Another big concern in the world of multimedia is color matching. Whether you are viewing or creating multimedia, it's important that colors are properly displayed on screen and in print, and the latest version of Apple's ColorSync provides more options than ever before in this area. ColorSync 2.5.1, part of the default Mac OS 8.5 installation, provides new monitor calibration features in place of the monitor gamma setting in the Monitors & Sounds control panel, as well as these new features:

- Photoshop plug-in support
- AppleScript support
- Multiprocessor support

A properly configured ColorSync profile will assist ColorSync-savvy applications interpret colors and display or print them accordingly. The Monitor Calibration Assistant will help you calibrate your system and generate a custom settings file (see Figure 9.7) that you can easily recall and use to switch among settings. This capability is useful in desktop publishing shops, where people share computers and work with dual-monitor workstations.

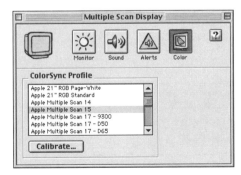

Figure 9.7   You can create and store ColorSync profiles to enhance color matching on Mac OS 8.5.

Immediate Solutions

The following sections describe how to configure the most important multimedia components that are part of the standard installation of Mac OS 8.5.

Configuring Monitors & Sound

Immediately after installing or upgrading to Mac OS 8.5, one of the first steps you should take is to configure the new Monitors & Sound control panel. Two examples are shown in Figure 9.8.

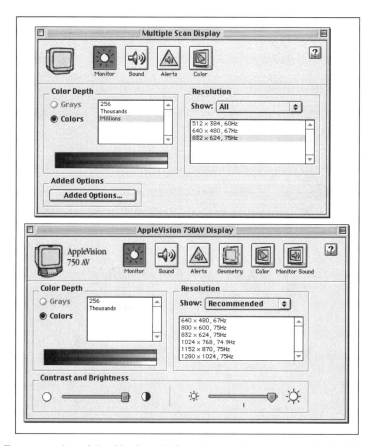

Figure 9.8   Two examples of the Monitors & Sound control panel, one of which has a substantial built-in AV capability.

9: Multimedia

Several elements in Monitors & Sound have changed since previous versions of Mac OS 8, and the options that are available will depend on the type of monitor you have attached to your computer (as in the previous figure). The first things you should notice are that the "Gamma" section is no longer present, that a new button named Color appears in the upper section of the window used to configure ColorSync, and that the Monitors & Sound window name is replaced with the title of your ColorSync profile. To configure Monitors & Sound, launch it from the Control panels folder and follow these steps:

1. In the Monitor section (refer to Figure 9.8), choose a color depth and resolution. Additional options may be present—depending on the type of monitor you have attached—such as contrast, brightness, and additional hardware options.

2. In the Sound section, choose the desired sound levels, input, and output options. Again, computers with additional AV hardware will have additional options in this section as well (see Figure 9.9).

3. In the Alerts section, choose a default system alert and sound level for the alert, which is independent of the computer system volume setting in the Sound section (see Figure 9.10).

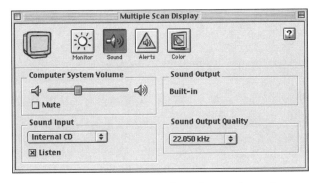

Figure 9.9   The Sound section of the Monitors & Sound control panel.

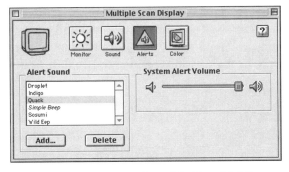

Figure 9.10   The Alerts section hasn't changed at all in Mac OS 8.5.

9: Multimedia

4. In the Color section, select a ColorSync profile and calibrate your display (see the "Configuring ColorSync" section below for details).

5. Configure any additional items that might be present in Monitors & Sound, such as the Geometry or Monitor Sound options, shown in Figure 9.11. You should note that many AV monitors will not be as tightly integrated with the Mac OS as are Apple's own AV monitors, and subsequent configuration might take place outside the Monitors & Sound control panel. This is probably the best argument for purchasing an Apple-brand monitor over other third-party displays.

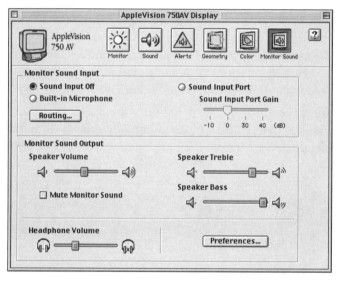

Figure 9.11   Different monitors will have different options in the Monitors & Sound control panel.

Configuring ColorSync

ColorSync isn't new to Mac OS 8.5, but some of the calibration options are new. It's a little complex for those of you who've never had occasion to change the old gamma settings in the Monitors or Monitors & Sound control panel, but fortunately for us, Apple provides well-documented configuration instructions.

To get started configuring ColorSync, open the ColorSync control panel and complete the following configuration options:

1. Select a System Profile from the 50 or so profiles contained in the ColorSync Profiles folder (located in the System Folder, as shown in Figure 9.12). ColorSync-savvy applications will take your profile into account

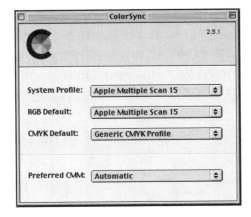

Figure 9.12   The ColorSync control panel.

when defining colors for viewing on the screen and in print. If your monitor comes with a different profile, follow the manufacturer's instructions on how to install it.

2. Select RGB and CYMK Default settings, which are used only when RGB- and CYMK-based files lack a profile of their own and request one from your computer.

3. Select a Preferred Color Matching Method (CMM).

The next step is to return to the Color section of the Monitors & Sound control panel and to calibrate your display in conjunction with a ColorSync profile:

1. Select the same ColorSync profile as in the ColorSync control panel, as shown in Figure 9.13.

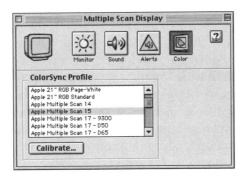

Figure 9.13   The next step in configuring ColorSync is to return to the Monitors & Sound control panel and calibrate your monitor.

9: Multimedia

2. Click on the Calibrate button, follow the instructions provided by the Monitor Calibration Assistant, and configure contrast, brightness, gamma, white point, and other color characteristics.

3. Save the profile, then return to the Color section of the Monitors & Sound control panel and select your new profile, as shown in Figure 9.14.

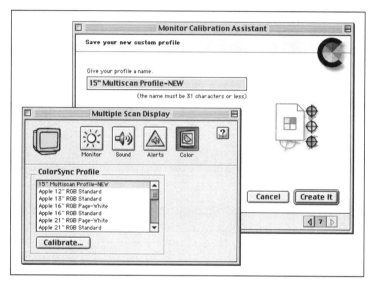

Figure 9.14   Save your profile, then select it in the Monitors & Sound control panel.

Using DigitalColor Meter

The DigitalColor Meter is a tool that allows you to sample on-screen images and translate the sampled area into industry-standard values as a means of color matching. A popular tool—called ColorPicker Pro by Mike McNamara and Rootworks, LLC—performs a similar task and is more friendly for HTML programmers. DigitalColor Meter, however, is designed for advanced color matching in the publishing industry. DigitalColor Meter matches an on-screen color to one of several industry standards, such as Pantone, CIE, and Tristimulus. Some matching features works in conjunction only with AppleVision and ColorSync monitors; RGB values, however, can be measured with any monitor.

To use the DigitalColor Meter to measure RGB color values of any element visible on your computer screen, follow these steps:

1. Launch the DigitalColor Meter application from the Monitors Extras folder in the Apple Extras folder.

9: Multimedia

2. Select the RGB (red, green, and blue) option.

3. Move the mouse pointer to any pixel on your display to display that pixel's RGB color value. For example, Figure 9.15 shows the DigitalColor Meter measuring the RGB value for the tip on the QuickTime penguin's left flipper, an enlargement of which is shown in the detail window on the left side of the DigitalColor Meter window.

RGB values can be interpreted as percentages, actual values, or hexadecimal values, which are used in HTML documents. DigitalColor Meter allows you to view a pixel's color value by using any of these methods.

Figure 9.15   Using the DigitalColor Meter to measure a pixel's RGB color value.

Configuring QuickTime

QuickTime is configured in two places, the QuickTime control panel and the QuickTime plug-in. Some configuration information is shared between the two; perhaps someday, Apple will combine them into one configuration utility or control panel. The control panel is used to configure all QuickTime settings except for Web-browser-specific settings, which we will describe in a section a bit further in this chapter.

9: Multimedia

To configure the QuickTime control panel, open the control panel and make the following selections:

1. In the AutoPlay section, enable or disable audio and CD-ROM AutoPlay, as in Figure 9.16. (Disabling AutoPlayis a good idea because of the AutoWorm virus, which spreads when these options are enabled.)

2. In the Connection Speed section, select an Internet connection speed to assist QuickTime in choosing from multiple files that have been optimized for streaming over the Internet (see Figure 9.17). Making an accurate decision here will allow you to view multimedia files more quickly.

3. In the Media Keys section, enter, edit, or delete any media keys that you have obtained to give you access to protected files (see Figure 9.18).

4. In the Music section, enter, edit, or delete music synthesizers installed on your computer. The QuickTime Music Synthesizer is installed by Mac OS 8.5 (see Figure 9.19).

5. In the QuickTime Exchange section, enable or disable the ability for QuickTime to automatically attempt to open multimedia files belonging to other computer platforms, such as AVI files created by Windows users. Checking this option is a good idea because many non-QuickTime files are readable using QuickTime.

6. Finally, click on the About QuickTime section to see information about what version of QuickTime you are using and about the technology partners companies Apple has partnered with to create QuickTime. Click on the Registration section to enter or reenter your QuickTime Pro registration information.

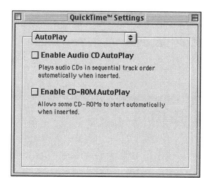

Figure 9.16   You should disable AutoPlay to prevent the AutoWorm virus from infecting your computer.

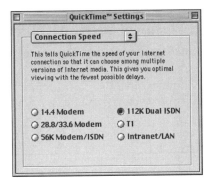

Figure 9.17   Choose the best connection speed for your computer.

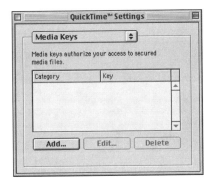

Figure 9.18   Media Keys configuration options.

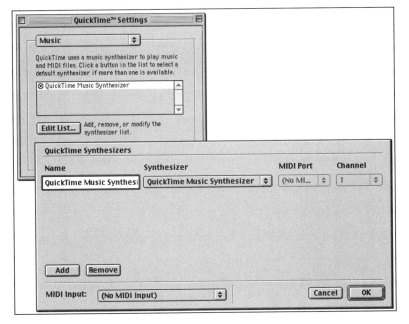

Figure 9.19   The default music synthesizer.

Playing QuickTime Movies With MoviePlayer

The best part about QuickTime is playing movies with the MoviePlayer and un-less you have the Pro version, playing movies is about all you can do. QuickTime allows the Mac OS to recognize the most popular multimedia file types and assign the MoviePlayer creator code (TVOD) to them for easier viewing with MoviePlayer.

To use MoviePlayer's basic functions, follow these steps:

1. Open a movie by double-clicking on its icon or by launching MoviePlayer and choosing File|Open and selecting a file, as in Figure 9.20.

2. Use the controls shown in Figure 9.21 to control the basic options for a movie, including the following:

Figure 9.20   A QuickTime movie viewed with MoviePlayer.

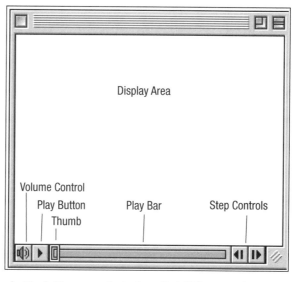

Figure 9.21   The basic MoviePlayer controls for a QuickTime movie.

- *Volume control*—Increase, decrease, or mute the volume of a movie or sound track (not all movies have sound tracks, however).
- *Play button*—Start and pause a movie or sound track.
- *Thumb*—Drag to move forward or backward; Shift-drag to select a section.
- *Step controls*—Step forward or backward through a movie or sound track; click and hold to fast-forward or fast-reverse.
- *Display area* (movie files only)—Area to view movie data.

Table 9.1   QuickTime import/export file types for the Mac OS.

Format	Import	Export
Video		
AVI	Yes	No
DV	Yes	Yes
MPEG	Yes	No
OpenDML	Yes	No
Audio		
AIFF/AIFC	Yes	Yes
Audio CD	Yes	No
DV	Yes	No
MPEG Layer 1 & 2	Yes	No
Sound Designer II	Yes	No
System 7 Sound	Yes	Yes
uLaw (AU)	Yes	Yes
WAV	Yes	Yes
Still Image		
3DMF	Yes	No
BMP	Yes	Yes
GIF	Yes	No
JPEG/JFIF	Yes	No
MacPaint	Yes	No
Photoshop	Yes	No
PICT	Yes	Yes

(continued)

9: Multimedia

Table 9.1   QuickTime import/export file types for the Mac OS (continued).

Format	Import	Export
PNG	Yes	No
QuickDraw GX	Yes	No
QuickTime	Yes	No
SGI	Yes	No
Targa	Yes	No
TIFF	Yes	No
Animation		
Animated GIF	Yes	No
FLC/FLI	Yes	No
PICS	Yes	No
MIDI		
Karaoke MIDI	Yes	No
Standard MIDI	Yes	Yes
Text		
Text	Yes	Yes

Table 9.2   QuickTime import/export file types for Microsoft Windows.

Format	Import	Export
Video		
AVI	Yes	No
DVCan	Yes	Yes
OpenDML	Yes	No
Audio		
AIFF/AIFC	Yes	Yes
DV	Yes	No
Sound Designer II	Yes	No
System 7 Sound	Yes	No
uLaw (AU)	Yes	Yes
WAV	Yes	Yes
Still Image		
3DMF	Yes	No
BMP	Yes	Yes

(continued)

9: Multimedia

Table 9.2   QuickTime import/export file types for Microsoft Windows (continued).

Format	Import	Export
GIF	Yes	No
JPEG/JFIF	Yes	No
MacPaint	Yes	No
Photoshop	Yes	No
PICT	Yes	Yes
PNG	Yes	No
QuickTime Image Format	Yes	Yes
SGI	Yes	No
Targa	Yes	No
TIFF	Yes	No
Animation		
Animated GIF	Yes	No
FLC/FLI	Yes	No
PICS	Yes	No
MIDI		
Karaoke MIDI	Yes	No
Standard MIDI	Yes	No
General MIDI	Yes	Yes
Text		
Text	Yes	Yes

Saving And Exporting Movies With QuickTime

The standard version of QuickTime doesn't allow you to save or export movies, but the Pro version does enable you to save files in several formats. Table 9.1 lists the import and export file types that QuickTime is capable of handling for the Mac OS; Table 9.2 lists these formats for Microsoft Windows.

To save a QuickTime movie after it has been opened in MoviePlayer, follow these steps:

1. Choose File|Save As, as shown in Figure 9.22, and select whether you want to save the movie *normally*—which creates a link to the actual data file—or as a self-contained QuickTime movie file.

2. Name the file and select a location for the new file.

9: Multimedia

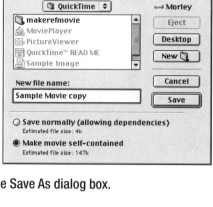

Figure 9.22   The QuickTime Save As dialog box.

To export the movie into another file format, take these steps:

1. Choose File|Export.

2. Choose from one of the export formats:
   - Movie to BMP
   - Movie to DV Stream
   - Movie to Picture
   - Movie to QuickTime Movie
   - Sound to AIFF
   - Sound to System 7 Sound
   - Sound to Wave
   - Sound to mLaw

3. Next, click on the Options button in the Export dialog window, and prepare to select from a long list of detailed configuration options (see Figure 9.23).

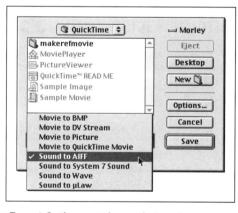

Figure 9.23   The primary Export Options settings window for exporting a QuickTime movie.

9: Multimedia

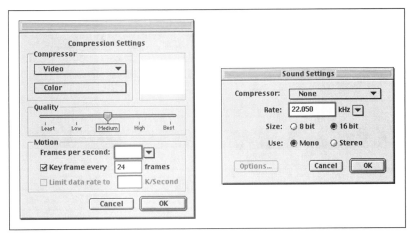

Figure 9.24   Export settings options for video and sound tracks.

Some of the many export options include decisions that must be made for video tracks as well as sound tracks. Figure 9.24 shows the different options present for these two kinds of tracks.

For software and tools to help you manage QuickTime files, see the QuickTime home page at **www.apple.com/quicktime** and the QuickTime FTP site at **ftp. apple.com/quicktime/developers/**.

Configuring QuickTime For Web Browsers

Once configured, using the QuickTime Web browser plug-in isn't much different from using the MoviePlayer application, although save and export features are limited in comparison. However, once saved as a QuickTime movie, you can always use MoviePlayer to perform any further conversions. Currently, the QuickTime Plug-in works with the following browsers: Macintosh: Navigator 3 and 4, Internet Explorer 3 and 4 and Windows: Navigator 3 and 4, Internet Explorer 3 and 4.

The plug-in isn't as flexible when viewing different file formats. Currently, it can support only the formats shown in Table 9.3. To configure the QuickTime Plug-in, follow these steps:

1. Make sure that the QuickTime Plug-in is in your Web browser's plug-ins folder, usually located in the browser's application folder. Both Netscape Navigator and Microsoft Internet Explorer use Netscape plug-ins, so don't be alarmed if the plug-ins in your Internet Explorer folder have Navigator icons.

2. Review your browser's file helper configuration options to ensure that QuickTime is properly defined as a file type. If not, open the Internet

Table 9.3   File formats supported by the QuickTime Plug-in.

Audio
AIFF
AU
MIDI
WAV

Video
AVI
FLC
MPEG (Mac only)
QuickTime

Animation
FLC

Image
BMP
MacPaint
Photoshop
PNG
SGI
Targa

control panel, shown in Figure 9.25, while in Advanced user mode and configure the File Mappings section with the settings shown in Figure 9.25.

3. Visit the QuickTime home page (**www.apple.com/quicktime/**) and load one of the movies on the Web listed in the QuickTime Showcase section. If it won't load, check your browser's preferences and make sure that it's configured to view QuickTime files via the QuickTime Plug-in, rather than trying to save the file to disk or viewing the movie with the Web browser.

4. If the QuickTime Plug-in is properly recognized by the browser, the movie will begin streaming, and the same QuickTime controls found in Movie-Player will be present, as shown in Figure 9.26, with one additional control.

5. To configure the QuickTime Plug-in, click on the triangle in the lower-right corner of the controls to reveal a menu, as shown in Figure 9.27.

6. These settings are straightforward: Just confirm a few general settings, your connection speed, and the MIME settings, and you're set (see Figure 9.28).

7. When you're ready to save a movie or sound file, just click on the triangle again and choose to save the files as a source (to preserve the original file format), or as a QuickTime file.

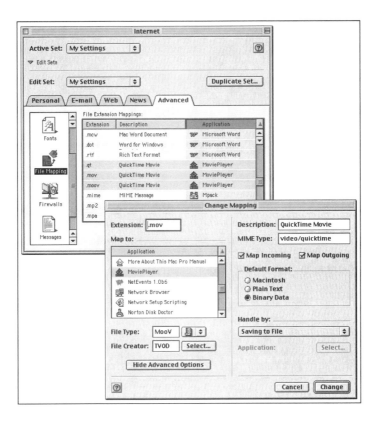

Figure 9.25   Your Web browser may need some assistance in recognizing QuickTime files, although the presence of the QuickTime Plug-in should be sufficient.

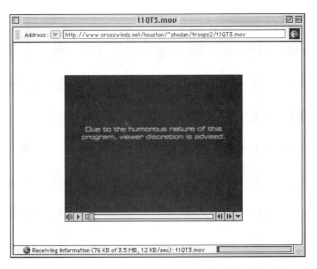

Figure 9.26   A streaming QuickTime movie view with the QuickTime Plug-in and Internet Explorer.

Figure 9.27   Accessing the QuickTime Plug-in's settings.

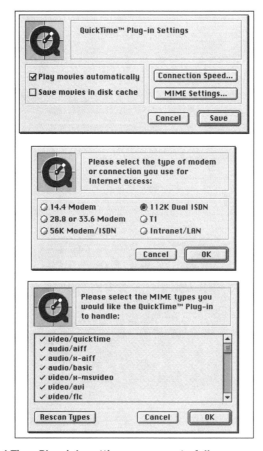

Figure 9.28   The QuickTime Plug-in's settings are easy to follow.

9: Multimedia

Viewing QuickTime VR Files

As we mentioned previously, QuickTime VR is now part-and-parcel with QuickTime, the QuickTime Plug-in, and the MoviePlayer application. Now, you can view QTVR files with any QuickTime 3-savvy application or plug-in, just as you view a QuickTime movie (see Figure 9.29).

However, because QTVR files are panoramas through and around which you may navigate, the controls are a bit different. Rather than stopping and starting a QTVR movie, use the controls shown in Figure 9.30 to do the following:

* *Back*—Step backwards to the previous hot spot.
* *Zoom out*—Move further away from the image.

Figure 9.29   A QuickTime VR movie viewed in a Web browser.

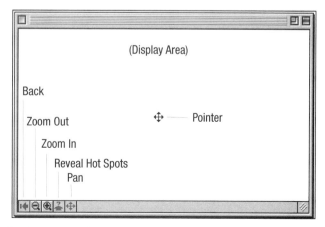

Figure 9.30   The basic controls for a QuickTime VR panorama.

- *Zoom in*—Move closer to the image.
- *Reveal hot spots*—Reveal a files hotspots.
- *Pan*—Move up, down, left, or right.

Viewing Images With PictureViewer

PictureViewer is a great addition to the QuickTime family because it serves as a no-frills helper application for general Internet use. You can do some basic image manipulation, such as change the size and rotate the image, as well as export images into the following formats:

- BMP
- JPEG
- Photoshop
- PICT
- QuickTime Image

To export an image using PictureViewer, take these steps:

1. Open an image in PictureViewer and make any changes, as shown in Figure 9.31.
2. Choose File|Export, select a file format, name, and location, then select Save. All changes you make in size or perspective will be saved.

Figure 9.31   Using PictureViewer to make changes to an image.

9: Multimedia

Operating AppleCD Audio Player

The AppleCD Audio Player, shown in Figure 9.32, has been around for a long time, and it hasn't changed a lick in Mac OS 8.5. You can mount and play an audio CD just as before, as well as customize the playlist.

To configure a playlist with the AppleCD Audio Player, follow these steps:

1. Insert an audio CD into your computer's internal or external CD-ROM player.

2. Click on the Track List show/hide triangle to reveal the track list, as shown in Figure 9.33.

3. Enter a title for the CD, as well as a name for each track in the playlist area. You can use any name.

The user interface is about as easy as it gets, because it mimics many household CD players. The upper-left buttons of the AppleCD Audio Player are (from left to right):

- *Normal*—Plays the track in its original order, then stops.

- *Shuffle*—Reorders the tracks randomly, then stops.

- *Prog*—Allows you to program the order in which the tracks are played, as shown in Figure 9.34.

- *Repeat*—Repeats the CD over and over without stopping.

The upper-right buttons use conventional icons to control the capability to start, stop, pause, jump to the previous or next track, scan forward and backward, as well as control volume. Also, clicking on the tracks pop-up menu allows you to skip to a specific track, as does double-clicking on a track number in the track list.

Note: *The playlists for your audio CDs, including programmed playlists, are stored in the Preferences folder in a file called CD Remote Programs. You should occasionally back up this file to preserve your playlists.*

Figure 9.32   The AppleCD Audio Player.

Figure 9.33   The AppleCD Audio Player's track list.

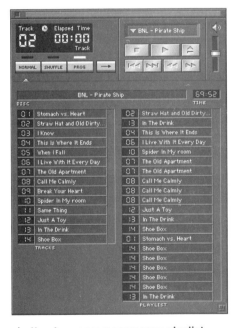

Figure 9.34   Use the Prog button to program your own playlist.

9: Multimedia

Manipulating QuickDraw 3D Objects

QuickDraw, QuickDraw 3D, and the QuickDraw 3D Meta File format are essential elements of Mac OS 8.5, and are installed as part of Mac OS 8.5 and QuickTime. QuickDraw-savvy applications tap into the power of the 2D and 3D rendering capabilities of QuickDraw, such as SimpleText and even the Scrapbook. For example, Figure 9.35 shows a SimpleText and a Scrapbook document with QuickDraw 3D objects embedded.

The QuickDraw controls, shown in Figure 9.36, are easy to use (much easier, in fact, than Netscape Navigator's LiveWorlds VRML controls):

- *Perspective*—See front, back, left, right, top, and bottom views
- *Zoom*—Zoom in or out
- *Rotate*—Move the object freely
- *Relocate*—Move the object to another region of the window
- *Home*—Restore the object's original perspective and position

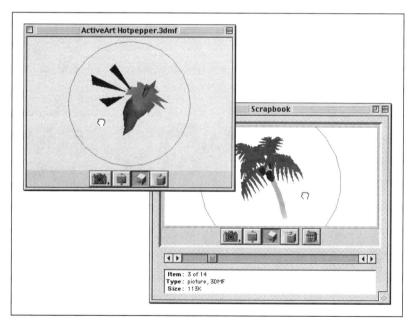

Figure 9.35   A couple of sample QuickDraw 3D objects.

9: Multimedia

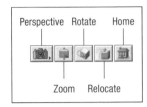

Figure 9.36   QuickDraw controls.

Enabling TV, Cable, Radio, DVD, And The Apple Video Player

Some models of Power Macintosh computers come with significantly more AV capabilities than others, and some are even cable-TV ready. Those that are cable ready will probably have the Apple Video Player—a nice piece of software—installed by default. It manages the AV hardware on your Mac and allows you to easily access cable TV, VCRs, regular TV and radio signals, camcorders, and other video- and audio-in sources. For example, Figure 9.37 shows a cable TV session, its controls, and an FM radio tuner.

Check your computer's specifications to see what AV hardware it came with and what types it can accept to enable some of these capabilities.

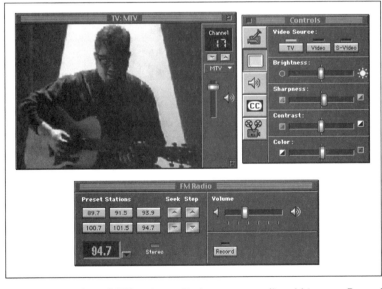

Figure 9.37   A few examples of AV hardware that you can easily add to your PowerMac and provide multimedia capabilities.

Playing Multimedia-Audio CD-ROMs

Finally, many new audio CD-ROMs come with a bonus multimedia track as well. It's no big surprise that the multimedia portion is based on QuickTime with a front-end created with Macromedia Director, one of the most popular CD-ROM gaming creation tools. Because these CD-ROMs are hybrid (audio and data) CDs, you can insert them into your Mac's CD-ROM drive and either play the audio portion by using the AppleCD Audio Player, or you can follow the directions on the data portion.

For example, Figure 9.38 shows a QuickTime movie placed in the center of the screen with Macromedia controls in the lower half of the screen that allow you to advance through the CD or return to the main menu.

Because Mac OS 8.5 installs the latest version of QuickTime, you usually don't need to install anything else; you can just double-click on the application icon and start watching, listening, or interacting with the CD, just like a Mac should!

Figure 9.38   An example of an audio CD, with a bonus multimedia track that features the band's videos and witticisms.

Chapter 10

Microsoft Windows Compatibility

In Depth

Windows Compatibility Issues

Why would you be interested in this chapter? More than 90 percent of computers run some version of Windows operating system. It's rare to find a predominantly Macintosh network, much less a network that contains only Macintosh computers. Most business environments, however, are diverse; if you are a network administrator, you may be supporting both platforms and need to provide server access to all users. Also, we are increasingly sharing and exchanging files electronically, unaware of what operating system is on the other end. Of course, perhaps the most important reason you are interested in this chapter is that you want access to all those great games.

File Problems

Sharing files between platforms is not an easy matter; it can be a huge headache. If you can acknowledge this fact up front, you can learn to deal with problems such as Windows applications that use identical file extensions, unfamiliar document extensions, and the DOS-based 8.3 naming convention.

File Extensions

Some file extensions are exclusive to certain applications. For example, in the PC world, the .xls extension indicates that the document is in some way associated with Microsoft Excel. Some extensions, on the other hand, can be associated with more than one application. The .txt extension indicates a plain-text file, which can be opened by any number of programs, from SimpleText to Microsoft Word 98. The monkey wrench appears when you have proprietary applications assigning similar document extensions. The .doc extension indicates a word-processing document. Although it is most commonly associated with Microsoft Word, the extension is also used with Lotus Word Pro. However, the files will not open cleanly between applications. Microsoft Word 98 doesn't even list Lotus Word Pro as a translation format.

Unknown Files

Occasionally, you will receive files with an extension that is not recognizable. If possible, contact the person who gave you the file for more information. Otherwise, you can open the file within a text editor and browse the file to look for hints about the application that created the file. Some Windows applications identify themselves near the top or bottom of the file. Later in this chapter, we discuss how you can educate your Mac to deal with new or unfamiliar file formats.

8.3 Naming Conventions

The number "8.3" is a reference to the DOS file-naming convention that limited you to eight characters in the file name, followed by a period and a three-character file extension. Your file name was not obligated to be this long or to even have an extension, but this was the maximum length of the file name. Windows 95 introduced long file names for the Windows community, but *fat32*—as it was known—was not understood by the Macintosh PC/DOS mounting software until Mac OS 8.1. More important, the naming convention is still needed because Windows 3.1 uses 8.3 file names, and there are still millions of Windows 3.1 users out there. You will also find this restrictive naming convention on CD-ROMs that use the ISO 9660 format. Level 1 of this standard used the 8.3 file name and was even more restrictive in its use of characters within the file name (the only characters allowed were the letters A through Z, the numbers 0 through 9, and the hyphen). Level 2 allowed long file names but still disallowed certain characters. To guarantee that the greatest number of users can view your documents, use the 8.3 naming convention.

File Format Issues

Exchanging files is one of the most common exchanges of information between Mac and Windows users. It is also often the greatest source of conflict. We exchange files in a variety of methods: We send them through email, hand them over on disk, save them on local servers, and FTP them to remote servers. In some situations, we print them and exchange hard copies. Whatever the method, many things can go wrong in the exchange. At some point, you and the other user need to find ways to coexist. Table 10.1 shows some "safe" file formats. By safe, we mean that these file formats have a greater success rate of manipulation between platforms.

Table 10.1   Safe file formats.

Application Type	File Format
Word Processors	RTF
Bitmapped Graphic	TIFF, GIF, and JPEG
Vector Art	Generic EPS or export as safe bitmap
Spreadsheet	Excel 3 or 4; DIF; dBASE3, tab- or comma-delimited
Database	Comma or tab delimited, dBASE3

First, if you know the platform, operating system, and even the software application of the other users, you should do your best to accommodate them. Save the file in a format they can easily read. While it is beyond the scope of this chapter to instruct you on every method of saving files, you will usually find a selection box in the Save As dialog box that lists other file formats. Figure 10.1 shows a listing of file formats available for GraphicConverter.

If the software application is developed on both platforms and the company releasing the software makes the best attempts to keep both platforms synchronized, then saving files in the appropriate format is easy. In many cases, the packages can open the file without any effort from you and save it in a special format. As the Windows platform has become dominant, however, the reality is that the Macintosh clients are often released well after the Windows clients.

What does this mean to you? In most cases, you can save the file normally and easily exchange it with your coworker, who is using the Windows version. Problems arise when you receive it back. Programs are written to be

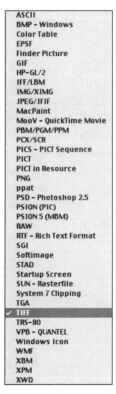

ASCII
BMP – Windows
Color Table
EPSF
Finder Picture
GIF
HP-GL/2
IFF/LBM
IMG/XIMG
JPEG/JFIF
MacPaint
MooV – QuickTime Movie
PBM/PGM/PPM
PCX/SCR
PICS – PICT Sequence
PICT
PICT in Resource
PNG
ppat
PSD – Photoshop 2.5
PSION (PIC)
PSION 5 (MBM)
RAW
RTF – Rich Text Format
SGI
Softimage
STAD
Startup Screen
SUN – Rasterfile
System 7 Clipping
TGA
✓ TIFF
TRS-80
VPB – QUANTEL
Windows Icon
WMF
XBM
XPM
XWD

Figure 10.1   An extensive listing of file formats.

backward-compatible, not forward-compatible. For example, Microsoft released the MS Office suite version 4.0 for Macintosh and Windows in 1995 (the Office suite contained Word 6.0, Excel 5.0, and PowerPoint 4.0). In 1997, Microsoft released the software suite Office 97 for Windows 95 users only. Mac users were still running Word 6.0 or even 5.1, which makes exchanging files between the two camps precarious. Microsoft did eventually write a translator that enabled Word 6.0 to open Word 97 files. However, Macintosh users couldn't save files in the Word 97 format. This created lapses in work productivity because files had to be constantly converted to the various formats. Finally, the scales were balanced in 1998 when Microsoft released Office 98 for the Macintosh.

Usually, you should prepare for the gaps between Windows and Mac versions of software. Excellent software applications are available that translate and convert files so that you can use them.

SuperDrive

The SuperDrive is actually the official name of your floppy drive. These drives are standard equipment on most Macintosh computers (with the exception of the iMac and some PowerBook computers). The SuperDrive is capable of reading data from, writing data to, and formatting several file formats, including the following:

- Macintosh

- ProDos

- DOS

The SuperDrive can also read from and write 1.6 megabyte formatted disks for Windows 95. Previous versions of PC Exchange, the utility used to mount non-Mac volumes, couldn't handle the long file-name format used by Windows 95 and NT. It instead displayed the truncated 8.3 naming convention. However, since Mac OS 8.1, PC Exchange can handle these names. If you have users who report problems with long file names, suggest that they upgrade to version 8.1 or later of the Mac OS.

File Exchange

Before we can discuss the Control Panel File Exchange, we need to explain a little history. When SuperDrives were first installed in Macs, in order to put information on the PC-formatted disks, you had to use a utility called Apple File Exchange. This was similar to the Font/DA mover utility. However, the PC disks would not mount on the desktop. Of course, users began clamoring for a way to utilize drag-and-drop functionality with these disks. PC Exchange was the answer because it enabled you to mount and manage the PC formatted disk. Figure

Figure 10.2   A DOS floppy disk on a Macintosh Desktop.

10.2 shows a PC formatted disk on the Desktop. Note that the initials "PC" are the only difference between a Mac and non-Mac disk icon.

Thanks to PC Exchange, you could easily mount DOS disks and media on the Desktop to be recognized and used within any application. This capability extended not only to floppy disks but also to other removable media, including Zip and Jaz disks, CD-ROMs, and Syquest removable hard drives. Also, remember that the SuperDrive can create DOS-formatted disks. Figure 10.3 shows the dialog box and available menu options when you choose to erase a disk. Actually, it isn't harmful to work exclusively with PC disks and media; in some settings, it's entirely appropriate (such as in a computer-lab environment, where you may need to use PCs, Macs, and even Sun computers).

However, that wasn't the limit of PC Exchange's usefulness. This utility also could be configured to open certain applications on your computer, depending on the file's extension. For example, you configure PC Exchange to launch Microsoft Excel when you double-click on files with an .xls extension. No matter how many new file extensions appeared, PC Exchange could be customized to open the correct program.

PC Exchange also worked hand-in-hand with another control panel named Mac OS Easy Open. This extension employed translation databases, such as those created by DataViz, to search and locate the application that could open the file. This is useful because so many different file extensions exist. You could spend hours customizing PC Exchange. With Mac Easy Open, the entire extension mapping was done for you. All you need to do is let the application search this database for the appropriate application. When it finds a match, it launches the correct software. When it cannot locate software to open the file (as shown in Figure

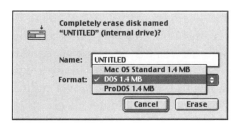

Figure 10.3   Formatting a floppy disk.

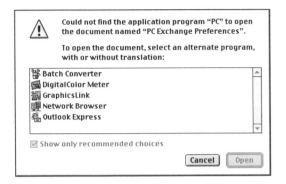

Figure 10.4   The Mac Easy Open Error dialog box.

10.4), it notifies you and suggests other possible applications for launching the program. This is especially helpful when you don't have the application that created the document installed on your computer.

In Mac OS 8.5, the File Exchange control panel is the combination of these two excellent utilities. It also uses some of the file mappings contained within Internet Config. Figure 10.5 shows the File Exchange control panel. The PC Exchange portion is distinguished by the tab of the same name. This has been improved to immediately contain a huge library of file extension mappings. As new programs are developed and released, you can still customize File Exchange to include the appropriate file mapping.

The File Translation tab contains many options that were original to Mac OS Easy Open. It allows you to set options for file translations as well as add new ones. Figure 10.6 shows the File Translation portion of the File Exchange control panel.

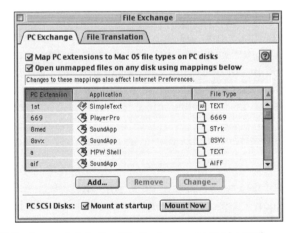

Figure 10.5   The PC Exchange tab In the File Exchange control panel.

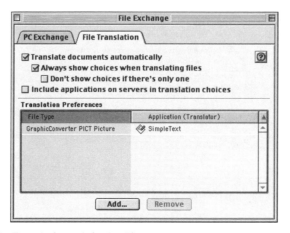

Figure 10.6   The File Translation tab in the File Exchange control panel.

MacLinkPlus

MacLinkPlus from DataViz is a commercial package that works in conjunction with File Exchange. It converts many different file formats, including image and HTML files. The greatest advantage of using MacLinkPlus is the extensive databases of file extensions built into the software that can locate the appropriate software to open the document. You may be aware that versions before Mac OS 8.5 bundled MacLinkPlus with the operating system. It is no longer included in the installation.

Graphic Converter

File Exchange is configured from the beginning to launch certain applications when you open a file with a particular extension. One of these applications, Graphic Converter, is a shareware utility that can import over 100 image file formats and can save files in roughly 40 formats. It can also perform some image editing functions, such as creating a transparent GIF image (*transparent* means that a certain color in the image disappears; in a Web page, this can eliminate the white box around a graphic). It can open and save several Windows file formats, including BMP, as well as the files understood across platforms, such as GIF and JPEG. It can do file conversions in batches and even manage some movie and animation files. If you don't have the time or money to spend on a big graphics-editing program, Graphic Converter is certainly an excellent tool to use.

Zip Files

More and more of us are retrieving files from the Internet. Macintosh files are compressed in many cases using StuffIt Deluxe from Aladdin Systems, Inc. You can recognize these archives by their file extension, which is usually .sit. For the PC world, the majority of files are compressed with PKZIP or WinZip; you can recognize these files by the .zip extension. For some of us, it is difficult to think of Zip files as anything other than applications which, of course, do not run on your machine. However, you can find huge sound archives that contain audio files that you can certainly use on your computer; these files may be zipped archives. You can also find sites that contain free clipart and images; these may also be zipped. As a Mac user, you know that you can easily download the file to your computer, but in the past, you may have moved the files to a disk and decompressed them on a PC. This is no longer necessary because excellent shareware and freeware utilities are available to unzip these files, including the following:

- Unzip—A free utility from Info-Zip, can effectively open the archived file. However, it cannot compress files or folders into Zip format.
- PKZIP Mac—From Ascent Solutions Inc., PKZIP Mac can open Zip files and can compress files into Zip archives. It can preserve the resource fork information, but this information will be lost if another decompression utility opens the archive. PKZIP is also recognized in the PC world for its compression capabilities.
- ZipIt—A shareware utility that also can decompress and compress Zip files. Figure 10.7 shows a sample extraction, using ZipIt.
- StuffIt Deluxe and Drop Stuff (with Expander Enhancer)—These two utilities can open Zip files as well as TAR and gzip files.

Unix Files

The other file format that you may need to decompress is often referred to as the *gzip format*. These are found in Unix systems; the archives may also be rather large. Utilities are available that can decompress and compress Unix files. Mac GZip is a freeware utility that can open archives and create new ones.

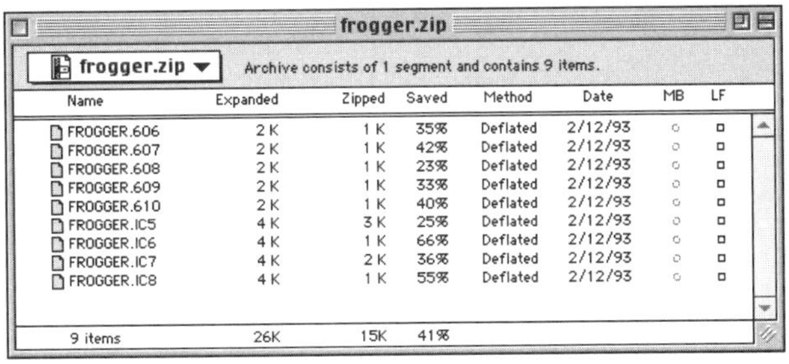

frogger.zip

frogger.zip Archive consists of 1 segment and contains 9 items.

Name	Expanded	Zipped	Saved	Method	Date	MB	LF
FROGGER.606	2 K	1 K	35%	Deflated	2/12/93	○	□
FROGGER.607	2 K	1 K	42%	Deflated	2/12/93	○	□
FROGGER.608	2 K	1 K	23%	Deflated	2/12/93	○	□
FROGGER.609	2 K	1 K	33%	Deflated	2/12/93	○	□
FROGGER.610	2 K	1 K	40%	Deflated	2/12/93	○	□
FROGGER.IC5	4 K	3 K	25%	Deflated	2/12/93	○	□
FROGGER.IC6	4 K	1 K	66%	Deflated	2/12/93	○	□
FROGGER.IC7	4 K	2 K	36%	Deflated	2/12/93	○	□
FROGGER.IC8	4 K	1 K	55%	Deflated	2/12/93	○	□
9 items	26K	15K	41%				

Figure 10.7 ZipIt in action.

Network Access

No man is an island; at least not in our networked environments. We either set up our own computers as servers or attach to one on the network. It's important to find ways to share this information as simply as possible and make it available to the broadest portion of your audience.

As you will see in Chapter 11, it is simple for you to set up your computer so that other Mac users can access your files. The difficulties arise when you need to access Windows or Novell servers. Programs run on these servers that allow you access to the file system. However, some environments may not be friendly to the AppleTalk protocol. If you cannot convince your system administrator to run the programs necessary for you to access the server, you can install applications and extensions that let you access the servers you need.

DAVE

DAVE is a software utility that uses the TCP/IP protocol to connect machines. TCP/IP has become the standard method of communication over the Internet. By focusing on this protocol, DAVE allows you to access Windows NT servers, as well as Windows 95 machines; it also allows Windows users to access your files. You can even access other Macintosh computers via a TCP/IP connection. Using the Network Browser, you can attach to other Windows machines. You can also use the Domain Logon feature to log on to an NT server domain, thus giving you access to the resources and servers in that domain. DAVE also features a messaging service that allows you to send and receive short messages in pop-up windows from other users. This is very useful for important messages regarding the server status. DAVE also supports AppleScripting. You can automate mounting and dismounting volumes.

Novell NetWare Client For Mac OS

While Windows NT servers are gaining in popularity, Novell servers are very common and have been active for a long time. In many cases, the administrator may have activated the netware-loadable modules necessary to allow Macintosh computers to access, read, and write files onto the server, as well as run applications from it. In some cases, however, this application may not have been enabled (some network administrators are skittish about confidential servers appearing in AppleTalk zones). By installing the Novell NetWare client, you can access any server for which you have been granted rights. The client enables your computer to speak the language of Novell—IPX. You also increase your functionality by using this client rather than relying on AppleTalk access.

Running Windows On A Mac

In the average business environment, you will find specialized software that is often customized for the company, enabling unique work processes to be performed efficiently. This type of innovation requires skill, hard work, and money. Unfortunately, Macintosh users definitely find themselves at a disadvantage when it comes to these specialized programs. In cases where Macintosh clients are created, they are often buggy and unstable. This happens because the program may have been created and customized for a Windows client, then "ported" to the Mac OS platform. Because the application wasn't written specifically for the Mac OS, you will find software that is often slow, unstable, and downright ugly. In fact, several software developers often label themselves as "enterprise" companies, which means their products are written to work on all popular platforms. Between the lines, you may see the very scenario we describe here. In fact, a site-license purchaser often has to balance the economical questions of a do-it-all package versus the "best of breed" (but more expensive) approach. In today's "do more with less" atmosphere, you can guess that the cheaper (but not-as-good packages) will usually win.

Worse yet, the Mac OS platform in many cases is not supported at all, leaving Mac users scrambling for a solution. Consequently, Macintosh users are finding that they must run Windows in some fashion. You can do so in two ways:

- You can run Windows using a client that emulates Windows, such as SoftWindows 98 or Virtual PC.

- You can run Windows by installing a PC card.

Emulation Clients For Productivity

The cheaper—but slower—solution is to run Windows in emulation mode. If you need to occasionally run a particular Windows application, you may want to consider this option. An *emulator* is a software application that runs Windows within your Mac OS environment. One of the oldest emulation packages was SoftPC (no longer available) from Insignia solutions. Insignia later created SoftWindows and SoftWindows95. The latter is excellent because it does include Windows 95 and certainly makes installation a little easier. However, the price of the software reflects this. Virtual PC from Connectix approaches emulation a little differently. It emulates the entire PC, not just a particular operating system, so you can run any operating system that will run on the PC. In fact, Virtual PC can run Windows NT, which is fast becoming the business user's operating system of choice. Provided you have a large amount of RAM and disk space as well as a fast processor, you can successfully run Windows 95 or NT while also performing tasks on your Mac. Figure 10.8 shows Virtual PC, running Windows 95.

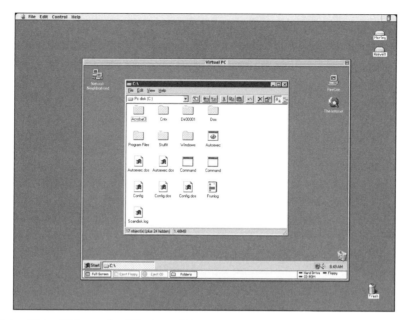

Figure 10.8   Virtual PC, running Windows 95.

Emulation Clients For Relaxation

We've gotten the business side out of the way; however, you can also use emulation clients for fun. In fact, one of the biggest reasons people want a DOS or Windows solution is so that they can play all the games that are out there. Some very economical solutions are available to do so.

Insignia, the makers of SoftWindows, also sells a product called Real PC. Although Real PC is capable of running any DOS or Windows application (provided you have purchased a Windows license), it is targeted for the recreational user who occasionally wants to play a game or two. Real PC, economically priced, includes several games.

Virtual PC, from Connectix, is also targeted toward the recreational user.

You can also find free emulation packages. For example, if you are in the grip of nostalgia and want to play some of the old arcade games, you can run an emulation package called MacMAME, which attempts to reproduce the 1980's experience of playing arcade games. It allows you to run hundreds of arcade games and it is frequently updated to add support for additional games. Figure 10.9 shows MacMAME, running the old "why did the frog cross the road" diversion.

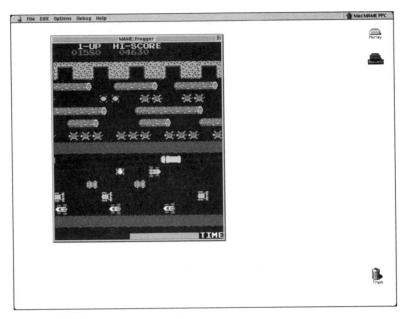

Figure 10.9   MacMAME, running an arcade game.

PC Cards

If you find that Windows is fast becoming a part of your daily life, but you just don't have the desk space for another computer, then you may want to consider a hardware solution. The biggest benefit of installing a PC card is the fact that it runs almost separately from the Mac OS—although information can be shared between the two environments. The PC card has its own memory and uses a portion of hard drive space allocated to it. Therefore, you could begin a process within the Windows environment, then switch to the Macintosh system and continue performing other tasks. PC cards also support separate monitors and even separate keyboards, as well as other peripheral devices such as joysticks.

PC card vendors include Radius and Orange Micro. Prices range from a few hundred dollars for low-end processors to Pentium Pro PC cards bundled with Windows NT. Expect to pay almost the cost of another computer for the high-end cards.

Client/Server Issues

Businesses often use the client/server model for productivity. Consequently, some platforms either do not receive the development needed to produce a decent application or are not supported at all. When this happens, users are often forced to use an operating system that they neither know nor like. They are advised to purchase emulators or PC cards or are told to switch platforms. However, if the affected user base is large enough, alternative solutions are available.

Browsers

One of the trends in the client/server industry is to develop clients with a Web browser interface. As long as the developer adheres to Internet standards, the resulting application should be accessible by Mac and Windows users via Web browsers. In the recent past, developers created applications for one platform (usually Windows) and ported to the other platforms (usually Mac and Unix). The results were mixed. Web browser client interfaces don't have to deal with this problem. As a side benefit, you aren't tied to one computer to be productive. As long as you can launch a Web browser, you can send information to and retrieve information from the server.

Java Applications

Some software companies are writing applications that will work effectively in a Web browser capable of running Java. By doing so, an application could truly be universal and not necessarily rely on a particular platform. Of course, this solution does require extensive programming, and Java standards seem to change daily. This approach looks promising, however, and Mac OS 8.5 continues to improve on its Java support. For more information on Java, please consult Chapter 15.

WinFrame

Several large companies that release specialized software have stated up front that they will not release software for a particular platform or operating system. In many cases, the Macintosh platform is the first item on the black list. However, these applications are also getting larger and larger. Even Windows users are finding that they need a better solution to these disk space and memory monsters. When you analyze this group of user needs, you will find an excellent solution is WinFrame by Citrix. Part of WinFrame is a thin client that is installed on your computer. The other piece of the puzzle is a WinFrame server. WinFrame is actually a customized version of the Windows NT server software. When launched, the client accesses a WinFrame server and then begins a session that appears to be running locally on the computer, but is actually executing from the server. WinFrame supports multiple platforms, including Macintosh and Windows 3.1. The WinFrame client is so thin that it barely takes any bandwidth on the network. It can even run successfully over a modem connection. Figure 10.10 shows a WinFrame session running within Mac OS 8.5.

The drawback to this solution is the expense. WinFrame requires a dedicated server and—depending upon your user base—you may want to have more than one server dedicated to WinFrame. However, if you have a large group of users frustrated by emulation and PC cards, you may want to consider this as an alternative.

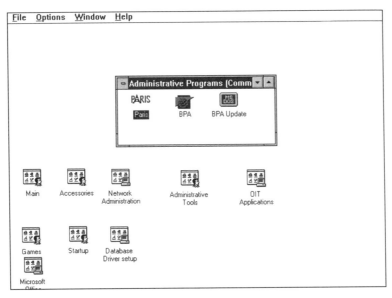

Figure 10.10   A WinFrame session.

WinFrame's Future

What is the future of WinFrame? The answer is Windows NT 5. The next NT release from Microsoft will include the capability to launch sessions on remote servers. The anticipated release of Windows NT 5 is the end of the first quarter of 1999. That's just in time for all the fun with the year 2000. Until then, WinFrame is an excellent solution that's available now.

Color Differences

One of the biggest and most-undisputed advantages you have as a Mac user is a uniform color table. Although there will always be differences viewing a particular color from Macintosh to Macintosh and even monitor to monitor, the Macintosh color palette has been standardized. This standardization gives you confidence as you prepare and exchange images with other Mac users, but the Windows color palette uses a different interpretation of color, so that the color *red* on your computer may look *orange red* on a PC. For this reason, if you are creating images for Web documents that will be viewed on Windows computer systems, check your Web page on the Windows platform. Be prepared for a shock. You may not like the results.

Macintosh Advocacy

Finally, a division of Apple is available that works with software developers and encourages them to begin or continue developing applications for the Macintosh platform. While not very many users at your business may be affected by the lack of Macintosh platform support, nationwide you could be a very persuasive group. By contacting Apple, you may be giving additional ammunition to justify the software development for the Macintosh platform.

Quick Reference Specifications

The following are the essential facts about Microsoft Windows compatibility:

- You can save files in a format appropriate for almost all recipients, negating the need for file conversion on their part.

- You can format disks both in Macintosh and PC format via the SuperDrive.

- PC Exchange enabled users to mount PC floppy disks on the Desktop and drag and drop files onto them.

- You can use a PC-formatted disk to save Macintosh data. In fact, in a computer-lab environment, doing so gives you more machine choices.

- The File Exchange control panel is the combination of the PC Exchange and Mac Easy Open control panels.

- File Exchange is installed with an extensive list of file extension and application mappings.

- ZIP is the compression format of choice for PC files.

- Emulator packages run a particular operating system from within the Mac OS.

- Hardware PC cards have a processor on the card, enabling the user to run a PC almost independently of the Mac OS.

- Many client applications are being ported to Java and bypassing the platform.

- Thin client applications allow you to run applications from a remote server and view the results on your computer screen.

Utilities To Use

The utilities or elements of the Mac OS discussed in this chapter are listed here as a memory aid for the busy user or system administrator:

- *SuperDrive*—The standard disk drive that comes with almost all Macintosh computers and allows multiple disk formats, including PC.

- *File Exchange*—The revised file translation control panel that opens the correct application for the selected file.

- *MacLink Plus*—A commercial package that works with and builds upon the File Exchange control panel.

- *Graphic Converter*—A shareware application with an extension-image import and export database included.

- *Unzip*—A free utility that decompresses PC Zip files.

- *ZipIt*—A shareware utility that decompresses existing and creates new Zip archive files.

- *PKZIP Mac*—The Macintosh version of the popular compression client that can open and create new Zip files.

- *Mac GZip*—A free utility that opens compressed Unix files.

- *DAVE*—A commercial package that allows Macintosh users to access Windows servers and share folders and resources.

- *Novell NetWare Client*—The official client from Novell that allows Macintosh users to access Novell servers if AppleTalk is not enabled on the server.

- *SoftWindows95 or SoftPC*—Emulation software from Insignia that allows the Mac OS to run the Windows operating system.

- *Real PC*—Emulation software from Insignia that is tailored to run DOS and Windows games on the Mac OS.

- *Virtual PC*—Emulation software from Connectix that runs any operating system written for the X86 chip, including Windows NT and OS/2.

- *MacMAME*—An emulation client that runs arcade games from the 1980s.

- *Orange Micro*—Hardware and software company that specializes in PC coprocessor cards.

- *WinFrame*—A modified version of Windows NT 3.51 server from Citrix that allows thin-client access.

- *ZapResForks*—A shareware utility that removes the resource fork from a Macintosh file.

Immediate Solutions

Formatting DOS Disks

If you anticipate sharing your information with anyone via disk, you should know how to create a DOS-formatted floppy disk in Mac OS 8.5. Your files will be handled just fine, and you can continue using the disk on your computer (just make sure that you back up the data; disks do not have a long life).

1. Insert a disk in the drive (make sure that it does not have files on it that you need to keep).

2. Go to the Special menu and select Erase disk as shown in Figure 10.11. Make sure that the disk icon is selected. (This menu selection will also work on other media, including hard drives.)

3. The Erase Disk dialog box will appear. Select DOS 1.4 MB and click on the Erase button, as shown in Figure 10.12.

4. You will see a series of messages informing you of the status of the formatting process. After the disk has been reformatted to a PC disk, the icon will change as shown in Figure 10.13. You can now store data on the disk.

Figure 10.11   Selecting Erase Disk from the Special menu.

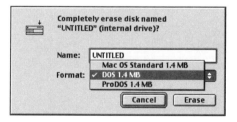

Figure 10.12   Choosing the correct format.

Figure 10.13   The on-screen disk icon, before and after.

Editing File Exchange Entries

The File Exchange control panel already contains an extensive library of file mappings. However, you may have a different application in mind for the particular file extension that is listed. You can edit the existing entries to launch your preferred application, as follows:

1. Go to the Apple menu and select Control Panels|File Exchange (if necessary, select the PC Exchange tab).

2. Click on the entry you wish to edit and click on the Change button (see Figure 10.14).

3. The application will search the hard drive for additional applications and display the dialog box shown in Figure 10.15. Choose the application you want to use to open the file and click on the Select button.

4. A dialog box displays that allows you to locate the application. Find it and click on the Select button.

5. Now add the application information. Click on the Change button to accept your changes.

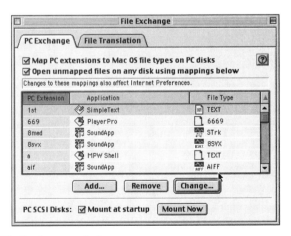

Figure 10.14   The File Exchange window.

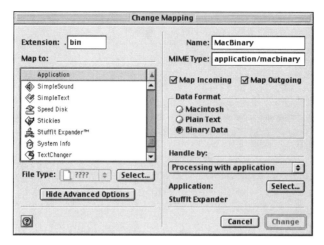

Figure 10.15   The Change Mapping window.

Adding File Exchange Entries

As new applications are written, you will need to add file extension mappings to the database already included with File Exchange. Follow these steps:

1. Go to the Apple menu and select Control Panels|File Exchange (if necessary, select the PC Exchange tab).

2. Click on the Add button.

3. Type the extension that you want to add (see Figure 10.16 for an example).

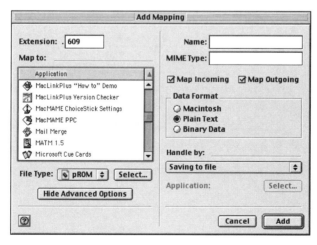

Figure 10.16   Entering the new extension.

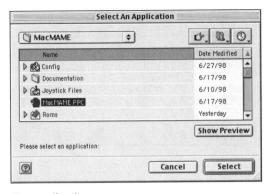

Figure 10.17   Locating the application.

4. Click on the Select button and locate the application that you want to open the file, as shown in Figure 10.17.

5. After you have located the application and it is highlighted, click on the Select button.

6. Click on the Add button to accept your new entry. Figure 10.18 shows the new addition listed with the other file extension mappings.

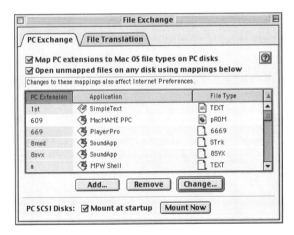

Figure 10.18   The new addition to the PC Exchange Panel.

File Exchange Advanced Options

When you begin adding file mappings to the PC Exchange section of the File Exchange control panel, you will notice a button labeled Show Advanced Options. Figure 10.16 has this option selected. You can indicate the MIME type and choose a data format. Moreover, if you would prefer to save the file rather than open it, you make changes in the Handle By menu.

File Exchange is improved over previous versions of PC Exchange in its handling of Windows NT and 95/98 disks and long file names. You can even mount PC SCSI drives to the desktop. All this improves your ability to collaborate with Windows colleagues.

Editing The File Translation In File Exchange

The File Translation part of File Exchange goes a step beyond file extension mapping. It also converts certain files to a particular file format, provided the file has a resource fork (this dictates that the file was created on another Mac). If the file is in the Windows format, File Exchange will attempt the translation based on the file extension. If it doesn't recognize the format, it will tell you that your only option is to open the file in the application that created it.

1. Go to the Apple menu and select Control Panels|File Exchange (if necessary, select the File Translation tab).

2. Click on the Add button. A dialog box prompts you to locate an example file. We've selected a GIF image as shown in Figure 10.19.

3. A window displays with the message shown in Figure 10.20. You should locate the application you want to be linked to the example file and click on Okay.

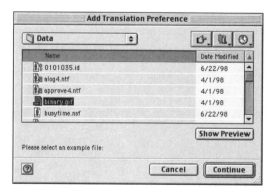

Figure 10.19   Selecting an example file.

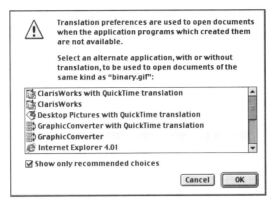

Figure 10.20   Selecting the appropriate file.

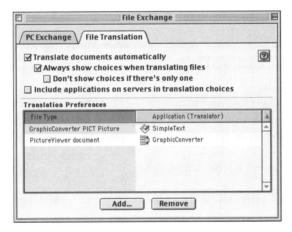

Figure 10.21   The new File Translation configuration.

4. When the process has finished, you should see the new File Translation option listed (see Figure 10.21).

Using MacLink Plus

If you really want to cover all the bases when it comes to file translation, you should definitely consider MacLinkPlus. It's worth the expense for the additional extension translations, and it is very easy to configure.

1. Go to the Apple Menu and select Control Panels|MacLinkPlus.

2. Look at the two options, but accept the defaults. See Figure 10.22 for the default configuration options (in case you do play with these drop-down menus and then forget what the default was).

3. MacLinkPlus is now ready for action.

Figure 10.22   MacLinkPlus.

Using Graphic Converter

Do you want to do a little image editing but don't have the money for a copy of Photoshop? An excellent shareware application is available that not only includes some nifty image editing features, but also can import and export a huge number of image formats. GraphicConverter can open just about any image file. If you locate a new format that the software can't handle, contact the author of the software. He really puts effort into keeping this utility up to date.

Just to get your feet wet, here is a simple file-import and -export session:

1. Launch GraphicConverter (you can also double-click on the image file in question).

2. Select File|Open. Locate your file, and open it with GraphicConverter.

3. The image will display in a window, similar to the window shown in Figure 10.23 (several other tool windows give you additional information about the image).

Figure 10.23   An open image in GraphicConverter.

4. Edit the image if you like, or go ahead and switch it to another format by choosing File|Save As to view the Save window.

5. Click on the drop-down menu beside the word "Format" to choose from over 40 file types. For Figure 10.24, we chose the GIF format.

6. If necessary, click on the Options button to choose additional settings for the image. See Figure 10.25 for some GIF options. When you have finished, click on Save to create the new image.

TIP: *GraphicConverter automatically adds the appropriate extension to your file. However, you can change this to suit your needs. For example, you can make the extension lowercase when you are creating Web graphics by simply retyping it.*

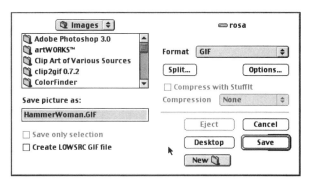

Figure 10.24   Choosing the GIF image format.

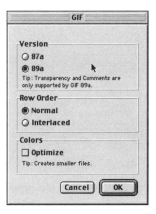

Figure 10.25   Additional GIF options.

Decompressing A ZIP File

The majority of PC files online or in network transfers are compressed, and you can recognize them by the .zip extension. Many of these files are universal, so you could use them on your machine. How about a cool desktop picture? Or some new system beeps? You don't have to run to a PC to get access. Stick with your Mac!

First, if you are frugal and don't anticipate needing to zip the files again, then Unzip may be the program for you. It's free, lean, and only does decompression. To decompress a zipped file, take these steps:

1. Download your file.

2. Launch Unzip. An empty status window will appear.

3. Go to the File menu and select Extract.

4. Locate your compressed file and choose Open.

Unzip decompresses your file and shows you the contents in the Status window (see Figure 10.26).

```
                               Unzip
unzip -aL dat-3103.zip ...

Archive:  dat-3103.zip
   inflating:  :file_id.diz      [text]
   inflating:  :reseller.txt     [text]
   inflating:  :whatsnew.txt     [text]
   inflating:  :clean.dat        [binary]
   inflating:  :internet.dat     [binary]
   inflating:  :names.dat        [binary]
   inflating:  :polyscan.dat     [binary]
   inflating:  :scan.dat         [binary]
   inflating:  :pkgdesc.ini      [text]
   inflating:  :validate.exe     [binary]
   inflating:  :packing.lst      [text]

Done
```

Figure 10.26   The Contents of a compressed PC archive, viewed with Unzip.

Creating A Zip File

Let's say that you need to create some archived or zipped files. As nice as Unzip is, it cannot compact files, so you need a utility that can compress files. Consider using another great utility written for the Macintosh—the shareware program ZipIt. You can use ZipIt to decompress files (like StuffIt Expander, it features drag-and-drop expanding) and create new archives. It can even preserve the resource fork in your files. Moreover, if you need to distribute your archive via floppy disks, ZipIt can break the archive into chunks that are more manageable. To create a Zip file, take these steps:

1. Launch ZipIt. An empty archive will appear. Use this window either to decompress zipped documents or to add files for an archive.

2. Go to the Zip menu and select Add.

3. The window in Figure 10.27 will appear. Choose the files or folders you want to add (you can continue adding all files for the archive within this dialog box). When you are finished, click on Done.

4. Go to the File menu and select Save.

5. If necessary change the name and click on the Save button (notice that ZipIt adds the .zip extension automatically).

You have now created an archive that can be opened from a PC. This is a useful tool for exchanging compressed files between Mac and PC users. Isn't it great to be so accommodating?

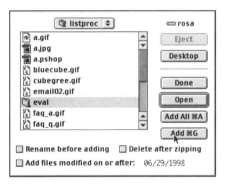

Figure 10.27   Adding items to the Zip archive.

Installing A PC Coprocessor Card

So, you've decided that you need to run Windows. However, you don't have the money or the desk space for two computers. If you choose to purchase a PC coprocessor card, you will find that it runs at competitive speeds and can put Windows access, even Windows NT, within reach. Orange Micro is the leading vendor of PC coprocessor cards and carries several products that have attractive prices. Orange Micro also writes excellent drivers for its products so that you can really work between the two environments. Figure 10.28 shows the PC side of the computer, running in a window within Mac OS 8.5.

Apple DOS Card Solutions

Apple used to sell DOS card solutions, including some bundled with certain PowerMacintosh models. You may still find some of these cards either installed or available for you to install in your CPU. The biggest difference between the Orange Micro cards and the Apple cards is the way the PC is set up: Apple uses extensions and a control panel, while Orange Micro uses an application. Between the two formats, the Orange Micro approach seems to be the more stable.

What follows are some general instructions for installing an OrangePC coprocessor card. If you already have the card, we recommend that you follow its enclosed instructions:

1. With the computer turned off, install the card in the expansion or PDS slot of your Power Macintosh computer. You may need to connect additional wiring such as video and sound cables to take advantage of multimedia processes.

2. Turn the computer on and install the software necessary for the Mac to access the Orange PC card.

3. Launch the application OrangePC and configure the PC environment (Figure 10.29 shows an example of the configuration options).

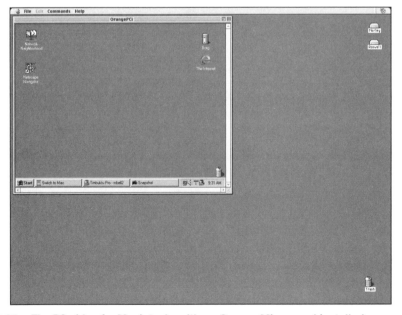

Figure 10.28   The PC side of a Macintosh, with an Orange Micro card installed.

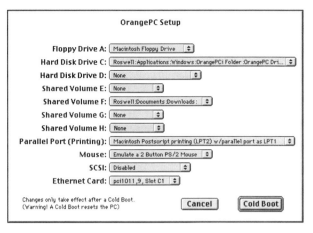

Figure 10.29   Setting up the OrangePC card.

4. Switch to the PC side of your Mac and install the operating system of choice, as well as any specialized drivers, for communicating with the Mac OS.

5. You should be able to run Windows and the Mac OS at the same time. To switch between the environments, you can use the menu shown in Figure 10.30 or see the next section for keystroke combinations.

Figure 10.30   The OrangePC Commands menu.

Key Combinations For PC Coprocessor Cards

The preferred method of accessing the PC environment from the Mac OS and vice versa is by using keystroke combinations. Use Table 10.1 on page 320 as a handy reference guide.

Table 10.1   Common keystroke combinations for PC cards.

Command	Function
Command+E	Eject a floppy disk (works on all PC cards)
Command+Y	Eject the CD (use with Apple-style DOS cards)
Command+Return	Switch between PC or Mac environment (use with Apple-style DOS cards)
Command+U	Eject the CD (use with the OrangePC)
Command+D	Switch between PC or Mac environment (use with the OrangePC)
Command+F	Select a floppy image file (use with the OrangePC)
Command+R	Reboot the OrangePC

Installing A Windows Emulator

While running an emulator may seem intimidating, you may want to remember that in reality, it is just one more software program running on your Mac. It just takes a little longer to set up, as follows:

1. Insert the software CD in the drive and run the installer program.

2. If necessary, reboot the computer and then launch the emulator application. It's that easy.

Emulators such as SoftWindows95 and Virtual PC come with an operating system so you can be productive immediately. You can install a different operating system, of course. Virtual PC can even run Windows NT.

Deleting Resource Forks

Files on the Mac OS are made up of two parts: the data fork and resource fork. The *data fork* contains the actual document information. The *resource fork* is the part of a file that contains Mac-specific information, such as the icon of the file and the creator and kind of file. Because this information is useful only within the Mac OS, you can remove it. Why would you want to do so? The answer is a simple one: Because the resource fork information can be merged into the data fork during the file compression or transmission process, it can hopelessly corrupt the file. Another reason to remove the resource fork is to decrease file size. For plain-text documents, this may not be as evident, but Photoshop places a large amount of extraneous information in the resource fork of a graphics file, making it appear much larger than it really is. For more information about data forks and resource forks, refer to Chapter 5.

You can remove the resource fork from documents that you need to exchange with Windows users. You can also use it to strip the resource fork informationfrom HTML files. Here are some instructions, using the shareware utility ZapResForks:

1. Click and drag the icon of the file over the ZapResForks icon.

2. The warning dialog box in Figure 10.31 displays and asks if you are *really* sure you want to do this.

3. Click on Okay to remove the resource fork.

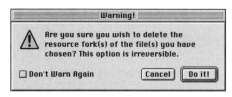

Figure 10.31   The Warning box in ZapResForks.

Using DAVE

DAVE is a utility that uses NetBIOS over the TCP/IP protocol to allow Macintosh computers to talk to other computers that also use NetBIOS over the TCP/IP protocol. Examples of these systems include Windows 95 computers and Windows NT servers. Normally, as a Mac user you would have to wait for the NT server administrator to enable the AppleTalk protocol enabling you to access the server. With DAVE, you can bypass this process and configure your computer to access Windows 95 or NT computers, as well as Macintosh computers, without additional software on the Windows computers. The best part is that the Windows machines won't even know you are a Macintosh. To them, you are just another Windows computer. You also can share printing devices and exchange pop-up messages.

DAVE is available from Thursby Software Systems, Inc. Contact them for more information on using DAVE.

To install and use DAVE, take these steps:

1. Use the standard installer to use the software (you will have to reboot).

2. Launch the NetBIOS control panel and enter the license key and user and machine information (see Figure 10.32).

3. Go to the Apple menu and choose DAVE Access. The icons in Figure 10.33 will appear. Click on the appropriate ones to log on to other servers in the domain.

Figure 10.32   The DAVE NetBIOS control panel.

Figure 10.33   The DAVE toolbar.

Connecting To A WinFrame Server

For many Macintosh users in large or specialized organizations, it is difficult to obtain a decent client to access the application server. Even worse, some of these software developers will not write a client for the Mac. In these cases, your solutions in the past were to use an emulator or purchase a PC coprocessor card.

However, a large enough disenfranchised group of users may be able to create the demand for a WinFrame Server. WinFrame from Citrix is a modified version of Windows NT 3.51. It is a thin client, which means that the local machine receives screen images of what is going on in the session on the WinFrame server. In most cases, servers are more powerful than local machines; because of this, some tasks actually run faster on the WinFrame server. WinFrame runs on a variety of platforms and can even perform in low-bandwidth situations, such as a modem connection.

To connect to a WinFrame server, take these steps:

1. Install the ICA client on your computer.

2. Launch the ICA client editor as shown in Figure 10.34.

3. Enter the IP address of the WinFrame server, and (if necessary) your login and password.

4. Click on the Connect button. The Citrix ICA client will launch and create a window on your desktop. Figure 10.35 shows the client session.

5. You can perform the functions within the client window. To bring up the Mac menu, hold down the Command key.

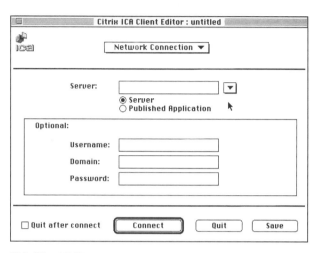

Figure 10.34   The ICA Client Editor.

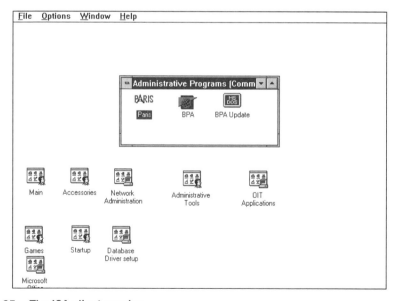

Figure 10.35   The ICA client session.

Chapter 11

Networking And File Sharing

In Depth

Creating a Local Area Network (LAN) of Macs is almost as easy as changing a Desktop pattern. Mac OS 8.5 supports all the most popular networking protocols, including TCP/IP, SNMP, and AppleTalk, as well as network cabling such as 10Base-2, 10Base-T, Ethernet, Fast Ethernet, and LocalTalk. This chapter explores the many ways to network Macs among themselves to share files, services, and applications.

Supported Networking Protocols

If you're a networking junkie like we are, then you might agree with us when we say that one of the greatest things about the Mac OS is that it continues to support all the most popular networking protocols, as well as limited support for a few less popular protocols. Open Transport 1.0 was introduced with the first line of PCI-bus PowerMacs and has since been through several revisions.

Mac OS 8.5 ships with Open Transport 2.0, which adds more robust networking support and improves support for several protocols, including:

- AppleTalk
- AppleTalk IP
- Transmission Control Protocol/Internet Protocol (TCP/IP)
- IRTalk
- Point-to-Point Protocol (PPP)
- Serial Line Interface Protocol (SLIP)
- Bootstrap Protocol (BootP)
- Dynamic Host Configuration Protocol (DHCP)
- Reverse Address Resolution Protocol (RARP)
- Apple Remote Access Protocol (ARAP)
- Open Transport Printer Access Protocol (OT PAP)

Mac OS 8.5 also adds support for another protocol called Simple Network Management Protocol (SNMP) that, although supported since 1993, is now bundled with Mac OS 8.5. The majority of you will use the AppleTalk and TCP/IP protocols, which are transmission protocols, in conjunction with non-transmission protocols such as BootP and DHCH, which are protocols that assist Open Transport in obtaining an IP address.

Modem users will most likely use PPP instead of SLIP, both of which are used to connect remote computers to a LAN or the Internet using a plain-old telephone service (POTS) line or an ISDN line.

It is still possible to use a tunneling protocol like AppleTalk IP and the Apple LocalTalk Bridge to communicate using TCP/IP via AppleTalk under Mac OS 8.5. For example, AppleTalk IP hides (or tunnels) TCP/IP packets over an AppleTalk network and delivers them to a TCP/IP-based network by using a gateway that connects both networks or devices. This kind of multi-protocol network is still in use today on networks that have many older Macs, such as in public school systems.

Supported Network Hardware

Most Mac users are connected these days via standard Ethernet running at 10Mbps, whereas in the early days they were connected via LocalTalk running at about 230Kbps. However, with the newest G3 PowerMacs, the standard networking speed is now 100Mbps. Mac OS 8.5 and Open Transport support the following networking hardware options:

- 10Mbps Built-in Ethernet
- 100Mbps Built-in Ethernet
- LocalTalk
- Infrared
- Third-party PCI- and PCMCIA Ethernet adapters (additional drivers required)

Note that Apple will no longer develop or test products to support Token Ring networks, including Token Ring adapters and TokenTalk drivers, however.

Apple has decidedly centered its networking and Internet strategy on TCP/IP instead of AppleTalk, and Fast Ethernet (100Mbps) over LocalTalk and standard Ethernet. This is welcome news because it makes Apple the first computer company to adapt the most widely used networking protocol (TCP/IP) and the fastest common hardware protocol (Fast Ethernet) in a home or business computer.

Other network hardware options are available, of course, from third-party vendors, such as Farallon (**www.farallon.com**) that make creating Mac-based LANs a snap. We recommend that when purchasing additional networking equipment such as Network Interface Cards (NICs), hubs, and switches, you should purchase products that support 100Mbps connections. This is where the computer industry as a whole is going and it's where Apple has already established its direction.

File Sharing

Built-in file sharing has also been a standard part of the Mac OS, along with support for multiple hardware and software protocols. Mac OS 8.5 supports built-in file sharing (sometimes called *personal file sharing*), as well as a file-sharing server called AppleShare IP. It also supports Web sharing via the personal Web server. Each method has its advantages and disadvantages.

Built-In File Sharing

Built-in file sharing uses the same interface for file sharing as in previous versions of Mac OS 8, as well as the same protocol (AppleTalk) with the same limitations (10 shared folders, 10 concurrent users, and 5 open files). Small networks may employ personal file sharing with little or no noticeable impact on the overall speed of a network or computers. Figure 11.1 shows the File Sharing and the Users & Groups control panels.

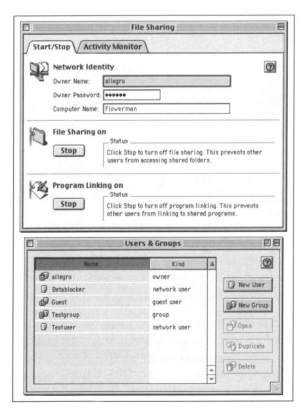

Figure 11.1   The File Sharing and the Users & Groups control panels work like those found in the previous version of Mac OS 8.

File sharing under the Mac OS is also the same as in the previous version of Mac OS 8 in terms of security. Passwords transmitted over AppleTalk and TCP/IP are encrypted on both ends so no one will see them, and they are case-sensitive. For more information on passwords and security, refer to Chapter 16.

AppleShare IP

Large networks will probably need the support of dedicated file sharing that runs AppleShare IP. This uses a much more robust protocol (TCP/IP) and has few restrictions on the number of users that it can support and the number of volumes, folders, and files it can serve. AppleShare IP also includes a Web and email server in addition to the file sharing capabilities, making it an ideal solution for small to medium sized LANs. Very large LANs or Wide Area Networks (WANs) will most likely require the support of several file servers. Figure 11.2 shows a Users and Groups Manager connection to an AppleShare IP 5 server.

Personal Web Sharing

Finally, Mac OS 8.5 allows you to share files using the Personal Web Server, which is installed by default, but disabled until activated through the Web Sharing control panel. Sharing files over the Web isn't as flexible as traditional file sharing, of course, but it may help meet the needs of some networking environments, such as those that do not support the AppleTalk protocol. See Chapter 12 for more information on providing Web services. Figure 11.3 shows an example of a folder that is shared via the Web.

Figure 11.2   You can remotely manage users and groups on an AppleShare IP server with the Users and Groups Manager application.

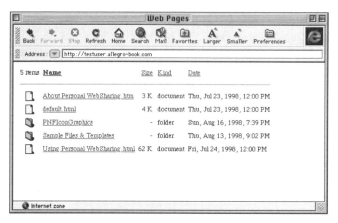

Figure 11.3   Personal Web sharing can meet the needs of some users to share files over a
LAN or the Internet.

File Servers

Small networks may not need a dedicated fileserver, but if you have more than a
few computers and you need to provide services such as backup, email, or Web,
having a dedicated file server is probably a good idea. Using individual Macs to
share files with each other is often called a *distributed* file-sharing network,
whereas a network with a dedicated file server is referred to as a *centralized*
network. Of course, having a dedicated Mac as a file server means that you have
one less workstation for use by someone on your LAN, but if it can provide several essential services, then it is a good investment.

Although you can use any Macintosh for traditional file serving or as an AppleShare
IP server, it's best to have at least an entry-level G3 Macintosh as a server. G3s
have several advantages over ordinary PowerMacs, including:

• A faster system bus (66Mhz)

• A much faster processor

• A faster hard drive (IDE)

You'll need a Network Operating System (NOS) for the server that is tuned for
serving files. The only options currently available are AppleShare IP, a TCP/IP-
based version of AppleShare, and MkLinux or LinuxPPC, freeware Unix deriva-
tives, created by Linus Torvalds and ported to the PowerPC by various groups. By
the fall of 1998, however, Apple is scheduled to release Mac OS X Server 1.0,
code-named Rhapsody, which will evolve into Mac OS X in 1999.

The pros and cons of these NOSs are as covered in the following sections.

AppleShare IP

- *Pros*—Easy to use, provides many services in addition to file sharing, large install base, supports Windows users and shows up in the Network Neighborhood, Web-based administration, many resources for support.

- *Cons*—Expensive, still uses OpenDoc for some features, file system is still a bottleneck.

MkLinux Or LinuxPPC

- *Pros*—Free, very fast, dedicated user support group, supports AppleTalk and most TCP/IP services.

- *Cons*—Difficult to administer, must compile own software, requires Unix experience.

Mac OS X Server

- *Pros*—Protected memory space, preemptive multitasking, completely PowerPC-native, supports AppleTalk and most TCP/IP services.

- *Cons*—Not yet tested, future development unsure at this time.

So, unless you are a Unix geek, AppleShare IP is the way to go. It isn't cheap (currently $1,349 for a 50-user license), but when you consider it provides Web, mail, FTP, and print services in addition to robust file sharing, it might be the right product for your LAN.

Apple Remote Access

Another resource for connecting Macs is Apple Remote Access (ARA), a client-server application developed several years ago by Apple to allow Macs to connect to a LAN and to each other using modems and share AppleTalk and TCP/IP resources. The current version of ARA (3.1) allows connections using AppleTalk and TCP/IP, in addition to direct-dial using a modem. The components of ARA include:

- Apple Remote Access Personal Server
- Apple Remote Access MultiPort Server
- Apple Remote Access Client

Mac OS 8.5 includes the ARA client, which uses either the Apple Remote Access Protocol (ARAP) or Point-to-Point Protocol (PPP) to connect to an ARA server running on a Macintosh. The ARA Personal Server is a single-user server that is designed to allow a remote connection to a Mac on a network and to access that computer's files and folders, as well as network volumes and printers. The ARA MultiPort Server is designed to run on a dedicated file server and supports up to 16 simultaneous users, who also have access to the ARA server's local resources, as well as all resources or services that may be available on the LAN to which the server is connected. Connecting to an ARA server using a modem, whether to a Personal or MultiPort server, enables the client to access the Internet as well as the LAN to which the server is attached, if the server is on the Internet. Visit the Apple Store on the Web at **store.apple.com** for current pricing and availability.

Timbuktu

A final method of networking Macs (as well as PCs) is by using Timbuktu from Farallon (**www.farallon.com**). Timbuktu is primarily used for screen sharing, but it provides multiple services, including:

- Screen sharing
- File exchange
- Chat
- Intercom
- ARA access

Timbuktu provides several unique benefits not found in other networking options that make it an excellent tool to have available on your network. The chief advantages include the ability to remotely control another computer to do anything but startup, as well as the ability to control a Windows-based PC with the same level of capability of a Mac. For example, Figure 11.4 shows a Timbuktu session with a PC running Windows 95.

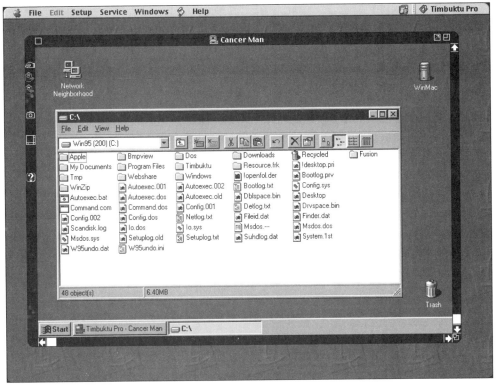

Figure 11.4   Use Timbuktu on your LAN to control Macs as well as PCs.

Immediate Solutions

11: Networking And File Sharing

The following sections explain how to perform the most common tasks relating to LAN creation and maintenance and to file sharing among computers connected to your LAN.

Selecting LAN Hardware

Since just about every Mac that is capable of running Mac OS 8.5 comes equipped with an Ethernet adapter, the hardware necessary to create a LAN falls into two categories:

- Cabling
- Hubs

Cabling

LocalTalk networks require cables that are used in no other networks that we are aware of, but Mac Ethernet networks use the same hardware as any other Ethernet network does. In general, these networks run at either 10Mbps or 100Mbps, the latter of which requires special cables, hubs, and repeating devices. Ethernet cabling comes in two basic types:

- *10Base-2*—(Also called ThinWire, or Thin Coax), a coaxial cable similar to the type that is used to connect a VCR to a TV.

- *10Base-T*—(Also called Twisted Pair), which looks like a telephone cable, but slightly bigger and having more pins.

No compelling reason exists to want to use 10Base-2 cabling anymore, unless it is in conjunction with an existing network. 10Base-T has been the standard for several years now. Both 10Base-2 and 10Base-T support 10Mbps throughput, but only 10Base-T supports 100Mbps, depending on the type of cable. 10Base-T cable comes in several levels, or categories, that measure throughput capacity, and the following levels are the ones you're most likely to encounter:

- *Category 3*—10Mbps
- *Category 5*—100Mbps

To identify which category (or *Cat*) of cable you are using, read the shielding and look for a description. If you don't find any description at all, throw it away and use confirmed Cat 5 cable.

When purchasing 10Base-T cabling, be sure to not confuse *straight-through* cables with *cross-over* cables. Straight-through cables are used to connect Ethernet ports or transceivers to ports on a hub. The pinout of a straight-through cable matches when viewed side-by-side and face-up, as shown in Figure 11.5.

Cross-over cables connect networking devices such as hubs, routers, and switches to one another and cannot be used to connect a Mac to a hub. However, a cross-over cable can be used to create a 2-node, hubless network by connecting the built-in Ethernet ports of two Macs. The pinouts of a cross-over cable will mirror one another when viewed side-by-side and face-up, as shown in Figure 11.6.

AppleTalk cable also comes in two flavors, one from Apple and another that uses standard indoor telephone cable (RJ11). Each has a special adapter on either end called a *LocalTalk connector* that plugs into the serial port (modem or printer); they both have the same 230Kbps throughput. RJ11-based LocalTalk connectors are usually cheaper than the traditional Apple-style connectors and the RJ11 wire is cheaper and easier to work with, making it our preference by a long shot.

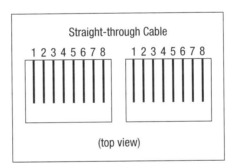

Figure 11.5   Diagram of a straight-through cable.

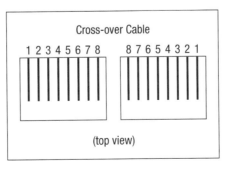

Figure 11.6   Diagram of a cross-over cable.

Hubs

A standard 10Base-T (10Mbps) hub is sufficient for most LANs, unless your Macs have Fast Ethernet capabilities and you have Cat 5 cabling. 100Mbps hubs are significantly more expensive than 10Mbps hubs, but prices are steadily dropping. For example, a typical 8-port 10Mbps hub sells for around $40, whereas a similar hub that supports 100Mbps might cost as much as $200. Also, in mixed environments (where you have both standard and Fast Ethernet), you'll have to purchase a switched 10/100Mbps hub to be able to accommodate both speeds, which is even more expensive.

Bridging LocalTalk And Ethernet Networks

Some LANs have LocalTalk segments that need to be connected to Ethernet segments. In large networked environments, such as schools and publishing corporations, many workstations may be located on LocalTalk segments, but need access to Ethernet segments and the Internet. Another common situation involves LocalTalk devices such as printers that are connected through LocalTalk ports on a Macintosh, but need to be accessible to other computers over an Ethernet network.

Several hardware and hardware/software options bridge the gaps between these two networks, but with the advent of Open Transport 2 in Mac OS 8.5, most of them will no longer work or are currently untested.

An example of a hardware bridge that connects AppleTalk and Ethernet networks is a GatorBox from Caymen (**www. caymen.com**), a highly configurable device that can connect an AppleTalk-based segment to an Ethernet segment that contains multiple AppleTalk zones.

Two examples of a software solution for bridging LocalTalk and Ethernet networks are Apple's LocalTalk and LaserWriter Bridge applications. LocalTalk Bridge allows connections to and from LocalTalk and Ethernet networks, including printers and TCP/IP services. LaserWriter Bridge provides access to a printer on a LocalTalk segment from an Ethernet segment. A simple control panel, shown in Figure 11.7, is all it takes to allow Ethernet users to print to a LocalTalk printer as if it were located on the Ethernet segment as a networked printer (it also appears to the host computer on the LocalTalk segment as a networked printer). The host computer is therefore serving as a print server and may take a performance hit if the printer is used heavily.

Figure 11.7   Apple's LaserWriter Bridge allows Ethernet users to access a LocalTalk-based
laser printer as a networked printer.

Other solutions exist for bridging LocalTalk and Ethernet networks, as well as
sharing LocalTalk devices (printers and modems), such as Stalker Software's
PortShare software (see **www.stalker.com/PortShare**).

Managing A Network Using SNMP

The Simple Network Management Protocol (SNMP) is implemented in the SNMP
Administrator, a tool included with Mac OS 8.5 that provides advanced AppleTalk
and TCP/IP management capabilities. SNMP works by allowing administrators to
create groups of computers that can be monitored using SNMP Administrator or
another tool that uses SNMP, such as SNMP Watcher from Dartmouth College
(**www.dartmouth.edu/pages/softdev/snmpwatcher.html**).

SNMP Administrator is not installed as part of the Easy Installation of Mac OS
8.5, but you can install it by choosing it from the Custom installation option from
the Mac OS 8.5 CD-ROM, shown in Figure 11.8.

Once installed, you can create customized groups of computers and monitor network activity for all computers that have the Open Transport SNMP extension
installed.

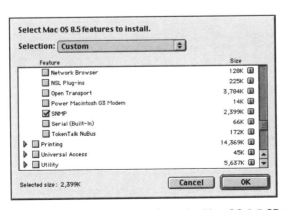

Figure 11.8   You can install SNMP Administrator from the Mac OS 8.5 CD-ROM.

TIP: *In order to be managed via SNMP, each Mac on your network must have the Open Transport SNMP extension installed.*

To create and monitor a group, follow these steps:

1. Launch SNMP Administrator and click on the New button to create a group, as in the New Community group shown in Figure 11.9.

2. Double-click on the new group to open and view the group's agent properties, as in Figure 11.10.

3. To view information about an agent, single-click the triangle beside an agent to expand it, or double-click an agent such as AppleTalk Agent, shown in Figure 11.11, to open it into a new window.

SNMP Administrator monitors just about every aspect of network activity for several protocols, including AppleTalk and TCP/IP. For example, you can monitor network activity by Ethernet hardware address, AppleTalk node or file sharing name, or by IP address or domain name. You can find most of these capabilities in SMTP Watcher as well, as shown in Figure 11.12.

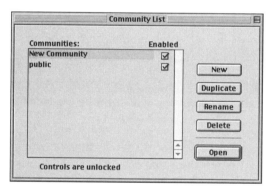

Figure 11.9   Creating a new group by using SNMP Administrator.

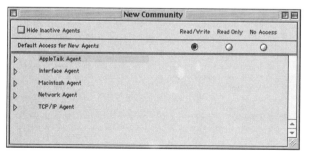

Figure 11.10   Selecting an agent to monitor in SNMP Administrator.

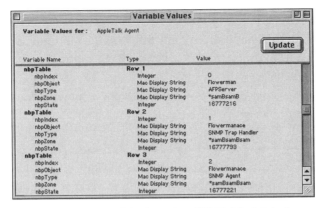

Figure 11.11 Monitoring AppleTalk activity by using SNMP Administrator.

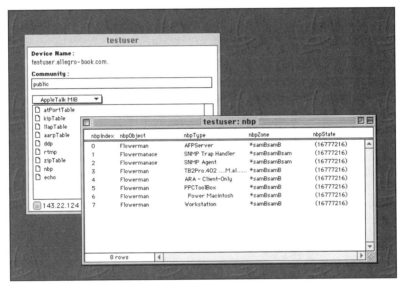

Figure 11.12 SMTP Watcher provides similar capabilities to Apple's SMTP Administrator.

Configuring File Sharing And Program Linking

Although file sharing and program linking are Open Transport-native under Mac OS 8.5, file sharing is still based on AppleTalk rather than TCP/IP and has limited capabilities when compared to AppleShare IP. We hope that future versions of the Mac OS will remove these limitations; for now, however, the file-sharing interface remains unchanged from previous versions of Mac OS 8.

To enable and disable file sharing and program linking:

1. Open the AppleTalk control panel, click on the Options button, and make sure that file sharing is enabled. File sharing cannot be enabled unless AppleTalk is active.

2. Open the File Sharing control panel and enter information for the Owner Name, Owner Password, and Computer Name in the Network Identity section of the Start/Stop tab, as in Figure 11.13. You must enter a unique name in the Computer Name field for each computer on your LAN. If your LAN is divided into zones, you can use the same name in different zones.

3. Click on the Start button to enable file sharing and/or program linking, then close the File Sharing control panel. This enables file sharing for the owner, but no one else.

4. To disable file sharing or program linking, open the File Sharing control panel and click on the Stop button for file sharing and/or program linking, as shown in Figure 11.14. You can individually enable or disable file sharing and program linking.

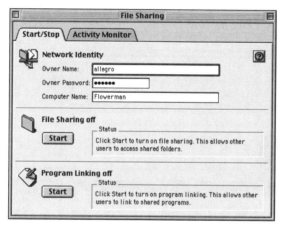

Figure 11.13   Configuring a Mac's identity on an AppleTalk network.

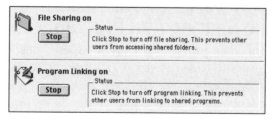

Figure 11.14   Stopping file sharing and program linking.

To monitor file sharing:

1. Open the File Sharing control panel and select the Activity Monitor tab, as shown in Figure 11.15.

2. The Sharing Activity progress bar will display the level of activity, and the Connected Users and Shared Items will provide quick access to disconnect users and to reconfigure shared folders.

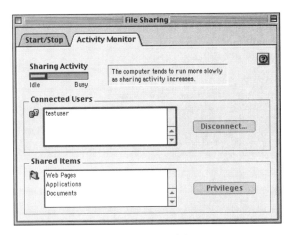

Figure 11.15   Monitoring the level of file-sharing activity.

Sharing Files And Folders

Mac OS 8.5 allows you to share 10 folders, host 10 concurrent users, or 5 open files to anyone on your AppleTalk LAN using file sharing. You may set individual privileges for each folder for the following entities:

- Owner

- Individual users or groups

- Guest (anonymous) access

When sharing an application, however, access is either enabled or disabled.

To share a folder and its contents, take these steps:

1. Open the Users & Groups control panel, shown in Figure 11.16, and click on the New User or New Group button.

2. Select a user account and give the account a name and password in the Identity section, shown in Figure 11.17. Check the Allow User To Change Password option if you want a user to be able to change his or her password.

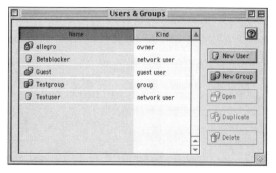

Figure 11.16   Creating user accounts.

Figure 11.17   The name and password options.

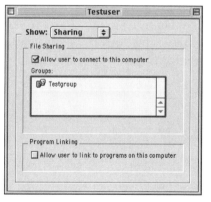

Figure 11.18   Enabling an account.

3. Select the Sharing portion of the configuration window and check the
    Allow User To Connect To This Computer to enable access, as shown in
    Figure 11.18. Deselect this option to disable access without deleting the
    account.

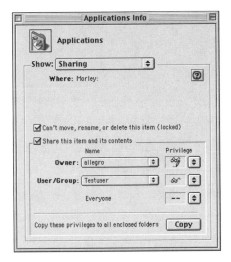

Figure 11.19 File sharing information for a folder.

4. Next, select a folder or volume to be shared, choose File|Get Info
(Command+I), and select the Show Sharing option, as in Figure 11.19. This
is the same result as if you were to select an item in the Activity Monitor of
the File Sharing control panel and click on the Privileges button.

5. Select from the following options to set the level of access for the folder:

   • *Can't move, rename, or delete this item (locked)*—Prevents users from
   deleting the folder, but not the contents of the folder.

   • *Share this item and its contents*—Enables others to access the folder
   (the owner always has access, as long as file sharing is enabled).

   • *Owner*—Enables you to grant ownership status to a user or group.
   Owners can then change access privileges for all others, but not add or
   delete users and groups themselves.

   • *User/Group*—Sets the level of access privileges for a particular user or
   group.

   • *Everyone*—Sets the level of access privileges for guests.

6. Select a privilege level for the owner, user or group; for guest access, select
from the options shown in Figure 11.20, which are as follows:

   • *Read & Write*—Allows you to read and modify existing files, add and edit
   new files and folders, delete files and folders, and view all the items in
   the folder and subfolder.

   • *Read only*—Allows you to read existing files and view the contents of the
   folder and subfolders, but not add, edit, or delete files or folders.

Figure 11.20   The various levels of access privileges in Mac OS 8.5.

- *Write only (Drop Box)*—Allows you to upload new files to a folder, but not view, edit, or delete files or folders.

- *None*—Denies the ability to mount or open the folder for a particular user or group.

File Sharing Concerns

You should be aware of a few peculiarities concerning file sharing under the Mac OS. First, file sharing isn't nearly as flexible in terms of access restrictions as other operating systems, most noticeably, Unix. For example, file sharing is really geared towards folder-based access rather than per-individual access. This means that you must configure access for each folder first, then maintain users and groups and assign access restrictions accordingly. A better system would allow you to create accounts for individual users on your Mac and then assign access privileges to sections of your hard drive as needed. Perhaps in future versions of the Mac OS, we'll see more robust file sharing.

Finally, here are a few tips to keep in mind when using file sharing:

- You cannot assign a higher level of access for guests than for users and groups, or the owner. If you do, the Mac OS will automatically grant that level of access to all others.

- You cannot share an individual file; you must share the parent folder containing that file instead.

- You cannot grant different levels of access to more than three entities: the owner, a particular user or group, and to guests. For example, if the owner has full access, user A has read-only access, and everyone has no access, you cannot also grant write access to user B.

Browsing File Servers With Network Browser

The most striking addition to the networking capabilities of Mac OS 8.5 is the Network Browser, which may eventually replace the venerable Choose for logging into AppleShare and AppleShare IP servers (but not for accessing printers).

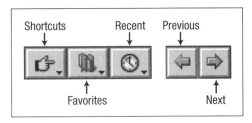

Figure 11.21   Use the Network Browser's navigational buttons to "browse" your network.

The Network Browser has many helpful features, described in a following section. The Network Browser's navigation buttons are explained in Figure 11.21.

To view the servers that are available on your network:

1. Launch the Network Browser and all available servers will appear in the Network window, shown in Figure 11.22. If your network is divided into zones, the zones will appear in the browser window.

2. Click on the triangle and enter the password to view the volumes that are available on a particular server, as in Figure 11.23.

To log in to an AppleShare server, double-click on a server or volume in the Network window, or select a server or volume and choose File|Open in Place, or

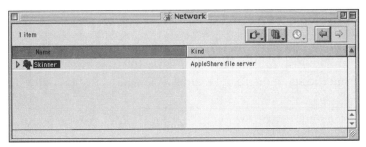

Figure 11.22   Using the Network Browser to view a list of available servers.

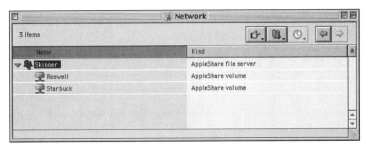

Figure 11.23   Use the Network Browser to view a list of volumes on an AppleShare server.

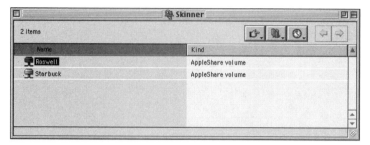

Figure 11.24   Open a server in a new window to see only the volumes located on that particular server.

select a server or volume and choose File|Open in New Window. Figure 11.24 shows a server and two volumes, opened in a new window.

To log in to an AppleShare IP server, follow these steps:

1. Choose Connect to Server from the Shortcuts button.

2. Enter the server's IP address or domain name. The server will appear like a regular AppleShare server in the Network window, as shown in Figure 11.25, which shows an AppleShare IP server with three volumes.

Finally, use the Network Browser's buttons to add server to a your list of favorite servers for easier access. When added to the list, a special type of alias is created in the Favorites folder located in the System Folder.

To add or select a favorite fileserver by using the Network Browser, log in to a fileserver and choose Add to Favorites from the Favorites menu button; select a favorite from the same menu, an example of which is shown in Figure 11.26.

TIP: You can create an alias to a fileserver from within the Network Browser by selecting File|Make Alias and following the instructions.

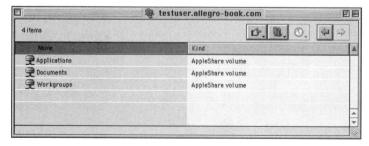

Figure 11.25   Browsing an AppleShare IP server.

Figure 11.26   Selecting a favorite fileserver from the Favorites menu.

To delete a favorite fileserver:

1. Choose Favorites|Remove From Favorites, and select a fileserver from the Remove Favorites window, shown in Figure 11.27.

2. Alternately, you can quit the Network Browser, then manually delete the server's entry from the Favorites folder. You can see examples of these in Figure 11.28.

Figure 11.27   Removing a favorite fileserver.

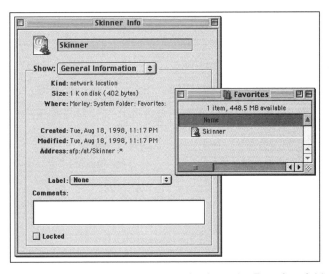

Figure 11.28   You may also manually delete a favorite from the Favorites folder.

Changing Passwords

Finally, you or the users on your network will want to change passwords on a regular basis as a security precaution, as described in Chapter 16. Be aware that file-sharing passwords are not sent across the network as clear text, but are encrypted when they travel across the network and when they are stored by the Mac OS on your hard drive.

To change a password of a user on your system, open the Users & Groups control panel, select a user, and type in the new password in the Password field. The password will remain in clear text until you press the Tab key, the Return key, or until you close the window.

To change a password on a remote server:

1. Open the Chooser and select a server.

2. Instead of logging in to the server, click on the Change Password button, shown in Figure 11.29.

3. In the password change window, shown in Figure 11.30, enter the old password, the new password, then click on the OK button.

4. Confirm the new password when prompted; any errors will result in your having to start over.

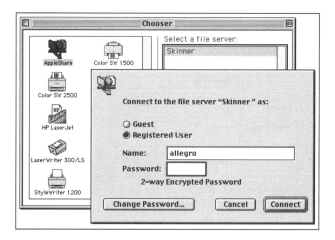

Figure 11.29   Changing a password on a remote file server.

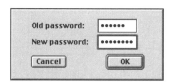

Figure 11.30   Entering old and new passwords.

Chapter 12

Internet Connectivity

In Depth

Internet Service Providers

The development of the World Wide Web has contributed to the desire for Internet access. Previous to the World Wide Web, you retrieved information available on the Internet using software applications specifically written for each kind of information. Databases required Gopher software or Telnet applications. Software archives required file transfer applications such as Fetch or Anarchie. Newsgroups required newsreaders like InterNews or NewsWatcher. And searching for specific information required patience and luck.

Then, a system of connected documents with hyperlinks was developed. Browsers were written that could display these documents and allow you to access additional documents by activating a hyperlink. These browsers not only made a new kind of information system available to the Internet, but they also handled existing information systems. Today, browsers can perform many tasks, such as accessing databases, transferring software, and reading newsgroups. They've also branched into new methods of communication such as chat and teleconferencing. Also, searching for information is much easier with the creation of Web search engines. All this makes Internet access a desirable computer feature. Businesses today routinely advertise Web addresses as an accepted form of communication and access. Most computers sold today feature Internet readiness; hardware and software are in place to connect to the Internet.

But that's just the first step. If you want to take advantage of the built-in Internet access features, you may need an *Internet Service Provider* or ISP. These are companies that allow you to dial a number and with proper authentication, establish a network connection over a phone line. Some ISPs provide additional services such as online magazine subscriptions and specialized discussion groups. America Online, Prodigy, and CompuServe each provide specialized services in addition to Internet access (in fact, these companies started out providing exclusive services and gradually added Internet access). These companies usually provide special software for accessing their services.

Some ISPs only provide Internet access. They may have a specialized dialer, but you can often use the software included with Mac OS 8.5 to establish network services over a phone line. These companies often cater to the savvy computer user or small business owner who is looking for high-speed access and reliable connection times. Many of the telephone companies are also ISPs; some of these include additional benefits such as server space for a Web site and the capability to have multiple email accounts. In fact, some ISPs specialize in setting up your own domain, enabling you to publicize a unique email address or Web site.

Which ISP is the best? That's for you to decide. While the nationally known ISPs are more familiar, a local company might better meet your needs. List what services you want and see what ISP can provide them for you at the best cost. You might find the Web site **www.ispfinder.com** helpful; it specializes in listing ISPs by area code.

Dialup Vs. Permanent Connections

Users who access the Internet fall into two groups (and depending on your financial position or job you may fall into both of them): those who use a modem and those who have a wired Ethernet connection. Modems have been around a long time; in the beginning, they were used to establish a terminal emulation session with a remote bulletin board service or database. Modems were slow because only text was exchanged. Files could be transferred, but the speed of the connection and the corruption rate hindered transfer success. Then, network protocols were developed that were capable of running over a telephone line. These protocols included *serial line interface protocol* (SLIP), the older protocol and still widely used, and *point-to-point protocol* (PPP), an improved version of SLIP. Apple also had *AppleTalk Remote Access* (ARA), which allowed Macs to communicate with each other and see AppleTalk zones over a telephone-line connection. These protocols demanded faster modems to be successful, so modem speed was increased. However, as fast as modems are, they cannot compete with the speed of a permanent Ethernet connection.

An Ethernet connection is 100 times faster than a dial-up connection. This type of permanent connection has a cable directly connected to your computer. The network cable is usually 10Base-T, although you do still see thin coaxial cable (this looks similar to cable television wire). The cable is connected to either a network interface card or a network port (newer systems including the Macintosh and iMac computers have the network interface wired on the motherboard). With the appropriate network software installed, the computer can send and receive data over the network wire. Permanent Internet connections are used mostly in businesses and educational institutions.

Hardware Requirements

In order to establish any kind of network connection, certain hardware elements must be in place. The hardware requirements also vary, depending on the connection you plan to establish.

Modem

For the average home user, the modem is the device used to remotely access the Internet. New technologies are on the horizon (which are discussed in the "New Technologies," a following section) that use different methods of remote access, but if you have limited funds, you'll use the modem. To establish a reliable connection, you need a fast modem. A productive PPP connection should be a minimum of 14.4Kbps (you can attempt a slower connection, but Web pages will load slowly). Watch for the other extreme, however. Some ISPs don't support K56 or V.90 speeds. You can easily determine if your ISP doesn't support these speeds by attempting to dial into the service. If your modem connects but "squeals" much longer than usual and never establishes a network connection, you can assume that your ISP doesn't support the K56 or V.90 standard. You need to adjust the modem script to force the modem to connect at slower speeds. Apple has just such a script for the iMac, available for download at **ftp.apple.com/Apple_ Support_Area/Apple_Software_Updates/US/Macintosh/iMac/**.

You also have the option of an internal or external modem. External modems are easier to configure, install, and upgrade. Just purchase a new one. However, an external modem is another peripheral and most external modems require a power supply. Internal modems make a neater desktop and both internal and external modems can serve as answering and fax machines. However, internal modems are more difficult to upgrade; you must pull the old card and replace it with the new card. Another problem with internal modems is that you must use special software to recognize the modem; this software occasionally conflicts with PPP connectivity.

Ethernet

Many businesses, schools, and organizations provide and maintain Ethernet networks for their employees. An Ethernet connection is much, much faster than a modem connection and provides fast access to information available on the Web. Also, if your system assigns static IP addresses, you can set up a computer as a Web server or email host.

For several years, Macintosh computers have included built-in Ethernet ports in two varieties. The port on most models (including older machines such as the Centris 610 and 650) is the Apple Attachment Unit Interface or AAUI port. This unusual port must have an additional hardware device, a *transceiver*, to access the network. When Apple began adding Ethernet capability to its computers, the cabling was not universal; some environments used 10Base-T cable while others used thin coax wire (other wiring solutions exist as well). The AAUI port allowed access to the network using a transceiver with the cable connection that matched the network environment. It wasn't necessary to adjust jumpers on a card or to change driver configurations. However, networks gradually moved to 10Base-T.

The second variety of Ethernet port is the 10Base-T port. It resembles a phone connection. 10Base-T is the more popular of the Ethernet wiring solutions, so Apple included it on its newer model computers. This port allows you to connect an Ethernet wire directly to your computer.

Some Macintosh computers, including several of the Performa computers, do not include Ethernet capability. If your computer is missing an AAUI or 10Base-T port, see if it has a free expansion slot. If so, you can purchase a network interface card with the appropriate connector for your environment. PowerBooks also have an expansion slot that can be filled by an Ethernet card; they also allow you to install a PCMCIA Ethernet card.

Software Requirements

The Mac OS includes the necessary software to connect to a permanent Ethernet connection or dial into a modem pool. It is also easy to set up either connection. However, if you purchased a PCMCIA card for your PowerBook, you will need to install the drivers for the card.

Protocol Software

Open Transport is the software suite of extensions and control panels that enables the computer to connect various types of networks. This software comes bundled with Mac OS 8.5. You may see vestiges of Classic Networking, especially within the control panels. *Classic Networking* is the term used to describe the network software previous to Open Transport. *Network* and *MacTCP* were used with the Classic Networking. The Open Transport control panels that replaced the Network and MacTCP control panels are AppleTalk and TCP/IP. If you have the newer Open Transport control panels, you can disable Network and MacTCP. Other control panels that you can use to establish Internet connectivity with Open Transport are DialAssist, Internet, Modem, and Remote Access. Some of the extensions used with Open Transport begin with *Open Transport* or *Open Tpt*. However, other extensions may not be labeled as such. For example, modem scripts are located in the Extensions folder.

These control panels and extensions work together to establish a network connection. However, other software packages are available for dial-up connectivity. FreePPP is a freeware connectivity package that is widely used because the Mac OS did not have a built-in connectivity software package for a PPP connection until System 7.6. FreePPP allows you to have multiple dial-up configurations and to adjust options such as the modem speed and initialization string. You can also have multiple configuration sets with the Modem control panel. However, you cannot change the modem speed or initialization string from the Modem control panel; you must manually edit the scripts or obtain updated dialing scripts from the modem manufacturer. For the average user who has struggled to find the correct initialization string, this is a blessing. Those used to the many options of FreePPP, however, may find this disconcerting.

ISP

Not only do you need hardware and software to access the Internet, you also need someone to let you into the Internet. Many institutions cover the cost of Internet access for their employees, but home users and small businesses must locate a company that provides Internet access. We mentioned the different kinds of ISPs at the beginning of this chapter. To access the Internet, you need to create an account with an ISP. Some ISPs are accessible via the Remote Access software included with Mac OS 8.5; others provide a dialer created for their users. Still others provide a complete Internet access package with proprietary email and Web browser software. Analyze what you need. How many hours per month will you be connecting to their services? Do you need unlimited access? Do you need multiple accounts? Does the ISP supply local access telephone numbers or toll-free access? Be aware that the cheapest ISP many not be the best one for your needs.

IP Number

An *IP number* is a unique number assigned to your machine that identifies you to the rest of the Internet. This number allows you to access Web sites, send email, and transfer files. Your number can also be used to set up Internet services such as email, Web, and FTP functions. Permanent Ethernet users may have a number assigned to the computer that usually does not change. In some settings, such as computer lab environments, you may see numbers assigned by a server. In this case, you don't need to remember the IP number; a server will assign one to the computer. Depending on the network configuration, the computer may have a new IP number each time the machine starts up and connects to the network or the number may last for several months. Dial-up connections usually receive a new number with each connection.

If your number is not unique, you will receive an error that the number is in use. It usually indicates the hardware address of the machine that is currently using the number. Figure 12.1 shows an example of this error. If your number is in use, you will not be able to access Internet services and you must either change IP numbers or locate and ask the offending computer user to change numbers.

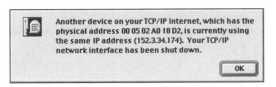

Another device on your TCP/IP Internet, which has the physical address 00 05 02 A0 18 D2, is currently using the same IP address (152.3.34.174). Your TCP/IP network interface has been shut down.

OK

Figure 12.1   A duplicate IP number error.

TIP: *Document the hardware address of your computer and your assigned IP number. If your IP number is ever stolen, you may be able to use it to track down your computer. In some networks, an administrator can provide the physical location of a computer on the network if the IP number is in use. You can also assign your IP number to a different computer and see if an error occurs, listing the stolen computer's hardware address. You can then alert your network administrators and the proper authorities that the stolen computer is in use.*

Another reason to document your IP number is so that you can easily reconfigure your computer if your hard drive crashes. You may be forced to configure your system from scratch.

New Technologies

Modems today are rather slow compared to a permanent Ethernet connection. Even Ethernet connections today could be faster. Emerging technologies might be available in your area that may change the way you access the Internet. Other high-bandwidth technologies are on the horizon, including wireless and satellite networking.

Fast Ethernet

Fast Ethernet refers to improved network cards, wire, and hubs capable of exchanging data packets at 100 megabits per second. Compare this to the common 10Base-T standard that passes data at 10 megabits per second. Fast Ethernet is available today, but before you can use it, your network hardware must be upgraded. You can purchase Macintosh computers today with Fast Ethernet, but unless the hubs and wires used in the network are also upgraded, you will not enjoy a speed increase. Fast Ethernet doesn't involve special software configuration. If the hardware elements are in place, you can use Fast Ethernet immediately.

ISDN

Integrated Services Digital Network (ISDN) promised to be the future of telephone communication. Not only could ISDN transmit voice, it could also transmit data simultaneously. ISDN is rather popular in several European and Asian countries, but is spotty in the United States because of competing telecommunication protocols and because the existing telephone lines may not support it.

ISDN may require that additional hardware be installed, some of which can be expensive. ISDN can transmit data faster than standard modem communication (up to 164Kbps), but not as fast as other competing technologies.

ADSL

Asymmetric Digital Subscriber Loop (ADSL) is a technology that radically improves the existing phone line communication so that you can talk on the telephone while accessing the Internet. With specialized hardware, you can achieve data exchange rates as a high 8MPS downstream and 1MPS upstream. The rationale behind this speed gap is that more users are pulling data down to their computers than putting data up on a remote server. ADSL may require an upgrade to your phone lines and requires a hardware device that interfaces with your computer.

Cable Modems

ISDN and ADSL are services provided by your local telephone company. Cable modems are provided by the cable television providers. Using the existing cable television line in your home, your cable provider can install a hardware device that transmits data over the cable line. As with ADSL, a speed discrepancy exists between downstream and upstream data transmissions. Downstream transmissions can equal 10Base-T speed. Upstream is much slower, but is still faster than standard modem speeds.

TIP: *One problem with the home or small-business network is that you seem to be locked into a single IP number if you use such technologies as ADSL or cable modems. Yet, you have multiple computers that need to access the Web simultaneously. An excellent company, Vicom Software, provides solutions not only to the small network but to the larger network. It offers several software solutions, ranging from SurfDoubler, which allows two Macs to access the Web using the same IP number, to Internet Gateway, which can connect small or large networks to the Internet. You can visit Vicom at www.vicomsoft.com.*

Quick Reference Specifications

The following are the essential facts about Internet Connectivity:

• You need an Internet Service Provider unless you have a proprietary server for network access.

• Some ISPs have unique software for accessing their services.

• A dial-up network connection is a temporary network connection, using a modem and telephone line to transport data packets.

- A permanent network connection contains hardware elements that are physically connected to network cabling and routers and that maintains a constant connection to the network.

- PPP (Point-to-Point Protocol) is a common network protocol in dial-up connections and is an improved method of SLIP (Serial Line Interface Protocol).

- ARA (Apple Remote Access) allows a Macintosh computer to access an AppleTalk network remotely.

- 10Base-T is a common network cabling option.

- The hardware requirements for Internet access are either a modem, a network card, or a built-in Ethernet port.

- The software requirement for Internet access is Open Transport networking software or a third-party dial-up software application.

- An IP number is a series of numbers that are unique to your machine and identify your computer to the Internet.

- You can have multiple configuration sets in many control panels.

- The Internet control panel is a descendent of Internet Config and stores Internet settings in a central location.

Utilities To Use

The utilities or elements of the Mac OS discussed in this chapter are listed here as a memory aid for the busy user or system administrator:

- *ISP* (Internet Service Provider)—A company that provides Internet access to customers.

- *SLIP* (Serial Line Interface Protocol)—A networking protocol capable of running within a modem connection.

- *PPP* (Point-to-Point Protocol)—An updated version of SLIP.

- *ARA* (Apple Remote Access)—An AppleTalk protocol capable of running within a modem connection.

- *AAUI* (Apple Attachment Unit Interface)—A generic Ethernet port that can accept transceivers for different network wiring environments.

- *Open Transport*—The multifaceted network software included with Mac OS 8.5.

- *FreePPP*—Third-party dial-up software used for creating a PPP connection.

- *Fast Ethernet*—An improved Ethernet network solution that increases data speeds to 100Mbps.

- *ISDN* (Integrated Services Digital Network)—A telecommunications protocol that provides faster data transfer speeds, but requires additional hardware that could be expensive.

- *Cable modems*—The technology presented by the cable television industry that provides fast Internet access via existing cable television wire.

- *ADSL* (Asymmetric Digital Subscriber Loop)—A modem technology that improves the efficiency of existing phone lines to allow speedier Internet access.

- *Internet Setup Assistant*—A software utility included with Mac OS 8.5 that configures the computer for Internet access based on answers provided by the user.

Immediate Solutions

Running The Internet Setup Assistant (Part 1—All Configurations)

When you first install Mac OS 8.5, you are given an opportunity to configure your Internet settings via a utility called the *Internet Setup Assistant*. This program asks a series of questions and uses your answers to configure control panels that control Internet access. If you close the Assistant when it first displays, you can launch the utility manually. If you launch a program that requires that these settings be in place, a dialog box displays, giving you the opportunity to launch the Internet Setup Assistant.

If you prefer to use the Internet Setup Assistant to configure your system, take the following steps:

1. Launch the Internet Setup Assistant.

2. The first dialog box directly asks if you want to get on the Internet. If you answer Yes, the utility continues. Answering No shuts down the utility.

3. The second dialog box asks if you already have an account on the Internet. If you answer No, you will be given an opportunity to create an account with an Internet Sevice Provider. If you answer Yes, you continue through the Internet Setup Assistant.

4. The window shown in Figure 12.2 displays. This is an introductory screen to the Internet Setup Assistant. Make sure that you know your DNS address, the type of connection you will be using, and your IP information, including the IP address, subnet router, and router address. In addition, if you are using a modem to connect, you need the number of your ISP, your name, and your password. If you have the required information, click on the right arrow in the bottom-right corner of the window.

5. In the next window, you are given an opportunity to name the configuration you are creating, as shown in Figure 12.3 (you can have multiple configurations). You also determine whether you are using a modem or network connection.

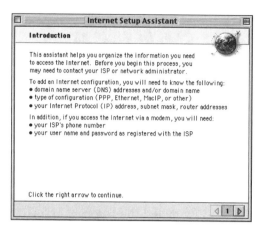

Figure 12.2   The Internet Setup Assistant introductory screen.

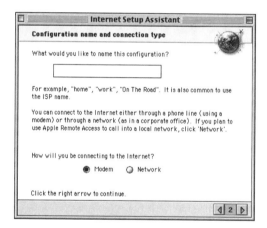

Figure 12.3   Naming your Internet configuration.

At this point, Internet Setup Assistant continues on a particular path that is based on the type of connection you are configuring. If you are using a modem to create an Internet connection, select it and click on the right arrow. Continue to the next section, "Running The Internet Setup Assistant (Part 2—Modem)" for the next steps. If you are using a permanent Ethernet connection, select Network and click on the right arrow. Proceed to the section, "Running The Internet Setup Assistant (Part 3—Network)" for further instructions.

Running The Internet Setup Assistant (Part 2—Modem)

If you have not done so, please make sure you have followed the steps in the previous section before you continue here. When you are finished, you should be able to connect to an ISP with Mac OS 8.5. Follow these steps:

1. You should see the window shown in Figure 12.4, which gives you the opportunity to indicate modem settings, such as the type of modem you're using and the port where the modem is connected. You can also indicate whether the phone line is capable of tone dialing and whether the dial tone should be ignored (non-U.S modems may require this setting in order to use the U.S. phone system and vice versa). After entering this information, click on the right arrow to continue.

2. In the next window, enter the telephone number and account information for your ISP, as shown in Figure 12.5. Then, click on the right arrow to continue.

3. Some ISPs require that a PPP connection script be used to access their services. If you have such a script, you must store it in a folder within the Extensions folder called PPP Connect Scripts. The window in Figure 12.6 shows the option of designating a PPP connection script. If you select No, you are taken to the section for setting up the IP information, continued in the section "Running The Internet Setup Assistant (Part 3—Network)" at Step 2. If you select No, you continue to the last step of this section. Choose an option and click on the right arrow to continue.

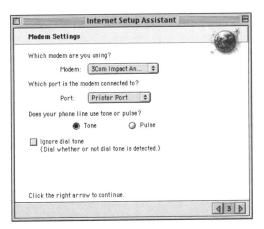

Figure 12.4   Configuring the modem within the Internet Setup Assistant.

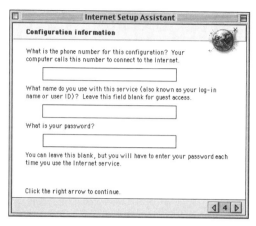

Figure 12.5   The ISP information.

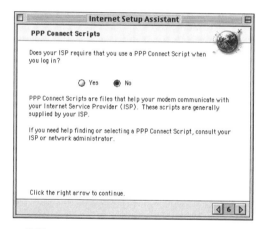

Figure 12.6   Do you use a PPP connect script?

4. Use this window (Figure 12.7) to indicate a connection script. If a script is present in the PPP Connect Scripts folder, you should be able to select it from the pop-up menu. If it is located elsewhere on the computer, you can use a navigator window to locate it and have the Internet Setup Assistant copy it to the proper folder. Choose a script and click on the right arrow to continue.

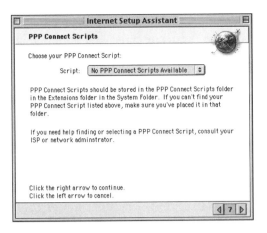

Figure 12.7   Choosing a connection script.

Running The Internet Setup Assistant (Part 3—Network)

If you have not done so, make sure you have followed the steps within the section "Running The Internet Setup Assistant (Part 1—All Configurations)." If you have, you should be ready to configure your network and IP information.

1. If you plan to use Apple Remote Access, you will be selecting the Network configuration route. Figure 12.8 shows the window that allows you to indicate whether you will be using Apple Remote Access to dial into a network. If you select Yes, you need to have access to some kind of network (LocalTalk, Ethernet, or Apple Remote Access) to set your Mac IP zone. Selecting No takes you to the IP configuration section.

Figure 12.8   Indicating the Apple Remote Access status.

2. Next, you are asked if you have an IP number assigned. Many permanent Ethernet connections do, while most dial-up connections don't. If you select No, go to Step 3. If you select Yes, you are prompted to enter your IP number. Go to Step 4.

3. If you selected No in the previous step, you must use a dynamic method of assigning an IP number. You are given two options as shown in Figure 12.9: You can choose MacIP or Other, which indicates another method such as DHCP or BootP. Choose the method, click on the right arrow, and skip to Step 6.

4. If you selected Yes when asked if you have an assigned IP number, you are given an opportunity to enter the number. Enter your IP number and click on the right arrow to continue.

5. Enter your Subnet Mask and Router address (see Figure 12.10). Then, click on the right arrow.

6. The next window requires you to enter DNS or Domain Name Server information (see Figure 12.11). A DNS server translates an IP number into an understandable host name (17.254.0.91 is translated to **www.apple. com**). Click on the right arrow to continue.

7. Next, you are prompted for email information, such as your published email address, password (optional), and the quoting character you prefer (the default is ">"). Enter the information and click on the right arrow to continue.

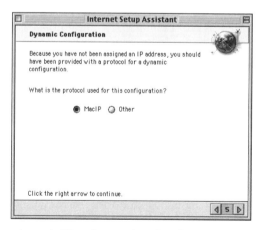

Figure 12.9   Selecting a dynamic IP assignment protocol.

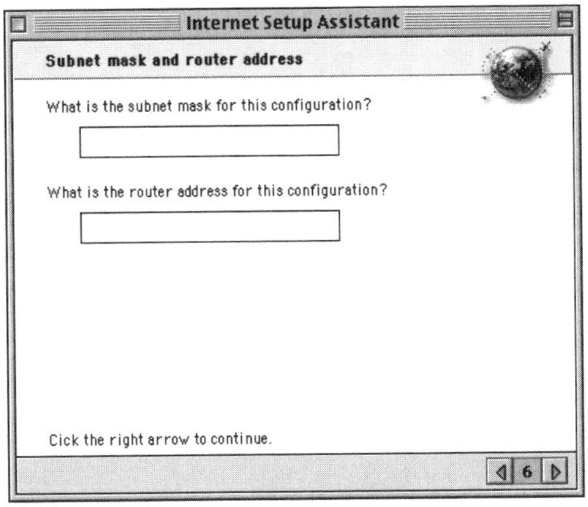

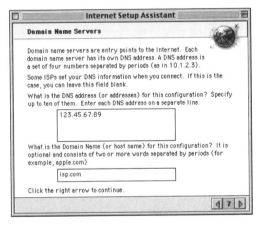

Figure 12.10   Entering the Subnet Mask and Router address.

Figure 12.11   Entering DNS information.

8. In Figure 12.12, you see an example of the next window in which you are prompted to enter your email account information. This could be different from the email address you indicated in Step 7. Also, enter the outgoing mail host. After you are finished here, click on the right arrow to continue.

9. Enter your news server host name (this step is optional). The news server provides Usenet groups to a software package that can display them (both Netscape Navigator and Internet Explorer have this capability). Click on the right arrow to continue when done.

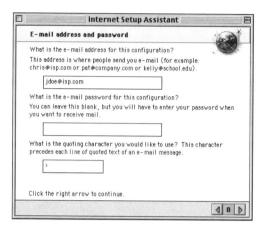

Figure 12.12   Email account information.

10. Your network may have security measures in place to prevent unauthorized access and may require you to use proxy servers. This window asks if you must use proxy servers. If you answer Yes and click on the right arrow, you are prompted to enter the information as shown in Figure 12.13. Enter the appropriate proxy server addresses and click on the right arrow. If you answer No, you skip this screen and continue to Step 11. Click on the right arrow to continue.

11. At this last window, you can select Go Ahead to finish the process and make the changes. If you want to verify your settings, you can click on Show Details for a list. After you click on Go Ahead, the Internet Setup Assistant will make the changes to the appropriate control panels and automatically quit. You are now ready to access the Internet.

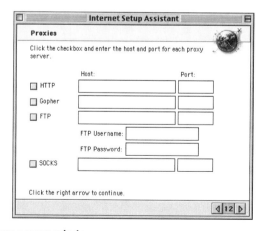

Figure 12.13   The proxy server window.

Configuring The Remote Access Control Panel

You can use the Internet Setup Assistant or you can manually configure the different control panels that allow you to access the Internet. The Remote Access control panel is used for modem connections. To configure the Remote Access control panel:

1. Open the Remote Access control panel (see Figure 12.14).

2. If applicable, enter your login name and password or click on the Guest radio button to remove these fields.

3. Enter your ISP telephone number.

4. Click on the Options button to access additional settings.

5. Click on the Redialing tab. You can access the pop-up menu to determine if redialing is enabled, how many times to redial, and if an alternate number should be used when redialing (see Figure 12.15).

Figure 12.14   The Remote Access control panel.

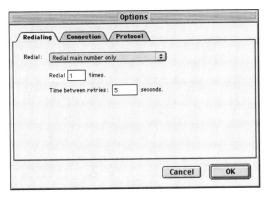

Figure 12.15   The Redialing tab within the Remote Access control panel.

12: Internet Connectivity

6. Click on the Connection tab (see Figure 12.16). You can turn on logging to troubleshoot connection problems. You can configure settings to remind you that you are connected, such as a flashing icon or a message every 10 minutes. You can also automatically disconnect yourself if you are idle for 10 minutes; this option is useful if you are billed for the time you are online.

7. Click on the Protocol tab. Determine the network protocol from the pop-up menu beside the Use protocol label. If you select Automatic, the control panel will choose the protocol to use. You can also choose ARAP for Apple Remote Access protocol. If you choose PPP, you will see the options shown in Figure 12.17.

8. You can set several options within the PPP tab, such as automatically connecting to an ISP when you launch TCP/IP applications. You can also indicate compression options. If you connect to an ISP via a command-line prompt, you can set the PPP option from this panel. You can also indicate a particular script to use when dialing the ISP.

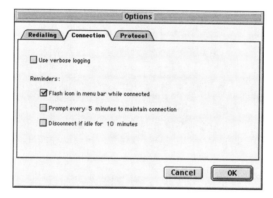

Figure 12.16   The Connection tab within the Remote Access control panel.

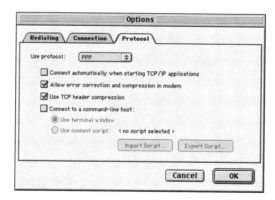

Figure 12.17   The PPP options in the Protocol tab.

When you have set your preferred options, you can click on Okay to return to the main window. You still must configure the Modem and TCP/IP control panels in order to access an ISP. These control panels can be accessed from the Remote Access menu in the Remote Access control panel.

Creating A Remote Access Script

In the preceding section, we explained how to configure the Remote Access control panel. For some ISPs, you connect via a command-line prompt, where you answer a series of prompts before you can establish a network connection. You can create a script that records this information automatically when you connect. It saves time and keystrokes.

1. Launch the Remote Access control panel.
2. Click on the Connect button to begin the PPP connection process.
3. When you connect to your ISP, you should be prompted with a terminal window. Click on the Settings button.
4. Activate the option Prompt To Save Connect Script On Close and click on Okay.
5. Enter your information as you normally would. When the PPP connection has been established, you are prompted to save the script. You don't have to save the script in a particular place. You just need to know where you saved it.
6. Click on the Options button. You should still be at the Protocol window.
7. Click on the radio button for Use Connect Script.
8. Click on the Import Script button, locate the script you created, and then click on OK.

The next time you connect to your ISP, you can test your script and see if you can automatically connect. You may have to repeat this process until the script is perfected. For example, some connections are noisy and insert additional characters at a command-line prompt. A quick work-around is to hit Enter to clear the characters. You should be given a clean prompt and can enter your information correctly.

Configuring The Internet Control Panel

The Internet control panel was developed from a software application called Internet Config. Without Internet Config, you were forced to enter the same information over and over again in the preferences of different TCP/IP applications. The Internet control panel, shown in Figure 12.18, contains information that can be referenced by TCP/IP applications such as email programs and Web browsers. You can set up multiple configuration sets with this control panel. See the following section "Creating Configuration Sets In The Internet Control Panel" for instructions.

You can set the following options with the Internet control panel:

- *Personal*—These settings are not used for accessing servers; they are just personal settings such as your name, email address, and organization. You can also create a signature file that will be appended to the end of your email and newsgroup messages.

- *Email*—These settings are used to access email servers. You can enter your user account, incoming and outgoing mail server addresses, and password. You can also set your options for email notification. Finally, by default Mac OS 8.5 uses Outlook Express as the default email application. You have the option of changing this to another application if you choose.

- *Web*—These settings are used with Web browsers such as Microsoft's Internet Explorer and Netscape Navigator. You can set your default home page and search engine. You can also designate a folder to contain files that you

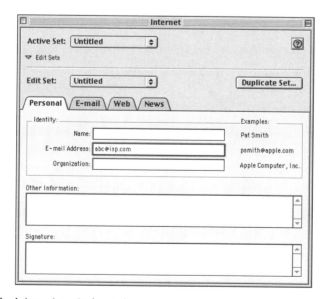

Figure 12.18   The Internet control panel.

download from the Internet. You can set Web browser colors and links defaults. Finally, Microsoft's Internet Explorer is the default Web browser; you can optionally select another browser.

- *News*—These options are used when reading Usenet newsgroups. You can set the news server address, your login options (if necessary), and select the preferred news reader (Microsoft's Outlook Express is the default reader).

TIP: *There is a hidden pane in the Internet control panel. If you go to the Edit menu and select User Mode, you can specify Advanced. When you close this window, you will have a new tab labeled Advanced. You will see all kinds of options you can set, including default FTP hosts, Helper Apps, Fonts, File Mapping, Firewalls, and Hosts.*

Creating Configuration Sets In The Internet Control Panel

The Internet control panel contains useful information about your Internet settings. But what if you share a workstation with another user? What if you have more than one email account? You will need more than one configuration set. You can use these sets as part of a shared workstation or with Location Manager to control different work environments. Follow these steps:

1. Launch the Internet control panel.

2. Go to File|New Set. If you need to make minor changes to an existing set, you can also click on the Duplicate Set button and select a new name for the set.

3. Fill in the appropriate fields or make changes to existing fields, then go to File|Save Settings.

4. If you would like to use the new set, click on the pop-up menu labeled *Active Set* and select the desired set. It will become active.

5. Close the Internet Control panel and, if you are prompted, save your settings.

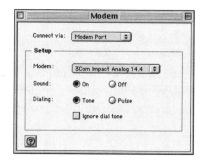

Figure 12.19   The Modem control panel.

Configuring The Modem Control Panel

The Modem control panel tells the Remote Access control panel how to dial the ISP. If these settings are inaccurate, you will not be able to successfully connect. Follow these steps to configure the Modem control panel:

1. Open the Modem control panel as shown in Figure 12.19.

2. Indicate the port you will use to communicate with the modem.

3. Click on the Modem pop-up menu and locate your modem model. If it is not listed, try using a generic script. You can also try installing the scripts from the software that came with the modem (scripts are also available from the manufacturer).

4. Use the radio button to turn on or off the dialing sound.

5. Use the radio button to indicate whether to use tone or pulse dialing.

6. If necessary, select Ignore dial tone.

Ignoring The Dial Tone

If you will be traveling out of the country and you anticipate dialing your ISP, you may need to enable this option. Modems are sensitive to the frequency of a telephone line. The frequency may be different in a particular country. You can tell immediately if you need to enable this option if you attempt to dial and can hear a dial tone, but receive an error message indicating that there is no dial tone. Turn this option on and attempt to connect. The Modem control panel will force the modem to ignore the apparent lack of connectivity and dial the ISP number.

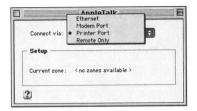

Figure 12.20   The AppleTalk control panel.

Configuring The AppleTalk Control Panel

The AppleTalk control panel is used with an Ethernet or LocalTalk network. Before you can configure the AppleTalk control panel, you must enable AppleTalk within the Chooser. If you launch this control panel while AppleTalk is inactive, you are prompted to turn AppleTalk on when you close the AppleTalk control panel. To configure the AppleTalk control panel for Ethernet:

1. Open Chooser and activate AppleTalk if it is inactive.

2. Launch the AppleTalk control panel (see Figure 12.20).

3. In the Connect Via pop-up menu, select Ethernet. If your network utilizes zones, you should see the current zone appear when you switch to Ethernet.

4. Close the control panel and save the settings.

Configuring The DialAssist Control Panel

The DialAssist control panel works with the Modem control panel. DialAssist helps when you are dialing under unusual conditions, such as long distance or from within a telephone network requiring special settings. In the past, you had to type long numeric strings separated by commas to accomplish such tasks as dialing a particular long-distance provider or inserting your calling card information. With DialAssist you can insert this information and use this control panel when you need additional numbers dialed to access your ISP or network. Be aware that not all settings must be completed to use DialAssist (you may only need to dial 9 for an outside line). To configure DialAssist, take these steps:

1. Launch the DialAssist control panel as shown in Figure 12.21 (note that all of the DialAssist settings reference the telephone number active within the Modem control panel).

Figure 12.21   The DialAssist control panel.

2. Optionally, indicate the area code of the number.

3. Select the country from the Country pop-up menu (if the country isn't listed, you can click on the Country button to add a new country to the listing).

4. Indicate a special prefix such as dialing a 9 for an outside line (if your prefix isn't listed, you can click on the Prefix button to add new ones).

5. Indicate your method of long-distance access (such as dialing 1+the area code) or a particular long-distance provider (if the provider isn't listed, click on the Long Distance button to add additional carriers).

6. Indicate your calling card or credit card number in the Suffix pop-up menu (if you select this option, you need to click on the Suffix button and edit the settings to include your card numbers).

TIP: If you do choose to add the Suffix option within DialAssist, don't worry that someone can retrieve your credit or calling card information by opening the Suffix settings. The numbers entered are protected in the same way passwords are protected—they are encrypted.

Configuring The TCP/IP Control Panel

TCP/IP settings are vital for successfully connecting to the Internet. If parts are configured incorrectly, you may see problems that range from the inability to connect to certain Web sites to the inability to connect to any site or server. The settings also vary depending on the type of Ethernet connection you will be using; it may be a permanent Ethernet connection or a remote access configuration. Follow these steps to configure the TCP/IP control panel for Internet access:

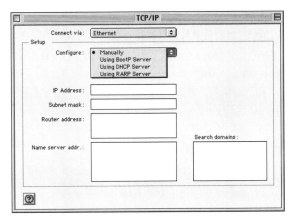

Figure 12.22   The TCP/IP control panel.

1. Launch the TCP/IP control panel as shown in Figure 12.22.

2. Select the connection protocol you will be using from the Connect Via pop-up menu. Each selection changes the options in the Setup portion of the TCP/IP control panel. You have several options that may include PPP, Ethernet, or MacIP.

3. Choose what configuration options you want; options include DHCP, BootP, PPP, or RARP server configurations. These selections are used if your computer is not assigned an IP number directly. Manually configure the TCP/IP control panel if you do have an assigned IP number. Figure 12.23 shows a TCP/IP manual configuration.

4. Close the control panel and click on Save Settings when prompted. You should be able to utilize TCP/IP applications. If you can't, try restarting your computer (especially if you had to edit an existing TCP/IP configuration).

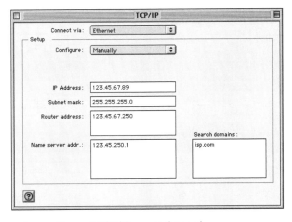

Figure 12.23   A manually configured TCP/IP control panel.

Creating And Saving Configuration Sets

The AppleTalk, Modem, Remote Access, and TCP/IP control panels all use the same method for creating different configurations. These configuration sets can be used with the Location Manager to control the network environment. You may be using a PowerBook that can use Ethernet at work and PPP connectivity at home. Follow these steps to create configuration sets:

1. Open the appropriate control panel.

2. Go to File|Configurations. The window shown in Figure 12.24 will appear.

3. Click on the Duplicate button and designate a new name for your configuration.

4. When you have created and named a set, click on the Make Active button to edit the configuration and save changes.

5. Go back into the control panel and make the changes so that your configuration set is unique.

6. Close the control panel and choose Save Settings.

7. You can now go back into the control panel and select Configurations to either make a different set active or create a new set.

TIP: You can also use the Configurations dialog box to import and export information. You can use these settings on multiple computers. Simply export the settings to a file, go to a new computer, and use the Configurations dialog box to import the settings. This is handy when you must configure and administer several computers. You also use the Configurations dialog box to delete old configuration sets.

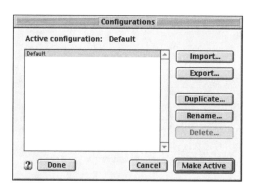

Figure 12.24   The Configurations window.

Chapter 13

Providing Internet, Intranet, And Extranet Services

In Depth

This chapter shows how you can provide Internet and intranet services on a Macintosh running Mac OS 8.5. The Mac OS has always been network-ready right out of the box since the first Macintosh was introduced in 1984. These first Macs communicated via AppleTalk as well as TCP/IP, and one of the first popular Web servers called MacHTTP ran on the Mac OS. The Mac OS 8.5 continues to be an inexpensive and incredibly easy operating system on which to provide all the most popular TCP/IP services over the Internet, as well as on intranets.

Internet, Intranet, And Extranet Services

Internet, intranet, and extranet services rely on the same transmission protocol, TCP/IP, and use the same wiring and routing technologies, such as frame relay, Ethernet, and ISDN. What makes them different, however, is the scope of their availability to the public. Internet services are usually made available to the general public as part of a commercial venture or a public service; intranet services are usually part of a private local area network (LAN), and are restricted to a specific group of users. Intranets that provide limited access to outside users are referred to as *extranets*. What, however, makes this discussion relevant in this book? The Mac OS, of course. If you're connected to the Internet, or a corporate intranet or extranet, on a full-time basis, you can provide services to users with your Macintosh.

Common TCP/IP Services

Many people think the Web is synonymous with Internet services, and that's not true at all. Internet services include the Web, for sure, but there are many more services you can provide with the Mac OS. It is possible—not to mention super easy—to provide multiple Internet services such as the following:

- Web (personal and commercial)
- Email
- Mailing list servers
- FTP
- Proxy and gateway
- Usenet News

- Domain Name Servers (DNS)
- Gopher
- Chat
- Talk
- Finger
- Whois
- Ident
- Audio

Until fairly recently, these Internet services have been provided almost exclusively by Unix computers, which required a resident computer expert to install and maintain, and more recently with Windows NT. Just about anyone can configure these Internet servers on a Mac. They all share in common a reliance on TCP/IP, as do many other services, and Mac users wanting to provide these services often have multiple options when it comes to choosing an application to provide these services.

Note: *To provide Internet services on most all computers, you will need one or more dedicated IP addresses.*

Hardware Requirements

Computers that are configured to provide Internet, intranet, and extranet services are typically faster and more expensive than your typical workstation. However, you can take a workstation and convert it into an efficient server without too much difficulty or expense, depending on the intended task. Of course, faster computers are usually better, but you might be surprised to learn that in some cases, speed is almost irrelevant and even the slowest Power Macintosh will be more than sufficient.

In general, look for the following hardware requirements or extras when selecting or building an Internet server:

- Fast PowerPC 604e or G3 processor (200Mhz or better)
- 7200 RPM or faster hard drive(s)
- RAID (redundant array of inexpensive disks)
- SCSI accelerator
- Fast Ethernet (100Mbps)
- L2 cache, if applicable

- Regular backup schedule
- UPS (uninterruptable power supply)
- Rebound or PowerKey (to restart the server)

Of course, don't forget the human requirements. Make sure that the procedures for operating your servers are well documented and that someone is always available who can step in as the primary caretaker. You never know when he or she may be hit by a name-brand beer truck on the way to work (not just any beer truck!).

Connectivity And Disaster Recovery Issues

Another consideration is the kind of connectivity you'll have to the Internet or on your internal network, and what to do in case your connection isn't stable or goes down for a prolonged period. Several utilities, discussed later in the chapter, help you monitor your servers and alert you to problems, but a good plan for providing online services includes a backup plan for a lost connection or a catastrophic hardware failure.

The most effective way to overcome prolonged downtime on a usable server is to have a redundant server co-located on another network. Maintaining two identical servers in different locations is a daunting task and may be overkill if your Internet service provider (ISP) is reliable enough to guarantee minimal downtime, making co-locating a second server unnecessary. In this case, having a redundant server on site is sufficient. Even maintaining two identical servers may be overkill; a backup Web server, for example, that provides basic services may be sufficient.

On the other hand, it is likely that you can find a peer institution or organization with which you can create a reciprocal agreement either for monitoring each others' servers or for co-locating backup servers. Mac people tend to stick together, so don't downplay the possibility of creating this type of arrangement.

Account Administration

Providing Internet, intranet, and extranet services involves the creation of user accounts, usage rules, and regular accounts maintenance. This is equally true for commercial services and personal or departmental intranet accounts; the more users you have, the more work the account will be to maintain. Tools and utilities are available to help with account maintenance, and some tools are worth the money when compared to shareware and freeware applications that perform some tasks adequately, but not others.

In addition to the drudgery of maintaining user and group access privileges, disk quotas, and user profiles, one area of account administration often overlooked is the creation and enforcement of rules for acceptable use. In our opinion, you're better off defining up front what users can and cannot do with your services than bickering with disgruntled users who have had their accounts restricted for misuse. When creating an acceptable user policy for your servers, consider the following for each account:

- Maximum levels of file transfer traffic
- Tech support limits
- Disk quotas
- Offensive language and flame wars
- Passing spam, chain letters, and the like
- Reselling of account resources
- Copyright laws and legal restrictions

It's a good idea to post your policies where everyone can read them and refer your user to the policies on a regular basis, perhaps with a monthly "help file" placed on a mailing list.

Immediate Solutions

Providing Personal Web Services

Personal Web servers aren't new to the Mac OS in version 8.5; several options have been available for a couple of years, with the two most popular servers coming from Apple and Microsoft. If you are connected to a LAN, then you may be more interested in running a Web server on your Mac than if you dial up to an ISP only on occasion. For part-time Internet users, a personal Web server might seem unnecessary.

Mac OS 8.5 includes a personal Web server capable of serving hundreds of thousands of "hits" per day, which is more than sufficient for most users. It is easy to set up and configure and includes a Finder-like interface to help make visitors to your Web site feel more like Mac users than Web surfers.

To configure your Mac as a personal Web server, open the Web Sharing control panel, shown in Figure 13.1, and follow these steps:

1. Select a folder to serve as the root folder for your Web server. Mac OS 8.5 installs a folder on your hard drive named Web Pages, which is the default (see Figure 13.2).

2. Select a default home page for your Web site. The default option is none, in which case the Web server uses Apple's Personal NetFinder to present the contents of your Web site to users. Figure 13.3 shows how the Personal NetFinder looks when viewed through Internet Explorer, and Figure 13.4 shows what the default.html page (supplied with the Web server) looks like.

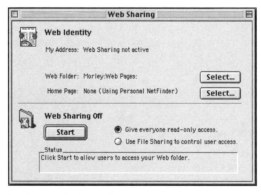

Figure 13.1   The Web Sharing control panel.

13: Providing Internet, Intranet, And Extranet Services

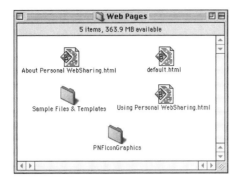

Figure 13.2   The default folder from which documents are served by Apple's personal Web server.

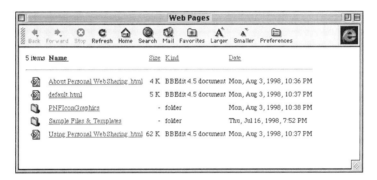

Figure 13.3   You can use the Personal NetFinder in place of a default HTML document for each folder in your Web server's folder hierarchy.

Figure 13.4   You can select your own default home page in place of the Personal NetFinder, or you can check out the page that's included, as you see here.

3. Open and edit the Preferences under the Edit menu, and make any necessary changes to the logging, port, access, memory, MIME, and actions settings (see Figure 13.5).

4. Return to the main window and click on the Start button to enable Web services; choose Stop to turn off the Web server.

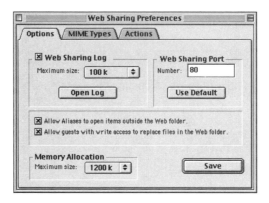

Figure 13.5   You can edit more settings through the Web Sharing Preferences window, accessible through the Edit menu.

Providing Commercial Web Services

Mac users have long had multiple software options for operating commercial or high-volume Web sites, but the field has really narrowed to only two commercial Web servers, WebSTAR from StarNine, and WebTen from Tenon Intersystems. WebSTAR is the more familiar of the two and has been around in one form or another for about eight years. It sports an easy to use interface and supports several million connections per day, depending on the hardware used. WebTen is a virtual Unix server that runs the Apache Web server, a public-domain server that is quickly becoming the most popular Web server on the Internet. WebTen is a bit more tricky to administer, but its performance is unmatched on the Mac OS and most other platforms. Running on a fast G3 computer, WebTen is capable of supporting 60 to 80 million hits per day, which ranks it as a first-class Web server by any standard. Both WebSTAR and WebTen cost around $500; a demo of WebTen is included on the companion CD-ROM.

The features of WebSTAR and WebTen are too numerous to cover in detail here. We will summarize them to help you decide which one might be better, if you're not using either one or if you are considering changing from one to another.

WebSTAR

WebSTAR 3 is a great improvement over earlier versions, providing faster performance, more features, and easier administration. WebSTAR is more than a Web server, however, and provides all the services you'll need to run multiple Web sites using a single server. Version 3 includes:

- Web server
- Proxy server
- FTP server
- SSL (Secure Sockets Layer)
- High-performance caching
- Virtual domain hosting
- Integrated search engine
- SSI (Server-Side Include) support
- Byte-server
- SMTP support
- Keep-alive support

This version is capable of running on a variety of Macs. However, to take advantage of all the plug-ins and services, you'll want a PowerMac, which is a requirement for Mac OS 8.5 anyway. Other requirements are as follows:

- System 7 or higher
- 3MB RAM minimum
- 20MB disk space, not including user files
- A dedicated IP address

To install and configure WebSTAR, download the latest version from **www. starnine.com** and follow these steps:

1. Run the WebSTAR Installer, reboot, and launch WebSTAR.
2. Go to the Edit menu and enter a password for administrative access.
3. Launch the WebSTAR Admin application and connect to your Web server using the server's IP address, port number, and administrative password.

The WebSTAR application has very few configuration options, and most of the real administration is accomplished through the WebSTAR Admin application. Figure 13.6 shows the WebSTAR Status window, which is automatically displayed on startup.

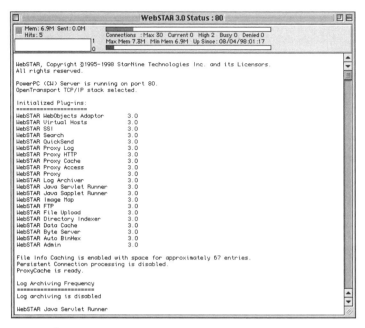

Figure 13.6   The WebSTAR application opens a status window automatically, but virtually all the administration is performed via the WebSTAR Admin application or over the Web using a Web browser.

Version 3 introduced a new user interface to WebSTAR Admin, making it much easier to administer WebSTAR and its user database. The Web Settings section of the Edit|Server Settings is shown in Figure 13.7.

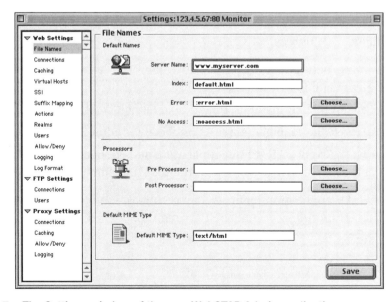

Figure 13.7   The Settings window of the new WebSTAR Admin application.

Here are some of the most important options in the Web Settings section:

- File Names—Set the default file names for index, error, and "no access" documents, pre- and post-processors, and the default MIME type.

- Connections—Set the number of maximum and persistent connections.

- Virtual Hosts—Configure virtual hosts, which allows your server to host multiple domains, such as www.debbie.com and www.mark.com, using one or more IP addresses and/or domain names.

- SSI (Server-Side Includes)—A series of commands that the Web server can execute that inserts items as page counters, time and date, and last modified information into Web pages.

- Suffix Mapping—Configures the Web server to serve files based on their file suffix and MIME type, such as QuickTime movies (which have the extension .mov or .moov).

- Actions—Configures plug-in and CGI scripts.

- Realms—The main security feature of WebSTAR, which allows you to password-protect files and folders, based on their names and paths.

- Users—Add, modify, and delete users, and assign access rights based on realms.

- Allow/Deny—Set global access restrictions based on visitors' IP and domain name information.

- Logging—Choose logging and log archiving options.

- Log Format—Select which elements are to be logged, such as date, time, and host name of visitors.

The FTP Settings and Proxy Settings sections of the Settings window control the FTP and Proxy servers by using interface designs similar to the Web Settings. This version of WebSTAR contains excellent documentation, which is easily accessible via the Web server, and contains an easy-to-use search engine. For example, it took us only about five minutes to learn how to create a search session, index the documentation folder, and perform a search on the term "MIME types" (see Figure 13.8).

WebTen

WebTen uses a very different approach to providing commercial Web services on the Mac platform. The makers of WebTen realized that to overcome certain limitations in the Mac OS's input/output and file systems, they could port elements of their virtual Unix operating system, *MachTen*, and port the freeware Web server, *Apache*, to this slimmed-down Unix server, and combine the two to create a hyperfast Web server. WebTen takes full advantage of the PowerPC processor, file caching, and an alternative replacement to Open Transport to create a Web server that is several times faster than WebSTAR.

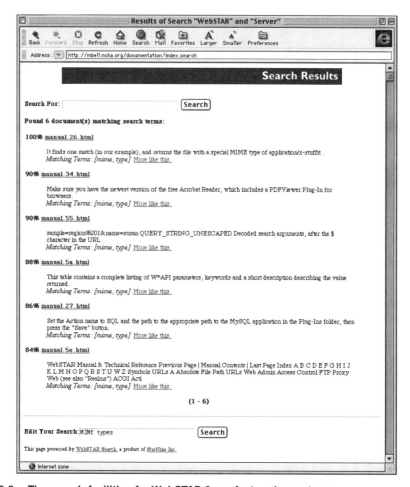

Figure 13.8 The search facilities for WebSTAR 3 are fast and easy to use.

The main features of WebTen include:

- Web server
- FTP server
- Proxy server
- DNS server
- NFS server
- Supports 1,000 hits per second
- High-performance caching
- Supports CGIs, Server-Side Includes (SSI), WebSTAR Plug-ins, AppleScript, Apache Plug-Ins, and Perl scripts

- True virtual hosting

- Supports multiple Ethernet adapters

However, the drawback is that WebTen is more complex to administer than WebSTAR and is not for the faint of heart. To install and configure WebTen, install it from the CD-ROM or visit **www.tenon.com**, then follow these steps:

1. Launch the WebTen application and fill in the WebTen Preferences, shown in Figure 13.9, which can be found under the File menu. (WebTen, however, should ask for these preferences the first time it is launched.)

2. Choose Admin|Set Admin Password and assign a username and password for access to the Administration Server.

3. Open a Web browser to the server and on the default home page, look for a link entitled "WebTen's Administration Server". Click on this link to access the Admin Server or enter www.*yourservername*.com/webten_admin. Figure 13.10 shows the main configuration page, after the username and password have been accepted.

The main configuration page is divided into two sections. The upper section is for system-wide configuration of the entire Web server, and the lower section is for the virtual domains that are hosted by the Web server. You can create multiple domains and configure each with its own preferences and settings, just like you can with WebSTAR.

The System-Wide Configuration section contains the following elements (reading top to bottom, left to right):

- Server Defaults—Settings for default file names and locations, logging, pre- and post-processors

- Plug-In Settings—Status and settings for any plug-ins, including WebSTAR and Apache plug-ins

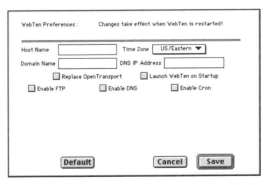

Figure 13.9 The first stop in configuring WebTen is to set the application's preferences.

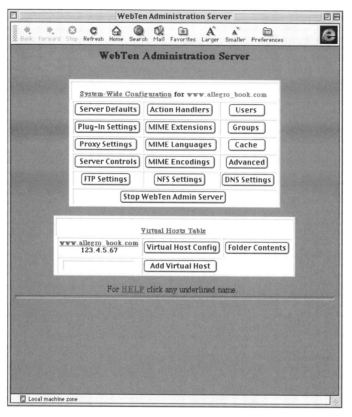

Figure 13.10   You configure WebTen, for the most part, by using a Web browser.

- Proxy Settings—Configuration options for proxy server

- Server Controls—View server status, error messages, as well as flush the cache and restart the server

- FTP Settings—Enable and disable FTP server, and configure logging

- Action Handlers—Configure plug-in and CGI scripts

- MIME Extension—Edit user-definable MIME extensions and assign actions to specific MIME extensions

- MIME Languages—Assign languages such as German or Italian to MIME extensions such as .de and .it

- MIME Encodings—Assign MIME encodings to provide "meta information" about document types, such as compressed files or PDF documents

- NFS Settings—Configure the Network File System (NFS) server to allow access to NFS volumes

- Users—Manage user accounts

- Groups—Manage groups of users

- Cache—Configure various cache settings

- Advanced—Configure various advanced settings that affect the performance of the Web server (see Figure 13.11)

- DNS—Configure DNS services

The Virtual Host Table section is where you'll add, modify, and delete virtual domains. For example, Figure 13.12 shows the settings for the default domain, called **www.allegro_book.com**.

Notice that many of the settings are inherited from the default host settings, so if you plan to add many virtual hosts in the future, make sure that you configure the System-Wide Settings with this in mind.

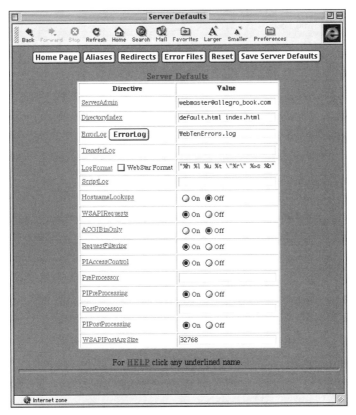

Figure 13.11   The Advanced Settings section of the WebTen Administration Server.

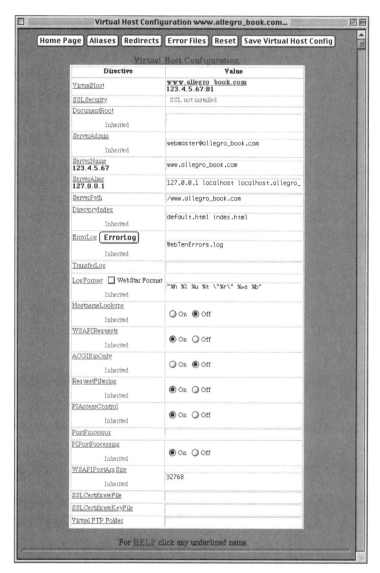

Figure 13.12   Virtual Host settings for the default domain.

Providing Email Services

Email is probably the most heavily relied on Internet service in use today. It may not take up the bandwidth and generate excitement like the Web, but it has become a standard form of communication vital to many organizations. You need to consider several issues when choosing an email server, including the email protocols

13: Providing Internet, Intranet, And Extranet Services

your server should use and the availability of email clients to access your server. Several email server solutions are currently available for the Mac OS, and many utilities and helper applications that enhance these servers.

POP Vs. IMAP

The most popular email protocols are Post Office Protocol (POP) and Internet Message Access Protocol (IMAP). Both POP and IMAP use Simple Mail Transfer Protocol (SMTP) to exchange data and connection information. SMTP is a server-to-server protocol, used to transfer email from a sending email server to a receiving email server. Most Unix-based computers employ SMTP in conjunction with sendmail, part of many Unix operating systems since the late 1970s, and are themselves email servers. Version 3 of POP (POP3) is the most popular Internet server protocol and is widely available on several platforms, including the Mac OS.

The POP protocol is structured as a "store and forward" or "store and download" email server, where email clients such as Qualcomm's Eudora log in to the server and then download the contents of a user's inbox to the hard drive. This makes the load on the email server minimal compared to IMAP-based email servers because POP-based email servers distribute email storage, processing, and other system-intensive tasks to the client. IMAP, on the other hand, keeps the user's email on the server and maintains a constant connection with its clients, which requires huge amounts of processor, RAM, and storage space. The greatest benefits of POP, therefore, are that it is much faster, isn't "chatty," and places less demand on the server. IMAP's greatest benefit is that a user's email is accessible from any IMAP email client from anywhere on the Internet because it isn't downloaded off the server to a local hard drive.

Eudora Internet Mail Server (EIMS)

The Eudora Internet Mail Server (EIMS), formerly the Apple Internet Mail Server (AIMS), is a feature-rich SMTP and POP3 email server for the Mac OS, which was acquired by Apple from Glen Anderson in 1995. EIMS is a complete server application that has minimal hardware and OS requirements, yet delivers everything needed to provide organizations of all sizes with robust Internet email services. To run this email server, your Mac needs only to meet the following requirements:

- A Mac LC or higher
- System 7 or higher
- Open Transport 1.1.2 or higher
- 1MB hard drive space (minimum)
- An Internet connection
- DNS services

Installing EIMS couldn't be any easier. Just launch the installer, reboot, launch the application, launch the EIMS Admin application, and configure the preferences.

The main configuration options found in the Admin|Preferences are as follows:

- General—Default expansion name and logging options.

- Connection Settings—EIMS uses three types of server processes—POP, SMTP, and Password—each of these uses one or more of the Mac OS network sockets. For small- to medium-sized offices, the default options will be adequate. Because POP uses a quick login-logout method of email retrieval, you don't need to increase the number of POP3 Server connections (unless your users are having to wait more than a few seconds to check their inboxes for new messages). The same holds true for SMTP, Password, and Ph server options (see Figure 13.13).

- Sending Setup—Queue and timeout values for each domain, including time to expire for messages that cannot be transmitted.

- Mail Routing—Routing options for each domain.

- Relay Restrictions—Rules for routing mail, on a domain basis.

- IP Range Restrictions—IP-based restrictions for POP3, SMTP, password, Ph, and mail relay services.

Adding or deleting email accounts and groups is easy. Figure 13.14 shows the properties for a user whose ID is *testuser*. Her account is active, and no limit exists on the forwarding of email or size limit on her Inbox, and she is a member of a group called Bookwriters.

By default, EIMS creates an account for the Postmaster, which is a requirement for email servers. The Postmaster account is used by the administrator of EIMS to receive email from users who need to contact the Postmaster without knowing the proper address to which to send a message. Someone should be designated to

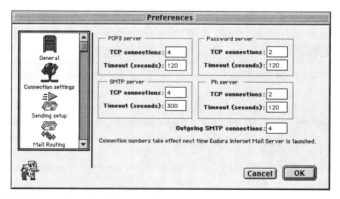

Figure 13.13   EIMS Connection Settings preferences.

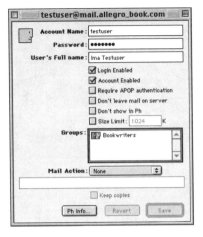

Figure 13.14   EIMS user account information.

either check for email sent to this account or to receive email that can be forwarded from the Postmaster account to his or her Inbox. Figure 13.15 shows the Forwarding options available to any user of the server.

EIMS maintains different configuration options for each domain it serves, making it very easy to maintain mail services for multiple domains. Figure 13.16 shows one of several domains that can be configured for each EIMS server, with several users and one group configured.

Other Email Servers

Several options are available for Mac OS email servers, but most are part of moderately priced commercial packages.

- NetTen from Tenon is an IMAP, POP3, DNS, and BIND server that uses a similar Unix virtual machine like WebTen to bring very high-performance mail services to Mac OS 8.5. See the demo copy on this book's CD-ROM, and visit **www.tenon.com/products/netten** for more information.

- Stalker Internet Mail Server from Stalker Software supports both POP3 as well as IMAP, and is reasonably priced at just a few hundred dollars. See **www.stalker.com/SIMS** for more information.

Figure 13.15   EIMS forwarding options.

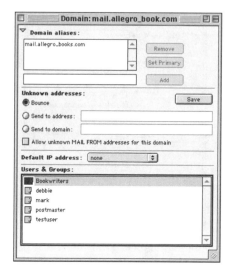

Figure 13.16   EIMS stores preferences and account information for each domain in its own window.

- Quarterdeck Mail from the makers of WebSTAR is a powerful, but costly, solution for providing email services on the Mac OS. See **www.starnine.com/ mail/mail.html** for more information.

Providing Mailing List Services

A *mailing list server*, often called a *listserv*, is a program that manages and sends email to lists of subscribers and provides email on demand. For example, you could have one email address such as **staff@mycompany.com** and be able to send a message to dozens, hundreds, or thousands of people by entering this single address. These mailing lists can be public or private, and can be configured to allow people to subscribe and unsubscribe themselves, as well as to post messages to the list. These servers can also allow you to provide email-on-demand services, which allow people to send email to the server and have the server reply to the requests with information, documents, and attachments.

EIMS and other mail servers contain basic mailing list capabilities, but they often are not robust enough to meet the needs of large or complex lists, and they do not offer email-on-demand and other services.

Macjordomo

Macjordomo is freeware, but don't be fooled because it is free: Macjordomo meets the needs of almost all organizations requiring an Internet list server. A product of Leuca Software and the Office of Academic Computing at Cornell Medical College, Macjordomo is extremely easy to set up and requires a POP3/SMTP email server (such as EIMS) to handle the actual mail delivery. Macjordomo serves as an intelligent email client that responds to email sent to one or more of its accounts. Its requirements include:

- 68K or PowerPC processor

- 2MB of application memory

- 1MB disk space, plus space for list messages and archives

- Internet connection

- POP3 server (such as EIMS)

See **leuca.med.cornell.edu/Macjordomo** for more information and software downloads.

The configuration options for Macjordomo are powerful and not nearly as complex as ListSTAR, which we'll discuss next. To use Macjordomo, download it from the Web, install it, and follow these steps:

1. Choose Edit|Prefrerences and make a few choices about message processing, character wrapping, and a few others (see Figure 13.17).

2. Choose Lists|New List to create a new mailing list, such as the one shown in Figure 13.18.

3. Edit the General settings for the new list, as well as any advanced settings that may be required for your needs.

4. Create an account on a mail server that will accept and distribute mail sent to and from the list, such as an EIMS account.

13: Providing Internet, Intranet, And Extranet Services

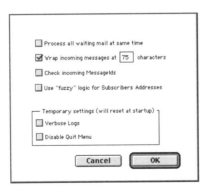

Figure 13.17   Macjordomo has few general preferences, making it a snap to get started.

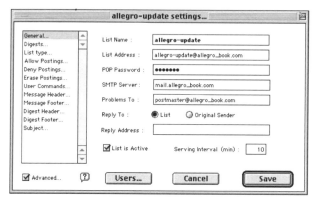

Figure 13.18   Creating lists is very easy with Macjordomo.

Macjordomo has a very easy-to-use interface not only for configuring mailing lists, but also for general listserv management. Figure 13.19 shows one such management option, the default error message that is sent to new subscribers of a mailing list. You may edit the text of the message, but you must not rename the LISTNAME variable because this response message is used with multiple subscriptions.

ListSTAR

StarNine, the makers of WebSTAR, offers two versions of its powerful and popular ListSTAR server, and demo versions are downloadable from its Web site at **www.starnine.com/liststar/liststar.html** (you must register for a demo key as well):

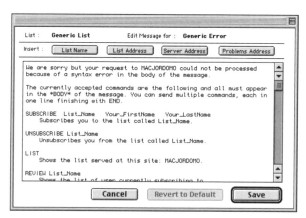

Figure 13.19   Macjordomo mailing list subscription response configuration, showing the default (but editable) error message.

- ListSTAR for SMTP

- ListSTAR for POP

The ListSTAR for SMTP version is the most powerful of the two; the estimated retail price is $499. ListSTAR for SMTP, shown in the examples that follow, is an incredibly powerful and highly configurable list server. Dozens and dozens of configuration options are possible, so rather than going into detail on all of them, we'll show you a few examples.

To get started, download a demo version, install it, and follow these steps:

1. Edit the ListSTAR Preferences by choosing Windows|General Preferences, as in Figure 13.20, and configure the listserver for logging, naming, enclosures, status window display options, and SMTP and TCP/IP configuration options.

2. Open the ListSTAR Services window and create a new SMTP (mailing list) or timer (time-based trigger) service.

3. Name the services and add rules for the processing of the list. Each list or timer can have many rules, and each rule has several sections.

Each mailing list or timer is governed by a set of rules that control which messages will be received by the server and how they will be acted upon. For example, Figure 13.21 shows one rule that tells the server what to do when someone sends mail to the list with the subject "subscribe digest" or "set digest".

The Content section of the rule looks for certain information in the header, body, or attachment of a message. Subsequent portions of the rule look for information in the address it is to or from, how to reply to the message sent to the list, which mailing list or timer the message might be associated with, and several miscellaneous rules that tell the server to stop processing a message or execute an AppleScript if certain conditions are met.

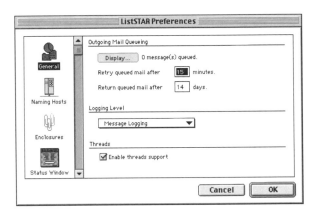

Figure 13.20   A few of the many general configuration options for ListSTAR.

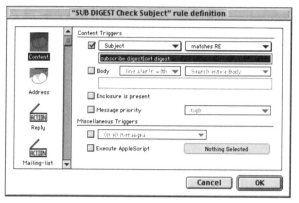

Figure 13.21   An example of one rule for a ListSTAR mailing list.

This gets complex, but it's necessary because ListSTAR can accommodate every imaginable situation relating to a mailing list. Basically, each list has many, many configuration options and—depending on what type of message is sent to the list—triggers one or more actions by the server. ListSTAR comes with some handy AppleScripts that assist in the creation of the most popular types of services (lists); after you have a few created, it's easy to copy the service and create new services based on the copied one.

The email-on-demand features of ListSTAR and Macjordomo are especially useful for communicating with people who may not have full Internet connectivity and access to the Web. By using email on demand and mailing lists, you can easily share most of the same information to which Web surfers have access with those (unfortunate) people who cannot surf. Many service providers and BBS operators don't provide the SLIP, PPP, and ISDN access needed to have full Internet access, so don't overlook advertising your listserv to these communities.

Providing FTP Services

FTP is used to transfer files from one computer to another using TCP/IP. FTP used to be the workhorse protocol on the Internet before the Web became the top dog. Several good FTP server options have been available for the Mac OS for many years; let's look at three that are sure to meet just about everyone's needs.

Better Telnet (NCSA FTP)

The easiest—and cheapest—FTP server is part of Better Telnet, formerly known as NCSA Telnet, which, though a little outdated, is still one of the few free FTP servers available. Better Telnet is easy to configure and has a minuscule memory footprint, taking only about a one megabyte of RAM. See **www.cstone. net/ ~rbraun/mac/telnet/** for the latest version, then follow these steps to provide FTP services:

1. Launch BetterTelnet and choose Edit|FTP Server, shown in Figure 13.22, and configure the FTP server. The NCSA FTP server has very basic control options and three levels of functionality:

   • Off

   • On, with no passwords needed

   • On, with username and passwords required

   It allows you to select the default text and binary transfer file creator type, as well as to use MacBinary II, which is helpful when communicating with older Macs.

2. Add users via Edit|FTP Users (see Figure 13.23). Users are assigned a unique username, encrypted password, and a default directory. Unlike more sophisticated FTP servers, however, it isn't possible to restrict users to certain areas of the server's hard drive.

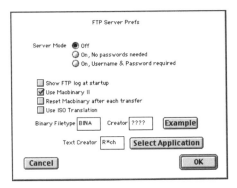

Figure 13.22 NCSA FTP server preferences.

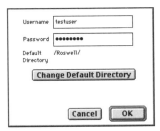

Figure 13.23 Adding a user to the NCSA FTP server.

Anonymous FTP

Anonymous FTP refers to an account on an FTP server that anyone can access. Anonymous FTP is very useful for distributing software and data files to the general public, but it also has its risks. If access restrictions are improperly configured, it is possible to accidentally grant too many privileges to tens of millions of Internet users, many of whom would like to see—and possibly erase—the contents of your server.

It's proper netiquette to request that anonymous FTP users employ the user ID "anonymous" and use their actual email address as a password. Most FTP servers keep a log file of anonymous visitors, so if anything goes wrong with their server, they have a detailed account of who was on their server, when, where they looked for information, and for how long. Of course, it's easy to misrepresent yourself when doing anonymous FTP by entering a false email address during login, but we wouldn't recommend this because a log file can contain visitors' IP names and numbers, which goes a long way toward tracking them down.

NetPresenz FTP Server

If you require a more secure FTP server, try Peter Lewis's $10 shareware program NetPresenz, formerly FTPd. NetPresenz is an FTP/Web/Gopher server that uses the Mac OS's built-in file sharing capabilities to control user access and restrictions through two programs, a setup application and an FTP daemon. To get the latest version of NetPresenz, see **www.stairways.com/netpresenz**, then follow these steps:

1. Because NetPresenz relies on Apple's file sharing for configuration and security, you must first go into the File Sharing control panel and configure your Mac for file sharing, then create a user in the Users & Groups control panel.

2. Next, launch NetPresenz and go to the FTP Setup window, where general access privileges and miscellaneous FTP-server settings are made, as shown in Figure 13.24. Note that users are categorized into three groups—Owner, Users, and Guests—as in file sharing, and that no place is available to edit usernames and passwords.

3. Go to the FTP Users configuration window, shown in Figure 13.25, where you can customize login directories and commands on a user-by-user basis.

4. Finally, review the Security options (Figure 13.26), where you have control over read, write, delete, and copy access to directories (defined through Apple file sharing) and files, as well as logging. One interesting feature is the capability to speak messages or play sounds during FTP sessions to inform the administrator about FTP activity!

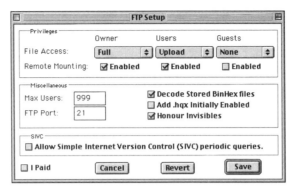

Figure 13.24   NetPresenz FTP Setup options.

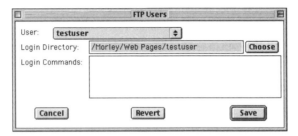

Figure 13.25   Customizing a user's login directory and commands.

Figure 13.26   NetPresenz security settings.

Note: *NetPresenz uses AppleShare's "Guest" account restrictions to control anonymous FTP.*

---

5. Launch the NetPresenz application.

Note that the Apple file sharing user Guest is the equivalent of an anonymous FTP user in NetPresenz, and that you must check the Remote Mounting checkbox (refer to Figure 13.23) to allow anonymous FTP.

Rumpus

The most powerful solution to providing FTP on the Mac OS is Rumpus from Maxum Development, a demo version of which is on this book's accompanying CD-ROM. Rumpus is unique among FTP servers for the Mac OS for several reasons:

- Rumpus is an Open Transport-native FTP server.
- It can use file sharing users and groups without File Sharing being turned on.
- It has the capability to automatically encode files, using MacBinary and Binhex.
- It supports more than 32 simultaneous connections.

Rumpus is easy to set up and provides for several different levels of FTP security. To get started using Rumpus, you'll need a computer running the Mac OS that meets the following criteria:

- System 7.5 or higher
- 3MB free RAM
- 1MB disk space for the application
- MacTCP or Open Transport

Rumpus is very easy to start using. Here's all you need to do:

1. Launch Rumpus and configure is the Basic Configuration tab, shown in Figure 13.27.

   This is where you'll set all the most important configuration options except the security options, discussed next. In the Basic tab, you need to decide the following:

   - The location of the root FTP directory, which can be anywhere on your system.

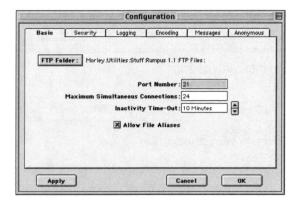

Figure 13.27   The Basic Configuration tab for Rumpus.

- The port that will be used by Rumpus (the default is 21).

- The maximum number of simultaneous connections Rumpus will accept before denying access to incoming connection requests. Version 1 of Rumpus allows up to 32 connections.

- The maximum number of simultaneous anonymous users, which should never be set to equal the total number of simultaneous connections because you need to reserve one or more authenticated connections for important persons like yourself or other FTP site administrators.

- Whether Rumpus will follow aliases outside the root FTP folder.

2. Open the Security tab, shown in Figure 13.28. Pay special attention because Rumpus provides a new paradigm for FTP server security. Rumpus acts more like a Web server because it uses a common folder from which files and aliases to folders are served, rather than strict file sharing. The Security tab allows you to select:

- Anonymous Login Only—This option tells Rumpus to ignore any or all File Sharing users and groups.

- Users & Groups Security—This option allows you to use the file-sharing database for authentication without having it running.

- Built-in Security—This option uses Rumpus's own security features.

3. Configure the Logging, Encoding, Messages, and Anonymous Configuration tabs.

4. If you use Built-In security, you need to open the Define Users window, shown in Figure 13.29, and create user accounts for each user.

Rumpus is easy to learn and really does provide much greater flexibility than do other FTP servers for the Mac OS.

Figure 13.28 The Security Configuration tab for Rumpus.

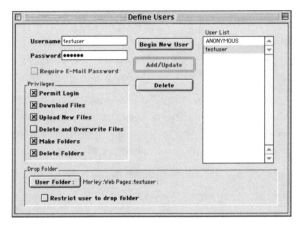

Figure 13.29   The Rumpus user account manager.

Providing Gopher Services

Gopher servers for the Mac aren't as plentiful as FTP and Web servers, and, once again, most of them come as part of a multi-server package. Gopher usage has been decreasing in proportion to the increase of Web server usage because the Web is capable of delivering the same file-searching and retrieving features with a more cross-platform interface. However, Gopher servers have their place on the Internet, and we think that you have at least two good options to choose from to host a Gopher server on your Mac: Peter Lewis's NetPresenz and GopherSurfer from the University of Minnesota.

Note: For the latest information on Internet Gopher servers and clients, see the University of Minnesota's Mother Gopher at **gopher://gopher.tc.umn.edu**.

NetPresenz Gopher Server

Configuring NetPresenz for Gopher access entails only one optional step more than for FTP access setup.

1. Launch the NetPresenz Setup application and select the Gopher Setup tab. Figure 13.30 shows the Gopher Setup options, which are all optional because these settings are read from the file-sharing setup.

2. Launch the NetPresenz application.

Note that, as with anonymous FTP, the Guest user account must be enabled in the Users and Groups Control Panel.

Figure 13.30   NetPresenz Gopher server setup.

GopherSurfer

GopherSurfer is a freeware Gopher server for the Mac OS from the University of Minnesota, home of the Gopher. See **gopher://boombox.micro.umn.edu:70/11/ gopher/Mac_server/** for the latest version.

GopherSurfer requires about 1MB of RAM and has several more configuration options than does NetPresenz.

To configure GopherSurfer, take these steps:

1. Launch GopherSurfer and select Gopher|Configure.

2. Configure the elements in the upper half of the window. Then, select the Other Preferences pop-up menu and configure any additional options. Figure 13.31 shows the main configuration options for GopherSurfer.

GopherSurfer allows from 1 to 50 simultaneous connections. Along with the host name and path to the base directory (Published Folder), these are the only settings you'll need to change to start running a Gopher server on your Mac when using GopherSurfer.

Host Name:	gopher.allegro_book.com
Host Port:	70 ☐ Run Gopher Server
Connections Allowed:	7 ⬦
Published Folder:	GopherSurfer1.1b3r2 folder
	Change
Other Preferences:	Gopher+ Server Attributes ⬦
Administrator:	Team Gopher, University of Minnesota +1
Organization:	Computer & Information Systems,
Site:	152 Shepherd Labs, 100 Union Street S.E.
Location:	Minneapolis, MN. 55455 USA
Latitude/Longitude:	44 58 48 N 93 15 49 W
Abstract:	Tell the world what is unique about your server in this box.

Figure 13.31   GopherSurfer Configuration preferences options.

13: Providing Internet, Intranet, And Extranet Services

Chapter 14

AppleScript

In Depth

Many people don't rely on AppleScript on a daily basis, but those of us that do just can't live without it. If you're one of these people, you can share the good news about AppleScript in Mac OS 8.5. Not only is it PowerPC-native, which makes it faster than previous versions, but it contains other improvements. This chapter explores all the fundamentals of AppleScript, as well as everything that's new in the latest version.

The Usefulness Of Scripting

Scripting has been around for a long time, and just about every major operating system has some type of scripting facility. Scripting under Mac OS 8.5 allows you to automate repetitive tasks and allows programmers to create intricate solutions and even build entire applications by using sophisticated scripts. Scripting also allows you to easily access application features such as printing, as well as to manage Finder elements such as files, folders, and windows.

For example, suppose that you have a Web site that contains a few thousand documents and you need to edit them to replace the name of your company's main product, SuperGizmo, with its new name, SuperUltraGizmo, Deluxe Edition. No problem, because AppleScript can handle that with ease. However, suppose you only want to change the name of the product in documents that also contain the name of your competitor's product, Very Fast Special Gizmo, Standard Edition. AppleScript can help you do this with the assistance of a special scripting addition called an Open Scripting Architecture Extension (OSAX) or with the assistance of an application that is scriptable, such as BBEdit.

More complex uses of AppleScript are everyday occurrences in the publishing industry, where AppleScripts are used with applications such as QuarkXPress to provide time-saving operations on image files. AppleScripts crop, filter, and apply special effects to batches of images, then send them to a printer. Tasks like these can take hours and require a graphic artist to stand by to make the operation continue, but an AppleScript can do it automatically and free up the artist to do other tasks.

Network managers can use AppleScripts to automate configuration tasks, delete unwanted files on users' computers, restore files that were unintentionally deleted, and perform any number of repetitive tasks. When combined with a *rapid*

14: AppleScript

application development (RAD) tool such as FaceSpan, you can even create entire applications by using AppleScript, complete with a user interface.

You also can use AppleScript to extract information from scriptable databases, such as FileMaker Pro, and to create Common Gateway Interfaces (CGIs) on Web servers.

Most users can see the immediate usefulness of AppleScript on a daily basis as a tool to create shortcuts for tasks such as finding a URL and opening the appropriate helper application, organizing files and folders, and controlling file sharing. The great thing about scripting, then, is that it is both powerful and very useful for even the most basic tasks.

What's New In AppleScript 1.3

Mac OS 8.5 includes version 1.3 of AppleScript, which is good news to those of us who were worried that Apple had forsaken further AppleScript development after version 1.1.2 and Mac OS 8.1. The latest version of AppleScript has several improvements and new features, which are summarized as follows:

- *PowerPC-native code*—AppleScript is now completely PowerPC-native and substantially faster than previous versions. The AppleEvents that are passed by the scripts to the Mac OS and scriptable applications, however, are not themselves PowerPC-native.

- *Revised dictionaries*—The scripting dictionaries for OS-level components such as the Finder have been streamlined and reorganized to make them easier to use.

- *Centralization of scripts*—You can now store all your scripts in the Scripts folder in the System Folder, where they are automatically moved when dropped onto the System Folder.

- *New scriptable components*—Several additional or new components have been made scriptable, including:
  - Appearance (control panel)
  - Apple Menu Options (control panel)
  - File Exchange (control panel)
  - Location Manager (control panel)
  - Application Switcher (extension)
  - ColorSync (extension)
  - Network Setup Scripting (faceless application)
  - Apple Help Viewer (application)

14: AppleScript

- Apple System Profiler (application)
- Desktop Printer Manager (application)
- Sherlock (application)

- *Consolidated OSAXen*—Scripting extensions (also called scripting additions) from Apple, such as Beep, Choose Application, and New File, have been consolidated into a single OSAX called Standard Additions.

- *New features*—The Standard Additions OSAX also includes several new features:

  - *Clipboard commands*—The clipboard, set the clipboard to, and clipboard information.

  - *Delaying a script*—Allows you to delay or pause a script without affecting other processes.

  - *List commands*—Present users with list-selection options.

  - *Mount remote volumes*—Mount one of more volumes on a server.

  - *Speech*—Have the computer speak from a script.

  - *Summarize text*—Reads and summarizes a document using a specific number of lines in the summary.

  - *Times dialogs*—Set the amount of time a dialog box will stay open before automatically closing.

- *New units of measurement*—Measure and convert between English and metric equivalents for length, weight, volume (liquid and solid), area, and temperature.

- *CGI suite*—Adds support for Common gateway Interface (CGI) events.

- *Folder actions*—Also known as attachable Finder folders, allow you to attach an AppleScript to a folder and have that script triggered when the folder is:

  - Opened
  - Closed
  - Added to
  - Deleted from
  - Moved or resized

- *Unicode support*

- *Path To commands*—Reserve many new folder names for System Folder contents for easier scripting, including Apple Menu, Apple Menu Items, Apple Menu Items Folder, Application Support, Application Support Folder, At Ease

Applications, At Ease Applications Folder, At Ease Documents, At Ease Documents Folder, Control Panels, Control Panels Folder, Control Strip Modules, Control Strip Modules Folder, Desktop, Desktop Folder, Desktop Pictures Folder, Editors, Editors Folder, Extensions, Extensions Folder, Folder Action Scripts, Folder Action Scripts Folder, Fonts, Fonts Folder, Frontmost Application, Help, Help Folder, Internet Plugins, Internet Plugins Folder, Launcher Items Folder, Modem Scripts, Modem Scripts Folder, Plugins, Preferences, Preferences Folder, Printer Descriptions, Printer Descriptions Folder, Printer Drivers, Printer Drivers Folder, Printmonitor, Printmonitor Folder, Scripting Additions, Scripting Additions Folder, Scripts Folder, Shared Libraries, Shared Libraries Folder, Shutdown, Shutdown Items, Shutdown Items Folder, Speakable Items, Startup (Startup Items), Startup Items Folder, Startup Disk, Stationery, Stationery Folder, System Folder, Temporary Items, Temporary Items Folder, Trash, Trash Folder, Voices, Voices Folder.

The only caveat with AppleScript 1.3 is that it is not backward-compatible with earlier versions of the Mac OS and AppleScript. Scripts that work in Mac OS 8.5 and AppleScript 1.3 are not guaranteed to work with previous versions of the Mac OS and AppleScript. AppleScript 1.3 will not work at all in earlier versions of the Mac OS.

AppleScript Components

Mac OS 8.5 has very few AppleScript components in Mac OS 8.5, but you can add many scripting additions and components from the Mac OS 8.5 CD-ROM and from third-party developers. The basic components of AppleScript include:

- *AppleScript extension*—Located in the System Folder, allows the Mac OS to interpret AppleEvents and AppleScripts.

- *AppleScriptLib extension*—Located in the System Folder, contains library routines necessary for AppleScript to function.

- *Scripting Additions folder*—Located in the System Folder; contains scripting extensions, additions, and applications used by AppleScript to provide added functionality (see Figure 14.1).

- *Scripts folder*—Located in the System Folder; serves as a central location for scripts (see Figure 14.2).

- *Script Editor*—Located in the AppleScript folder in the Apple Extras folder, writes, edits, and records AppleScripts and other Open Scripting Architecture (OSA)-compliant scripts (see Figure 14.3).

Figure 14.1   The Scripting Additions folder.

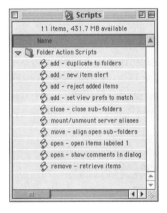

Figure 14.2   The Scripts folder.

Figure 14.3   The Script Editor (and sample scripts).

You can install additional scripting components—which we'll discuss later—in various locations on your hard drive, but for the most part, they will be automatically placed in the Scripts and Scripting Additions folders.

How AppleScript Works

AppleScript is actually an object-oriented programming language that works by interpreting English-like commands into AppleEvents and passing them to the appropriate application or to the Mac OS. The AppleScript commands are interpreted by the AppleScript extension and library, as well as any AppleScript extensions or additions (OSAXen) that are installed on your computer. Basic scripts that rely on the standard suite of OSAXen work on any computer with the full installation of AppleScript, but scripts that rely on special OSAXen do not function properly (or at all) on computers that lack these OSAXen.

AppleScripts work in conjunction with portions of the Mac OS and applications that have been written to be AppleScript-compatible. AppleScript compatibility has three levels:

- *Scriptable applications*—Applications that understand AppleScript commands.
- *Attachable applications*—Applications that contain elements to which AppleScripts can be attached, such as buttons.
- *Recordable applications*—Applications for which AppleScripts can be created by using the Record feature rather than having to write AppleScript code.

Few applications are recordable to the point of being truly useful, so most AppleScripts are written manually for applications that are scriptable or scriptable and attachable.

Scripting The Mac OS

Many elements of the Mac OS are scriptable, in addition to the new elements previously described, and many of the best applications for the Mac OS are scriptable in varying degrees. However, some elements of the Mac OS are still not scriptable. The AppleScript folder contains several example scripts that perform actions in the Finder and various control panels. The folders that contain these sample scripts are named *Automated Tasks*, and *More Automated Tasks*, as shown in Figure 14.4.

14: AppleScript

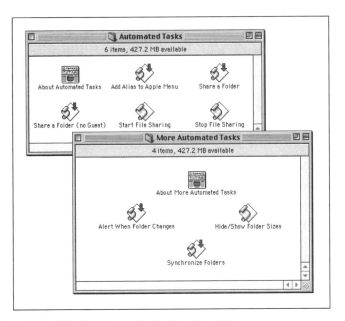

Figure 14.4   Sample AppleScripts for scripting the Mac OS.

Basic scripts can turn file sharing on and off and select user-interface configuration preferences such as themes, fonts, and Desktop patterns. However, most users will want to explore the new folder action scripts listed previously. We'll look at these in detail later in the "Immediate Solutions" part of this chapter. In addition to the Finder, which is scriptable, Table 14.1 lists the control panels and their scriptability in a standard Desktop installation of Mac OS 8.5:

We'll look at several elements of the Finder that are scriptable shortly, but assume for now that future releases of the Mac OS will probably incorporate more scriptability.

Scripting Applications

Many applications for the Mac OS that are current have been made scriptable, including Microsoft Internet Explorer and Outlook Express, but others have not. It is up to the individual software developer to decide whether to support AppleScript, but if you or your organization rely on AppleScript, choose products that are scriptable and let vendors know that AppleScript is a critical feature.

Table 14.1   Control panels in Mac OS 8.5 and their scriptability.

Control Panel	Scriptable?
Appearance	Yes
Apple Menu Items	Yes
AppleTalk	No
ColorSync	No
Control Strip	No
Date & Time	No
DialAssist	No
Energy Saver	No
Extension Manager	No
File Exchange	Yes
File Sharing	Yes
General Controls	No
Internet	No
Keyboard	No
Location Manager	Yes
Launcher	No
Memory	No
Modem	No
Monitors & Sound	No
Mouse	No
Numbers	No
QuickTime Settings	No
Remote Access	No
Speech	No
Startup Disk	No
TCP/IP	No
Text	No
Users & Groups	Yes
Web Sharing	Yes

14: AppleScript

Alternatives To AppleScript

Currently, only one alternative to AppleScript that is also OSA-compliant is available, Frontier from UserLand (**www.userland.com**), but it is now more a Web-based solution than an alternative to AppleScript. Another product that uses AppleScript is FaceSpan (**www.facespan.com**), a robust application development environment that allows developers to place Mac-like interfaces, including dialog boxes and windows, on top of AppleScripts. FaceSpan is a very cool tool to have if you want to distribute AppleScript-based solutions to others and if you need users to have a familiar user interface environment.

Several alternatives to Apple's Script Editor are also available. This editor is very basic when compared to programs such as Scriptor from Main Event (**www.mainevent.com**). Scriptor is our editor of choice because it goes well beyond the capabilities of Script Editor, especially in its capability to debug scripts. We'll look at Scriptor alongside Script Editor later in the chapter.

Immediate Solutions

The following sections explain how to perform the most common tasks in AppleScript and discuss several tools that are essential for scripting under the Mac OS.

Identifying Scriptable Applications

Since not all applications and elements of the Mac OS are scriptable, one of the first tasks you need to perform is to identify what is scriptable and what is not. You can currently employ several ways to identify scriptability in an application or the Mac OS using Script Editor or another editor, such as Scriptor. Each of these methods entails opening the application's scripting dictionary where the scripting commands are stored.

Open The Dictionary Using Script Editor

The Script Editor can open a scripting dictionary in two ways. The first way is through the File menu, as follows:

1. Launch Script Editor and choose File|Open Dictionary.

2. Select an application or OS component that appears in the Open dialog, as in Figure 14.5.

3. The dictionary will open in Script Editor (see Figure 14.6).

Only those items containing dictionaries will appear in the dialog window. For example, if you choose File|Open Script instead of File|Open Dictionary, nothing will appear.

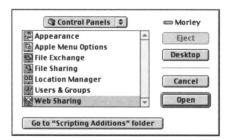

Figure 14.5   Opening a scripting dictionary by using Script Editor.

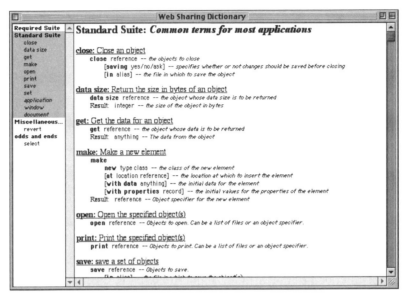

Figure 14.6   An example of a scripting dictionary, with several elements selected.

You can also drag and drop an application or OS component onto the Script Editor icon to determine if it is scriptable. If it is scriptable, the dictionary will open in the Script Editor. If it is not, an information dialog box will open with an error message, such as the one shown in Figure 14.7.

Open The Dictionary Using Scriptor

You can also use Scriptor to open a scripting dictionary, which does a much better job displaying the information than does Script Editor. To open a scripting dictionary:

1. Launch Scriptor and choose Apps|Other Dictionary.

2. Like Script Editor, Scriptor only displays selection options for items that are scriptable. Select an item.

3. The dictionary opens in Scriptor (see Figure 14.8).

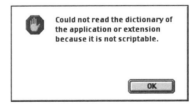

Figure 14.7   Unscriptable applications generate this error when dropped onto the Script Editor application icon.

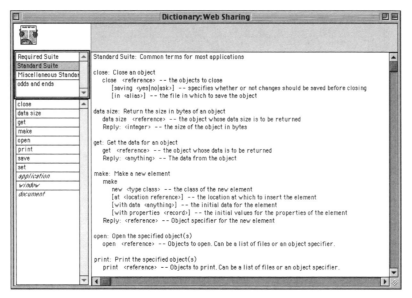

Figure 14.8   Scriptor displays scripting dictionaries in a more intuitive way than does Script Editor.

Working With Editors

Once you've identified an application's scripting dictionary, you can proceed to write, edit, and record scripts using an editor such as Script Editor or Scriptor. AppleScript has been around long enough for you to be familiar with Script Editor, which hasn't changed much over the past few years. If you're new to Scriptor, however, pay attention because it is an essential tool to have for any level of user: beginner, intermediate, or advanced.

Working With Script Editor

Script Editor is a very basic scripting tool that lets you perform the following tasks:

• View dictionaries

• Create, edit, and save scripts

• Do basic debugging

Figure 14.9 shows a sample script in the Script Editor that activates file sharing and performs several steps along the way.

14: AppleScript

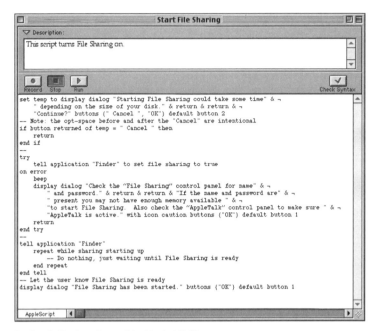

Figure 14.9   An AppleScript viewed in Script Editor.

The Script Editor has a simple interface and using it to edit a script is straightforward. The editor window is divided into two sections. The top portion of the window is used to write a description of the script, or whatever the script's author wants to include, such as instructions or background notes.

The lower portion of the window contains the script, as well as buttons for the following:

- Recording a script
- Stopping recording or playing back a script
- Running the current script
- Checking the syntax of the script

Working With Scriptor

Scriptor is much more powerful than Script Editor and has dozens of features, too many in fact to even begin to cover here. When comparing it to Script Editor, you'll quickly see that it is a comprehensive scripting tool, not just a script editor. For example, Figure 14.10 shows the same script as in the previous figure opened in Scriptor.

Figure 14.10   A sample script in Scriptor.

Scriptor allows you to perform all the same tasks as in Script Editor, and it allows you to do the following:

- Debug scripts in detail

- Build custom scripting additions

- Build databases of coding shortcuts

- Customize your scripting environment with multiple palettes for shortcuts and assembly tools

- Perform mature search and replace

- Do multiple undos

The demo version of Scriptor that comes on the companion CD-ROM for this book is fully functional, except that it will not allow you to save your work. However, you can use its many features, including:

- *The application bar*—Adds quick access to your favorite scriptable applications, such as BBEdit.

- *Builders*—Builds scripting additions for an application (see Figure 14.11).

- *A tools palette*—Shortcuts to commonly used scripting tools and commands, such as commenting and searching scripts.

- *Collection*—A central location for your more frequently used scripts (see Figure 14.12).

- *Command tool*—Executes a short command quickly as a reference tool to help debug scripts (see Figure 4.13).

14: AppleScript

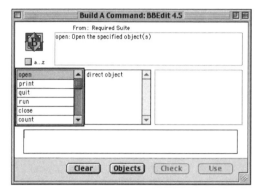

Figure 14.11   A builder for BBEdit in Scriptor.

Figure 14.12   Use the Collection feature to store your frequently used scripts for quick reference or execution.

Figure 14.13   The Command tool.

Recording Scripts

The best way for new users of AppleScript to learn how it works is to create a script by recording a few simple Finder actions. Remember, the Finder is scriptable as well as recordable, so creating a script is very easy. The following examples create a script that performs several actions on a folder in the Finder.

Recording In Script Editor

To record a script using Script Editor, follow these steps:

1. Open the Apple Extras folder on your hard drive and select ViewlAs Icons, then move it so it is easily visible on the Desktop.

2. Launch Script Editor and click on the Record button that appears in the window of the untitled window, as in Figure 14.14.

3. Select the Apple Extras folder on the Desktop.

4. Choose ViewlAs List.

5. Click on the Zoom box in the Apple Extras folder window.

6. Choose ViewlAs Pop-up Window.

7. Click on the Close box.

8. Return to the Script Editor by choosing it from the Application menu or by clicking anywhere in the open script.

9. Click on the Stop button to end recording.

Script Editor will automatically check the syntax of the script and display the results of your recording in the untitled window, shown in Figure 14.15.

Because not all actions are recordable in the Finder or in any application, some of your actions may not be recorded and will therefore not appear in your script. All the actions in this example are recorded, however.

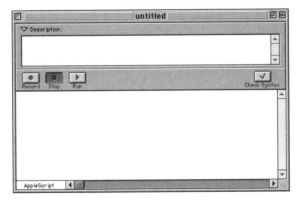

Figure 14.14   Preparing to record a script.

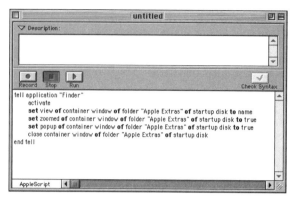

Figure 14.15   A newly recorded AppleScript.

Recording In Scriptor

Scriptor records scripts just as Script Editor does, but uses different commands. To perform the same task as in the previous example, follow these steps:

1. Launch Script Editor and choose Script|Record.

2. Follow the same Finder actions in the example above.

3. Return to Script Editor and choose Script|Stop. Figure 14.16 shows the results of the recording, which produces exactly the same script code as does Script Editor.

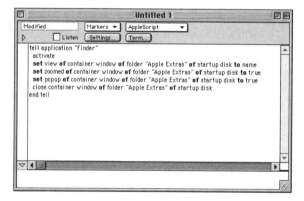

Figure 14.16   Recording a script in Scriptor.

Writing Scripts

AppleScripts can be very easy or they can be sufficiently complex that only a seasoned programmer can completely understand them. We've already mentioned the sample scripts that come as part of the standard AppleScript installation (Automated Tasks and More Automated Tasks). They give a good overview of the basics of AppleScript usage, but the mechanics of a script rely on at least three things:

- The level of scriptability programmed into an application by its creators

- The scripting dictionary and documentation of its scripting commands

- Any scripting additions or extensions that may be present and can influence the scriptability of an application

For example, look at the result of the script we just recorded:

```
tell application "Finder"
  activate
  set view of container window of folder "Apple Extras" of startup disk to
  name
  set zoomed of container window of folder "Apple Extras" of startup disk to
  true
  set popup of container window of folder "Apple Extras" of startup disk to
  true
  close container window of folder "Apple Extras" of startup disk
end tell
```

AppleScript is referred to as an *object-oriented language*, which means it uses commands (such as open, close, change, or print) to act upon objects (such as windows, selected words, or interface features). These commands are listed in the scripting dictionary and the objects are grouped into logic units referred to as *object classes*. Commands and objects are described by using *expressions* (collections of values) and are capable of performing simple (*unary*) and complex (*binary*) operations, such as simple math or algebraic calculations.

In our example, the Finder is commanded to change the *value* (view as name) of certain *objects* (windows) and then perform other commands as well (close container window). So, on one hand, AppleScript is easy enough to learn to record basic scripts, but it's also a highly complex object-oriented programming language that is most powerful when used by experienced programmers; it's limited only by the software developers who choose to make their products scriptable.

14: AppleScript

Debugging Scripts

Because AppleScript is a programming language, you must ensure that your code is free of all errors before your scripts can be properly used. Errors can occur as the result of several things, including:

- Bad syntax and inaccurate usage of commands
- Misplaced variables
- Typographical errors
- Circular logic

Fortunately for most of us, Script Editor and Scriptor provide various levels of debugging to help programmers correct problems such as these.

Debugging In Script Editor

Script Editor provides only a very basic level of code debugging execution error reporting called *syntax checking*. To generate some test errors, take these steps:

1. Make the Apple Extras folder into a pop-up window, then check the syntax of the script. Because the folder is already a pop-up window, the script will fail because it doesn't contain any IF-THEN logic to take into account that the folder is already a pop-up window.

2. Open the script we just recorded.

3. Click on the Run button and Script Editor will generate an error like the one shown in Figure 14.17.

In addition to this warning, you can also view the Event Log, which logs both successful and unsuccessful scripting activities. To view the Event Log:

1. Run the script.

2. Choose Controls|Open Event Log, an example of which is shown in Figure 14.18.

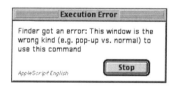

Figure 14.17   A typical execution error warning from Script Editor.

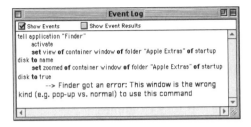

Figure 14.18   Errors are recorded in the Event Log.

Script Editor also has a basic syntax-checking feature, which you can use by following these steps:

1. Open the script we just recorded.

2. Change the first instance of the command **set** to a nonsensical term like **setter**.

3. Click on the Check Syntax button and Script Editor will generate an error like the one shown in Figure 14.19.

Finally, you can use one other feature in Script Editor called the *Result window* to debug your scripts. To view the Result window:

1. Open any script.

2. Run the script.

3. Choose Controls|Show Result.

The Result window will only display the result of successful scripts, which can help you refine steps taken in the script and optimize it accordingly (see Figure 4.20).

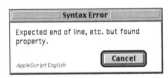

Figure 14.19   Script Editor's syntax checking feature returns results like this.

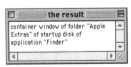

Figure 14.20   The Result window.

Debugging In Scriptor

Scriptor has all the capabilities of Script Editor—and more—when debugging. Our favorite feature is its capability to step through a script one line at a time, checking syntax and debugging along the way. To debug a script in Scriptor:

1. Open a script that either contains a known error or performs an illegal operation, as in the previous examples.

2. Choose Script|Step to step through the script one line at a time, or Script|Auto Step to move through the script automatically until it encounters an error. Figure 14.21 shows the script window with an arrow beside the last line to be successfully executed.

3. When Scriptor encounters an error, a dialog appears asking you to bring Scriptor to the foreground, then another dialog details the error.

4. When you switch back to Scriptor, a red X points to the line that contains the error, as shown in Figure 14.22.

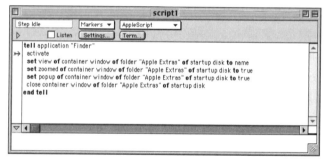

Figure 14.21   Scriptor uses visual clues like this arrow to indicate good and bad lines of code.

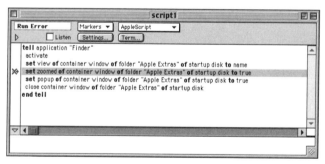

Figure 14.22   Scriptor reports errors like this to help identify problematic code.

Saving Scripts

One of the cooler things about AppleScript is that you can create several different type of scripts from the same code base. In AppleScript 1.3, you can create:

- *Scripts*—ASCII text files that other editors can open in their native dialect.

- *Applications*—Standalone programs that can be launched and executed (like any other application for the Mac OS), and that are editable in their original dialect.

- *Compiled scripts*—Scripts that have had their dialect removed so that they are executed by AppleScript in a more AppleScript-native format. AppleScript 1.3 only supports the English dialect.

- *Run-Only scripts*—Scripts that are not editable, only executable.

To save a script in Script Editor or Scriptor:

1. Open a script and choose File|Save As or File|Save as Run-Only (Script Editor).

2. In the Save dialog box, select Application, Compiled Script, or Text.

For example, Figure 14.23 shows a script being saved as an application.

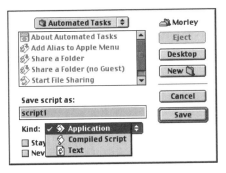

Figure 14.23   Saving a script as an application.

Expanding AppleScript

AppleScript has the wonderful capability to provide a framework that allows programmers, amateur and professional, to create sophisticated inter-application communication. Here are two useful resources for expanding AppleScript that you can download from Apple's Web site. The two resources in the following section, "AppleScript CD-ROM Extras," are included on the Mac OS 8.5 CD-ROM.

14: AppleScript

Apple Data Detectors

Apple Data Detectors (**applescript.apple.com/data_detectors**) is an Apple-Script-based technology that recognizes certain types of data, such as URLs, and provides additional options to users when selected in the Finder or an application such as BBEdit. It is also a framework that allows developers to create different types of detectors—not just URL detectors—that can also be available across applications and in the Finder.

Apple Data Detectors consists of a contextual menu and a control panel that allows you to customize what helper applications to use with the various types of data it can detect. Apple Data Detectors automatically install a module called Internet Address Detectors that can detect several types of URLs, including the following:

- Email addresses
- Web addresses
- Newsgroups
- FTP addresses
- Host addresses

It is easy to install and works by allowing you to select text in an application and activate the contextual menu; then, it displays a set of options. For example, Figure 14.24 shows some text with multiple URLs, one of which is selected to be open with Internet Explorer.

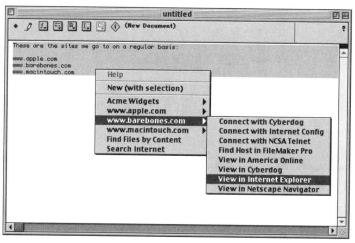

Figure 14.24   An example of how AppleScript and Apple Data Detectors work together to provide easy access to URLs.

14: AppleScript

Acme Contextual Menu Manager

Another cool use of a technology that relies on AppleScript is a collection of Acme Contextual Menu Manager (CMM) Widgets from Acme Technologies (**www.acmetech.com**). Like the Apple Data Detectors, the Acme CMM Widgets provide several additional features to the Contextual menus that are becoming one of the most favored new features of Mac OS 8 and 8.5. For example, the Acme CMM Widgets provide several additional menu options under the Acme Widgets option, which are shown in Figure 14.25, that are very useful for Web developers and Webmasters.

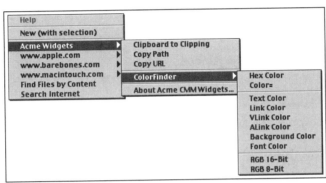

Figure 14.25   The new Contextual menu options added by the Acme CMM Widgets.

AppleScript CD-ROM Extras

The Mac OS 8.5 installation CD-ROM includes three additional items that you can install to learn more about the capabilities of AppleScript. They are not installed by default, so you'll have to locate them on the CD and install them manually (unless they were previously installed as part of a custom installation).

OSA Menu Lite

OSA Menu Lite by Leonard Rosenthol is a program that adds a script menu to all elements of the Mac OS and all applications, even if they have their own script menu (as is the case with BBEdit). Figure 14.26 shows the menu when viewed while in the Finder.

If you rely on AppleScript in your daily work, this is an excellent feature to have.

Script Sets

Another optional installation consists of three collections of scripts that provide functionality and examples for the OSA Menu. The script sets are:

14: AppleScript

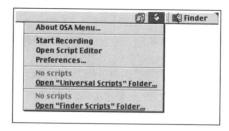

Figure 14.26   The OSA Menu, an optional installation with Mac OS 8.5.

- *Finder Scripts*—Scripts that work in conjunction with the Finder, files, folders, and windows.
- *Script Editor Scripts*—Various scripts for the Script Editor and Finder.
- *Universal Scripts*—Miscellaneous scripts for going to a Web site or selecting a folder or window, for example.

Figure 14.27 shows some of the additional OSA Menu options that are available with the addition of the scripts.

Additional Scripts

Finally, the AppleScript CD-ROM Extras installs a folder entitled More Folder Actions that contains three additional scripts that work in conjunction with the approximately ten scripts installed by AppleScript.

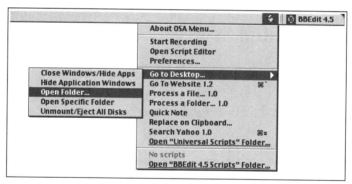

Figure 14.27   Additional OSA Menu options.

Scripting Resources

AppleScript is a huge subject to attempt to cover in this book, so we encourage you to explore the following resources for additional information.

- Apple Computer's AppleScript Web site: **www.apple.com/applescript**
- Everything CD for Macintosh Scripting: **www.isoproductions.com/cd/macscripting**
- ScriptWeb Web site: **www.scriptweb.com**
- The AppleScript Sourcebook Web site: **oasis.bellevue.k12.wa.us/cheeseb/index.html**
- MacScripting Mailing List: **www.dartmouth.edu/info/macscript/mailing-list.html**
- *AppleScript Applications: Building Applications With FaceSpan and AppleScript* (AP Professional, John Schettino, et al, 1996)
- *AppleScript Complete: The Complete Guide for Users and Developers* (MacIntosh Inside Out, Dan Shafer, 1995)
- *AppleScript Finder Guide: English Dialect* (Apple Computer, 1994)
- *AppleScript for Dummies* (IDG, Tom Trinko, 1995)
- *AppleScript Language Guide* (Apple Computer, 1994)
- *AppleScript Scripting Additions Guide* (Apple Computer, 1994)
- *AppleScript Visual Quickstart Guide: AppleScript for Your Desktop and the Internet* (Peachpit Press, Ethan Wilde, 1998)
- *Everyday AppleScript: Connecting Applications Computers and Users* (Addison-Wesley, Christopher Allen, 1996)
- *The Complete AppleScript Handbook* (Addison-Wesley, Danny Goodman, 1993)
- *The Tao of AppleScript* (Hayden Books, Derrick Schneider, 1994)

14: AppleScript

Chapter 15

Java

In Depth

This chapter introduces Java and the Mac OS Runtime for Java. Java is a very important language because it is cross-platform and can be used from the Internet. Java has received more press and public review than any other computer language in history, which has helped Java grow to an even safer and more robust language. The number of developers that have already switched to programming in Java is unprecedented in any language, and the simplicity of Java seems to be attracting those who wouldn't otherwise be programmers. As a result, a huge body of software is available for use by developers and users alike, with more to come in the next few years.

Introducing Java

Java is an object-oriented programming language that is cross-platform because of the *Virtual Machine*, a program that runs Java programs. Just like any other program, the Virtual Machine had to be written differently for Unix, Windows, and the Macintosh. Even so, it has a consistent interface for Java Programs, as shown in Figure 15.1. Java will run on any platform as long as a Virtual Machine is written for that platform. Other programming languages, such as C++, will also run on different platforms. However, with C++, a program must be written with great care for the underlying operating system. Rewriting code for different operating systems, or *porting*, involves a significant time investment. The amount of effort is large because the programmers have to know two operating systems. Using Java, a program has to be written only once rather than being ported to multiple operating systems; also, the Virtual Machine takes care of running the Java application on each specific platform. The Virtual Machine can be considered the operating system, but the Virtual Machine runs on top of the other operating systems and can also be thought of as a co-operating system. A *translator* is a common analogy used to explain the role of a virtual machine. The Virtual Machine has the role of translating calls made from Java into calls on the native operating system. This analogy is useful, but not technically correct. Many scripting languages use a program called a translator that performs this function. Java, however, is compiled into *bytecodes*, which are similar to machine code instructions for a computer chip, except that the bytecodes are designed for the Virtual Machine. The Virtual Machine has its own registers, instruction stack, and Garbage Collector; things that translators don't have. These differences, however, are relatively unimportant to anyone except the computer programmers.

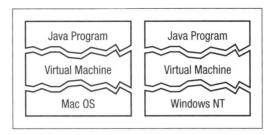

Figure 15.1 Virtual Machine, which takes care of the differences between platforms.

The major Internet browser companies embedded Virtual Machines into the browser itself, allowing Java programs to be run directly from Web pages. Programs that are run in this way are called *applets*, and they are under certain restrictions for security reasons. These restrictions protect the user from malicious applets. They are important and will be discussed in full later in this chapter.

Aside from the Virtual Machine, Java provides a large library of functionality for developers that is referred to as the *Class Library*. Within it, developers find pieces of software that they can easily use to create programs. This library keeps the wheel from having to be reinvented. It also speeds up Internet delivery, because large program elements are already on the your computer. The Class Library was created by taking a cross section of the functionality provided by programming libraries on major operating systems like Macintosh, Windows, and Unix.

Another important Java concept is the *Just In Time Compiler* (JITc), shown in Figure 15.2. This program optimizes Java code as it is running by compiling parts of the Java program into platform-specific code.

The final important concept of Java is the *Native Interface*. This allows Java Programmers to make system calls from Java code, which is especially important to the Mac for several reasons that we will describe in the following section. Allowing system calls from Java removes the capability to transfer from platform to

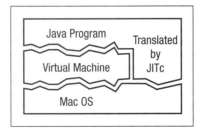

Figure 15.2 The Just In Time Compiler translates cross-platform Java code into platform-specific code. Bypassing the Virtual Machine in this way gives a drastic performance increase.

platform, but not completely. The framework and user interface of a program are still primarily written in Java, with smaller parts of the program specific to the operating system.

Several competing standards for the Native Interface exist. The first edition of Java used a technique known as *Native Methods* to achieve the same thing. The problem was that the Native Methods code was not very portable. Native Methods written for one Virtual Machine would not work on another Virtual Machine, even if the machines were on the same platform. Netscape came out with a solution named *Java Raw Interface* (JRI), and Microsoft released its own solution, *Raw Native Interface* (RNI). RNI's problem is that it is Microsoft-specific; code written with this interface is not portable. Sun gathered a committee, including Microsoft, and created a specification named *Java Native Interface* (JNI). It is largely based on Microsoft's RNI, except that the code written with JNI is portable among Virtual Machines on the same platform. For some reason, although they participated in its creation, Microsoft continues to push developers to use RNI.

Other features of Java include easy-to-use networking, connectivity to databases, and internationalization, which is the ability of a program to automatically display itself in a different way—or even in different languages—for other cultures. All of these enterprise features are keys to a quantum leap in the current state of the Internet.

Mac OS Runtime For Java

Mac OS Runtime for Java (MRJ) is not simply an implementation of Java for the Macintosh. The Runtime environment provides not only the Java Runtime Libraries, but a standalone Apple Applet Runner as well. The Apple Applet Runner program allows you to use applets without having to use a Web browser. This is convenient for several reasons, the foremost being that it takes a relatively long time for the average Web browser to start.

Security is also a concern. When you run an applet from your hard drive, you probably aren't too concerned that it could be harmful, so you will run it without constraints. When you surf the Internet, you want those constraints on. You might easily forget to apply the constraints if you have to switch back and forth. It is best to have a separate program dedicated to running applets. Another advantage is that the Apple Applet Runner is frequently updated. MRJ gives a major advantage to browser users on the Macintosh platform. The internal Virtual Machine of Internet Explorer can be dynamically replaced with the MRJ Virtual Machine. This is important because it enables users to see applets that are developed with the latest technology without needing to wait for a new version of the Web browser.

The only technology that comes close to this one on other platforms is the Java Plugin (sometimes called Java Activator). This technology also enables the user to switch the Virtual Machine, but is inferior because it requires applet distributors to rewrite their HTML files by using plugin syntax rather than the applet tag.

MRJ includes several development tools that might make Mac the premier development platform for Java. Accessing these features requires downloading and installing the MRJ SDK. This chapter is not intended solely for those who are interested in learning Java on the Mac; however, it is easier to understand what is going on if you understand the pieces involved. Here is a list of those pieces:

- Java programs can be packaged as Macintosh programs so that you will not have to do anything special to make them run. The *JBindery* performs this packaging.

- The functionality of the Macintosh is made available to Java developers through standard channels, but also with an easier, alternate interface named JDirect.

- Even when Java is run in its pure form, MRJ includes techniques to allow Java applications to fulfill the Human Interface Guidelines. These guidelines establish the way that a program should act and historically served as the launching point for Graphic User Interfaces in general. The MRJToolkit provides these techniques.

JBindery is a technology that allows developers to make Java applications double-clickable. Although this may not seem like much of a feat, most Java software is not currently distributed in such a way. Although Java has a full class library of graphic interface tools, most Java applications are not tightly integrated with the systems they are delivered on. JBindery doesn't remove the portability of Java code; it merely produces a Macintosh wrapper around the Java code to benefit the user. Although you can develop wrapper code by hand, you will find JBindery a wonderful convenience.

JDirect allows Java code to directly call Macintosh Toolbox Routines. This destroys the portability of the Java code, but it ultimately allows many developers access to the Mac that they wouldn't otherwise have. The Java Native Interface allows developers to call underlying native functions, but provides no support for maintaining the object-oriented state of the system. JDirect makes a Java wrapper around the Macintosh System Calls so that developers can easily integrate those calls with their own Java code. This is so great because the Macintosh provides a rich set of libraries, many of which are not available directly from Java, especially without loss of performance. The JDirect Interface not only makes these libraries available, but also makes them easy to use. Java programs can more directly access the Macintosh hardware. This encourages developers to

15: Java

develop for the Macintosh platform. The greatest fear of many programmers is specializing in technology that soon becomes obsolete. JDirect allows developers to use the cross-platform strengths of Java while concentrating the platform specifics into smaller pieces of the program. It's much easier to convert a program to another platform when the majority of the program is written with Java.

If you want to write a Java program that will remain portable to other platforms yet have all the behavior of a good Macintosh program, you can use the MRJToolkit. This toolkit is written in Java, so it does not limit the developer to one platform. A book printed by Apple, *The Human Interface Guidelines*, describes exactly how every computer program should act. For example, it outlines that every program should have a File menu that would allow the user to quit. The MRJToolkit allows Java applications to respond to Apple Events so that these signals will be caught. Users will be more comfortable with familiar keyboard combinations. Soon, QuickTime support will be another benefit of the MRJToolkit. *Project Biscotti* is another name for the integration of the QuickTime APIs with Java. The MRJToolkit also allows Java applications to manipulate file creators and types.

Java Vs. JavaScript

Many users are still somewhat confused about the differences between Java and JavaScript, as well as Microsoft's implementation of JavaScript—*JScript*—and ActiveX. These technologies are all used to add interactivity to Web pages, yet some of them have nothing else to do with each other.

Java is a programming language that is cross platform. A compiler is used to change Java code into *byte codes* that are kept on the server. A Web page can contain a reference to a specific kind of Java program called an *applet*. When this occurs, the Web browser reading the Web page downloads the byte codes and runs the Java program inside the Web page. Special security restraints within the browser keep Java from doing any harm by putting a limit on the Applet's capabilities. This is known as running Java *in the sandbox*. Java also has a server-side functionality called *Servlets*. These programs work in a manner similar to CGI and are created to replace PERL as the *de facto* server language of choice.

JavaScript, created by Netscape, is a scripting language for browsers. It is interwoven with HTML within Web pages and is not compiled. It is loosely based on the syntax of Java, although its sole concern is the browser. A server-side JavaScript also exists, with a database-access functionality called *LiveWire*. This is the same JavaScript, except that the objects deal with server activities rather than browser activities. This is similar to Active Server Pages, which we discuss in a following section of this chapter.

15: Java

JScript is Microsoft's version of JavaScript; it is nearly identical to JavaScript. Some differences, however, affect compatibility. Recent updates to JScript are more concerned with ActiveX objects, which is a divergence with JavaScript. VBScript is another Microsoft scripting language, although it is based on Visual Basic instead of JavaScript. It is somewhat similar in syntax, except that it lacks the object model and handles user events in a different manner.

ActiveX is a *component technology*—software that comes in pieces. Components are linked to form bigger components, but no running components exist. These components are generally used either to create applications or they are embedded in a container (such as a Web page) and scripted with another language (in this case, JScript or VBScript). Although many comparisons were made between ActiveX and Java Applets when the two were first becoming known, these comparisons were invalid. The Java component model is called *JavaBeans*. ActiveX components embedded in Web pages are inherently more dangerous than Java Applets. The reason for this is twofold. First, ActiveX components do not have a sandbox: They have no security restrictions when they are run within a user's Web browser. The second is the bytecode verifier. A Java Virtual Machine checks downloaded code to make sure that it is valid before it runs that code. ActiveX takes no such precautionary measures.

Java Development Environments

If you're a programmer for the Mac OS, consider exploring the various development environments that are available for use in the Mac OS. Development environments are useful, providing several features not available from text editors. These environments will automate the tasks that programmers face. One important feature of development environments is that they sometimes present information in a way that makes it easier to understand and manipulate. Programmers should, therefore, pick the tool that is the most comfortable and intuitive. Almost all of the most common development tools provide demo versions that are free for download. It is advisable to try several tools before you buy one. Too many development tools exist to try to list all of them; I must apologize to those that I leave out. These products are mentioned because of either their widespread use, their usefulness, or their unique nature. Some of these tools include the following:

- *Metrowerks CodeWarrior Pro*—CodeWarrior is a widely excepted programming environment. It features many languages and built-in support for development across platforms and with many other types of devices. It is robust and fairly intuitive. This is a good platform to use as a measuring stick for other environments.

15: Java

- *Symantec Visual Café*—A new wave in software development involves using prebuilt components to assemble applications. You can create programs visually, without writing very much code. This reuse of software is sometimes called *Rapid Application Development*, or RAD. Java uses a model named JavaBeans for components. Developers can use the components written by other developers and never see the actual code. Visual Cafe uses this model.

- *GenieWorks SpotCheck*—SpotCheck is the editor that "knows the Java language." This editor pursues rapid development in a different manner. The use of components for visual development is compelling, but severely limiting. SpotCheck takes the opposite strategy: Rather than hiding information from developers, SpotCheck provides more information. Most programming environments can detect certain kinds of errors, such as spelling or syntax. SpotCheck, however, detects higher-level programming errors that are usually checked by compiler. This speeds development not only by reducing compile time, but also by preventing the developer from pursuing an erroneous line of thought. SpotCheck also provides fast options for common tasks, such as writing common loop structures.

- *Zero G's InstallAnywhere Now!*—This installer program allows you to create installer programs in six steps. The installers work on Macintosh, Windows, and Unix. The best part about this great package (which was voted one of the top 10 Java packages by the Java Report) is that it is included free with the MRJ SDK. The SDK itself is also free.

15: Java

Immediate Solutions

This section covers all the important details for installing and using MRJ 2.0 in conjunction with Mac OS 8.5. Please note that MRJ is scheduled for an update about the time this book goes to press. The authors recommend that you check the Web sites listed later in the chapter for more information about how to obtain the latest version.

Installing Mac OS Runtime For Java

Mac OS Runtime for Java may not have been installed from the Mac OS 8.5 CD-ROM. You can find out by looking in your Extensions folder. If you find the MRJLibraries folder, it is already installed. Highlight one of the icons in this folder and press Command+I to get information. Make sure that the extensions are at least version 2. If they are not, run the installer from the CD-ROM again. Make sure that MRJ is selected. After the installation is complete, your system should have a new folder (Mac OS Runtime for Java), and additions to the System Folder and the Extensions folder.

A folder called "Mac OS Runtime for Java" is in the Apple Extras folder. It contains the following data:

- An *About MRJ readme file*—Gives a general overview of Mac OS Runtime for Java.

- *A License Agreement folder*—Contains a license agreement in the appropriate language.

- *The Apple Applet Runner folder*—Contains the Apple Applet Runner and an Applets folder. (We will explore these in the following section.)

In the System Folder, you'll find the following:

- *The Text Encodings folder*—Contains mappings to other character sets, such as Chinese and Cyrillic.

In the Extensions Folder, you see these items:

- *Text Encoding Converter Extension*

- *MRJ Libraries folder*—This folder is in the Extensions folder, and it contains all of the remaining files and folders shown in this bullet list.

- *Lib folder*—Contains properties files that store the Java preferences. These are not regenerated like Macintosh Preferences, so don't delete them.

- *MRJ PPC JITc*—The new Just In Time Compiler for the Macintosh PowerPC platform. This extension is responsible for the performance of the Mac Java Virtual Machine.

- *MRJLib*—This extension contains functions used by the Virtual Machine.

- *MRJClasses folder*—This folder contains the JDKClasses.zip, MRJClasses.zip, and Properties.zip.

- *JDKClasses.zip*—Contains the core Java Class Libraries.

- *MRJClasses.zip*—Contains the specialized Java classes that allow Java files to use Macintosh resources, respond to Apple Events, and call Macintosh System Functions. These are the classes that make up JManager, JBindery, the Java Native Interface, and other helper classes, such as those that provide mapping between the Mac and Java fonts.

- *Properties.zip*—Programmers need to use several standard tools, such as compilers, to make programs. The MRJ SDK comes with several development tools, such as the Java compiler called *javac*. This zip file contains text files that are used by Java helper tools. For example, the error messages that javac produces are stored in this file.

Launching Java Applets

The MRJ installation routine installed several example Java applets on your hard drive. These applets and the Apple Applet Runner are good examples of the capabilities of Java. For those who would like to learn Java programming, these programs are an invaluable aid. They not only demonstrate the capabilities of Java, but they also include all the source code so you can see exactly how each applet was written. To launch a Java applet, you can open the applet by using the Apple Applet runner or by using a Java-enabled Web browser, such as Netscape Navigator or Microsoft Internet Explorer.

Apple Applet Runner

The Applet Runner is easy to use because it works like any other application for the Mac OS. To launch an applet, take these steps:

1. Launch the Apple Applet Runner application, located in the Mac OS Runtime for Java folder in the Apple Extras folder.

2. You can choose an applet from the following options:

   • Select an item from the Applets menu

   • File|Open URL (Command+N)

   • File|Open Local HTML File (Command+O)

3. Once the applet has been loaded, choose from several options on the Applet menu (Suspend Applet or Resume Applet, for example), as well as close the applet or quit the Apple Applet Runner application.

You can also drag and drop the HTML file containing the applet onto the Applet Runner icon or double-click on the HTML file. (The creator code is that of the Apple Applet Runner, so they will be automatically opened by that application instead of a Web browser or HTML editor, such as BBEdit).

Also, the File|Open URL option is similar to the choice for opening a local file, except that remote files are opened with security settings automatically on, as you will see in the following section. Apple also included a convenient feature in the Open URL menu item. The dialog box remembers frequently accessed URLs and lets you choose one of them rather than having to retype the URL (see Figure 15.3).

Little more is involved in running the Apple Applet Runner. It's merely a shell for Java applets, so it is fairly simple.

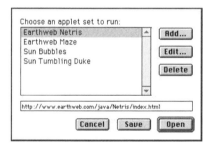

Figure 15.3   The Open URL dialog box.

Previewing Some Sample Applets

The following previews highlight some of the sample applets that are installed as part of Mac OS Runtime for Java, as well as a few observations about the applets.

• *Animator*—The Animator applet (see Figure 15.4) shows several increasingly complex animations. The word "Java" is formed out of coffee beans while

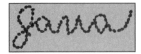

Figure 15.4   The Animator applet.

sounds play in the background. The first version is shown in Figure 15.4. It shows the developer how to play sounds, how to display pictures, and most important, how to double-buffer animations.

- *ArcTest*—The ArcTest applet shown in Figure 15.5 takes user input and displays an arc, depending on what you enter. This exposes the drawing primitives within the Java language, which are very similar to those of Microsoft's DirectDraw, or OpenGL. This code is a good introduction to two-dimensional graphics for beginning developers.

- *BarChart*—The BarChart, pictured in Figure 15.6 is actually a useful applet for business, reads numbers from the HTML file that it is embedded in and uses those numbers to generate a bar chart. You can put this applet in your Web site to display statistics in a graphical format.

- *BlinkingText*—The applet in Figure 15.7 is fun to look at, but it actually serves a higher purpose. The code is written to be multithreaded, which is considered one of the hardest things to learn. This is a wonderfully simple example for beginning programmers. If you want to customize this applet, replace the value associated with "lbl" with your own text. You can also change the number associated with "speed" to change the rate of display. All these values are parameters in the HTML text and don't require that the applet be recompiled or changed in any other way. You will find, however,

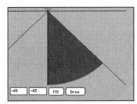

Figure 15.5   The ArcTest applet.

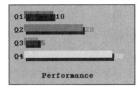

Figure 15.6   The BarChart applet.

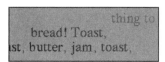

Figure 15.7   The BlinkingText applet.

that if you don't restart the browser when you change those values, it will often crash.

- *CardTest*—The CardTest Applet is of no use to anyone except as an example of Java's capabilities or as an exercise to developers to learn how layouts work in the Java Abstract Window Toolkit. The buttons are rearranged in different orders, depending on which buttons you press. Figure 15.8 shows one of the layouts.

- *Clock*—Figure 15.9 shows a clock. It is fairly straightforward, and takes no HTML parameters. You can insert it directly onto a Web page. For beginning developers, this applet should follow the ArcTest Applet because it uses similar techniques.

- *DitherTest*—This applet isn't pictured because it is highly dependent on color. This applet is a good learning tool for more advanced graphics programmers and for nonprogrammers who are interested in graphic design.

15: Java

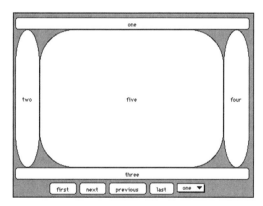

Figure 15.8   The CardTest applet.

Figure 15.9   The Clock applet.

Experiment with different numbers and colors, and you will soon understand what is going on. It helps if you choose a solid (unchanging) alpha value and let some other color vary. Then, gradually shift the color and alpha values so that you can follow the way the color changes. This is a good introduction to using RGB color values with an Alpha channel.

- *DrawTest*—Figure 15.10 shows an applet that acts as a coloring book. You can draw in different colors. This applet shows beginning programmers how to handle events, such as mouse clicks and drags, within Java programs.

- *Fractal*—The applet shown in Figure 15.11 uses a simple technique of repetitive division to draw a fractal.

- *GraphicsTest*—The applet shown in Figure 15.12 continues the study of drawing figures and shapes, this time with a literal twist. The addition of colors and overlay to create stripes makes this more fun.

- *GraphLayout*—The applet shown in Figure 15.13 is one of a series of four applets. These applets demonstrate mathematical concepts of computational geometry. They are also fun to drag around.

Figure 15.10   The DrawTest applet.

Figure 15.11   The Fractal applet.

Figure 15.12   The GraphicsTest applet.

Figure 15.13   The GraphLayout applet.

- *ImageMap*—This applet takes a fun approach to something that comes up in Web design fairly often: how to make a picture into a tool for navigation. This applet allows you to supply your own picture and behaviors, but you still have to figure out the coordinates. Look at the HTML and you will see what you need. Figure 15.14 shows a cute example that will get you started.

- *JumpingBox*—This applet is another exercise in event handling. It is impossible to click on the box, which you see in Figure 15.15. Variations of this program open by saying, "click here for your $1,000 raise...".

- *MoleculeViewer*—This program takes a series of numerical coordinates and converts them into models of molecules. What makes this even more exciting is that you can click on the molecule and drag to make it rotate in different directions. Figure 15.16 shows one of the several examples included with this applet.

- *NervousText*—You can open the HTML file associated with the applet in Figure 15.17 and replace the text value with your own, then watch it shake. This applet uses multithreading to make the text do the Mamba.

Figure 15.14   The ImageMap applet.

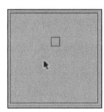

Figure 15.15   The JumpingBox applet.

Figure 15.16   The MoleculeViewer applet.

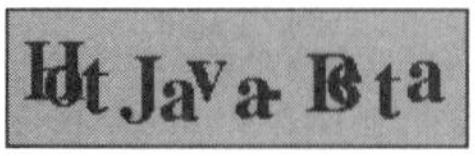

Figure 15.17   The NervousText applet.

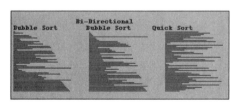

Figure 15.18   The SimpleGraph applet.

- *SimpleGraph*—The graph that displays (see Figure 15.18) is created by adding certain mathematical functions. This applet only takes about five lines of code to create.

- *SortDemo*—When working with large amounts of data, programmers want to deal with the data in the quickest way possible (*optimization*). This applet shows three ways of sorting data that programmers commonly use. This graphical depiction could be quite useful in a programming course. The fastest of these three sort techniques is the Quick Sort algorithm. The Bi-Directional Bubble Sort is second, and the regular Bubble Sort comes in last. You can watch each one run by clicking on it. Figure 15-19 shows a sample run.

- *SpreadSheet*—Figure 15.20 is a functional applet, useful in the same way that the bar graph was useful. You can insert the data in the HTML; the cells that are based on functions instead of actual values are automatically calculated. The cells that are to be given actual values are marked with a "v" and the cells

Figure 15.19   The SortDemo applet.

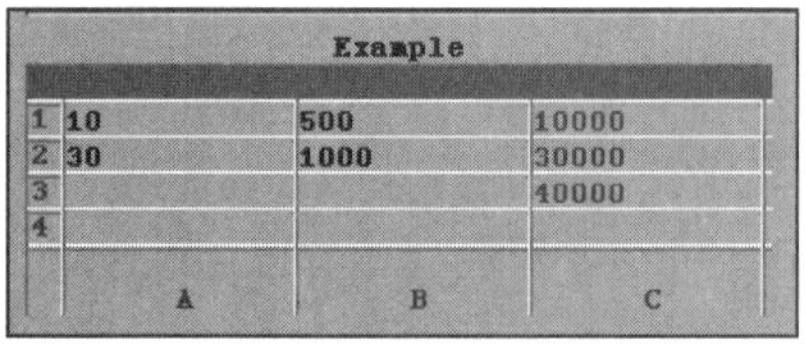

Figure 15.20   The SpreadSheet applet.

15: Java

that will be calculated from functions are designated by an "f". This is all in the HTML for this example.

- *TicTacToe*—The applet in Figure 15.21 is the TicTacToe game. Although it might seem the silliest of the applets we're describing, it is probably the most difficult to program of all these applets. It makes a fun addition to a Web page and doesn't require any special parameters in the HTML. The program takes time to understand, but is well worth the effort for those who aspire to learn programming. This is the only program that approaches a typical software project in complexity. This sort of rule-based logic is a useful programming example.

- *WireFrame*—The wireframe models in this applet look impressive. You can manipulate them by dragging your mouse across them. Dragging the mouse makes these models rotate around the X, Y, or Z axis. They are created with a coordinate system somewhat similar to the one used for the molecule models. This system names all vertices in the model, listing the coordinates. Then, these coordinates are used to define lines, faces, and other structures. If you have the inclination, you could create a model without any Java programming. This applet can still be used by simply referring to the model that you create in the HTML file, replacing the current value that is next to the model parameter name. The HTML file used to create Figure 15.22 used the coordinates of a helicopter model.

Figure 15.21   The TicTacToe applet.

Figure 15.22   The WireFrame applet-helicopter model.

Configuring Java Security

We should bring a few security concerns to your attention. We have previously mentioned the *Applet Sandbox*, which prohibits certain activities when code is loaded over a network. It's time to take a closer look at what goes on in the sandbox.

Whenever you load a Java class into the Virtual Machine, an internal object called the *ClassLoader* inspects the class. If the class comes from an untrusted source (such as the Internet), the class will be under restrictions.

Major Restrictions Placed On Untrusted Code (*The Sandbox*)

Untrusted code has the following major restrictions:

- You are not allowed to read or write files.

- You are not allowed to control the threads that do not belong to it.

- You cannot start any other processes.

- You are not able to use native methods (which we discussed a little bit earlier in the "Introducing Java" section).

- You cannot create network connections to anywhere except the server from which the applet was downloaded.

  You can see in Figure 15.23 how Microsoft's Internet Explorer allows you to choose how much of the sandbox you want in place. You can decide to give applets full network connectivity, if you want.

With these restrictions in place, it is safe to interact with executable content on the Web. The problem is that these restrictions are very limiting. Other techniques used for security allow users to trust code that wouldn't otherwise be trusted.

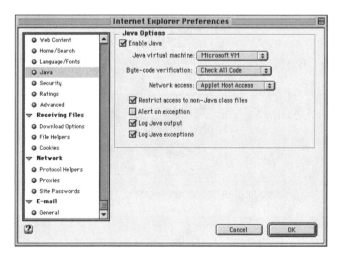

Figure 15.23   The Microsoft Internet Explorer Preferences dialog box, showing the Java preferences area.

Digital Signatures And The Trust Model

Sometimes when computer consultants describe security, they talk about the *trust model*. This refers to the fact that you can inherently trust code that you wrote yourself, but inherently not trust code that you download from a Web site. Everything else falls somewhere in between. When security consultants refer to *untrusted* code, they aren't placing blame or casting aspersions. Untrusted simply means that no way exists to determine whether someone modified the code to contain a virus or did some other malicious act. Trusted code has all of the following traits:

- *Authenticity*—The creator of the code can be reliably determined.

- *Integrity*—The code could not have been altered in transit.

- *Nonrepudiation*—The creator of the code cannot later deny having created the code.

One way to get this much security is by using *digital signatures*—a special way of processing a file so that nobody can tamper with it, in any way, without changing the signature. This assures the receiver that nobody has infected the original file with a virus. A danger still exists that the original creator of the file embedded a virus in the file, but if this happened, the digital signature would prove that the creator was responsible.

Digital signatures are made possible through large organizations known as *Certificate Authorities*. You can see the ones that your browser supports by opening the security preferences (see Figure 15.24 and Figure 15.25). When a person uses a digital signature, it has the same effect as getting a co-signature from one of these Certificate Authorities. You must have the same Certificate Authority that the digital signer used listed in your browser's security preferences.

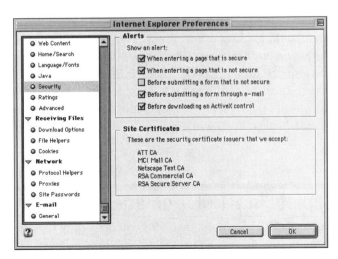

Figure 15.24   The Microsoft Internet Explorer Security Preferences dialog box.

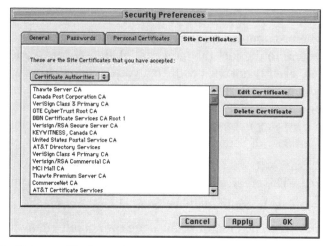

Figure 15.25   The Netscape Navigator Security Preferences dialog box.

Figure 15.26   Editing a Certificate Authority.

If you want to learn more about a particular certificate, such as its expiration date, press the Edit button. You shouldn't actually edit the certificate, but you can see information about it (see Figure 15.26).

ActiveX uses the trust model for security. When you go to a Web page that has an ActiveX control, a dialog box opens and tells you the name of the signer of the code and asks if you want to trust that person. If anything goes wrong, you know exactly whom you can blame. The problem with ActiveX is that there is no other option. You can either trust other people completely or not trust them at all. Java allows you to use the trust model, but also allows partial trust by using the Java Sandbox. It is the best of both worlds.

Inserting Applets In HTML Documents

Now that you've seen what applets can do, you are ready to start putting applets into Web pages yourself. You will need some knowledge of HTML. If you just want to experiment, you can alter only one of the pages from the example section.

The JAR File Format

Before we discuss the applet HTML tag, let's look at one more element that you'll encounter. It's a new type of file known as a *Java Archive* (JAR) file; it employs the .zip format created by PKWare. You should use JAR files for the following reasons:

- Operating systems have different rules about the lengths of names. No limit exists for the length of a file name within an archive.

- When files are transferred over a network, fewer transactions (and, consequently, better performance) occur when just one big file is transferred. JAR also allows for compression, which can reduce network transfer times even more.

- Digital Signatures are only possible on archive files, because they store information about the signature within the archive itself.

The MRJ SDK comes with a tool for creating JAR files. You can extract files from a JAR file with any commercial decompression utility that understands the zip format, such as Aladdin's StuffIt Expander. Most modern browsers can make use of JAR files.

Embedding Applets In Web Pages

The <APPLET> tag is the mechanism used to embed applets in Web pages. Suppose that the applet is in a file named Test.class, and we want the applet to be centered in a red page. The width of the applet is 200 pixels, and the height is also 200 pixels. Here is a sample:

```
<HTML>
<HEAD>
<TITLE>The First Applet</TITLE>
</HEAD>
<BODY bgcolor="#800000" text="#FFFFFF">
<CENTER>
<H3> This is a Test Applet <H3>
<APPLET CODE=Test.class HEIGHT=200 WIDTH=200>
I can write stuff here that will only appear
if the applet doesn't work, or if Java applets
aren't supported by the browser.
</CENTER>
</BODY>
</HTML>
```

15: Java

In the following example, we are still using Test.class, but this time we have stored Test.class in a different directory, so we need to specify that it is located somewhere else. We do this by using the CODEBASE attribute. Just to make things interesting, we will say that it's actually located on a different computer, and rather than listing a different directory, it will be an entirely different URL.

```
<HTML>
<HEAD>
<TITLE>The First Applet</TITLE>
</HEAD>
<BODY bgcolor="#800000" text="#FFFFFF">
<CENTER>
<H3> This is a Test Applet </H3>
<APPLET CODE=Test.class WIDTH=200 HEIGHT=200
CODEBASE=www.otherserver.com>
Notice that the height and width are in a
different order than they were last time.
It doesn't matter!  They work either way.
BUT THEY ALWAYS HAVE TO BE PRESENT!
</CENTER>
</BODY>
</HTML>
```

If you read the code closely, you saw the comment about HEIGHT and WIDTH. Those two tags, along with CODE, are the only things that are required to be in every <APPLET> tag. This time around, we have stored Test.class in a JAR file named codefiles.jar.

```
<HTML>
<HEAD>
<TITLE>The First Applet</TITLE>
</HEAD>
<BODY bgcolor="#800000" text="#FFFFFF">
<CENTER>
<H3> This is a Test Applet </H3>
<APPLET CODE=Test.class WIDTH=200 HEIGHT=200
CODEBASE=www.otherserver.com
ARCHIVE=codefiles.jar>
</CENTER>
</BODY>
</HTML>
```

Now that you know how to put a Java applet in a Web page, you just need to know how to send information to the applet, so that you can customize the applet to your own needs. The exact parameters that each applet needs vary, depending on the developer. You will need documentation with an applet to find out what names the applet is expecting.

If you are developing an applet for widespread distribution, you should make it as customizable as possible, without becoming too complicated. In this example, we will assume that the developer lets us customize the applet's background by sending in a color and that there is a line of text that we can also customize. If you want to see an example of this in practice, modify the HTML file of the BlinkingText example.

```
<HTML>
<HEAD>
<TITLE>The First Applet</TITLE>
</HEAD>
<BODY bgcolor="#800000" text="#FFFFFF">
<CENTER>
<H3> This is a Test Applet </H3>
<APPLET CODE=Test.class WIDTH=200 HEIGHT=200
CODEBASE=www.otherserver.com
ARCHIVE=codefiles.jar>
<PARAM NAME=BGCOLOR VALUE="red">
<PARAM NAME=textstring VALUE="this is my line of text">
</CENTER>
</BODY>
</HTML>
```

Exploring Additional Java Resources

Many online resources are available for exploring and developing Java applets, including Web sites, newsgroups, and mailing lists. Too many really exist to do the subject justice, but here are some favorites that can get you started:

MRJ Mailing List

- **www.lists.apple.com/mrj.html**

MRJ Specific Websites

- **www.apple.com/macos/java/**

Frequently Asked Questions

- **www.ping.be/beta9/MRJ-FAQ.html**
- **gemma.apple.com/java/text/faq.html**

Other Java And Mac Development Websites

- **devworld.apple.com/java/**
- **developer.apple.com/techpubs/mac/mac.html**
- **java.sun.com/products/**
- **developer.javasoft.com/developer/jdchome.html**
- **www.javaworld.com/**
- **www.ibm.com/java/**
- **www.gamelan.com/**
- **javaboutique.internet.com/**
- **java.oreilly.com/news/knudsen/**
- **www.cupojoe.com/**
- **www.javacats.com/**
- **www.teamjava.com/**
- **www.javology.com/javology/**
- **www.javareport.com/**
- **www.javalobby.com/**
- **www.sys-con.com/java/**

Java Newsgroups

- **comp.lang.java.advocacy**
- **comp.lang.java.api**
- **comp.lang.java.beans**
- **comp.lang.java.corba**
- **comp.lang.java.databases**
- **comp.lang.java.gui**
- **comp.lang.java.help**
- **comp.lang.java.machine**
- **comp.lang.java.misc**
- **comp.lang.java.programmer**
- **comp.lang.java.security**
- **comp.lang.java.softwaretools**
- **comp.lang.java.tech**

15: Java

Chapter 16

System Security

In Depth

Security Issues

A computer is vulnerable, just like a person, depending on his or her situation. A person working on a ship in the middle of the Atlantic, for example, is at a greater risk of drowning or sinking than someone working in construction in Arizona. Computers face different security issues that vary according to their situations. A computer that is not networked and has no method of networking is not as vulnerable to hacking as a computer that is in an Ethernet environment. Yet, that same isolated computer may face serious problems if no data backup strategy exists and the hard drive fails. You need to analyze all areas where your computer may be vulnerable and utilize both built-in Mac OS 8.5 security features and third-party applications to protect your system's hardware and software.

You should also recognize the limitations of security programs. The best security plan includes a mixture of physical devices and password protection.

Physical Security

This is one of the most obvious, yet ignored security issues. So many people assume that because a lock is on their door, they do not need to physically secure their computer system, yet computers are a desirable theft item. PowerBooks are especially vulnerable, as the insurance industry well knows. Billions of dollars in claims are filed each year for stolen computer property. And it's not just the office computer that is the target; a thief is just as likely to walk off with a computer as with your VCR. The amazing thing is that most Macintosh computers include a slot in the back that can connect to inexpensive security cables. While they don't provide complete physical security, these cables will at least make it more difficult to steal the computer. You can include more physical security options such as alarm systems and video surveillance devices; with the appropriate configuration, even a QuickCam video camera can serve in this capacity.

Many software-based security programs, especially shareware or freeware, can be bypassed by booting from an alternate medium. Physical devices are available that lock the floppy and CD-ROM drives so that they cannot be used. If your funding is limited, you can try a simpler measure, such as removing your keyboard and mouse and locking them in a separate location.

16: System Security

Configuration Preservation

Most computers are one-person machines. Other computers are shared among a small group of users. Still others are used by a large group of people. Computers used by large groups of people are often in either a lab or another, similar cluster setting. Without the appropriate security software, these machines can be accidentally or deliberately disabled. For example, a person may install a program that removes necessary system extensions (such as TCP/IP) and then replaces it with an incompatible TCP/IP stack. In this case, the goal of the administrator of these computers is usually either to preserve or restore a particular system configuration. Unfortunately, this capability is not completely included with Mac OS 8.5. However, third-party security programs can help reduce or remove the risk of computer mangling.

Mac OS 8.5 Security Options

You can take a few measures to protect some important settings from curious users. Several control panels, including AppleTalk, TCP/IP, and Modem, have an option called Administrator (see Figure 16.1). When this option is enabled, you can lock particular settings within the control panel. When you save the settings and lock them with a password, a user can view but cannot change the settings. Of course, an experienced user simply has to delete the preference for the control panel, and this option is immediately disabled. To really protect settings, you need third-party software.

Apple Network Administrator Toolkit

This software application from Apple is a suite of network administrator tools that helps control computer configurations and aids in day-to-day maintenance. This suite includes At Ease for Workgroups, Apple Network Assistant, and Apple User and Group Manager.

At Ease controls basic System configuration, determines who can and cannot access the computer, and what the user can see and do while using the computer. At Ease requires an AppleShare server, which many lab or cluster environments already have.

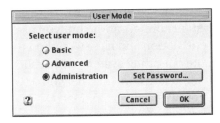

Figure 16.1   The Administrator window in the AppleTalk control panel.

The Apple Network Assistant remotely accesses the computers and allows an administrator to control the computer, install or remove software, or display the user's screen on the other computers in the network. This tool does not require a server and is especially useful in a learning environment.

The Apple User and Group Manager manages user accounts across AppleShare servers (this utility also requires an AppleShare server).

MacPrefect

MacPrefect from Hi Resolution is a security program that locks down areas of the computer and disallows changes to be made to protected areas. In fact, to bypass this security you must launch the MacPrefect software and enter an appropriate password. You can hide certain control panels so that they are not visible from the Apple menu. A user who attempts to add or remove components from areas that you have locked receives an error message and is unable to complete the task. You can also limit printing options and installation of new software. You can stop users from pirating software by disabling the copy capability of certain files or folders. And MacPrefect can be installed on a single machine or a cluster of computers as a method of protecting the hard drive; no server is required.

One final benefit of MacPrefect is that it cannot be bypassed. You cannot boot from another medium, such as a floppy or CD-ROM, and disable the security software. Therefore, MacPrefect cannot be disabled like other security programs.

Assimilator

Assimilator is a shareware utility that is used to create an "image" of a hard drive. It takes a while to create this image, but when you have finished creating it you can store it on a server and use it to restore a computer's original configuration. This utility is especially useful for creating computers with almost identical configurations. You may not have the resources or need for complex network administration tools, but Assimilator is an economical alternative and can simplify the initial setup of a new office computer.

Data Security

Not only do you need to concern yourself with the physical security of the computer as well as the system configuration, but you also need to protect your data from prying eyes and corruption and have a method to recover it, should disaster strike. In many ways, the operating system and applications are expendable. You can always reinstall them. But documents that you or your users create are unique, vulnerable, and even confidential. Again, Mac OS 8.5 includes only limited data protection. For stronger protection, you need to invest in additional software and hardware.

File And Folder Locking

You can protect files within the Mac OS by locking them. Within the Get Info window for General Information, an option is available to lock a file. After the file has been locked, you can open it, but you cannot make changes to it. You cannot even use Save As to replace the existing file. If a locked file is dragged to the trash, the Empty Trash action cannot delete the locked file. You must unlock the file or hold down the Alt key as you select the Empty Trash option. A locked file is not safe, especially for the experienced hacker. No password protection exists for the Get Info window, and you can simply deselect the Lock option, which makes the file open to changes and deletion.

You can protect a folder from being deleted, moved, or renamed. If File Sharing is enabled, you can access the Sharing options from the Get Info window. Simply select the option that restricts folder actions such as moving, renaming, or deleting the folder. It even says "Locked". This provides some protection for folders, because no option is available to lock them the way you can lock a file. Of course, someone who is at your computer can easily disable this protection. For better protection, you need to invest in other software applications.

FolderBolt Pro

FolderBolt Pro from Citadel is a software program that sets access privileges to files and folders. It has four levels of access, from Deadbolt, which allows no access at all (it even prevents copying) to read-only access. FolderBolt Pro also includes encryption software for sensitive data and the capability to make a deleted file unrecoverable, even by file recovery utilities. FolderBolt Pro settings on files and folders are maintained even when placed on a computer without FolderBolt Pro installed. However, FolderBolt Pro has some compatibility problems with Mac OS 8. It must have a special update patch installed and this patch inhibits the use of File Sharing on the Mac.

Encryption

When you have a confidential phone conversation, you certainly take measures to ensure your privacy. If you use a cordless phone, you may hold the conversation in a closed room or use scrambling technology. Similarly, if you have confidential information, you may want to protect a file from being opened and viewed by unauthorized users.

We mentioned encryption briefly in the previous section. Passwords have used encryption for years, and email applications use various methods of encryption to protect messages. PGP or Pretty Good Privacy is an excellent encryption method that is unreadable without the appropriate unlocking key. It works in two parts. It has a public key that you can distribute freely. A user who wants to send you information simply looks up your public key and encrypts the information using this key. This information cannot be opened without the corresponding private key, which only you know and do not distribute.

PGP for Personal Privacy from PGP Inc. is an encryption package that can not only be used with email, it can also encrypt files and folders. You can download free versions from the Internet. Be aware, however, that PGP can only be used in the United States and Canada. It may be illegal in other countries. A Macintosh version, MacPGP, is available from MIT at **bs.mit.edu:8001/pgp-form.html**.

Back Up

If you faithfully back up your computer, you may never need data recovery. If you never back up, you or your users are living dangerously. Databases can become corrupted and unusable. A user can accidentally overwrite a file and need to recover the original. A hard drive can completely crash, and a backup copy of the drive would save time restoring the configuration.

A backup program is a worthwhile investment in data protection. The Iomega drives include backup software. Programs are also widely respected by the industry that can back up entire offices. Retrospect from the Dantz Corporation can be configured to run automatically and can back up both Macs and Windows machines. It can send messages to the system administrator when the backup program has started or finished, and send notification if a particular tape or media is needed. With high-capacity storage devices such as tape drives, you can make sure that if disaster strikes, you can put things almost back to normal.

Viruses

Someone is out to attack you, with the intention of causing problems with your computer's functioning. It may be an innocuous saying that flashes on your screen, but does little else. It may eat away at your hard drive or memory. Or, it may attempt to completely destroy your configuration. Does this person know you? Probably not. It's just some strange individual who has learned how to write a program. These programs are called *viruses*. Multimillion-dollar companies exist solely to provide virus protection for computer users. The vast majority of computer viruses are written for DOS and Windows applications (viruses are already showing up, specifically aimed at Windows 98). Mac users have at least one benefit of being the minority platform—fewer malicious programs have been written for attacking computers. However, the viruses out there are quite vicious and virus-protection software should be included on every computer.

16: System Security

The Millenium Bug

The Millennium or Y2K (Year 2000) Bug is not a virus; it's a situation that may occur on January 1, 2000. Many devices, computers, and programs use an abbreviated field for the year; *90* for example, instead of *1990*. As a result, some of the BIOS chips and systems may become confused on January 1, 2000 and treat this date as January 1, 1900. Several operating systems and applications may also have trouble with this date and cause the computer to malfunction. If a computer, operating system, or application has been tested and found to operate normally on this date, then it is called "Year 2K compliant."

The Macintosh computer is Year 2K compliant. The hardware and operating system can count correctly past the year 2000. However, some software applications may not use the system's clock and may malfunction. You also may have created databases that use the abbreviated date format and, therefore, may be vulnerable. To test your Mac to see if problems will develop on January 1, 2000, visit the Year 2000 Web site at **www.apple.com/macos/info/2000.html**.

Macro Viruses

Macro viruses are different because they can cross platforms. In most cases, PC viruses do not affect Macintosh computers and vice versa. However, macro viruses were developed from the macro files for Microsoft Word 6 and Excel 5. If you did not use these software applications, you did not need to worry about macro viruses. However, if you consider that these software applications are the biggest-selling word-processor and spreadsheet applications for the Mac, then you know that the threat of damage is real. Many virus-protection packages can remove and repair virus-infected files, and the Office 98 suite now allows you to disable the automatic launching of macros.

Autostart Virus Or Autostart Worm

For several years, the macro viruses were the biggest virus concern of Mac users; true Macintosh viruses just weren't being written, and the ones that existed were handled by a free virus-protection program called Disinfectant (Disinfectant is no longer being updated because it could not address macro viruses). All this changed with the discovery of the Autostart Worm. This hidden file runs when QuickTime is set to autoplay CD-ROMs. The virus is then passed on to different volumes across the computer, from floppies to Zip disks and remote volumes. In fact, one symptom of this virus is that the computer suddenly reboots when a disk is inserted. Another symptom is computer or network activity every 30 minutes. If your computer seems to be crashing frequently or just behaving strangely, you should run a virus-detection program and remove all viruses present. You should also disable the QuickTime setting that automatically launches CD-ROM applications. If you don't have the virus, these steps will give you a measure of protection. The virus has many variations, but several commercial companies can recognize and remove the Autostart Worm as well as other known viruses. Some packages are available that not only detect existing viruses, but also monitor the system for virus-like activity.

Kerberos

Kerberos is a method of authentication in a multiserver environment. Frequently, you have to log in to one server and log in again on a different server. In some cases, security breaches can occur when passwords are entered so frequently. Kerberos is a process that runs on a Unix server. This server is a *trusted server* (a user can enter secure information to this server, verifying who he or she is). The server then grants the user a ticket that can be used to access other servers that support Kerberos authentication. This reduces the need to log in so frequently to multiple servers. Kerberos was developed at MIT and requires a Kerberos server and client software to function.

MacLeland from Stanford is an excellent Kerberos client; however, it requires editing the resource fork with ResEdit to be used at locations other than Stanford. MacLeland has the side benefit of locking the Mac and permitting the user to locally mount remote AFS volumes.

Quick Reference Specifications

The following are the essential facts about System Security:

- Mac OS 8.5 includes limited security options.
- Macintosh computers contain built-in ports for security cables to lock down the computer.
- Control panels with the Edit|User Mode option can have portions of the control panels locked against changes.
- You must purchase third-party software to secure the Macintosh against unwanted changes in a lab or cluster environment.
- Some security programs require an AppleShare server.
- You can lock files with the Get Info menu option.
- You can use file sharing to lock a folder against changes.
- You can use PGP encryption with email to encrypt files on your computer.
- You can use a backup process and program to protect against data loss, which then can be used to restore corrupted or overwritten files.

- You must install a third-party virus-protection program to protect your computer against viruses. Most viruses are passed by floppies or downloaded files.

- Systems, computers, and files that operated correctly when the year 2000 occurs are "Year 2K compliant."

- Passwords should not be any recognizable word or identification associated with you; they should be a minimum of six characters, and you should change them frequently.

- Some applications, such as Microsoft Word 98, included the capability to password-protect a file.

- You can activate the System and Applications folders protection with the General Controls control panel.

- You can disable automatic receiving of cookies if you are concerned about privacy.

Utilities To Use

The utilities or elements of the Mac OS discussed in this chapter are listed here as a memory aid for the busy user or system administrator:

- *Apple Network Administrator Toolkit*—A software package from Apple that secures a network of Macintosh computers and provides computer remote control capability.

- *MacPrefect*—A security program that locks down and hides portions of the computer against user damage.

- *Assimilator*—A program that creates an ideal computer configuration image that can be stored on a server and placed on a computer with an incorrect system configuration.

- *FolderBolt Pro*—A security program that grants access rights to files and folders on the computer.

- *MacPGP*—A free program from MIT that creates PGP encryption keys and is used to protect files.

- *Retrospect*—Backup software from Dantz.

- *MacLeland*—Software that works with a Kerberos server to provide authentication to multiple servers.

- *Sesame*—A shareware program that provides password access to the Mac OS at startup.

- *Virex*—Virus-protection software from Dr. Solomon that can scan and repair files against computer viruses.

- *After Dark*—A commercial screen saver program that provides password protection at startup and after the screen saver has been activated.

Immediate Solutions

Enabling Password Protection With Sesame

One benefit of accessing a remote server is the password protection that the server enjoys. Even when you enable File Sharing, you can configure it so that a password is entered before the volume is mounted. It would be convenient and secure to require that a password be entered before the computer will boot. The only Macintosh computer with built-in password protection is the PowerBook; for other Macintosh computers, you must install a third-party driver. Several applications perform these functions quite effectively. StartUp Lock is a freeware control panel that does just that; it locks the computer until an appropriate password is entered. Sesame is a shareware application that functions differently from StartUp Lock. It provides more features than StartUp Lock, including the capability to disable the Shift key while the computer is booting; also, Sesame can be enabled any time to lock the computer. However, Sesame can be deactivated by holding down the Spacebar during startup or by booting from another disk. Sesame is available from the standard software archive sites.

To install and configure Sesame:

1. Launch the Sesame installer and install the application on your startup disk.

2. Sesame aliases will be installed in the Startup Items folder and the Apple Menu. Restart the computer.

3. After the computer has booted, you will be prompted to enter a password. The first time Sesame is run, no password exists. You can click on Okay, as shown in Figure 16.2.

4. Sesame warns you that no password has been set, and gives you the option to create one. You can create a new password. Sesame Password prefer-

Figure 16.2   The Sesame login window.

Figure 16.3   The Sesame Password Preferences window.

ences will be launched at this time. Figure 16.3 shows the Password window that allows you to enter a new password and to determine whether the passwords will be clear text. Enter a password.

5. Figure 16.4 shows the Sesame Preferences categories; they include Presentation (you can insert a company graphic in the login screen) and Screen (which determines the look of the Finder window while Sesame is active). If you want to make sure that no one can disable Sesame during the boot process, select Advanced Security.

6. Enable the option to prevent inactivation by the Shift key. You should also make sure that the option to disable the force-quit key combination for Sesame is selected.

TIP: *If you should enable the option to disable the Shift key during the boot process but delete Sesame, make sure that you disable this option before deleting Sesame or you will not be able to turn extensions off during troubleshooting processes.*

---

7. If you want to use this application in a networked environment, you can set an administrator password that will allow you to access the computer regardless of the personal password. Select the Administrator category and set an administrator password.

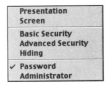

Figure 16.4   The Sesame Preferences categories.

16: System Security

Choosing A Good Password

No matter how excellent your security software is, if you do not have a secure password, a good hacker can bypass your security measures. For this reason, use the following suggestions to create a good password:

- Make sure that your password is not a common word; you should never use a word that is in the dictionary.

- Do not use your initials, name, or a relative's name.

- Do not use your home address, telephone number, or any other piece of information about you that can be easily retrieved.

- Make sure that the password is long. The recommended minimum length for a password is six characters or longer. The more important the data, the longer the password.

- Mix numbers with letters in the alphabet.

- Mix case if you are on a case-sensitive system.

- Change your password routinely. Every three to six months would be a good guideline.

- Do not write your password down; memorize it.

- Do not share your password with anyone.

Locking Files

Mac OS 8.5 provides some limited security measures. In some cases, these options don't necessarily protect your files from malicious hacking, but they do prevent important files from being accidentally overwritten. One option you can easily activate is the setting to lock a file. A knowledgeable Macintosh user can disable it, but—like leaving the front light on in a darkened house to scare away burglars—this option may deter some users. To lock a file, take these steps:

1. Click once on the file you want to lock.

2. Select File|Get Info and choose General Information.

3. Enable the option to lock the file.

When you open this file within a software application and attempt to make changes to the file or use the Save As option to overwrite it, you will receive an error message. Locked files that are placed within the trash cannot be deleted by the Empty Trash command unless the files are unlocked or the user presses the Alt key while emptying the trash.

Locking Folders

Technically, you cannot lock a folder in the same way that you can a file (by using the Get Info window within Mac OS 8.5). However, you can lock a folder through the Sharing option without ever sharing the folder's contents. This will provide some measure of security to your folders. You should be aware that a knowledgeable Macintosh user could easily disable this setting. To lock a folder with File Sharing, take these steps:

1. Enable File Sharing (if you are unsure of this process, refer to Chapter 11).

2. Select the folder you want to lock.

3. Select File|Get Info and choose Sharing.

4. Enable the option for "Can't move, rename, or delete this item (locked)", as shown in Figure 16.5.

5. Close the window to initiate the changes.

Figure 16.5   Locking a folder through the Sharing window.

Enabling Administrative Mode In Control Panels

Several Control panels including AppleTalk, Internet, Modem, Remote Access, and TCP/IP have an option to lock certain parts of the control panel. When these sections are locked you cannot make changes to the protected sections. You must initiate Administrator mode by way of a password to open and change these sections. Of course, the Mac OS is very open and an experienced Mac user can simply remove the preference for the particular control panel to disable the locks. For the purposes of this exercise we will lock the AppleTalk control panel, but the instructions apply to any control panel with an option under the Edit menu named User Mode. To enable administrative mode, take these steps:

1. Open the AppleTalk control panel.

2. Choose Edit|User Mode.

3. The User Mode window appears as shown in Figure 16.6. You have three options: Basic, Advanced, and Administration. Choose Administration.

4. The Set Password button becomes active. Click on this button, enter an appropriate password, and retype it in the Verify field.

5. Click on Okay to exit the User Mode window. The AppleTalk window will now be changed to allow you to lock certain portions of the control panel.

6. Click on the Lock button for any part of the control panel that you want to protect, as shown in Figure 16.7. The Open Lock icon will change to a closed lock.

7. Close the control panel and save the settings. A user will not be able to make changes to the locked portions of the control panel.

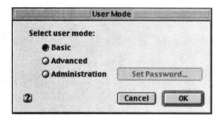

Figure 16.6   The User Mode window.

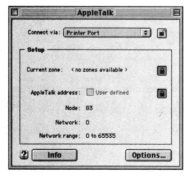

Figure 16.7   Locking AppleTalk options.

16: System Security

8. To disable the security, open the AppleTalk control panel and select Edit|User Mode.

9. Select Administration and enter the administrator password when prompted, then click on Okay.

10. Click on Okay to return to the AppleTalk window. You will now have the opportunity to unlock locked options. When you are finished, close the window and save the settings.

Securing Documents Within Applications

Some applications provide an option to password-protect a file. When you attempt to open a protected file, you will be prompted for a password. The Microsoft Office suite offers this kind of protection. For the purposes of this example, we will use Microsoft Word 98 for Macintosh. Word 98 has several layers of protection that you can employ. Follow these steps:

1. Open an existing file or create a new one within Microsoft Word 98.

2. Select File|Save As.

3. Designate a name for the file and click on the Options button, as shown in Figure 16.8.

4. The preferences for saving a file will appear. Locate the File sharing options for file name section.

5. If you want to mark the file as read-only, place a check in the "Read-only recommended" checkbox. This action locks the file against changes.

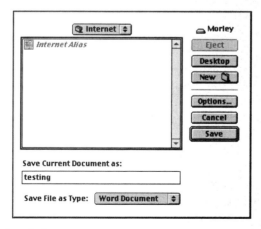

Figure 16.8   The Save As window.

6. If you want to create a password for opening the file, enter a password in the field under "Password to open". This forces a user to enter a password, but after the correct password is given, the user has complete access to the file.

7. For a second level of protection, you can designate a separate password for making changes to a file by entering a password in the "Password to modify" field. A user who doesn't know this password can only view the file, but he or she cannot make changes to it. Figure 16.9 shows these options enabled.

8. When you have determined and entered your settings, click on Okay. If you entered passwords, you will be prompted to verify them. You can now save the file.

This password protection applies only when the creator application is used to open the file. You can open these files using another word processor, but the documents will be very difficult to read. Additionally, if you save the file in another format such as text only, then you will lose the password protection.

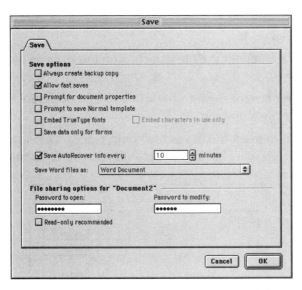

Figure 16.9   The Save preferences with password protection enabled.

Using Virus Protection

If a user is complaining of strange computer activity or poor performance, one of the first actions you should take is to run a virus check. If you don't have virus software installed, you can install a free version named Disinfectant. This program doesn't detect Microsoft Word macro viruses as well as some Trojan Horse programs, but it does detect several system viruses that are rather dangerous, and it can repair the files effectively.

TIP: *A Trojan Horse program is different from a virus. A Trojan horse is a file that "pretends" to be a specific kind of program, but when run, really does something else. For example, a Trojan horse program exists that masquerades as a program named FontFinder. When the program is launched, however, it makes the files on the hard drive inaccessible.*

To really protect your hard drive, you will need to invest in a commercial virus-protection program. Several are available, but for the purposes of our example, we'll discuss Virex, from Dr. Solomon. Virex was one of the first commercial programs to address the Autostart Worm. Figure 16.10 shows the main Virex application window.

You need to run only a few options to clean your computer:

- *Scan or diagnosis for viruses*—This option does not repair infected files, but it operates faster than the Repair infected files option, and it reports the viruses it finds.

- *Repair infected files*—This option runs slower than a scan, but if it encounters viruses, it can repair the files. Depending on the preferences chosen, it repairs the files with or without immediate notification and generates a report at the end of the process.

- *Automatically scan floppies*—For a long time, it was the floppy that was the major source of virus infection. Today, files from the Internet are also major virus carriers. A good virus-protection program will automatically scan removable media such as floppies and Zip disks, as well as compressed files that you download.

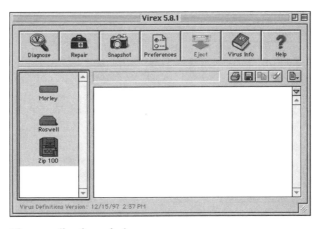

Figure 16.10   The Virex application window.

- *Schedule virus scanning*—If you have a large hard drive, a virus scan can take several minutes. During that scan you should allow the program to run uninterrupted. A good virus-protection package will allow you to schedule virus scanning and repair. This is helpful because you are not interrupted and also don't have to remind yourself to perform a virus check.

In addition to these options, some programs will watch certain files and report if questionable changes occur within the files' structure.

Protecting The Applications And System Folders

Mac OS 8.5 includes limited protection for the System Folder and the Applications folders. When this protection is enabled, a user cannot manually make changes to these folders. However, installer programs will be able to install software within these folders, and programs will be able to generate and update items in the Preferences folder. The greatest benefit of enabling this folder protection option is that it protects you (and your users) from deleting important items accidentally. To enable System Folder or Applications folder protection, take these steps:

1. Launch the control panel General Controls. The window shown in Figure 16.11 appears.

2. Locate the Folder Protection section.

3. Enable the appropriate protection. You can choose to protect the System Folder, Applications folder, or both.

4. Close the control panel.

Be aware that the error message that appears when you try to make changes to protected folders tells you how to disable the protection (see Figure 16.12). To

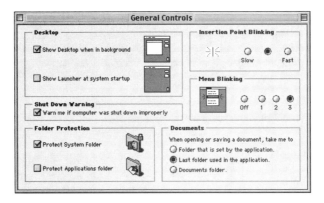

Figure 16.11   The General Controls window.

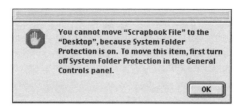

Figure 16.12　The error message for changing a protected folder.

really protect files and folders, you need to invest in a third-party security package, such as MacPrefect from Hi Resolution.

Screen-Saver Security

The Energy Saver control panel contains no option to prompt for a password when the system is "awakened" from sleep mode. If you want protection while your computer is inactive, you can download many free screen savers or purchase a commercial version. After Dark from Berkeley Systems is a very popular screen-saver package. You can easily require a password to cancel the screen saver by following these instructions:

1. Launch the After Dark control panel.
2. Click on the Setup button. The window shown in Figure 16.13 will appear.
3. Select the Password section.
4. Determine if a password will be required during Wakeup and/or Startup.
5. Click on the Set Password button, and then enter and confirm your password. Click on Okay twice to close the Setup options.
6. Close the After Dark control panel.

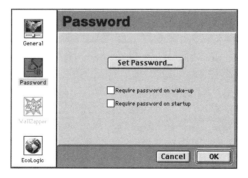

Figure 16.13　The Setup options in the After Dark screen saver.

16: System Security

> **TIP:** Did you notice that you can require a password at startup? If you want password protection when your computer is started, select this option. If a user cannot enter the appropriate password, the computer immediately goes into the screen saver program and cannot be accessed. This protection can be disabled by the Shift key.

Secure Internet Access

You are probably most vulnerable to security breaches when you access the Internet. Your information passes through several routers on its journey to a server or Web site. You may be attempting to buy a new hard drive at bargain prices, but unscrupulous people can access your credit card number. You need to take steps to protect the information you submit or at least be warned that your connection is not secure. Most Web browsers include security options. For the purpose of this discussion, we'll look at the security options in Internet Explorer, the default Web browser of Mac OS 8.5.

To view the security options in Internet Explorer, follow these steps:

1. Launch Internet Explorer.
2. Go to Edit|Preferences.
3. If it is not expanded, click on the arrow beside the Web Browser category on the left to produce more options.
4. Select Security to view the window, as shown in Figure 16.14.

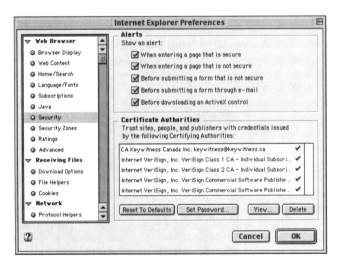

Figure 16.14   The Security options in Internet Explorer.

5. Select the options you want active during a browsing session. By default, they are all enabled. If you only want to be notified, for example, that you are entering an insecure site, you can disable the option to show an alert when entering a page that is secure.

This window also contains information on Certificate Authorities; these are companies who issue secure certificates to users, usually for a fee. When a user submits information by using a certificate from a certifying authority, Internet Explorer accepts or trusts the information, if it is received from one of the companies on this list. You can disable or delete any of the companies listed. A certificate can protect information that you submit over the Web.

Deleting Cookies

One of the great debates of the Web community is the use of cookies. If you use a Web browser, a text file is created that browsers and Web sites use to store information about you. For example, if you have a login and password that you use to read a popular newspaper via the Web, you can have that information stored in the cookie file so that you don't have to keep entering it to read the daily news. Some Web sites use Java applets to load different images each time you access a Web site and this information is also stored in the cookie file. The debate centers on the privacy of the user. Some users feel uncomfortable that some Web sites use cookie information to target advertising banners. While cookies are not inherently dangerous to your system and do not contain viruses, some users want the ability to disable them or at least know when a cookie is being placed on their system. You can disable cookies in several ways. These instructions are based on Internet Explorer's settings:

1. Launch Internet Explorer.
2. Go to Edit|Preferences.
3. Go to the section heading Receiving Files and select Cookies.
4. Figure 16.15 shows the Cookies settings. Servers that have placed cookies on your computer will be listed. You can delete any or all of these submissions.
5. Set the action you want taken when cookies are received and click on Okay. Figure 16.16 shows the available options.

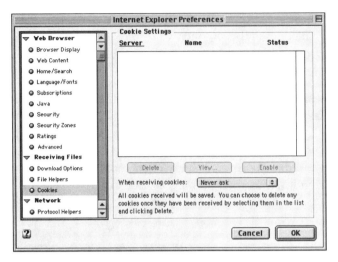

Figure 16.15   The Cookies settings in Internet Explorer.

Figure 16.16   The options in Internet Explorer for receiving cookies.

Generating A MacPGP Key

We could write an entire chapter on PGP or Pretty Good Privacy and its Macintosh client MacPGP. It is a versatile program that can generate public and private keys and encrypt files. You can send a file to someone by encrypting it with a correspondent's public PGP key. You can send the file over conventional email and only the recipient can open the file; even then, they must use their password to gain access to the file. Some email programs support PGP encryption, including Eudora and Simeon. MacPGP can be retrieved from the MIT Web site at **bs.mit.edu:8001/pgp-form.html**. It is not freely available from other Web sites because this kind of encryption can only be distributed to the United States and Canada (the encryption is *that* good, and in some countries it's illegal for ordinary citizens to use this technology).

For this discussion, you will learn how to create a PGP key and how to encrypt a file. If you would like to learn more about the program, MacPGP includes an extensive Help section. To create your own PGP key, take the following steps:

1. Launch MacPGP.

2. Go to Key|Generate Key. The window in Figure 16.17 will appear.

16: System Security

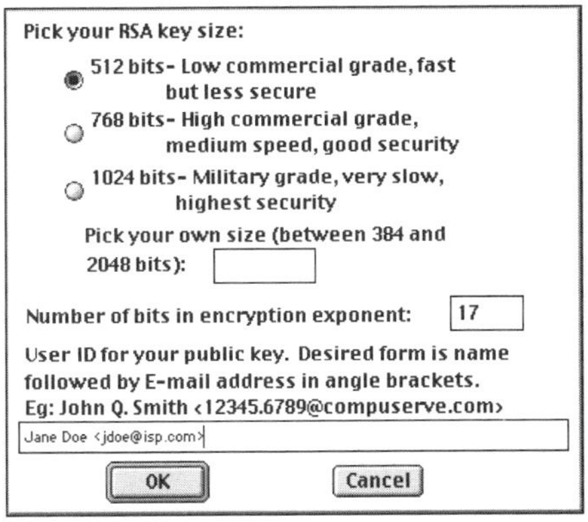

Pick your RSA key size:

○ **512 bits**– Low commercial grade, fast
but less secure

○ **768 bits**– High commercial grade,
medium speed, good security

○ **1024 bits**– Military grade, very slow,
highest security

Pick your own size (between 384 and
2048 bits): [   ]

Number of bits in encryption exponent: [17]

User ID for your public key. Desired form is name
followed by E-mail address in angle brackets.
Eg: John Q. Smith <12345.6789@compuserve.com>

[Jane Doe <jdoe@isp.com>]

[OK]   [Cancel]

Figure 16.17   The MacPGP key-creation window.

3. Decide on your key size. The larger the key, the more secure the encryption, but the longer it takes to generate it. You can choose from the preset options or manually enter your key size preference.

4. Enter the User ID for your public key. Unlike standard logins, this information can contain spaces. MacPGP suggests you use your name followed by your email address.

5. Click on Okay. You will be prompted to enter the private passkey. Unlike a password, this field can be much longer (even a sentence) and contains spaces as well as upper- and lowercase.

6. You may be prompted to type random characters on the keyboard to generate the passkey. After the process is finished, two files will be created: pubring.pgp and secring.pgp. The pubring.pgp file can be exchanged with other users so that information can be sent to you only. The secring.pgp ring is confidential and should not be shared.

Encrypting A File Using MacPGP

After you generate a key, you can exchange this key with other people with whom you correspond. However, you can use this program to password-protect files on your hard drive. This prevents the casual snooper from viewing your files without you having to resort to extensive encryption. Follow these steps:

1. Launch MacPGP.

2. Go to File|Conventional Encrypt.

3. Locate the file you wish to encrypt and select Open.

4. Set your encryption options (see Figure 16.18). You can export the file as ASCII text for easy exchanging. Click on the Do It button to encrypt the file.

5. You will be prompted to enter a pass phrase. This does not need to match your private passkey (and in fact, should not match it) so that your encryption key is not compromised.

6. The encryption process will create a new file with the .pgp extension. This file cannot be opened without the pass phase you designated.

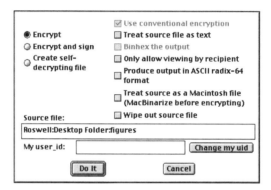

Figure 16.18   The Conventional Encryption window.

Chapter 17

Event And System Monitoring Tools

In Depth

Monitoring System Performance

As you are working on your computer you experience a drag in system performance. Many things could be causing this. Did you just send a long document to print? Is someone accessing your computer via file sharing? Do you have an application running that periodically takes over system resources? Are you running multiple applications? How long has it been since you've defragmented your hard drive? Any of these could be true. The problem lies in determining *what* is causing this lag in processing power. You have to ask yourself or the user what applications are running, how the applications are configured, if virtual memory is active, if the Mac is connected to a network, and if unexpected services are being used. Mac OS 8.5 includes some basic programs that show what applications are running, who is accessing the computer, and how the computer is configured. In this first section, we will be covering monitoring utilities included with Mac OS 8.5. We'll cover third-party utilities that can perform some of these functions better in "Choosing The Right Tools."

The Application Menu

The Mac OS has frequently used graphical objects as menus; for example, until Mac OS 8, the Help menu was located under a question mark. For many years, you accessed the Apple menu to instantly launch applications or utilities. Now, you use the Application menu, located in the top right of the screen. It changes depending on the active application, and you can switch to any open application by selecting it from this menu. You can also hide or show open applications. Figure 17.1 shows the Application menu.

Figure 17.1   The Application menu.

17: Event And System Monitoring Tools

However, many users are not even aware of this menu because it doesn't display the word "Application" for them to click on. They launch huge applications like Microsoft PowerPoint or Excel and close document windows without choosing File|Quit when they are finished. They click on the Desktop and suddenly lose the menus that applied to the previous program, so they don't have a reminder or even an option to quit the open application. Soon, they begin to experience memory errors. In the past, frustrated systems administrators have installed programs such as Tilery or GoMac to give users visual reminders of what was running. In Mac OS 8.5, the Application menu has been updated. You can still click on it to see a list of running programs, but now you can optionally drag the menu onto the Desktop. When it is in this state, it is called the *Application Switcher*. The menu now changes into a strip with an icon button and/or title for each running program. You can simply click on the desired application to switch to it and perform new tasks or to quit the program. Figure 17.2 shows the Application menu placed on the Desktop.

By clicking on the Zoom box located within the title bar, you can collapse the buttons to graphic icons or expand the buttons to include the application title. You can drag the Application Switcher to any part of the Desktop by dragging its title bar. The Application Switcher also behaves like the AppleGuide windows: It stays to the forefront no matter what application is active; therefore, it's always visible. It remains in this state even after you restart your computer. The Application Switcher is also AppleScriptable. You can write a script that indicates the location and look of the Application Switcher and use it to preserve your settings or the settings of another user. The one problem with the Application Switcher is that you can close it and lose the visual reminders of running applications. For this reason, you may want to consider using some of the other tools we will discuss in this chapter, such as GoMac and Tilery.

File Sharing Monitor

File sharing has many benefits. It allows you to collaborate with a coworker easily without exchanging floppy disks or asking a server administrator to create a shared directory. You can also access your own computer from another computer on the network. However, it can deplete your system performance, especially if someone is doing processor-intensive actions such as copying a file. If you experience a sudden reduction in system performance, you should see if file

Figure 17.2   The Application menu on the Desktop.

sharing is active. Check the Control Strip File Sharing icon or open the File Sharing control panel. If file sharing is active, you need to find out if someone else is accessing your computer. The File Sharing control panel has a second panel called *Activity Monitor*; It indicates who is connected to your computer, the level of activity, and what items are currently being used. If you are working on an extremely important document and need every bit of computer power, you can disconnect users that are attached by clicking on the Disconnect button. You can detach users immediately or give them a grace period and allow them to detach themselves. Figure 17.3 shows the Activity Monitor.

You can also determine the access privileges of a user who is accessing your computer. For example, you may notice that someone has logged on as *Guest*, but seems to be accessing your hard drive. You may be witnessing a security breach in progress. Someone may have changed file-sharing privileges at your computer while you were away and is now grabbing all kinds of information from your computer without your permission. In other cases, you can see if a particular user has logged on to give you information in an appropriate shared folder. Whatever the case, you can see quickly who is using your computer resources.

About This Computer

When you are experiencing memory errors, one of the first places you should go to begin the troubleshooting process is the About This Computer window. This application is located under the Apple menu. Notice that it can only be accessed within the Finder. About This Computer gives a dependable view into the allocation of memory and it shows you not only how memory is generally allocated, but also how each application is utilizing that partition. The amount of built-in memory and virtual memory are added to provide the total memory available. About This

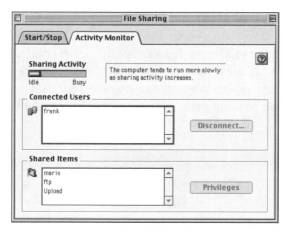

Figure 17.3   The Activity Monitor within the File Sharing control panel.

17: Event And System Monitoring Tools

Figure 17.4   The About This Computer window.

Computer also indicates what applications are currently running on your computer. Figure 17.4 shows the About This Computer window.

As a knowledgeable Mac user, one of the first things you probably do when an application crashes due to an error of a specific type is to increase the memory allocated to the application. However, it is not always memory that is the problem. Later, you may determine that it was a corrupted document or another problem; yet, you leave the increased memory allocation available to the application when it is not really needed. The About This Computer window shows the total block of memory allocated to an application and how much of the allocation the program actually uses. Remember that this allocated block of memory is unavailable to other programs. You should periodically check About This Computer to see if a particular application was allocated too much memory so that you don't waste memory.

Choosing The Right Tools

The Mac OS provides adequate programs and menus for monitoring activities within the system. Sometimes, however, you need more information than these utilities provide. The information is often there; you just need the right software to reach it. Tools are available that show open applications and reveal exactly how the memory is being distributed. Tools are also available that restart your computer in the event of a system or application crash. You can even purchase programs that show you exactly what processes are running (even processes usually hidden within the System). Many of these programs are commercially available. You can download several from software archives; some of these applications are free (Okey Dokey, for example, is freeware).

Application Monitoring

While the detachable Application menu is a handy method of viewing and switching among open applications, you can purchase third-party programs that not only provide this view, but also allow you to easily retrieve important program information. In fact, until Mac OS 8.5 you had to use a third-party utility to view open applications as buttons on a task bar. Each monitoring program has its strengths, and one of them even allows you to monitor how long you have been using an application, which would be helpful if you need to bill a customer for your computer time.

Tilery

Tilery is an application monitoring program that has been available for some time and is still being updated with each new Mac OS release. Tilery is an application, not a control panel or extension. To have it launch each time the computer is booted, you must put an alias of the Tilery program in the Startup Items folder. Tilery displays open applications as buttons or bars, with or without the application name. Clicking on a Tilery button provides a contextual menu that allows you quick access to the Get Info window as well as information on the application's memory usage. Tilery also has an extensive online help system. Additionally, Tilery differentiates itself from other programs of its kind by featuring *remembered tiles*. These tiles are actually buttons for programs not currently running (this feature is similar to the Launcher control panel). To launch the application, simply click on its button within Tilery. Tilery is a shareware program that you can download from most software archives, including **www.shareware.com**.

GoMac

GoMac is a control panel that gives the Mac OS a taskbar similar to the one available in Windows 95/98. This taskbar appears across the bottom of the screen and displays a button for each running application. GoMac also creates a folder named Start Menu Items within the System Folder. You can place aliases to applications within this folder. When you click on the Start button located on the GoMac taskbar, you will see these items listed within its menu (an extensive listing is automatically created when you install and restart your computer). You can also add new items to the Start menu by dragging an icon over the Start menu button (an alias will be placed within the Start Menu Items folder). As with Tilery, shortcut menus are available when you click on a button within the taskbar. The menu allows you to perform such tasks as minimizing, hiding, and quitting a running application. You can also see how much memory the application is using within this shortcut menu. And GoMac allows you to use Command+Tab to switch among open programs. GoMac is a shareware program that you can download from most software archives, including **www.shareware.com**.

One Click

One Click from Westcode Software is a commercial program that provides a method for seeing exactly what applications are running. One Click gives you extra functionality in managing the open programs including hiding, showing, and quitting the selected application from the toolbars. One Click uses a task toolbar with buttons that represent the applications currently running and also provides a launcher toolbar you can use to launch files, applications, and folders. What makes One Click an excellent addition to your system is its extensive scriptability. The One Click Web site at **www.westcodesoft.com** includes a large library of buttons that have useful scripts attached. You can also record and write scripts to reduce the steps you take in often-repeated tasks. You truly can do many system functions with just One Click.

MultiTimer Pro

Occasionally, you may need to track the time you spend on a particular project. You can use the MultiTimer application to perform this task. You can then use the log information in monthly reports, in billing records, or as a gauge for the time it takes to complete different kinds of projects. You can create, save, and delete different modules within MultiTimer that allow you to organize the tracking information. After you have created a module, you can click on the Stopwatch button to begin the timer. You can note any applications or tasks that you perform while the timer is running in a log file for the module. You can also designate certain files to open automatically if the module's timer is activated. MultiTimer also displays a floating window when the timer is activated as a reminder while you are working. MultiTimer can also sense when idle time occurs during a timed session and ask you if you want to remove it from the recorded minutes for that module. MultiTimer is a shareware utility also available from most software archives. Figure 17.5 shows the MultiTimer Pro window.

Memory Monitoring

Although adequate information about memory allocation exists in the About This Computer utility, more information is available that can help you manage memory better or determine if you need to restart your computer to defragment your memory. Perhaps an application has not completely released its memory, or several applications have been launched so that large blocks of memory are no longer available. In either case, applications exist that provide more information about what is going on with your computer's memory.

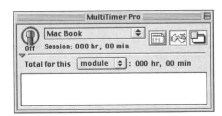

Figure 17.5   The MultiTimer Pro window.

MATM

More About This Macintosh (MATM) is an application that you can launch at any time to report on the state of memory allocation on the Mac. It shows the actual division of memory between System and Finder. It also shows the blocks of available memory. If it finds several of these free blocks, rather than one large empty one, this indicates fragmented memory. MATM warns you if this condition exists. You can also determine which applications would be most beneficial to quit in order to free the greatest amount of memory. MATM also provides volume and system information. Figure 17.6 shows the MATM application window in action. Refer to Chapter 2 for more information about MATM.

Ram Doubler

Ram Doubler is a commercial program that uses methods at the system level to increase memory performance. This program has an added benefit of comprehensive memory usage reports. You can not only see how much memory is allocated versus how much is actually used, but you can also determine how the memory in each application is being used. Figure 17.7 shows the Ram Doubler application pane. For more information about Ram Doubler, see Chapter 6.

System And Server Crashes

Macintosh computers are wonderful, but they are not perfect. Applications hang and the system crashes. In all cases, this is frustrating. You usually must restart the computer to restore it to working order. However, there may be mission-critical computers, such as network servers that users access to run applications that must stay in good working order. Another example is a company Web server that

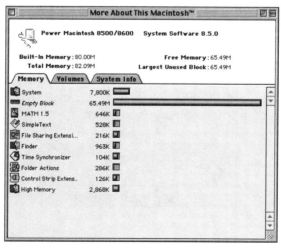

Figure 17.6   The MATM memory window.

17: Event And System Monitoring Tools

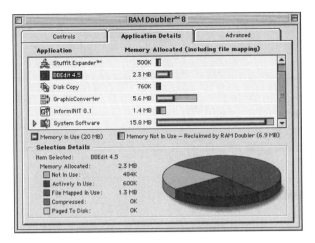

Figure 17.7   Ram Doubler memory monitoring.

must stay up. In many situations, the server is located in a protected room, and crash messages may not be immediately visible, or the crash may occur after hours and force a server administrator to return to work to reboot the computer. The following utilities help forewarn of a crash or automatically reboot in the event of one.

Norton CrashGuard

Norton CrashGuard from Symantec is a simple program included with Norton Utilities that helps prevent crashes and gives you a few more options in the event of an application crash. Norton CrashGuard requires almost no configuration. Simply install and run it to enable the protection. CrashGuard now watches for application instability. If it detects problems, CrashGuard displays an alert window, allowing you the options of quitting the application, fixing the application, or restarting the computer. The safest option is to quit the application. You should attempt to fix the application only if the problem application contains unsaved work. If CrashGuard is successful, you should save the data under a different name to prevent corruption, then restart your computer. If you do not restart, you may cause an error that even CrashGuard cannot bypass. When crashes do occur, CrashGuard makes an entry in the log file. You can use this log file to diagnosis problems on the computer, such as determining if the same application is always crashing.

Norton DiskLight

Norton DiskLight is a component of Norton Utilities from Symantec. DiskLight is a control panel that provides a simple functionality. It displays a tiny icon in the corner of the screen that indicates what type of disk is processing information.

Figure 17.8   The DiskLight control panel.

The icon also indicates if data is being written to the disk and identifies the SCSI ID of the device. Figure 17.8 shows the DiskLight control panel.

PowerKey

Although this application doesn't have much to do with monitoring system performance, Sophisticated Circuits provides an excellent hardware and software solution that enables you to keep mission-critical machines running as well as remotely turn on your Macintosh. For example, PowerKey Pro is a sophisticated power strip with an ADB port. You can plug your computer's power cords into this strip (including the peripheral devices such as scanners and Zip drives). You can then use an ADB cable to connect your computer to the PowerKey Pro ADB port. What does this do for you? You can start all your devices with one push of your power button. With some products, you can "call" your computer and, by a series of telephone rings, initiate the command to turn the computer on.

What makes the PowerKey Pro and PowerKey Rebound! software/hardware solution really practical is that the hardware can determine if the computer has crashed. If so, it can send a signal to restart the computer. This is especially useful if the crash occurs when you are not at the office. You can find more information about PowerKey products at **www.sophisticated.com**.

AutoBoot

AutoBoot is a shareware utility that performs a specific function: It restarts a Mac after a system crash or bomb. It doesn't detect application crashes or hangs (Keep It Up performs that task). This utility is wonderful if you have a computer that must stay up and running in good order. When the system crashes, AutoBoot displays an alert message that a crash has occurred (it might also display a bomb). In most cases, enough system resources are available to cause AutoBoot to restart the computer. (This helps eliminate cross-town trips back to work to restart the computer.) When AutoBoot is activated, it keeps a log file so you can

17: Event And System Monitoring Tools

determine the cause of the crash (be aware that this information might be lost in the restart; in this case, the log file gives the reason as "cause unknown"). AutoBoot is available at most software archives.

Keep It Up

Keep It Up is a shareware utility that you can configure to check certain applications for activity. If a certain period passes without a monitored application interacting with the system because the application crashed or because you quit the application, Keep It Up restarts the monitored application. If the program cannot be launched again, Keep It Up displays a warning dialog box and restarts the computer. You can configure Keep It Up to automatically disable itself during certain periods of the day and schedule automatic computer restarts. Keep It Up is available at most software archives.

MacsBug

MacsBug is a programming utility that provides detailed system information to programmers. An entire chapter could be written on this utility and much of what it does is outside the scope of this chapter. MacsBug gives you detailed information on what is happening in Mac OS 8.5. Much of it will only make sense to developers and system engineers. If it is installed in the System Folder, the MacsBug window will appear when an application or the system experiences a crash. You may also accidentally enter the MacsBug window. The window is completely text-based and includes a prompt for entering text-based commands. Common MacsBug commands will be covered in the section "Using MacsBug" later in this chapter. MacsBug may be included on your system. If not, you should be able to retrieve it from **www.apple.com**.

System Processes

Today, many work environments interact heavily with the network. You may be running multiple Internet and client applications simultaneously. Suppose that you are working on your computer when you notice that at a regular interval it seems to hang for several seconds. You might have a problem identifying which application is taking over system processes. Prime candidates could be email programs checking for new mail, word processors performing an automatic save, or a client program interacting with its server. You can use utilities to see exactly what is happening with the system. You may also see situations where a dialog box appears on your monitor while you are away from your computer (perhaps during booting). The dialog box continues to sit there waiting for your input and halting the proper operation of the system. A utility is available that can automatically respond to these dialog boxes and allow system processes to continue.

17: Event And System Monitoring Tools

Peek-A-Boo

Peek-a-Boo is a shareware utility that monitors and displays information about system processes. It displays information available in the Process Manager that has been included in the Macintosh operating system since System 7. Peek-a-Boo can tell you how the system memory is being allocated, the CPU activity generated by an application, and precisely what system resources a process is using. This utility is useful if you routinely experience a degradation in system performance and are unsure of the culprit application. Some client applications are notorious for polling with the server at incredibly short intervals and monopolizing system resources during this communication. Peek-a-Boo provides great detail about these applications or processes, including history graphs, and even allows you to "kill" a process from within Peek-a-Boo. Kill will issue the **quit** command to the application or process, allowing it to exit properly. Peek-a-Boo is available from most software archives. Figure 17.9 shows a sample Peek-a-Boo window.

Okey Dokey Pro

Okey Dokey Pro is a free control panel that performs a very simple function: In dialog boxes that are left unattended, it accepts the default option and clears the window. You can configure Okey Dokey Pro to clear the dialog window after a certain time has elapsed, provide a countdown to when Okey Dokey Pro will accept the default, and keep a log of missed dialogs. This program is valuable in restarting crashed servers by answering the dialog box to restart the computer. You can also list certain applications that either are ignored by Okey Dokey Pro or are the only applications handled by Okey Dokey Pro. Okey Dokey Pro is available from most software archives.

Quick Reference Specifications

The following list shows the essential facts about event and system monitoring tools:

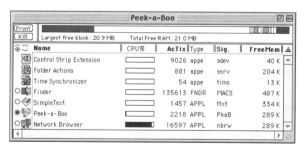

Figure 17.9   The Peek-a-Boo window.

17: Event And System Monitoring Tools

- Mac OS 8.5 includes limited system monitoring options.

- You can detach the Application menu. In this state, it is called the Application Switcher.

- The Application Switcher window stays in the foreground.

- You can monitor file-sharing use by using both the File Sharing control panel and Control Strip button.

- A program may not use all the memory allocated to it. You can determine this from the About This Computer window.

- The Tilery application-monitoring program can also act as an application launcher.

- You can add additional items to the GoMac Start menu by dragging an icon over the Start menu button.

- Memory can become fragmented so that the total unused memory may not contain a large enough block to meet the memory allocation of a launching application.

- Applications that are running make periodic calls to the operating system.

- Some client applications are programmed to interact with the server on a regular basis and could monopolize your available system resources.

- You can log application activity with MacsBug.

Utilities To Use

The utilities or elements of the Mac OS discussed in this chapter are listed here as a memory aid for the busy user or system administrator:

- *Application Switcher*—Term for the Application menu when it has been detached from the menu bar and placed on the Desktop.

- *About This Computer*—The application included with Mac OS 8.5 that provides memory usage information.

- *File Sharing*—The control panel included with Mac OS 8.5 that monitors file-sharing activity.

- *The Tilery*—A program that displays a button for open and remembered applications.

- *GoMac*—A control panel that provides a taskbar similar to Windows 95/98 for the Mac OS.

- *MultiTimer*—A software program that times and logs projects and applications.

17: Event And System Monitoring Tools

- *MATM*—A program with an interface similar to About This Computer that provides additional memory information.

- *Ram Doubler*—A commercial program that increases the performance of installed memory and provides tools for monitoring memory usage.

- *Norton CrashGuard*—A commercial program included with Norton Utilities that warns you and provides additional options if a system or application crash is looming.

- *Norton DiskLight*—A commercial program included with Norton Utilities that displays an icon of the active volume.

- *AutoBoot*—A program that restarts your computer in the event of a system crash or bomb.

- *Keep It Up*—An application that monitors applications and launches them again if the monitored programs crash or are manually exited.

- *MacsBug*—Debugging software that provides detailed information about system processes.

- *Peek-a-Boo*—A software program that displays information about the processes running on a computer; it maintains a history of CPU usage.

- *Okey Dokey Pro*—A control panel that automatically accepts the default option of dialog boxes after a certain period of time has elapsed.

Immediate Solutions

Monitoring Applications In The Finder

Apple includes an excellent and simple method of determining what applications are running. It is called the *Application menu*, and it is located in the top-right corner of the screen. You can also detach it and display it on the Desktop. Follow these steps to detach the Application menu:

1. Click on the Application menu.

2. Drag it to the end of the window and wait for the outline of a box to appear on the Desktop.

3. Release the mouse where you want the Application Switcher to appear.

4. Click on the Zoom box to reduce the Application Switcher to small buttons. Figure 17.10 shows the Application Switcher sized both large and small.

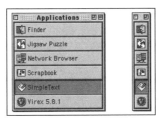

Figure 17.10　The two sizes of the Application Switcher.

Monitoring Memory In About This Computer

Whether you are encountering memory errors or need to see what operating system is running on a Mac, you can use the About This Computer utility to retrieve this information. You can determine if your memory is allocated efficiently, how much memory is on the machine, how much memory is free, and what operating system is running on the computer. To access About This Computer, follow these steps:

1. Go to the Application menu and select Finder.

2. Select Apple menu|About This Computer.

17: Event And System
Monitoring Tools

501

3. Look in the top-right corner of this window for operating system information.

4. Look under the Mac OS Computer graphic for built-in, virtual, and free memory information.

Each open application is listed within the About This Computer window and memory usage is represented by a box progress bar. The more the progress bar fills the box, the more the application is using the memory allocated to it. Figure 17.11 shows the About This Computer window.

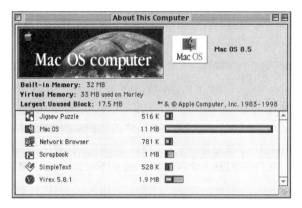

Figure 17.11   The About This Computer window.

Using The File Sharing Activity Monitor

If you have file sharing active and suddenly notice a lot of hard drive activity on your computer—especially if you take a significant performance hit—someone might be accessing your computer. Several ways exist within Mac OS 8.5 to help you determine if this is happening:

1. Go to Apple Menu|Control Panels and select File Sharing.

2. Click on the Activity Monitor tab.

3. Look at the box listing connected users. If it is empty, no one is accessing your computer. If the box does contain a list of users, check the Sharing Activity level to determine if that is causing the increased activity on your computer. Figure 17.12 shows the File Sharing Activity Monitor window.

TIP: *You can easily see if someone is accessing your computer from the Control Strip: The File Sharing icon adds the image of a person on the folder. You can then click on the File Sharing button and see the connected users. Figure 17.13 shows the changed folder and menu that lists connected users.*

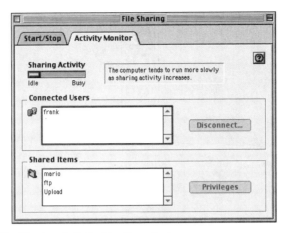

Figure 17.12　The File Sharing Activity Monitor window.

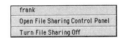

Figure 17.13　The File Sharing Control Strip showing attached users.

Using The Tilery

The Application Switcher in Mac OS 8.5 shows only the applications that are running. It is not even configured for contextual menus. Tilery, however, is a third-party application that goes beyond just listing what applications are running. You can see how much memory the programs are using, create buttons to launch favorite programs, and easily access the Get Info window for a particular application. Follow these steps for using the Tilery:

1. Launch the Tilery application (add the Tilery alias to your Startup Items folder to have Tilery launch automatically).

2. All open applications should appear as buttons on your Desktop as shown in Figure 17.14. To change the style of these buttons go to Tiles|Tile Styles.

3. If you don't like the location of the tiles, go to Tiles|Tile Placement to set the location of the beginning tile and the orientation and space between the tiles.

4. As you launch applications you can configure Tilery to display a button for the program, even when it's not running. Click on the Tilery button for the application and wait for a menu to appear, then select Remember Tile (see Figure 17.15).

Figure 17.14   The Tilery buttons on the Desktop

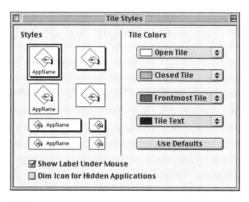

Figure 17.15   The Tilery button menu.

Using GoMac

GoMac is a third-party control panel that provides you with a taskbar similar to Windows 95/98 (actually, it mimics this taskbar very closely). Applications that are running will appear as buttons on the taskbar; a Start menu provides fast access to specified applications. GoMac also includes a clock and built-in calendar. Clicking on the buttons on the taskbar brings up menus for that application. To install and use GoMac:

1. Drag the GoMac control panel over the System Folder to install GoMac with the other control panels.

2. Restart your computer. You should see a welcome screen for the GoMac control panel providing some quick tips and reminding you to pay for the product. GoMac will initiate the creation of a folder in the System Folder called Start Menu Items.

3. If GoMac has successfully loaded, a taskbar will appear at the bottom of the screen with a button for each open application.

4. By default, the Start menu contains links to the Applications folder and several Apple Menu folders. You can manually add items to this folder or drag an icon over the Start menu button to add items to the Start menu. Figure 17.16 shows the default Start menu.

5. Each application button on the taskbar has a menu. Click on this menu to retrieve information about the program (such as memory usage) as well as to quit the program from GoMac.

Figure 17.16   The GoMac default Start menu.

Using MultiTimer

If you need to track the time it takes to complete a project or you need to provide billing records for your time, you may want to use MultiTimer. This application enables you to create "modules" and record all activity associated with that module. You can use this information for reporting or billing. You can also configure MultiTimer to launch certain applications and documents when a module is selected and activated. Follow these steps for using MultiTimer:

1. Launch MultiTimer. The window in Figure 17.17 appears.

2. Go to File|New Module and designate a name for your project.

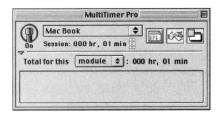

Figure 17.17   The MultiTimer Pro window appears.

3. If you want certain documents or applications to be opened when a module's timer is activated, select File|Auto-Open Files.

4. Click on the Add Files button and add the appropriate applications or documents (you can also drag items from Finder into the window). You can add up to five items.

5. Click on the stop-watch button icon to start the timer. Any activity you do on the computer while the timer is running will be recorded in a log file for the module. You can use this information to create billing records or reports.

Using MATM

The About This Computer window does provide adequate information for the average user, but sometimes you need more information. MATM is an application that provides the same information as About This Computer and also expands on it. MATM can show when memory is fragmented and also provide volume and system information. Follow these steps for using MATM:

1. Launch MATM. The window in Figure 17.18 appears.

2. If memory is fragmented, MATM warns you, even suggesting that you restart your computer to repair your memory.

Blue bars appear to the right of all open processes and applications. Red bars indicate a free memory block. You may see more than one red bar if the memory is fragmented.

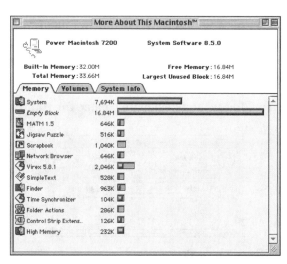

Figure 17.18   The MATM window.

17: Event And System Monitoring Tools

Using AutoBoot

AutoBoot is a program comprised of a system Extension and a control panel. AutoBoot can restart your computer in the event of a system crash or bomb. This kind of utility is useful for important computers and servers that must be up and running at all times. AutoBoot works in conjunction with Keep It Up to make sure that your computer or server is operational without forcing you to return to work just to reboot the system. Be aware that you should not run AutoBoot and Norton CrashGuard at the same time. To use AutoBoot:

1. Select the AutoBoot control panel and Extension, and drag them over the System Folder. Allow the System Folder to place the files.

2. Restart your computer.

3. Go to Apple Menu|Control Panels and select AutoBoot (see Figure 17.19).

4. Set your options for AutoBoot (you can even indicate what should trigger AutoBoot to restart the computer and the length of the delay before the computer is restarted).

If you are adventurous (or skeptical) and want to test AutoBoot, you can launch some applications included with AutoBoot that are located within the Bomb folder. These programs should generate a system error and cause the computer to restart.

Figure 17.19   The AutoBoot control panel.

Using Keep It Up

Keep It Up is a shareware utility that monitors a defined set of applications. If Keep It Up determines that a program is no longer running or functioning, it restarts the program after a predetermined time has elapsed. All running applications communicate with the operating system, even when they are in the background and not being actively used. Keep It Up monitors the system calls of the applications you have configured it to monitor and if Keep It Up notices that an application is no longer communicating with the system it will attempt to restart. The application in question may have crashed or you may have quit the application. You can also configure Keep It Up to restart the computer on a regular schedule. Follow these steps to configure Keep It Up:

1. Launch Keep It Up (place an alias of Keep It Up in your Startup Items folder to automatically launch Keep It Up when your computer is restarted).

2. A folder will be created in the Preferences folder called Keep It Up Items. Add aliases to all applications or documents that you want Keep It Up to monitor. Be aware that Keep It Up is only activated by an application quitting, not a document closing.

3. Switch to the Keep It Up program and go to File|Preferences. The window in Figure 17.20 will appear.

4. Set the appropriate preferences for Keep It Up. Make sure you set a delay for the idle time for activation or applications that are exited will immediately be launched again. Also, be aware that some applications take as long as 10 minutes between system calls, yet could still be active (remember that the lack of system calls is what activates Keep It Up).

5. You can also disable the option to restart the computer if Keep It Up cannot launch the monitored application. However, if Keep It Up is on a server, you should leave this setting enabled.

6. Set the Background Speed option; this determines how often Keep It Up monitors the system calls of the monitored applications. The Slow setting takes fewer system resources, but it may miss system calls.

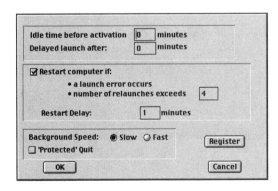

Figure 17.20   The Keep It Up Preferences window.

7. If desired, select Protected Quit; this option disables the option to exit Keep It Up (you can hold down the Shift key to access the Quit option if this is selected).

8. After you have set the desired options for Keep It Up, click on the Okay button.

When Keep It Up is active, a small window appears that contains the Keep It Up icon.

Using MacsBug

MacsBug is a free developer's tool for debugging programming. This program gives detailed technical information that is useful for fixing problems in software. You can obtain it from Apple's software archive at **www.apple.com**. For the average user, MacsBug is confusing, intimidating, and downright frightening after the simplicity of the graphical user interface. But it can allow you to document errors with an application or system process and give this information to the appropriate developer.

You may see MacsBug on two occasions: because you activated it accidentally or because an application has crashed. When MacsBug is activated, the screen is filled with text information, and a prompt is available for entering commands. Table 17.1 shows the text-string commands that a non-programmer would use within MacsBug.

Table 17.1   Useful MacsBug commands.

Command	Result
Command+Power Key	Activates the MacsBug interface (often done accidentally).
Esc	Toggles between the Finder and MacsBug interfaces.
g	Returns the user to the Finder interface.
help	When typed at the command prompt, displays MacsBug help information.
help miscellaneous	Provides listing and result of common MacsBug commands.
ea	Restarts the current application.
es	Forces the running application to quit (you should restart after this command).
rs	Unmounts all volumes except the server and restarts the computer.
rb	Unmounts everything and restarts.
stdlog	Logs the current application's activity.

17: Event And System
Monitoring Tools

You can provide a software developer with information about a buggy application by using the **stdlog** command. Simply invoke MacsBug, type "stdlog", go back into the Finder, and then launch the problem application. When the application crashes, a log file is created with detailed information you can give to the developer.

Using Peek-A-Boo

Occasionally, you may be curious about what is really going on in the operating system, or you may have an unknown process hogging system resources. Peek-a-Boo is a shareware program that provides information on all processes running and how much of the system resources each process is using. Peek-a-Boo displays information that you normally cannot see and you can use this information to pinpoint troublesome programs. Follow these steps to use Peek-a-Boo as a diagnostic tool:

1. Launch the Peek-a-Boo application. See Figure 17.21 for an example window.

2. Watch the CPU% bar for the different processes.

3. If you think you have identified a problem application or process, go to Processes|CPU% History. A small window will appear and after a period of time a graph will be drawn indicating the activity history of the process (see Figure 17.22)

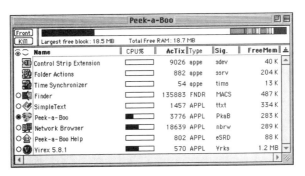

Figure 17.21   The Peek-a-Boo process monitoring window.

Figure 17.22   A history graph of an application monitored by Peek-a-Boo.

17: Event And System Monitoring Tools

Using Okey Dokey Pro

Suppose that your computer has crashed, and you had to force it to restart. You run out for a drink of water and end up in a conversation with a colleague. When you return to your computer, you find that a dialog box is displayed, which warns you to properly shut down your computer and which has held up the rest of the boot process. Okey Dokey Pro is a free control panel that can take care of these situations. It automatically answers dialog boxes that appear. You can set the delay time before Okey Dokey Pro will auto-answer and display a countdown. You can create a set of applications that can be treated differently by Okey Dokey Pro depending on the setting you choose (you can choose whether Okey Dokey Pro answers or doesn't auto-answer dialog boxes from these applications). To install and configure Okey Dokey Pro:

1. Drag the Okey Dokey Pro control panel to the System Folder and install the control panel.

2. Restart your computer.

3. Go to Apple menu|Control Panels and select Okey Dokey Pro. The window shown in Figure 17.23 appears.

4. Set the amount of time that will pass before Okey Dokey Pro is activated.

5. You can display a countdown by clicking the button beside Display Remaining Time.

6. Select Keep Snapshot Log if you want a record of the dialog boxes answered by Okey Dokey Pro.

7. If desired, click on the Special Apps button to designate applications affected or not affected by Okey Dokey Pro (you have the options Inactive or Active only in special apps).

Changes in Okey Dokey Pro take place when you close the window.

Figure 17.23   The Okey Dokey Pro control panel window.

Chapter 18

Troubleshooting

In Depth

Even the most complex computer system needs occasional attention and maintenance. The Macintosh computer is no exception. The Mac OS is constantly under revision and with each new release comes a new set of possible problems. The Macintosh platform underwent a major shift a few years ago with the switch to the RISC (Power PC) chip. When this happened, old software did not run on the new processor chip. Gradually, software developers made the switch to the Power Macintosh platform so that today, most software for the Macintosh requires that the computer be Power Macintosh. Later releases of the Mac OS (including Mac OS X) will be written explicitly and tested for the G3 chip. Even this will not remove the possibility that memory will be fragmented, that hard drives will need maintenance, and that extensions will fail to load.

This chapter will not cover every troubleshooting situation in depth. In fact, entire books have been written on this subject. We'll give you tips to speed up the general troubleshooting process and cover some of the common situations you may face.

Steps In Troubleshooting

When you have a problem with your system, one of the most frustrating aspects is the amount of time you waste when you realize the solution was simple. For example, a user was using a common word-processor program and as she typed, strange formatting changes would occur. After a system upgrade and other hardware improvements, the behavior still occurred. The eventual cause of the problem was a workstation chair that was too low, causing the user's hands to accidentally push the Control key while typing.

Whether you are dealing with a problem on your own computer or providing support for a user in your department, you can use the following series of steps to understand the problem and narrow your scope of solutions.

Get The Details

If you are experiencing problems with your computer, one of the first things you need to do is document the details of the problem. Ask yourself if you installed any new software, made changes to the configuration of a control panel, or performed a system upgrade. Note the last time you successfully performed the task

18: Troubleshooting

that now is failing. Document the operating system environment when the problem occurs. Pay attention to any system error messages; they often tell you what is wrong. For example, suppose that Netscape Navigator seems to run out of memory after extensive Internet browsing. Determine the version of operating system you are using, the version of Netscape Navigator, the amount of available memory, and how long you were able to browse the Web before the failure occurred. If the problem seems to be widespread across multiple applications, you may want to keep a journal that lists error messages and crashes. You may be surprised to discover that a pattern really does exist in the crashes.

If you are dealing with a user or customer who is experiencing computer problems, the most important thing you can do is listen carefully to his or her description of the problem. You are not listening if you think ahead of possible solutions, or of the next customers. For now, let him or her explain what is going wrong and ask them key questions such as, "Did you change anything on the computer?" and "When was the last time you could perform this task?" If you have an unreliable memory, write down the information. When you have the details, you can begin to isolate the problem and look for solutions.

Duplicate The Problem

Use the information you retrieved. Then, try to duplicate the problem. In some cases, this may be easy. If the computer freezes when it boots, you should be able to verify the problem easily. Some problems may be more difficult to duplicate. For example, a user has reported that everything on his computer seemed to crash at once. He had to restart the computer, but was concerned because he was working on a document at the time. You may have to observe him at work or ask him to maintain a diary until you can see if some action or system process could be causing the problem. After you duplicate the problem, you can analyze the process causing the problem.

Check The Obvious

Suppose that a user has an external Zip drive and she reports trouble mounting the disk. Check the system to ensure that the necessary components are in place and check the physical connection. In this case, the Zip drive was terminated when the termination should have been disabled.

In another example, a Power Macintosh 6100 is turned on and makes a startup sound, but the monitor never displays an image. Check the obvious. Are the video cables securely connected? Can you hear the hard drive spinning? Will the computer boot from another system disk? You may want to try some quick fixes at this point such as running Disk First Aid, rebuilding the Desktop file, or running a virus check.

Check the obvious before exploring the obscure. Make sure that control panel settings are correct. In the first example, we could have wasted a lot of time downloading the latest drivers and playing with extension sets when the problem was an incorrect hardware setting.

Find The Cause

If all the obvious components are in place, you should begin the process of isolating the cause of the problem. Note every process that takes place before the problem occurs. Try some general solutions and document if the problem has been fixed. Don't try several solutions at once. For example, you may try rebuilding the Desktop file. At this point, rather than zapping the PRAM, see if the problem continues.

Start with general solutions before going to the specific. If you suspect an extension conflict, enable only the Mac OS 8.5 necessary extensions and see if the problem continues. You can then get more specific by enabling a few extensions at a time until you can isolate the problem.

Repair The Problem

Now that you have a general idea of what is causing the problem, you can suggest ways to repair it. In some cases, you can update software or device drivers. You can rearrange the load order of extensions. Whatever the solution, make sure that you document it for future reference. If you have the means, make the solution available to other users who may face the same situation.

Common Problems

Check out the Tech Info Library at **til.info.apple.com** and you'll see that this database contains hundreds—if not thousands—of documented problems and solutions. However, some common solutions can help you resolve the majority of your computer problems.

Sound But No Picture

Suppose that a user has pressed the power button on his computer, but he sees no booting activity. Nothing displays. Check how much of the power process is occurring. Verify that a startup sound occurred. If the CPU has an indicator light, see if it is lit. (A Macintosh computer may not make a startup sound if the volume is turned completely down.) If the indicator light is off, check the hardware connections, especially the keyboard. (The keyboard passes the signal to activate the computer, but if the keyboard connection has become loose, the signal will not reach the computer.)

If the indicator light is lit, check the monitor light. Today's energy saver monitors usually have an amber-colored indicator light when no video signal emits from the CPU or when the system is in energy-saver mode. When a signal is received, the amber light changes to a green light. If this doesn't happen but the CPU indicator light is active, check the monitor connections. If you do find a loose monitor cable and reconnect it, you may have to restart the system before the CPU and monitor can communicate.

If all connections are in place, restart the computer and listen for system activity. If it is absent, you could be looking at a hardware problem. Try switching monitors; if the monitor works on another computer, the problem is localized to the CPU. If not, a monitor problem exists. If the problem lies with the CPU, check the video card. Also, some older model Macintosh computers produce a startup sound but produce no other system activity when the battery is dead. If none of these options work, you should probably have an Apple-authorized repair shop look at the computer.

Problems Getting Started

Suppose that you have a Macintosh that does start, but cannot seem to progress to the Welcome screen for the Mac OS. Examine the display icons for clues. Identify if an icon appears at all. If you see only a gray screen, check for SCSI devices attached to the computer. If they are present, turn off the computer and remove the SCSI cable at the back of the computer, then restart the computer. If it boots, check the termination of the SCSI devices and make sure that they have unique identifying numbers. This may involve reattaching the devices one at time and booting the computer.

If your computer does display an icon but it is not the Happy Mac, inspect the icons closely. The Sad Mac indicates that the computer did an initial system check and discovered a problem. Try booting with the system software CD-ROM or a system disk. If you see this icon again, a possible hardware problem is present. If the computer can boot with another disk, a software problem, such as an incorrect System installed may exist. (Users may cause this by doing a copy of a System Folder, rather than actually running the installation program.) You can run Disk First Aid or Norton Utilities to fix the problem or install a correct operating system.

A disk icon with a blinking question mark indicates that a bootable system cannot be located or used. Try booting with a system CD-ROM or floppy disk. If the computer boots without error, try running Disk First Aid on the hard drive. (Apple suggests that you run the program several times.) Be aware that although Disk First Aid may initially say that it cannot repair the drive, it may be able to do so.

18: Troubleshooting

You may also want to run Norton Utilities or TechTool Pro for faster results. If the computer boots with an alternate system disk, but reports that the hard drive needs to be initialized, try running Disk First Aid. It may report that the disk cannot be repaired, but in many cases the computer will recognize the hard drive and allow you to boot from it. If so, you have a chance to back up your data before running serious programs, such as Norton Utilities, to diagnose and fix the disk. You may need to reinitialize the disk to fix it.

Hanging During Startup

Your computer does start successfully but cannot seem to finish the boot process. You may have an extension conflict or a problem with a particular extension. If your computer freezes while booting, restart it with extensions disabled. Verify that the computer can boot. If it cannot boot, you need to use another system disk such as a CD-ROM or floppy and run Disk First Aid on your computer. If the computer can launch, try enabling the Mac OS 8.5 base set in the Extensions Manager and restart. If the computer cannot boot, try booting from another media and running Disk First Aid. If the computer can boot, begin enabling extensions gradually (you probably will restart the computer multiple times). Make sure that you don't load huge batches of extensions; it's difficult to pinpoint the conflict to a particular file. You may also want to observe where the booting process hangs. Extensions and control panels load in alphabetical order. If the computer stops suddenly, check the last extension icon to successfully load; it can be an indicator of which extension is giving you trouble. Be aware that many of these files do not exhibit an icon during the boot process, so don't assume that the icon frozen on the screen is the culprit program.

If your computer seems to hang just before the end of the boot process, you need to see if a program in the Startup Items folder is causing the problem. You can disable items within this folder from the Extensions Manager.

Memory Trouble

You launch an application only to experience a system error, indicating that not enough memory is available. One of the first places you need to check is the About This Computer window. Locate the figure that indicates the largest free block of memory and compare it to the total memory used. If these figures added together do not equal your total memory, the memory is fragmented. You may be able to quit other open applications to create a large enough block for the application you want to open. Restarting the computer will also clear memory fragmentation. Errors may occur when a process is launched in the background and memory is not available for the process (for example, sending an item to print). Quitting open applications should clear enough memory to enable the process.

18: Troubleshooting

You may need to adjust the memory allocated to an application. While the application is closed, select File|Get Info|Memory and increase the preferred memory size. If you have an application that suddenly quits because an error has occurred—usually indicated with a numeric code—see if allocating more memory can improve the application's performance.

If you have several applications that need to be open at the same time and you do not have enough built-in memory, go to the Memory control panel and allocate hard drive space as Virtual Memory. (Virtual Memory is enabled by default.) Remember that increasing the Virtual Memory allocation reduces System performance (the hard drive memory partition is much slower than actual RAM). If you are constantly running out of memory, consider a physical memory upgrade.

Printing Problems

A user reports a Mac that is unable to complete the boot process. You learn that she had sent a document to print, but experienced a system crash and had to force the computer to restart. Now, the computer immediately hangs as the printing software attempts to pick up where it left off: printing the document. Remove the document from the print queue, then start the computer with extensions disabled. The desktop printer icons will now display large X's through them, as shown in Figure 18.1. Double-click on the icon of the printer driver that was in use during the system crash. Although printing software is disabled, you can still remove documents from the print queue.

Another common printing problem is that the printer cannot be found. To resolve this error, go to the Chooser and select the printer again. If the printer is not listed in the Chooser, check the printer's indicator light and cabling to make sure that the printer is on and connected to the computer or network. If the printer is on and correctly connected, turn the printer off for 10 seconds, then turn it back on to reinitialize it. If you still cannot see the printer, you may need to turn the printer and computer off and then restart the devices. You should be able to choose the printer and print your document.

If you are experiencing memory errors when printing, go to the Desktop Print Monitor application located in the Extensions folder. You can increase the memory allocated to the Desktop Print Monitor. You may also be sending a large and complex document to print. In this situation, it's a good idea to quit all open applications so that the bulk of the computer's resources can be used to print the document.

Figure 18.1   A disabled desktop printer icon.

Document Dilemmas

Suppose that a user has previously created and saved a file, but now cannot locate it. This is most often due to user error. The first time a file is saved, many applications default to the application's home folder. Users may not pay attention to this and select the Save option without switching to a documents folder. Mac OS 8.5 now provides an option for Favorite folders. Applications that support the new Save and Open dialog boxes make it easier for the user to locate files. You can also use the Find utility to search for the missing file by name, date created, date modified, kind, type, and even creator.

Another common document problem occurs when a user double-clicks on a document, but the application that created it cannot be found. You should first verify that the application is installed on the computer. If it is not, you have several options:

- Install the missing application.
- Ask the person who supplied the document to save it in a format your computer can open, such as Rich Text Format or TIFF.
- If you have an application similar to the missing one, see if translators are available that can open the document in question. For example, you have Microsoft 6.0, but receive a document from a colleague that is in Word 97 format. The Microsoft Web site has a translator you can download that allows Word 6.0 to open Word 97/98 documents. You may also get better results if you launch the application first, then open the file in question.

If you double-click on the document and the application is installed on your computer, rebuild the Desktop file. This corrects the file and document association problem. If you need to open the document immediately, try launching the application first, then the file from within the application.

Useful Tools

Whether you support only your own Macintosh computer or an entire organization, you need a library of software that you can use when troubleshooting. Mac OS 8.5 includes only limited utilities, so you need to invest in commercial software utilities to effectively maintain and support the Macintosh computer. Several excellent programs are available; we'll discuss the most common ones.

Disk First Aid

Disk First Aid is a free utility that is included with Mac OS 8.5. When you create a boot disk (such as a floppy startup disk), Disk First Aid is included. It can repair many, but not all, disk problems, so when you experience disk problems try running Disk First Aid first. Many Mac users use this utility as their only disk repair software.

Figure 18.2 shows the Disk First Aid window. Its options are simple: Select a disk to examine and choose to Verify or Repair the disk. The difference between these two actions is that Verify scans the disk and generates a report that indicates what repairs are needed and whether Disk First Aid can repair them. The Repair option also scans the disk and generates a report; then, it repairs problems if possible. Don't despair if Disk First Aid says it cannot repair a disk problem. Run Disk First Aid multiple times; the program may actually be fixing the problems bit by bit. This option is even recommended by Apple.

Disk First Aid can repair Mac OS Extended format disks. An improved version included with Mac OS 8.5 can repair the startup disk while it is active. In fact, if you improperly shut down or restart your Macintosh, Disk First Aid automatically scans the disk upon restart. Although Disk First Aid lacks the features of the commercial and shareware programs, it can repair many disk problems and is installed with the operating system.

Norton Utilities

Norton Utilities from Symantec is one of the most recognized of the disk repair and maintenance programs. It can do much more than Disk First Aid and has an excellent library of programs that helps you recover data, improve disk performance, and protect against crashes.

The most well-known utility in the Norton Utility suite is Disk Doctor. For many users, disk protection is an afterthought. Suddenly strange things happen to their

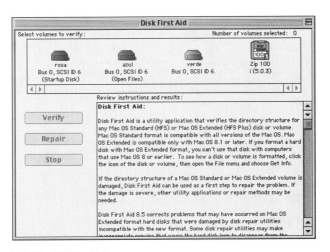

Figure 18.2   The Disk First Aid window.

computers that Disk First Aid cannot fix. Almost in desperation, they run out and purchase Norton Utilities just to run Disk Doctor and fix their disks. The good news is that Disk Doctor can usually save the day. But Norton Utilities can do much more. Figure 18.3 shows the Norton Utilities program window.

All of its elements are useful for troubleshooting, but some of the most commonly used of the Norton Utilities are the following:

- *DiskDoctor*—The mainstay of the utilities, it repairs damaged disks and volumes. Make sure that you get version 4 or later if you have drives with the Macintosh Extended Format.

- *Unerase*—Recovers files that have been deleted from the hard drive. It works best with FileSaver.

- *Volume Recover*—A final-resort program that is used on extremely corrupted or damaged disks. You usually should not run this utility unless Norton Disk Doctor has suggested it.

- *FileSaver*—Catalogs disks and volumes and saves the information to a file. When you need to run Unerase, you have the best chance of data recovery if the volume has been cataloged by FileSaver.

- *System Info*—Tests your system and gives you information on its performance. You can use this information to see if you have an under-performing system or need an upgrade.

Norton Utilities includes many other components that provide information about your system at its most basic level. It is a valuable program to include in your software library.

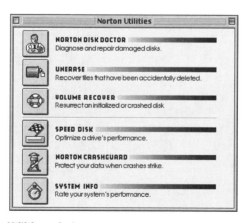

Figure 18.3   The Norton Utilities window.

TechTool Pro

TechTool Pro from Micromat is an extensive hardware and system testing utility program. It can run a battery of tests on your computer and advise you of problems with your system. It can test many of your hardware components, including your floppy drive, Zip drive, modem, mouse, and system. TechTool Pro has two interfaces to tailor the program toward the needs of the user:

- *The Standard interface*—This has preconfigured the system testing so that even a beginner can check the computer. If TechTool Pro finds a problem, it informs you and indicates whether it can make the repair. TechTool Pro can also let you know whether you need to have hardware elements repaired.

- *The Expert interface*—This is geared toward a knowledgeable user who wants to control the testing and even limit it to a particular device. For example, if a user is having trouble with a modem, you can test the modem only. TechTool Pro tests not only the modem, but also the integrity of the telephone line. TechTool Pro can conduct over 300 tests on the system and its many components.

For a long time, TechTool Pro has endeavored to provide the same functionality as Norton Utilities, plus provide extensive hardware testing that Norton Utilities lacks. TechTool Pro's strength is in its hardware testing programs and extensive information about the system. However, Norton Utilities has been slow to provide support for the Mac OS Extended format disk structure which was released with Mac OS 8.1. TechTool Pro grabbed the opportunity and included support for Extended format volumes. It cannot defragment these volumes, but TechTool Pro can perform file recovery functions on disks with the Mac OS Extended format. TechTool Pro is an excellent addition to your software library for its extensive hardware testing as well as its support of the Mac OS Extended format. A freeware version of this software called TechTool is also available; it can do some of the same functions.

Conflict Catcher

One of the most difficult problems to diagnosis with the Mac OS is an extensions conflict. Apple includes Extensions Manager to assist you, but sometimes you need more. You may need the commercial utility Conflict Catcher from Casady & Green. If you are experiencing an extensions conflict, you can make Conflict Catcher do all the tedious work of restarting the computer and testing the extensions. It will identify the extensions that don't seem to get along, as well as the program that seems to make your system crash. Conflict Catcher provides useful information about each extension and control panel, including the version number, type of file, and even links to the company that developed the program. If your computer is configured to load many extensions and control panels, consider adding Conflict Catcher to your software library.

Where To Get Help

You may know a lot about your system and how it functions. But at some point you will encounter a situation where none of your "tricks" work. You need to know where to go to get help. An extensive listing of helpful resources is included in Appendix G and the Mac OS includes an excellent online Help Viewer that has been completely revamped. If you want an extensive resource of troubleshooting information for the Mac OS as well as many Macintosh models, you may want to consult *Sad Macs, Bombs, and other Disasters* by Ted Landau and published by Peachpit Press. Many practical solutions, as well as in-depth information, are included in this volume. Ted Landau also maintains a Web site at **www.macfixit.com** that provides troubleshooting information for the Macintosh computer and Mac OS.

Quick Reference Specifications

The following are the essential facts about Event And System Monitoring Tools:

- You should pay attention to the details when troubleshooting and listen carefully to the problem if you are supporting other users.

- Duplicate the problem, if possible, so you can analyze the process.

- Try obvious solutions before going to extreme solutions such as a complete system installation.

- Check the wealth of information for Macintosh technical support at **til.info.apple.com**.

- A Sad Mac icon visible during startup may not indicate a hardware problem. Reboot with another system disk to determine if the problem is truly a hardware problem.

- A disk with a blinking question mark indicates that a suitable operating system could not be found on the disk.

- When a computer hangs during the startup process, the most common cause is an extension conflict.

- When you double-click on a document that can be opened with an application on your hard drive but Finder reports that the application that created the document could not be found, you need to rebuild the Desktop file.

- The Web site at **www.macfixit.com** contains up-to-date Macintosh technical support information.

- Use the Shift key during startup to disable extensions.

- Rebuild the Desktop file by holding down the Option+Command keys during startup.

- Strange system behavior may require that you delete and re-create the Finder preference.

- Use the Option+Command+P+R keys during startup to clear the PRAM.

- An inability to preserve the correct date on a computer is an indication of a dying battery, especially when the date resets to the years 1956 or 1904.

- You may need to run Disk First Aid multiple times to correct a disk problem.

Utilities To Use

The utilities or elements of the Mac OS discussed in this chapter are listed here as a memory aid for the busy user or system administrator:

- *Disk First Aid*—Free disk repair from Apple that is included with Mac OS 8.5.

- *Extensions Manager*—The control panel that controls what extensions load during startup.

- *Norton Utilities*—A commercial program from Symantec that specializes in disk repair and optimization.

- *Disk Doctor*—One of the utilities with the Norton Utilities that repairs disks.

- *Unerase*—A program within Norton Utilities that recovers deleted files.

- *Volume Recover*—A recovery utility with Norton Utilities that recovers data from hopelessly corrupted volumes.

- *FileSaver*—A function of Norton Utilities that catalogs files on a disk and saves the information to make recovery of deleted files more successful.

- *System Info*—One of the programs in Norton Utilities that provides information about system performance and what your system should be doing.

- *TechTool*—A free utility from Micromat that does some basic troubleshooting, tasks such as zapping the PRAM and rebuilding the Desktop file.

- *TechTool Pro*—A commercial suite of hardware and software utilities from Micromat that specializes in testing and diagnosing hardware problems and fixing Macintosh extended format disks.

- *Conflict Catcher*—A commercial utility from Casady & Greene that manages extensions and resolves conflicts.

18: Troubleshooting

Immediate Solutions

Resolving Startup Conflicts

If your computer cannot complete the booting process and it has displayed the Happy Mac icon, a conflict probably exists between extensions, or it has a problem launching an application. Follow these steps to troubleshoot an extension conflict:

1. Restart the computer and hold down the Shift key to disable all extensions.

2. Go to Apple Menu|Control Panels.

3. Open Extensions Manager, and click on the Extensions set pop-up menu to select the Mac OS 8.5 base set, as shown in Figure 18.4.

4. Restart the computer. If the system will not boot, you have a problem with the basic Mac OS 8.5 installation. Run Disk First Aid and perhaps rebuild the Desktop file. You may need to reinstall the operating system.

5. If the computer will boot with the basic set of Mac OS 8.5 extensions, launch the Extensions Manager and enable a few of the programs (perhaps those closely related, such as telecommunication software), and restart the computer. Repeat this process until you experience the conflict.

6. When you locate the extension that is causing the problem, determine if the extension is needed. If it is, you may want to rearrange when the

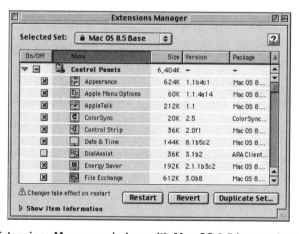

Figure 18.4   The Extensions Manager window with Mac OS 8.5 base extensions selected.

extension loads by changing its name (you can insert a number or space at the beginning of the file name to force it load earlier or a tilde or bullet to force it to load later). Check also that the software has been updated to be compatible with Mac OS 8.5.

7. In some cases, you may find that you can enable all extensions and no longer have a conflict. You should still observe the system closely to see if the problem reoccurs.

TIP: *If you have a lot of extensions, consider purchasing Conflict Catcher. It can automate much of the process of determining the source of an extension conflict.*

Fixing Corrupted Preferences

Suppose that a user is experiencing strange problems within an application. He cannot launch the spell checking function within the program. He or she may have a corrupted preference file. (Preferences can become corrupted and hamper the effective functioning of an application, extension, or even the Finder.) The best course of action is to remove and delete the corrupted preference and allow the application to create a new one. Follow these steps for locating, deleting, and re- creating a preference file:

1. Quit the application that may have a corrupted preference.

TIP: *Be aware that if the Finder or an extension or control panel has a corrupted preference that you will achieve the best results by booting from another startup disk to completely purge the preference information from memory.*

---

2. Open the Preferences folder that is housed in the System Folder or use the Find utility.

3. Locate the malfunctioning program's preference file and drag it to the trash. Be aware that some applications store entire folders of information in the Preferences folder (Netscape Navigator, for example) so you may need to open additional folders to access the preference. Make sure that you remove only the preference in these cases. The application may store other important information in this folder that you don't want to lose (in a Web browser, for example, your bookmarks and e-mails are stored in this folder).

TIP: *Some applications store their preferences within the same folder as the application. Check in the application folder if the preference is not stored in the Preferences folder.*

---

4. If the preference file you removed belonged to an application, you should be able to start the application and re-create the preference. You may have to reconfigure some settings or enter the program's serial number.

5. If the preference file you removed belonged to the Finder or a system component, restart the computer to re-create the preference. Remember that you will not completely remove the corruption of the Finder unless you restart the system with a different system disk.

Rebuilding The Desktop File

If you have a computer that is not performing as well as it should, you may need to rebuild the Desktop file, a database that remembers the association of a document to a program. This database can become rather convoluted. One specific symptom of a corrupted Desktop file occurs when you double-click on a document associated with a program on your computer, but receive an error that the application that created the document could not be found. Networking problems are also associated with a corrupt Desktop file. Follow these steps to rebuild the Desktop file:

1. Restart the computer with extensions off by holding down the Shift key.

2. When the startup screen appears that says the extensions are off, release the Shift key and hold down the Option+Command keys until the dialog box appears that is shown in Figure 18.5.

3. Release the keys and allow the computer to rebuild the Desktop file.

4. After the computer has completed the rebuild process and finished booting, restart the computer and allow it to boot normally. The computer will rebuild the Desktop file one more time on its own.

If you have purchased TechTool Pro, you can use this program to rebuild the Desktop file more efficiently. TechTool Pro completely removes the existing Desktop file and creates a new one. You can also perform this function with the free utility TechTool from **www.micromat.com**.

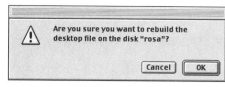

Figure 18.5   The dialog box that asks if you want to rebuild the Desktop file.

18: Troubleshooting

Zapping The PRAM

Suppose you have an application that you must use every day, but the program is poorly written and in spite of your best efforts, this program causes an application crash on a daily basis. As these crashes continue, your PRAM begins to develop problems. Symptoms include poor system performance and problems with basis system settings, such as the sound level. When this happens, zap the PRAM or clear out and reset the PRAM settings. Follow these steps to zap the PRAM:

1. Hold down these keys during startup: Command+Option+P+R.

2. Hold down the key combination described in Step 1 until the computer restarts again; this indicates that the PRAM has been cleared. Some groups recommend holding down the key combination until the Mac has restarted several times, but Apple indicates that two starts should be adequate.

When you zap the PRAM, some basic system settings are reset to the factory defaults. For example, the system alert sound and highlight color will return the original settings, and your AppleTalk port connection may default to the printer port.

TechTool has the capability to completely clear the PRAM. If the PRAM is not cleared, some of the corruption can remain and continue to cause problems. If the keystroke combination given in this solution does not solve your problem, download TechTool from **www.micromat.com** or purchase TechTool Pro.

Fixing Common Printing Problems

Printing is often a critical task on a computer. A user who can't print may be upset if the problem is not solved. Fortunately, you can follow some common procedures to resolve the problem:

1. If you receive an error message that the document failed to print and you are offered the option to print again, try printing again. Your document may print.

2. If you tried again to print and failed, cancel the print job and see if the printer is still visible within the Chooser. You may have lost your network connection and need to restore it. Or the printer may no longer be visible on the network.

3. For locally attached printers, check your cables and make sure the correct port is chosen in the Chooser.

18: Troubleshooting

529

4. If you still cannot print or if a networked printer is not visible on the network, turn the printer off and on.

5. If necessary, restart your own computer and the printer and attempt to print.

6. If you still cannot print, try removing the printer preference, restarting the computer, and generating a new preference for the preferred printer.

7. Check the indicator lights on the printer and verify that the printer does not have a hardware problem.

Identifying A Bad Battery

Suppose that you are working, accidentally click on the time on the menu bar, and notice that you are living in the past, to be precise, in the year 1956 (or 1904). This is one of the most common symptoms of a failing battery on your motherboard. Other symptoms may appear similar to a corrupted PRAM because the battery preserves the contents of the PRAM. When the battery begins to die, the PRAM settings are frequently lost. In extreme cases, your computer may not be able to boot.

Apple warns that replacing the battery could void your warranty on your computer, but your computer usually is no longer under warranty when the battery dies. If you want to replace your battery on your own, the Web site **www.academ. com/info/macintosh/** provides instructions for replacing the battery in most Macintosh models.

Using Disk First Aid

Disk First Aid is a free utility written by Apple that provides some disk repair options. Disk First Aid is very easy to run and has been written to perform the task of disk repair, so you should be able to instruct users on how to run this utility on their own if they experience problems. Disk First Aid is usually found in the Utilities folder. To use Disk First Aid, take these steps:

1. Launch Disk First Aid. A window will appear similar to that shown in Figure 18.6.

2. All data volumes will appear, including hard drives, CD-ROMs, floppies, and Zip disks.

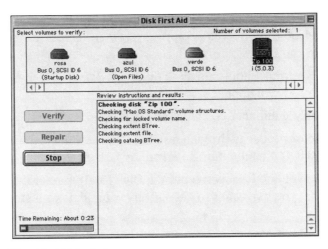

Figure 18.6   The Disk First Aid window.

3. Select the disk you want repaired. Note that in previous versions of Disk First Aid you have to boot from another system disk to verify the startup volume. Mac OS 8.5 now allows you to repair the primary volume while its system is active.

4. Select Verify or Repair (some folks are nervous about doing a repair immediately and run Verify to see what problems they are facing with the disk in question). Verify only checks the volume for problems and creates a report. Repair identifies the problems and attempts to fix them.

5. If Disk First Aid reports that it cannot fix the volume, run Disk First Aid again and again. Although it may report that it cannot fix the disk, in some cases it actually is fixing the problem in small bits.

If Disk First Aid really cannot repair your volume, invest in a commercial utility that specializes in disk repair, such as Norton Utilities from Symantec or TechTool Pro from Micromat.

Using Norton Utilities Disk Doctor

If a user experiences strange errors on the computer, and you have tried all the free solutions such as desktop rebuilds and Disk First Aid, you may want to run Norton Utilities.

Norton Utilities includes an excellent disk repair program called Disk Doctor. Disk Doctor takes longer to run than Apple's Disk First Aid but it does a careful examination of the system at a basic level, including the disk media and volume structure, and analyzes every file on the system for errors and problems. Follow these steps to run Disk Doctor:

1. Launch Norton Utilities and click on the Disk Doctor button. The window in Figure 18.7 will appear.

2. Select the volume that you want analyzed.

3. Disk Doctor proceeds through a series of tests and programs, as shown in Figure 18.8. If it encounters an error, it will alert you.

4. When the volume has been repaired, Disk Doctor generates a detailed report that you may want to keep if this volume has a history of the same problems.

5. If Disk Doctor cannot repair the volume, the disk may be in extremely poor condition. At this point Disk Doctor may recommend using Volume Recover to recover the data to another volume. Only do this if Disk Doctor recommends it.

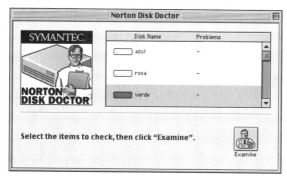

Figure 18.7   Norton Disk Doctor.

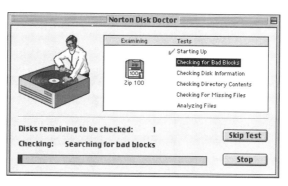

Figure 18.8   Norton Disk Doctor repairing a volume.

18: Troubleshooting

Using Norton Utilities Unerase

You have a user standing before you with desperation in his eyes. He has deleted a document, but now desperately needs it back. Here is your chance to be a hero. Norton Utilities includes a program named Unerase that can recover files that have been deleted. Remember that when a file is deleted, only the "directory" information is gone. The file itself is still on the hard drive and will remain there until new data needs to be written. Logic dictates that the more free space you have on your disk, the longer the files will remain. However, if you have nearly filled the hard drive, run Unerase as soon as possible to recover the files. Follow these instructions to run Unerase:

1. Launch Norton Utilities.

2. Click on the Unerase button.

3. If you have File Sharing enabled, you will be warned to disable it to effectively use Unerase. You should disable File Sharing.

4. A window appears allowing you to choose the volume that contains the information you want recovered (see Figure 18.9). Choose the volume you want and click on the Search button.

5. Unerase scans the drive and presents you with a list of files it located and their chances of being recovered (some files have a poor chance of recovery because they are fragmented and portions of the file may be overwritten by other data).

6. Select the file you want to recover and click on the Recover button.

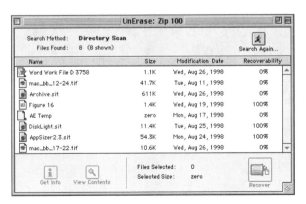

Figure 18.9   The Norton Utilities Unerase window.

18: Troubleshooting

Using TechTool Pro

Suppose that you have a computer that has a corrupted PRAM. You've attempted to zap the PRAM manually, but are still experiencing errors. You may want to give TechTool or TechTool Pro a chance. The difference between TechTool and TechTool Pro is in the capabilities of their software. TechTool is limited to only a few functions, such as rebuilding the Desktop file and zapping the PRAM. TechTool Pro has over 300 tests, both hardware and software, that can be performed on your system. TechTool Pro can also perform disk repair. Both TechTool and TechTool Pro are known for their hardware testing capabilities. For the purposes of this example, we'll look at what TechTool Pro can do. To use it, take these steps:

1. Launch TechTool Pro.

2. The window in Figure 18.10 will appear. This is the default setting for TechTool Pro, which is known as the Standard Interface. TechTool Pro has already selected the appropriate tests to run that give you a general overview of the condition of your computer. If you are not familiar with TechTool Pro, use this interface to make sure that the appropriate tests are run.

3. You can choose to test only a part of your system by removing the check marks by system categories or by each individual test. Decide what system categories to check, what tests to disable, or leave the settings as they are.

4. When you are ready to begin, click on the Run button. The tests will begin running on your system. You can pause or stop the testing if necessary.

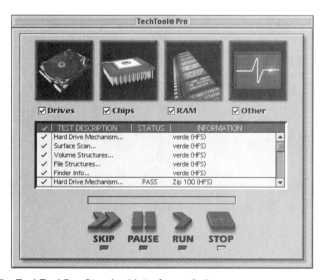

Figure 18.10   The TechTool Pro Standard Interface window.

5. As each test is finished, the status for the item being tested indicates whether it passed or failed. When the battery of tests is complete, TechTool generates a report of test results.

6. You can also switch to the Expert Interface by selecting Interface|Expert. The window changes and allows you to manually determine what tests should be run (see Figure 18.11).

7. You can select a category from the list at the right or use the scroll bar to select a category from the window tabs. Choose a category and the test you want to run.

8. Click on the Run button to start the test.

9. TechTool Pro runs the diagnostics and generates a report. In some cases, TechTool Pro repairs the problem. For hardware, TechTool Pro generates a report and indicates if a trip to the computer shop is necessary.

Figure 18.11   The Expert Interface window in TechTool Pro.

Appendix A
Shortcuts And Tricks

Overview

Sometimes you just want the facts—or as this appendix is entitled—the shortcuts. This section covers some of the hints and tricks that you should know as you support Macintosh computers. You may even find some gems that have not been covered previously in this book.

Starting The Computer

Use some of these tricks and diagnosis tools to help your system start properly.

Power Key Vs. CPU Power Button

The most common and proper method for turning on your Macintosh computer is to use the power key on the keyboard. This sends a signal to the computer to turn on and begin loading the system.

Some models, such as the 6100, have a button located on the front of the computer. If you press the keyboard power button and nothing happens, you may want to confirm the model. However, you should know that you cannot start a limited number of Macs from the keyboard, including the early Macs (such as the Classic, the Centris, and the Quadra 610) up to the 6100 Power Macintosh. You also must start some Performa models by pressing a power switch.

Zapping The PRAM

If your computer has been crashing and you have had to improperly restart it or shut it down multiple times, then you may want to clear the PRAM. The PRAM contains some very basic system configurations, including the display bit depth, system sound, and the date and time. When the system crashes, it affects the PRAM, causing the system to malfunction even more. Therefore, this circle of trouble feeds on itself. Zapping the PRAM sets everything back to normal (in some cases resetting some of these settings to the factory default).

To zap the PRAM, restart the computer while holding down Control+Command+P+R keys. When the computer reaches the point where the welcome screen should appear, the computer will restart. Some Mac gurus recommend that you let the computer restart this way a second or third time, then release the keys and let the system boot normally.

Sounds easy, doesn't it? Not quite. The hard part is getting your fingers in position. Our technique is to prepare to hold down the Control+Command keys with the left hand and use the right hand to restart the computer. Immediately press the left-hand keys down and use your right hand to press the P+R keys. Hold all these keys until the PRAM has been zapped.

You should also know that there is an excellent freeware utility called TechTool. This program can zap the PRAM effectively so that you don't have to scramble for the keystroke combination.

Startup Screens

The first image you see on your screen is usually the small computer. The second image welcomes you to the Macintosh. This second screen is the *startup screen*. It has changed over the various versions of the Macintosh operating system to the simple, yet elegant and modern art version you see today. You, however, can display an alternate image in its place. Two methods are available.

First, you can retrieve ready-made startup screens from software archives, including Info-Mac. These files may have names such as "cutepuppy" or "laketahoe" when you transfer them to your computer. Some images are photographs, some are original artwork, and many are an attractive replacement to the standard welcome image. The most important thing about these files is that—except for one small change—they are ready to use.

Second, you can create your own startup screens. You may want to see the happy face of your dog or perhaps a great vacation photo. No matter what your choice of image, you need to save it in PICT format, with an ID of zero. If you have the wonderful image utility called Graphic Converter, you can save files as a startup screen. Other imaging programs also have this capability. If, however, you are adventurous, you can use ResEdit to change the resource ID to zero.

After you have the file with the correct resource ID, you can finish the process by renaming the file "StartupScreen" and placing it in the System folder. The next time your system launches, the new image will be the startup screen.

One note of caution: For whatever reason, some startup screens can wreak havoc. You will know this immediately, because your system will hang and you will be unable to boot. The only solution is to remove the startup screen from the System folder. You will have to restart the computer and boot from another disk, such as a CD-ROM or floppy disk with a system installed. You can then remove the offending file and boot the computer normally.

Starting With Extensions Off

You can start your system with only the basic system components loaded by starting with extensions off. You might do this either when you install new software or when your system is unable to boot normally.

To start the computer with extensions off, turn on or restart the computer as you normally would, but hold down the Shift key until the welcome screen appears. In addition to the normal image, it should say "Extensions Off". Release the Shift key (if you have installed a startup screen, then you can also release the Shift key at this time).

Your system will be very limited at this point, but if you are having extension conflicts, you can begin the diagnosis process. If this is why you have booted by using this method, we recommend that you next start with only the basic Mac OS 8.5 extensions loaded. This will help determine if the system itself is the problem or if you are dealing with a problem third-party driver.

Calling The Extensions Manager

You may restart the computer, but forget to press the Shift key to disable extensions. You still have a second chance. As long as extensions have not begun loading, you can hold down the spacebar until the Extensions Manager Control Panel is launched. You can disable one, several, or all of the extensions and then allow the system to continue booting.

Rebuilding The Desktop Folder

The Desktop folder is hidden, but it performs important functions: It contains the icons on the Desktop and keeps a "road map" of file and creator associations. Occasionally, this road map becomes incorrect and confused; files take longer to open or lose their distinctive icon. One of the biggest symptoms of Desktop folder problems is manifested when you double-click a file, expecting it to open with the correct application; instead, an error message appears, indicating that the application that created the document could not be found.

For problems like these, as well as generally poor system performance, you should rebuild the Desktop folder. For the best results, restart the computer with extensions off (hold down the Shift key). After the welcome screen indicates extensions are disabled, release the Shift key and press the Command+Option keys. Continue holding them down until you are asked if you want to rebuild the Desktop folder; this will occur for every volume or disk partition that you have mounted. You should rebuild at least your hard drive partitions.

After you have rebuilt the Desktop folder with the extensions disabled, restart the computer. You will notice that one more Desktop folder rebuild will occur automatically. After this has finished, your computer is now ready for work.

You may also want to use TechTool for rebuilding the Desktop folder. It completely removes the folder and re-creates it, thus eliminating the possibility that corrupted data could survive the standard method for rebuilding the desktop folder.

Startup Items

Do you use the same programs every time you start your computer? You may want to put aliases of these programs in your Startup Items folder. They will launch in alphabetical order, but you can control this by using numbers or special characters to control the launch sequence. If you expect to quit some of these applications during your computer session, then have them listed near the end of the list. When you exit the application, it will free up valuable memory. On the other hand, the first applications that launched often cause fragmented memory when you quit them.

Disk And File Management

Use the following tricks, shortcuts, and diagnosis tools for handling files, folders, and disks.

Changing An Icon

Occasionally, you may not like the icon of a file. For example, you've been editing an application configuration file in a particular word processor. When you saved the file, it took the icon of the word processor instead of matching the other files associated with the application. It's easy to change it to the correct or favored icon. First, locate the icon that you want the file to use, click on it once and select File|Get Info. Click once on the icon that appears in this window and press Command+C to copy the icon. Now, close the Get Info window and click once on the offending file. Again select File|Get Info and click on the icon within this window. This time, press Command+V to paste the new icon.

Deleting A File

To delete a file, you must first drag it to the trash can. Once there, you must go to the Special menu and select Empty Trash to delete everything in the trash can. To recover files that you have deleted, you will need to use disk utility software such as Norton Utilities.

If you don't like dragging files to the trash, you can select the file and use the keystroke combination Command+Delete to move the file to the trash. You can also access the contextual menu by clicking on the file while holding the Control key.

You can also delete a whole range of files by using the Sherlock or Find utility. Simply search for the files that you want to delete (for example, every file that contains the words "Backup copy" in the file name). You can then take the files directly from the results window and drag them to the trash.

Copying With Drag And Drop

Dragging and dropping a file onto another partition or volume will result in an automatic copy. However, when you click on a folder or file and drag it to a location on the same partition, it will move the file rather than copy it. To force it to copy the file, hold down the Option key while you are dragging. When you release the mouse it will copy the file rather than move it. You can even do this within the same window (the duplicate file will have the word "copy" after the file name).

Disabling The Trash Warning

Have you been annoyed by the dialog box telling you how much trash you have and asking if you are sure you want to delete it? Although it's nice to know how much disk space you'll recover and you may appreciate a chance to cancel the Empty Trash command, you'll find that most power users hate the delay this dialog box causes. You can easily disable this warning. Simply click once on the trash can icon, then press Command+I for the Get Info window. At the bottom of the window, the option to Warn Before Emptying displays. Remove the check in the box and you won't see the warning any more.

Determining File Or Folder Size

If you perform housecleaning functions on your hard drive, you know that it helps to see the size of files and folders. You can find out this information in several ways, one of which is the Get Info window. Simply click once on the icon of the file or folder and press Command+I. You should see the file size in this window.

You can also see file size by viewing the contents of a window as a list rather than viewing by icon. If the folder size doesn't display, you can turn it on by going to the View menu and selecting View Options. Enable the option to calculate folder sizes. After you click on Okay and close this window, you should see folder sizes listed. Be careful with this option because it does affect system performance (information will be slower to display in the Finder windows); you may want to enable it only for short periods.

Repairing A Damaged Disk

It's distressing to insert a Zip disk, only for the Mac to tell you it doesn't recognize the disk and offer you the option to either eject or initialize. Don't panic and format the disk. This dialog box also appears when a disk needs repair. Simply launch Disk First Aid, then insert the Zip disk (or any removable media that needs repair). You can attempt to fix the disk and at least recover the data.

Once this warning does appear, you may want to exercise caution with the media in question. Move the data to a secure medium and then format the disk. Even then, the disk may not be reliable and probably should be discarded.

The Finder

The Finder has been greatly improved in Mac OS 8.5. We've listed just a few of the great things Finder can do.

Organizing Columns In Views

Maybe it's the fault of spreadsheet applications, but people want to control columns in a list view. It's been on the wish list for Mac OS improvements and finally appears in Mac OS 8.5. You can rearrange the columns and control their width. Simply move your cursor to the headers that label the columns. To move the column, click on the header and drag it where you want it (the cursor changes to the shape of a hand). To control the width, move the cursor to the end of the header where the columns meet. The cursor will change to the resize cursor, and you can adjust the column width.

Hiding The Desktop

If you want to see only application windows, you can activate a setting that hides the Finder or Desktop whenever it is not active. Go to the General Controls Control Panel, deactivate the option Show Desktop When In Background, and close the window. In fact, some users enable this accidentally and report this as a problem. To see the Finder again, you can either go to the Application menu and select Finder or go back to the General Controls window and activate the Show Desktop option.

Labeling Files

Users who are not organized tend to use file labels to turn icons into pretty colors. This is perfectly acceptable, but you can also use labeling to organize files according to importance, subject matter, or level of completion. Simply edit the file labels to reflect your organizational method. Go to the Edit menu and select Preferences. Select the Label tab and edit the text. You can also change the label colors from here.

To apply a label to a file or folder, simply select it and go to the File|Label menu. Choose your label—it's that easy. You can display file views by labels as well and search by label within the Sherlock utility.

Indexing With Sherlock

As a Mac OS 8.5 user, you can now search files by content. To expedite this process, index the volumes that you'll be searching. You can arrange automatic scheduling and manual indexing from the Sherlock Utility. Click on the Search By Content tab to set your options and conduct searches.

Highlight Colors

The system default highlight color is black. When you select a file by clicking once on the icon graphic, it darkens and the name of the file becomes white text on a black background. If you actually click on the name of the file to change it, you'll notice that it becomes white text on a black background as well, but with a small white border. This file name is in *highlight* or *editing* mode. One of the first things you should do is change the highlight color to something other than black to make the icon state more obvious. Go to the Appearance Control Panel and select the Appearance tab. You can change your highlight color to something other than black (it's usually a good idea to go with a lighter color, because the text will remain black if you choose a color other than black).

Scolling Without Scroll Bars

One of the cool additions to Mac OS 8.5 is the ability to see the window's hidden contents without scrolling. Click anywhere in the window while holding down the Command key. Your cursor becomes a grabbing hand and you can move the window contents in realtime (you don't have to wait until the display redraws the window).

Aliases

Aliases are found all over your system; even installation programs create aliases to give you easy access to the original.

Creating An Alias

Use an alias to access a common folder from multiple locations or to provide access to a program without duplicating it. Simply click once on the item that needs an alias and select Make Alias from the File menu. An icon will appear with an italic typeface and the word "alias" appended to the file name. Move the alias to any location. If you know where you want to put the alias, you can click once on the original, hold down the Option+Command keys, and drag the icon to its destination folder. When you release the mouse, an alias will be placed in the folder with the exact name of the original. This second method is preferable because you don't have to edit the file name and remove the word "alias".

Finding The Original

Many software installations place aliases on the Desktop or in the Apple menu. If you want to find the file that the alias is referencing, go to File|Show Original. Finder will locate the original application. This option is also available by holding the Control key as you click.

Selecting A New Original

If you have an alias on the Desktop or in the Apple menu that should now point to a new original (perhaps you've upgraded the software in a new folder), you now have the option to point the alias to a new application. Click once on the alias and go to File|Get Info. Select General Information and click the button at the bottom of the window, Select New Original. You can use the browser window to redirect the alias to a new original.

Memory Management

Use these tips for improving your system performance with effective memory management.

Increasing An Application's Memory Allocation

If you find that an application seems to be malfunctioning with regularity, one of the first steps you should take is to allocate more memory to the program. Make sure that the program is not running, and then click once on the application icon. Go to File|Get Info and select Memory. Manually increase the preferred memory size. Use your judgment on how much more memory to allocate.

Virtual Memory

By default, virtual memory is enabled; this helps decrease the memory needs of some applications. However, some programs—usually games—don't behave well with virtual memory. To disable virtual memory, go to the Memory Control Panel. Locate the virtual memory section and click on the Off radio button. You can also go to the Memory Control Panel and increase the virtual memory allocation: The larger the virtual memory partition, the more performance is affected. If you find that your installed memory is not enough, try installing additional RAM instead of increasing virtual memory.

Disk Cache

Some system functions or commands are done more frequently than others. The disk cache keeps a record of as many of these commands as possible so that the system won't have to retrieve this command information from the hard drive. Interaction with the hard drive is always slower than interaction with memory. In Mac OS 8.5, the disk cache is automatically set using the calculation of 32 kilobytes per megabyte of memory. You can customize this to a larger size, but a smaller cache will affect system performance.

Determining Available Memory

As you are working, you may need to know how much memory you have available and whether you can launch another application. Switch to the Finder and select About This Computer from the Apple menu. You will see the memory allocation for each application that is running, as well as the system allocation. Occasionally, programs "leak" memory or use it to the point that it cannot be reallo-cated, even when you quit the application. Utilities such as More About This Macintosh (MATM) will show fragmented memory blocks. In most cases, only a system restart will restore all memory.

Printing

Printing tips could cover a whole chapter (in fact, they do, in Chapter 8). Here are a few ideas you can use when printing.

Switching Printers

When you changed printers in previous systems, you had to go through the Chooser. Then, System 7.5 introduced Desktop Printing; this places the icon of a printer on the desktop each time you select a new printer within the Chooser so that you can switch printers on the fly. If you already have the printer icon on the Desktop, you can make it your default printer by clicking on the icon and access-ing the Print menu. This menu appears only when you select a printer icon. Choose the Set Default Printer option. The default printer icon will have a heavy black border.

You can also drag a document to any Desktop printer icon. The application that created the document will launch and send the document to the printer you se-lected. Then, it will automatically exit.

Faster Printing

If the quality of the printing is not important, you can increase your printing speed by choosing a black-and-white scheme rather than grayscale.

Windows Compatibility

As a Mac user, use these tips to work with PC users. After all, we are in the minor-ity in the computer world.

Formatting A Disk For Windows

You can use a PC-formatted floppy disk on both Macintosh- and Windows-based systems. You can even purchase disks that are IBM formatted and use them on the Mac. However, you cannot use Macintosh disks on Windows systems without special utilities. To format a disk for the PC, simply insert it in the drive and select Erase Disk from the File menu. Choose DOS 1.4 MB instead of the Macintosh format. When finished, you can use the disk on almost any system, including Sun computers.

Universal File Formats

When you are creating files that may be exchanged with other users and you are not sure of the word processor or version of the software, save the file in Rich

Text Format. Most applications can translate this type of file, which preserves special features such as bold and italic formatting and font type. If you want users to view your file exactly the way you intended, from the graphics to the alignment, then you may want to purchase Adobe Acrobat. Files saved in this format are called Portable Document Format (PDF). The user can read the file or print it, but cannot make changes to the document without special software (namely, Acrobat Exchange).

Networking

Not everyone enjoys an Ethernet network, but here are some tips for those that do.

Accessing A Server

Mac OS 8.5 has greatly improved network server access with the inclusion of the Network Browser. Accessing a server is as simple as a double-click and you save many steps compared to server access from the Chooser. If you access a server on a regular basis, add it to your Favorites list for easy access even from the Open and Save dialog boxes. Items in the Favorites list are accessible from the Favorites option in the Apple menu.

Organizing Favorites

You can place anything in the Favorites folder. After all, the items in Favorites are only aliases. You can have links to server volumes, shared disks, or files and applications on your hard drive. After a while, however, this list can become quite long. You can organize items in the Favorites folder by opening the folder, either by selecting Apple Menu|Favorites or by opening the System Folder and locating the Favorites folder (the Favorites item in the Apple Menu is itself an alias). After the window is open, you can create new folders and organize the items within it (perhaps, by servers or by application). Use an organizational method that you prefer.

Custom AppleTalk Configurations

You can have multiple AppleTalk configurations that can be used in the Location Manager. This can allow you to easily change your network settings, depending on your environment. When you configure your AppleTalk Control Panel for network access, these settings are saved to a default configuration. Go to the File menu and choose Configurations. Duplicate the current configuration and rename it. You can have several configurations including sets for Ethernet and remote access.

Custom Remote Access Configurations

If you access multiple Internet service providers or must try several numbers to establish a connection, you can save these configurations in the Remote Access

Control Panel. Duplicate the current configuration, make changes to it, and then give it a distinctive name. You can switch between configurations and use the different files within the Location Manager.

Creating A Remote Access Script

If you connect to an Internet Service Provider (ISP) by using a command line prompt, you can record your keystrokes and save them to a script. Initiate the connection and when you are shown the terminal window, choose the Settings button. You can elect to save the connect script when the terminal window closes. When it's completed, you can change the settings in the Protocol tab from Use Terminal Window to Use Connect Script and locate the file you just created, making connecting to an ISP a little easier.

Internet

The Internet contains a vast storehouse of information and communication. Use the shortcuts and diagnosis tools to facilitate your Internet surfing.

Internet Config

A wonderful utility included with Mac OS 8.5 is Internet Config. You can record common Internet settings within such things as your email address and server, SMTP gateway address, and news server address. Many Internet and Web applications such as email clients and Web browsers can retrieve your settings from Internet Config so that you don't have to keep entering the same information in different applications.

Internet Clippings

Mac OS 8.5 continues to support the text-clipping feature. Select text in an application that supports this—such as SimpleText—and drag the text to the Desktop. A small file appears with the contents of the selection. However, Mac OS 8.5 improves this feature to support intelligent clippings. If you clip and drag text that contains an email address, the icon will change to indicate its contents. There are special icons for text clippings, such as Web page addresses, news groups, email addresses, and FTP sites.

Using Sherlock To Search The Internet

The Sherlock application within Finder now includes the ability to search the Internet. (You can also search within a browser, but the Sherlock utility launchers much faster and can produce the same results.)

Troubleshooting

If it were a perfect world, our computers would always start, would never hang while booting, and would never crash. Unfortunately, things can go wrong at any moment during a computer session.

Computer Will Not Turn On

If you press the power button on the keyboard but the indicator light on the CPU does not light up, make sure the power strip and outlet are active. Check the keyboard connections and all power cords. Use the power button on the CPU to see if the computer will turn on. If not, you may have a hardware problem.

Monitor Will Not Display An Image

If the computer has begun to boot but you cannot see an image on the monitor, make sure the power button has been depressed. Check the power cables, as well as the monitor connection to the computer. If necessary, wait until enough time has lapsed for the computer to boot, then push the power button on the keyboard to bring up the Shutdown dialog window. Even though you cannot see it, you can press the R key to restart the computer. Some of the more sophisticated monitors will not display an image if they were not turned on before the computer. Restarting should display the image. If nothing else works, switch monitors to rule out hardware problems.

Computer Will Not Boot

If you see any other icon than the smiling computer, you have computer problems. A disk with a blinking question mark indicates the computer cannot locate an operating system. Try inserting a boot disk or CD-ROM to see if the computer can boot by another medium.

A sad or sick Mac icon or a different startup sound usually indicates hardware problems. You can try to use a boot disk to determine if the problem is with the hard drive or the components on the motherboard.

Computer Cannot See The Network

Watch the computer as it is booting. The network icon is one of the first to appear. If the icon has a large red X, the network hardware—such as a bad cable—is the problem. If the icon appears to be normal, you should be able to establish a network connection, provided the appropriate hardware and connectivity are in place.

If you cannot see AppleTalk zones in the Network Browser or Chooser, make sure that AppleTalk is active. If it is, go to the AppleTalk Control Panel and confirm that Ethernet is the chosen protocol. If it is, but lists no zones available, try rebuilding the Desktop file. If you still cannot access the network, you may need to reinstall the network software.

General System Crankiness

If your applications seem to freeze or take longer to launch, or if icons seem to switch to generic ones, you should rebuild the Desktop file. It will improve system performance and speed up application launching.

A Hanging Application

If you still have mouse movement, but you cannot select other options within the application or switch to the Finder, then you may have an application that is no longer responding or functioning. Make sure that adequate time has passed. Some database clients must interact with the server and this may take some time. If you feel the application has stopped responding, you will need to force the program to quit. Use the Option+Command+Escape keystroke combination. When you force an application to quit, you should restart the computer. The system may be unreliable and could lead to a crash.

System Freezes Or Crashes

If you do not have mouse movement or if you receive a dialog box with a system bomb or restart prompt, these are serious indicators that you are dealing with a system crash. If you are given the opportunity to restart, use this option. If the system freezes, you will have to restart using the reset button (if one is installed). If not, you can press Control+Command+the keyboard power button to restart the computer.

You can also attempt to access the system debugger by pressing the Command+Power keys. You can type "RS" to restart the system or "G FINDR" to quit the Finder.

Shortcut Key Combinations

Use the keystroke combinations shown in Table A.1 to reduce the need to reach for a mouse and speed up productivity.

Table A.1   Shortcut key combinations and results.

Keystroke Combination	Result
Shift	During startup, loads system with extensions off
Option+Command+P+R	During startup, resets PRAM
Shift+Option+Command+Delete	Forces a boot from another SCSI device
C	During startup, will boot from a System CD
Spacebar	During startup, opens the extensions manager
Option+Command	Rebuilds the Desktop file
Command+.	Cancels a command
Command+O	Opens a file or folder
Command+W	Closes a window
Command+N	Creates a new folder within the Finder

(continued)

Table A.1   Shortcut key combinations and results (continued).

Keystroke Combination	Result
Command+Z	Undoes previous action
Command+P	Prints
Command+X	Cuts
Command+C	Copies
Command+V	Pastes
Command+Q	Quits
Command+S	Saves
Command+A	Selects all
Command+I	Gets info
Command+M	Makes an alias
Command+F	Launches Sherlock
Command+E	Ejects disk
Command+Y	Puts away
Command+?	Launches Help
Command+Delete	Moves item to the trash
Command+Option+Escape	Forces an application to quit
Control+Command+Power	Forces a computer restart
Command+Shift+3	Captures a PICT file of the desktop
Command+Shift+4	Captures a PICT file of the currently active window

Appendix B

Administrative Features
And Tools

The Mac OS has been network-ready from the very start, and we're lucky that so many administrative tools are available to help us manage groups of networked computers. We've used many administrative tools over the past decade to administer small, medium, and very large groups of computers, and we've found the following tools and features of Mac OS 8.5 to be the most useful. We'll point out what you can do in Mac OS 8.5 to make your users' computers more secure, then we'll touch on several utilities and programs to make your job as easy as possible.

Mac OS 8.5 Administrative Features

Mac OS 8.5 has several built-in features that system administrators can use to prevent unwanted tampering by users and would-be saboteurs. The configuration features found in the General Controls, AppleTalk, and TCP/IP control panels allow you to provide basic levels of protection for several aspects of a computer, as does the Simple Finder option.

General Controls

The General Controls control panel, shown in Figure B.1, allows you to select three options that will help you administer a Macintosh. Although these aren't earth-shattering administrative options, they will be useful for many environments and help prevent low-level users from deleting files and installing unwanted software:

- Shut Down Warning
- System Folder Protection
- Application Folder Protection

The Shut Down Warning simply displays a warning dialog to users when the computer is improperly restarted. Mac OS 8.5 incorporates a new warning dialog window from previous versions of the Mac OS and then runs Disk First Aid to search for, and repair, possible errors in the file system. It performs these tasks before loading any system extensions and the OS itself.

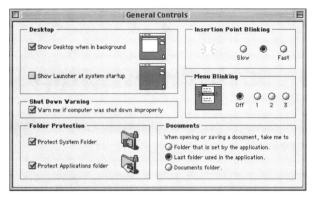

Figure B.1   The General Controls control panel offers basic administrative assistance.

The folder protections options affect only the System Folder and the Applications folder (which is created when Mac OS 8.5 is installed), under the following conditions:

• Only on the startup disk

• Only if File Sharing is turned off

You will know a folder is protected and that its contents cannot be moved or added to in two ways. First, a warning dialog displays when changes to the folder are attempted. Second, the contents of the folder appear with a small icon of a padlock in the lower-left corner. See Figure B.2 for examples of these types of warnings.

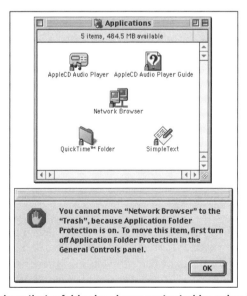

Figure B.2   Two visual clues that a folder has been protected by using the General Contols control panel.

AppleTalk Password Protection

In a networked environment, you usually don't want users taking their computers off the network without good reason and without telling you first. This is especially true if a computer is hosting a printer or some other networked device that is accessible to other users over AppleTalk. You can prevent users from disabling certain AppleTalk features by following these steps:

1. Open the AppleTalk control panel and choose Edit|User Mode.

2. Choose Administration, shown in Figure B.3, and enter an administrative password.

3. Lock down any available options, such as Connect via Ethernet, shown in Figure B.4. Toggle between locked and unlocked by clicking on the Padlock icon.

4. Quit AppleTalk, saving the changes when prompted to do so.

Users cannot re-enter Administration mode without first entering the password. They can, however, change mode between Basic and Advanced, as well as turn AppleTalk off (let's hope Apple revises these capabilities in the next release).

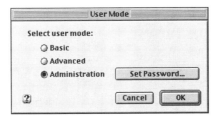

Figure B.3   Choose Administration from the User Mode menu option.

Figure B.4   You can selectively lock certain parts of the AppleTalk control panel while in Administration mode.

TCP/IP Password Protection

The TCP/IP control panel works just like the AppleTalk control panel to protect certain features via password protection. It uses a different administrative password than does the AppleTalk control panel (although you may set them to be the same). To configure the TCP/IP control panel, take these steps:

1. Open the TCP/IP control panel and choose Edit|User Mode.

2. Choose Administration and enter an administrative password.

3. Lock down any available options.

4. Quit TCP/IP, saving the changes when prompted to do so.

As with the AppleTalk control panel, users will not be able to re-enter Administration mode without first entering the password, but they will be able to change modes between Basic and Advanced, as well as turn TCP/IP off entirely. Figure B.5 shows the TCP/IP control panel in Basic mode (top) and Administration mode (bottom), illustrating which options may be locked.

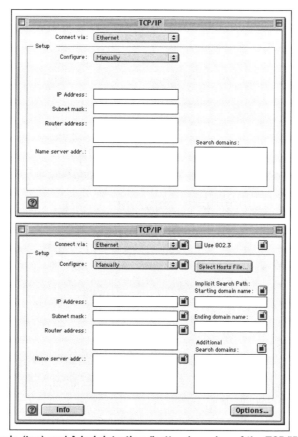

Figure B.5   The Basic (top) and Administration (bottom) modes of the TCP/IP control panel.

TIP: *It is possible, however, to simply replace the TCP/IP Preferences file instead of edit it, which is a means of bypassing the password security feature.*

Simple Finder

The Simple Finder option, shown in Figure B.6, provides fewer options to users, which will decrease the number of questions and user-interface issues you are likely to encounter. This option works by hiding menu options and disabling their respective features.

To activate the Simple Finder:

1. Choose Edit|Preferences in the Finder.

2. Select the General tab.

3. Check the Simple Finder option and close the window.

The biggest difference users will notice is the absence of menu options and key-board-command equivalents, including such things as Command+Delete to throw a selected item into the trash, as well as the inability to create pop-up windows. Figure B.7 shows how checking the Simple Finder option affects the File and View menus.

Apple Network Administrator Toolkit

The Apple Network Administrator Toolkit (ANAT) is a collection of three applications from Apple that assists in the management of networked Macintosh computers. These applications provide a very wide array of options, which is why the ANAT is expensive (about $400 for a 10-user license) and possibly, the only tool

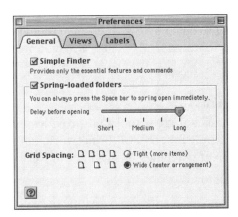

Figure B.6   The Simple Finder option.

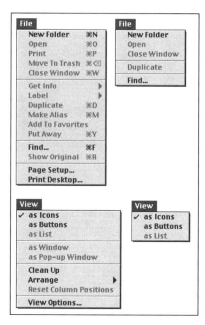

Figure B.7   The Simple Finder option affects the user experience by limiting menu options, such as the File and View options.

you'll need to administer a large number of computers. The three tools are shown in the following list:

• Network Assistant

• At Ease for Workgroups

• User and Group Manager

These three applications have easily over one hundred options and benefits among them, too many in fact to cover even a fraction of them here. Instead, we'll review each below, list their features, and discuss why you would want to use them on your network.

Network Assistant

The Network Assistant is a great tool that provides essential levels of control over clients over an AppleTalk or TCP/IP network, allowing you to perform the following tasks on client machines from a central Network Assistant server:

• Check software versions.

• Compare the differences in software versions between the Network Assistant server and clients, including applications, control panels, extensions, fonts, shutdown items, and startup items.

- Search client hard drives.
- Obtain system software information.
- Copy items between client and server.
- Open an application on a client from the server.
- Restart a client either immediately, or after allowing the client to save open documents.
- Share a client or the server screen with one of the clients.
- Lock a client screen after presenting it with a message.
- Observe a client screen.
- Control a client screen.
- Announce or talk with a client.
- Copy or delete items or a hard disk to or from a client.
- Change system settings, TCP/IP address, or Internet settings.
- Empty a client's trash, rebuild the Desktop, or rename the client.

Network Assistant has a good user interface and is easy to use. It allows you to create up to 20 lists of clients, with up to 250 clients in each list, and perform actions on one or more clients in a list or lists. For example, to poll a client for its system information, you would follow these steps:

1. Launch Network Assistant.
2. Open a list of clients and select a client.
3. Choose Reports|System Information, or click on the Sys Info button from the Network Assistant toolbar.
4. Choose from the many options for reported system information, including All, Memory, Hardware, Network, and Info. Figure B.8 shows how we've selected five items from the All menu option.
5. Click on the Get Report button, and the Network Assistant server will poll the client and quickly generate a report that you may export. For example, Figure B.9 shows a list with one computer named 7200, with a customized System Information Report screen in the foreground.

At Ease For Workgroups

At Ease for Workgroups is a comprehensive client/server application that allows you to secure up to 4,000 clients and prevent users from changing, adding, or deleting information from a computer without your permission or knowledge.

B: Administrative
Features And Tools

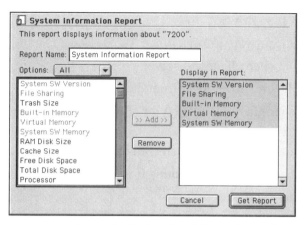

Figure B.8   Create custom reports about client system information, using Network Assistant.

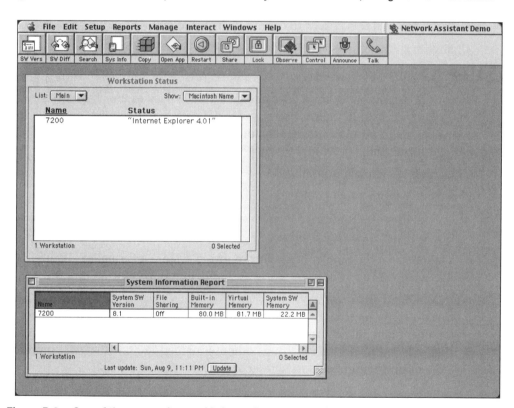

Figure B.9   One of the many pieces of information you can obtain from a Network Assistant
client is a computer's system information.

You can create several different levels of administrative privileges to allow other administrators to manage users and groups. The types of users are:

- *Administrator*—Full access
- *Teacher*—Full or limited access
- *Student*—Limited access
- *Guardian*—Limited access

Administrators have the ability to control just about any kind of resource on a client computer, including:

- Documents
- Folders
- Applications
- Entire hard drives
- AppleTalk servers
- Printers
- Access to removable media
- System Folder contents

In addition to creating administrative rights and client access restrictions, At Ease also provides services that are useful in educational settings, such as classrooms and training clusters:

- Access to documents over the Internet.
- Use drop boxes to hand out information or submit documents.
- Manage Web browser preferences and bookmarks.
- Assign helper applications for use in conjunction with a Web browser.
- Set up multiple configurations (up to 200), making it easy to manage different classes using one cluster of computers.
- Limit the amount of space on a hard drive for personal use.
- Restrict login capabilities by date and time.
- Log usage.

User And Group Manager

The User and Group Manager is a simple application that allows you to perform administrative tasks on the following types of servers:

- AppleShare IP

- AppleShare (version 3 or later)

- At Ease for Workgoups (version 4 or later)

- First Class

The actions you can take with the User and Group Manager are limited in comparison to the other two applications that constitute the Apple Network Administrator Toolkit. They include:

- Add users and groups.

- Delete users and groups.

- Modify existing users and groups.

- Compare groups of users.

- Export user and group information among different types of servers, as well as among similar servers.

- Import and export lists of users and groups as ASCII text.

Apple LAN Utility

The Apple LAN Utility assists administrators with only one specific task: Ethernet and Token Ring hardware address management. Every network interface card (NIC) has a unique hardware address (12 hexadecimal digits) that identifies it on a network, including built-in Ethernet, Ethernet or Token Ring transceivers, adapters, and PCMCIA cards. Administrators should keep lists of which computer uses what hardware address as a means of locating computers that misbehave on a network. By misbehaving, we mean hacking, disrupting network traffic, or just spewing bad packets and flooding the network.

Most advanced network administrators will have a means of identifying hardware addresses, because IP addresses can be faked or spoofed, whereas hardware addresses are rarely faked (although it is possible). Also, once in a blue moon, two hardware adapters will broadcast the same hardware address, which will cause them both to report serious errors.

The Apple LAN Utility has three basic features. First, it reports the computer's hardware address, which is the same information that can be found in the Get Info section of the TCP/IP control panel, as shown in Figure B.10.

Second, it can save a computer's hardware address along with the following information, to a tab-delimited text file:

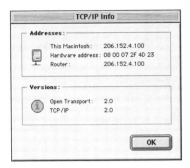

Figure B.10   You can obtain your computer's hardware address from the TCP/IP control panel.

- Computer model
- Computer name
- User name
- Location of NIC
- Type of address (burned-in or local)

Finally, you can replace the burned-in hardware address with a locally administered address, which is useful in Simple Network Administration (SNA) or DECNet environments.

To view or change a computer's hardware address:

1. Launch the Apple LAN Utility.
2. Record or export the hardware address, shown in Figure B.11.
3. To change the address, choose Edit|Allow Changes and enter the new address, as in Figure B.12.

Figure B.11   The Apple LAN Utility.

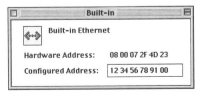

Figure B.12   Entering a locally administered hardware address.

Timbuktu

Timbuktu is an essential tool for persons administering remote servers, such as co-located Web servers or fileservers located in remote buildings or computer rooms. It can also be equally valuable for providing support in computer clusters, training rooms, and for general remote technical support. Timbuktu costs about $50 per seat, doesn't require a server, and provides the following services:

- Screen sharing
- Remote control
- File transfer
- Intercom
- File synchronizing
- AppleScript support
- Conferencing capabilities

The best thing about Timbuktu is that it is very cross-platform compatible. The following operating systems are supported:

- Timbuktu Pro for Mac OS
- Timbuktu Pro for Mac OS with Application Sharing
- Timbuktu Pro 32 for Windows NT and Windows 95/98 (32-bit)
- Timbuktu Pro for Windows 3.x, 95 and NT (16/32-bit)
- Timbuktu Pro for Enterprise

Timbuktu is easy to install, very secure (it provides robust password encryption), and requires little system resources. To run Timbuktu, you'll need the following:

- System 7.5 or higher
- 68040 or PowerPC processor
- 8MB of physical RAM (total)
- AppleTalk, TCP/IP, or modem connection

The actual requirements for the two versions of Timbuktu for the Mac OS (standard and Application Sharing) will vary, depending on the features you want to use. The two most popular features provided by Timbuktu are remote control and file exchange. To remotely control another computer (either Mac or Windows), install Timbuktu and follow these steps:

1. Launch Timbuktu and choose File|New to open a new connection, called a control connection.

2. Choose a connection method (Personal Address Book, AppleTalk, or TCP/IP).

3. Enter a username and password, if requested. The remote computer will open in a framed window, as shown in Figure B.13.

To exchange files with the same computer once a control connection has been established:

1. Choose Service|Exchange.

2. A username and password will not be required once you have opened a control connection and not closed out of it before opening the exchange connection. Figure B.14 shows an example of an exchange connection.

In addition to control and exchange connections, you may also open the following types of connections:

- Observation (view only)

- Chat (text exchange)

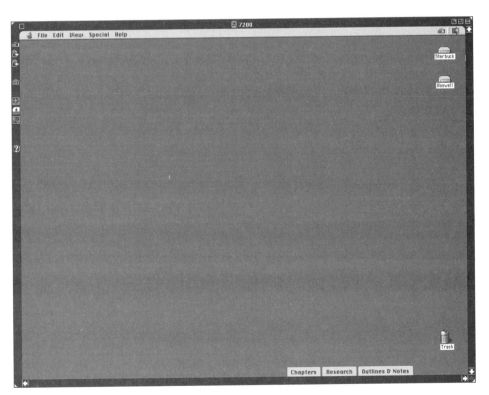

Figure B.13   A remote connection by using Timbuktu.

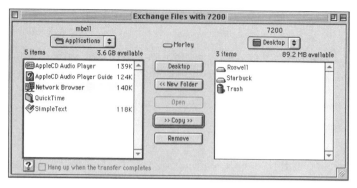

Figure B.14   A Timbuktu exchange connection.

- Notify (when a client becomes available)
- Intercom (voice exchange)
- Invitation (to open a connection)

Retrospect

No Mac administrator should be without Retrospect from Dantz, the leading client/server backup program for the Mac OS. After all, what good is a well-administered network of computers if they aren't backed up on a regular basis? Dantz provides several options for backing up one or more Mac or Windows computers, including:

- *Retrospect*—Back up server
- *Retrospect Express*—Personal backup
- *Retrospect Network Backup Kit*—Back up server plus 10 clients for the Mac OS

Retrospect is capable of backing up most Mac OS or Windows clients to a wide array of storage devices (over 150, according to Dantz). These devices include file servers, CD-R, tape, and removable drives from ADIC, DEC, Exabyte, HP, Quantum, Seagate, and Sony. A few of Retrospect's features include the following:

- Full or incremental backup
- Automated or on-demand backup of the server itself or a remote client
- Quick, one-step restoration of a remote volume
- Archiving of client data
- Data encryption

B: Administrative Features And Tools

The approach we've always taken to backing up our computers with retrospect follows these steps:

1. Full backup once per week.

2. Incremental backups every day, excluding Web browser cache files and other files that aren't necessary for the restoration of a client (see Figure B.15).

3. Maintain four archived sets of backups, so we can restore a client to its original state for any day in the previous 30 days.

It's not necessary to back up a client hard drive in its entirety, but if users are allowed to install their own software and customize their computers, this isn't a bad idea. If, however, you want to back up only the Documents folder, for example, and feel comfortable reinstalling the OS and any applications manually, a more limited backup is acceptable. Remember that you and your users need to first understand what is being backed up and what is not.

Client configuration is performed in two steps. First, the client software is loaded, the server administrator assigns an activator code to each client, and the server is told which volumes are to be backed up (see Figure B.16). Second, open the Retrospect control panel (shown in Figure B.17), and make all necessary customizations, such as waiting for the next scheduled backup before shutting down the computer or notification if the computer isn't backed up on schedule.

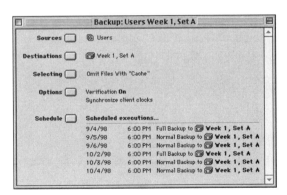

Figure B.15   A Retrospect script that excludes files that contain the word "Cache" from being backed up.

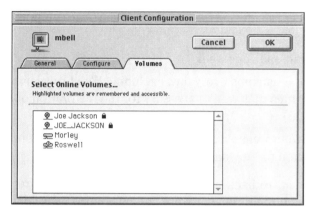

Figure B.16   Selecting which client volumes are to be backed up (note that some types of volumes, such as audio CD-ROMs, are excluded by default).

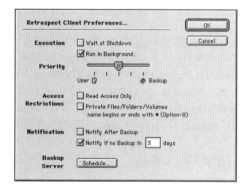

Figure B.17   The Retrospect Client Preferences control panel.

Appendix C

Mac OS Changes And Enhancements

The Mac OS has undergone many changes over the years, and the future of the Mac OS appears to be even more exciting. Mac OS 8.5 incorporates many significant changes over earlier versions of the OS; future versions will have even more impressive features while retaining backward-compatibility to all applications that will run under Mac OS 8.5. Because the first version of Mac OS X (Mac OS X Server) wasn't yet released at the time this book went to press, we aren't exactly sure what will be included in a final release. However, it has been in beta for most of the year, and we have a good idea of what it will bring in terms of features and underlying technology. Table C.1 illustrates the major components of the Mac OS and how they were (or will be) implemented in three major versions of the OS: System 7, Mac OS 8.5, and Mac OS X.

Table C.1   The major features of the Mac OS.

	7.0	8.5	X
File System	HFS	HFS+	UFS?
Tasking	Cooperative multitasking	Multithreaded, cooperative multitasking	Preemptive multitasking
Processor	Single 68K processor	Limited PPC multiprocessor	Symmetric multiprocessor PPC G4
Memory Protection	No	No	Yes
Virtual Memory	Optional	Optional	Mandatory
Networking	MacTCP, AppleTalk, TCP/IP	Open Transport, AppleTalk, TCP/IP	Berkeley Sockets, Open Transport, AppleTalk, TCP/IP
Multimedia	QuickDraw	QuickDraw, ColorSync, QuickDraw 3D, QuickTime	ColorSync, QuickTime, Display Postscript, or enhanced QuickDraw
File Sharing	File sharing	File sharing, Web sharing	File sharing, Web sharing, NFS?
Java	n/a	MRJ	Tightly integrated
Users	Single user	Single user	Multiuser

The following sections describe these versions in greater detail. They will give you a better idea of the historical significance of Mac OS 8.5 and of what lies ahead.

Pre-System 7

Prior to System 7, several versions of operating systems ran on the first Apple computers (Apple I, II, II+, IIe, III) and the Lisa. When the first Macintosh was released in January 1984 (remember the famous Super Bowl commercial?), Apple introduced System 1.0. It (the original Macintosh) was able to run many versions of the operating system, up through the first releases of System 7. Each version of the OS fixed bugs, added features, and increased performance and stability. These versions include the following:

- System 1.0
- System 1.1
- System 2.0
- System 2.0.1
- System 5.0
- System 5.1
- System 6.0

- System 6.0.1
- System 6.0.2
- System 6.0.3
- System 6.0.4
- System 6.0.5
- System 6.0.7
- System 6.0.8

The next family of the Mac OS introduced even more features.

System 7

No other major version of the Mac OS has had as many version changes as System 7 (which eventually became Mac OS 7.6.1). This is probably so because System 7 introduced several important features that required updating and patching to keep pace with advances in hardware, such as the move by users from monochrome to color and the migration from the 68000 family of processors to the PowerPC processor. New features such as virtual memory, increased physical memory addressing, multi-gigabyte storage space, PowerPC native code, Open Transport networking, and multithreading required numerous updates to the OS, producing the following versions:

- System 7.0
- System 7.0.1
- System 7.1
- System 7.1 P

- System 7.5
- System 7.5.1
- System 7.5.2
- System 7.5.3

C: Mac OS Changes And Enhancements

- System 7.1.1
- System 7.1.2
- System 7.1.2 P

- System 7.5.5
- System 7.6
- System 7.6.1

Mac OS 8

When the Mac OS 8 and 8.1 arrived, things started to look a lot simpler when it came to versions of the OS. Still, many changes were under the hood, including the multithreaded and PowerPC-native Finder, improved Open Transport networking, the new Apple Platinum appearance, Web sharing, Java, and updated versions of QuickTime, QuickDraw, and many other peripheral OS components.

Mac OS 8.5, on the other hand, updates numerous features and incorporates several additions, including the following:

- More PPC-native code
- Virtual memory improvements
- Feature-rich content
- User-interface themes and sounds
- Font smoothing (anti-aliasing)
- Icons in Window title bars
- Multiple scroll bar options (double scroll and proportional thumbs)
- New Find command powered by V-Twin engine allows you to find-by-content, search the Internet, index a local drive, and use script
- Revised Applications menu supports tear-off menus, is sizable, and is scriptable
- PPC-Native AppleScript 1.3 has more scriptable applications
- Open Transport 2.0 supports SNMP and better DHCP
- Control Strip 2.0
- New navigational services (Open/Save dialogs)
- QuickDraw rewrite
- Font smoothing
- AppleGuide Help in HTML and new Help menu items
- Unicode and European character support by LaserWriter 8
- Desktop printer browser
- Network Browser for file server and TCP/IP services

- Personal Web server update
- Application Switcher
- List View enhancements
- Monitors and Sounds rewrite
- Monitor Calibration rewrite
- New icons for files and folders
- JPEG files that are dropped onto the System folder are redirected to the Desktop Pictures folder
- New Get Info window
- Disk-cache improvements
- Date & Time control panel rewrite adds synchronizing and time server capabilities
- File Exchange control panel replaces Mac OS Easy Open and PC Exchange
- File sharing
- General Controls
- Internet control panel integrates Internet Config 2.0 capabilities
- Keyboard
- Launcher
- Revised Location Manager control panel
- Revised Memory control panel
- Modem
- Revised Monitors & Sound control panel
- Mouse
- Numbers
- PowerBook/Energy saver replaces several PB control panels
- QuickTime settings
- Remote Access control panel/Apple Remote Access 3.1 replaces OT/PPP and ARA 2.1

It is anticipated that Apple will update Mac OS 8.5 at least twice before moving on to the next generation of OS named Mac OS X (Ten), with versions 8.6 and 8.7.

Mac OS X

The future of Mac OS X is actually now, with the impending release of Mac OS X Server, which is essentially Rhapsody 1.0 for PowerPC and Intel. However, as soon as OS X Server is released, it will form the basis of Mac OS X, a modern OS that will finally bring all the features of a modern OS to the Mac platform, such as the following:

- Memory protection

- Preemptive multitasking

- Symmetric multiprocessing

- Robust virtual memory

To take advantage of these features, Apple culled through the more than 8,000 Application Programming Interfaces (APIs) that are found in Mac OS 8 and discarded those that would prevent applications and the OS from enabling these kinds of features, including 68K code. The remaining PowerPC-native APIs (a.k.a. Carbon APIs) are placed atop the Mach kernel, which provides a hardware abstraction layer to most physical devices, such as the processor, RAM, SCSI and IDE devices, and schedules the tasks the processor must handle. The result is serious protection against system freezes and crashes and a rock-solid OS that will be backward-compatible with all applications that currently run under Mac OS 8.5. The only foreseeable drawback is that Mac OS X will probably only support G3 and later PowerMacs. Finally, a new set of APIs (the Yellow Box APIs) has been specified so developers can create even more sophisticated—and possibly cross-platform—applications, including Java-based software. These applications will possibly run on Win32-enabled Microsoft Windows platforms, including Windows 95, NT, and 98.

Appendix D

Mac OS Error Codes

The numeric error codes returned by the Mac OS can be cryptic, frustrating, and often unhelpful. Most of you have probably encountered a few of the more popular errors, such as Type 11, bus, or FPU. Usually, you can't do anything about the errors, because they are the result of a programming mistake with an application or within the Mac OS. However, knowing a little about what caused the error can go a long way in helping you make decisions on how to correct the problem.

The following error codes were compiled by Caerwyn Pearce and exported from his shareware program, SysErrors. This useful program, which is included on this book's accompanying CD-ROM, is a great resource. We encourage you to check it out and register your copy with Caerwyn.

Mac OS 8.5 System Errors

You may encounter the following error codes while using the Mac OS, using a debugger such as MacsBug, or in an application. Programmers will be familiar with many of these errors, but they can help anyone to better understand what caused the error in Mac OS, and, hopefully, fix it.

Table D.1   Mac OS 8.5 System error codes.

Code	System Error	Description
1	dsBusError	bus error
2	dsAddressErr	address error
3	dsIllInstErr	illegal instruction error
4	dsZeroDivErr	zero divide error
5	dsChkErr	check trap error
6	dsOvflowErr	overflow trap error
7	dsPrivErr	privilege violation error
8	dsTraceErr	trace mode error

Code	System Error	Description
9	dsLineAErr	line 1010 trap error (A-line)
10	dsLineFErr	line 1111 trap error (F-line)
11	dsMiscErr	miscellaneous hardware exception error
12	dsCoreErr	unimplemented core routine error

(continued)

Table D.1   Mac OS 8.5 System error codes (continued).

Code	System Error	Description	Code	System Error	Description
13	dsIrqErr	uninstalled interrupt error	41	dsFinderErr	can't load the Finder error
14	dsIOCoreErr	IO Core Error	42	dsBadStartupDisk	unable to mount boot volume (sad Mac only)
15	dsLoadErr	Segment Loader Error			
16	dsFPErr	Floating point error	42	shutDownAlert	handled like a shutdown error
17	dsNoPackErr	package 0 not present [List Manager]	43	dsSystemFileErr	can't find System file to open (sad Mac only)
18	dsNoPk1	package 1 not present [Reserved by Apple]	51	dsBadSlotInt	unserviceable slot interrupt
19	dsNoPk2	package 2 not present [Disk Initialization]	81	dsBadSANEopcode	bad opcode given to SANE Pack4
20	dsNoPk3	package 3 not present [Standard File]	83	dsBadPatchHeader	SetTrapAddress saw the "come-from" header
21	dsNoPk4	package 4 not present [Floating-Point Arithmetic]	84	menuPrgErr	happens when a menu is purged
22	dsNoPk5	package 5 not present [Transcendental Functions]	85	dsMBarNFnd	SysErr — cannot find MBDF
23	dsNoPk6	package 6 not present [International Utilities]	86	dsHMenuFindErr	SysErr — recursively defined HMenus
24	dsNoPk7	package 7 not present [Binary/Decimal Conversion]	87	dsWDEFnFnd	Could not load WDEF
			88	dsCDEFnFnd	Could not load CDEF
			89	dsMDEFnFnd	Could not load MDEF
25	dsMemFullErr	out of memory!	90	dsNoFPU	"FPU instruction executed, but machine has no FPU"
26	dsBadLaunch	can't launch file			
27	dsFSErr	file system map has been trashed	98	dsNoPatch	Can't patch for particular Model Mac
28	dsStknHeap	stack has moved into application heap	99	dsBadPatch	Can't load patch resource
30	dsReinsert	request user to reinsert offline volume	101	dsParityErr	memory parity error
31	dsNotThe1	not the disk I wanted (obsolete)	102	dsOldSystem	System is too old for this ROM
33	negZcbFreeErr	ZcbFree has gone negative	103	ds32BitMode	booting in 32-bit on a 24-bit sys
40	dsGreeting	welcome to Macintosh greeting	104	dsNeedToWrite	need to write new boot BootBlocks blocks

(continued)

D: Mac OS Error Codes

Table D.1   Mac OS 8.5 System error codes (continued).

Code	System Error	Description	Code	System Error	Description
105	dsNotEnough RAMToBoot	need at least 1.5MB of RAM to boot 7.0	20003	dsRemoveDisk	request user to remove disk from manual eject drive
106	dsBufPtrTooLow	bufPtr moved too far during boot	20004	dsDirtyDisk	request user to return a manually ejected dirty disk
20000	dsShutDown OrRestart	user choice between ShutDown and Restart			
20001	dsSwitchOff OrRestart	user choice between Switch off or Restart	20109	dsShutDown OrResume	allow user to return to Finder or ShutDown
20002	dsForcedQuit	"allow the user to ExitToShell, return if Cancel"	20010	dsSCSIWarn	Portable SCSI adapter warning
			32767	dsSysErr	general system error (catch-all used in DSAT)

Post-MacsBug System Errors

System Errors are used after MacsBug is loaded to put up dialogs, because they shouldn't cause MacsBug to stop; negative numbers add to an existing dialog without putting up a whole new dialog.

Table D.2   Post-MacsBug error codes.

Code	System Error	Description	Code	System Error	Description
-10	dsMacsBugInstalled	say "MacsBug Installed"	-2	vTypErr	invalid queue element
-11	dsDisassemblerInstalled	say "Disassembler Installed"	-3	corErr	core routine number out of range
-12	dsHD20Installed	say "HD20 Startup"	-4	unimpErr	unimplemented core routine
-13	dsExtensionsDisabled	say "Extensions Disabled"	-5	SlpTypeErr	invalid queue element
General System			-8	seNoDB	no debugger installed to handle debugger command
1	evtNotEnb	event not enabled at PostEvent			
0	noErr	0 for success			
-1	qErr	queue element not found during deletion			

(continued)

Table D.2   Post-MacsBug error codes (continued).

D: Mac OS Error Codes

Code	System Error	Description	Code	System Error	Description
Color Manager			-23	openErr	"Requested read/write permission doesn't match driver's open permission, or Attempt to open RAM SerD failed"
-9	iTabPurgErr	from Color2Index/ ITabMatch			
-10	noColMatch				
-11	qAllocErr	from MakeITable			
-12	tblAllocErr				
-13	overRun		-24	closErr	Close failed
-14	noRoomErr		-25	dRemovErr	tried to remove an open driver
-15	seOutOfRange	from SetEntry			
-16	seProtErr		-26	dInstErr	DrvrInstall couldn't find driver in resources
-17	i2CRangeErr				
-18	gdBadDev				
-19	reRangeErr		-27	abortErr	IO call aborted by KillIO
-20	seInvRequest				
-21	seNoMemErr		-27	iIOAbortErr	IO abort error (Printing Manager)
I/O System			-28	notOpenErr	Couldn't rd/wr/ctl/ sts cause driver not opened
-17	controlErr	Driver can't respond to Control call			
			-29	unitTblFullErr	unit table has no more entries
-18	statusErr	Driver can't respond to Status call	-30	dceExtErr	dce extension error
			File System		
-19	readErr	Driver can't respond to Read call	-33	dirFulErr	Directory full
			-34	dskFulErr	disk full
			-35	nsvErr	no such volume
-20	writErr	Driver can't respond to Write call	-36	ioErr	I/O error (bummers)
			-37	bdNamErr	there may be no bad names in the final system!
-21	badUnitErr	Driver ref num doesn't match unit table			
			-38	fnOpnErr	File not open
-22	unitEmptyErr	Driver ref num specifies NIL handle in unit table	-39	eofErr	End of file

(continued)

Table D.2   Post-MacsBug error codes (continued).

Code	System Error	Description	Code	System Error	Description
-40	posErr	tried to position to before start of file (r/w)	-58	extFSErr	volume in question belongs to an external fs
-41	mFulErr	memory full (open) or file won't fit (load)	-59	fsRnErr	file system internal error: during rename the old entry was deleted but could not be restored
-42	tmfoErr	too many files open			
-43	fnfErr	File not found	-60	badMDBErr	bad master directory block
-44	wPrErr	diskette is write protected			
-45	fLckdErr	file is locked	-61	wrPermErr	write permissions error
-46	vLckdErr	volume is locked			
-47	fBsyErr	File is busy (delete)	**Font Manager**		
-48	dupFNErr	duplicate file name (rename)	-64	fontDecError	error during font declaration
-49	opWrErr	file already open with write permission	-65	fontNotDeclared	font not declared
			-66	fontSubErr	font substitution occurred
-50	paramErr	error in user parameter list	-32615	fontNotOutlineErr	bitmap font passed to routine that does outlines only
-51	rfNumErr	refnum error			
-52	gfpErr	get file position error			
-53	volOffLinErr	volume not on line error (was Ejected)	**Disk**		
			-64	lastDskErr	I/O System Errors
			-64	noDriveErr	drive not installed
-54	permErr	permissions error (on file open)	-65	offLinErr	r/w requested for an offline drive
-55	volOnLinErr	drive volume already online at MountVol	-66	noNybErr	couldn't find 5 nybbles in 200 tries
-56	nsDrvErr	no such drive (tried to mount a bad drive num)	-67	noAdrMkErr	couldn't find valid addr mark
			-68	dataVerErr	read verify compare failed
-57	noMacDskErr	not a Mac diskette (sig bytes are wrong)	-69	badCksmErr	addr mark checksum didn't check

D: Mac OS Error Codes

(continued)

Table D.2   Post-MacsBug error codes (continued).

Code	System Error	Description	Code	System Error	Description
-70	badBtSlpErr	bad addr mark bit slip nibbles	-86	clkWrErr	time written did not verify
-71	noDtaMkErr	couldn't find a data mark header	-87	prWrErr	parameter ram written didn't read-verify
-72	badDCksum	bad data mark checksum	-88	prInitErr	InitUtil found the parameter ram uninitialized
-73	badDBtSlp	bad data mark bit slip nibbles	-89	rcvrErr	"SCC receiver error (framing, parity, OR)"
-74	wrUnderrun	write underrun occurred			
-75	cantStepErr	step handshake failed	-90	breakRecd	Break received (SCC)
-76	tk0BadErr	track 0 detect doesn't change	**AppleTalk**		
-77	initIWMErr	unable to initialize IWM	-91	ddpSktErr	error in socket number
-78	twoSideErr	tried to read 2nd side on a 1-sided drive	-92	ddpLenErr	data length too big
			-93	noBridgeErr	no network bridge for non-local send
-79	spdAdjErr	unable to correctly adjust disk speed	-94	lapProtErr	error in attaching/detaching protocol
-80	seekErr	track number wrong on address mark	-95	excessCollsns	excessive collisions on write
-81	sectNFErr	sector number never found on a track	-96	portNotPwr	serial port not currently powered
-82	fmt1Err	can't find sector 0 after track format	-97	portInUse	driver Open error code (port is in use)
-83	fmt2Err	can't get enough sync	-98	portNotCf	driver Open error code (parameter RAM not configured for this connection)
-84	verErr	track failed to verify			
-84	firstDskErr	I/O System Errors			
"Serial Ports, PRAM/Clock"			**Speech Manager**		
-85	clkRdErr	unable to read same clock value twice	-240	noSynthFound	
			-241	synthOpenFailed	

(continued)

D: Mac OS Error Codes

Table D.2   Post-MacsBug error codes (continued).

Code	System Error	Description		Code	System Error	Description
-242	synthNotReady			-117	memLockedErr	trying to move a locked block (MoveHHi)
-243	bufTooSmall					
-244	voiceNotFound			**HFS**		
-245	incompatibleVoice			-120	dirNFErr	Directory not found
-246	badDictFormat					
-247	badInputText			-121	tmwdoErr	No free WDCB available
Scrap Manager						
-100	noScrapErr	No scrap exists error		-122	badMovErr	Move into offspring error
-102	noTypeErr	No object of that type in scrap		-123	wrgVolTypErr	Wrong volume type error: not supported for MFS
Memory Manager						
-99	memROZErr	hard error in ROZ				
-99	memROZError	hard error in ROZ		-124	volGoneErr	Server volume has been disconnected
-99	memROZWarn	soft error in ROZ				
-108	memFullErr	Not enough room in heap zone		-127	fsDSIntErr	Internal file system error
-108	iMemFullErr	Not enough room in heap zone (Printing Error)		-1300	fidNotFound	no file thread exists
-109	nilHandleErr	Master Pointer was NIL in HandleZone or other		-1301	fidExists	file id already exists
				-1302	notAFileErr	directory specified
-110	memAdrErr	"address was odd, or out of range"		-1303	diffVolErr	files on different volumes
-111	memWZErr	WhichZone failed (applied to free block)		-1304	catChangedErr	catalog has been modified
-112	memPurErr	trying to purge a locked or non-purgeable block		-1305	desktopDamagedErr	desktop database files are corrupted
				-1306	sameFileErr	can't exchange a file with itself
-113	memAZErr	Address in zone check failed		-1307	badFidErr	file id is dangling or doesn't match file number
-114	memPCErr	Pointer Check failed		-1308	notARemountErr	when _Mount allows only remounts and doesn't get one
-115	memBCErr	Block Check failed				
-116	memSCErr	Size Check failed				

(continued)

Table D.2   Post-MacsBug error codes *(continued)*.

Code	System Error	Description	Code	System Error	Description
-1309	fileBoundsErr	file's EOF offset mark or size is too big	-149	insufficientStackErr	not enough stack space for the necessary buffers
-1310	fsDataTooBigErr	file or volume is too big for system	-150	cMatchErr	Color2Index failed to find an index
Menu Manager			-151	cTempMemErr	failed to allocate memory for temporary structures
-126	dsMBarNFnd	system error code for MBDF not found			
-127	dsHMenuFindErr	could not find HMenu's parent in MenuKey	-152	cNoMemErr	failed to allocate memory for structure
-128	userCanceledErr	user canceled the operation	-153	cRangeErr	range error on colorTable request
HFS FileID			-154	cProtectErr	colorTable entry protection violation
-130	fidNotFound	no file thread exists			
-131	fidNotAFile	directory specified	-155	cDevErr	invalid type of graphics device
-132	fidExists	file id already exists	-156	cResErr	invalid resolution for MakeITable
Color Quickdraw			-157	cDepthErr	invalid pixel depth
-125	updPixMemErr	insufficient memory to update a pixmap	-158	cParmErr	invalid parameter
			-500	rgnTooBigErr	region too big error
-145	noMemForPictPlaybackErr		-1000	noMaskFoundErr	Icon Utilties Error
-147	rgnOverflowErr	"Region accumulation failed, rgn may be corrupt"	-11000	pictInfoVersionErr	wrong version of the PictInfo structure
-147	rgnTooBigError	"Region accumulation failed, rgn may be corrupt"	-11001	pictInfoIDErr	the internal consistancy check for the PictInfoID is wrong
-148	pixMapTooBigErr	passed pixelmap is too large	-11002	pictInfoVerbErr	the passed verb was invalid
-149	nsStackErr	not enough stack space for the necessary buffers	-11003	cantLoadPickMethodErr	unable to load the custom pick proc

(continued)

D: Mac OS Error Codes

Table D.2   Post-MacsBug error codes (continued).

Code	System Error	Description
-11004	colorsRequestedErr	the number of colors requested was illegal
-11005	pictureDataErr	the picture data was invalid
Resource Manager		
-185	badExtResource	extended resource has a bad format
-186	CantDecompress	resource bent (the bends) can't decompress a compressed resource
-188	resourceInMemory	Resource already in memory
-189	writingPastEnd	Writing past end of file
-190	inputOutOfBounds	Offset of Count out of bounds
-192	resNotFound	Resource not found
-193	resFNotFound	Resource file not found
-194	addResFailed	AddResource failed
-195	addRefFailed	AddReference failed
-196	rmvResFailed	RmveResource failed
-197	rmvRefFailed	RmveReference failed
-198	resAttrErr	attribute inconsistent with operation
-199	mapReadErr	map inconsistent with operation

Code	System Error	Description
Sound Manager		
-200	noHardwareErr	No hardware support for the specified synthesizer
-201	notEnoughHardwareErr	No more channels for the specified synth
-203	queueFull	No more room in queue
-204	resProblem	Problem loading resource
-205	badChannel	Invalid channel queue length
-206	badFormat	Handle to 'snd' resource was invalid
-207	notEnoughBufferSpace	could not allocate enough memory
-208	badFileFormat	"was not type AIFF or was of bad format, corrupt"
-209	channelBusy	the Channel is being used for a PFD already
-210	buffersTooSmall	cannot operate in the memory allowed
-211	channelNotBusy	
-212	noMoreRealTime	not enought CPU cycles left to add another task
-220	siNoSoundInHardware	no Sound Input hardware
-221	siBadSoundInDevice	invalid index passed to Sound In Get Indexed Device

(continued)

D: Mac OS Error Codes

Table D.2   Post-MacsBug error codes (continued).

D: Mac OS Error Codes

Code	System Error	Description
-222	siNoBufferSpecified	nil buffer passed to synchronous SPBRecord
-223	siInvalidCompression	invalid compression type
-224	siHardDriveTooSlow	hard drive too slow to record to disk
-225	siInvalidSampleRate	invalid sample rate
-226	siInvalidSampleSize	invalid sample size
-227	siDeviceBusyErr	input device already in use
-228	siBadDeviceName	input device could not be opened
-229	siBadRefNum	invalid input device reference number
-230	siInputDeviceErr	input device hardware failure
-231	siUnknownInfoType	driver returned invalid info type selector
-232	siUnknownQuality	invalid quality selector returned by driver

Midi Manager

Code	System Error	Description
-250	midiNoClientErr	no client with that ID found
-251	midiNoPortErr	no port with that ID found
-252	midiTooManyPortsErr	too many ports already installed in system
-253	midiTooManyConsErr	too many connections made
-254	midiVConnectErr	pending virtual connection created

Code	System Error	Description
-255	midiVConnectMade	pending virtual connection resolved
-256	midiVConnectRmvd	pending virtual connection removed
-257	midiNoConErr	no connection exists between specified ports
-258	midiWriteErr	couldn't write to all connected ports
-259	midiNameLenErr	name supplied is longer than 31 characters
-260	midiDupIDErr	duplicate client ID
-261	midiInvalidCmdErr	command not supported for port type

Notification Manager

Code	System Error	Description
-299	nmTypErr	Wrong queue type

Start Manager

Code	System Error	Description
-290	smSDMInitErr	SDM could not be initialized
-291	smSRTInitErr	Slot Resource Table could not be initialized
-292	smPRAMInitErr	Slot Resource Table could not be initialized
-293	smPriInitErr	Cards could not be initialized
-300	smEmptySlot	No card in slot
-301	smCRCFail	CRC check failed for declaration data
-302	smFormatErr	FHeader Format is not Apple's

(continued)

Table D.2   Post-MacsBug error codes (continued).

Code	System Error	Description	Code	System Error	Description
-303	smRevisionErr	Wrong revision level	-317	smIntTblVErr	An error occurred while trying to initialize the Slot Resource Table
-304	smNoDir	Directory offset is Nil			
-305	smDisabledSlot	This Slot is disabled	-318	smNoJmpTbl	SDM jump table could not be created
-305	smLWTstBad	This Slot is disabled (Old mnemonic)	-319	smBadBoardId	"BoardId was wrong, re-init the PRAM record"
-306	smNosInfoArray	No sInfoArray. Memory Mgr error			
			-320	smBusErrTO	BusError time out
-307	smResrvErr	Fatal reserved error. Reserved field <> 0	-330	smBadRefId	Reference Id not found in List
			-331	smBadsList	Bad sList: Id1<Id2<Id3… format is not followed
-308	smUnExBusErr	Unexpected BusError			
-309	smBLFieldBad	ByteLanes field was bad	-332	smReservedErr	Reserved field not zero
-310	smFHBlockRdErr	Error occurred during _sGetFHeader	-333	smCodeRevErr	Code revision is wrong
-311	smFHBlkDispErr	Error occurred during _sDisposePtr (Dispose of FHeader block)	-334	smCPUErr	Code revision is wrong
			-335	smsPointerNil	"LPointer is nil From sOffsetData. If this error occurs, check sInfo rec for more information"
-312	smDisposePErr	DisposePointer error			
-313	smNoBoardsRsrc	No Board sResource			
-314	smGetPRErr	Error occurred during _sGetPRAMRec (See SIMStatus)	-336	smNilsBlockErr	Nil sBlock error (Don't allocate and try to use a nil sBlock)
			-337	smSlotOOBErr	Slot out of bounds error
-315	smNoBoardId	No Board Id	-338	smSelOOBErr	Selector out of bounds error
-316	smIntStatVErr	The InitStatusV field was negative after primary or secondary init	-339	smNewPErr	_NewPtr error
			-340	smBlkMoveErr	_BlockMove error

(continued)

Table D.2   Post-MacsBug error codes (continued).

Code	System Error	Description
-341	smCkStatusErr	Status of slot = fail
-342	smGetDrvrNamErr	Error occurred during _sGetDrvrName
-343	smDisDrvrNamErr	Error occurred during _sDisDrvrName
-344	smNoMoresRsrcs	No more sResources
-345	smsGetDrvrErr	Error occurred during _sGetDriver
-346	smBadsPtrErr	Bad pointer was passed to sCalcsPointer
-347	smByteLanesErr	NumByteLanes was determined to be zero
-348	smOffsetErr	"Offset was too big (temporary error, should be fixed)"
-349	smNoGoodOpens	No opens were successful in the loop
-350	smSRTOvrFlErr	SRT overflow
-351	smRecNotFnd	Record not found in the SRT

Device Manager

Code	System Error	Description
-360	slotNumErr	invalid slot # error
-400	gcrOnMFMErr	gcr format on high density media error

Edition Manager

Code	System Error	Description
-450	editionMgrInitErr	edition manager not inited by this app

Code	System Error	Description
-451	badSectionErr	not a valid SectionRecord
-452	notRegisteredSectionErr	not a registered SectionRecord
-453	badEditionFileErr	edition file is corrupt
-454	badSubPartErr	cannot use sub parts in this release
-460	multiplePublisherWrn	A Publisher is already registered for that container
-461	containerNotFoundWrn	couldn't find editionContainer now
-462	containerAlreadyOpenWrn	container already opened by this section
-463	notThePublisherWrn	different publisher was first registered for that container

SCSI Manager

Code	System Error	Description
-470	scsiBadPBErr	invalid field(s) in the parameter block
-471	scsiOverrunErr	attempted to transfer too many bytes
-472	scsiTransferErr	write flag conflicts with data transfer phase
-473	scsiBusTOErr	bus error during transfer
-474	scsiSelectTOErr	scsiSelTO exceeded (selection failed)
-475	scsiTimeOutErr	scsiReqTO exceeded

(continued)

D: Mac OS Error Codes

Table D.2   Post-MacsBug error codes *(continued).*

Code	System Error	Description	Code	System Error	Description
-476	scsiBusResetErr	"the bus was reset, so your request was aborted"	-602	appModeErr	"memory mode is 32-bit, but app not 32-bit clean"
-477	scsiBadStatus	non-zero (not Good) status returned	-603	protocolErr	app made module calls in improper order
-478	scsiNoStatusErr	device did not go through a status phase	-604	hardwareConfigErr	hardware configuration not correct for call
-479	scsiLinkFailErr	linked command never executed	-605	appMemFullErr	application SIZE not big enough for launch
-489	scsiUnimpVctErr	unimplemented routine was called	-606	appIsDaemon	"app is BG-only, and launch flags disallow this"
Debugger SysErrs			-607	bufferIsSmall	error returns from Post and Accept
-490	userBreak	user debugger break	-608	noOutstandingHLE	
-491	strUserBreak	user debugger break display string on stack	-609	connectionInvalid	
			-610	noUserInteractionAllowed	no user interaction allowed
-492	exUserBreak	user debugger break execute commands on stack	**Memory Dispatch**		
			-620	notEnoughMemoryErr	insufficient physical memory
TextEdit			-621	notHeldErr	specified range of memory is not held
-501	teScrapSizeErr	scrap item too big for text-edit record			
O/S			-622	cannotMakeContiguousErr	cannot make specified range contiguous
-502	hwParamrErr	bad selector for _HWPriv	-623	notLockedErr	specified range of memory is not locked
Process Manager					
-600	procNotFound	no eligible process with specified descriptor	-624	interruptsMaskedErr	don't call with interrupts masked
-601	memFragErr	not enough room to launch app w/ spec requirements	-625	cannotDeferErr	unable to defer additional functions

(continued)

D: Mac OS Error Codes

D: Mac OS Error Codes

Table D.2   Post-MacsBug error codes (continued).

Code	System Error	Description	Code	System Error	Description
-626	noMMUErr	no MMU present	-854	hmBadHelpData	from HMShow MenuBalloon if menu and item is same as last time
Database Access			-854	hmSameAsLastBalloon	from HMShow MenuBalloon if menu and item is same as last time
-800	rcDBNull				
-801	rcDBValue		-855	hmHelpManager	HMGetHelp MenuHandle if help menu not setup
-802	rcDBError				
-803	rcDBBadType				
-804	rcDBBreak				
-805	rcDBExec		-856	hmBadSelector	
-806	rcDBBadSessID		-857	hmSkippedBalloon	Helpmsg specified a skip balloon
-807	rcDBBadSessNum	bad session number for DBGetConnInfo			
			-858	hmWrongVersion	Help mgr resource was the wrong version
-808	rcDBBadDDEV	bad ddev specified on DBInit			
			-859	hmUnknownHelpType	Help msg record contained a bad type
-809	rcDBAsyncNotSupp	ddev does not support async calls			
			-860	hmCouldNotLoadPackage	
-810	rcDBBadAsyncPB	tried to kill a bad pb	-861	hmOperation Unsupported	Bad method passed to HMShowBalloon
-811	rcDBNoHandler	no app handler for specified data type			
			-862	hmNoBalloonUp	No balloon visible when HMRemove Balloon called
-812	rcDBWrongVersion	incompatible versions			
-813	rcDBPackNotInited	attempt to call other routine before InitDBPack	-863	hmCloseViewActive	CloseView active when HMRemove Balloon called
Help Manager			**PPC Toolbox**		
-850	hmHelpDisabled	"Show Balloons mode off, call to routine ignored"	-900	notInitErr	PPCToolBox not initialized
-851	hmResNotFound		-902	nameTypeErr	Invalid or inappropriate locationKind Selector in locationName
-852	hmMemFullErr				
-853	hmBalloonAborted	if mouse was moving or mouse wasn't in window port rect			

(continued)

Table D.2   Post-MacsBug error codes (continued).

Code	System Error	Description	Code	System Error	Description
-903	noPortErr	Unable to open port or bad portRefNum	-917	sessClosedErr	session was closed
-904	noGlobalsErr	"The system is hosed, better re-boot"	-919	badPortNameErr	PPCPortRec malformed
-905	localOnlyErr	Network activity is currently disabled	-922	noDefaultUserErr	user hasn't typed in owners name in Network Setup Control Panel
-906	destPortErr	Port does not exist at destination	-923	notLoggedInErr	The default userRefNum does not yet exist
-907	sessTableErr	"Out of session tables, try again later"	-924	noUserRefErr	unable to create a new userRefNum
-908	noSessionErr	Invalid session reference number	-925	networkErr	"An error has occurred in the network, not too likely"
-909	badReqErr	bad parameter or invalid state for operation	-926	noInformErr	PPCStart failed: dest didn't have inform pending
-910	portNameExistsErr	port is already open (perhaps another app)	-927	authFailErr	unable to authenticate user at destination
-911	noUserNameErr	user name unknown on destination machine	-928	noUserRecErr	Invalid user reference number
-912	userRejectErr	Destination rejected the session request	-930	badServiceMethodErr	"illegal service type, or not supported"
-913	noMachineNameErr	user hasn't named his Macintosh in the Network Setup Control Panel	-931	badLocNameErr	location name malformed
-914	noToolboxNameErr	"A system resource is missing, not too likely"	-932	guestNotAllowedErr	destination port requires authentication
-915	noResponseErr	unable to contact destination	**AppleTalk NBP**		
			-1024	nbpBuffOvr	Buffer overflow in LookupName
-916	portClosedErr	port was closed	-1025	nbpNoConfirm	Name not confirmed on ConfirmName

(continued)

D: Mac OS Error Codes

Table D.2   Post-MacsBug error codes (continued).

Code	System Error	Description
-1026	nbpConfDiff	Name confirmed at different socket
-1027	nbpDuplicate	Duplicate name exists already
-1028	nbpNotFound	Name not found on remove
-1029	nbpNISErr	Error trying to open the NIS

AppleTalk ASP

Code	System Error	Description
-1066	aspBadVersNum	Server cannot support this ASP version
-1067	aspBufTooSmall	Buffer too small
-1068	aspNoMoreSess	No more sessions on server
-1069	aspNoServers	No servers at that address
-1070	aspParamErr	Parameter error
-1071	aspServerBusy	Server cannot open another session
-1072	aspSessClosed	Session closed
-1073	aspSizeErr	Command block too big
-1074	aspTooMany	Too many clients (server error)
-1075	aspNoAck	No ack on attention request (server err)

AppleTalk ATP

Code	System Error	Description
-1096	reqFailed	SendRequest failed: retry count exceeded
-1097	tooManyReqs	Too many concurrent requests
-1098	tooManySkts	Too many concurrent responding-sockets

Code	System Error	Description
-1099	badATPSkt	Bad ATP-responding socket
-1100	badBuffNum	Bad response buffer number specified
-1101	noRelErr	No release received
-1102	cbNotFound	Control Block (TCB or RspCB) not found
-1103	noSendResp	AddResponse issued without SendResponse
-1104	noDataArea	No data area for request to MPP
-1105	reqAborted	SendRequest aborted by RelTCB
-3101	buf2SmallErr	Buffer too small error
-3102	noMPPErr	No MPP error
-3103	ckSumErr	Check sum error
-3104	extractErr	Extraction error
-3105	readQErr	Read queue error
-3106	atpLenErr	ATP length error
-3107	atpBadRsp	ATP bad response error
-3108	recNotFnd	Record not found
-3109	sktClosedErr	Socket closed error

AppleTalk ADSP driver control ioResults

Code	System Error	Description
-1273	errOpenDenied	open connection request was denied
-1274	errDSPQueueSize	send or receive queue is too small
-1275	errFwdReset	read terminated by forward reset

(continued)

D: Mac OS Error Codes

Table D.2   Post-MacsBug error codes (continued).

Code	System Error	Description	Code	System Error	Description
-1276	errAttention	attention message too long	-5021	RangeOverlap	Attempt to lock some of an already locked range
-1277	errOpening	open connection request was denied			
-1278	errState	Bad connection state for this operation	**AppleTalk AFP**		
			-5000	afpAccessDenied	AFP access denied
-1279	errAborted	control call was aborted	-5001	afpAuthContinue	AFP authorization continue
-1280	errRefNum	bad connection refNum	-5002	afpBadUAM	AFP bad UAM
			-5003	afpBadVersNum	AFP bad version number
Print Manager w/LaserWriter			-5004	afpBitmapErr	AFP bit map error
-4096	???	No free Connect Control Blocks available	-5005	afpCantMove	AFP can't move error
-4097	???	Bad connection reference number	-5006	afpDenyConflict	AFP deny conflict
-4098	???	Request already active	-5007	afpDirNotEmpty	AFP dir not empty
-4099	???	Write request too big	-5008	afpDiskFull	AFP disk full
-4100	???	Connection just closed	-5009	afpEofError	AFP End-of-File error
-4101	???	"Printer not found, or closed"	-5010	afpFileBusy	AFP file busy
			-5011	afpFlatVo	AFP flat volume
File Manager Extensions			-5012	afpItemNotFound	AFP item not found
-5000	accessDenied	Incorrect access for this file/folder	-5013	afpLockErr	AFP lock error
			-5014	afpMiscErr	AFP misc error
-5006	DenyConflict	Permission/Deny mode conflicts with the current mode in which this fork is already open	-5015	afpNoMoreLocks	AFP no more locks
			-5016	afpNoServer	AFP no server
			-5017	afpObjectExists	AFP object already exists
			-5018	afpObjectNotFound	AFP object not found
-5015	NoMoreLocks	Byte range locking failure from Server	-5019	afpParmErr	AFP parm error
-5020	RangeNotLocked	Attempt to unlock an already unlocked range	-5020	afpRangeNotLocked	AFP range not locked
			-5021	afpRangeOverlap	AFP range overlap

D: Mac OS Error Codes

(continued)

Table D.2   Post-MacsBug error codes (continued).

Code	System Error	Description	Code	System Error	Description
-5022	afpSessClosed	AFP session closed	-5041	afpPwdTooShortErr	the password being set is too short: there is a minimum length that must be met or exceeded
-5023	afpUserNotAuth	AFP user not authorized			
-5024	afpCallNotSupported	AFP call not supported			
-5025	afpObjectTypeErr	AFP object type error	-5042	afpPwdExpiredErr	the password being used is too old: this requires the user to change the password before login can continue
-5026	afpTooManyFilesOpen	AFP too many files open			
-5027	afpServerGoingDown	AFP server going down			
-5028	afpCantRename	AFP can't rename	-5043	afpInsideSharedErr	folder being shared is inside a shared folder
-5029	afpDirNotFound	AFP directory not found			
-5030	afpIconTypeError	AFP icon type error	-5044	afpInsideTrashErr	folder being shared is in the trash folder
-5031	afpVolLocked	Volume is Read-Only			
-5032	afpObjectLocked	Object is M/R/D/W inhibited	-5060	afpBadDirIDType	
			-5061	afpCantMountMoreSrvre	
			-5062	afpAlreadyMounted	
-5033	afpContainsSharedErr	folder being shared has a shared folder	-5063	afpSameNodeErr	

SysEnvirons

Code	System Error	Description
-5034	afpIDNotFound	
-5035	afpIDExists	
-5036	afpDiffVolErr	
-5037	afpCatalogChanged	
-5038	afpSameObjectErr	
-5039	afpBadIDErr	
-5040	afpPwdSameErr	someone tried to change his or her password to the same password on a mandatory password change

Code	System Error	Description
-5500	envNotPresent	SysEnvirons trap not present (returned by glue)
-5501	envBadVers	Version non-positive
-5502	envVersTooBig	Version bigger than call can handle

Gestalt

Code	System Error	Description
-5550	gestaltUnknownErr	Gestalt doesn't know the answer

(continued)

Table D.2   Post-MacsBug error codes (continued).

Code	System Error	Description
-5551	gestaltUndefSelectorErr	Undefined code was passed to Gestalt
-5552	gestaltDupSelectorErr	Tried to add entry that already existed
-5553	gestaltLocationErr	Gestalt function ptr wasn't in sysheap

LaserWriter Driver

Code	System Error	Description
-8132	????	Manual Feed time out
-8133	????	General PostScript Error
-8150	????	No LaserWriter chosen
-8151	????	Version mismatch between LaserPrep dictionaries
-8150	????	No LaserPrep dictionary installed
-8160	????	Zoom scale factor out of range

Thread Manager

Code	System Error	Description
-617	threadTooManyReqsErr	
-618	threadNotFoundErr	
-619	threadProtocolErr	

Power Manager

Code	System Error	Description
-13000	pmBusyErr	Pmgr never ready to start handshake
-13001	pmReplyTOErr	Timed out waiting for reply
-13002	pmSendStartErr	"During send, pmgr did not start hs"
-13003	pmSendEndErr	"During send, pmgr did not finish hs"

Code	System Error	Description
-13004	pmRecvStartErr	"During receive, pmgr did not start hs"
-13005	pmRecvEndErr	during receive pmgr did not finish hs configured for this connection

MacTCP

Code	System Error	Description
-23000	ipBadLapErr	Bad network configuration
-23001	ipBadCnfgErr	Bad IP configuration error
-23002	ipNoCnfgErr	Missing IP or LAP configuration error
-23003	ipLoadErr	Error in MacTCP load
-23004	ipBadAddr	Error in getting address
-23005	connectionClosing	Connection in closing
-23006	invalidLength	
-23007	connectionExists	Request conflicts with existing connection
-23008	connectionDoesntExist	Connection does not exist
-23009	insufficientResources	Insufficient rsrcs to perform request
-23010	invalidStreamPtr	
-23011	streamAlreadyOpen	
-23012	connectionTerminated	
-23013	invalidBufPtr	
-23014	invalidRDS	
-23014	invalidWDS	
-23015	openFailed	
-23016	commandTimeout	

D: Mac OS Error Codes

(continued)

Table D.2   Post-MacsBug error codes (continued).

D: Mac OS Error Codes

Code	System Error	Description
-23017	duplicateSocket	
-23030	ipOpenProtErr	"Can't open new protocol, table full"
-23031	ipCloseProtErr	Can't find protocol to close
-23032	ipDontFragErr	Packet too large to send w/o fragmenting
-23033	ipDestDeadErr	Destination not responding
-23034	ipBadWDSErr	Error in WDS format
-23035	icmpEchoTimeoutErr	ICMP echo timed-out
-23036	ipNoFragMemErr	No memory to send fragmented pkt
-23037	ipRouteErr	Can't route packet off-net
-23041	nameSyntaxErr	
-23042	cacheFault	
-23043	noResultProc	
-23044	noNameServer	
-23045	authNameErr	
-23046	noAnsErr	
-23047	dnrErr	
-23048	outOfMemory	

Internal File System

Code	System Error	Description
1	chNoBuf	no free cache buffers (all in use)
2	chInUse	requested block in use
3	chnotfound	requested block not found
4	chNotInUse	block being released was not in use

Code	System Error	Description
16	fxRangeErr	file position beyond mapped range
17	fxOvFlErr	extents file overflow
32	btnotfound	record not found
33	btexists	record already exists
34	btnospace	no available space
35	btnoFit	record doesn't fit in node
36	btbadNode	bad node detected
37	btbadHdr	bad BTree header record detected
48	cmnotfound	CNode not found
49	cmexists	CNode already exists
50	cmnotempty	directory CNode not empty (valence = 0)
51	cmRootCN	invalid reference to root CNode
52	cmbadnews	detected bad catalog structure
53	cmFThdDirErr	thread belongs to a directory not a file
54	cmFThdGone	file thread doesn't exist
64	dsBadRotate	bad BTree rotate

Slot Declaration ROM Manager

Code	System Error	Description
1	siInitSDTblErr	slot int dispatch table couldn't be initialized
2	siInitVBLQsErr	VBLqueues for all slots couldn't be initialized

(continued)

Table D.2   Post-MacsBug error codes (continued).

Code	System Error	Description	Code	System Error	Description
3	silnitSPTblErr	slot priority table could not be initialized	48	invalidResp	First byte in response packet was wrong
10	sdmJTInitErr	SDM Jump Table could not be initialized	49	sqncNumErr	Sequence number in response packet was wrong
11	sdmInitErr	SDM could not be initialized	50	dNumberErr	Drive number in response packet was wrong
12	sdmSRTInitErr	Slot Resource Table could not be initialized	64	noResp	No response packet ever received
13	sdmPRAMInitErr	Slot PRAM could not be initialized	**SCSI Manager (obscure)**		
14	sdmPriInitErr	Cards could not be initialized	2	scCommErr	Communications error (operations timeout)
HD20 Driver			3	scArbNBErr	Arbitration failed during SCSIGet—Bus busy
16	wrtHsLw	HSHK low before starting	4	scBadparmsErr	Bad parameter or TIB opcode
17	wrtHSLwTO	Timeout waiting for HSHK to go low	5	scPhaseErr	SCSI bus not in correct phase for operation
19	wrtHSHighTO	Timeout waiting for HSHK to go high	6	scCompareErr	SCSI Manager busy with another operation when SCSIGet was called
32	rdHsHi	HSHK high before starting			
33	rdSyncTO	Timeout waiting for sync ($AA) bye	7	scMgrBusyErr	SCSI Manager busy with another operation when SCSIGet was called
34	rdGroupTO	Timeout waiting for group			
36	rdHoffSyncTO	Timeout waiting for sync after holdoff	8	scSequenceErr	"Attempted operation is out of sequence—e.g., calling SCSISelect before doing SCSIGet"
37	rdHsHiTO	Timeout waiting for HSHK high			
38	rdChksumErr	Checksum error on response packet			

(continued)

Table D.2   Post-MacsBug error codes (continued).

Code	System Error	Description	Code	System Error	Description
9	scBusTOErr	Bus timeout before data ready on SCSIRBlind and SCSIWBlind	10	scComplPhaseErr	SCSIComplete failed—bus not in Status phase

Primary Or Secondary Init Code

The following errors are for primary or secondary init code. The errors are logged in the vendor status field of the sInfo record. Normally the vendor error is not Apple's concern, but a special error is needed to patch secondary inits.

Table D.3   Primary and secondary error codes.

Code	System Error	Description	Code	System Error	Description
-32768	svTempDisable	Temporarily disables card but runs primary init	-415	btRecNotFnd	Record cannot be found
-32640	svDisabled	Reserve -32640 to -32768 for Apple temp disables	-416	btKeyLenErr	Maximum key length is too long or equal to zero
Dictionary Manager			-417	btKeyAttrErr	There is no such a key attribute
-410	notBTree	The file is not a dictionary	-20000	unknownInsertModeErr	There is no such an insert mode
-413	btNoSpace	Can't allocate disk space	-20001	recordDataTooBigErr	The record data is bigger than buffer size (1024 bytes)
-414	btDupRecErr	Record already exists	-20002	invalidIndexErr	The recordIndex parameter is not valid

D: Mac OS Error Codes

Table D.4   Apple event manager error messages.

Code	System Error	Description	Code	System Error	Description
AppleEvent Manager			-1714	errAENotASpecial Function	there is no special function for/with this keyword
-1700	errAECoercionFail	bad parameter data or unable to coerce the data supplied	-1715	errAEParamMissed	a required parameter was not accessed
-1701	errAEDescNotFound		-1716	errAEUnknown AddressType	the target address type is not known
-1702	errAECorruptData		-1717	errAEHandlerNotFound	no handler in the dispatch tables fits the parameters to AEGetEvent-Handler or AEGet-CoercionHandler
-1703	errAEWrongDataType				
-1704	errAENotAEDesc				
-1705	errAEBadListItem	the specified list item does not exist			
-1706	errAENewerVersion	need newer version of the AppleEvent manager	-1718	errAEReplyNotArrived	the contents of the reply you are accessing have not arrived yet
-1707	errAENotAppleEvent	the event is not in AppleEvent format	-1719	errAEIllegalIndex	index is out of range in a put operation
-1708	errAEEventNotHandled	the AppleEvent was not handled by any handler	**OSL Error Codes**		
-1709	errAEReplyNotValid	AEResetTimer was passed an invalid reply parameter	-1720	errAEImpossibleRange	A range like 3rd to 2nd or 1st to all
-1710	errAEUnknown SendMode	mode wasn't NoReply WaitReply or QueueReply or Interaction level is unknown	-1721	errAEWrongNumberArgs	Logical op kAENOT used with other than one term
-1711	errAEWaitCanceled	in AESend the user cancelled out of wait loop for reply or receipt	-1723	errAEAccessorNotFound	Accessor proc matching wantClass and containerType or wildcards not found
-1712	errAETimeout	the AppleEvent timed out	-1725	errAENoSuchLogical	Something other than AND OR or NOT
-1713	errAENoUserInteraction	no user interaction is allowed			

(continued)

D: Mac OS Error Codes

Table D.4   Apple event manager error messages (continued).

Code	System Error	Description	Code	System Error	Description
-1726	errAEBadTestKey	Test is neither typeLogical-Descriptor nor type CompDescriptor	-1761	errOSAComponent Mismatch	Parameters are from 2 different components
-1727	errAENotAnObjSpec	Param to AEResolve not of type 'obj'	-1762	errOSACantOpen Component	Can't connect to scripting system with that ID
-1728	errAENoSuchObject	e.g. Specifier asked for the 3rd but only two exist, for example— basically this indicates a runtime resolution error	-10000	errAEEventFailed	
			-10001	errAETypeError	
			-10002	errAEBadKeyForm	
			-10003	errAENotModifiable	
			-10004	errAEPrivilegeError	
			-10005	errAEReadDenied	
			-10006	errAEWriteDenied	
-1729	errAENegativeCount	CountProc returned negative value	-10007	errAEIndexTooLarge	
			-10008	errAENotAnElement	
			-10009	errAECantSupplyType	
-1730	errAEEmptyListContainer	Attempt to pass empty list as container to accessor	-10010	errAECantHandleClass	
			-10011	errAEInTransaction	
			-10012	errAENoSuchTransaction	
-1731	errAEUnknown ObjectType	available only in version 1.0.1 or greater	-10013	errAENoUserSelection	
			-10014	errAENotASingleObject	
			-10015	errAECantUndo	
-1732	errAERecordingIs AlreadyOn	available only in version 1.0.1 or greater	-10016	errAELocalOnly	

OSA API Errors

QuickTime

Code	System Error	Code	System Error
-1750	errOSASystemError	-2000	couldNotResolveDataRef
-1751	errOSAInvalidID	-2001	badImageDescription
-1752	errOSABadStorageType	-2002	badPublicMovieAtom
-1753	errOSAScriptError	-2003	cantFindHandler
-1754	errOSABadSelector	-2004	cantOpenHandler
-1756	errOSASourceNotAvailable	-2005	badComponentType
-1757	errOSANoSuchDialect	-2006	noMediaHandler
-1758	errOSADataFormatObsolete	-2007	noDataHandler
-1759	errOSADataFormatTooNew	-2008	invalidMedia
		-2009	invalidTrack
		-2010	invalidMovie

(continued)

D: Mac OS Error Codes

Table D.4   *Apple event manager error messages (continued).*

Code	System Error	Description	Code	System Error	Description
-2011	invalidSampleTable		-2043	dataNotOpenForWrite	
-2012	invalidDataRef		-2044	dataAlreadyOpenForWrite	
-2013	invalidHandler		-2045	dataAlreadyClosed	
-2014	invalidDuration		-2046	endOfDataReached	
-2015	invalidTime		-2047	dataNoDataRef	
-2016	cantPutPublicMovieAtom		-2048	noMovieFound	
-2017	badEditList		-2049	invalidDataRefContainer	
-2018	mediaTypesDontMatch		-2050	badDataRefIndex	
-2019	progressProcAborted		-2051	noDefaultDataRef	
-2020	movieToolboxUninitialized		-2052	couldNotUseAnExistingSample	
-2020	noRecordOfApp		-2053	featureUnsupported	
-2021	wfFileNotFound		-2054	noVideoTrackInMovieErr	QT for Windows error
-2022	cantCreateSingleForkFile	happens when file already exists	-2055	noSoundTrackInMovieErr	QT for Windows error
-2023	invalidEditState		-2056	soundSupportNotAvailableErr	QT for Windows error
-2024	nonMatchingEditState		-2057	unsupportedAuxiliaryImportData	
-2025	staleEditState		-2058	auxiliaryExportDataUnavailable	
-2026	userDataItemNotFound		-2059	samplesAlreadyInMediaErr	
-2027	maxSizeToGrowTooSmall		-2062	movieTextNotFoundErr	
-2028	badTrackIndex		-2201	digiUnimpErr	feature unimplemented
-2029	trackIDNotFound		-2202	qtParamErr	"bad input parameter (out of range, etc)"
-2030	trackNotInMovie				
-2031	timeNotInTrack		-2203	matrixErr	bad matrix digitizer did nothing
-2032	timeNotInMedia				
-2033	badEditIndex				
-2034	internalQuickTimeError		-2204	notExactMatrixErr	warning of bad matrix digitizer did its best
-2035	cantEnableTrack				
-2036	invalidRect				
-2037	invalidSampleNum		-2205	noMoreKeyColorsErr	all key indexes in use
-2038	invalidChunkNum				
-2039	invalidSampleDescIndex		-2206	notExactSizeErr	Can't do exact size requested
-2040	invalidChunkCache				
-2041	invalidSampleDescription				
-2042	dataNotOpenForRead				

(continued)

D: Mac OS Error Codes

Table D.4   Apple event manager error messages (continued).

Code	System Error	Description
-2207	badDepthErr	Can't digitize into this depth
-2208	noDMAErr	Can't do DMA digitizing (i.e. can't go to requested dest)
-2209	badCallOrderErr	Usually due to a status call being called prior to being set up first
-8960	codecEr	
-8961	noCodecErr	
-8962	codecUnimpErr	
-8963	codecSizeErr	
-8964	codecScreenBufErr	
-8965	codecImageBufErr	
-8966	codecSpoolErr	
-8967	codecAbortErr	
-8968	codecWouldOffscreenErr	
-8969	codecBadDataErr	
-8970	codecDataVersErr	
-8971	scTypeNotFoundErr	codecExtension Not FoundErr
-8972	codecConditionErr	
-8973	codecOpenErr	
-8974	codecCantWhenErr	
-8975	codecCantQueueErr	
-8976	codecNothingToBlitErr	
-9400	noDeviceForChannel	
-9401	grabTimeComplete	
-9402	cantDoThatInCurrentMode	
-9403	notEnoughMemoryToGrab	
-9404	notEnoughDiskSpaceToGrab	
-9405	couldntGetRequiredComponent	
-9406	badSGChannel	
-9407	seqGrabInfoNotAvailable	

Code	System Error	Description
-9408	deviceCantMeetRequest	
-9994	badControllerHeight	
-9995	editingNotAllowed	
-9996	controllerBoundsNotExact	
-9997	cannotSetWidthOfAttachedController	
-9998	controllerHasFixedHeight	
-9999	cannotMoveAttachedController	
Display Manager		
-6220	kDMGenErr	Unexpected Error
-6221	kDMMirroringOnAlready	Returned by all calls that need mirroring to be off to do their thing
-6222	kDMWrongNumber OfDisplays	Can only handle 2 displays for now
-6223	kDMMirroringBlocked	DMBlock Mirroring() has been called
-6224	kDMCantBlock	Mirroring is already on can't Block now (call DMUnMirror() first)
-6225	kDMMirroringNotOn	Returned by all calls that need mirroring to be on to do their thing
-6226	kSysSWTooOld	Missing critical pieces of system software
-6227	kDMSWNotInitializedErr	Required software not initialized (e.g., windowmanager or display mgr).
-6228	kDMDriverNot DisplayMgrAwareErr	Video Driver does not support display manager

(continued)

Table D.4   Apple event manager error messages (continued).

Code	System Error	Description	Code	System Error	Description
-6229	kDMDisplayNotFoundErr	Could not find item (will someday remove)	-4212	cmNoGDevicesError	Begin/End Matching—no gdevices available
-6229	kDMNotFoundErr	Could not find item	-4213	cmInvalidProfile Comment	Bad profile comment during drawpicture
-6230	kDMDisplay AlreadyInstalledErr	Attempt to add an already installed display	-4214	cmRangeOverFlow	One or more output color value overflows in color conversion
-6231	kDMMainDisplay CannotMoveErr	Trying to move main display (or a display mirrored to it)	**Colour Picker**		
			-4000	invalidPickerType	
-6231	kDMNoDevice TableclothErr	Obsolete	-4001	requiredFlagsDontMatch	
Colour Sync			-4002	pickerResourceError	
-4200	cmElementTagNotFound		-4003	cantLoadPicker	
-4201	cmIndexRangeErr	Index out of range	-4004	cantCreatePickerWindow	
-4202	cmCantDeleteElement		-4005	cantLoadPackage	
-4203	cmFatalProfileErr		-4006	pickerCantLive	
-4204	cmInvalidProfile	A Profile must contain a 'cs1 ' tag to be valid	-4007	colorSyncNotInstalled	
			-4008	badProfileError	
-4205	cmInvalidProfileLocation	Operation not supported for this profile location	-4009	noHelpForItem	
			Translation Manager		
-4206	cmInvalidSearch	Bad Search Handle	-3025	invalidTranslationPathErr	Source type to destination type not a valid path
-4207	cmSearchError		-3026	couldNotParse SourceFileErr	Source document does not contain source type
-4208	cmErrIncompatibleProfile				
-4209	cmInvalidColorSpace	Profile colorspace does not match bitmap type	-3030	noTranslationPathErr	
			-3031	badTranslationSpecErr	
-4210	cmInvalidSrcMap	Source pix/bit map was invalid	-3032	noPrefAppErr	
			Component Manager		
-4211	cmInvalidDstMap	Destination pix/bit map was invalid	-3000	invalidComponentID	
			-3001	validInstancesExist	
			-3002	componentNotCaptured	
			-3003	componentDontRegister	

(continued)

D: Mac OS Error Codes

D: Mac OS Error Codes

Table D.4   Apple event manager error messages (continued).

Code	System Error	Description
Apple Guide		
-2900	kAGErrUnknownEvent	
-2901	kAGErrCantStartup	
-2902	kAGErrNoAccWin	
-2903	kAGErrNoPreWin	
-2904	kAGErrNoSequence	
-2905	kAGErrNotOopsSequence	
-2906	kAGErrReserved06	
-2907	kAGErrNoPanel	
-2908	kAGErrContentNotFound	
-2909	kAGErrMissingString	
-2910	kAGErrInfoNotAvail	
-2911	kAGErrEventNotAvailable	
-2912	kAGErrCannotMakeCoach	
-2913	kAGErrSessionIDsNotMatch	
-2914	kAGErrMissingDatabaseSpec	
-2925	kAGErrItemNotFound	
-2926	kAGErrBalloonResourceNotFound	
-2927	kAGErrChalkResourceNotFound	
-2928	kAGErrChdvResourceNotFound	
-2929	kAGErrAlreadyShowing	
-2930	kAGErrBalloonResourceSkip	
-2931	kAGErrItemNotVisible	
-2932	kAGErrReserved32	
-2933	kAGErrNotFrontProcess	
-2934	kAGErrMacroResourceNotFound	
-2951	kAGErrAppleGuideNotAvailable	
-2952	kAGErrCannotInitCoach	
-2953	kAGErrCannotInitContext	
-2954	kAGErrCannotOpenAliasFile	
-2955	kAGErrNoAliasResource	
-2956	kAGErrDatabaseNotAvailable	
-2957	kAGErrDatabaseNotOpen	
-2958	kAGErrMissingAppInfoHdl	

Code	System Error	Description
-2959	kAGErrMissingContextObject	
-2960	kAGErrInvalidRefNum	
-2961	kAGErrDatabaseOpen	
-2962	kAGErrInsufficientMemory	
Code Fragment Manager		
0	fragNoErr	
-2800	fragContextNotFound	contextID was not valid
-2801	fragConnection IDNotFound	connectionID was not valid
-2802	fragSymbolNotFound	symbol was not found in connection
-2803	fragSectionNotFound	section was not found
-2804	fragLibNotFound	library name not found in Frag registry
-2805	fragDupRegLibName	registered name already in use
-2806	fragFormatUnknown	fragment container format unknown
-2807	fragHadUnresolveds	"loaded fragment had 'hard' unresolved imports"
-2808	fragUnused1	unused
-2809	fragNoMem	out of memory for internal book-keeping
-2810	fragNoAddrSpace	out of memory in user's address space for loadable section
-2811	fragNoContextIDs	no more context id's

(continued)

Table D.4   Apple event manager error messages (continued).

Code	System Error	Description	Code	System Error	Description
-2812	fragObjectInitSeqErr	order error during user initialization function invocation	-2824	fragInvalid FragmentUsage	an application fragment or accelerated resource has no entry point or termination routine
-2813	fragImportTooOld	import library was too old and therefore incompatible	-2899	fragLastErrCode	last reserved error code number
-2814	fragImportTooNew	import library was too new and therefore incompatible	**Script Manager**		
-2815	fragInitLoop	circularity detected in mandatory initialization order	-2720	errASCantConsider AndIgnore	Runtime
			-2721	errASCantCompare MoreThan32k	Runtime
-2816	fragInitRtnUsageErr	boot library has initialization routine	-2760	errASTerminology NestingTooDeep	Parser/Compiler error
-2817	fragLibConnErr	error connecting to library (error occurred in sub prepare)	-2761	errASIllegalFormal Parameter	Parser/Compiler error
			-2762	errASParameter NotForEvent	Parser/Compiler error
-2818	fragMgrInitErr	error in initialization of this manager	-2763	errASNoResultReturned	Parser/Compiler error
-2819	fragConstErr	internal inconsistency	Dialect specific script errors:		
-2820	fragCorruptErr	fragment container corrupted (known format)	-2780		-2780 thru -2799 is reserved for dialect specific error codes
-2821	fragUserInitProcErr	user initialization routine did not return noErr	-2799		Error codes from different dialects may overlap
-2822	fragAppNotFound	no application found in cfrg (for Process Manager)	-2780	errASInconsistentNames	English
			Text Services Manager		
-2823	fragArchError	fragment targeted for an unacceptable architecture	0	tsmComponentNoErr	component result no error
			-2500	tsmUnsupScriptLanguageErr	
			-2501	tsmInputMethodNotFoundErr	
			-2502	tsmNotAnAppErr	not an application error

(continued)

D: Mac OS Error Codes

Table D.4   Apple event manager error messages (continued).

Code	System Error	Description	Code	System Error	Description
-2503	tsmAlreadyRegisteredErr	want to register again error	-2519	tsmUnknownErr	any other errors
			Drag Manager		
-2504	tsmNeverRegisteredErr	app never registered error (not TSM-aware)	-1800	errOffsetInvalid	
			-1801	errOffsetIsOutsideOfView	
-2505	tsmInvalidDocIDErr	invalid TSM documentation id	-1810	errTopOfDocument	
			-1811	errTopOfBody	
-2506	tsmTSMDocBusyErr	document is still active	-1812	errEndOfDocument	
			-1813	errEndOfBody	
-2507	tsmDocNotActiveErr	document is *NOT* active	-1850	badDragRefErr	unknown drag reference
-2508	tsmNoOpenTSErr	no open text service	-1851	badDragItemErr	unknown drag item reference
-2509	tsmCantOpen ComponentErr	can't open the component	-1852	badDragFlavorErr	unknown flavor type
-2510	tsmTextServiceNot FoundErr	no text service found	-1853	duplicateFlavorErr	flavor type already exists
-2511	tsmDocumentOpenErr	there are open documents	-1854	cantGetFlavorErr	error while trying to get flavor data
-2512	tsmUseInputWindowErr	not TSM aware because we are using input window	-1855	duplicateHandlerErr	handler already exists
			-1856	handlerNotFoundErr	handler not found
-2513	tsmTSHasNoMenuErr	the text service has no menu	-1857	dragNotAcceptedErr	drag was not accepted by receiver
-2514	tsmTSNotOpenErr	text service is not open	**Telephony Manager (ISDN)**		
-2515	tsmComponentAlready OpenErr	text service already opened for the document	-1001	isdnError	
			-1002	isdnBadBufferLength	
			-1003	isdnBadNetBufferLength	
-2516	tsmInputMethodIsOldErr	returned by Get DefaultInputMethod	-1004	isdnBadBufferSpecified	
			-1005	isdnBadNetBufferSpecified	
-2517	tsmScriptHasNoIMErr	script has no input method or is using old IM	-1006	isdnBadcsCode	
			-1007	isdnCannotLoadLocalRPTask	
			-1008	isdnCannotLoadNetworkRPTask	
-2518	tsmUnsupportedTypeErr	unSupported interface type error	-1009	isdnCardNotRunning	
			-1010	isdnCANotInValidState	

(continued)

Table D.4   Apple event manager error messages (continued).

Code	System Error	Description
Telephony Manager		
-1	telGenericError	
0	telNoErr	
8	telNoTools	no telephone tools found in extension folder
-10001	telBadTermErr	invalid TELHandle or handle not found
-10002	telBadDNErr	TELDNHandle not found or invalid
-10003	telBadCAErr	TELCAHandle not found or invalid
-10004	telBadHandErr	bad handle specified
-10005	telBadProcErr	bad msgProc specified
-10006	telCAUnavail	a CA is not available
-10007	telNoMemErr	no memory to allocate handle
-10008	telNoOpenErr	unable to open terminal
-10010	telBadHTypeErr	bad hook type specified
-10011	telHTypeNotSupp	hook type not supported by this tool
-10012	telBadLevelErr	bad volume level setting
-10013	telBadVTypeErr	bad volume type error
-10014	telVTypeNotSupp	volume type not supported by this tool
-10015	telBadAPattErr	bad alerting pattern specified

Code	System Error	Description
-10016	telAPattNotSupp	alerting pattern not supported by tool
-10017	telBadIndex	bad index specified
-10018	telIndexNotSupp	index not supported by this tool
-10019	telBadStateErr	bad device state specified
-10020	telStateNotSupp	device state not supported by tool
-10021	telBadIntExt	bad internal external error
-10022	telIntExtNotSupp	internal external type not supported by this tool
-10023	telBadDNDType	bad DND type specified
-10024	telDNDTypeNotSupp	DND type is not supported by this tool
-10030	telFeatNotSub	feature not subscribed
-10031	telFeatNotAvail	feature subscribed but not available
-10032	telFeatActive	feature already active
-10033	telFeatNotSupp	feature program call not supported by this tool
-10040	telConfLimitErr	limit specified is too high for this configuration
-10041	telConfNoLimit	no limit was specified but required

(continued)

D: Mac OS Error Codes

Table D.4   Apple event manager error messages (continued).

Code	System Error	Description	Code	System Error	Description
-10042	telConfErr	conference was not prepared	-10063	telDisplayModeNotSupp	display mode not supported by tool
-10043	telConfRej	conference request was rejected	-10064	telNoCallbackRef	no call back reference was specified but is required
-10044	telTransferErr	transfer not prepared	-10070	telAlreadyOpen	terminal already open
-10045	telTransferRej	transfer request rejected	-10071	telStillNeeded	terminal driver still needed by someone else
-10046	telCBErr	call back feature not set previously	-10072	telTermNotOpen	terminal not opened via TELOpenTerm
-10047	telConfLimitExceeded	attempt to exceed switch conference limits	-10080	telCANotAcceptable	" CA not 'acceptable' "
-10050	telBadDNType	DN type invalid	-10081	telCANotRejectable	" CA not 'rejectable' "
-10051	telBadPageID	bad page ID specified	-10082	telCANotDeflectable	" CA not 'deflectable' "
-10052	telBadIntercomID	bad intercom ID specified	-10090	telPBErr	parameter block error bad format
-10053	telBadFeatureID	bad feature ID specified	-10091	telBadFunction	bad msgCode specified
-10054	telBadFwdType	bad fwdType specified	-10101	telNoTools	unable to find any telephone tools
-10055	telBadPickupGroupID	bad pickup group ID specified	-10102	telNoSuchTool	unable to find tool with name specified
-10056	telBadParkID	bad park id specified	-10103	telUnknownErr	unable to set config
-10057	telBadSelect	unable to select or deselect DN	-10106	telNoCommFolder	Communications/ Extensions f not found
-10058	telBadBearerType	bad bearerType specified			
-10059	telBadRate	bad rate specified	-10107	telInitFailed	initialization failed
-10060	telDNTypeNotSupp	DN type not supported by tool	-10108	telBadCodeResource	code resource not found
-10061	telFwdTypeNotSupp	forward type not supported by tool	-10109	telDeviceNotFound	device not found
-10062	telBadDisplayMode	bad display mode specified			

(continued)

Table D.4   Apple event manager error messages (continued).

Code	System Error	Description
-10110	telBadProcID	invalid procID
-10111	telValidateFailed	telValidate failed
-10112	telAutoAnsNotOn	autoAnswer in not turned on
-10113	telDetAlreadyOn	detection is already turned on
-10114	telBadSWErr	Software not installed properly
-10115	telBadSampleRate	incompatible sample rate
-10116	telNotEnoughdspBW	not enough real-time for allocation
NameRegistry		
-2536	nrLockedErr	
-2537	nrNotEnoughMemoryErr	
-2538	nrInvalidNodeErr	
-2539	nrNotFoundErr	
-2540	nrNotCreatedErr	
-2541	nrNameErr	
-2542	nrNotSlotDeviceErr	
-2543	nrDataTruncatedErr	
-2544	nrPowerErr	
-2545	nrPowerSwitchAbortErr	
-2546	nrTypeMismatchErr	
-2547	nrNotModifiedErr	
-2548	nrOverrunErr	
-2549	nrResultCodeBase	
-2550	nrPathNotFound	a path component lookup failed
-2551	nrPathBufferTooSmall	buffer for path is too small
Mixed Mode Manager		
-2526	mmInternalError	
1010	dsBadLibrary	Bad shared library
1011	dsMixedModeFailure	Internal Mixed Mode Failure

Code	System Error	Description
ENET Errors		
-92	eLenErr	Length error ddpLenErr
-91	eMultiErr	Multicast address error ddpSktErr
SQL Errors		
-4	SQL_NO_TOTAL	
-2	SQL_INVALID_HANDLE	"Function failed due to an invalid handle, indicates a programming error"
-1	SQL_ERROR	Function failed
0	SQL_SUCCESS	"Function completed successfully, no additional information is available"
1	SQL_SUCCESS_WITH_INFO	"Function completed successfully, possibly with a nonfatal error"
2	SQL_STILL_EXECUTING	A function that was started asynchronously is still executing
99	SQL_NEED_DATA	"While processing a statement, the driver determined that the application needs to send parameter data values"
100	SQL_NO_DATA_FOUND	All rows from the result have been fetched

D: Mac OS Error Codes

(continued)

Table D.4   Apple event manager error messages (continued).

Code	System Error	Description	Code	System Error	Description
OT/PPP (Preliminary)			-7112		An unexpected error with no useful information has occurred
-7102		OT/PPP did not load properly at system startup			
-7103		OT/PPP could not set up a port	-7113		One or more of the installed OT/PPP files is damaged
-7104		OT/PPP is out of memory			
-7105		The requested action is not supported	-7114		The requested action could not be performed because OT/PPP was busy
-7106		One or more resources are missing from OT/PPP's installed files			
			-7115		The OT/PPP logical port is in an unknown state
-7107		"The 'Remote Access Connections' file is not compatible with the installed version of OT/PPP"	-7116		The OT/PPP logical port is in an invalid state
			-7117		The OT/PPP logical port has detected an invalid serial protocol
-7108		An action requiring a connection was requested when there was no connection	-7118		Login is disabled for the given user
			-7120		The server administrator requires the user to enter a password
-7109		The connection attempt or established connection was terminated by the user			
			-7122		OT/PPP could not initialize Open Transport
-7110		The user name is unknown	-7123		The requested action could not be performed because OT/PPP is not fully initialized yet
-7111		The password is invalid			

(continued)

D: Mac OS Error Codes

Table D.4   Apple event manager error messages (continued).

Code	System Error	Description	Code	System Error	Description
-7124		TCP/IP is inactive and cannot be loaded	-7140		There is a pre-existing file using an OT/PPP type or creator
-7125		TCP/IP is not yet configured	-7141		There is a pre-existing folder using an OT/PPP folder name and location
-7126		PPP is not selected as the TCP/IP interface in the current TCP/IP configuration			
			-7142		"The 'Remote Access Connec-tions' file is not open"
-7128		The requested PPP protocol was rejected by the PPP peer			
			-7144		An unknown PPP control protocol type was received
-7129		PPP authentica-tion failed	-7145		PPP received a packet with an invalid length
-7130		PPP negotiation failed			
-7131		PPP was disconnected locally	-7146		PPP received a negotiable option with an invalid value
-7132		The PPP peer disconnected unexpectedly			
			-7147		PPP received a negotiable option with invalid flags
-7133		The PPP peer is not responding			
-7134		The OT/PPP log file is not open	-7148		PPP ran out of memory while negotiating with the peer
-7135		The OT/PPP log file is already open			
			-7152		PPP encountered an error with no useful information
-7136		The OT/PPP log entry could not be retrieved			
			-7153		PPP is in an invalid state
-7138		OT/PPP cannot locate the active System folder	-7163		The user canceled the password entry dialog
-7139		OT/PPP cannot locate its preferences folder			

(continued)

Table D.4   Apple event manager error messages (continued).

Code	System Error	Description	Code	System Error	Description
-7164		The user did not respond to the password entry dialog in time	8	cmNoTools	
			9	cmUserCancel	
			11	cmUnknownError	
-7165		An unknown Open Transport serial port was referenced	**CTB File Transfer**		
			-1	ftGenericError	
			0	ftNoErr	
			1	ftRejected	
-7166		The OT/PPP logical port is not configured	2	ftFailed	
			3	ftTimeOut	
-7167		No AppleTalk services endpoints are available	4	ftTooManyRetry	
			5	ftNotEnoughDSpace	
			6	ftRemoteCancel	
-7168		The modem script ASK or manual dialing dialog was canceled by the user	7	ftWrongFormat	
			8	ftNoTools	
			9	ftUserCancel	
			10	ftNotSupported	
			11	ftUnknownError	

CTB Terminal

Code	System Error
-1	tmGenericError
0	tmNoErr
1	tmNotSent
2	tmEnvironsChanged
7	tmNotSupported
8	tmNoTools
11	tmUnknownError

CTB Connection

Code	System Error
-1	cmGenericError
0	cmNoErr
1	cmRejected
2	cmFailed
3	cmTimeOut
4	cmNotOpen
5	cmNotClosed
6	cmNoRequestPending
7	cmNotSupported

D: Mac OS Error Codes

Appendix E

Apple Spec Chart

The information in the following tables is reproduced with the permission of Apple Computer. The Apple Spec Chart (November 1997 edition) lists all makes and models of Apple hardware through the end of 1997. We have changed the format of the chart for publication in this book and updated a few items to list currently shipping products. Due to space limitations, we did not include printer specifications. If you also need complete printer information, point your Web browser to **support.info. apple.com/applespec/applespec.taf**. We take full responsibility for any errors contained herein.

Desktop Computers

Table E.1   Macintosh Plus, SE Classic, and II.

Macintosh Plus and SE			
Processor	68000	System Software	System 6.0.5
Speed	8 MHz	System Enabler	–
PMMU	–	RAM	1MB
FPU	–	Maximum RAM supported	4MB
AV technologies and multimedia options	–	RAM on logic board	–
		Memory slots	Four 30-pin SIMM
Video RAM	–	Level 2 Cache	–
Networking	LocalTalk	Internal Hard Disk	None/20MB or 40MB
Slots	None/1 PDS		

(continued)

Table E.1   *Macintosh Plus, SE Classic, and II (continued).*

Macintosh Classic

Processor	68000	System Software	System 6.0.7
Speed	8 MHz	System Enabler	–
PMMU	–	RAM	1MB or 2MB
FPU	–	Maximum RAM supported	4MB
AV technologies and multimedia options	–	RAM on logic board	1MB
		Memory slots	Two 30-pin SIMM
Video RAM	–	Level 2 Cache	–
Networking	LocalTalk	Internal Hard Disk	None or 40MB
Slots	–		

Macintosh Classic II

Processor	68030	System Software	System 7.0.1
Speed	16 MHz	System Enabler	–
PMMU	Integrated	RAM	2MB or 4MB
FPU	–	Maximum RAM supported	10MB
AV technologies and multimedia options	–	RAM on logic board	2MB
		Memory slots	Two 30-pin SIMM
Video RAM	–	Level 2 Cache	–
Networking	LocalTalk	Internal Hard Disk	40MB or 80MB
Slots	–		

Macintosh Color Classic

Processor	68030	System Software	System 7.1
Speed	16 MHz	System Enabler	401
PMMU	Integrated	RAM	4MB
FPU	Optional 68882	Maximum RAM supported	10MB
AV technologies and multimedia options	–	RAM on logic board	4MB
		Memory slots	Two 30-pin SIMM
Video RAM	265K to 512K	Level 2 Cache	–
Networking	LocalTalk	Internal Hard Disk	40MB, 80MB, or 160 MB
Slots	1 LC PDS		

(continued)

E: Apple Spec Chart

Table E.1   Macintosh Plus, SE Classic, and II (continued).

Macintosh SE/30

Processor	68030	System Software	System 6.0.5
Speed	16 MHz	System Enabler	–
PMMU	Integrated	RAM	1MB
FPU	68882	Maximum RAM supported	32MB
AV technologies and multimedia options	–	RAM on logic board	2MB
		Memory slots	Eight 30-pin SIMM
Video RAM	–	Level 2 Cache	–
Networking	LocalTalk	Internal Hard Disk	40MB or 80MB
Slots	1 SE/30 PDS		

Macintosh II and IIx

Processor	68020/68030	System Software	System 6.0.5
Speed	16 MHz	System Enabler	–
PMMU	Optional/Integrated	RAM	1MB
FPU	68881/68882	Maximum RAM supported	32MB
AV technologies and multimedia options	–	RAM on logic board	2MB
		Memory slots	Eight 30-pin SIMM
Video RAM	–	Level 2 Cache	–
Networking	LocalTalk	Internal Hard Disk	40MB or 80MB
Slots	6 NuBus		

Macintosh IIsi

Processor	68030	System Software	System 6.0.7
Speed	20 MHz	System Enabler	–
PMMU	Integrated	RAM	1MB
FPU	Optional 68882	Maximum RAM supported	17MB
AV technologies and multimedia options	–	RAM on logic board	1MB
		Memory slots	Four 30-pin SIMM
Video RAM	IMB DRAM	Level 2 Cache	–
Networking	LocalTalk	Internal Hard Disk	40MB or 80MB
Slots	1 PDS or 1 NuBus		

(continued)

E: Apple Spec Chart

Table E.1   *Macintosh Plus, SE Classic, and II (continued).*

Macintosh IIcx and IIci

Processor	68030	System Software	System 6.0.5
Speed	16 MHz /25 MHz	System Enabler	–
PMMU	Integrated	RAM	1MB
FPU	68882	Maximum RAM supported	32MB
AV technologies and multimedia options	–	RAM on logic board	–
		Memory slots	Eight 30-pin SIMM
Video RAM	None/1MB DRAM	Level 2 Cache	–
Networking	LocalTalk	Internal Hard Disk	40MB, 80MB, or 230 MB
Slots	3 NuBus		

Macintosh IIvi and IIvx

Processor	68030	System Software	System 7.1
Speed	16 MHz /32 MHz	System Enabler	001
PMMU	Integrated	RAM	4MB
FPU	Optional 68882/ 68882	Maximum RAM supported	20MB or 68MB
		RAM on logic board	4MB
AV technologies and multimedia options	–	Memory slots	Four 30-pin SIMM
		Level 2 Cache	–
Video RAM	512K to 1MB	Internal Hard Disk	40MB, 80MB, 230 MB, or 400MB; one expansion bay
Networking	LocalTalk		
Slots	3 NuBus, 1 PDS		

Macintosh IIfx

Processor	68030	System Software	System 6.0.5
Speed	40 MHz	System Enabler	–
PMMU	Integrated	RAM	4MB
FPU	68882	Maximum RAM supported	128MB
AV technologies and multimedia options	–	RAM on logic board	4MB
		Memory slots	Eight 64-pin SIMM
Video RAM	–	Level 2 Cache	–
Networking	LocalTalk	Internal Hard Disk	40MB, 80MB, or 160MB
Slots	6 NuBus, 1 PDS		

E: Apple Spec Chart

Table E.2   Macintosh Centris and Macintosh Quadra systems.

Macintosh Centris 610

Processor	68LC040	System Software	System 7.1
Speed	20 MHz	System Enabler	040 1.0
PMMU	Integrated	RAM	4MB
FPU	–	Maximum RAM supported	68MB
AV technologies and multimedia options	–	RAM on logic board	4MB
		Memory slots	Two 30-pin SIMM
Video RAM	512K to 1MB	Level 2 Cache	–
Networking	LocalTalk, optional Ethernet	Internal Hard Disk	80MB, 230MB, or 500MB; one expansion bay
Slots	One 7" NuBus or 1 PDS		

Macintosh Centris 650

Processor	68040	System Software	System 7.1
Speed	25 MHz	System Enabler	040 1.0
PMMU	Integrated	RAM	4MB
FPU	Optional 68882	Maximum RAM supported	136MB
AV technologies and multimedia options	–	RAM on logic board	4MB or 8MB
		Memory slots	Four 72-pin SIMM
Video RAM	512K to 1MB	Level 2 Cache	–
Networking	LocalTalk, optional Ethernet	Internal Hard Disk	80MB, 230MB, or 500MB; one expansion bay
Slots	3 NuBus, 1 PDS		

Macintosh Quadra 605

Processor	68LC040	System Enabler	065
Speed	50/25 MHz	RAM	4MB
PMMU	Integrated	Maximum RAM supported	36MB
FPU	–	RAM on logic board	4MB
AV technologies and multimedia options	–	Memory slots	Four 72-pin SIMM
		Level 2 Cache	–
Video RAM	512K to 1MB	Internal Hard Disk	80MB, 230MB, or 500MB; one expansion bay
Networking	LocalTalk		
Slots	1 LC III PDS		
System Software	System 7.1		

(continued)

E: Apple Spec Chart

Table E.2   Macintosh Centris and Macintosh Quadra systems (continued).

Macintosh Quadra 610

Processor	68040	System Software	System 7.1
Speed	50/25 MHz	System Enabler	040 1.1
PMMU	Integrated	RAM	4MB
FPU	Optional 68882	Maximum RAM supported	68MB
AV technologies and multimedia options	–	RAM on logic board	4MB
Video RAM	512K to 1MB	Memory slots	Two 72-pin SIMM
Networking	LocalTalk, Ethernet	Level 2 Cache	–
Slots	One 7" NuBus or 1 PDS	Internal Hard Disk	160MB or 230MB

Macintosh Quadra 630

Processor	68040	Slots	1 LC PDS, 1 CS, 1 video
Speed	66/33 MHz	System Software	System 7.1.2 P
PMMU	Integrated	System Enabler	405
FPU	Integrated	RAM	4MB
AV technologies and multimedia options	Works with Apple Video System, Apple Presentation System, and Apple TV/ Video System	Maximum RAM supported	36MB
		RAM on logic board	4MB
Video RAM	1MB DRAM	Memory slots	One 72-pin SIMM
Networking	LocalTalk, optional Ethernet	Level 2 Cache	–
		Internal Hard Disk	160MB or 230MB

Macintosh Quadra 650

Processor	68040	System Enabler	040 1.1
Speed	66/33 MHz	RAM	4MB
PMMU	Integrated	Maximum RAM supported	132MB
FPU	Integrated	RAM on logic board	4MB or 8MB
AV technologies and multimedia options	–	Memory slots	Four 72-pin SIMM
Video RAM	512K to 1MB	Level 2 Cache	–
Networking	LocalTalk, Ethernet	Internal Hard Disk	250MB or 500MB; one expansion bay
Slots	3 NuBus, 1 PDS		
System Software	System 7.1		

(continued)

Table E.2   Macintosh Centris and Macintosh Quadra systems (continued).

Macintosh Centris and Quadra 660AV

Processor	68040 with DSP	System Software	System 7.1
Speed	50/25 MHz	System Enabler	088
PMMU	Integrated	RAM	8MB
FPU	Integrated	Maximum RAM supported	68MB
AV technologies and multimedia options	GeoPort, PlainTalk		
		RAM on logic board	4MB
Video RAM	1MB	Memory slots	Two 72-pin SIMM
Networking	LocalTalk, Ethernet	Level 2 Cache	–
Slots	One 7" NuBus or 1 PDS	Internal Hard Disk	230MB or 500MB; one expansion bay

Macintosh Quadra 700

Processor	68040	System Enabler	–
Speed	50/25 MHz	RAM	4MB
PMMU	Integrated	Maximum RAM supported	20MB
FPU	Integrated		
AV technologies and multimedia options	–	RAM on logic board	4MB
		Memory slots	Four 30-pin SIMM
Video RAM	512K to 2MB	Level 2 Cache	–
Networking	LocalTalk, Ethernet	Internal Hard Disk	80MB, 230MB, or 400MB
Slots	2 NuBus, 1 PDS		
System Software	System 7.0.1		

Macintosh Quadra 800

Processor	68040	System Enabler	040
Speed	66/33 MHz	RAM	4MB
PMMU	Integrated	Maximum RAM supported	136MB
FPU	Integrated		
AV technologies and multimedia options	–	RAM on logic board	8MB
		Memory slots	Four 72-pin SIMM
		Level 2 Cache	–
Video RAM	512K to 2MB	Internal Hard Disk	230MB, 500MB, or 1GB; one expansion bay
Networking	LocalTalk, Ethernet		
Slots	3 NuBus, 1 PDS		
System Software	System 7.1		

(continued)

E: Apple Spec Chart

Table E.2   Macintosh Centris and Macintosh Quadra systems (continued).

Macintosh Quadra 840AV

Processor	68040 with DSP	System Enabler	088
Speed	80/40 MHz	RAM	8MB
PMMU	Integrated	Maximum RAM supported	128MB
FPU	Integrated		
AV technologies and multimedia options	GeoPort, PlainTalk	RAM on logic board	–
		Memory slots	Four 72-pin SIMM
		Level 2 Cache	–
Video RAM	1MB to 2MB	Internal Hard Disk	230MB, 500MB, or 1GB; one expansion bay
Networking	LocalTalk, Ethernet		
Slots	3 NuBus		
System Software	System 7.1		

Macintosh Quadra 900

Processor	68040	System Software	System 7.1
Speed	50/25 MHz	System Enabler	–
PMMU	Integrated	RAM	4MB
FPU	Integrated	Maximum RAM supported	64MB
AV technologies and multimedia options	–		
		RAM on logic board	–
		Memory slots	16 30-pin SIMM
Video RAM	1MB to 2MB	Level 2 Cache	–
Networking	LocalTalk, Ethernet	Internal Hard Disk	160MB or 400MB
Slots	5 NuBus, 1 PDS		

Macintosh Quadra 950

Processor	68040	System Enabler	–
Speed	66/33 MHz	RAM	8MB
PMMU	Integrated	Maximum RAM supported	256MB
FPU	Integrated		
AV technologies and multimedia options	–	RAM on logic board	–
		Memory slots	16 30-pin SIMM
		Level 2 Cache	–
Video RAM	1MB to 2MB	Internal Hard Disk	230MB, 500MB, or 1GB; three expansion bays
Networking	LocalTalk, Ethernet		
Slots	5 NuBus, 1 PDS		
System Software	System 7.1		

E: Apple Spec Chart

Table E.3   Macintosh LC systems.

Macintosh LC

Processor	68020	System Software	System 6.0.7
Speed	16 MHz	System Enabler	–
PMMU	–	RAM	4MB
FPU	–	Maximum RAM supported	10MB
AV technologies and multimedia options	–	RAM on logic board	2MB
		Memory slots	Two 30-pin SIMM
Video RAM	256K-512K	Level 2 Cache	–
Networking	LocalTalk	Internal Hard Disk	80MB
Slots	1 LC PDS		

Macintosh LC II

Processor	68030	System Software	System 7.0.1
Speed	16 MHz	System Enabler	–
PMMU	Integrated	RAM	4MB
FPU	–	Maximum RAM supported	10MB
AV technologies and multimedia options	–	RAM on logic board	2MB or 4MB
		Memory slots	Two 30-pin SIMM
Video RAM	256K-512K	Level 2 Cache	–
Networking	LocalTalk	Internal Hard Disk	40MB or 80MB
Slots	1 LC PDS		

Macintosh LC III and LC III+

Processor	68030	System Software	System 7.1
Speed	25/33 MHz	System Enabler	003
PMMU	Integrated	RAM	4MB
FPU	Optional 68882	Maximum RAM supported	36MB
AV technologies and multimedia options	–	RAM on logic board	4MB
		Memory slots	One 72-pin SIMM
Video RAM	512K to 768K	Level 2 Cache	–
Networking	LocalTalk	Internal Hard Disk	80MB or 160MB
Slots	1 LC III PDS		

(continued)

E: Apple Spec Chart

Table E.3   Macintosh LC systems (continued).

Macintosh LC 475

Processor	68LC040	System Software	System 7.5
Speed	50/25 MHz	System Enabler	065
PMMU	Integrated	RAM	4MB
FPU	–	Maximum RAM supported	36MB
AV technologies and multimedia options	–	RAM on logic board	4MB
		Memory slots	One 72-pin SIMM
Video RAM	512K to 1MB	Level 2 Cache	–
Networking	LocalTalk	Internal Hard Disk	160MB or 250MB
Slots	1 LC III PDS		

Macintosh LC 520

Processor	68030	System Software	System 7.1
Speed	25 MHz	System Enabler	403
PMMU	Integrated	RAM	4MB
FPU	Optional 68882	Maximum RAM supported	36MB
AV technologies and multimedia options	–	RAM on logic board	4MB
		Memory slots	One 72-pin SIMM
Video RAM	512K-768K	Level 2 Cache	–
Networking	LocalTalk	Internal Hard Disk	80MB or 160MB
Slots	1 LC PDS		

Macintosh LC 550

Processor	68030	System Software	System 7.1
Speed	33 MHz	System Enabler	403
PMMU	Integrated	RAM	4MB
FPU	Optional 68882	Maximum RAM supported	36MB
AV technologies and multimedia options	–	RAM on logic board	4MB
		Memory slots	One 72-pin SIMM
Video RAM	512K to 768K	Level 2 Cache	–
Networking	LocalTalk	Internal Hard Disk	160MB
Slots	1 LC PDS		

(continued)

Table E.3   Macintosh LC systems (continued).

Macintosh LC 575

Processor	68LC040	System Software	System 7.5
Speed	66/33 MHz	System Enabler	065
PMMU	Integrated	RAM	4MB
FPU	–	Maximum RAM supported	36MB
AV technologies and multimedia options	–	RAM on logic board	4MB
		Memory slots	One 72-pin SIMM
Video RAM	512K-1MB	Level 2 Cache	–
Networking	LocalTalk, optional Ethernet	Internal Hard Disk	160MB or 320 MB; one expansion bay
Slots	1 LC PDS, 1 CS		

Macintosh LC 580

Processor	68LC040	System Software	System 7.5
Speed	66/33 MHz	System Enabler	–
PMMU	Integrated	RAM	8MB
FPU	–	Maximum RAM supported	52MB
AV technologies and multimedia options	Works with Apple Video System, Apple Presentation System, and External Video Connector	RAM on logic board	4MB
		Memory slots	Two 72-pin SIMM
		Level 2 Cache	–
		Internal Hard Disk	500MB; one expansion bay
Video RAM	1MB DRAM		
Networking	LocalTalk, optional Ethernet		
Slots	1 LC PDS, 1 CS, 1 video		

(continued)

E: Apple Spec Chart

Table E.3   Macintosh LC systems (continued).

Macintosh LC 630

Processor	68LC040	System Software	System 7.1.2 P
Speed	66/33 MHz	System Enabler	405
PMMU	Integrated	RAM	4MB
FPU	–	Maximum RAM supported	36MB
AV technologies and multimedia options	Works with Apple Video System, Apple Presentation System, and Apple TV/ Video System	RAM on logic board	4MB
		Memory slots	One 72-pin SIMM
		Level 2 Cache	–
Video RAM	1MB DRAM	Internal Hard Disk	250MB or 350MB; one expansion bay
Networking	LocalTalk, optional Ethernet		
Slots	1 LC PDS, 1 CS, 1 video		

Macintosh LC 630 DOS Compatible

Processor	68LC040 and 486DX2	Slots	1 CS, 1 video
		System Software	System 7.5.1
Speed	66 MHz for both processors	System Enabler	–
		RAM	8MB; 4MB
PMMU	Integrated	Maximum RAM supported	52MB; 32MB
FPU	–	RAM on logic board	4MB
AV technologies and multimedia options	Works with Apple Video System, Apple Presentation System, and Apple TV/ Video System	Memory slots	Two 72-pin SIMM, plus one DOS Compatibility card
		Level 2 Cache	–
Video RAM	1MB DRAM	Internal Hard Disk	500MB; CD-ROM drive
Networking	LocalTalk, optional Ethernet		

Table E.4   Macintosh Performa systems.

Macintosh Performa 400, 405, 410, and 430

Processor	68030	RAM	4MB
Speed	16 MHz	Maximum RAM supported	10MB
FPU	–		
Video RAM	256K or 512K	RAM on logic board	2MB
Networking	LocalTalk	Memory slots	One 30-pin SIMM
Slots	1 LC PDS	Level 2 Cache	–
System Software	System 7.1 P	Internal Hard Disk	80MB-120MB

Macintosh Performa 450

Processor	68030	RAM	4MB
Speed	25 MHz	Maximum RAM supported	36MB
FPU	Optional 68882		
Video RAM	512K	RAM on logic board	2MB
Networking	LocalTalk, optional Ethernet	Memory slots	One 72-pin SIMM
		Level 2 Cache	–
Slots	1 LC III PDS	Internal Hard Disk	80MB-160MB
System Software	System 7.1 P		

Macintosh Performa 460 Series

Processor	68030	RAM	4MB
Speed	33 MHz	Maximum RAM supported	36MB
FPU	Optional 68882		
Video RAM	512K-768K	RAM on logic board	2MB
Networking	LocalTalk	Memory slots	One 72-pin SIMM
Slots	1 LC PDS	Level 2 Cache	–
System Software	System 7.1 P	Internal Hard Disk	80MB or 160MB

Macintosh Performa 475 and 476

Processor	68LC040	RAM	4MB
Speed	33 MHz	Maximum RAM supported	36MB
FPU	–		
Video RAM	512K-1MB	RAM on logic board	2MB
Networking	LocalTalk	Memory slots	One 72-pin SIMM
Slots	1 LC III PDS	Level 2 Cache	–
System Software	System 7.5	Internal Hard Disk	160MB or 230MB

E: Apple Spec Chart

(continued)

Table E.4   Macintosh Performa systems (continued).

Macintosh Performa 550 and 560

Processor	68030	RAM	4MB
Speed	33 MHz	Maximum RAM supported	36MB
FPU	Optional 68882		
Video RAM	512K-768K	RAM on logic board	4MB
Networking	LocalTalk	Memory slots	One 72-pin SIMM
Slots	1 LC PDS	Level 2 Cache	–
System Software	System 7.1 P	Internal Hard Disk	160MB

Macintosh Performa 570 Series

Processor	68LC040	RAM	4MB
Speed	66/33 MHz	Maximum RAM supported	36MB
FPU	–		
Video RAM	512K-1MB	RAM on logic board	4MB
Networking	LocalTalk, optional Ethernet	Memory slots	One 72-pin SIMM
		Level 2 Cache	–
Slots	1 LC PDS, 1 CS	Internal Hard Disk	250MB or 320MB; CD-ROM drive
System Software	System 7.1 P		

Macintosh Performa 580

Processor	68LC040	RAM	8MB
Speed	66/33 MHz	Maximum RAM supported	52MB
FPU	–	RAM on logic board	4MB
Video RAM	1MB DRAM	Memory slots	Two 72-pin SIMM
Networking	LocalTalk, optional Ethernet	Level 2 Cache	–
		Internal Hard Disk	500MB; CD-ROM drive
Slots	1 LC PDS, 1 CS, 1 video		
System Software	System 7.5		

(continued)

E: Apple Spec Chart

Table E.4   Macintosh Performa systems (continued).

Macintosh Performa 600 Series

Processor	68030	RAM	4MB
Speed	32 MHz	Maximum RAM supported	68MB
FPU	Optional 68882	RAM on logic board	4MB
Video RAM	512K or 1MB VRAM		
Networking	LocalTalk, optional Ethernet	Memory slots	Four 72-pin SIMM
		Level 2 Cache	–
Slots	3 NuBus, 1 PDS	Internal Hard Disk	160MB
System Software	System 7.1 P		

Macintosh Performa 630 Series

Processor	68LC040	RAM	4MB
Speed	66/33 MHz	Maximum RAM supported	36MB or 52MB
FPU	–		
Video RAM	1MB DRAM	RAM on logic board	4MB
Networking	LocalTalk, optional Ethernet	Memory slots	One or two 72-pin SIMM
Slots	1 LC PDS, 1 CS, 1 video	Level 2 Cache	–
		Internal Hard Disk	250MB-500MB
System Software	System 7.1.2 P or 7.5		

Macintosh Performa 630 DOS Compatible and 640CD DOS Compatible

Processor	68LC040 and 486DX2	RAM	8MB; 4MB
Speed	66 MHz for both processors	Maximum RAM supported	52MB; 32MB
		RAM on logic board	4MB
FPU	–	Memory slots	Two 72-pin SIMM, plus one on DOS Compatibility card
Video RAM	1MB DRAM		
Networking	LocalTalk, optional Ethernet		
		Level 2 Cache	–
Slots	1 CS, 1 video	Internal Hard Disk	500MB; CD-ROM drive
System Software	System 7.5.1		

(continued)

E: Apple Spec Chart

Table E.4   Macintosh Performa systems (continued).

Macintosh Performa 5200 CD Series

Processor	PowerPC 603 RISC	RAM	8MB
Speed	75 MHz	Maximum RAM supported	64MB
FPU	Integrated		
Video RAM	1MB DRAM	RAM on logic board	–
Networking	LocalTalk, optional Ethernet	Memory slots	Two 72-pin SIMM
		Level 2 Cache	256K
Slots	1 LC PDS, 1 CS, 1 video	Internal Hard Disk	500MB or 1G; CD-ROM drive
System Software	System 7.5.1		

Macintosh Performa 5260CD

Processor	PowerPC 603e RISC	RAM	8MB
Speed	100 MHz	Maximum RAM supported	64MB
FPU	Integrated		
Video RAM	1MB DRAM	RAM on logic board	–
Networking	LocalTalk, optional Ethernet	Memory slots	Two 72-pin SIMM
		Level 2 Cache	–
Slots	1 LC PDS, 1 CS, 1 video	Internal Hard Disk	800MB
System Software	System 7.5.3		

Macintosh Performa 5300CD

Processor	PowerPC 603e RISC	RAM	16MB
Speed	100 MHz	Maximum RAM supported	64MB
FPU	Integrated		
Video RAM	1MB DRAM	RAM on logic board	–
Networking	LocalTalk, optional Ethernet	Memory slots	Two 72-pin SIMM
		Level 2 Cache	256K
Slots	1 LC PDS, 1 CS, 1 video	Internal Hard Disk	1.2GB; CD-ROM drive
System Software	System 7.5.1		

(continued)

E: Apple Spec Chart

Table E.4   *Macintosh Performa systems (continued).*

Macintosh Performa 6100 Series

Processor	PowerPC 601 RISC	Maximum RAM supported	72MB
Speed	60 MHz	RAM on logic board	8MB
FPU	Integrated	Memory slots	Two 72-pin SIMM
Video RAM	DRAM video	Level 2 Cache	–
Networking	LocalTalk, Ethernet	Internal Hard Disk	250MB, 350MB, 500MB, or 700MB; one expansion bay
Slots	One 7" NuBus or 1 PDS		
System Software	System 7.5		
RAM	8MB		

Macintosh Performa 6200CD Series

Processor	PowerPC 603 RISC	RAM	8MB
Speed	75 MHz	Maximum RAM supported	64MB
FPU	Integrated	RAM on logic board	–
Video RAM	1 MB DRAM	Memory slots	Two 72-pin SIMM
Networking	LocalTalk, optional Ethernet	Level 2 Cache	256K
Slots	1 LC PDS, 1 CS, 1 video	Internal Hard Disk	1GB; CD-ROM drive
System Software	System 7.5.1		

Macintosh Performa 6300CD Series

Processor	PowerPC 603e RISC	RAM	8MB
Speed	100 MHz /120 MHz	Maximum RAM supported	64MB
FPU	Integrated	RAM on logic board	–
Video RAM	1 MB DRAM	Memory slots	Two 72-pin SIMM
Networking	LocalTalk, optional Ethernet	Level 2 Cache	256K
Slots	1 LC PDS, 1 CS, 1 video	Internal Hard Disk	1.2GB; 4x-speed CD-ROM drive
System Software	System 7.5.1		

(continued)

E: Apple Spec Chart

Table E.4   Macintosh Performa systems (continued).

Macintosh Performa 6360

Processor	PowerPC 603e RISC	Maximum RAM supported	136MB
Speed	160 MHz	RAM on logic board	8MB
FPU	Integrated	Memory slots	Two 168-pin DIMM
Video RAM	1 MB DRAM	Level 2 Cache	Optional 256K
Networking	LocalTalk, optional Ethernet	Internal Hard Disk	1.2GB; 8x-speed (maximum) CD-ROM drive
Slots	1 PCI, 1 CS, 1 video		
System Software	System 7.5.3		
RAM	16MB		

Macintosh Performa 6400/180 and 6400/200

Processor	PowerPC 603e RISC	RAM	16MB
Speed	180 MHz /200 MHz	Maximum RAM supported	136MB
FPU	Integrated	RAM on logic board	8MB
Video RAM	1 MB	Memory slots	Two 168-pin DIMM
Networking	LocalTalk, optional Ethernet	Level 2 Cache	Optional 256K/256K
Slots	2 PCI, 1 CS, 1 video	Internal Hard Disk	1.6GB or 2.4GB; 8x-speed (maximum) CD-ROM drive
System Software	System 7.5.3		

Table E.5   Power Macintosh systems.

Power Macintosh 5200/75 LC

Processor	PowerPC 603 RISC	System Software	System 7.5.1
Speed	75 MHz	System Enabler	406
FPU	Integrated	RAM	8MB
AV technologies and multimedia options	Works with Apple Video System, Apple Presentation System, and Apple TV/ Video System	Maximum RAM supported	64MB
		RAM on logic board	–
		Memory slots	Two 72-pin SIMM
Video RAM	1MB DRAM	Level 2 Cache	256K
Networking	LocalTalk, optional Ethernet	Internal Hard Disk; CD-ROM	500MB; 2x-speed CD-ROM drive
Slots	1 LC processor-direct slot (PDS), 1 communications slot (CS), 1 video	Other Features	–

(continued)

Table E.5   Power Macintosh systems (continued).

Power Macintosh 5260/100, 5260/120, and 5300/100 LC

Processor	PowerPC 603e RISC	System Software	System 7.5.3/7.5.1
Speed	100 MHz /120 MHz	System Enabler	None/406
FPU	Integrated	RAM	16MB
AV technologies and multimedia options	Works with Apple Video System, ApplePresentation System, and Apple TV/ Video System	Maximum RAM supported	64MB
		RAM on logic board	–
		Memory slots	Two 72-pin SIMM
		Level 2 Cache	Optional 256K/256K
Video RAM	1MB DRAM	Internal Hard Disk; CD-ROM	800MB/1.2GB; 4x-speed CD-ROM drive
Networking	LocalTalk, optional Ethernet		
Slots	1 LC PDS, 1 CS, 1 video	Other Features	–

Power Macintosh 6100/60 and 6100/66

Processor	PowerPC 601 RISC	System Enabler	PowerPC 1.0/1.1.1
Speed	60 MHz /66 MHz	RAM	8MB
FPU	Integrated	Maximum RAM supported	72MB
AV technologies and multimedia options	Optional video output, GeoPort, PlainTalk	RAM on logic board	8MB
		Memory slots	Two 72-pin SIMM
		Level 2 Cache	256K
Video RAM	DRAM video	Internal Hard Disk; CD-ROM	160MB or 250MB/ 350MB or 500MB; optional CD-ROM drive
Networking	LocalTalk, Ethernet		
Slots	One 7" NuBus or 1 PDS		
System Software	System 7.1.2/7.5	Other Features	–

(continued)

E: Apple Spec Chart

627

Table E.5   Power Macintosh systems (continued).

Power Macintosh 6100/66 DOS Compatible

Processor	PowerPC 601 RISC, 486DX2	RAM	8MB; 0MB
		Maximum RAM supported	72MB; 32MB
Speed	60 MHz for both processors	RAM on logic board	8MB
FPU	Integrated	Memory slots	Two 72-pin SIMM, plus one on DOS Compatibility CARD
AV technologies and multimedia options	Optional video input / output, GeoPort, PlainTalk		
		Level 2 Cache	256K
Video RAM	DRAM video	Internal Hard Disk; CD-ROM	500MB; 2x-speed CD-ROM drive; one expansion bay
Networking	LocalTalk, Ethernet		
Slots	–		
System Software	System 7.5/MS-DOS	Other Features	–
System Enabler	PowerPC 1.1.1		

Power Macintosh 7100/66 and 7100/80

Processor	PowerPC 601 RISC	RAM	8MB
Speed	66 MHz; 80 MHz	Maximum RAM supported	136MB
FPU	Integrated	RAM on logic board	8MB
AV technologies and multimedia options	Optional video input / output, GeoPort, PlainTalk	Memory slots	Four 72-pin SIMM
		Level 2 Cache	Optional 256K/256K
Video RAM	1MB to 2MB	Internal Hard Disk; CD-ROM	250MB or 500MB/ 500MB or 700MB; CD ROM drive; one expansion bay
Networking	LocalTalk, Ethernet		
Slots	3 NuBus		
System Software	System 7.1.2/7.5	Other Features	–
System Enabler	PowerPC 1.0/1.1.1		

(continued)

E: Apple Spec Chart

Table E.5   Power Macintosh systems (continued).

Power Macintosh 7200/75, 7200/90, and 7200/120

Processor	PowerPC 601 RISC	RAM	8MB or 16MB
Speed	75 MHz /90MHz / 120 MHz	Maximum RAM supported	256MB
FPU	Integrated	RAM on logic board	–
AV technologies and multimedia options	GeoPort, PlainTalk	Memory slots	Four 168-pin DIMM
		Level 2 Cache	Optional 256K
Video RAM	1MB to 4MB	Internal Hard Disk; CD-ROM	500MB or 1.2GB; 4x-speed CD-ROM drive; one expansion bay
Networking	LocalTalk, Ethernet		
Slots	3 PCI		
System Software	System 7.5.2/7.5.3	Other Features	Upgradable to Power Macintosh 7600/120
System Enabler	701 1.1/none		

Power Macintosh 7200/120 PC Compatible

Processor	PowerPC 601 RISC, Pentium	System Software	System 7.5.3; MS-DOS 6.22
Speed	120 MHz and 100 MHz	System Enabler	None
		RAM	8MB; 8MB
FPU	Integrated	Maximum RAM supported	256MB
AV technologies and multimedia options	GeoPort, PlainTalk	RAM on logic board	–
		Memory slots	Four 168-pin DIMM
Video RAM	1MB, expandable to 4MB; 1MB DRAM	Level 2 Cache	Optional 256K
Networking	LocalTalk, Ethernet; supports ODI and NDIS; multiple support for simultaneous connections	Internal Hard Disk; CD-ROM	1.2GB; 4x-speed CD-ROM drive; on expansion bay
		Other Features	Upgradable to Power Macintosh 7600/120
Slots	3 PCI (one accompanied by PC Compatibility card)		

(continued)

E: Apple Spec Chart

Table E.5   Power Macintosh systems (continued).

Power Macintosh 7500/100

Processor	PowerPC 601 RISC	RAM	8MB or 16MB
Speed	100 MHz	Maximum RAM supported	512MB
FPU	Integrated		
AV technologies and multimedia options	GeoPort, PlainTalk, video input, audio line input /output	RAM on logic board	–
		Memory slots	Eight 168-pin DIMM
		Level 2 Cache	Optional 256K
Video RAM	2MB, expandable to 4MB	Internal Hard Disk; CD-ROM	500MB or 1.2GB; 4x-speed CD-ROM drive; one expansion bay
Networking	LocalTalk, Ethernet		
Slots	3 PCI		
System Software	System 7.5.2	Other Features	Processor on separate card
System Enabler	701 1.2		

Power Macintosh 8100/80, 8100/100, and 8100/110

Processor	PowerPC 601 RISC	RAM	8MB
Speed	80 MHz /100 MHz / 110 MHz	Maximum RAM supported	264MB
FPU	Integrated	RAM on logic board	8MB
AV technologies and multimedia options	Optional video input / output, GeoPort, PlainTalk	Memory slots	Eight 72-pin SIMM
		Level 2 Cache	256K
Video RAM	2MB, expandable to 4MB	Internal Hard Disk; CD-ROM	250MB, 500MB, 1GB/700MB, 1GB, or 2GB; 2x-speed CD-ROM drive; one expansion bay
Networking	LocalTalk, Ethernet		
Slots	3 NuBus		
System Software	System 7.1.2/7.5	Other Features	Upgradable to Power Macintosh 8500
System Enabler	PowerPC 1.0/1.1.1		

(continued)

E: Apple Spec Chart

Table E.5   Power Macintosh systems (continued).

Power Macintosh 4400/200

Processor	PowerPC 603e RISC	System Enabler	827
Speed	200 MHz	RAM	16MB
FPU	Integrated	Maximum RAM supported	160MB
AV technologies and multimedia options	GeoPort, PlainTalk	RAM on logic board	–
		Memory slots	Three 168-pin DIMM
Video RAM	2MB EDO VRAM	Level 2 Cache	256K
Networking	LocalTalk, Ethernet	Internal Hard Disk; CD-ROM	2GB; 12x- or 24x-speed (maximum) CD-ROM drive
Slots	3 PCI (one 7" and one 12")		
System Software	System 7.5.3		

Power Macintosh 4400/200 PC Compatible

Processor	PowerPC 603e RISC; Cyrix PR166	System Software	System 7.5.3; MS-DOS 6.22
Speed	200 MHz and 166 MHz (Performance Rated)	System Enabler	827
		RAM	32MB; 16MB
FPU	Integrated	Maximum RAM supported	160MB; 80MB
AV technologies and multimedia options	GeoPort, PlainTalk	RAM on logic board	–
		Memory slots	Three 168-pin DIMM
Video RAM	2MB and 1MB	Level 2 Cache	256K
Networking	LocalTalk, Ethernet	Internal Hard Disk; CD-ROM	2GB; 12x-speed (maximum) CD-ROM drive
Slots	2 PCI (the 12" slot is occupied by the PC Compatibility card)		

(continued)

E: Apple Spec Chart

Table E.5   Power Macintosh systems (continued).

Power Macintosh 5400/120 and 5400/180

Processor	PowerPC 603e RISC	System Enabler	410
Speed	120 MHz /180 MHz	RAM	16MB
FPU	Integrated	Maximum RAM supported	136MB
AV technologies and multimedia options	Works with Apple Video Systems, Apple Presentation System, and Apple TV/ Video System	RAM on logic board	8MB
		Memory slots	Two 168-pin DIMM
		Level 2 Cache	Optional
Video RAM	1MB DRAM	Internal Hard Disk; CD-ROM	1.2GB or 1.6GB; 4x- or 8x-speed (maximum) CD-ROM drive
Networking	LocalTalk, Ethernet		
Slots	1 PCI; 1 CS; 1 video		
System Software	System 7.5.3		

Power Macintosh 5400/200

Processor	PowerPC 603e RISC	System Enabler	–
Speed	200 MHz	RAM	24MB
FPU	Integrated	Maximum RAM supported	136MB
AV technologies and multimedia options	Works with Apple Video Systems, Apple Presentation System, and Apple TV/ Video System	RAM on logic board	8MB
		Memory slots	Two 168-pin DIMM
		Level 2 Cache	Optional
Video RAM	1MB DRAM	Internal Hard Disk; CD-ROM	1.6GB; 8x-speed (maximum) CD-ROM drive
Networking	LocalTalk, Ethernet		
Slots	1 PCI; 1 CS; 1 video		
System Software	System 7.5.5		

(continued)

Table E.5   Power Macintosh systems (continued).

Power Macintosh 5500/225 and 5500/250

Processor	PowerPC 603e RISC	System Enabler	411/none
Speed	225 MHz /250 MHz	RAM	32MB
FPU	Integrated	Maximum RAM supported	128MB
AV technologies and multimedia options	Works with Apple Video Systems, Apple Presentation System, and Apple TV/ Video System	RAM on logic board	–
		Memory slots	Two 168-pin DIMM
		Level 2 Cache	Optional
Video RAM	2MB	Internal Hard Disk; CD-ROM	2GB; 12x- or 24x-speed (maximum) CD-ROM drive
Networking	LocalTalk, Ethernet		
Slots	1 PCI; 1 CS; 1 video		
System Software	System 7.5.5/ Mac OS 8		

Power Macintosh 6400/200

Processor	PowerPC 603e RISC	System Software	System 7.5.3
Speed	200 MHz	System Enabler	410 x1.1
FPU	Integrated	RAM	16MB
AV technologies and multimedia options	GeoPort, PlainTalk; works with Apple Video Systems, Apple Presentation System, and Apple TV/ Video System	Maximum RAM supported	136MB
		RAM on logic board	8MB
		Memory slots	Two 168-pin DIMM
		Level 2 Cache	256K
Video RAM	1MB DRAM	Internal Hard Disk; CD-ROM	2.4GB; 8x-speed (maximum) CD-ROM drive
Networking	LocalTalk		
Slots	2 PCI; 1 COMM II, TV, video		

(continued)

Table E.5   Power Macintosh systems (continued).

Power Macintosh 6500 Series			
Processor	PowerPC 603e RISC		Mac OS 8
Speed /	225 MHz /250 MHz	System Enabler	410 or none
	275 MHz /300 MHz	RAM	32MB, 48MB, 64MB
FPU	Integrated	Maximum RAM supported	128MB
AV technologies and multimedia options	Works with Apple Video Systems, Apple Presentation System, and Apple TV/ Video System	RAM on logic board	–
		Memory slots	Two 168-pin DIMM
		Level 2 Cache	256K or 512K
Video RAM	2MB	Internal Hard Disk; CD-ROM	2GB, 3GB, 4GB, or 6GB; 12x- or 24x-speed (maximum) CD-ROM drive; optional Zip drive
Networking	LocalTalk, Ethernet		
Slots	2 PCI; 1 COMM II, TV, video		
System Software	System 7.5.5/		

Power Macintosh 7300 Series			
Processor	PowerPC 604e RISC	System Enabler	702
Speed	180 MHz /200 MHz	RAM	16MB or 32MB
FPU	Integrated	Maximum RAM supported	512MB
AV technologies and multimedia options	GeoPort, PlainTalk, audio line input / output	RAM on logic board	–
		Memory slots	Eight 168-pin DIMM
Video RAM	2MB to 4MB	Level 2 Cache	256K or 512K
Networking	LocalTalk, Ethernet	Internal Hard Disk; CD-ROM	2GB; 12x-speed (maximum) CD-ROM drive
Slots	3 PCI		
System Software	System 7.5.5		

(continued)

E: Apple Spec Chart

Table E.5   **Power Macintosh systems (continued).**

Power Macintosh 7300/180 PC Compatible

Processor	PowerPC 604e RISC, Pentium	System Software	System 7.5.5; MS-DOS 6.22
Speed	180 MHz and 166 MHz	System Enabler	702
		RAM	32MB; 16MB
FPU	Integrated	Maximum RAM supported	512MB; 80MB
AV technologies and multimedia options	GeoPort, PlainTalk, video input; audio line input /output	RAM on logic board	–
		Memory slots	Eight 168-pin DIMM
Video RAM	2MB	Level 2 Cache	256K and 256K
Networking	LocalTalk, Ethernet	Internal Hard Disk; CD-ROM	2GB; 12x-speed (maximum) CD-ROM drive
Slots	3 PCI (one occupied by PC Compatibility card)		

Power Macintosh 7600/120 and 7600/132

Processor	PowerPC 604 RISC	System Enabler	None
Speed	120 MHz /132 MHz	RAM	16MB
FPU	Integrated	Maximum RAM supported	512MB
AV technologies and multimedia options	GeoPort, PlainTalk, video input, audio line input /output	RAM on logic board	–
		Memory slots	Eight 168-pin DIMM
Video RAM	2MB; supports up to 4MB	Level 2 Cache	256K
Networking	LocalTalk, Ethernet	Internal Hard Disk; CD-ROM	1.2GB; 4x-speed (maximum) CD-ROM drive; one expansion bay
Slots	3 PCI		
System Software	System 7.5.3		

(continued)

E: Apple Spec Chart

Table E.5   Power Macintosh systems (continued).

Power Macintosh 8500/120, 8500/132, 8500/150, and 8500/180

Processor	PowerPC 604 or 604e RISC	System Enabler	701 1.2 or none
		RAM	16MB or 32MB
Speed	120 MHz /132 MHz / 150 MHz /180 MHz	Maximum RAM supported	512MB
FPU	Integrated	RAM on logic board	–
AV technologies and multimedia options	GeoPort, PlainTalk, audio line input / output	Memory slots	Eight 168-pin DIMM
		Level 2 Cache	256K
Video RAM	2MB; supports up to 4MB	Internal Hard Disk; CD-ROM	1.2GB or 2GB; 4x- or 8x-speed (maximum) CD-ROM drive; one expansion bay
Networking	LocalTalk, Ethernet		
Slots	3 PCI		
System Software	System 7.5.2/7.5.3		

Power Macintosh 8600 Series

Processor	PowerPC 604e RISC	System Enabler	702
Speed	200 MHz /250 MHz / 300 MHz	RAM	32MB
		Maximum RAM supported	512MB
FPU	Integrated	RAM on logic board	–
AV technologies and multimedia options	GeoPort, PlainTalk, audio line input / output	Memory slots	Eight 168-pin DIMM
		Level 2 Cache	256K/1MB
Video RAM	2MB to 4MB	Internal Hard Disk; CD-ROM	2GB or 4GB; 12x- or 24x-speed (maximum) CD-ROM drive; Zip drive
Networking	LocalTalk, Ethernet		
Slots	3 PCI		
System Software	System 7.5.5/ System 7.6.1/ Mac OS 8		

(continued)

E: Apple Spec Chart

Table E.5   Power Macintosh systems (continued).

Power Macintosh 9500/120, 9500/132, 9500/150, and 9500/200

Processor	PowerPC 604 or 604e RISC	System Software	System 7.5.2/7.5.3
		System Enabler	701 1.2 or none
Speed /	120 MHz /132 MHz	RAM	16MB or 32MB
	150 MHz /200 MHz	Maximum RAM supported	768MB
FPU	Integrated	RAM on logic board	–
AV technologies and multimedia options	GeoPort, PlainTalk	Memory slots	Twelve 168-pin DIMM
		Level 2 Cache	512K
Video RAM	2MB to 4MB (requires graphics card)	Internal Hard Disk; CD-ROM	1GB or 2GB; 8x-speed (maximum) CD-ROM drive; one expansion bay
Networking	LocalTalk, Ethernet		
Slots	6 PCI		

Power Macintosh 9500/180MP

Processor	Two PowerPC 604e RISC	System Enabler	–
		RAM	32MB
Speed	180 MHz	Maximum RAM supported	768MB
FPU	Integrated		
AV technologies and multimedia options	GeoPort, PlainTalk	RAM on logic board	–
		Memory slots	Twelve 168-pin DIMM
Video RAM	2MB to 4MB (requires graphics card)	Level 2 Cache	512K
		Internal Hard Disk; CD-ROM	2GB; 8x-speed (maximum) CD-ROM drive
Networking	LocalTalk, Ethernet		
Slots	6 PCI		
System Software	System 7.5.3		

(continued)

E: Apple Spec Chart

Table E.5   Power Macintosh systems (continued).

Power Macintosh 9600 Series

Processor	PowerPC 604e RISC	System Enabler	702/none
Speed	200 MHz /233 MHz /300 MHz /350 MHz	RAM	32MB or 64MB
FPU	Integrated	Maximum RAM supported	768MB
AV technologies and multimedia output options	GeoPort, PlainTalk, audio line input /	RAM on logic board	—
		Memory slots	Twelve 168-pin DIMM
Video RAM	4MB to 8MB (requires graphics card)	Level 2 Cache	256K/1MB
		Internal Hard Disk; CD-ROM	4GB; 12x- or 24x-speed (maximum) CD-ROM drive; Zip drive
Networking	LocalTalk, Ethernet		
Slots	6 PCI		
System Software	System 7.5.5/ System 7.6.1/ Mac OS 8		

Power Macintosh 9600/200MP

Processor	Two PowerPC 604e RISC	System Enabler	702
		RAM	32MB
Speed	200 MHz	Maximum RAM supported	768MB
FPU	Integrated		
AV technologies and multimedia options	GeoPort, PlainTalk	RAM on logic board	—
		Memory slots	Twelve 168-pin DIMM
Video RAM	4MB (requires graphics card)	Level 2 Cache	1MB
		Internal Hard Disk; CD-ROM	4GB; 12x-speed (maximum) CD-ROM drive
Networking	LocalTalk, Ethernet		
Slots	6 PCI		
System Software	System 7.5.5		

(continued)

Table E.5   Power Macintosh systems (continued).

Power Macintosh G3 Series Desktop

Processor	PowerPC G3 RISC	System Enabler	770
Speed	233 MHz /266 MHz /300 MHz	RAM	32MB or 64MB
		Maximum RAM supported	192MB
FPU	Integrated		
AV technologies and multimedia options	GeoPort, PlainTalk, audio line input / output	RAM on logic board	–
		Memory slots	Three 168-pin DIMM
		Level 2 Cache	512K Backside
Video RAM	2MB; supports up to 6MB	Internal Hard Disk; CD-ROM	4GB or 6GB; 24x-speed (maximum) CD-ROM drive; optional Zip drive
Networking	LocalTalk, Ethernet		
Slots	3 PCI; 1 Personality		
System Software	Mac OS 8.1		

Power Macintosh G3 Series Mini Tower

Processor	PowerPC G3 RISC	System Enabler	770
Speed	266 MHz /333 MHz / 366 MHz	RAM	32MB or 64 MB
		Maximum RAM supported	384MB
FPU	Integrated		
AV technologies and multimedia options	GeoPort, PlainTalk, video input /output, audio line input / output	RAM on logic board	–
		Memory slots	Three 168-pin DIMM
		Level 2 Cache	512K or 1MB Backside
Video RAM	2MB; supports up to 6MB	Internal Hard Disk; CD-ROM	2GB/6GB/8GB; 24x-speed (maximum) CD-ROM drive; Zip drive
Networking	LocalTalk, 10/100 BASE-T Ethernet		
Slots	3 PCI; 1 Personality		
System Software	Mac OS 8.1		

(continued)

E: Apple Spec Chart

Table E.5   Power Macintosh systems (continued).

iMac Series			
Processor	PowerPC G3 RISC	Ports	2 USB, 1 4MbpsInfrared IrDA
Display	15" Multi-resolution (1,024 x 768 maximum)	System Software	Mac OS 8.1
		System Enabler	–
Speed	233 MHz	RAM	32MB
FPU	Integrated	Maximum RAM supported	128MB
AV technologies and multimedia options	Built-in speakers	RAM on logic board	–
		Memory slots	Three 168-pin DIMM
Video RAM	2MB; supports up to 4MB	Level 2 Cache	512K Backside
Networking Modem	LocalTalk, 10/100 BASE-T Ethernet, 56K Internal	Internal Hard Disk; CD-ROM	4GB; 24x-speed (maximum) CD-ROM drive; optional Zip drive
Slots	1 PCI		

Portable Computers

Table E.6   Macintosh PowerBook systems.

Macintosh Portable			
Processor	68000	RAM on logic board	1MB
Speed	16 MHz	Memory slots	One
PMMU	–	Internal Hard Disk	None or 40MB
FPU	–	Weight	15.8 lb.
Networking	LocalTalk	Display type	10" active-matrix LCD
Slots	1 modem slot		
System Software	System 6.0.5	Display resolution	640x400 pixels
System Enabler	–	Grays/Colors	Monochrome
RAM	1MB		
Maximum RAM supported	8MB		

(continued)

E: Apple Spec Chart

Table E.6   Macintosh PowerBook systems (continued).

Macintosh PowerBook 100

Processor	68HC000	Maximum RAM supported	8MB
Speed	16 MHz		
PMMU	–	RAM on logic board	2MB
FPU	–	Memory slots	One
Networking	LocalTalk	Internal Hard Disk	20MB or 40MB
Slots	1 modem slot	Weight	5.1 lb.
System Software	System 7.0.1	Display type	10" backlit supertwist
System Enabler	–	Display resolution	640x400 pixels
RAM	2MB	Grays/Colors	Monochrome

Macintosh PowerBook 140

Processor	68030	Maximum RAM supported	8MB
Speed	16 MHz		
PMMU	Integrated	RAM on logic board	2MB
FPU	–	Memory slots	One
Networking	LocalTalk	Internal Hard Disk	20MB or 40MB
Slots	1 modem slot	Weight	6.8 lb.
System Software	System 7.0.1	Display type	10" backlit supertwist
System Enabler	–	Display resolution	640x400 pixels
RAM	2MB or 4MB	Grays/Colors	Monochrome

Macintosh PowerBook 145

Processor	68030	Maximum RAM supported	8MB
Speed	25 MHz		
PMMU	Integrated	RAM on logic board	2MB
FPU	–	Memory slots	One
Networking	LocalTalk	Internal Hard Disk	20MB or 40MB
Slots	1 modem slot	Weight	6.8 lb.
System Software	System 7.0.1	Display type	10" backlit supertwist
System Enabler	–	Display resolution	640x400 pixels
RAM	4MB	Grays/Colors	Monochrome

(continued)

E: Apple Spec Chart

Table E.6   Macintosh PowerBook systems (continued).

Macintosh PowerBook 145B

Processor	68030	RAM on logic board	4MB
Speed	25 MHz	Memory slots	One
PMMU	Integrated	Internal Hard Disk	40MB, 80MB, or 120MB
FPU	–		
Networking	LocalTalk	Weight	6.8 lb.
Slots	1 modem slot	Display type	10" backlit supertwist
System Software	System 7.1	Display resolution	640x400 pixels
System Enabler	–	Grays/Colors	Monochrome
RAM	4MB		
Maximum RAM supported	8MB		

Macintosh PowerBook 150

Processor	68030	Maximum RAM supported	40MB
Speed	33 MHz		
PMMU	–	RAM on logic board	4MB
FPU	–	Memory slots	One
Networking	LocalTalk	Internal Hard Disk	250MB
Slots	1 modem slot	Weight	5.5 lb.
System Software	System 7.1.1 or 7.5 (7.5 with more than 4MB of RAM)	Display type	9.5" backlit FSTN passive matrix
		Display resolution	640x400 pixels
System Enabler	PowerBook 150	Grays/Colors	4 levels of gray
RAM	4MB		

Macintosh PowerBook 150

Processor	68030	Maximum RAM supported	40MB
Speed	33 MHz		
PMMU	–	RAM on logic board	4MB
FPU	–	Memory slots	One
Networking	LocalTalk	Internal Hard Disk	250MB
Slots	1 modem slot	Weight	5.5 lb.
System Software	System 7.1.1 or 7.5 (7.5 with more than 4MB of RAM)	Display type	9.5" backlit FSTN passive matrix
		Display resolution	640x400 pixels
System Enabler	PowerBook 150	Grays/Colors	4 levels of gray
RAM	4MB		

(continued)

Table E.6   Macintosh PowerBook systems (continued).

Macintosh PowerBook 165

Processor	68030	Maximum RAM supported	14MB
Speed	33 MHz		
PMMU	Integrated	RAM on logic board	4MB
FPU	–	Memory slots	One
Networking	LocalTalk	Internal Hard Disk	80MB or 160MB
Slots	1 modem slot	Weight	6.8 lb.
System Software	System 7.1	Display type	10" backlit supertwist
System Enabler	131	Display resolution	640x400 pixels
RAM	4MB	Grays/Colors	16 levels of gray

Macintosh PowerBook 165c

Processor	68030	RAM on logic board	4MB
Speed	33 MHz	Memory slots	One
PMMU	Integrated	Internal Hard Disk	40MB, 80MB, or 120MB
FPU	68882		
Networking	LocalTalk	Weight	7.0 lb.
Slots	1 modem slot	Display type	10" backlit passive-matrix color
System Software	System 7.1		
System Enabler	131	Display resolution	640x400 pixels
RAM	4MB	Grays/Colors	256 colors
Maximum RAM supported	14MB		

Macintosh PowerBook 170

Processor	68030	RAM on logic board	2MB
Speed	25 MHz	Memory slots	One
PMMU	Integrated	Internal Hard Disk	40MB or 80MB
FPU	68882	Weight	6.8 lb.
Networking	LocalTalk	Display type	10" backlit active matrix
Slots	1 modem slot		
System Software	System 7.0.1	Display resolution	640x400 pixels
System Enabler	–	Grays/Colors	16 levels of gray
RAM	4MB		
Maximum RAM supported	8MB		

(continued)

E: Apple Spec Chart

Table E.6 Macintosh PowerBook systems (continued).

Macintosh PowerBook 180

Processor	68030	RAM on logic board	4MB
Speed	33 MHz	Memory slots	One
PMMU	Integrated	Internal Hard Disk	80MB or 120MB
FPU	–	Weight	6.8 lb.
Networking	LocalTalk	Display type	10" backlit active matrix
Slots	1 modem slot		
System Software	System 7.1	Display resolution	640x400 pixels
System Enabler	131	Grays/Colors	16 levels of gray
RAM	4MB		
Maximum RAM supported	14MB		

Macintosh PowerBook 180c

Processor	68030	RAM on logic board	4MB
Speed	33 MHz	Memory slots	One
PMMU	Integrated	Internal Hard Disk	80MB or 160MB
FPU	68882	Weight	7.1 lb.
Networking	LocalTalk	Display type	8.4" backlit passive-matrix color
Slots	1 modem slot		
System Software	System 7.1	Display resolution	640x400 pixels
System Enabler	131	Grays/Colors	256 colors
RAM	4MB		
Maximum RAM supported	14MB		

(continued)

E: Apple Spec Chart

Table E.6   Macintosh PowerBook systems (continued).

Macintosh PowerBook 190/66

Processor	68LC040	Maximum RAM supported	36MB or 40MB
Speed	66/33 MHz		
PMMU	Integrated	RAM on logic board	4MB or 8MB
FPU	–	Memory slots	One
Networking	LocalTalk; optional infrared technology; optional Ethernet through PC card	Internal Hard Disk	500MB; one expansion bay
		Weight	6.0 lb.
		Display type	9.5" passive matrix (diagonal)
Slots	2 PC card slots		
System Software	System 7.5.2	Display resolution	640x480 pixels
System Enabler	PowerBook 5300/190	Grays/Colors	16 levels of gray
RAM	4MB or 8MB		

Macintosh PowerBook 190cs/66

Processor	68LC040	Maximum RAM supported	36MB or 40MB
Speed	66/33 MHz		
PMMU	Integrated	RAM on logic board	4MB or 8MB
FPU	–	Memory slots	One
Networking	LocalTalk; optional infrared technology; optional Ethernet through PC card	Internal Hard Disk	500MB; one expansion bay
		Weight	6.3 lb.
		Display type	10.4" dual-scan color (diagonal)
Slots	2 PC card slots		
System Software	System 7.5.2	Display resolution	640x480 pixels
System Enabler	PowerBook 5300/190	Grays/Colors	256 colors
RAM	4MB or 8MB		

(continued)

E: Apple Spec Chart

Table E.6   Macintosh PowerBook systems (continued).

Macintosh PowerBook Duo 210

Processor	68030	Maximum RAM supported	24MB
Speed	25 MHz		
PMMU	Integrated	RAM on logic board	4MB
FPU	–	Memory slots	One
Networking	LocalTalk	Internal Hard Disk	80MB
Slots	1 modem slot	Weight	4.2 lb.
System Software	System 7.1	Display type	9" backlit supertwist
System Enabler	PowerBook Duo Enabler 1.0	Display resolution	640x400 pixels
		Grays/Colors	16 levels of gray
RAM	4MB		

Macintosh PowerBook Duo 230

Processor	68030	Maximum RAM supported	24MB
Speed	33 MHz		
PMMU	Integrated	RAM on logic board	4MB
FPU	–	Memory slots	One
Networking	LocalTalk	Internal Hard Disk	80MB, 120MB, or 160MB
Slots	1 modem slot		
System Software	System 7.1	Weight	4.2 lb.
System Enabler	PowerBook Duo Enabler 1.0	Display type	9" backlit supertwist
		Display resolution	640x480 pixels
RAM	4MB	Grays/Colors	16 levels of gray

Macintosh PowerBook Duo 250

Processor	68030	Maximum RAM supported	24MB
Speed	33 MHz		
PMMU	Integrated	RAM on logic board	4MB
FPU	–	Memory slots	One
Networking	LocalTalk	Internal Hard Disk	200MB
Slots	1 modem slot	Weight	4.2 lb.
System Software	System 7.1	Display type	9" backlit supertwist
System Enabler	PowerBook Duo Enabler 1.0	Display resolution	640x400 pixels
		Grays/Colors	16 levels of gray
RAM	4MB		

(continued)

E: Apple Spec Chart

Table E.6   Macintosh PowerBook systems (continued).

Macintosh PowerBook Duo 270c

Processor	68030	RAM on logic board	4MB
Speed	33 MHz	Memory slots	One
PMMU	Integrated	Internal Hard Disk	240MB
FPU	68882	Weight	4.8 lb.
Networking	LocalTalk	Display type	8.4" backlit active-matrix color
Slots	1 modem slot		
System Software	System 7.1	Display resolution	640x400 or 480 pixels
System Enabler	PowerBook Duo Enabler 1.0		
		Grays/Colors	256 colors
RAM	4MB		
Maximum RAM supported	24MB		

Macintosh PowerBook Duo 280

Processor	68LC040	Maximum RAM supported	40MB
Speed	66/33 MHz		
PMMU	Integrated	RAM on logic board	4MB
FPU	–	Memory slots	One
Networking	LocalTalk	Internal Hard Disk	240MB
Slots	1 modem slot	Weight	4.2 lb.
System Software	System 7.1.1	Display type	9" backlit active matrix
System Enabler	PowerBook Duo Enabler 2.0		
		Display resolution	640x480 pixels
RAM	4MB	Grays/Colors	16 levels of gray

Macintosh PowerBook Duo 280c

Processor	68LC040	Maximum RAM supported	40MB
Speed	66/33 MHz	RAM on logic board	4MB
PMMU	Integrated	Memory slots	One
FPU	–	Internal Hard Disk	320MB
Networking	LocalTalk	Weight	4.8 lb.
Slots	1 modem slot	Display type	8.4" backlit active-matrix color
System Software	System 7.1.1		
System Enabler	PowerBook Duo Enabler 2.0	Display resolution	640x400 pixels
		Grays/Colors	256 colors
RAM	4MB		

E: Apple Spec Chart

(continued)

Table E.6   Macintosh PowerBook systems (continued).

Macintosh PowerBook 520

Processor	68LC040	Maximum RAM supported	36MB
Speed	50/25 MHz		
PMMU	Integrated	RAM on logic board	4MB
FPU	–	Memory slots	One
Networking	LocalTalk, Ethernet	Internal Hard Disk	240MB
Slots	1 modem slot, 1 PDS	Weight	6.3 lb.
System Software	System 7.1.1	Display type	9.5" passive matrix
System Enabler	PowerBook 500 Series Enabler	Display resolution	640x480 pixels
		Grays/Colors	16 levels of gray
RAM	4MB		

Macintosh PowerBook 520c

Processor	68LC040	Maximum RAM supported	36MB
Speed	50/25 MHz		
PMMU	Integrated	RAM on logic board	4MB
FPU	–	Memory slots	One
Networking	LocalTalk, Ethernet	Internal Hard Disk	240MB or 320MB
Slots	1 modem slot, 1 PDS	Weight	6.4 lb.
System Software	System 7.1.1	Display type	9.5" dual-scan color
System Enabler	PowerBook 500 Series Enabler	Display resolution	640x480 pixels
		Grays/Colors	256 colors
RAM	4MB		

Macintosh PowerBook 540

Processor	68LC040	Maximum RAM supported	36MB
Speed	66/33 MHz		
PMMU	Integrated	RAM on logic board	4MB
FPU	–	Memory slots	One
Networking	LocalTalk, Ethernet	Internal Hard Disk	240MB
Slots	1 modem slot, 1 PDS	Weight	7.1 lb.
System Software	System 7.1.1	Display type	9.5" active matrix
System Enabler	PowerBook 500 Series Enabler	Display resolution	640x480 pixels
		Grays/Colors	64 levels of gray
RAM	4MB		

(continued)

E: Apple Spec Chart

Table E.6   Macintosh PowerBook systems (continued).

Macintosh PowerBook 540c

Processor	68LC040	RAM on logic board	4MB
Speed	66/33 MHz	Memory slots	One
PMMU	Integrated	Internal Hard Disk	320MB or 500MB
FPU	–	Weight	7.3 lb.
Networking	LocalTalk, Ethernet	Display type	9.5" active-matrix color
Slots	1 modem slot, 1 PDS		
System Software	System 7.1.1	Display resolution	640x400 or 480 pixels
System Enabler	PowerBook 500 Series Enabler	Grays/Colors	256 or thousands of colors
RAM	4MB		
Maximum RAM supported	36MB		

Macintosh PowerBook Duo 23000c/100

Processor	PowerPC 603e RISC	RAM on logic board	8MB
Speed	100 MHz	Memory slots	One
PMMU	Integrated	Internal Hard Disk	750MB or 1.1GB
FPU	Integrated	Weight	4.8 lb.
Networking	LocalTalk	Display type	9.5" active-matrix color (diagonal)
Slots	1 modem slot		
System Software	System 7.5.2	Display resolution	640x400 or 480 pixels
System Enabler	PowerBook 5300/ 2300/190 Enabler	Grays/Colors	256 or thousands of colors
RAM	8MB or 20MB		
Maximum RAM supported	56MB		

(continued)

E: Apple Spec Chart

649

Table E.6   Macintosh PowerBook systems (continued).

Macintosh PowerBook 5300/100

Processor	PowerPC 603e RISC	Maximum RAM supported	64MB
Speed	100 MHz		
PMMU	Integrated	RAM on logic board	8MB
FPU	Integrated	Memory slots	One
Networking	LocalTalk; infrared technology; optional Ethernet through PC card	Internal Hard Disk	500MB; one expansion bay
		Weight	5.9 lb.
		Display type	9.5" dual scan (diagonal)
Slots	2 PC card slots		
System Software	System 7.5.2	Display resolution	640x480 pixels
System Enabler	PowerBook 5300	Grays/Colors	16 levels of gray
RAM	8MB		

Macintosh PowerBook 5300cs/100

Processor	PowerPC 603e RISC	Maximum RAM supported	64MB
Speed	100 MHz		
PMMU	Integrated	RAM on logic board	8MB or 16MB
FPU	Integrated	Memory slots	One
Networking	LocalTalk; infrared technology; optional Ethernet through PC card	Internal Hard Disk	500MB or 750MB; one expansion bay
		Weight	6.2 lb.
		Display type	10.4" active-matrix color (diagonal)
Slots	2 PC card slots		
System Software	System 7.5.2	Display resolution	640x480 pixels
System Enabler	PowerBook 5300	Grays/Colors	256 colors
RAM	8MB or 16MB		

(continued)

Table E.6   Macintosh PowerBook systems (continued).

Macintosh PowerBook 5300c/100

Processor	PowerPC 603e RISC	Maximum RAM supported	64MB
Speed	100 MHz		
PMMU	Integrated	RAM on logic board	8MB or 16MB
FPU	Integrated	Memory slots	One
Networking	LocalTalk; infrared technology; optional Ethernet through PC card	Internal Hard Disk	500MB or 750MB; one expansion bay
		Weight	6.2 lb.
		Display type	10.4" active-matrix color (diagonal)
Slots	2 PC card slots		
System Software	System 7.5.2	Display resolution	640x480 pixels
System Enabler	PowerBook 5300	Grays/Colors	256 or thousands of colors
RAM	8MB or 16MB		

Macintosh PowerBook 5300ce/117

Processor	PowerPC 603e RISC	Maximum RAM supported	64MB
Speed	117 MHz		
PMMU	Integrated	RAM on logic board	16MB
FPU	Integrated	Memory slots	One
Networking	LocalTalk; infrared technology; optional Ethernet through PC card	Internal Hard Disk	1.1GB; one expansion bay
		Weight	6.2 lb.
		Display type	10.4" active-matrix color SVGA (diagonal)
Slots	2 PC card slots		
System Software	System 7.5.2	Display resolution	800x600 pixels
System Enabler	PowerBook 5300	Grays/Colors	Thousands of colors
RAM	32MB		

(continued)

E: Apple Spec Chart

Table E.6   Macintosh PowerBook systems (continued).

Macintosh PowerBook 1400cs/117

Processor	PowerPC 603e RISC	RAM on logic board	12MB or 16MB
Speed	117 MHz	Memory slots	One expansion slot for two memory cards
PMMU	Integrated		
FPU	Integrated	Internal Hard Disk	750B; optional 6x- or 8x-speed (maximum) CD-ROM drive
Networking	LocalTalk; infrared technology; optional Ethernet through PC card		
		Weight	6.7 lb.
Slots	2 PC card slots	Display type	11.3" dual-scan color SVGA (diagonal)
System Software	System 7.5.3		
System Enabler	PowerBook 1400	Display resolution	800x600 pixels
RAM	12MB or 16MB	Grays/Colors	Thousands of colors
Maximum RAM supported	64MB		

Macintosh PowerBook 1400c/117

Processor	PowerPC 603e RISC	Maximum RAM supported	64MB
Speed	117 MHz		
PMMU	Integrated	RAM on logic board	16MB
FPU	Integrated	Memory slots	One expansion slot for two memory cards
Networking	LocalTalk; infrared technology; optional Ethernet through PC card		
		Internal Hard Disk	1GB; 6x-speed CD-ROM
		Weight	6.6 lb.
Slots	2 PC card slots	Display type	11.3" active-matrix color SVGA (diagonal)
System Software	System 7.5.3		
System Enabler	PowerBook 1400	Display resolution	800x600 pixels
RAM	16MB	Grays/Colors	Thousands of colors

(continued)

E: Apple Spec Chart

Table E.6   Macintosh PowerBook systems (continued).

Macintosh PowerBook 1400cs/133

Processor	PowerPC 603e RISC	RAM on logic board	–
Speed	133 MHz	Memory slots	One expansion slot for two memory cards
PMMU	Integrated		
FPU	Integrated	Internal Hard Disk	1.3GB; 8x-speed CD-ROM
Networking	LocalTalk; infrared technology; optional Ethernet through PC card		
		Weight	6.9 lb.
		Display type	11.3" dual-scan color SVGA (diagonal)
Slots	2 PC card slots		
System Software	System 7.6.1	Display resolution	800x600 pixels
System Enabler	None	Grays/Colors	Thousands of colors
RAM	16MB		
Maximum RAM supported	64MB		

Macintosh PowerBook 1400c/133

Processor	PowerPC 603e RISC	RAM on logic board	16MB
Speed	133 MHz	Memory slots	One memory slot and one expansion slot for two memory cards
PMMU	Integrated		
FPU	Integrated	Internal Hard Disk	1GB or 1.3GB; 6x- or 8x-speed (maximum) CD-ROM
Networking	LocalTalk; infrared technology; optional Ethernet through PC card		
		Weight	6.6 lb.
Slots	2 PC card slots	Display type	11.3" active-matrix color SVGA (diagonal)
System Software	System 7.5.3		
System Enabler	PowerBook 1400	Display resolution	800x600 pixels
RAM	16MB	Grays/Colors	Thousands of colors
Maximum RAM supported	64MB		

(continued)

E: Apple Spec Chart

Table E.6   Macintosh PowerBook systems (continued).

Macintosh PowerBook 1400cs/166

Processor	PowerPC 603e RISC	Maximum RAM supported	64MB
Speed	166 MHz		
PMMU	Integrated	RAM on logic board	–
FPU	Integrated	Memory slots	One expansion slot for two memory cards
Networking	LocalTalk; infrared technology; optional Ethernet through PC card	Internal Hard Disk	1.3GB; 12x–speed (maximum) CD-ROM
		Weight	6.9 lb.
Slots	2 PC card slots	Display type	11.3" dual-scan color SVGA (diagonal)
System Software	Mac OS 8		
System Enabler	None	Display resolution	800x600 pixels
RAM	16MB	Grays/Colors	Thousands of colors

Macintosh PowerBook 2400c/180

Processor	PowerPC 603e RISC	Maximum RAM supported	80MB
Speed	180 MHz		
PMMU	Integrated	RAM on logic board	16MB
FPU	Integrated	Memory slots	One
Networking	LocalTalk; infrared technology; optional Ethernet through PC card	Internal Hard Disk	1GB
		Weight	4.3 lb.
		Display type	10.4" active-matrix color SVGA (diagonal)
Slots	2 PC card slots	Display resolution	800x600 pixels
System Software	Mac OS 8	Grays/Colors	Thousands of colors
System Enabler	None		
RAM	16MB		

(continued)

E: Apple Spec Chart

Table E.6   Macintosh PowerBook systems (continued).

Macintosh PowerBook 3400c/180

Processor	PowerPC 603e RISC	RAM on logic board	16MB
Speed	180 MHz	Memory slots	One memory slot; supports EDO RAM
PMMU	Integrated		
FPU	Integrated	Internal Hard Disk	1.3GB; optional 6x-speed CD-ROM drive
Networking	LocalTalk; infrared technology; optional Ethernet through PC card		
		Weight	7.2 lb.
		Display type	12.1" active-matrix color SVGA (diagonal)
Slots	2 PC card slots		
System Software	System 7.6	Display resolution	800x600 pixels
System Enabler	PowerBook 3400	Grays/Colors	Thousands of colors
RAM	16MB		
Maximum RAM supported	144MB		

Macintosh PowerBook 3400c/200

Processor	PowerPC 603e RISC	RAM on logic board	16MB
Speed	200 MHz	Memory slots	One memory slot; supports EDO RAM
PMMU	Integrated		
FPU	Integrated	Internal Hard Disk	2GB; 6x-speed CD-ROM drive
Networking	LocalTalk; infrared technology; Ethernet		
		Weight	7.2 lb.
Slots	2 PC card slots	Display type	12.1" active-matrix color SVGA (diagonal)
System Software	System 7.6		
System Enabler	PowerBook 3400	Display resolution	800x600 pixels
RAM	16MB	Grays/Colors	Thousands of colors
Maximum RAM supported	144MB		

(continued)

E: Apple Spec Chart

Table E.6   Macintosh PowerBook systems (continued).

Macintosh PowerBook 3400c/240

Processor	PowerPC 603e RISC	RAM on logic board	16MB
Speed	240 MHz	Memory slots	One memory slot; supports EDO RAM
PMMU	Integrated		
FPU	Integrated	Internal Hard Disk	1.3GB; optional 12x-speed CD-ROM drive
Networking	LocalTalk; infrared technology; Ethernet		
Slots	2 PC card slots	Weight	7.2 lb.
System Software	System 7.6	Display type	12.1" active-matrix color SVGA (diagonal)
System Enabler	PowerBook 3400		
RAM	16MB	Display resolution	800x600 pixels
Maximum RAM supported	144MB	Grays/Colors	Thousands of colors

Macintosh PowerBook G3

Processor	PowerPC G3	RAM on logic board	32MB
Speed	250 MHz	Memory slots	One memory slot
PMMU	Integrated	Internal Hard Disk	5GB; 20x-speed (maximum) CD-ROM drive
FPU	Integrated		
Networking	LocalTalk; infrared technology; Ethernet		
Slots	2 PC card slots	Weight	7.5 lb.
System Software	Mac OS 8	Display type	12.1" active-matrix color SVGA (diagonal)
System Enabler	PowerBook G3 1.0		
RAM	32MB	Display resolution	800x600 pixels
Maximum RAM supported	160MB	Grays/Colors	Thousands of colors

(continued)

E: Apple Spec Chart

Table E.6   Macintosh PowerBook systems (continued).

Macintosh PowerBook G3 Series 12.1"

Processor	PowerPC G3	RAM on logic board	None
Speed	233 MHz	Memory slots	Two memory slots
PMMU	Integrated	Internal Hard Disk	2GB IDE; 20x-speed (maximum) CD-ROM drive
FPU	Integrated		
Networking	LocalTalk; infrared technology; Ethernet	Weight	7.2 lb.
Slots	2 PC card slots	Display type	12.1" STN (dual-scan passive matrix) color SVGA (diagonal)
System Software	Mac OS 8.1		
System Enabler	PowerBook G3 1.0	Display resolution	800x600 pixels
RAM	32MB	Grays/Colors	Thousands of colors
Maximum RAM supported	192MB		

Macintosh PowerBook G3 Series 13.3"

Processor	PowerPC G3	RAM on logic board	None
Speed	233 MHz /250 MHz	Memory slots	Two memory slots
PMMU	Integrated	Internal Hard Disk	2GB or 4GB IDE; 20x-speed (maximum) CD-ROM drive
FPU	Integrated		
Networking	LocalTalk; infrared technology; Ethernet	Weight	7.6 lb.
Slots	2 PC card slots	Display type	13.3" TFT (active-matrix) color SVGA (diagonal)
System Software	Mac OS 8.1		
System Enabler	PowerBook G3 1.0	Display resolution	1,024x768 pixels
RAM	32MB	Grays/Colors	Thousands of colors
Maximum RAM supported	192MB		

(continued)

E: Apple Spec Chart

Table E.6   Macintosh PowerBook systems (continued).

Macintosh PowerBook G3 Series 14.1"

Processor	PowerPC G3	RAM on logic board	None
Speed	233 MHz /292 MHz	Memory slots	Two memory slots
PMMU	Integrated	Internal Hard Disk	2GB or 8GB IDE; 20x-speed (maximum) CD-ROM drive
FPU	Integrated		
Networking	LocalTalk; infrared technology; Ethernet	Weight	7.8 lb.
Slots	2 PC card slots	Display type	14.1" TFT (active-matrix) color SVGA (diagonal)
System Software	Mac OS 8.1		
System Enabler	PowerBook G3 1.0		
RAM	32MB	Display resolution	1,024x768 pixels
Maximum RAM supported	192MB	Grays/Colors	Thousands of colors

Servers

Table E.7   Network Server systems.

Network Server 500/132

Processor	PowerPC 604	Server Software	Trial version of several third-party products (may vary)
Speed	132 MHz		
FPU	Integrated	RAM	32MB of parity RAM
Networking	Ethernet; optional Fast Ethernet, FDDI, and ATM	Maximum RAM supported	512MB
Slots	6 PCI	Level 2 Cache	512K
SCSI devices supported	2 Fast/Wide SCSI-2 channels support up to 7 internal and (with optional PCI expansion cards) 70 external devices; SCSI-1 channel supports up to 7 external devices	Internal Hard Disk; CD-ROM	1GB or 2GB; up to six 4GB drives for 24GB (expandable to 256GB total using external disk arrays and subsystems); CD-ROM drive
System Software	AIX 4.1 (sold separately)	Tape backup drive	Optional

(continued)

Table E.7   Network Server systems (continued).

Network Server 700/150 and 700/200

Processor	PowerPC 604 or 604e RISC	Server Software	Trial version of several third-party products (may vary)
Speed	150 MHz / 200 MHz		
FPU	Integrated	RAM	32MB or 48MB of parity RAM
Networking	Ethernet; optional Fast Ethernet, FDDI, and ATM	Maximum RAM supported	512MB
Slots	6 PCI	Level 2 Cache	512K
SCSI devices supported	2 Fast/Wide SCSI-2 channels support up to 7 internal and (with optional PCI expansion cards) 70 external devices; SCSI-1 channel supports up to 7 external devices	Internal Hard Disk; CD-ROM	1GB or 2GB; up to six 4GB drives for 24GB (expandable to 256GB total using external disk arrays and subsystems); CD-ROM drive
		Tape backup drive	Optional
System Software	AIX 4.1 (sold separately)		

Table E.8   Workgroup Server systems.

Workgroup Server 95

Processor	68040	Server Software	AppleShare Pro
Speed	33 MHz	RAM	32MB or 48MB
FPU	Integrated	Maximum RAM supported	256MB
Networking	LocalTalk, Ethernet	Level 2 Cache	256K or 512K
Slots	5 NuBus, one 040 PDS	Internal Hard Disk; CD-ROM	250MB or 2GB
		Tape backup drive	Included
SCSI devices supported	Up to 20		
System Software	A/UX 3.1		

(continued)

E: Apple Spec Chart

Table E.8   Workgroup Server systems (continued).

Workgroup Server 6150/66

Processor	PowerPC 601 RISC	Server Software	AppleShare 4.1
Speed	66 MHz	RAM	16MB
FPU	Integrated	Maximum RAM supported	72MB
Networking	LocalTalk, Ethernet	Level 2 Cache	256K
Slots	One 7" NuBus or 1 PDS	Internal Hard Disk; CD-ROM	250MB
		Tape backup drive	–
SCSI devices supported	Up to 7		
System Software	System 7.5.1		

Workgroup Server 7250/120

Processor	PowerPC 601 RISC	RAM	16MB
Speed	120 MHz	Maximum RAM supported	256MB
FPU	Integrated		
Networking	LocalTalk, Ethernet	Level 2 Cache	256K
Slots	3 PCI	Internal Hard Disk; CD-ROM	1.2GB; CD-ROM drive; one expansion bay
SCSI devices supported	Up to 7		
System Software	System 7.5.3		
Server Software	Server Solutions CD/ AppleShare 4.2.1 Internet Server Solutions	Tape backup drive	–

Workgroup Server 7350/180

Processor	PowerPC 604e RISC	RAM	48MB
Speed	180 MHz	Maximum RAM supported	512MB
FPU	Integrated		
Networking	LocalTalk, Ethernet	Level 2 Cache	256K
Slots	3 PCI	Internal Hard Disk; CD-ROM	4GB; CD-ROM drive
SCSI devices supported	Up to 14		
System Software	System 7.6.1	Tape backup drive	–
Server Software	AppleShare 5.0		

(continued)

E: Apple Spec Chart

Table E.8   Workgroup Server systems (continued).

Workgroup Server 8150/110

Processor	PowerPC 601 RISC	Server Software	AppleShare 4.1
Speed	110 MHz	RAM	16MB
FPU	Integrated	Maximum RAM supported	264MB
Networking	LocalTalk, Ethernet		
Slots	3 NuBus, 1 PDS	Level 2 Cache	256K
SCSI devices supported	Up to 9	Internal Hard Disk; CD-ROM	Up to 2 1GB, 2GB, or 4GB
System Software	System 7.5.1	Tape backup drive	Optional

Workgroup Server 8550/132 and 8550/200

Processor	PowerPC 604 or 604e RISC	RAM	24MB
		Maximum RAM supported	512MB
Speed	132 MHz / 200 MHz		
FPU	Integrated	Level 2 Cache	512K
Networking	LocalTalk, Ethernet	Internal Hard Disk; CD-ROM	2GB; CD-ROM drive; one expansion bay
Slots	3 PCI		
SCSI devices supported	Up to 8	Tape backup drive	Optional
System Software	System 7.5.3		
Server Software	Server Solutions CD/ AppleShare 4.2.1 Internet Server Solutions		

Workgroup Server 9150/120

Processor	PowerPC 601 RISC	Server Software	AppleShare 4.1
Speed	120 MHz	RAM	16MB
FPU	Integrated	Maximum RAM supported	264MB
Networking	LocalTalk, Ethernet		
Slots	4 NuBus, 1 PDS	Level 2 Cache	1MB
SCSI devices supported	Up to 14	Internal Hard Disk; CD-ROM	Up to five 1GB, 2GB, or 4GB
System Software	System 7.5.1	Tape backup drive	Optional

(continued)

E: Apple Spec Chart

Table E.8 Workgroup Server systems (continued).

Workgroup Server 9650/233

Processor	PowerPC 604e RISC	Server Software	AppleShare IP 5.0
Speed	233 MHz	RAM	64MB
FPU	Integrated	Maximum RAM supported	268MB
Networking	LocalTalk, Ethernet		
Slots	6 PCI	Level 2 Cache	512K
SCSI devices supported	Up to 21	Internal Hard Disk; CD-ROM	One or two 4GB; CD-ROM drive
System Software	System 7.6.1	Tape backup drive	Optional

Workgroup Server 9650/350

Processor	PowerPC 604e RISC	RAM	64MB
Speed	350 MHz	Maximum RAM supported	768MB
FPU	Integrated		
Networking	LocalTalk, Ethernet	Level 2 Cache	1MB Inline cache
Slots	6 PCI	Internal Hard Disk; CD-ROM	Two 4GB / 24x-speed (maximum) CD-ROM drive
SCSI devices supported	Up to 21		
System Software	System 7.6.1 or Mac OS 8	Tape backup drive	Optional
Server Software	Server Solutions CD/ AppleShare IP 5.0 Internet Server Solutions		

Apple Displays

Table E.9 Apple Displays

Macintosh 12" Monochrome Display

Maximum resolution	640x480 pixels; 256 levels of gray	Screen refresh rate	67 Hz
		Stripe/Dot pitch	480 lines
Viewable image size	11.5" (diagonal)		

Macintosh 12" RGB Display

Maximum resolution	512x348 vertical line; color	Screen refresh rate	60 Hz
		Stripe/Dot pitch	0.28 mm
Viewable image size	11.5" (diagonal)		

(continued)

E: Apple Spec Chart

Table E.9   Apple Displays (continued).

Apple High-Resolution Monochrome Monitor

Maximum resolution	640x480 pixels; monochrome	Screen refresh rate	67 Hz
		Stripe/Dot pitch	480 lines
Viewable image size	11" (diagonal)		

Apple Color High-Resolution RGB Monitor (13")

Maximum resolution	640x480 pixels; color	Screen refresh rate	67 Hz
Viewable image size	12.8" (diagonal)	Stripe/Dot pitch	0.26 mm

Apple Basic Color Monitor (14")

Maximum resolution	640x480 pixels; color	Screen refresh rate	60 Hz
		Stripe/Dot pitch	0.39 mm
Viewable image size	13" (diagonal)		

Apple Performa Display (14")

Maximum resolution	640x480 pixels; color	Screen refresh rate	67 Hz
		Stripe/Dot pitch	0.39 mm
Viewable image size	13" (diagonal)		

Apple Performa Plus Display (14")

Maximum resolution	640x480 pixels; color	Screen refresh rate	67 Hz
		Stripe/Dot pitch	0.29 mm
Viewable image size	11.9" (diagonal)		

Apple Color Plus Display (14")

Maximum resolution	640x480 pixels; color	Screen refresh rate	67 Hz
		Stripe/Dot pitch	0.28 mm
Viewable image size	11.9" (diagonal)		

Macintosh Color Display (14")

Maximum resolution	640x480 pixels; color	Screen refresh rate	67 Hz
		Stripe/Dot pitch	0.26 mm
Viewable image size	11.5" (diagonal)		

AudioVision Display (14")

Maximum resolution	640x480 pixels; color	Screen refresh rate	67 Hz
		Stripe/Dot pitch	0.26 mm
Viewable image size	11.5" (diagonal)		

E: Apple Spec Chart

(continued)

Table E.9 Apple Displays (continued).

Macintosh Portrait Display (15")

Maximum resolution	640x870 vertical lines; monochrome	Screen refresh rate	75 Hz
		Stripe/Dot pitch	870 lines
Viewable image size	14.2" (diagonal)		

Apple Multiple Scan 15 Display

Maximum resolution	Up to 832x624 pixels (Mac OS)	Screen refresh rate	60 to 75 Hz
		Stripe/Dot pitch	0.28 mm
Viewable image size	13.3" (diagonal)		

Apple Multiple Scan 15 Display

Maximum resolution	Up to 832x624 pixels (Mac OS)	Screen refresh rate	60 to 75 Hz
		Stripe/Dot pitch	0.28 mm
Viewable image size	13.3" (diagonal)		

Macintosh 16" Color Display

Maximum resolution	832x624 pixels; color	Screen refresh rate	75 Hz
		Stripe/Dot pitch	0.26 mm
Viewable image size	16" (diagonal)		

Macintosh 21" Color Display

Maximum resolution	1152x870 vertical lines; color	Screen refresh rate	75 Hz
		Stripe/Dot pitch	0.26 mm
Viewable image size	19" (diagonal)		

Apple 2-Page Monochrome Monitor

Maximum resolution	1152x870 vertical lines; monochrome	Screen refresh rate	75 Hz
		Stripe/Dot pitch	870 lines
Viewable image size	–		

Apple Multiple Scan 14 Display

Maximum resolution	Up to 832x624 pixels (Mac OS)	Screen refresh rate	60 to 75 Hz
		Stripe/Dot pitch	0.28 mm
Viewable image size	12.4" (diagonal)		
Picture tube	Shadow mask		

(continued)

Table E.9   Apple Displays (continued).

Apple Multiple Scan 15AV Display

Maximum resolution	1024x768 pixels	Screen refresh rate	60 to 75 Hz
Viewable image size	13.75" (diagonal)	Stripe/Dot pitch	0.26 mm
Picture tube	Shadow mask		

Apple Multiple Scan 17 Display

Maximum resolution	640x480 to 1024x768 pixels (Mac OS)	Picture tube	Trinitron
		Screen refresh rate	60 to 75 Hz
		Stripe/Dot pitch	0.26 mm
Viewable image size	16.1" (diagonal)		

Apple Multiple Scan 1705 Display

Maximum resolution	1024x768 pixels	Screen refresh rate	60 to 75 Hz
Viewable image size	15.8" (diagonal)	Stripe/Dot pitch	0.28 mm
Picture tube	Shadow mask		

Apple Multiple Scan 720 Display

Maximum resolution	1280x1024 pixels	Screen refresh rate	60 to 85 Hz
Viewable image size	16" (diagonal)	Stripe/Dot pitch	0.28 mm
Picture tube	Shadow mask		

AppleVision 1710 Display

Maximum resolution	1280x1024 pixels	Screen refresh rate	60 to 75 Hz
Viewable image size	16.1" (diagonal)	Stripe/Dot pitch	0.26 mm
Picture tube	Trinitron		

AppleVision 1710AV Display

Maximum resolution	1280x1024 pixels	Screen refresh rate	60 to 75 Hz
Viewable image size	16.1" (diagonal)	Stripe/Dot pitch	0.26 mm
Picture tube	Trinitron		

Apple ColorSync 750 Display

Maximum resolution	1600x1200 pixels	Screen refresh rate	60 to 85 Hz
Viewable image size	16.1" (diagonal)	Stripe/Dot pitch	0.25 mm
Picture tube	Trinitron		

(continued)

E: Apple Spec Chart

Table E.9   Apple Displays (continued).

Apple ColorSync 750AV Display

Maximum resolution	1600x1200 pixels	Screen refresh rate	60 to 85 Hz
Viewable image size	16.1" (diagonal)	Stripe/Dot pitch	0.25 mm
Picture tube	Trinitron		

Apple Multiple Scan 20 Display

Maximum resolution	640x480 to 1024x768 pixels (Mac OS)	Picture tube	Trinitron
		Screen refresh rate	60 to 75 Hz
Viewable image size	19.1" (diagonal)	Stripe/Dot pitch	0.26 mm

Apple ColorSync 850 Display

Maximum resolution	1600x1200 pixels	Screen refresh rate	75 to 85 Hz
Viewable image size	19" (diagonal)	Stripe/Dot pitch	0.25 mm
Picture tube	Trinitron		

Apple ColorSync 850AV Display

Maximum resolution	1600x1200 pixels	Screen refresh rate	75 to 85 Hz
Viewable image size	19" (diagonal)	Stripe/Dot pitch	0.25 mm
Picture tube	Trinitron		

Appendix F

HTML Resource Guide

The Mac OS is the premier operating system for the creation of HTML documents and management of Web sites. To help you fulfill your potential, we're including a slightly modified version of the *HTML Resource Guide*, by Jeremy Hall. The *HTML Resource Guide* is a great solution for a good and quick HTML reference for the novice HTML user.

Introduction

When I was beginning to learn a bit about HTML, I always wondered why I could not find a straightforward list of tags and what they did. The books always seemed too long, and the online information always seemed too hard to follow. Therefore, I decided to put something together that fills that niche. Yes, it does contain a mixture of tags from different levels of HTML standards and not necessarily all the tags that have been introduced. I'll leave it up to you to decide which you will and will not use, according to your personal preferences. There are many improvements to this version of the guide, so be sure to see the version history in the "Contact Information" section for these updates.

This is a document that you can contribute to. If you see any part that could use some correction, improvement, or that otherwise needs help, please contact me using the information included in this document. If you find mistakes, let me know what they are. If I ever find the time, I'll also write an HTML primer much like this guide.

How To Use This Guide

In this version of the guide, you'll find the following sections:

- Introduction
- How To Use this Guide
- A Quick HTML List

- Description Of Tags
- Additional Resources
- Contact Information
- Licensing Information
- Shameless Plug
- Version History

The only section not included in this guide is a collection of examples, which you can find in older versions, including the DocMaker version on this book's accompanying CD-ROM that contains links to examples on the Web that are no longer available. The following abbreviations are used in all the versions of the *HTML Resource Guide* to indicate browser compatibility:

- (NS) Netscape Navigator
- (IE) Internet Explorer
- (NS/IE) Netscape Navigator and Internet Explorer

A Quick HTML List

This section lists the HTML tags that are described in more detail in the subsequent section. Please see the DocMaker version of this guide for hyperlinks to online examples of these tags.

General

```
<HTML>...</HTML>
<HEAD>...</HEAD>
<TITLE>...</TITLE>
<BODY>...</BODY>
<!DOCTYPE>
```

Formatting

```
<B>...</B>
<I>...</I>
<U>...</U>
<S>...</S> OR <STRIKE>...</STRIKE>
<TT></TT>
<BLINK></BLINK>
<BASEFONT SIZE=x>
<FONT></FONT>
```

F: HTML Resource Guide

```
<Hx></Hx>
<CITE></CITE>
<CODE></CODE>
<DFN></DFN>
<EM></EM>
<KBD></KBD>
<XMP></XMP>
<PRE></PRE>
<STRONG></STRONG>
<SAMP></SAMP>
<VAR></VAR>
<ADDRESS></ADDRESS>
<SMALL></SMALL>
<BIG></BIG>
<SUB></SUB>
<SUP></SUB>
```

Alignment

```
<Hx ALIGN=y></Hx>
<P ALIGN=x></P>
<BLOCKQUOTE></BLOCKQUOTE>
<CENTER></CENTER>
```

Links And Images

```
<A HREF="document.html"></A>
<A HREF="#target"></A>
<A NAME="target"></A>
<IMG SRC="image.gif"  ALIGN=x>
<MAP>...</MAP>
```

Dividers

```
<BR>
<P>
<HR SIZE=x WIDTH=y>
<NOBR></NOBR>
<WBR>
```

Lists

```
<OL>...</OL>
<UL>...</UL>
```

F: HTML Resource Guide

```
<DL>...</DL>  including <DT> and <DL>
<DIR>...</DIR>
<MENU>...</MENU>
<LI>
<DT>
<DD>
```

Tables And Columns

```
<TABLE>...</TABLE>
<CAPTION ALIGN=x>...</CAPTION>
<TR>...</TR>
<TH>...</TH>
<TD>...</TD>
<MULTICOL> or <COLGROUP>
```

Forms

```
<FORM ACTION="action URL" METHOD=GET/POST>...</FORM>
<INPUT NAME="name" VALUE="value" TYPE=x SIZE=y MAXLENGTH=z>
<TEXTAREA NAME="name" ROWS=x COLS=y>...</TEXTAREA>
```

Miscellaneous

```
<FRAMESET>...</FRAMESET> (All frame tags and modifiers)
<!-- -->
<META>
<SPACER>
<MARQUEE>
<EMBED>
<OBJECT>
```

Description Of Tags

The following section describes the previously listed HTML tags in brief detail. Please see the DocMaker version of this guide for hyperlinks to online examples of these tags.

General

```
<HTML>...</HTML>
```

The <HTML> tag tells the Web-browsing software that the document it's looking at is indeed an HTML page. Make sure that you place <HTML> at the top of every

HTML document you create. Similarly, place a </HTML> tag at the bottom of every document.

`<HEAD>...</HEAD>`

The head tag tells the browser what part of the document is the top section, or the head. This section holds the title, meta information, and also can hold JavaScript information.

`<TITLE>...</TITLE>`

The title contains the text that appears in the title bar of your browser window. This is located within the <HEAD> container.

`<BODY>...</BODY>`

The largest part of your HTML document is the body, which contains the document content (shown within the display area of your browser window).

Attributes (on all the following, the default colors will be used if omitted):

- *TEST*—Sets the base color for the normal text within the document.
- *LINK*—Sets a specific color for text links.
- *ALINK*—Sets a specific color for an active link.
- *VLINK*—Sets a specific color for a visited link.
- *BGCOLOR*—Sets a specific background color (all the color attributes are best if set equal to a hexadecimal number equivalent).
- *BACKGROUND*—Specifies a graphic file to be tiled for the background. If a BGCOLOR is also set, the page will appear in that color until the background graphic is loaded.
- *BGSOUND*—Loads and plays a sound file in the background; also requires the sound to be EMBEDDED if Netscape is the browser. (NS3/IE2)
- *BGPROPERTIES*—When set to fixed, locks the background image into place as a watermark. (IE)
- *LEFTMARGIN/TOPMARGIN*—Defines size of the margins in pixels. (IE)

`<!DOCTYPE>   Document Type Declaration`

Specifies the version of HTML used in the document. !DOCTYPE is the first element in any HTML document and is a required element for any HTML 3.2-compliant document.

F: HTML Resource Guide

Formatting

`<B>...</B>  Bold`

Bolds text. Often, this reproduces the same effect as the <STRONG> emphasis tag.

`<I>...</I>  Italics`

Italicizes text.

`<U>...</U>  Underline`

Underlines text; not widely supported, because underlining typically is associated with links, though NS3 began supporting it.

`<S>...</S>  or <STRIKE>...</STRIKE>  Strikeout`

Displays the text with a line through the middle, striking it out.

`<TT>...</TT>  Typewriter Text`

Used for typewriter text, a fixed-width font supposedly like a typewriter.

`<BLINK>...</BLINK>  Blinking Text  (NS/IE)`

Causes all the text that appears between these tags to blink incessantly. (A somewhat annoying option when overused.)

`<BASEFONT SIZE=x>  Base Font Size`

Sets the font size of your entire document to be a specified size in relation to what has been set in the user's browser. The x equals a number between 1 and 7.

`<FONT>...</FONT>  Font Modification  (NS/IE)`

This font tag makes temporary changes in text attributes within the body of your document. A big advantage to this tag is that you can make changes in mid-sentence, not forcing a new line break like the heading tag.

Attributes:

- *SIZE*—Changes the size of the text. The size can be set as an absolute value or proportional, that is, '+' or '-' a certain number between 1 and 7.

F: HTML Resource Guide

- *COLOR*—A newer attribute that (in some browsers) allows you to change the test color. Use a hexadecimal number or certain names, for example: red, blue, green, and so forth. This option is ignored by non-capable browsers.
- *FACE*—Sets the font. You can specify a list of font names. If the first font is available on the system, it will be used; otherwise, the second will be tried, and so on. If none are available, a default font will be used. (NS3/IE3)

`<Hx>...</Hx>  Heading`

HTML has six levels of headings. The symbol x equals numbers 1 through 6, with 1 being the top level. Headings are displayed in larger and/or bolder fonts than normal body text. The first heading in each document should ideally be tagged <H1>.

Attributes:

- *ALIGN*—Aligns the heading text either left, right, or center.

`<CITE>...</CITE>  Citation`

Used for titles of books, films, and so on. Typically displayed in italics.

`<CODE>...</CODE>  Code`

Used for computer code. Displayed in a fixed-width font.

`<DFN>...</DFN>  Definition`

Emphasizes a definition. No recognizable change in most browsers.

`<EM>...</EM>  Emphasis`

Used for emphasis. Typically displayed in italics.

`<KBD>...</KBD>  Keyboard Entry`

Used for user keyboard entry. Typically displayed in plain fixed-width font.

`<XMP>...</XMP>  Preformatted - No tags`

Preformatted without tags. Handy for showing HTML tags on screen if you are explaining how tags work.

```
<PRE>...</PRE>  Preformatted
```

The <PRE> tag (which stands for "preformatted") generates text in a fixed-width font. This tag also makes spaces, new lines, and tabs significant (multiple spaces are displayed as multiple spaces, and lines break in the same locations as in the source HTML file). This is useful for program listings, among other things.

```
<STRONG>...</STRONG>  Strong Emphasis
```

Used for strong emphasis. Typically displayed in bold.

```
<SAMP>...</SAMP>
```

Used for a sequence of literal characters. Displayed in a fixed-width font.

```
<VAR>...</VAR>  Variable
```

Used for a variable, where you replace the variable with specific information. Typically displayed in italics.

```
<ADDRESS>...</ADDRESS>  Address
```

Generally used to specify the author of a document, a way to contact the author (for example, an email address), and a revision date. It is usually the last item in a file.

```
<SMALL>...</SMALL>  Small Text  (NS/IE)
```

A bit of an obvious tag. The text enclosed within this container appears smaller in relation to the surrounding text. Basically the same effect as reducing the font size by -1.

```
<BIG>...</BIG>  Big Text  (NS/IE)
```

The text enclosed within this container appears larger in relation to the surrounding text. Basically the same effect as increasing the font size by +1.

```
<SUB>...</SUB>  Subscript  (NS/IE)
```

The text enclosed within this container appears as a subscript. This is very useful for creating footnotes or endnotes or doing mathematical formulas. The text will be one font size smaller and half a line below the rest of the text.

F: HTML Resource Guide

```
<SUP>...</SUP>  Superscript  (NS/IE)
```

The text enclosed within this container appears as a superscript. This is very useful for creating footnotes or endnotes or doing mathematical formulas. The text will be one font size smaller and half a line above the rest of the text.

Alignment Tags

```
<Hx ALIGN=y></Hx>  See previous entry under "Alignment."
```

```
<P ALIGN=y></P>  See entry in "Links and Images"
```

```
<BLOCKQUOTE>...</BLOCKQUOTE>  Block Quotation
```

Use the <BLOCKQUOTE> tag to include lengthy quotations in a separate block on the screen. Most browsers generally indent from both margins for the quotation to offset it from surrounding text.

```
<CENTER>...</CENTER>  Center
```

Centers text and—even objects—on your screen.

Links And Images

```
<A>...</A>  Anchor
```

Gives interactivity to an HTML document and creates links to other Internet pages, documents, and downloadable files. Anything that appears between the begin and end anchor tags takes you to the specified destination when clicked.

Attributes:

- *HREF*—The basic attribute to an anchor tag that tells the destination of the link. This can specify a link within the current document or outside the document or file. Outside links can be absolute (name the full URL, including http, mailto, and so on) or relative (within the same folder or directory on the WWW server).
- *MAILTO*—Used within an HREF reference to create a hyperlink for emailing.
- *NAME*—Specifies the location and name of an internal link.
- *TARGET*—If you are using frames, this specifies what frame or window to load the link into. See the following entry under frames.

`<IMG>  Image`

To include an image in a Web document, you need to use an <IMG> tag. Make certain the file name ends with ".gif" or .jpg" for GIF or JPEG images. By default, the bottom of an image is aligned with the text. There are numerous attributes for the <IMG> tag.

Attributes:

- *SRC*—The basic and necessary element of an image tag that specifies the location of the image file to be displayed.

- *WIDTH*—Specifies the width of the image. Optional, but recommended for faster page layout. This can stretch or shrink the display of the image.

- *HEIGHT*—Specifies the height of the image. Same description as WIDTH.

- *BORDER*—Specifies a border width (in pixels) when an image is used as a hyperlink. Set the border width to zero if you want no border to appear. (It is good etiquette to also include a text version of the link as well.)

- *ALIGN*—Aligns the image to the left, right, middle, bottom, and top. When defining the alignment, the image appears where specified and the text wraps to the other side.

- *ALT*—Lists optional text to appear if a browser viewer is not loading images or is using a non-graphical browser.

- *LOWSRC*—An optional image that loads first and faster to give a feel for the page before the larger image loads. If using this feature, be sure the LOWSRC is much smaller than the larger image that loads after it.

- *USEMAP*—If using a client-side image map, this specifies what coding to refer to.

`<MAP>...</MAP>  Client-Side Image Map  (NS2/IE2)`

A wonderful feature that allows the use of a graphic as an image map without the use of server image maps. You need to make several modifications for this tag to work. First, you must find the coordinates around the sections to be clickable. Then, set up the code to work according to those clickable points. You must also include the USEMAP attribute in the <IMG> tag.

Attributes:

- *NAME*—Essential attribute giving the code a name to be referenced by for the image tag.

- *USEMAP*—Included with the image tag to specify what coding to refer to.

F: HTML Resource Guide

`<AREA>` `Client-Side Image Map (cont'd)` `(NS2/IE3)`

Part of the <MAP> tag; much like the <LI> is to a list. Specifies the different areas that are clickable, and where they take a viewer.

Attributes:

- *SHAPE*—Determines the shape of the clickable area being defined; can be rectangle (rect), polygon (poly), circles (circle), and default (default). Default defines an action for those parts of the image that do not have a shape given.
- *COORDS*—Sets the coordinates of the area. For a rectangle, they are "left, top, right, bottom." A circle is defined as a center point and then a radius (for a total of three numbers).
- *HREF*—Same use as in an anchor tag; specifies the action when the area is clicked.
- *NOHREF*—Specifies an area to be non-clickable, or to have no action associated with it.
- *TARGET*—If frames are used, this specifies what frame or window to load the link into. See the entry under "Frames."

Dividers

`<BR>` `Line Break`

Forces a line break with no extra (white) space between lines.

Attributes:

- *CLEAR*—Discontinues wrapping next to an inline graphic and continues one line below the graphic. Can be set equal to left, right, and center.

`<P>...</P>` `Paragraph`

Creates a line break and starts a new paragraph. Without <P> tags, the document becomes one large paragraph. You can omit the </P> closing tag, because it implies that there is an end to the previous paragraph.

Attributes:

- *ALIGN*—Aligns text; can be set equal to left, center, or right.

```
<HR>  Horizontal Rule
```

Produces a horizontal line the width of the browser window. It's often used as a way to break up information in your document. You can use the WIDTH and SIZE attributes with <HR> individually or together.

Attributes:

- *NOSHADE*—Forces the line to be solid, rather than shadowed or 3D. (NS/IE)
- *WIDTH=X*—Designates the width of the rule with x equaling the rule's percentage (or absolute pixel width) to the size of the browser window. (NS/IE)
- *SIZE=X*—Designates the thickness of the rule with x equaling the number of pixels.
- *ALIGN*—Aligns the line to the left, center, or right. (NS/IE)

```
<NOBR>...</NOBR>  No (Line) Break  (NS/IE)
```

Forces text to stay on the same line, much like the PRE tag, but does not start on a new line at the beginning of the tag or force the text to a fixed font. Good for poetry that requires a particular appearance.

```
<WBR>  Word Break  (NS/IE)
```

Used inside of the NOBR tag to specify breaking points, or when to start a new line.

Lists

```
<OL>  Ordered List
```

A numbered list (also called an *ordered list*, from which the tag name derives) is identical to an unnumbered list, except it uses <OL> instead of <UL>. The items are tagged using the same <LI> tag. These lists can be nested to form an outline format, automatically assigning different numbering formats for the nested lists.

Attributes:

- *TYPE*—Specifies numbering type; can be set to disc, square, or circle.

F: HTML Resource Guide

`<UL>...</UL>` Unnumbered (unorganized) List

Makes an unnumbered, bulleted list. Each item in the list appears between the UL tags, and is preceded by an <LI> tag. These lists can be nested to form an outline format, automatically assigning different symbols for the nested lists.

Attributes:

- *TYPE*—Specifies bullet type; can be set to disc, square, or circle.

`<DL>...</DL>` Definition List

A definition list usually consists of alternating a definition term (coded as <DT>) and a definition (coded as <DD>). Web browsers generally format and indent the definition on a new line.

`<DIR>...</DIR>` Directory List

No longer frequently used, but acts the same as an unnumbered list. You can use it to help organize your coding.

`<MENU>...</MENU>` Menu List

No longer frequently used, but acts the same as an unnumbered list. You can use it to help organize your coding.

`<LI>` List Item

Each item in a numbered or unnumbered list is preceded by an <LI> tag. The closing </LI> tag is optional.

`<DT>` Definition Term

Within a definition list (<DL>), specifies the term or stem of the list item. Starts on a new line of text.

`<DD>` Definition Data

Within a definition list (<DL>), specifies the definition or body of the list item. Usually appears on the following line of text and indented from the left margin.

F: HTML Resource Guide

Tables

`<TABLE> ... </TABLE>   Table`

Defines a table in HTML. Tables are very useful for controlling the layout of a page so that it appears exactly as intended. Tables were introduced by Netscape, but are now widely supported by other browsers.

Attributes:

- *BORDER*—Specifies a visible border width for a table. A border of 1 pixel width is the default if you do not specify the width. Use BORDER=0 if you do not want to show a border.

- *CELLSPACING*—Specifies a pixel width for spacing between cells, visible if a border >1.

- *CELLPADDING*—Specifies a pixel width/value for spacing from the cell border to the cell contents.

- *WIDTH*—Gives pixel dimensions or percentage for the width of the entire table.

- *BORDERCOLOR*—Specifies a color for the table border (hex, rgb, name). (IE)

- *BORDERCOLORLIGHT*—Specifies a light color for the 3D table border (hex, rgb, name). (IE)

- *BORDERCOLORDARK*—Specifies a dark color for the 3D table border (hex, rgb, name). (IE)

`<CAPTION> ...</CAPTION>   Table Caption`

Defines the caption for the title of the table. The default position of the title is centered at the top of the table. You can use any kind of markup tag in the caption.

Attributes:

- *ALIGN*—Specifies whether the caption appears at the top or bottom of the table.

`<TR> ... </TR>   Table Row`

Specifies a table row within a table. All table cells and headings will be contained within a table row.

F: HTML Resource Guide

Attributes:

- *ALIGN*—Specifies default alignment for the entire row of cells, including left, right, center.

- *VALIGN*—Default vertical alignment for the entire row, including top, bottom, middle.

`<TH> ... </TH>` `Table Heading`

Defines a table header cell. By default, the text in this cell is bold and centered. Table header cells may contain other attributes to determine the characteristics of the cell and/or its contents. See following Table Attributes for more information.

Attributes:

- *ALIGN*—Specifies default alignment for the contents of the cell, including left, right, center.

- *VALIGN*—Vertical alignment for the contents of the cell, including top, bottom, middle.

- *WIDTH/HEIGHT*—Dimensions for the cell; may be in pixel value or percentage of the table.

- *COLSPAN*—Specifies how many columns for the current cell to span or cross.

- *ROWSPAN*—Specifies how many rows for the current cell to span or cross.

- *BGCOLOR*—Sets the background color for the table cell. (NS3/IE)

`<TD> ... </TD>` `Table Data (cell)`

Defines a table data cell. By default, the text in this cell is aligned left and centered vertically. Table data cells may contain other attributes to determine the characteristics of the cell and/or its contents. See the following Table Attributes for more information.

Attributes:

- *ALIGN*—Specifies default alignment for the contents of the cell, including left, right, center.

- *VALIGN*—Vertical alignment for the contents of the cell, including top, bottom, middle.

- *WIDTH/HEIGHT*—Dimensions for the cell; may be in pixel value or percentage of the table.

- *COLSPAN*—Specifies how many columns for the current cell to span or cross.

- *ROWSPAN*—Specifies how many rows for the current cell to span or cross.

- *BGCOLOR*—Sets the background color for the table cell. (NS3/IE)

`<MULTICOL> ... </MULTICOL>  Multiple Columns  (NS)`

The <MULTICOL> tag is a container, and all the HTML between the starting and ending tags will be displayed in a multicolumn format. The tag can be nested. Internet Explorer uses a format much different within tables. (You'll find more information on this in a later version of this guide.)

Attributes:

- *COLS*—Mandatory attribute that controls the number of columns the display will be split into. Layout will attempt to flow elements evenly across the columns to make each column about the same height. Unless the WIDTH attribute is specified, column width is adjusted to fill the available view.

- *GUTTER*—Controls the amount of space between columns. It defaults to a value of 10 pixels.

- *WIDTH*—Specifies the width of an individual column in pixels.

Forms

`<FORM>...</FORM>  Form`

The basic element of the form, this tag begins and closes the area enclosing the form elements. You can contain any HTML coding within the form area to enhance the look of your form. There are attributes within the FORM tag that are required to tell your browser where to send the information and how to do it.

Attributes:

- *ACTION*—Tells your browser what URL to send the information to; this is typically a CGI program of some kind.

- *METHOD*—There are two options, GET or POST. The difference between these two options is actually somewhat complicated, but basically, GET encodes all the information into the URL that is sent, and POST sends the data separately from the actual call to the script. Which do you use? Typically, you will be using a set program someone else has created that will tell you which one to use.

F: HTML Resource Guide

`<INPUT>  Input (Variables)`

INPUT is the most common element within the form area. This allows you to specify text-input fields, radio buttons, checkboxes, selection lists, and perhaps more as it is developed.

Attributes:

- *NAME*—Specifies the field or variable name; must be included.
- *VALUE*—Specifies the default value for the variable when sent to the CGI program. You can specify this as hidden to send information that you do not want the user seeing. This text appears within the field, and the user can delete and/or replace it.
- *TYPE*—Specifies what type input you are looking for, either text, radio, checkboxes, or selection menus. Be sure to see the coding examples for how to use these options.
- *SIZE*—Gives the length of a text-input field (width in characters).
- *MAXLENGTH*—Specifies how many characters the user input is limited to in a text-input field.
- *SELECTED*—Determines which button is selected by default (be sure to select only one) in a radio field.
- *CHECKED*—Specifies which box(es) are selected in a checkbox field.

`<TEXTAREA>...</TEXTAREA>  Form Text Area`

When you are asking a user to input a large amount of text, use the text area element instead of a small one-line text input box. You can assign the dimensions of the text area to help determine how much the user types. Text entered between the opening and closing tags will appear within the text area and can be deleted and/or replaced by the user.

Attributes:

- *NAME*—Specifies the field or variable name; must be included.
- *VALUE*—Specifies the default value for the variable when sent to the CGI program.
- *ROWS*—Determines how long the text area will be (length in text lines).
- *COLS*—Determines how wide the text area will be (width in characters).
- *WRAP*—Specifies how you would like the text to wrap within the text area, usually *virtual* if you do anything, but optional.

Miscellaneous

Frames (NS2/IE3)

You may wonder why frames was not put in its own section, as were tables and lists. Although popular, frames are memory- and bandwidth-intensive and usually not utilized very well. You should take care when using them, and always offer a noframe alternative. Even though I may be a little biased against them, there are good uses for frames, and therefore, let's get on to explaining them.

```
<FRAMESET>...</FRAMESET>  Frame Container  (NS2/IE3)
```

This is the main container for a frame. When creating a frame "defining" page, leave out the <BODY> tag and use this tag for each frame. You can nest frames within frames, much like a table. <FRAMESET> is comparable to rows or columns in a table.

Attributes:

- *ROWS*—A value that assigns how much of the screen each row is allotted; this is given in fixed pixels, percentage number, or '*' (meaning it takes up the remaining space).

- *COLS*—Follows same format as rows, only assigns the screen sections horizontally.

- *BORDERCOLOR*—Sets a default color for the border of the frames. See the following explanation under "Individual Frame" for conflicting situations. (NS)

```
<FRAME>  Individual Frame  (NS2/IE3)
```

This tag defines a single frame in a frameset. It is not a container, so it has no matching end tag.

Attributes:

- *SRC*—Defines the source URL to be displayed in the frame. If omitted, a blank space is displayed in the size of the frame.

- *NAME*—Defines a name for the window. Although this is not displayed, it is useful for targeting particular windows with links.

- *MARGINWIDTH*—Gives control of the margin width within a frame, defined in pixels.

- *MARGINHEIGHT*—Gives control of the margin height within a frame, defined in pixels.

F: HTML Resource Guide

- *SCROLLING*—Determines whether the frame contains a scroll bar, defined as *yes*, *no*, or *auto*. Be sure to include if your page might not fit within the frame display area.

- *NORESIZE*—Specifies that the user cannot change the size of the frame. There is no value associated with the tag; it's inclusion only. This is optional and all frames are resizable by default.

- *FRAMEBORDER*—Specifies the presence of a 3D border for the frame. (NS) uses the options of YES or NO, (IE) uses the options of 1 or 0.

- *BORDERCOLOR*—Sets a specific color for the frame border. This can run into difficulties when two frames have conflicting border colors. Netscape defines the solution: "The attribute in the outer FRAMESET has the lowest priority. This in turn is overridden by the attribute used in a nested FRAMESET tag. Finally, the BORDERCOLOR attribute used in a FRAME tag overrides all previous FRAMESET tags."

```
<NOFRAMES>...</NOFRAMES>  No Frame Option  (NS2/IE3)  (but for other
browsers)
```

Option included on the primary frame document that provides information or alternate page layout for non-frames-capable browsers. This is necessary if you are interested in reaching the portions of the Web that choose not to use frames-capable browsers.

```
TARGET - Targeting Links Within Frames  (NS2/IE3)
```

This is an option for pointing your links into specific frames. These targets can be contained within the anchor tag, area tag of a client-side image map, or within the base tag for an overall default destination.

TIP: *Before using frames, be sure you understand how to target links and how to make a link fill the whole window when it leaves your site.*

Values (set target equal to these within the anchor tag):

- *window name*—Sets the target equal to the name of the window to load into.

- *blank*—Causes the link to always load in a new blank window.

- *self*—Causes the link to always load in the same window that the anchor was clicked in.

- *parent*—Makes the link load in the immediate <FRAMESET> parent of this document. This defaults to acting like "*_self*" if the document has no parent.

- *top*—Makes the link load in the full body of the window. This is how you exit from your frames when leaving your site.

Other

`<!--  -->  Comments`

Allows you to place comments within the code of your HTML documents that do not appear when loaded into a browser. This is handy for placing markers or reminders to yourself in a highly changing document.

`<META>  Meta Indexing`

Embedding information for the server. Used for several options, especially for passing indexing information to search engines (both internal and the larger popular ones) and for automatic reloading or reloading to a different URL of your page (client-pull).

Attributes:

- *HTTP-EQUIV*—Set this equal to a URL and time to be reloaded.
- *NAME*—Name of the document/HTML file or descriptor for a search engine (such as description, keywords, or author).
- *CONTENT*—A short description of the content of the page.

`<SPACER>  Invisible Spacer  (NS3)`

The <SPACER> tag enhances page formatting. A simple use of the tag would be to indent a paragraph. Use this tag much like an image, with height, width, and align attributes.

Attributes:

- *TYPE*—Can be horizontal, vertical, and block.
- *WIDTH*—Specifies the width of the invisible space to be blocked off.
- *HEIGHT*—Specifies the height of the invisible space to be blocked off.
- *ALIGN*—Aligns the invisible space much like an image; most used as left or right.

`<MARQUEE>  Scrolling Marquee  (IE)`

Creates a scrolling text marquee. This is only supported by Internet Explorer, though a popular Java applet has been widely used making it available for

F: HTML Resource Guide

Netscape. Use this with care; it can become as annoying as the <BLINK> tag has become.

Attributes:

- *ALIGN*—Specifies how the surrounding text should align with the marquee. The align type can be top, middle, or bottom.

- *BEHAVIOR*—Specifies how the text should behave. The possible values are:

  - *scroll*—Start completely off one side, scroll all the way across and completely off, and then start again. This is the default.

  - *slide*—Start completely off one side, scroll in, and stop as soon as the text touches the other margin.

  - *alternate*—Bounce back and forth within the marquee.

- *BGCOLOR*—Sets a specific background color (all the color attributes are best if set equal to a hexadecimal number equivalent).

- *DIRECTION*—Specifies in which direction the text should scroll. The direction can be LEFT or RIGHT. The default is LEFT, which means scrolling to the left from the right.

- *HEIGHT/WIDTH*—Specifies the height and width of the marquee, either in pixels or as a percentage of the screen (a % sign is required).

- *HSPACE/VSPACE*—Specifies the horizontal and vertical margin or buffer around the marquee.

- *LOOP*—Specifies how many times the marquee message will loop. This can be a whole integer or INFINITE.

- *SCROLLAMOUNT*—Specifies the number of pixels between each successive draw of the marquee text.

- *SCROLLDELAY*—Specifies the number of milliseconds between each successive draw of the marquee text.

`<EMBED>` Embeds an Object (NS/IE)

Indicates an embedded object. OBJECT is the preferred element for inserting objects for (IE), but <EMBED> is also supported by (IE). The OBJECT attributes are very similar, but also add several other options for specific types of objects.

Attributes:

- *SRC*—Location of the object data, just like any other link or image.

- *HEIGHT/WIDTH*—The height or width of the object specified in pixels.

- *NAME*—The name used by other objects or elements to refer to this object.
- *PALETTE*—Sets the color palette to the foreground or background color.
- *AUTOSTART*—Determines if a sound that is played starts automatically (true/false).
- *LOOP*—If a sound file, designates the number of times to loop.

Additional Resources

Hexadecimal Color Codes

Figuring out the correct hexadecimal equivalent for colors can be a real pain. Jack Wilson is a co-worker and friend of mine and has taken the time to make a color chart to use with this guide. There are two formats that you can use:

- The first is created using table cells and BGCOLOR information, which requires that you have either IE2+ or NS3 to view it.
- The second is basically a screen capture of this chart, but can be viewed with any graphics program that supports the JPEG or GIF format.

Both the HexChart and screen captures are included on this book's accompanying CD-ROM.

Contact Information

As previously mentioned, I would be happy to hear about any improvements that could be made to this document. I know that not all the latest and greatest "proposed" tags are in this document, either. If you think a tag should be included or better explained, let me know. Also, if you would like to see a primer included or as a separate standalone document, let me know as well. I really would like this to be a useful guide.

Big thanks go to Vince Shrader as the primary co-author and editor of this document. Thanks to Jack Wilson for creating the Hex Color Chart and his constant help throughout. Also, thanks to all those who emailed in your suggestions...keep 'em coming.

Thanks for all your comments to help make this a great resource for Macintosh HTML users.

Jeremy Hall

email: **jeremy@idiglobal.com**

Vince Shrader

email: **shraderv@ed.byu.edu**

home page: **www.qi3.com/vince**

Jack Wilson

email: **wilsonj@ed.byu.edu** (Hex Color Chart)

Snail Address:

205 MCKB
BYU
Provo, UT 84604

Licensing Information

This document is "emailware," "postcardware," and "helpmeware." First off, send either of us an email to let us know if this was helpful in any way. Second, if you are feeling kind, send us a postcard. Last and most important, please email us any suggestions to improve the functionality and content of this document. Of course, if you feel extremely kind, I would never refuse monetary donations!

Shameless Plug

I (Jeremy) do Web-page design (both graphical design and page layout) and would be more than happy to develop your page or Web site. Contact me via email for a quote that will meet your needs and available resources.

Version History

Version 1.1

- Added Netscape (NS) and Internet Explorer (IE) indicators. On some, the version number is included, showing when the tag began to be supported.

- Added new tags not as widely supported or recently released.

- Added chapter on special (ISO) characters in response to many requests.

- Fixed several typos and some explanations.

Version 1.0

- Initial public release, much more response and use than expected—a pleasant surprise.

Appendix G
Additional Resources

We've covered a lot of information in this book, but we may not have addressed some issues. An occasion may occur when this book may not be able to answer your question. This appendix provides information and resources where you can find additional help.

New Online Help

One of the most useful, yet ignored sources of assistance is the Mac OS online help. AppleGuide, a help application that combined a definition database with an online tutorial, provided the previous interface. AppleGuide was well organized and could help even the most naïve computer user perform system tasks. Step-by-step instructions told you what to do and helpful screen hints were provided, such as a red marker circling an object or special highlighting within a menu. The AppleGuide window also stayed in the foreground, unlike other application windows, allowing you to continue following the steps without bringing the window to the front.

Online help has been revamped in the 8.5 release. Now called the Help Center, the application has an interface that resembles a simple Web browser (the browser is called Help Viewer). Topics are arranged by category with links to other relative documents. The online help is divided into two main categories: Mac OS and AppleScript assistance. You can access system assistance directly by selecting Mac OS Help from the Help menu.

Is the AppleGuide still included with the system? Sort of. Many software applications did take advantage of AppleGuide and wrote their own help modules in this format. For this reason, the engine is still included in Mac OS 8.5. You may also be able to invoke AppleGuide within specific control panels.

One other help tool included with Mac OS 8.5 is Balloon Help. If you have a question about a menu option or button and a short definition will suffice, you can enable Balloon Help by selecting it from the Help menu. When Balloon Help is active, you will see small balloons containing text that appear next to balloon-sensitive items. For example, if you enable Balloon Help within the Finder and move the mouse over the Edit menu, the following text will appear within a balloon: "Edit menu—Use this menu to undo an action, work with text and graphics, or set Finder preferences". Not all applications support Balloon Help and you may only be able to keep it active for a minute or two before it begins to irritate you. But in a pinch, it can help define a button or clarify a menu option, eliminating the necessity of launching the entire Help Center application.

TIP: *We could be cruel and let you suffer through the balloons a little longer, but we will put you out of your misery. To turn off Balloon Help, select Hide Balloons from the Help menu. (This menu option changes depending on the state of Balloon Help, allowing you to hide balloons when they are active or show balloons when they are inactive.)*

One final note about online help: most applications—including Microsoft software programs—place their versions of online help under the Help menu. Microsoft has its own help method, as do many other packages. However, you may see the odd application that places its help files in a different location, such as under the Apple Menu or within the About This Application window. You may even find that Help is a totally separate application that you will need to launch. Before you begin using the program, locate the online help. Then use it; you might save valuable time.

Web Sites

The Internet contains a lot of good information. Whether it is the Tech Info library from Apple or the Info-mac shareware archives at MIT, sites are available that can answer your question or provide software to fix your problem. The one downside of the Web (and it's a big one) is that you may not know the reliability of the site. When was the last time it was updated? How knowledgeable is the author? Is this legal? We'll list some of the best sites available and a description of their contents. However, links die daily and we can't guarantee that these addresses will still be active. If you should find that the information listed is not at the address provided, use your favorite Web search engine to see if the site has relocated or if another Web page can meet your needs. Also, while we've tried to list a wide variety of sites, you'll find that many of these pages contain links to other great Macintosh sites.

Apple

All of these sites are supported and maintained by Apple Computer:

G: Additional Resources

- **til.info.apple.com**—The Technical Information Library for Apple. This site is constantly changing to include new and old technical information for Mac computers. If you provide support for Macs you should bookmark this site.

- **support.info.apple.com/info.apple.com/manuals/manuals.qry**—The Product Documentation Archive. You can locate and browse the user manual for many Apple products from this site (if you don't enter a search string, the results will list all manuals available online).

- **support.info.apple.com/info.apple.com/te/te.taf**—The Tech Exchange. This site is an excellent starting point for several categories of support pages, including the Apple Spec database, Printers & Imaging, and basic trouble-shooting.

- **www.info.apple.com/swupdates/**—Apple Software Updates. This is a software archive site containing software utilities and updates for Macintosh computers as well as some PC files. Archives of older Macintosh operating systems are also available to download freely.

- **mirrors.apple.com/**—The Apple Mirror software site. Mirrors of popular software archives are contained here on a very fast server.

- **www.apple.com/documents/publications.html**—Apple Online Publications. This page includes links to online publications both by and relating to Apple computing.

- **www.macsoftware.apple.com/**—Macintosh Products Guide. This is a searchable database of over 12,000 hardware and software products for the Macintosh.

- **devworld.apple.com/devworld.shtml**—Apple Developer World. The Web site devoted to Macintosh developers.

- **www.aspn.apple.com/**—Apple Solutions Professional Network. This Web page could be useful if you need to locate an Apple consultant near you.

- **powerbook.apple.com**—Apple's resource page for PowerBook users.

- **applescript.apple.com**—Apple's online resource for AppleScript programmers. This site contains links to online manuals as well as AppleScript tutorials.

News And Publications

If you want to find out what's happening in the world of Macintosh, then consult these sites:

- **www.macsurfer.com**—*Mac Surfer*. This site provides an overview of several popular Macintosh news pages on a daily basis. It's a site you should bookmark.

- **www.tidbits.com**—*Tidbits*. This is one of the original and best online magazines.

- **www.macintouch.com**—*MacInTouch*. This is Ric Ford's Macintosh site (Ric Ford is a Macintosh guru). You can find reliable technical information and late-breaking information as well as links for other Macintosh sites.

- **www.zdnet.com/mac/**—*ZDNet Mac*. Ziff Davis, the publishers of *MacWorld*, have an online site that includes news and information from *MacWeek* and *MacWorld*, software, help, and even investing information.

- **www.macaddict.com**—*MacAddict*. This is the online version of this popular Macintosh magazine.

- **www.macnn.com**—*Mac News Network*. This is an excellent site for tips, information, and sneak previews of upcoming software releases.

- **www.maccentral.com**—*Mac Central*. Check this site for reviews and tips for Macintosh software and hardware.

- **macworld.zdnet.com**—*MacWorld*. This is the online version of the popular *MacWorld* magazine.

- **macweek.zdnet.com**—*MacWEEK*. This is the only version of this popular magazine. The published version of *MacWEEK* has changed to *eMedia Weekly*.

- **www.mactech.com**—*MacTech*. The *MacTech* site contains technical and developer information.

- **www.machome.com**—*MacHome*. The online version of the *MacHome* magazine is geared toward the home user, but its news information is updated hourly, which is beneficial to any Mac user.

- **mactoday.com**—*Mac Today*. This is a tart online magazine that may be a good tension reliever.

- **www.macosrumours.com**—Macintosh rumours site. This site is not always right, but it is accurate a fair amount of time and is a good place to check if you are interested in the bleeding edge of Mac information.

- **deal-mac.com**—Macintosh Deals. This site locates the best deals on Macintosh systems, hardware, and software.

Software

These addresses link to Macintosh software archives, including freeware, shareware, and demo software:

- **www.pht.com/info-mac/**—The Info-Mac software archive. This is one of the oldest and best software archives on the Internet.

G: Additional Resources

- **download.com and shareware.com**—CNet software archive. This is a huge repository of software and is maintained by CNet.

- **www.zdnet.com/mac/download.html**—Ziff Davis Macintosh software archive. This is a searchable Macintosh software archive.

- **www.tucows.com**—Tucows. This is a comprehensive Internet software archive.

- **www.mac-conflicts.com/**—The Complete Conflict Compendium. If you have an extension conflict, this is the site to check.

- **www.macwindows.com/**—MacWindows. This is a great site for Mac and Windows compatibility.

- **www.pixelfoundry.com/**—The Pixel Foundry. This is a great graphics design archive and includes Kai's power tips and tricks.

- **www.kindground.com/gui_junky/**—GUI Junky. Check out this site for some great ways to spruce up your Desktop.

- **www.insanely-great.com/**—Insanely Great Mac. This is a diverse Web page with software downloads, reviews, and links to other great Mac sites.

- **cafe.ambrosiasw.com/DEF/**—The Mac Pruning Pages and InformINIT. This is an excellent resource for finding out exactly the function of an extension or control panel.

- **www.powerbook.org/army/CSM/csm.html**—CSM Collection. This is a collection of control strip additions (it's also a PowerBook resource).

- **www.versiontracker.com/**—VersionTracker. This is an excellent tool to keep you up-to-date on the latest versions of popular utilities.

- **www.kaleidoscope.net/greg/**—Greg's Shareware. Greg Landweber has written Aaron and Kaleidoscope, control panels that allowed the Mac user interface to be customized.

Hardware

These sites are geared to hardware solutions (although software may be referenced):

- **www.xlr8yourmac.com/**—Accelerate Your Mac. Use this site as a reference for hardware information and tips to increase Mac performance.

- **www.macevolution.com/**—Macintosh Evolution. This page lists information on a wide variety of Macintosh systems.

- **www.macpconline.com/**—MacPC. This online source for Windows emulation on a Mac covers software and hardware solutions.

G: Additional Resources

- **www.everymac.com/**—Every Mac. This detailed Web site contains information on every Macintosh and Mac compatible in the world.
- **www.macspeedzone.com/**—MacSpeedZone. This site is *the* resource for CPU clock speeds as well as upcoming chip information.
- **www.ogrady.com**—The O'Grady's PowerPage. This Web site is devoted to information about the Macintosh PowerBook.

iMac

These links provide information about the iMac, Apple's consumer Internet computer:

- **www.iMac2Day.com/**—iMac2Day. This site provides information for the iMac computer, including USB peripherals.
- **www.theimac.com/**—The iMac. This site provides information about the iMac.

Repair

Use these sites to help repair some common Macintosh problems:

- **macfixit.pair.com/**—MacFixIt. This is an excellent resource for fixing problems—both hardware and software related—on your Macintosh.
- **www.academ.com/info/macintosh/**—The Macintosh Battery Web Page. This site provides complete information and directions to handle almost any battery problem that you may encounter.
- **www.mainelink.net/~deceiver/phoenixmacrepair.html**—Phoenix Macintosh Repair. This site contains helpful information for repairing and configuring your Mac.
- **www.nowonder.com/**—No Wonder Computer Support. This is a free Macintosh support site.

Mailing Lists

Mailing lists are excellent sources of information, and they have an advantage over Web pages. You don't have to visit a page to get information; it's delivered to your email account. Mailing lists also provide you the opportunity to get help from other knowledgeable Mac users (many of whom live for the opportunity to either help a user in need or show off their superior knowledge):

- **support.info.apple.com/support/supportoptions/lists.html**—This Web page allows you to subscribe to several mailing lists sponsored by Apple, including Information Alley, press releases, developer news, and software updates.

- **info-mac.starnine.com/**—Subscribe to the Info-Mac digest.

- **Majordomo@cc.gatech.edu**—Mac Wizards (post questions for difficult problems and receive an answer in about a day). Send an email to **Majordomo@cc.gatech.edu** and in the body of the message type "subscribe mac-wizard *YOUR NAME*".

- **LISTSERV@LISTSERV.UTA.EDU**—IO MUG (a worldwide Mac Users Group). Send a message to **listserv@listserv.uta.edu** and in the body of the message type "subscribe IO-MUG *YOUR NAME*".

- **lyris@clio.lyris.net**—MAC-L (a mailing list for discussing Mac issues and information). Send a message to **lyris@clio.lyris.net** and in the body of the message type "subscribe Mac-L *YOUR NAME*".

- **majordomo@r8ix.com**—Mac Talk (a mailing list geared toward advanced topics: "newbies" are discouraged). Send a message to **majordomo@r8ix.com** and in the body of the message type "subscribe MacTalk *YOUR NAME*".

- **emod.starnine.com/list-maintenance/Address-List-Editor.html**—Mailing lists for Macintosh Webmasters who use WebSTAR software to run Macintosh Web servers.

- **lists.apple.com**—This site has an index of many mailing lists either run by Apple or discussing Apple hardware or software. There are literally hundreds of mailing lists that may discuss a topic of interest to you.

Newsgroups

Newsgroups are discussion boards. Users post messages which are freely viewable by other newsgroup users. Most of these newsgroups are in a hierarchy that is accepted by most news servers. The **comp** area of Usenet (the term for the collection of these newsgroups) is devoted to computing discussions. These groups discuss Macintosh issues, both software- and hardware-related. You must use special software applications called *newsreaders* to view these groups and your ISP must have access to or maintain its own news server. You can download newsreaders from software archives. The newsgroups are:

- **comp.sys.mac.advocacy**—The Macintosh computer, compared to other platforms.

- **comp.sys.mac.announce**—Announcements for Mac users (moderated).

- **comp.sys.mac.apps**—Macintosh applications.

- **comp.sys.mac.comm**—Macintosh communications.

- **comp.sys.mac.databases**—Macintosh database systems.

- **comp.sys.mac.digest**—Macintosh information and uses, but no programs (moderated).

- **comp.sys.mac.games**—Games on the Macintosh (a large hierarchy exists within the **mac.games** newsgroups).

- **comp.sys.mac.graphics**—Macintosh graphics issues.

- **comp.sys.mac.hardware**—Macintosh hardware issues (a hierarchy exists within the **mac.hardware** group that discusses particular hardware issues).

- **comp.sys.mac.hypercard**—Macintosh Hypercard information and discussion.

- **comp.sys.mac.misc**—General discussions about the Mac.

- **comp.sys.mac.portables**—Discussion about Mac portables.

- **comp.sys.mac.printing**—Mac printing issues.

- **comp.sys.mac.programmer**—Apple programming (a large hierarchy exists under **mac.programmer** to discuss programming specifics).

- **comp.sys.mac.scitech**—Scientific and technical Macintosh uses.

- **comp.sys.mac.system**—Macintosh system software.

- **comp.sys.mac.wanted**—Items wanted for the Mac.

- **misc.forsale.computers.mac**—Macintosh-related computer items for sale.

User Groups

User groups are groups of people who join together to discuss a particular application, platform, or functions (such as Web servers). Several Mac users groups exist; they usually abbreviate their names to the acronym *MUG (the star being replaced by their geographical location). For example, one of the more famous Mac user groups is the Los Angeles Mac Users Group (LAMUG).

If you would like to locate a user group near you, go to **www.apple.com/ usergroups/** for a listing of Mac users groups. If you don't find one, maybe you should consider starting one in your area.

Glossary

32-bit addressing—Allows a Mac to use more than 8MB of memory. This option must be checked within the Memory Control Panel for System 7.5.3 or earlier to efficiently use large memory blocks.

Accelerator—Additional hardware that is installed when the existing software cannot perform particular functions at an acceptable speed. Graphic and floating-point accelerators are the most common.

Access Privileges—The permissions a user is given to access a particular server, folder, or file.

ADB—(Apple Desktop Bus) The port on the Macintosh that connects peripheral devices, such as a keyboard or mouse.

Adobe Acrobat Reader—A free utility from Adobe that views PDF files. (See also *PDF File*.)

Adobe Type Manager—A commercial utility from Adobe that smoothes screen text.

AIFF—(Audio Interchange File Format) A Windows sound file format that is one of the most flexible formats found on the Internet.

Alias—A small file that references or points to an original file.

Allow—To give access or rights (usually to a server).

America Online—A large commercial Internet provider service.

Analog—Data transmission format that uses wave technology.

Anarchie—A Macintosh archie client (archie clients search file archives).

Animated GIF—A GIF file containing a series of images that appear one-at-a-time in sequence, causing the image to appear as if it is moving and changing. (See also *GIF*.)

Anonymous FTP—The ability to log on to a file archive server without an account.

Anti-aliasing—The effect of removing jagged edges from images and fonts. This is also a new feature of Mac OS 8.5.

Appearance—The Control Panel that you can use to alter the look and sound of the Desktop interface.

Apple Computer Corp.—The company responsible for the Mac OS and the Macintosh computer.

Apple Guide—A component of the online help program that is activated by certain links. It takes the user step-by-step through various system tasks.

Apple Menu—A menu represented by the small colorful apple that you can customize. Applications or aliases placed in the Apple menu execute when selected and folders show items.

AppleCD Audio Player—The desk accessory that controls audio CDs, including song order and volume.

AppleEvents—The Mac OS's method of interapplication communication.

AppleScript—The high-level scripting and programming utility included with the Mac OS that allows you to control functions within both the system and certain applications.

AppleShare—Networking services included in the Mac OS that allow you to access other Macintosh computers, printers, and servers.

AppleTalk—A networking protocol developed and included in the Macintosh operating system.

AppleVision—Product name for the better Apple monitors.

Application—A file that, when launched, enables you or the computer to perform a task.

Application Menu—The menu located in the top-right corner of the screen. The Application Menu lists all applications running and allows you to hide particular programs. In Mac OS 8.5, you can "tear off" the Application Menu and drag it to any part of the Desktop.

Application Switcher—The term for an application menu that has been torn from the menu bar.

ARA—(Apple Remote Access) The modem software that allows a Macintosh to access other Macintosh computers remotely.

Archie—A utility that can perform searches on FTP file archives.

ASCII—(American Standard Code for Information Interchange) The standard character set for plain-text files.

Assistants—Programs included with Mac OS 8.5 that automate the system and Internet configuration.

Automated Tasks—A folder under the Apple menu that contains ready-to-use AppleScript applications.

AVI—(Audio Video Interleave) An audio and video compression format for the Windows operating system.

Background Application—An application that launches and runs in the background without interfering with applications running in the foreground.

Backward Compatibility—Refers to an application that includes the capability to manage data from a previous version of the software.

Balloon Help—The component of the online help application that provides quick descriptions of particular icons or menus in the format of speech balloons.

Bandwidth—The amount of data a network can carry. Bandwidth is usually defined in bits per second.

Base Directory—A Web server's default directory; also called the root directory.

BBEdit—A text editor from Bare Bones Software that includes HTML and programming components.

Binary—The primary building block for the storage of data; it represents data as a series of ones and zeros.

BinHex—A method of encoding files, especially mail attachments. BinHex is used most often with Macintosh files to protect the integrity of the resource and data fork during Internet transmission.

Bitmap—A method of representing an image or font by filling squares or pixels. This often results in an image or a font with jagged edges. This was an early format used for images and printing, before PostScript was released.

Bitstream—The amount of data that can pass through for processing.

Bookmarks—Netscape Navigator term for a list of sites that a user either frequently visits or wants to remember as a reference. Internet Explorer refers to this list as Favorites.

Browser Cache—The amount of hard-disk space reserved for storing images, text, and previously visited links when using a Web browser. Caching is used to decrease the time it takes to load a Web page.

Buffer—A portion of memory reserved for storing data.

Buttons—A view within the Mac OS that changes the icons to buttons, allowing one-click launching or opening of documents, applications, or media.

CD-R—A format of compact disk on which data can be written if the user has the appropriate drive.

CD-ROM—A compact disk that can store large amounts of data and is read-only, thus protecting the contents from inappropriate changes. Most software today is released on CD-ROM. Also often referred to as *CD*.

cdevs—A Control Panel device. This is the creator code for the file.

CGI—(Common Gateway Interface). A standard for sending data to and from a Web server to another application running on the server.

Chooser—A utility found under the Apple menu that allows you to access other computers or printers.

CISC—(Complex Instruction Set Computer) A chip that stores a large variety of complex instructions. This format of processing is found in the Motorola 68040 and Intel X86 and Pentium chips.

Clean Install—To install a new system folder rather than update an existing one. If you are having problems attempting to update a system, you may want to perform a clean installation of the operating system.

Client—A computer that requests information or services from another computer, usually a server.

Client/Server—Describes the relationship between computers that are requesting services of each other.

Clipboard—The temporary buffer that stores copied or cut information, saving it until you place new information on the clipboard or turn off or restart the computer.

Clipping—A file that contains any information that has been selected and dragged to a different location. You can then drag the icon of the clipping into a new document or application. Not all applications support clippings.

Close Box—The small box on the top-left corner of a window in Mac OS 8.5 that closes the window.

CMYK—(Cyan Magenta Yellow Key) The system used by printers to produce color output. The K also stands for blacK. K was selected for this acronym so that it didn't conflict with RGB.

Collapse Box—The small box in the top-right corner of a window that hides the window contents and displays only the title bar.

Color Picker—Launched when you select Other from a color-listing menu. Color Picker contains several ways to choose custom colors.

ColorSync—The software used by Apple to match the color on a monitor screen with the color output of a printer. Because the two systems use different methods for color reproduction, the results often do not match. ColorSync helps reduce color conflict.

Command key—The key located next to the spacebar on most Macintosh keyboards. The Command key is used heavily in keyboard shortcut combinations (for example, Command+Q = quit).

Comments—Additional information about a file or folder that you enter or access by selecting Get Info from the File menu while you are operating within the Finder.

Compression—The method or algorithm of reorganizing the data bit structure of a file to shrink its size. This saves disk space or reduces file transmission time.

CompuServe—A large commercial Internet service provider that also includes proprietary database access.

Computer Name—Entered in the File Sharing Control Panel, this is the name the computer broadcasts over an AppleTalk network.

Conseil Européen pour la Recherche Nucléaire (CERN)—The European Laboratory for Particle Physics, where the World Wide Web was developed.

Contextual Menu—A menu that is accessed by holding down the Control key and clicking the mouse. Depending upon the application or view, the menu may have different options. Not all applications support contextual menus.

Control Panels—A collection of customizable extensions that control the function or look of the system.

Control Strip—A small strip, usually located at the bottom of the screen, that contains buttons for quick access to different applications. Most of the buttons access control panels. If the strip is not visible, you may need to go to the Control Strip Control Panel to make it visible.

Convergence—Refers to the overlapping of red, green, and blue signals to produce a sharp image. If convergence is off, monitor output appears blurred or you may see rainbow effects around the edges of images on the screen.

Crayon Picker—A method of selecting colors via crayon images. Crayon Picker is found when you access the Color Picker application by electing to choose a color.

Creator Code—A four-digit identification that indicates what application created the file. You can use this code while conducting searches with the Find utility.

Cursors—The on-screen graphical representation, usually in the shape of an arrow, that indicates the active selection point. The cursor can also be in the shape of a watch, counting hand, or insertion point.

Daemon—An application that lies dormant until the conditions are met that cause it to execute or become active.

Data Fork—Part of the file that contains the file contents. Depending upon the file type, the data fork can be read on multiple platforms.

Decompression—The act of interpreting compression information, allowing the file to expand to original state and size.

Dedicated Server—A computer reserved for specific server applications. A dedicated server should not double as a workstation.

Defragmentation—The act of optimizing a disk by rearranging the files to remove the gaps between them.

Degauss—The act of correcting monitor screen distortions caused by magnetic interference from other devices, including monitors placed too close together, left on for a long period, or moved while powered up. Newer monitors degauss automatically when they are turned off and on; older monitors have a switch in the back usually located next to the power button.

Desk Accessories—Utilities included in the Mac OS that perform simple system functions. Examples of desk accessories are the Audio CD Player, Stickies, Notepad, and Scrapbook. Desk Accessories are usually found on the Apple menu.

Desktop—Refers to the background area where hard drives, removable media, and the trashcan are displayed, as well as any other icons a user places on it. The Finder is responsible for displaying the Desktop and its contents.

Desktop Printing—The method of placing printer icons on the Desktop and allowing you to access the printer immediately for print job information, as well as print to printers other than the one selected in the Chooser.

Disk Cache—A portion of RAM allocated to store frequently used commands, information, or functions. In Mac OS 8.5, the disk cache is set in the Memory Control Panel.

Disk First Aid—An Apple utility that performs checks on media, including hard drives, zip disks, and floppies. Disk First Aid can repair many problems with disks. You may be able to fix other problems that are beyond its capability by using a third-party utility, such as TechTool Pro or Norton's Disk Doctor.

DNS—(Domain Name System) A database system that translates numeric Internet addresses into user-friendly names (for example, 123.45.67.89 would be my.computer.domain.com).

DOS—(Disk Operating System) The familiar name for the command-line operating system used to operate PCs. There are various flavors, including MS-DOS, PC DOS, and others.

Dotted Octet—The naming convention for IP numbers represented by four groups of numbers that contain one, two, or three numbers in each group.

Double-Scroll Arrows—A new window feature in Mac OS 8.5 that can place an up and a down scroll arrow together at the bottom or bottom and top of a scroll bar pane.

Drag and drop—The ability to select an object, drag it, and drop it onto a new location such as a new folder or disk.

Drag Lock—The ability to view hidden areas of the window by holding down the Control key, grabbing an area of the window, and moving the entire pane. This is a new feature of Mac OS 8.5.

Drive Setup—A utility released by Apple for formatting and partitioning hard drives. Later versions of Drive Setup include the capability to format a disk with the new Macintosh Extended format.

Drivers—Programs that run in the system and enable the computer to perform functions, as well as talk to peripheral devices such as printers, scanners, and external drives.

Droplets—Mini-applications created in AppleScript that perform certain functions. Examples of droplets are included in the Automated Tasks folder located under the Apple menu.

DVD-ROM—The next generation in removable optical disk media. DVD-ROMs can hold more than double the capacity of a CD-ROM disk.

Dynamic Data Exchange—A communication protocol in a client/server model that exchanges data between programs. This is especially used in the Windows operating system.

Easy Access—A control panel that contains options for customizing the Mac OS for users with special needs.

Easy Open—Also known as Mac OS Easy Open. This control panel performs file translations and can be configured to included new formats.

Eject Disk—When selected, ejects the media selected, such as a floppy disk or CD-ROM. In previous systems, the Eject Disk menu option would eject the disk but keep its contents in memory.

Email—The generic term for the electronic exchange of messages.

Email Address—The unique address that allows electronic messages to be sent from one address to another.

Empty Trash—Found under the Special menu, this command empties the contents of the trashcan. Files within the trashcan are not deleted until you select Empty Trash.

Emulator—An application that runs one environment on top of another. Macs utilize emulator programs to run Windows, DOS, and Unix.

Energy Saver—The control panel that configures when the computer will put the system to sleep. Energy Saver also has settings for scheduling routine system shutdown and startup.

Erase Disk—Found under the Special menu, this command reformats any formattable media you select.

Ethernet Network—A popular Local Area Network that transfers data via several network protocols, including TCP/IP, IPX, AppleTalk, and NetBEUI.

Eudora—A popular Internet email package that uses the POP and IMAP protocols.

Extended Desktop—Increasing the Desktop space by using two monitors instead of one. This feature requires that an additional video card be installed.

Extensions—Programs that increase the functionality or repair or improve parts of the Mac OS.

Extensions Manager—Control panel that controls the loading and unloading of control panels, extensions, and startup and shutdown items.

EZ Drive—A Syquest removable media drive.

FAT—(File Allocation Table) Refers to the database on a PC disk that keeps information on all files saved on the disk.

Favorites—In Mac OS 8.5, the list of commonly accessed servers and Web sites. This term is also used in Internet Explorer.

Fetch—The Macintosh FTP tool from Dartmouth that allows users to retrieve and place files on file archives.

File Exchange—The Control Panel that controls file translation and extension mapping.

File Sharing—Allows other Macintosh computers to access the user's computer. File Sharing is activated from the File Sharing Control Panel.

Find By Content—A new feature of the Sherlock utility included in Mac OS 8.5 that allows the searching of file contents. Find By Content can also index drives for routine searching.

Finder—The part of the system that opens and closes windows, displays the Desktop, and keeps a directory of the files on a disk.

Firewall—One method of defending a network from outside hackers. Firewalls can also refer to a configuration to limit a user's access to the Internet from within a network.

FireWire—A new high-speed serial bus that supports the transfer of large amounts of data. FireWire supports digital devices such as digital video cameras.

Floppy Disk—Refers to the 3.25" removable disks. Floppy disks can be double density (800K) or high density (1.44MB).

Folder—An item used to organize files and data. Folders have no size in themselves, but act as containers and dividers for other files.

Fonts—A set of images representing letters in a character set.

Force Quit—The act of forcing an application that has ceased to respond to shut down.

Form—A Web page with fields that allow you to input information to the server.

Fragmentation—Gaps in a drive's storage system. Fragmentation is caused by the act of saving, changing, and deleting files.

Frames—Special Web pages that are written to display several HTML files at once.

Freeware—Software that is available without charge. Freeware is usually found at public file archive sites such as **www.download.com/**.

FTP—(File Transfer Protocol) The method used for transferring files over the Internet.

Gateway—A device that connects networks using different protocols.

Geometry—The section of the Monitors and Sound Control Panel that controls advanced features of AppleVision monitors.

Get Info—Provides information about a selected object including the size, data created and modified, and path.

GIF—(Graphics Interchange Format) The image compression method developed by CompuServe and denoted by the .gif extension. GIF is also a file format that is limited to 256 colors.

Gopher—A document retrieval system that has been largely superseded by the World Wide Web.

Graphing Calculator—A desk accessory included with Mac OS 8.5 that visually displays mathematical formulas and equations.

Grid Spacing—Activating an invisible grid within Finder. Grid spacing grabs icons and places them in the appropriate space if the icon is moved.

Groups—A part of the Users and Groups Control Panel that allows the creation of lists of approved users. The lists can then be selected when sharing an item.

GUI—(Graphical User Interface) This commonly refers to the front end of any operating system that utilizes images rather than a command line prompt.

Hackers—Persons who attempt unauthorized and often illegal access to a server or system.

Header—Information in an email message that includes the path of the message and special identifiers. Much of this information is hidden unless you activate the option to view full headers.

Help Viewer—The revamped online help system included with Mac OS 8.5. The Help Viewer now has a browser-like interface, rather than relying completely on AppleGuide.

Hierarchical submenus—Menus that branch out from a menu selection and can often extend several layers. The Apple menu supports submenus.

Home Page—The main or index page at a Web site. Other pages at the site are accessed via links from the home page.

Host—A machine containing services that it makes available to other computers.

Hot Swappable—The ability to switch hardware while the system is enabled. Several Apple PowerBooks have hot swappable CD and floppy drives.

HTML—(Hypertext Markup Language) The language used to write hypertext documents that can be displayed by Web browsers.

HTTP—(Hypertext Transfer Protocol) The method for transferring Web documents between servers and clients.

Hub—A device that connects computers to a network.

Hyperlinks—Areas of text within an HTML document that access another document when clicked or selected.

Icon—A graphic used to represent a file or document.

Image Map—A graphic within a Web page with areas assigned to hyperlinks.

IMAP— (Internet Message Access Protocol) Email protocol that allows a client to access mail stored on a server. IMAP differs from POP in that messages are stored on a server instead of locally.

Inactive Window—A window that is visible, but lies in the background.

Index—A file containing information about all the files on a volume. Indexing is used heavily in the Find By Content section of the Sherlock utility.

Infrared—A specialized technology that utilizes a frequency below visible light to transfer information. Infrared is the primary component of some wireless networks.

INITs—Refers to extensions and control panels that load within the system.

Inline Image—An image displayed in an HTML document.

Insertion Point—The cursor commonly seen in word processing programs. It is sometimes referred to as the "I" bar because of its shape.

Internet—A collection (or network) of networks connected by routers. The Internet refers to the largest collection of networks.

Internet Config—The utility that houses user Internet preferences such as email address, SMTP server, news host, and so on. In Mac OS 8.5, Internet Config has become part of the Internet Control Panel.

Internet Explorer—The Web browser released by Microsoft.

Internet Service Provider—Also know as an ISP, provides Internet access to customers, usually for a fee.

Internet Setup Utility—A program included with Mac OS 8.5 that asks basic questions of a user and uses the information to configure the computer for Internet and network access.

Intranet—Term used for a network that provides services to its users similar to those found on the Internet without necessarily being connected to it.

IP—(Internet Protocol) The session layer of the TCP/IP protocol.

IP Address—The unique number assigned to a computer that is on the Internet. An IP number allows the computer to access other Internet services.

IP Name—The user-friendly name that is bundled with the IP number.

IPX—(Internetwork Packet eXchange) A protocol used by Novell to provide clients access to a server.

IrDA—(Infrared Data Association) Refers to the infrared industry standard for infrared data transmission.

IRTalk—The AppleTalk infrared data transmission protocol.

Java Applet—An attachment in a World Wide Web document that performs simple Java actions. Most browsers restrict what Java applets can do for security reasons.

JavaScript—A programming language developed by Sun Microsystems that allows Web browsers to handle complex operations.

Jaz Drive—A removable media drive manufactured by Iomega that can handle cartridges in one and two gigabyte sizes.

JPEG—(Joint Photographic Experts Group) An algorithm that compresses images and is commonly used for photographic images (be warned that JPEG files degrade after repeated saves).

Kaleidoscope—A third-party utility that provides a way to change the look of the Mac OS. Some of the Kaleidoscope themes work with the Mac OS 8.5 Appearance Control Panel.

Key Caps—A desk accessory that provides a keyboard-like interface for seeing all characters in a font set.

L2 Cache—A protected area of memory that increases the system performance.

Label—An option to assign a color and organizational name to an icon. You can customize the label names and colors.

LAN—(Local Area Network) Refers to a small network of computers.

LaserWriter Bridge—An Apple utility that allows a computer with a locally attached LaserWriter to still run the AppleTalk protocol.

Launcher—A control panel that contains buttons for single-click launching of programs. You can customize the Launcher window.

LocalTalk—An implementation of AppleTalk that allows Macintosh computers and printers to communicate.

Location Manager—A control panel that allows you to keep different network configurations based upon your location. Examples include a profile for work using an assigned IP address and remote access at home using an Internet Service Provider.

Locked File—A file that has the Lock option enabled from the Get Info window.

Low Level Format—A type of format that completely wipes all data from a disk. A low-level format also takes much longer than a standard format.

Mac Clone—A computer that is capable of running the Mac OS, but is not a Macintosh computer.

Mac OS Extended—Refers to the new file format released with Mac OS 8.1 that increases the allocation bits to allow accurate representation of file size.

Mac OS Standard—Term used to describe the normal file allocation format on Macintosh disks.

Mac OS X Server—The operating system developed by Apple that combines the OpenStep and Macintosh operating systems. Mac OS X Server is a server operating system.

MacBinary—A method of file compression that results in a smaller file size than other compression methods.

Macintosh—The name given for the computer models released from the Apple Company.

MacsBug—A debugging utility that allows you to accurately determine what caused a system or application crash. You can also access MacsBug to perform system functions from a command line.

MacTCP—The classic TCP/IP Control Panel that you can configure for Internet access.

Marquee Selection—The term used to describe the box that appears within Finder when the mouse button is held down to perform a click and drag function. Within certain applications such as Photoshop, the selection box appears to move in a marquee fashion.

Memory—The colloquial term for RAM. Memory is measured in megabytes. In OS 8.5, also the Control Panel that controls disk cache and virtual memory options as well as the size of a RAM disk.

Memory Allocation—The amount of memory an application is allowed to use. You can change the allocation amount in the Get Info window.

Menu Blinking—When selected within the General Controls Control Panel, Menu Blinking causes a menu item to flash several times, indicating that the command has been chosen.

Microkernel—Resides between the operating system and the hardware, and forms a layer that translates the communication between the two.

MIME—(Multipurpose Internet Mail Extensions) A method of encoding email attachments.

MkLinux—A Macintosh-compatible version of Linux.

Monitor Calibration Assistant—A utility that correctly configures and calibrates certain monitor models, including the AppleVision brand displays.

Motorola—The manufacturer of the RISC-based processor used in Power Macintosh computers.

Mouse Keys—Set with the Easy Access Control Panel, this option allows you to control the mouse by keys rather than by dragging.

MPEG—(Motion Picture Experts Group) This includes both the organization and the video and audio file format.

MRJ—(Macintosh Runtime for Java) A component of the operating system that allows the execution of Java applets and applications.

Multimedia—The term used to describe files and applications that contain elements of media, including sound and graphics.

Multitasking—The capability of the operating system to run and work with several applications at once.

Native Applications—Used to refer to applications that contain code specifically written for the Power Macintosh.

Navigation Services—The Open and Save dialog boxes in Mac OS 8.5. These have been improved to include server access and a favorites list.

Netscape Navigator—The Web browser from Netscape Communications Corporation.

Network—The generic term used to refer to computers that are connected and communicate with each other.

Network Browser—The new utility from Mac OS 8.5 that allows you to browse the network in the same way that you browse your hard drive. You can connect to servers from within the browser and also keep a list of favorite servers.

Network Identity—A method for giving network devices unique names, including IP numbers and Ethernet numbers.

Network Interface Card—The card that allows a computer to connect to a network. Network cards usually run the Ethernet protocol.

Network Time Server—Used by the Date and Time Control Panel to keep the system clock accurate.

Newsgroup—A discussion forum on Usenet where messages are posted and accessed.

NeXT—The computer developed by the NeXT Corporation that ran the OpenStep operating system. The OpenStep technology was purchased by Apple and developed as part of the Mac OS X Server operating system.

Node—A computer or device on a network.

Norton Utilities—A third-party disk-management utility from Symantec that can perform disk defragmentation, disk repair, and recover deleted files.

NotePad—The desk accessory that can hold text information that you input.

Novell—The makers of NetWare, a popular server operating system.

NTP Time Servers—(Network Time Protocol Time Servers) Publicly accessible servers that can be used to keep the system clock accurate. The servers are selected in the Date and Time Control Panel.

OLE—(Object Linking and Embedding) Utilized heavily with Microsoft products, it allows the applications to share and link information with documents.

Open Transport—The networking protocol currently used by Mac OS 8.5. Open Transport includes Ethernet and modem connectivity functions and uses AppleTalk, PPP, and TCP/IP network protocols.

OpenStep—The operating system purchased by Apple and incorporated into the Rhapsody operating system.

OS/2—The operating system released from IBM.

Owner Name—The setting with the File Sharing Control Panel that determines the owner login account.

Packet—A unit of data that is transferred across a network.

PANTONE®—A commercial color indexing system that allows the precise reproduction of particular colors. PANTONE® is used in the printing process.

PC Coprocessor Card—A third-party card that allows a Macintosh computer to simultaneously run a PC operating system such as Linux, Windows, and DOS.

PC Disk—The term used to describe a floppy disk that has been formatted for a PC.

PC Exchange—The portion of the File Exchange Control Panel that allows PC disks to be mounted within the Mac OS Desktop.

PCI Card—(Peripheral Component Interconnect Card) A hardware device that plugs into the PCI slot on desktop computers. Common PCI cards are video and sound capture devices.

PCMCIA Card—Hardware devices used primarily in mobile computers that provide modem, Ethernet, and storage solutions.

PDD Files—Printer Description documents that contain information about certain printers. Without the correct PDD file, you cannot take advantage of the special functions of the printer.

PDF File—(Portable Document Format) Files that were created by using Adobe Acrobat, these files can be viewed on multiple platforms, including Macintosh and PCs (in Windows). These files cannot be modified without specialized software, but they can be easily viewed by using Adobe's freeware application, Acrobat Reader.

PICT—An Apple graphics format that can be opened by most image editing applications as well as SimpleText.

Plain text—Files that contain only ASCII characters.

Platform—Refers to the type of operating system that runs on a computer.

Plug-in—Special applications that run within an application and provide additional functionality. Web browsers use plug-ins to allow special functions to run, including streaming video and QuickTime movies.

POP—(Post Office Protocol) An email protocol that keeps mail on a server until the user accesses the mail via a POP email client. Mail is moved to the local machine and managed, unless you choose to keep a copy on the server.

Pop-up Menu—A menu that is only viewable if you click on the menu name.

PostScript—A technology developed by Adobe that radically improved printing. Prior to PostScript, printed images and especially fonts produced jagged edges. PostScript enabled the smooth printing of text and images.

Power Macintosh—Refers to the line of Macintosh computers using the RISC processor (also known as the PowerPC chip).

PowerBook—The line of portable computers from Apple.

PowerPC—Computers that use a RISC-based processor.

PPP—(Point-to-Point Protocol) Network protocol used over a modem line that allows the computer to connect to the Internet.

PRAM—(Parameter RAM) A small memory in a Macintosh with a battery power supply that stores system information, including the Desktop pattern, screen resolution, system alert sound, and so on, when the computer is not running.

Preferences—Files stored within the System folder that contain settings for an application.

Print Queue—The holding space that lines up print jobs in order of print submission. The print jobs stay within the queue until the printer is ready to print the file.

Print Spooling—The act of preparing and submitting a file to a print queue for printing.

PrintMonitor—The utility used to monitor the progress of print jobs. If the system is using Desktop printing, then PrintMonitor is disabled.

Program Linking—A setting in the File Sharing Control Panel that allows other Macintosh computers to run applications from the host machine.

Proportional Scroll Boxes—The tab within a scroll bar that changes size depending upon how much of the contents of the window are visible. Proportional scroll boxes or "thumb tabs" are a new feature of Mac OS 8.5.

Protocols—A standard for the transmission of data over a network.

Proxy Server—A server that is configured to allow computers not on a particular network to access protected servers and information.

Put Away—The menu option within the Finder under the File menu that dismounts and ejects a disk.

QuickDraw—The technology used by the Mac OS to draw the graphical user interface.

QuickTime—Apple's standard for video.

QuickTime VR—A function of QuickTime that allows a series of still images to be interfaced into a seamless picture, creating the illusion of three-dimensional imaging.

RAM—(Random Access Memory) The hardware within the computer that stores the system, as well as any information that is launched or input. This storage is temporary and the data input must be transferred to a storage device to be kept permanently.

RAM Disk—A portion of the RAM set aside as a storage device. RAM disks are used most commonly on mobile computers to increase battery life.

Recalibrate—Used with high-quality monitors to correct and optimize the color display.

Remote Access—Any method used to access a server while not directly connected to it. Remote Access most commonly refers to dial-up access.

Removable Media—Any of the various storage media that are not installed and stored within the computer casing. Removable media include floppy disks, Zip, Jazz, CD-ROMs, DVD-ROMs, and removable hard drives.

Repeater—An unintelligent device that repeats any network signal it intercepts.

ResEdit—A utility that you can use to edit the resource fork of a file or application.

Resize Handle—The small box located at the bottom right of a window that allows you to drag the window to the desired size.

Resolution—The number of pixels displayed in an inch of screen area. Larger numbers produce larger Desktops and smaller icons.

Resource Fork—The part of a file that contains information relevant only to the Mac OS, such as the creator type and icon (however, files can be opened without a resource fork). Resource forks for applications contain information governing how the program should run, Therefore, applications cannot run without a resource fork.

Restart—The one-step act of bringing down and then relaunching the Mac OS. Restart is also called a warm reboot.

RGB—(Red Green Blue) The color system that is used for screen color reproduction.

RISC—(Reduced Instruction Set Computer) Refers to a type of processor that contains limited system instructions allowing for faster computing with a cooler chip. RISC processors are used in the Power Macintosh and PowerPC computers.

Router—A device that forwards network traffic between networks.

Scrapbook—The desk accessory that stores any information pasted into it including text, images, and sound files.

Script—A file that contains instructions for a system or application. When executed, the instructions within the script are performed.

Scroll Arrow—Small tabs at the bottom and top of a scroll bar that contain triangles, which allow the navigation of a window where not all of the content can be seen within the window.

SCSI—(Small Computer System Interface) A small chain of devices that contains a unique number between zero and seven. SCSI devices include hard drives, scanners, Zip drives, and external hard drives. Pronounced "Scuzzy."

SCSI ID Conflict—A situation involving the devices on a SCSI chain where two devices have been assigned the same number.

Search Engine—A Web site that allows a user to search the Internet. These sites use different methods for searching and cataloging the World Wide Web.

Server—A computer that provides information or applications to clients that are running on other computers.

Shared Folder—A folder that has been configured to allow other computers on the network to access the contents of the folder.

Shared Libraries—Common code libraries shared by multiple applications allowing programs to use the code without re-creating it.

Shareware—Software that has been written by developers and released with the request for a nominal fee. Shareware programs either rely on the honor system or put limits within the application until the software has been purchased.

Sherlock—Also referred to as the Find utility. Utility included in Mac OS 8.5 that searches a disk. Search parameters can include the file name, size, date created or modified, creator type, and so on (See also *Find By Content.*)

Show Original—A menu option within Finder under the File menu that shows the original document or file for an alias. The alias must be selected to run this menu option.

Simple Finder—A setting within the Finder preferences that displays only the basic menus in the Finder.

Simple Player—A sound and video playback utility.

SimpleText—The text editing application included on all Mac OS systems as well as installer programs. Files saved in SimpleText are in plain-text format.

Sleep Mode—The act of ceasing the activity of the system without shutting it down entirely. Sleep mode is used most often on mobile computers.

SLIP—(Serial Line Interface Protocol) A networking protocol often used over modem connections.

Slow Keys—A setting in the Easy Access Control Panel that decreases the sensitivity of the keyboard, causing the computer to take longer to register a keystroke. This eliminates repeating characters for users with special needs.

SMNP—(Simple Network Administration Protocol) A standard network management protocol included with Mac OS 8.5 that manages network nodes such as computers, routers, and other devices in a simplified way.

SMTP Gateway—(Simple Mail Transfer Protocol Gateway) A machine that processes email to be delivered to other mail systems.

Sneakernet—Colloquial term that refers to the act of manually handing a file on removable disk to another user.

SoftPC—The emulation software from Insignia that allows you to run DOS from within the Mac OS.

Speech—The capability of the Macintosh to speak or read information back to the user. With additional software, the user can speak commands to the computer.

Speech Manager—The control panel that controls the settings for the speech abilities of the Macintosh.

Spring-Loaded Folders—A system function initiated during the act of moving or copying a file within Finder. During the dragging process, when the mouse is held over a folder or storage device for a short time, the folder spontaneously opens, and the process can continue until the end of the hierarchy has been reached.

SSL—(Secure Sockets Layer) The protocol designed for the secure transfer of information between the client and server.

Startup Disk—The device selected to boot the computer.

Startup Items—Files or aliases that are placed in the Startup Items folder. These items launch when the system is started.

Stationary—A file format used for creating templates.

Steve Jobs—The co-developer of the first personal computer. Steve Jobs was also a co-founder of Apple computer and is currently Interim CEO of Apple Computer.

Stickies—A desk accessory that is a utility for storing text information in small colored windows. Information stored in Sticky notes is kept even when the application has been closed.

Sticky Keys—A setting in the Easy Access Control Panel that increases the sensitivity of the keyboard.

Streaming—A method of distributing video and audio so that you can begin listening to and viewing the file contents while the file is still downloading. Streaming is also used for live Web events to maintain a constant connection with the multimedia server.

StuffIt—A utility from Aladdin software that compresses files so that they are reduced in size.

StuffIt Expander—A free utility from Aladdin software that decompresses files not only compressed with StuffIt, but also with MacBinary, BinHex, and Compact Pro. StuffIt Expander is also available for the Windows platform.

Subnet Mask—Used to identify the portion of the IP number that corresponds to the network address. Subnet masks are also determined by the class of the IP address.

Suffix Mapping—The act of programming the File Exchange Control Panel to open certain applications when files with a particular extension are opened.

SuperDrive—Refers to the floppy drive installed in most Macintosh and Mac clone computers. SuperDrives are characterized by their capability to eject a floppy disk without using an eject button.

Syntax—The structure of the strings in a scripting language.

System—The file that contains resources necessary to run the computer and other applications.

System Folder—The folder on a startup disk that contains the information for launching the operating system as well as extensions, preferences, fonts and other components of the operating system.

System Heap—An area of RAM set aside for components such as fonts and desk accessories.

System Requirements—A list of system specifications that must be met before an application or program will run on a particular computer.

Tags—Refers to text enclosed in brackets in an HTML file that gives instructions to the browser for handling and displaying the file.

TCP/IP—(Transmission Control Protocol over Internet Protocol) A protocol used over Ethernet networks to transport and encapsulate data packets. TCP/IP is the primary network protocol of the Internet.

Tear Away Menu—A special function of certain menus that allows you to drag items from the menu bar to any location on the Desktop. The Application menu, for example, has this functionality. When torn away, it *becomes* the Application Switcher.

TechTool Pro—A commercial disk-management utility from Techworks that can repair disks beyond the capability of Disk First Aid.

Telnet—An application that accesses a remote server and initiates a terminal connection.

Templates—Specialized files that are saved with certain data intact but are protected so that you are prompted to choose a different name for the file.

TIFF—(Tagged Image File Format) An image file format for image bitmaps.

Timbuktu—Commercial software that allows one computer to control another computer remotely.

Title Bar—The top portion of a window that contains the title of the disk or folder.

Token Ring—A networking protocol developed by IBM.

Trackpad—A pointing device that moves the cursor around the screen by gliding a finger over the surface. Most PowerBooks contain a trackpad.

Trash—The container (indicated by a small "garbage can" icon) on the Desktop that stores items dragged to it until they are removed or deleted. Also referred to as a "trashcan"

TrueType—A font technology originally developed in competition to PostScript fonts. Unlike PostScript technology, TrueType is limited to fonts.

Unix—A powerful and flexible operating system. The Unix OS includes the capability to be a server, and it provides protected memory and a very stable environment.

URL—(Uniform Resource Locator) Used to specify the location of an object on the World Wide Web.

USB—(Universal Serial Bus) Refers to devices that can be connected to USB ports while the system is still active. The iMac computer employs USB ports for the keyboard and mouse, as well as other peripheral devices as they become available.

Usenet—An organization of discussion areas organized into groups. Messages are posted to Usenet groups and are available for anyone to read who has the appropriate software.

User Mode—Classes of access to certain extensions, such as the TCP/IP Control Panel. Administrative access can set privileges so that a user cannot change sensitive areas of the control panel.

Video Mirroring—On a computer with two monitors attached, the act of displaying the same image or Desktop on both monitors.

Video Player—A desk accessory that displays video and television images. Additional hardware must be installed to use this utility.

Views—Different methods of displaying the information in a window. Folder contents can be viewed by such methods as by icon or list.

Virtual Memory—Reserving a part of the hard drive to function as memory. It is often necessary to enable virtual memory for the system to function efficiently, although some programs such as game applications may generate errors or slow down when virtual memory is activated.

Virtual PC—Emulation software from Connectix that allows the Mac OS to run any application that will run on an Intel Pentium II chip within the operating system in an application window.

Volumes—Often refers to divisions in a storage device that has been partitioned.

VRAM—(Video Random Access Memory) Refers to memory allocated for the video operations of the system. Expanded VRAM allows the display of thousands or millions of colors in multiple resolutions.

WAN—(Wide Area Network) Describes a large network inclusive of smaller Local Area Networks.

WAV—An audio file type used most often in the Windows operating system.

Web—Colloquial term used to describe the World Wide Web.

Web Browser—An application used to retrieve content and information from the World Wide Web.

Web Sharing—A function of the Mac OS that allows you to set up a computer as a Web server.

Windows 95, 98, NT 4.0—GUI operating systems developed and released by Microsoft. MS Windows and its variations are the most popular operating systems running on computers today.

Windows NT Server—An installation of Windows NT 4.0 that provides server access and applications for remote clients.

WindowShade—The action of decreasing a window so that only the title bar is shown. This action can occur by either clicking the collapse box or double-clicking on the title bar.

WorldScript—Unifies script-specific behavior as defined by tables in the system resources.

WWW—(World Wide Web) The term for the network of computers sharing information via the HTTP protocol.

Y2K—Colloquial term for the year 2000 when many computers as well as devices with an internal calendar may fail. An application or operating system that will not malfunction on January 1, 2000 is considered Y2K-compliant. The Mac OS is completely compliant.

Zip Drive—An external disk drive that uses 100MB disks. Zip drives are manufactured by Iomega.

Zones—Refers to AppleTalk zones or the logical grouping of computers into small networks. AppleTalk zones are often determined by routers on the network.

Zoom Box—The small box in the top right of a window that expands or shrinks the window to display the contents.

Index

Numbers

3D objects, 264, 288
3DMF format, 264
5xxx/6xxx Tester, 106, 118
8.3 naming convention, 295
10Base-2 cables, 336-337
10Base-T cables, 336-337

Symbols

• (bullet), controlling launch order, 41
~ (tilde), controlling launch order, 41

A

AAUI (Apple Attachment Unit Interface), 359
Abnormal endings. *See* crashes; freezes; hangs.
About This Computer
    definition, 36, 173
    displaying available resources, 42-43
    monitoring memory, 501-502
    performance monitoring, 490-491, 499
About This Macintosh. *See* About This
    Computer; MATM (More About
    This Macintosh).
Accelerator cards, 105
Acme Contextual Menu Manager, 434-435
ACTION Files!, 100-101
ActiveX, 444-445, 458
Address blocks, 674
Administrative features. *See* system
    administrator features.
Administrator mode control panel, 475-477
Administrator window, 465
ADSL (Asymmetric Digital
    Subscriber Loop), 358, 360
AFS volumes
    remote, mounting locally, 470

After Dark, 471
AIMS (Apple Internet Mail Server). *See* EIMS
    (Eudora Internet Mail Server).
Alias icons
    arrow on, 8-9
    identifying, 8-9
    illustration, 11
    italicized labels, 8
Aliases
    creating, 157-158, 543
    definition, 142
    finding the original, 543
    fixing broken, 158
    selecting a new original, 544
    visual cues to, 10-11
Anchors, 675
Animations, Java script sample, 449-450
Animator, Java script sample, 449-450
Anonymous FTP, 404
AppDisk, 173, 187
Appearance control panel, 16-17
Appearance Manager, 6, 12-13, 76-81
Appearances. *See also* Desktop; themes.
    changing, utility for, 16
    definition, 17
Apple Applet Runner, 448-449
Apple Attachment Unit Interface (AAUI), 359
Apple Data Detectors, 433-434
Apple DOS cards, 320
Apple Extras folder, 58
Apple Internet Mail Server (AIMS). *See* EIMS
    (Eudora Internet Mail Server).
Apple LAN Utility, 560-561
Apple menu, configuring
    BeHierarchic utility, 71-73
    GoMac utility, 74-76
Apple Menu Items folder, 33
Apple Network Administrator Toolkit
    definition, 471
    At Ease for Workgroups, 557-559

B

C

N

O

P

U

V

X

X-ray exposure, and PowerBooks, 212

Y

Y2K problem, 469-470
Yank utility, 117

Z

Zapping the PRAM, 29, 529, 534-535, 537-538
ZapResForks utility, 309, 322-323
Zero G's InstallAnywhere Now!, 446
Ziff-Davis Publishing Company, 192-194
Zip disk driver, 144